UMI ANNUAL SUNDAY SCHOOL LESSON
COMMENTARY

PRECEPTS FOR LIVING

2000-2001

UMI ANNUAL SUNDAY SCHOOL LESSON COMMENTARY

PRECEPTS FOR LIVING

2000-2001

International Sunday School Lessons

published by

URBAN MINISTRIES, INC.

A. Okechukwu Ogbonnaya, Ph.D., Editor

Melvin E. Banks, Sr., Litt.D., *CEO*

A. Okechukwu Ogbonnaya, Ph.D., *Vice President of Editorial*
Kathryn Hall, *Managing Editor*

VOLUME 3

Urban Ministries, Inc.

CONTRIBUTORS

Vice President of Editorial
A. Okechukwu Ogbonnaya, Ph.D.

Layout & Design
Larry Taylor, Vice President,
Creative Services

Bible Illustrations
Fred Carter

Editorial Staff
Kathryn Hall, Managing Editor
Shawan Brand, Production Manager
Kim Brooks, Publications Assistant
Cheryl Wilson-Carter, Publications
Assistant

Contributing Writers
Essays
Dr. Melvin Banks, Litt.D.
Rev. Donald L. Bean, Jr., B.S., M.Div.
Rev. Luke Benton, III, Th.D.
Youssouf Dembele, Ph.D.
James Estep, D.Min., Ph.D.
Carlyle Fielding Steward, III, Ph.D.
Praitha Hall, Ph.D.
Georgia Kurko, Ph.D.
Rev. Dr. Joel D. Taylor

Rev. Carol McIlwain Edwards
A. Okechukwu Ogbonnaya, Ph.D.
Judith St.Clair-Hull, Ph.D.
Carl Jeffrey Wright, J.D.

Bible Study Guides
Evangeline Carey
Olivia Cloud
Victoria Johnson
Rev. Raedorah Stewart-Dodd
Jerii Rodman
Philip Rodman

More Light On The Text
Stephanie Crowder
Luther Hicks
Amanda Johnson
Koala Jones
Rev. Mary S. Minor
A. Okechukwu Ogbonnaya, Ph.D.
Alfonzo Surrett
Rev. Alajemba Reuben Unaegbu

Unless otherwise indicated, all
Scripture references are taken
from the authorized King James
Version of the Bible.

A LETTER FROM THE EDITOR

Dear Brothers and Sisters in Christ,

We here at UMI are in the business of spreading the gospel of Jesus Christ and equipping the church for an effective ministry in the world. We are especially concerned with providing relevant tools to the church which will make her Divine witness to the Lord among God's children of African descent more effective. We believe that it is through the knowledge of the Word that God's people can be healed and restored to their true place in the heart of God.

PRECEPTS FOR LIVING is one of the tools which we believe will help Christians to become more effective communicators of the Word of God. This is the first Sunday School Lesson Commentary written from an African American perspective. In this we continue the UMI tradition of giving relevant gifts to the body of Christ as it seeks to reach the people of African descent for our Lord.

This Sunday School annual commentary is unique. One unique contribution of this work has already been stated, the fact it is written from an African-American Christian perspective. Second, it provides deep analysis of scriptural passages in both the IN DEPTH section and in the new and unique feature appropriately titled MORE LIGHT ON THE TEXT. The MORE LIGHT ON THE TEXT section is linguistic and cultural exposition of the text. It takes the passages verse by verse and comments on them from the perspective of the original language and culture. Another important aspect of the work is that the TEACHING TIPS section precedes each lesson. This section is important for those in the church who teach Sunday School and Bible studies. It gives direction and suggests activities which may help you as you teach God's Word.

PRECEPTS FOR LIVING is a useful tool for Pastors in sermon preparation and Bible study tips, Church School teachers, Sunday school superintendents and all Christians who are interested in a deeper understanding of the Word of God. We here at UMI have put much prayer into this Sunday School Annual. We know that God will use it to bless you in your walk.

Peace be with you,

A. Okechukwu Ogbonnaya, Ph.D.
Vice President, Editorial

TABLE OF CONTENTS

v

CYCLE OF 1998-2004

Arrangement of Quarters According to the

Church School Year, September through August

	1998 - 1999	1999 - 2000	2000 - 2001	2001- 2002	2002- 2003	2003- 2004
Sep Oct Nov	God Calls a People to Faithful Living (Old Testament Survey) (13)	From Slavery to Conquest (Exodus, Leviticus, Numbers, Deuteronomy, Joshua) (13)	The Emerging Nation (Judges, 1,2, Samuel [1 Chronicles], 1 Kings 1-11 [2 Chronicles 1-9]) (13)	Jesus' Ministry (Parables, Miracles Sermon on the Mount) (13)	Judgment and Exile (2 Kings 18-25 [2 Chronicles 29-36] Jeremiah, Lamentations, Ezekiel, Habakkuk, Zephaniah) (13)	Faith Faces the World (James, 1,2, 2 Peter, 1,2,3, John, Jude) (13)
Dec Jan Feb	God Calls Anew in Jesus Christ (New Testament Survey) Christmas Sun. (12/20) (13)	Emmanuel: God with Us (Gospel of Matthew) Christmas Sun. (12/19) (13)	Good News of Jesus (Gospel of Luke) Christmas Sun. (12/24) (13)	Light for All People (Isaiah 9:1-7, 11:1-9; 40-66; Ruth, Jonah, Naham) Christmas Sun. (12/23) (13)	Portraits of Faith (Personalities in the New Testament) Christmas Sun. (12/22) (13)	A Child is Given (4) (Samuel, John the Baptist, Jesus [2]) Lessons from Life (9) (Esther, Job, Ecclesiastes, Song of Solomon) Christmas Sun. (12/21)
Mar Apr May	That You May Believe (Gospel of John) Easter (4/4) (13	Helping a Church Confront Crisis (1, 2 Corinthians) Easter (4/23) (13)	Continuing Jesus's Work (Acts) Easter (4/15) (13)	The Power of the Gospel (Romans, Galatians) Easter (3/31) (13)	Jesus: God's Power in Action (Gospel of Mark) Easter (4/20) (13)	Jesus Fulfills His Mission (6) (Passion Narratives) Living Expectantly (7) (1,2 Thessalonians, Revelation) Easter (4/11)
Jun Jul Aug	Genesis: Beginnings (Genesis) (13)	New Life in Christ (Ephesians, Philippians, Colossians, Philemon) (13)	Division and Decline (1 Kings 1-17, [2 Chronicles 10-28], Isaiah 1-39, Amos, Hosea, Micah) (13)	Worship and Wisdom for Living (Psalms, Proverbs) (13)	God Restores a Remnant (Ezra, Nehemiah, Daniel, Joel, Obadiah, Haggai, Zechariah, Malachi) (14)	Hold Fast to the Faith (8) (Hebrews) Guidelines for the Church's Ministry (5) (1,2 Timothy, Titus)

* Parenthetical numerals indicate number of sessions.

A PRAYER FOR MY RISING

A. OKECHUKWU
OGBONNAYA, PH.D.

FATHER

Work thy marvel in my heart
Even in this heart of mine
Move me to the core of my marrow bone
Shake out the dust
Refine me as gold is refined
Draw me away from that which blots
Prune me as a fruit tree is pruned
and cause me to bear fruit that will forever abide.

MY GOD

I ask for your perpetual presence
If I must go through the fire.
O that it will be the fire of your love.
If I must go through the water
May it be the water of your purification.
If I must walk these long ways
Provide for my feet a pair of sandals.
If I must go through death
May it be the door to my resurrection.

MY LORD

I leave behind this world's falsehood
I embrace your refining fire
I am done with mediocrity
I live no longer to maintain the status quo
But to create newness
No longer shall my spirit praise those who stand still
and call their stagnation creativity
I revolt, I embrace a spiritual revolution
My God, with you I am no longer afraid
I know my being shall resurrect.

INTRODUCTION TO THE SEPTEMBER 2000 QUARTER

This quarter's study follows the theme "The Emerging Nation." Sessions are taken from Judges, 1 and 2 Samuel, 1 Kings, and 1 and 2 Chronicles. The study deals with the most significant events and persons from the time of Israel's first years in the Promised Land through the reign of Solomon.

The Quarter at-a-Glance

RULERS OF ISRAEL

UNIT 1. JUDGES OF ISRAEL

Unit 1 consists of four sessions from Judges and 1 Samuel. Lesson one focuses on the story of Deborah, who inspired Barak to defeat the army of Sisera. Lesson two deals with Gideon, whom God called to deliver Israel from the Midianites. Session three is a study of Samson, who revealed the secret of his strength and died as a result of his weakness. Lesson four deals with Samuel's call from God and Samuel's leadership as the last of the judges.

LESSON 1: September 3
Deborah
Judges 4:2-3, 4-9, 14-15, 22

The Biblical content of this lesson emphasizes the fact of Israel's roller coaster relationship with the Lord. Israel's unfaithfulness to God often led to their oppression from foreign rulers. In this lesson we study the oppressive rule of King Jabin and his general Sisera. We also learn of Deborah, a prophetess, who was leading Israel at this time. She held court to hear the people's disputes. We will learn how Deborah instructed Barak, at the Lord's command, to take ten thousand soldiers to Mount Tabor where the Lord would deliver Jabin's army into Barak's hands. We will study Barak's refusal to do battle with Jabin's army unless Deborah, who represented God's favor, went with him. We see the courage of Deborah as she agreed to go with Barak. (vv. 8-9) Through Deborah's encouragement, Barak launched an attack on Sisera, and God gave Barak the victory. (vv. 14-15) As you study this lesson

you will see another woman used by God to spur Israel on to victory. Jael, the Kenite, sealed defeat of Sisera by Israel when she destroyed him. (v. 22)

This lesson points to the fact that we all need encouragement. If you feel the need of support because you are facing dangerous situations or just a tough decision, this lesson calls you to be willing, like Barak, to receive encouragement from God's people. This lesson also encourages us to respond positively to strong leadership. As you study this lesson hopefully you will encourage those around you to take advantage of unexpected opportunities, and you will also allow others to encourage you in your journey.

LESSON 2: September 10
Gideon
Judges 6:11-14; 7:1-3, 20-21

In this lesson the content of the scriptural passage deals with the appearance of the angel of the Lord to Gideon. The text tells us that the angel of the Lord was present with Gideon and addressed Gideon as a mighty warrior. (6:11-12) We also see Gideon, the great man of God, questioning how the Lord's power could deliver God's people into the hands of the Midianites, their enemy. (v. 13) The text also points out how even in his reflectiveness and questioning, God still commissioned Gideon to deliver the people from Midian. (v. 14) As we proceed, the text reveals how God insisted that Gideon must reduce the number of his troops so that all would know that the coming victory would be of God. (7:1-3) Finally, the text shows us the paradigm of divine cooperation as we study the shouts of Gideon's men, the smashing of the jars, and the trumpets blowing, resulting in the flight of the Midianites. (20-21)

In this lesson we will look at one of life's major concerns, obedience. Many adults are reluctant to obey. Obedience is especially difficult when we face unfavorable odds and risky situations. Through this lesson we hope that you will find creative and unusual ways of attaining the goal of scriptural obedience. Because as humans we all like to win, this lesson teaches how obedience to the Lord can put us on the winning side. It is only through obedience to the divine will, as in the case of Gideon, that we can overcome feelings of inadequacy. Obedience is a sign of faith. When we obey the Lord—even in difficult situations in which we feel abandoned by God—it is a sure sign that we have faith in God. Hopefully, through this lesson you and I will learn to obey the voice of the Lord even in difficult situations.

LESSON 3: September 17
Samson
Judges 16:4-5, 17, 19-22, 28-30

The biblical content of this lesson deals with Samson, a judge and leader of Israel dedicated to the Lord by his parents at birth. Samson's lover, Delilah, agreed—for a price—to deliver the secret of Samson's strength to the Philistine lords. (vv. 4-5) After much persuasion, Samson revealed that the source of his strength was in keeping the Nazarite vow of not cutting his hair. Having discovered this information Delilah had Samson's head shaved while he slept. (vv. 17, 19) Further along in the text we study how Samson sought to fight the Philistines and was captured. Once he was enslaved, they put out his eyes and forced him into labor. (vv. 20-21) While in prison Samson's hair began to grow again. Subjected to public ridicule, Samson called on God to help him. God restored Samson's strength, and he pulled down the pillars of the temple that held him captive. (vv. 28-30)

This lesson helps believers to understand the biblical concept of faithfulness, and warns us of the painful results of irresponsible and faithless behavior. The faithful one does not have to seek revenge when hurt or betrayed because vengeance belongs to the Lord. Hopefully this lesson will lead believers to be faithful and not depend on their own means to get where God wants them to be.

LESSON 4: September 24
Samuel
1 Samuel 3:2-9, 19-20; 7:3-5, 12

In this lesson we observe how Samuel, a young man serving under Eli the priest, is called by God. (3:2-9) As Samuel grew, the people listened to his advice and recognized him as a prophet from the Lord. (vv.19-20) As Israel mourned, Samuel told

them that if they would return to the Lord and no longer worship false gods, the Lord would deliver them from the Philistines. This act of repentance resulted in Israel becoming exemplary in her walk with God. (7:3-4) Finally, Samuel gathers all Israel together to petition the Lord in prayer, erecting a memorial stone at Mizpeh called Ebenezer which means, "Thus far the Lord has helped us." (vv. 5, 12)

A major concern among the people of God is finding someone who can, in times of confusion, exemplify ways to walk in the will of the Lord. This lesson shows us that we are called to particular tasks as children of God. It calls those who are leaders to be genuine and sincere in displaying exemplary characteristics. Hopefully as you study this lesson you will learn from Samuel and choose to be an example that will honor the Lord.

UNIT 2. SAUL AND DAVID

Unit 2 consists of five sessions from 1 and 2 Samuel and 1 Chronicles that focus on Israel's first two kings. Lesson one tells the story of God's choosing Saul. Lesson two reports Saul's failure as king and his rejection by God in favor of David. Lesson three looks at David's song of lamentation over the deaths of Saul and Jonathan. Lesson four explores the circumstances surrounding David's becoming king of all Israel. Lesson five discusses God's covenant with David to found the Davidic dynasty.

LESSON 5: October 1
Saul Becomes King
1 Samuel 9:1-2; 10:17-26

This lesson concentrates on the selection of Saul as the first king of Israel. Scripture describes Saul as tall and handsome and from a wealthy family. (9:1-2) Samuel called the people to Mizpeh together and told them they had rejected God by demanding a king to rule over them. This rejection was viewed as a rejection of the Divine kingship of God over Israel. (10:17-19) In this text we observe the human tendency to view people based on their external characteristics. The people proclaimed Saul king because of his physical attributes instead of examining his spiritual characteristics. The passage tells us that the people sought Saul, who was exceptionally tall, and found him as he hid among the baggage, trying to avoid this call. (vv. 22-24) We find Samuel explaining the duties of the king and writing these duties in a book before dismissing the people. (v. 25) Afterwards, Saul returns to Gibeah with a band of warriors whose hearts God had touched. (v. 26)

Today's lesson deals with the challenge of change. Change is a life concern for many believers. Many believers seek to conform to widely accepted customs instead of the will of God, but for change to be healthy it must be grounded in God's will. This lesson deals with the human desire to change simply for the sake of change. This type of change can cause one to pursue a course of action against the will of God even when warned it is wrong. Also noted here is that our quest for change may, at the root, be a desire to avoid responsibility or attention. If our change involves submission to divine authority as well as a call to act responsibly, then this is a change we as believers must embrace. However, we must be aware of changes which come mainly because we seek to conform to the patterns of an ungodly world.

LESSON 6: October 8
Saul Rejected and David Anointed
1 Samuel 16:1-7, 11-13

The content of this lesson emphasizes the transition of leadership from Saul to David, concentrating on the rejection of one and the choosing of the other. Here we see that after the Lord rejected Saul as king He instructs Samuel to go to Bethlehem to anoint a son of Jesse to be king. Samuel feared that Saul would kill him for this, so God told Samuel to carry out his assignment while conducting religious services in Bethlehem. (vv. 2-3) It was through obedience to the will of God that Samuel received the revelation of the new king. Being human, Samuel wanted to choose Eliab based on outward appearance. God responded that outward appearance does not matter—only what is in the heart. (vv. 6-7) We see how God rejects each of Jesse's seven sons and David, the youngest son, is sent for and God chooses him. On God's command Samuel anoints David in the presence of his brothers, and the Spirit of the Lord fell on David from that day forward. (vv. 12-13)

In this lesson the focus is on the challenge to listen for the voice of God when making choices in life. How do we, as believers, know whom God has

chosen to lead or carry out the work of the Lord? Leaders of the church are concerned about the choices they make because they know that their choice will affect the entire church. Many of life's choices are often swayed by outward appearances. When presented with a task we may choose to plan prudently the best means of accomplishing that task, or we may choose to act merely on impulse. This lesson teaches us to choose based on divine guidance. If we are tempted to choose based on outward appearance alone, this lesson teaches us that we need to recognize it is what's inside a person that matters. In this way we will not discount the potential of those whom God may be calling to work in the divine vineyard. Hopefully, we will learn through this lesson to make our choices based on divine guidance and revelation.

LESSON 7: October 15
David Mourns Saul and Jonathan
2 Samuel 1:17-20, 22-27

The biblical content for this lesson concentrates on David mourning for Jonathan and Saul. David orders that a song of lamentation be composed and thus be taught to the people. (vv. 17-18) David states that Israel's glory was slain with the death of Saul and Jonathan, and he did not want the Philistines to know about and consequently exult in their deaths. (vv. 19-20) In his lamentation David acknowledged that Saul had brought prosperity to the people, and he called on them to mourn Saul's death. (v. 24) Overall, the text is David's expression of personal grief over the death of his friend, Jonathan. (vv. 25-27)

If you have experienced the death of someone you love this lesson will help you understand that grieving is not a sign of weakness. As people struggle for words to express grief know that David's behavior, in his time of grief, is an example to all. With this text we are called to understand the importance of grieving appropriately over deep losses. If you have experienced loss, listen to David as he mourns—yet he is empowered by the Spirit of the Most High.

LESSON 8: October 22
David Becomes King of All Israel
2 Samuel 2:1-7; 5:1-5

This passage of Scripture begins with David

seeking guidance from the Lord. As instructed by God David took his family and all his men to Hebron. (2:1-3) As a result of seeking the Lord the people of Judah anointed David as their king. (v. 4) David blessed the people of Jabesh-Gilead for burying Saul, and he promised to reward them for their act of loyalty. (4-7) After years of strife under Saul's leadership, the northern tribes and the elders of Israel came to David in Hebron to anoint him king over all of Israel. (5:1-3) At the age of 30 David began a 40-year reign; he ruled seven and a half years over Judah at Hebron, and from Jerusalem 33 years over all Israel. (4-5)

This lesson examines leadership. As believers we must be concerned with the type of leaders we choose to follow. Leadership must be earned. Leaders should be selected on the basis of merit and qualifications, not merely on a hunch. Often, the problem most Christians have with leadership is becoming frustrated and impatient when goals are not quickly attained. In this lesson we learn how to respond positively to the opportunities for leadership God sends our way. Finally, this lesson teaches us not to abuse the authority we have over others.

LESSON 9: October 29
God's Covenant with David
2 Samuel 7:1-13

This lesson is based on the story of David's desire to build a permanent structure for the Ark of God. (vv. 1-2) In response to this Nathan told David to do as he wished, but that same night, God directed Nathan to tell David not to build the house. (vv. 3-7) To make sure that David understood this instruction, God told Nathan to remind David of how He changed him from a shepherd to a prince and how God had protected him. (vv. 8-9) God promises to make David's name great, ensure the people's security and safety in the land, and establish David's dynasty. (vv. 9-11) In addition to the promise of rulership, God promised to give David a son who would build the temple and establish his kingdom forever. (vv. 12-13)

In this lesson we study the challenge of God's promise. As we seek ways to express appreciation and praise to God, we must remember our security and longevity is based on God's Word to us. If

we keep this in mind then we will be careful not to confuse our good intentions with the will of God. One thing the lesson will teach us is that our good intentions are sometimes ill-timed. God's promise to protect and care for us in the present and in the future is always secure, whether we do all that we desire for God or not. We will learn that God's promise also applies to our children and the dreams we have for a greater tomorrow.

UNIT 3. DAVID AND SOLOMON

Unit 3 consists of four sessions from 2 Samuel, 1 Kings, and 1 and 2 Chronicles that focus on the reigns of David and Solomon. Lesson one considers the relationship of David and Bathsheba and the resulting sin and repentance of David. Lesson two deals with David's charge to his son Solomon and Solomon's prayer for wisdom in ruling the people. Lesson three addresses Solomon's prayer regarding the Temple and God's response to him. Lesson four examines Solomon's errors that resulted in the division of the kingdom.

LESSON 10: November 5
David and Bathsheba
2 Samuel 11:2-5, 14-18, 26-27; 12:13-15

During the spring after David sent Joab to fight his enemies, from the rooftop of his palace David saw a beautiful woman bathing. (11:2) David learned that the woman was Bathsheba, wife of Uriah; he sent for her and she became pregnant with his child. (vv. 3-5) After David's attempt to hide his adultery failed, he arranged to have Uriah killed in battle. (vv. 14-18) As we proceed in the text, we read that after Bathsheba mourned the death of her husband David brought her to the palace to be his wife, and she gave birth to their son. (vv. 26-27) Nathan the prophet told David a story to confront him with the fact that he had stolen Uriah's wife. (11:27—12:7) David acknowledged his guilt and because of his repentance Nathan said that David would not die as a result of his sin, but the baby would not survive. (vv. 13-15)

The focus of this lesson deals with the fall of believers. As human beings we have the tendency to satisfy selfish desires and sometimes take advantage of other people. It also deals with human intoxication with power and the abuse of that power which often places us and others in compromising situations. We are also shown the tragedy that occurs when those in power seek to cover up their own sins, resulting in grief for loved ones and for innocent people. Finally, this lesson teaches us the meaning of repentance.

LESSON 11: November 12
Solomon Succeeds David
1 Kings 2:1-4; 3:3-4, 5-10

The content of this lesson is taken from the passage dealing with the death of David. Shortly before his death, King David instructed his son Solomon to walk in the way of the Lord so as to assure the succession of his house. (2:1-4) Solomon loved the Lord and followed in the way of David, except he sacrificed and offered incense at the high places. (3:3) At Gibeon the Lord appeared to Solomon in a dream and invited him to ask for a gift from God. (vv. 4-5) Solomon asked for the gift of wisdom to rule Israel, and God was pleased. (vv. 6-10)

In this lesson we learn that when our tasks overwhelm us it is needful for the elders to give sound advice to help younger people succeed in life. Also, the lesson also calls believers to follow the good examples of our ancestors who walked with the Lord. It teaches us to that God is a reliable source when we feel overwhelmed by responsibilities. God is able to give us more than we expect or request in the time of our need.

LESSON 12: November 19
Solomon Builds the Temple
1 Kings 6:37-38; 8:22, 27-30; 9:1-5

The focus of this text is on Solomon's seven-year process of building the temple. (6:37-38) Here we see that Solomon acknowledged that God's presence was not limited to the temple. (8:22, 27) We are also treated to the prayer of Solomon for the blessing of the temple. (vv. 28-30) After Solomon had finished the temple, the Lord appeared again to him in a dream. (9:1-2) In response to Solomon's prayer God promises to consecrate the temple and put His name, eyes, and heart there for all time. (v. 3) In this passage God renewed the promise made to David and to Solomon. God insisted that if Solomon and his

descendants were faithful to God, they would continue to reign in Israel. (vv. 4-5)

From this lesson we learn that as many of us work for years to attain a goal, we must keep the Lord at the forefront of our consciousness. This means that we must not let our works overshadow the presence of God in our worship experience. This lesson calls us to acknowledge the completion of works of spiritual significance but more importantly to dedicate them to God, who has helped us thus far. This lesson also encourages us to desire to achieve something which will endure beyond our lifetime, remembering that our actions will have a strong effect on future generations.

LESSON 13: November 26
Solomon's Mistakes
1 Kings 11:1-13

This scriptural text highlights the mistakes of Solomon, the King of Israel. The first act that led Solomon down the path of destruction was disobedience to the command of the Lord. Contrary to God's commands, Solomon married foreign women who worshiped their own gods. (vv. 1-2) Solomon was not as faithful to God as David his father was; in his old age Solomon worshiped the gods of his wives. (vv. 3-6) Instead of remaining steadfast to God, Solomon built places of worship for foreign gods so his wives could worship them in Israel. (vv. 7-8) God was angry that Solomon had turned away to worship other gods. (vv. 9-10) He told Solomon that because he had not kept the divine covenant, he would lose his throne. We read that because of God's love for David and Jerusalem, the punishment would fall upon Solomon's son, who would rule over a greatly reduced kingdom. (vv. 11-13)

The focus of this lesson is that spiritual compromise causes ruin. Caution should be given to relationships that cause problems in our walk with God. Relationships that cause conflict with our commitment to God need to be discarded. This lesson calls us to consider the far-reaching consequences of our actions, especially those that do not conform to the will of God or prevent us from keeping promises made to God.

KEYS TO SUCCESSFUL CHRISTIAN EDUCATION

C. Jeffrey Wright, J.D.

Introduction

Mental, moral and spiritual development in the Christian context is a principle objective of the work of the church. Some churches are blessed with large facilities, a full-time Christian education staff and a department including trained individuals with seminary or divinity school degrees in Christian Education. Others have only one or two volunteers and a commitment to study the Word. In either case, these three keys will help unlock the door to a successful Christian Education program: (1) the full commitment of the Pastor or Elders of your church; (2) an effective process for the recruitment, selection, and training of teachers or facilitators; and (3) a deliberate approach to help maximize the effectiveness of the available physical space for teaching.

Leadership of the Pastor or Elders

Of the many roles of the pastor or elders of a church, that of teacher or Christian educator is perhaps the most important. Effective teaching is embodied in virtually all pastoral responsibilities. Over half of all African American pastors surveyed in a recent national research project indicated that their spiritual gift was teaching as well as preaching. Yet despite this report, many pastors are completely uninvolved in the Christian education program or Sunday School activity of their church. Without the active and effective involvement and the physical presence of the leader of a congregation in its Christian education activities, the results will be severely limited. Although the church's program may appear successful, it could be much better with pastoral support and endorsement.

If the pastor's authority to direct that members participate in the church's Sunday School or Christian education activity is not exercised, then an important key to the successful program is lost. A pastor should use the biblical authority and directives of Scripture constantly to admonish the people to build the Word into their lives and build their lives on the Word. This is the purpose of the Christian education program of the church and should be a part of the pastor's vision.

A church without a vision of excellence in Christian education is a church with an incomplete vision. The words of the prophet Hosea ring true yet today that "[our] people are destroyed from lack of knowledge." It is unfortunate, but true, that today many view church growth solely from the context of Sunday morning service and soul-winning without regard to the long-term development and discipling of new members. The right hand of fellowship should include not just a completed new members class certificate but also a commitment regularly and diligently to attend Sunday School and the Christian education program activities of the church. If the pastor says it, the people will do it. At least most of them will. If the pastor says it and participates himself, you may even get the wayward sheep to follow along.

There is no substitute for the consistent, visible, physical presence of the pastor in the Sunday School and Christian education program of the church. If Sunday School is going on and the pastor is in the church building, being present and involved in the activity is one of the best ways to enhance the program. The temptation to turn over the Sunday School to a trusted deacon or

1

elder and then completely drop out of the program is tempting but should be avoided. While many pastors do "close out" the Sunday School general assembly time, others have learned that the total program is strengthened when they do one or more of the following:

1. build the preaching ministry around the Sunday school lesson themes or scriptures;
2. teach a class, usually an adult class or an elective;
3. visit each class for a few minutes of participation or observation;
4. hold teacher's prayer meeting before class sessions;
5. visit each class in its entirety over successive weeks;
6. serve teachers and administrators in support capacities, "washing feet" by providing supplies or other tools for teaching and solving the small problems that come up.

Many pastors would be shocked at what is taught or said in the Sunday School and Christian education programs of their church. But the purpose of physical presence is not quality control of the program, but rather leading by example. Making sure teaching is on target is best done through a well-thought-out teacher recruitment and training program.

Recruiting and Training Teachers and Facilitators

Teaching Sunday School is one of the most rewarding experiences in the church. This great secret has had two unintended consequences in many churches. Many of those who should teach don't, because they don't know what they are missing. And many people who should not be teaching try to hold on forever because despite their limited competence, it is so rewarding they don't want to stop. School teachers are notorious for expressing the sentiment that "since I teach all week, I wouldn't have the energy to teach on Sunday." Professional teachers who also teach Sunday School will often testify that their inspiration to teach during the week grows out of their service to God on Sunday or in an evening class.

Here are some pointers which may help lead your church to an effective teacher recruiting and training process and develop a more systematic approach to Christian education. Here are some questions that can help you.

Who Do We Have In Our Church?

1. Profile all members getting accurate records on jobs held, special interests and abilities, education, hobbies, and volunteer work.
2. Categorize the many professional teachers or educational administrators you have and what ages and grades they have taught. Examine membership to see if you have any members who teach teachers or are involved in school curriculum design and decision making.
3. Do a skill inventory to see which members have presentation skills (not talking skills) that are used in their employment. Professional sales people or those who have jobs in sales training can be of great help.

How Do We Choose?

1. Decide on the current teachers. State reasons for choosing them. Never elect teachers through political process. (Bad idea!)
2. Do not rely on the old habit of choosing Sunday School teachers based on the three "Ts": talkers, tenure, and tithers. Verbal ability and faithfulness in attendance and giving are important but not necessarily the best reasons for choosing a teacher; particularly if the person lacks bible knowledge or a basic understanding of teaching methods.
3. Develop a process for evaluating effectiveness and removing ineffective teachers.

What Do We Do To Train And Prepare?

1. Develop a library of teacher training resources such as books on teaching methods, Christian education fundamentals, reference materials such as Bible dictionaries, concordances and commentaries.
2. Take steps that allow a person to teach and that protect from exposing to doctrinal error or poor teaching methods such as lecture-only teaching.
3. Have weekly teachers' meetings, "Certify" teachers periodically with evaluations, tests or

other feedback tools. Ask the students to evaluate the teachers.

Often despite the best recruiting and available training, we still find that we do not have the people or resources necessary to have an effective training program. Defining the leaders as "facilitators" is one way to address this problem. Facilitators assist the group in the learning process while learning themselves. Removing the authority inherent in the defined role of "teacher" and using leaders' guides which give step-by-step instructions on facilitating a learning session can allow for almost anyone to be effective in the Christian education leadership role. Many resources are now available for facilitators who do not have significant teaching experience.

Effective Use of Available Space

A place to teach and hold class sessions is frequently a major concern of the Christian education or Sunday School department. The environment within which you teach can either be at war with the learning process or it can make learning easy and enjoyable. Rather than give up because your class in the choir loft is drowned out by the mens' class number two on the deacons' bench, get creative. Consider alternatives rather than be locked into tradition. Daniel provides an excellent example of developing a creative alternative to a seemingly insurmountable problem (see Daniel 1). By proposing a comparative experiment in creative eating rather than simply complaining about the problem presented, he was able to continue a kosher diet even in the captivity of Babylon. To get the needed space to conduct an effective Christian educa-

tion program, be sure to consider the following:

    a) use of schools or facilities near the church

    b) use of different times for different classes

    c) giving the best spaces to the children who are less tolerant of poor teaching space

    d) planning for educational activities when doing building projects; classrooms and meeting spaces often get two to three times more use than sanctuary or auditorium space

    e) moveable partitions can be very effective to create privacy and are often available from used office equipment dealers at prices that would surprise you

Don't forget to decorate the teaching environment. Scripture Scene posters, maps, wall charts and other visual aids can be very effective in the creating the atmosphere for learning. School supply stores often have resources that are suitable for the Christian education learning environment.

Conclusion

There are many keys to Christian education success but these three will open the door to an effective program. A leader that embraces the program, a plan for teacher success, and an environment that makes learning a pleasure will be honored by God as you "Do your best to present yourself to God as one approved, a workman who does not need to be ashamed and who correctly handles the word of truth" (2 Timothy 2:15).

EVANGELIZING AFRICAN AMERICANS

Rev. Dr. Joel D. Taylor

I have come today to suggest to each of us who read this article that the theme of evangelism is one of the most important themes in the African-American community and for the entire church of Jesus Christ. I hope as the African American people of God, we have truly made evangelism a part of our lives. When I begin to look critically at our African-American churches, homes, neighborhoods, streets and communities, I realize that there needs to be a revival. I am a leader who certainly feels that our evangelism and missionary work needs to be carried across the sea, but many unsaved folk are right on the steps of our churches. Honestly, most of our churches have many empty pews that need to be filled. Most of our churches have become so busy with church work that somehow they have forgotten the work of the church. The church has become so busy meeting that we have failed to understand why we meet and what we are supposed to do until we meet again. In the simplest terms, the work of the church is to save lost souls.

The Lord is depending on you to share the message of salvation. I thought about how important it is for each of us to make up our minds that we will be concerned about the lost at any cost. "This year in America 2.2 million people will die."[1] When you look at research from surveys, more than 1 million of those people will die and go to hell. These people will end up in eternal damnation from the hot fires of a place called hell. We can accept physical death because Jesus is coming back for us in the rapture. You can eat right and exercise, but you are still going to die. The catastrophe and calamity for me is that these people will die without having cashed in on eternal life; people will die—miss heaven and go to hell. Surveys suggest that "262 million people live in America and 187 million have not accepted Jesus Christ as their personal

Savior."[2] Where are all of these unsaved people? Do you know any unsaved people? They sit on the padded pews of our churches. They live right on the doorsteps of our churches. They sleep in the bed with us each and every night. They live under the same roof as we do. These unsaved people live next door and down the street. These unsaved people are among your family your friends. The words Jesus spoke were correct when He said, "the harvest is great, but the laborers are few." I argue that it is time for the people of God to become active in their evangelistic efforts. In this article I want to share from a personal perspective about the evangelistic message, methods and mentality.

EVANGELISTIC MESSAGE

The word of God tells us in Mark 16:15, "And he said unto them, Go ye into all the world and preach the gospel to every creature." It is here that Jesus gives the message of the great commission for the world of evangelism, along with the promise of salvation to those who believe. This great commission is the message of the good news. The word for preach, here in this text, is *kerusso*, which in Greek signifies to be a herald, or in general, "proclaim to preach the Gospel as a herald." Jesus wants us to share the Gospel or the Good News. The New Testament Gospel denotes the good tidings of the kingdom of God and of salvation through Christ, to be received by faith, on the basis of His expiatory death, His burial, resurrection, and ascension.

All believers must share this message. This is a command given to the church by Jesus Christ for the church and all believers. Many of us treat this message as if God only wants a few people to share the Good News. We act as if the Word of God is not for us to share. Jesus here did not discuss excuses for sharing this Gospel message; this was an uncompromising demand. I come to report that as

God loved the world and Christ came into it, so are Christians to go into the world as spokesmen for Christ. The question is not, are you going to be a witness? The fact is if you are a Christian, then you are a witness.

The Lord wants us to go into the entire world and spread the Gospel message. The Lord wants us to go to every land, every people, every nationality, every home, every community, every street, and every block to share the Good News. No land is to be neglected and no people are to be ignored. The believers must be audacious, undaunted, unafraid, and undismayed from their sharing of the great commission. Have you as a follower of Christ responded to the call of God to "go ye into all the world"? Have you become one of the believers who are willing to share the Good News? The world needs us to be a witness.

EVANGELISTIC METHODS

When I think about evangelism, I am aware that there are various methods that can be employed by the Christian who has responded to the call of evangelism. In Acts 20:20 it states, "but have shewed you, and have taught you plublicly and from house to house." Another way of stating this is "I have evangelized to you and taught you, from house to house." It is here that I see Paul proclaimed the message of Jesus publicly as well as privately. This was a method that he employed in order to share the good news about the Lord.

I suggest that there are many ways and methods used to spread the message of the risen Savior, but only one message. People can share the Good News personally, as a corporate body, door to door, through street corner preaching, evangelistic tent revivals, broadcast evangelism, cell groups, community development, tracts, mass mailing, or with family, friends and associates. I tell the members of the church where I serve that if you make yourself available to the Lord, He will give you a method to use that is suitable to the gifts that God has given you. God can use anyone to spread the Good News. You do not have to talk like somebody else, just use what God has given you.

One of the problems is some people do not want to do evangelism; some people do not want to have a method. Moreover, some of our methods may need to be updated to deal with a new generation. Remember, whenever you talk about change

people become nervous; however, I did not say change the message. We need to update the message and tailor it to our personal growth. Your message about Christ should continue to grow and your methods of sharing the Good News about Christ should also grow.

EVANGELISTIC MENTALITY

The writer of Proverbs tells us that "he that winneth souls is wise." Thank God that I can say there are many wise believers. But on the other hand, many of the believers who come to church every week show no signs of being wise. I am cognizant of the fact that Satan uses ignorance in order to stop believers from doing what "thus said the Lord." If you do not win souls, you can consider yourself as being senseless, witless, imprudent and injudicious as a soul winner. This reminds me of a man who said, "I will build me a church." The man bought the land, hired an architect and a contractor to build the church. The man placed a Hammond organ, grand piano, sound system, pews, carpet, and an elevator in the building. He hired a musician, janitor, and secretary and bought supplies for the building. He opened the church for worship and went to the pulpit to preach and remembered he had forgot about having members for the church. The pastor had a building, pews and place to worship, but he did not have any members.

I come to report today that we need to have an evangelistic mentality. If your church is empty, you need to make evangelism a priority. If family members are lost, you need to win souls. If your block is deplorable, you need to win souls. If your job is Satan's den, you need to win some souls. If your church is full of hell, you need to win some souls. God needs somebody who will go into the hedges and the highways. God needs somebody to seek the lost at any cost. God needs somebody, for the harvest is great but the laborers are few. Jesus needs somebody to follow Him so that He can make you a fisher of men. The Gospel must be preached to all nations, people, communities, children, adults, singles, and couples—the lost, hurting, and helpless.

1. George Barna, *Evangelism that Works* (Ventura, California; Regal Books, 1995), p.11.

2. *Ibid.*, p.22.

RULERS OF ISRAEL: THE EMERGING NATION

Judith St.Clair Hull, Ph.D.

The people of Israel arrived in the Promised Land as twelve nomadic tribes held together by the strong leadership of Joshua, who had just replaced Moses. Joshua was victorious over the loose confederation of Canaanite tribes which had populated the Promised Land, but large pockets yet to be conquered by the individual tribes of Israel were left after the death of Joshua. Many of the Canaanite people were still in the land, along with their perverse idolatry. Prostitution and child sacrifice were part of their religion. The Israelites waffled back and forth between assimilating these evil practices and following the true God and His commands for holiness. When the people sinned, God allowed the sinful Canaanite people surrounding them to harass them, steal from them, enslave them, and conquer them, but when the people cried in anguish to God, He delivered them through divinely-appointed leaders known as the judges. For the most part these leaders operated locally, with none of the judges acting as a strong leader to unite all of the tribes of Israel. Although the narratives of the various judges follow one after the other, their ministries often overlapped one another in time.

The office of judge was not inherited, nor was a judge elected or appointed in any official way. The judges were charismatic leaders raised up by the Lord. Their primary role was leading the people to freedom from those who oppressed them; thus, they were truly judges whose main responsibility was bringing about justice for the people of God. They were often very flawed people. Samson is the first to come to mind. He seemed to be obsessed with becoming sexually involved with pagan women. Even Gideon, who became a brave warrior leading a group of three hundred men to victory using pitchers, torches, and swords, became involved in establishing a new idolatrous religion at the end of his days. Deborah, who begins our quarter, was an unlikely leader in a very male-oriented culture, yet she seemed to exemplify the ideal as a judge. Deborah modeled the role of judge of civil disputes as she sat under a palm tree judging the people. Her spirituality was evident by her designation as a prophetess and through her songwriting and leading of a great praise hymn to God. And even though she deferred to a man in the role of military leader, she ended up going along with him to lead the army to victory over Sisera. The judges were not simply leaders of the judicial aspects of government. They were also executive leaders in all areas of civil law as well as military leaders. Above all, they were Spirit-empowered leaders.

The three hundred or so years when Israel was led by the judges were marked by political, moral, and spiritual deterioration and anarchy. Because the people did "as they saw fit," rather than obeying the Lord God, they missed the many blessings that God desired to give them. Towards the end of this period, sinfulness was so great that even the sons of Eli, the high priest, had completely turned away from God and were using their position for their own greed and lustful pursuits. Just when it seemed that Israel had fallen beyond redemption, God answered the prayers of a woman named Hannah and sent her a son named Samuel who would turn the federation of tribes back to the Lord God.

Samuel was the last and greatest of the judges. He functioned as judge, prophet, and priest. But in spite of all this power, he was still not the king. As Samuel reached an old age, the people saw that his sons were corrupt and incapable of providing the leadership needed to provide military security. They looked at the people surrounding them and threatening to overcome them and they desired a king to protect them. They lacked the trust in God to wait for Him to raise up a leader who could conquer their enemies. Samuel thought that the people were rejecting his leadership, but the people were rejecting God.

The Books of Samuel cover the period of Israel's history in transition from judgeship to monarchy, from loose tribal affiliation to strong central government. The Books of 1 and 2 Samuel were named after Samuel, the judge who is the major character in most of 1 Samuel. Samuel is thought to have written much of this history himself or at least have supplied the information. No one is certain who wrote the rest of these two books, which were considered one document in the earliest Hebrew manuscripts. Towards the end of the narrative concerning Samuel, the emphasis shifts to Saul, the first king of Israel, and then to King David. Israel asked God for a king. This request was not in itself wrong. In Genesis 17:6, 16; 35:11; and Deuteronomy 17:14-20, God revealed that His plan for Israel was that they should have a king. But the people of Israel were asking for the right thing at the wrong time and with the wrong motives. They asked for a king to be like the other nations and thus they were denying God, the true Sovereign King of His people, the right to provide the government for them.

Saul was just the sort of man that the people would want as a king. He seemed shy, sincere, and very likable. His appearance (head and shoulders taller than anyone else in the crowd) convinced the people that he was the one. But he had some character deficiencies that soon surfaced. In the beginning he appeared to be a spiritual man; the Spirit of the Lord came upon him and he was called one of the prophets for a brief time. But he was spiritually shallow. He lived less than five miles from Samuel's home, but he had not even heard of him or known of his ministry. Early in his reign he did not seem to realize the seriousness of his sin in taking upon himself the role of priest as he offered sacrifice to God instead of waiting for Samuel. Late in his reign he consulted divination; again he just did not understand the theological implications of such a move. And when he was called upon to make the kind of decisions a king needed to make, he lacked important discernment. Saul just did not have the necessary spiritual depth or political sense to make a good and godly king.

By the time David was anointed as King, it is obvious that God's timing and choosing of the king had come to fruition. David was the king God had promised in Genesis 49:10 and Numbers 24:17. David had a genuine heart for God, he was a great military leader, and he was an astute politician. But Scripture does not overlook his faults, which were also great. Although David knew what was the right thing to do, he sometimes erred in impulsive action without thinking about the consequences. But when David sinned, he confessed and God forgave him. (However, the consequences of his sins could not be avoided.) Because of David's genuine love for God, God established His covenant with him. We are the recipients of the blessings of this covenant, for from the lineage of David has come our Saviour, the eternal King.

First Kings takes over where 2 Samuel leaves off, recounting the succession of King Solomon to the throne of his father, King David. The period of Israel's history under the reigns of Saul, David, and Solomon is considered the era of the united kingdom, because this was the only time in which both Israel and Judah were united under one king.

Solomon was the sort of king of which legends are made. Under Solomon the Kingdom of Israel expanded its borders further than ever before or since. The wisdom of Solomon was proverbial. He made alliances that expanded not only the borders of Israel, but also catapulted Israel into becoming a major business and trading power from Africa to the Middle East to the Mediterranean. Although the Israelite people were saddled with great taxes and were enlisted in Solomon's massive building projects, they became a strong nation of which they could be proud. But Solomon's downfall came as a result of some of the very things which had built up the nation. The heavy taxation wearied the people by the time his son, Rehoboam, was ready to assume the throne. The alliances and marriages to foreign women caused Solomon to turn from his devotion to God and build temples to worship idols and the sun, moon, and stars. When Solomon turned away from single-hearted love for God and obedience to the Father, he planted the seeds for the kingdom to fall apart.

Israel's leaders from initial entrance into the Promised Land through the establishment of a strong monarchy were as diverse a group as could be. In them we observe the best of leadership and the worst. We see severe character flaws in the best leaders and surprising trust in God in the worst. But from this diverse group of leaders, God built a strong nation.

Toussaint L'Ouverture
(1749-1803)

Pierre Francois Dominique was one of the most important leaders of the slave revolt of St. Domingue (later called Haiti). The insurrection later led to the independence of Haiti. His father, Gaou-Guinou, was the son of an African king. Toussaint labored as a slave on a sugar plantation. He learned French, Latin, geometry, and the Roman Catholic religion.

The Spanish brought slaves to St. Domingue in 1512. The French came in 1630 and controlled the western side of St. Domingue. Through the use of free slave labor, their territory became the richest colonial possession. They were able to send abundant supplies of sugar, indigo, and cotton back to France. By the end of the seventeenth century, there were at least 2,000,000 Blacks, 50,000 mulattoes and 20,000 Frenchmen. Outnumbering their masters by such a large margin created a very uneasy balance on the island. Sadly, class and caste systems deeply divided these groups, creating feelings of arrogance on one hand and bitterness on the other. In contrast, France was filled with the talk of freedom, equality, and fraternity. While in France the people fought to obtain the rights of man, on the island the French ruled the slaves with cruelty and no thought of dealing fairly with the Haitians. The slaves produced great wealth for the French while enduring harsh treatment, and the mulattoes, while permitted to own land, had no recognized social or political position. The lofty ideals of the French Revolution found no root in the hearts of the French overseers.

On August 1, 1789, a voodoo priest named Boukmann held a meeting with various leaders. Pierre Dominique Toussaint was invited because of his reputation for wisdom and respect for his level of education. Plans were laid for a revolt. On August 9, the sound of hundreds of drums signaled the beginning of the attack. Thousands of slaves swept through village after village burning property and killing French people. More than 6000 coffee plantations and 200 sugar refineries were destroyed, but the French fought back and killed the slave leader, Boukmann.

Toussaint became the leader of the slaves. At the same time, France had declared war on Spain and England. Toussaint shrewdly joined the Spanish and fought the French again. The Spanish equipped Toussaint's rebels, who drove 3,000 French soldiers from the northern and eastern parts of the island. He later left the Spanish and fought his way through French territory, overcoming the enemy forces in town after town. His many victories won him the nickname of L'Ouverture (the Opener). He then established himself as governor-general of St. Domingue and began to develop the island's natural resources and foreign trade. Showing that he was not blinded by bitterness, he began trade with France and sent his two sons to study in Paris. He saw the revolt as directed against the institution of slavery rather than against the French people.

In the meantime, Napoleon had conquered much of Europe and determined to recapture St. Domingue and all its rich resources. He had 86 ships built to carry 22,000 soldiers back to the island. In February, 1802, the powerful armada arrived. Captain-General LeClerc was the commander and declared that all plantations be returned to their former French owners and that slavery be reinstituted. LeClerc attacked Cap Francois, which was burned by Henri Christophe, one of Toussaint's governors. Realizing the futility of having to continually face further insurrections, LeClerc declared an end to slavery. He offered Christophe a generalship in the French army. Toussaint was captured in June 1802 and sent to France. He died there in prison on April 7, 1803.

St. Domingue again erupted in a bloody revolt. The slaves and mulattoes drove the French into the sea. St. Domingue was proclaimed a Republic and given the Indian name of Haiti. Haitian independence was declared on January 1, 1804.

Toussaint L'Ouverture was an extraordinary leader who worked to free the slaves. He was a champion of freedom and independence.

(Source: Russell Adams, Great Negroes Past and Present, Chicago: Afro-Am, pp. 16-19)

September 3
Bible Study Guide 1

1. Words You Should Know

A. Judge (Judges 4:4) Hebrew *Shphat*—To decide or judge; to be an arbitrator; to govern and rule. The term is especially used to refer to heroic Israelite leaders who delivered their people from the oppression of neighboring nations between the time of Joshua and Samuel.

B. Host (4:2) Hebrew *Tsava*—A mass of persons especially for war; a campaign, army, or troops assembled in military service, warfare, or hardship.

2. Teacher Preparation

A. To familiarize yourself with lessons for the entire quarter, read the QUARTER-AT-A-GLANCE and the introductory material for Unit 1.

B. Take time to read Bible Study Guide 1 and highlight important points that you plan to emphasize in your teaching time today.

C. Be sure you have studied and read through the FOCAL VERSES, perhaps from several translations of the Bible.

D. Materials needed: Bible, index cards, paper and pencils.

3. Starting the Lesson

A. Open the class with prayer. Thank God for all of the students who have returned from their summer vacations and are ready to learn biblical truths.

B. Take at least 10 minutes to review what students learned from last quarter and how they applied it to their lives over the past three months.

C. Ask a student to read the FOCAL VERSES and the IN FOCUS sections of the lesson. Then ask, "Why is it important that we have encouragers in our lives?"

4. Getting into the Lesson

A. Pass out the index cards or paper, and have students write down what it means to be an encourager. Then ask the students how their definition relates to Deborah.

B. Have three students read the FOCAL VERS-ES, using the AT-A-GLANCE outline as a guide for reading. Have several students comment on what the verses are saying and how they might apply the ideas to their specific lives.

C. Have a student read the BACKGROUND section. Discuss the implications behind Israel's "treadmill" lifestyle and whether or not the church today is similar or different in our relationship with God.

5. Relating the Lesson to Life

A. Review the SEARCH THE SCRIPTURES questions together.

B. Use the DISCUSS THE MEANING questions to get the students to focus on their own relationship with the Lord.

C. After they have answered the questions, ask volunteers to comment on their answers and how they plan to apply what they learned to their own lives.

6. Arousing Action

The MAKE IT HAPPEN assignment challenges students to find someone they can encourage this week. Have them find at least one person in church they can encourage before or after the morning service is over. Ask them to report on their activity in next week's class.

WORSHIP GUIDE

For the Superintendent or Teacher
Theme: Deborah
Theme Song: "I'll Be a Witness"
Scripture: Luke 1:46-55
Song: "My Help Comes from the Lord"
Devotional Thought: Dear Lord, thank You for encouraging me to do Your will at all times. Help me to be an encourager for someone else this week. In Jesus' name, Amen.

DEBORAH

Bible Background • JUDGES 4-5
Printed Text • JUDGES 4:2-3, 4-9, 14-15, 22
Devotional Reading • PSALM 68:1-6

LESSON AIM

By the end of the lesson, students will be able to appreciate Deborah's role as an encourager; explain what; it means to be an encourager; and commit to encourage one person this week.

KEEP IN MIND

"And Deborah said unto Barak, Up; for this is the day in which the LORD hath delivered Sisera into thine hand: is not the LORD gone out before thee?" (Judges 4:14).

FOCAL VERSES

Judges 4:2 And the LORD sold them into the hand of Jabin kin of Canaan, that reigned in Hazor; the captain of whose host was Sisera, which dwelt in Harosheth of the Gentiles.

3 And the children of Israel cried unto the LORD: for he had nine hundred chariots of iron; and twenty years he mightily oppressed the children of Israel.

4 And Deborah, a prophetess, the wife of Lapidoth, she judged Israel at that time.

5 And she dwelt under the palm tree of Deborah between Ramah and Bethel in mount Ephraim: and the children of Israel came up to her for judgment.

6 And she sent and called Barak the son of Abinoam out of Kedesh-napthtali, and said unto him, Hath not the LORD God of Israel commanded, saying, Go and draw toward mount Tabor, and take with thee ten thousand men of the children of Naphtali and of the children of Zebulun?

7 And I will draw unto thee to the river Kishon

LESSON OVERVIEW

LESSON AIM
KEEP IN MIND
FOCAL VERSES
IN FOCUS
THE PEOPLE, PLACES,
AND TIMES
BACKGROUND
AT-A-GLANCE
IN DEPTH
SEARCH THE SCRIPTURES
DISCUSS THE MEANING
LESSON IN OUR SOCIETY
MAKE IT HAPPEN
FOLLOW THE SPIRIT
REMEMBER YOUR THOUGHTS
MORE LIGHT ON THE TEXT
DAILY BIBLE READINGS

Sisera, the captain of Jabin's army, with his chariots and his multitude; and I will deliver him into thine hand.

8 And Barak said unto her, If thou wilt go with me, then I will go: but if thou wilt not go with me, then I will not go.

9 And she said, I will surely go with thee: notwithstanding the journey that thou takest shall not be for thine honour; for the LORD shall sell Sisera into the hand of a woman. And Deborah arose, and went with Barak to Kedesh.

4:14 And Deborah said unto Barak, Up; for this is the day in which the LORD hath delivered Sisera into thine hand: is not the LORD gone out before thee? So Barak went down from mount Tabor, and ten thousand men after him.

15 And the LORD discomfited Sisera, and all his chariots, and all his host, with the edge of the sword before Barak; so that Sisera lighted down off his chariot, and fled away on his feet.

4:22 And, behold, as Barak pursued Sisera, Jael came out to meet him, and said unto him, Come, and I will shew thee the man whom thou seekest. And when he came into her tent, behold Sisera lay dead.

IN FOCUS

Deborah Willard is an investigative reporter for WUSA-TV Channel 9 in Washington, D.C. Known for her tenacious reporting, Deborah has won many awards for stories she has covered, including political corruption and gang-related murders.

Someone asked Deborah whether she would rather be a news anchor than an investigative reporter. Deborah quickly replied that investigating was in her "blood" and she could never give it up to sit behind a desk and become a "talking head."

"When I help expose a crooked politician, close a crack-house, or provide the community with vital information that other reporters may not have, I feel that I am encouraging the people to believe that Channel 9 makes a difference. Plus, I know my work is not in vain," said Deborah.

Deborah Willard is determined to work to make her community better. In today's lesson we will meet another Deborah who also worked to make her community, Israel, better by bringing them out of bondage into the glorious liberty of light.

THE PEOPLE, PLACES, AND TIMES

Ramah. A name given alone and in combination with other words to several places in Palestine. Ramah of Benjamin, which is identified with modern er-Ram, was located about five miles north of Jerusalem and west of Geba and Michmash on the border of Israel and Judah. Although the site has been excavated, surface exploration indicates occupation began about the twelfth century B.C.

Ramah can be associated with a number of Old Testament passages. Deborah judged between Ramah and Bethel (Judges 4:5). Baasha, King of Israel, fortified Ramah, but by an alliance with Ben-Hadad of Damascus, Asa of Judah tore it down (1 Kings 15:17-22). According to Isaiah 10:29, the Assyrians advanced toward Jerusalem through Ramah. Ramah is mentioned in Hosea's cry against Israel (Hosea 5:8), and Jeremiah was set free there (Jeremiah 40:1).

(Harper's Bible Dictionary, Paul J. Achtemeier, General Editor, San Francisco: Harper and Row Publishers, 1986, p. 852.)

Bethel. An important biblical city on the north-south mountain road north of Jerusalem. Bethel had few natural defenses, but it did have plentiful water from nearby springs. It also stood at the intersection of the north-south road that passed through the central hill country and the main east-west road that led from Jericho to the Mediterranean Sea.

(Harper's Bible Dictionary, pp. 105-106.)

BACKGROUND

Israel's journey to the Promised Land was not an easy ride. There were many battles yet to fight by each tribe before they could take their rightful place in Canaan. Though Joshua died, God still intended for the people to follow His instructions to the letter in conquering Canaan and destroying everything, including the people. But Israel chose to do "what was right in [their] own eyes" (Judges 17:6) and left many of the enemy intact. Thus, the Children of Israel assimilated the cultures of the Canaanites, Hittites, Amorites, Perizzites, Hivites, and Jebusites, and these people became a snare unto Israel. The result is that the Book of Judges is a story of repeated compromises by God's people.

Israel's history in Canaan became a destructive "treadmill." Here is the pattern: The people settled into the Promised Land and fell into apostasy by bowing down to the other gods. God raised up an enemy to punish them for their rebellion. After they had suffered and repented, Israel cried out to God for His help. The Lord sent a judge who was responsible for delivering the people out of their oppression into victory. Once the people were saved, they returned to their rebellious ways and the "treadmill" began again. Thus, the Book of Judges is a history of Israel's life between the conquest of Canaan and the monarchy. God raised up a total of 13 judges (eleven are named in the Book of Judges) to help the people understand what God shared with us in Deuteronomy—obedience brings blessings, disobedience brings cursing (Deuteronomy 28).

In today's lesson we meet Deborah, the only woman judge that God sent to assist Israel.

AT-A-GLANCE

1. The Lord Sells Israel (Judges 4:2-3)
2. The Lord Chooses Deborah (vv. 4-9)
3. The Lord Uses Deborah (vv. 14-15, 22)

IN DEPTH

1. The Lord Sells Israel (Judges 4:2-3)

After the death of Ehud, Israel's second judge, the people returned to their idolatrous ways, being influenced by the Canaanites. Because Israel refused to wholly follow the Lord, God's anger against the people resulted in their release "into the hands of spoilers that spoiled them" (Judges 2:14). This time, the "spoiler" was Jabin, a Canaanite king who reigned in Hazor (v. 2). The word "Jabin" actually means "intelligent" in Hebrew, so it was probably a title for the king, rather than his name, just as Pharaoh was a title for Egyptian kings. Hazor was a strategic city in the northern part of Canaan. It is here that Joshua defeated Jabin and his allies by cutting the tendons of their horses and burning their chariots. Joshua also set Hazor on fire and killed all of the kings who had joined Jabin in his revolt against God's people (see Joshua 11:1-15).

Assisting Jabin in "spoiling" the Israelites was Sisera, who served as captain of the Canaanite army. Sisera's headquarters were in Harosheth, which was strategically located near Mount Carmel, near the plain of Esdraelon, which separated Galilee from Samaria in Jesus' time.

Two things are significant about Sisera: He commanded a huge army, consisting of nine hundred chariots; and his oppression of Israel lasted twenty years—almost as long as some of Israel's judges ruled the people.

2. The Lord Chooses Deborah (vv. 4-9)

While Sisera enjoyed his heavy-handed rule over Israel, God demonstrated His mercy toward the people by raising up a deliverer who would be strategic in bringing down Sisera (see Judges 2:18). For the first time in Israel's history, God chose a woman who would lead the people out of bondage into freedom. Deborah was given the assignment to be both a judge and prophet by God. Not only did she render legal decisions for the people who came to her, but she also developed a strategic plan for victory.

Deborah is a prime example of how God can use women for the work of the kingdom. Joel affirms that in the last days, God will pour out His Spirit on everyone, man and woman alike (Joel 2:28). We must be careful that our personal biases don't overshadow God's Word by subjecting women to the "back row."

Deborah's jurisdiction stretched approximately 20 miles, from Ramah to Bethel near mount Ephraim. Although Deborah's husband is mentioned in Scripture, it is obvious that he was not in a position of leadership, since she is the one who "judged Israel at that time" (v. 4).

The name Deborah means "bee" and perhaps emphasized the way this woman organized God's people for battle. Having heard the cries of the people, Deborah sent for Barak, the son of Abinoam and a member of the tribe of Naphtali. Her plan was simple: Barak was to muster an army of 10,000 men from the tribes of Naphtali and Zebulun and lead them to the Kishon River. In the meantime, Deborah would use her considerable influence to draw Sisera and his army to the river, and there, and God would demonstrate His power by helping Barak destroy Sisera's chariots.

The Kishon River is a stream bed that flows westward through Esdraelon and Mount Tabor. The Kishon was muddy and swampy during this time, which made it easier for Barak and his men to overcome Sisera's army (Judges 5:21).

Barak not only understood protocol, but also divine government. He recognized that Deborah was God's spokesperson and the one whom the Lord had chosen to rule Israel. Therefore, he insisted that the only way he would abide by Deborah's plan was if she would go with him into the battle. We can learn a lesson from Barak in our churches today. Some people feel that following leadership is not important, and instead they prefer to do their own thing. However, God has established godly leadership in our local churches, and it would be wise for us to follow their directions—especially as our leaders follow Jesus Christ.

Deborah must have felt frustrated because of Barak's refusal to go to war unless she accompanied him. Even though she had already given him specific instructions on how the battle was to be waged, Barak needed assurance. Deborah's "assurance" came in a form that may not have been pleasing to Barak. In essence she said, "Sure, Barak, I'll go with you. But when the victory comes, you will not receive the honor. The

14

Lord will slay Sisera by the hand of a woman because you refused to follow the specific instructions of another woman" (Judges 4:9, paraphrased).

3. The Lord Uses Deborah (vv. 14-15, 22)

Just as Deborah said, Sisera was drawn to the Kishon River with his army. Barak and his 10,000 men met Sisera at the river. Not only did Sisera encounter Barak, but also the Lord God Himself. The battle was so intense that Sisera left his men and ran away to safety.

Where did Sisera go? He fled to Jael, the wife of Heber, one of Jabin's allies. Just as Deborah predicted, Jael was responsible for killing Sisera. First, she lured him into her tent for "safety" away from the pursuing Israelites. Next, she gave him some milk to drink so that he might become comfortable and fall asleep. Finally, Jael took a hammer and drove a nail into Sisera's temples so by the time Barak arrived, Israel's enemy was dead at the hand of Jael.

Deborah's determination and willingness to be used by God helped her to become an important encourager in the life of Israel while she served as prophetess and judge. Can God use you to be an encourager today?

SEARCH THE SCRIPTURES

1. Who sold the Children of Israel into the hands of Jabin, King of Canaan? (Judges 4:2)
2. What was Deborah's role as leader of Israel? (vv. 4-5)
3. Who did Deborah call and give instructions to regarding Israel's liberation? (v. 6)
4. Why did Barak refuse to obey Deborah? (v. 9)
5. How was Sisera killed? (v. 22)

DISCUSS THE MEANING

1. What is the purpose of a judge in Israel?
2. How does Deborah's position as a judge and prophetess contradict the belief that God doesn't use women in His kingdom?
3. Why do you think Barak insisted that Deborah go with him?
4. Describe and discuss the significance of leaders in the life of the church today.

LESSON IN OUR SOCIETY

With the rise of many women in leadership positions around the country, are women on an equal footing with men today? How does having men and women on the same social and economic level affect our communities, men-women relationships, and so-called traditional family values? Discuss.

MAKE IT HAPPEN

This week, ask God to help you be an encourager to someone who may be afraid to face the future. Perhaps you can share two or three points of today's lesson with that person. You may even help them to see that no matter what the situation, God will enable them to overcome any struggles and battles when they put their trust in Him. Next week, be prepared to share your experience with the class.

FOLLOW THE SPIRIT

What God wants me to do:

_____

_____

REMEMBER YOUR THOUGHTS

Special insights you have learned:

_____

_____

MORE LIGHT ON THE TEXT
Judges 4:2-3, 4-9, 14-15, 22

4:2 And the Lord sold them into the hand of Jabin king of Canaan, that reigned in Hazor; the captain whose host was Sisera, which dwelt in the Harosheth of the Gentiles.

The verse begins "And the Lord sold them into the hand" (Hebrew *Wayimkareem Yahweh bayad*). God "sold" Israel, or handed Israel over as one would a slave, because of their disobedience. The word *wayimkareem* has within it the word *makar*, which is the Hebrew word translated "to sell," but literally it means to turn something into commodity. Thus rather than being grounded in divine autonomy, they became merchandisable and as such merely things. One could also read this to mean that God surrendered them to the enemy. They were sent away from the presence of God.

Note also the use of the phrase "into the hand" (Hebrew *bayad*). Israel was supposed to be in the hands of God (Hebrew *yad*, pronounced **yawd**), which means that God's door was to be always open to them as God's anointed ones. It also indicates the availability of divine power, means, direction, and confidence. By extension the word *yad* can mean to consecrate or to have credit or to be in one's custody. But as used here, it implies dominion, forced fellowship or labor conjoined with pain derived from misuse of power. God sold them into the hand of a human being. They were sold into the hand of Jabin, or *Yabiyn*, which in Hebrew probably means the "clever one." Note the progression: They left the hand of God, were sold or transferred into a human hand and were given over into the hands of the nations. In other words, God was going to allow Jabin and his people to oppress Israel as punishment for sin. This action is the essence of what we find in Galatians 6:7, 8 of the New Testament where the Bible speaks of "sowing and reaping." Whenever believers disobey God, we are voluntarily placing ourselves outside of His will. Thus, without God's protection, we will suffer from harmful situations which result as natural consequences or from His punishment (see Hebrews 12:5-7).

The city of Hazor was located within the land of the tribe of Naphtali. Hazor was near the eastern border which adjoined the land of the tribe of Mannasseh. The land of the tribe of Zebulun was adjacent to the southwest border of Naphtali. Obviously, non-Hebrew people lived in various areas on the land which was captured by Israel under Joshua. Therefore, Sisera's base of operations in Harosheth was located among the northern tribes of Israel, and he could easily reach out to torment them. The king named Jabin in this text is a descendant of another king, also named Jabin, who had previously been defeated by Joshua (see Joshua 11:1, 10). This passage marks the beginning of the cycle of rebellion, punishment, and restoration that the Children of Israel will go through for the next millennium.

3 And the children of Israel cried unto the LORD: for he had nine hundred chariots of iron; and twenty years he mightily oppressed the children of Israel.

Sisera had a great advantage in battle due to many iron chariots. His men could drive through a swarm of Israelite foot soldiers and kill them with swords or trample them with their horses. They also had sharp blades attached to the wheels to injure the enemy as they turned. Sisera's men were therefore less vulnerable because of the iron protection surrounding them. The mismatch in weaponry must have become appealing to Sisera because for "twenty years he mightily oppressed the children of Israel."

Israel was true to the pattern they had established and begged the God whom they had rejected to help them out once again. One might wonder if they tacked a familiar modern-day refrain onto their plea, i.e., "Lord, if you help us out of this jam, we'll never disobey You again." Many a Christian has said those words only to repeat the same destructive behavior again and again. Some things never change.

The text reads "And the children of Israel cried unto the LORD" (Hebrew *wayitsaquw beney-y'Israel el-Yahweh*) Here we see the reaction which will become a dominant theme of the book of Judges: "the children of Israel cried unto the Lord." The word "cry" here is more than shedding tears of regret. The Hebrew phrase *wayitsaquw* meaning "they cried" has as its root the word *tsa`aq* (pronounced, **tsaw-ak'**), which means to shriek or to cry out in pain in such a way that this proclamation of one's hurt calls together an assembly. One could read this verse as "they cried out bitterly with a bitter cry." The next part of the verse shows that this reading is correct as it says "he mightily oppressed the children of Israel" (*wahu lachaats et-beney y'Israel bachaazaqaah esriym shaanaah*). Note that the reason for this mighty cry—this shrieking, this deep sobbing, this convulsion of the whole body of Israel which shook heaven's door—was because of the enemy's might (Hebrew *chezqah*, pronounced **khez-kaw'**), which was grounded in technological superiority. But it must be remembered that their prevailing power was not because of their technology but because the Lord had allowed them to prevail over Israel. Israel was so overwhelmed with the war machine of Jabin and Sisera that they had to cry out to the Lord. The pain had become too much to bear. As the passage suggests, after they had walked out of God's hand into the hand of God's enemy, they found themselves without a place to stand.

4 And Deborah, a prophetess, the wife of Lapidoth, she judged Israel at that time.

Deborah is described in this passage with three words a "prophetess" and a "wife" and a "judge." The first title related to God's direct call upon her life, the second spoke to their familial relationship, and the third related to her role as the leader of Israel. This tri-dimensional relationship speaks to all of us today who are called to fulfill more than one role. It speaks especially to sisters who in this day have to work and be mother and assume spiritual leadership both in the church and at home. Deborah is called prophetess, *ishaah nabiyaah.* She is among the many women of Scripture (such as Miriam in Exodus 15:20, and Hulda the wife of Shallum in 2 Kings 22:14) whose gifts were so powerful that they could not be ignored by the establishment. We read that she was "a wife of Lapidoth." Reading this from our current liberal world view, we may miss the radical nature of this statement. Being a prophetess and a wife were not mutually exclusive. Furthermore, she was chosen by God to judge the nation of Israel (*shoop-a-taah Y'Israel*). This was not a transitional position of leadership until God could find someone else more suitable; she was the permanent ruler or established leader of Israel. She was the chief judge of the supreme of court of Israel. Whenever there was a dispute among the people that heads of the villages were unable to settle, it was appealed to her presence. This was in line with the process established by Moses under the influence of his father-in-law Jethro (Deuteronomy 17:8).

God chose a woman to be the judge of Israel during Jabin's period of oppression. This should at least humble, if not silence, anyone who says that God will not choose a woman to accomplish any particular divine purpose. Some scholars maintain that the name "Deborah" means "the bee" in Hebrew. This association may arise from her exhibited industriousness and her untiring service to her people. But it must be remembered that the ending "rah" or "ra" is an Egypto-African

ending of names with divine significance. Thus, we may want to read Deborah's name as meaning God's sting. As a prophetess, God chose to have a very intimate relationship with her. He revealed His thoughts and wisdom to her through the power of His Spirit as He would with any male prophet.

5 And she dwelt under the palm tree of Deborah between Ramah and Bethel in mount Ephraim: and the children of Israel came up to her for judgment.

Deborah dwelt under the palms between Ramah (er RÉm; see Joshua 18:25) and Bethel in the tribe of Benjamin, upon the mountains of Ephraim. The Hebrew text begins with *W'hiy yoshebet,* translated "and she dwelt." The word "dwelt" is the translated from the Hebrew *yoshebet* rooted in the word *yashab yaw-shab* meaning to sit down as a judge. It could also mean to set out in ambush against enemies. This wording could also mean that Deborah remained in the land when everyone was leaving. But here it can also mean that she married and settled down. Not only did Deborah continue to dwell where others had left because of oppression, she also endured much hardship in order to establish her habitation. There is another meaning which may also be derived from the use of the Hebrew word *yawshab* which is to be still and to keep one's house in order. This is a spiritualism in Israel as in many African cultures for seeking the face of God and preparing for direction from the Most High.

The Bible also gives us the location of Deborah's dwelling. We are told that she dwelt under the Deborah-palm between Ramah (er RÉm; see Joshua 18:25) and Bethel (Joshua 7:2) in the tribe of Benjamin, upon the mountains of Ephraim. The palm where she sat in judgment (cf. Psalm 9:5) was named after her, the Deborah-palm or the palm tree of Deborah. The Israelites went up to her there to obtain justice. The expression "came up" is applied here (as in Deuteronomy 17:8) to the place of justice as a spiritual height, independent of the fact that the place referred to here really stood upon an eminent mountain.

Palm trees were significant in ancient times

because they supplied many things. They bore edible fruit after six to eight years, and were productive for a century. Their sap could be made into wine, and their leaf fibers were woven into ropes and riggings. These activities still exist among west Africans. Palm trees were good for timber, and their leaves also were used to make brushes, mats, bags, baskets, and roofs. Deborah's base under a palm tree could also be used to symbolize God's purpose for her life and the fact that her life would sustain Israel, like the palm tree in those days.

We read further "and the children of Israel came up to her for judgment" (Hebrew *waya'aluw eeleyha'a baneey Y'Israel lamispaat*). The idea that they went up may refer to the fact that her location was on the hill. The Hebrew `alah (pronounced **aw-law'**) means primarily to ascend or to be in a high place. In fact, it represents the act of mounting to a higher level both literally and figuratively. Therefore, this phrase may also mean that the Children of Israel exalted her. In other words, she was excellent. When used of a judge, it could also carry with it the sense of taking one's case to higher authority. So the phrase "went up" could be similar to our modern process of taking a case up to the Supreme Court. Thus, it can have both a literal and figurative meaning in this verse.

They did not just go up, they went up for a purpose. They went for "judgment" according to the King James Version. The Hebrew word translated "judgment" is the word *mishpat* (**mish-pawt'**) which means a proper verdict pronounced by a judge. She was there specifically to give a sentence regarding guilt or innocence as it relates to human or divine law. Her authority defined which act deserved what penalty. The Israelites went to Deborah for justice. The people had faith in her judgment, apparently recognizing that God spoke to her quite intimately. They sought her guidance on civil and spiritual issues. Perhaps, they even went up to ask her to intercede with God to relieve the oppression that their actions had produced.

6 And she sent and called Barak the son of Abinoam out of Kedesh-naphtali, and said unto him, Hath not the LORD God of Israel commanded, saying, Go and draw toward mount Tabor, and take with thee ten thousand men of the children of Naphtali and of the children of Zebulun?

As a prophetess and spokesperson for God, Deborah could speak for God and relate God's promise to answer the prayers of His people. We read that "she sent and called Barak" (Hebrew *Watishlach watiqraa l'a Baaraaq*). Note that the word "sent," translated from *watishlach* which has its root in the word *shalach* (pronounced **shaw-lakh'**), can mean that she sent away for Barak. It could also mean that in her capacity as judge she appointed Barak. In traditional African cultures, especially among ancient Ibos, warriors lived in the forest to protect the community from their violent tendencies. This may have been the case here, especially considering the fact that at this time any Israelite warrior was a threat to the oppressor. Thus, this phrase can mean that Deborah searched the stretch of the land to find this warrior.

Not only did Deborah send for him, but it was a specific call. The Hebrew word *watiqraa*, root word *qara* (pronounced **kaw-raw'**) has the idea of accosting a person. Since Barak was a warrior, it took more than a mere word to call him out. The word for "call" can also mean that they cried to Barak. But there is also a sense of honor implied in this call. Barak was being invited to divine fame. He was being called to be God's warrior guest. By sending for Barak in this way, Deborah was showing a willingness to share her power with this warrior for the salvation of her people.

Barak "was the son of Abinoam out of Kedesh Naphtali;" this phrase is an important identity trait. It was important in those days to know one's family lineage. He came out of "Kedesh" (Hebrew *Qedesh*, **keh'-desh**), which according to scholars may be derived from the Hebrew word *qadash* meaning a sanctum. This was probably one of those places of refuge God commanded Moses to build for those who were guilty of manslaughter (Numbers 35:10-15). Barak was probably in a protected place of refuge. The name Barak means a shooting swiftness, lightning, or flashing sword. Note also that dwelling in the forest sanctum of Naphtali, Barak was closer to the enemy. He probably had been through some skirmishes with the enemy, thus earning the name Barak. Napthali was an ideal location for war with Sisera'a army. By the grace of God, the hills of Naphtali gave Israel a natural advantage.

Deborah did not just send for Barak, but she sent a word from the Lord: "Hath not the LORD God of Israel commanded" (Hebrew *watomer ilayu halo tsiwah Yahweh Eloheey Israeel*). The Hebrew word *watomer* contains within it the word *amar* (pronounced **aw-mar'**) meaning to say or to answer. However, it is often used by the prophets to indicate divine appointment. When it is used in the same sentence as the name of God, it becomes a divine challenge or charge. Deborah's statement implies a command, a divine imperative. This Hebraism would not have been lost on Barak. Barak must listen because what she asked him to do was what the Lord had determined and willed expressly. As judge, Deborah could have said, "Barak, your people need saving, go do it!" But she invoked the most high God, the same God to whom the Children of Israel had been praying. Her statement implied that God had answered their prayer. The way Deborah spoke to Barak also implied that God had already spoken to Barak about defending his people. The statement "Hath not the LORD God of Israel commanded" suggested that Barak was disobeying the command of the Lord. We do not know when God first spoke or called Barak, but we know that Deborah was implicitly using her status as judge to pass sentence on Barak. The sentence was "you are living in disobedience to God's command."

In verse 8, we can see that Barak was not surprised by being commissioned by God as others were, such as Moses (see Exodus 3:11; 4:10) and Gideon (see Judges 6:15). Barak was probably like many Christians today who desire to do great things for God but need a "confirmation" of God's agreement with their plans. Many times God confirms His will in a more subtle fashion than He employed with Barak. We must grow in the knowledge of God through His Word so that we can clearly discern those times when He is silently screaming volumes of confirmation. What has the Lord God "said, and in saying commanded"? The first part of the command was "Go and draw toward Mount Tabor." Barak was to walk and to

carry himself to a different place (*yalak*, pronounced **yaw-lak'**). Not only was he commanded to depart, this Hebrew word can also imply that he was to grow to the point where he could lead. He was to let down his guard and trust someone other than himself. So far his fighting has been as an individual. He was a lone warrior, but now he must spread the burden of deliverance. Note also the word "draw" from the Hebrew *mashak* (**mawshak'**) can mean to plant oneself or to make a prolonged sound as in a musical arrangement. In Israel's military history, this is similar to the use of the ram's horn to call the people into battle. The word translated "draw" can also refer to the process of developing a theme. Militarily, it can mean a tactical delay meant to confuse the enemy while one continues a different course of action. But *mashak* can mean to scatter as in sowing seeds. In this sense, the word "draw" could also refer to the number of people Barak must draft into his army. He was commanded to gather 10,000 men from that tribe and the neighboring tribe of Zebulun to vanquish Sisera's "host" (v. 2) or "multitude" (v. 7).

The tone of this whole passage suggests that Barak had already demonstrated that he was a great strategist. Thus this call to arms was a prophetic confirmation of God's choice. God's method of selection differs from ours because He knows what lies on the "inside" (see 1 Samuel 16:7).

7 And I will draw unto thee to the river Kishon Sisera, the captain of Jabin's army, with his chariots and his multitude; and I will deliver him into thine hand.

In verse 6 God told Barak to draw 10,000 men. Barak was to use his charisma to draw others to do battle for the Lord. But here, God is the one who draws. God says "I will draw unto thee . . . ." The Hebrew phrase *umishaaktiy eleeka* is a divine promise. This "I will" is directed both to God's power over the enemy and to His concern for the people. God will not only draw Sisera to Barak, but God will make sure that his formidable weapons of warfare are left intact. The second promise of "I will" in verse 7 is directed to both Barak and Sisera, "I will deliver him" (Hebrew *untatiyhu*) referring to Sisera and "into your hand" (Hebrew *bayadeaka*) referring to Barak. Note the double edge of this deliverance. The deliverance of Sisera into the hand of Barak contained an implicit promise for the deliverance of Barak from the hand of Jabin and Sisera.

8 And Barak said unto her, If thou wilt go with me, then I will go: but if thou wilt not go with me, then I will not go.

So far, we have heard from Deborah whose message came directly from God. Now in this verse we hear from Barak. Note that Barak does not say anything directly about the Lord in this response. Rather Barak says "if you go with me, I will go" (Hebrew *Im teelkiy imiy wahaalaakatiy*). Remember that in this period of Israel's history, Deborah was the mouthpiece of God. Barak's statement derives from the belief that God was with Deborah; it was a sign that God was going with him. Barak's statement is similar to the one made by Moses after God told him to take the people into the Promised Land, but that he would not go with them (Exodus 33:1-16). There was an issue of faith involved here. If Deborah had really heard from God and truly believed her own message, then she should have no problem joining Barak on the battlefield. In that context, his statement would challenge Deborah to prove the reliability of her predictions. Barak's whole reply indicates his desire for God's presence and wise counsel in battle.

God's Spirit was obviously working in Deborah. To have her near would be like having a spirit-filled, mature, and obedient Christian at our side today. For, in Old Testament times, the Holy Spirit "came upon" individuals whom God anointed for a particular purpose (see Judges 3:10; 13:25; 14:6, 19; 15:14; and 16:14 for examples). By contrast, we now have the Holy Spirit permanently within us in order to lead us, teach us, and guide us (see 1 Corinthians 6:19 and John 14:16, 17, 26). So, a case can be made that Barak was merely seeking a tangible way to have God near in a moment of great need.

9 And she said, I will surely go with thee: notwithstanding the journey that thou takest shall not be for thine honour; for the LORD shall sell

Sisera into the hand of a woman. And Deborah rose, and went with Barak to Kedesh.

Deborah responds to Barak with "I will surely go with thee" (Hebrew *haalok eeleek imak*). The word "surely" is translated from the primitive root which may be related to the word *halak* and is probably connected with the Hebrew word *yalak* meaning "to walk." It could mean to behave oneself in a specific manner. It can also signal a commitment to be another's continual confidant. This indicates an exercise in self-confidence. It indicates that some promise, either positive or negative, is about to follow. In relationship to the word "walk," it speaks to the surefootedness with which one walks a known path. Thus when Deborah begins with "surely" Barak anticipates a promise. It is a Hebraism similar to Jesus' use of the phrase "verily, verily." This word "surely" is followed with a promise which mimics divine blessing: "I will go with thee." Though Deborah does not invoke the name of the Lord here, these conversations must be understood in the context of what God had said to Barak through the mouth of Deborah. Her firm response was indicative of her certainty that God would always do what He promised. Numbers 23:19 says, "God is not a man, that he should lie." And, by now, every maturing Christian should know the obvious answer to God's question in Jeremiah 32:27, i.e., "Behold, I am the Lord, the God of all flesh: is there any thing too hard for me?" Of course, the answer to that question is a resounding, "No!" Deborah knew her God. But note that Deborah adds to the promise a rebuke for Barak's lack of faith.

Note the way Deborah uses words here: "notwithstanding the journey that thou takes shall not be for thine honor" (*epes kiy lo tihayeh tipaartakaa al haderek asher ataah holeek*). The promise to go contains the idea of walking which refers to the ability of the foot to hold firm to ground. But the word "notwithstanding" (Hebrew *'ephesh eh'-fes*) metaphorically refers to cessation, or to the ankle without the foot. It could also mean "less than nothing" or "to make a thing nought." Thus we could read this passage to say "you are taking this journey for naught." He was about to take a journey without believing in the God who commanded. One wonders if Barak's failure to believe God had something to do with the fact that Deborah was a woman. The word "journey," as used here, is taken from the Hebrew word *haderek* derived from *derek* (**deh'-rek**), which is akin to saying "this road you are about to travel." It is a figure of speech for a course of life or mode of action undertaken for a specific purpose. In Israel, as in other ancient cultures, war was a journey undertaken for personal glory or honor. The goal of war was not just deliverance but the glorification of the successful warrior. The Hebrew word for "honor" is *tipharah* (pronounced **tif-aw-raw'**). Some scholars connect it with *tiph'ereth* (**tif-eh'-reth**), which mean to decorate or ornament literally or figuratively. This war will not result in Barak's decoration. It can also mean that Deborah was trying to warn him that he would not be praised for bravery by other warriors if he allowed a woman to lead the battle. Barak would be unable to boast about his victory, as was the custom in those days, "for the LORD shall sell Sisera into the hand of a woman." No matter what Barak's religious motive may have been, Deborah was also concerned about how Barak would be perceived. This is evident by her expression of care for the reputation of Barak. In verse 9, the oppression of Israel at the hand of Jabin comes full circle. Deborah says "the Lord shall sell Sisera . . . ." Note that Judges 4:2 began with the fact that God "sold Israel into the hand" of Jabin, the warrior but here in a prophetic move the Lord will "sell" (*makar*, pronounced **maw-kar'**) or merchandise and surrender the enemy back into the hand of an Israelite woman. Deborah's prophetic statement was fulfilled and the victory was won by another woman.

Deborah, the judge and prophetess of God, had no secondthoughts about what she should do. "And Deborah rose, and went with Barak to Kedesh." The King James Version reads "Deborah arose and went" but the Hebrew does not include the word "arose"; rather, it uses the word `alah (**aw-law'**) meaning to ascend or to mount. Deborah rose. Her decisive action should be a reminder to modern Christians to be willing to help our brothers and sisters shoulder any load they face. This willing attitude combined with quick action will become evidence of our commitment as Christians to act as one body in Christ (see 1 Corinthians 12:14-26 and Romans 15:1, 2).

14 And Deborah said unto Barak, Up; for this is the day in which the LORD hath delivered Sisera into thine hand: is not the LORD gone out before thee? So Barak went down from mount Tabor, and ten thousand men after him.

In this verse, Deborah continues to speak to Barak. This time the words are not those of consultation but of command. The command was "Up" (Hebrew *quwm*) meaning to rise and to take a stand. Barak was now being commanded to become powerful or to go to the scene of the conflict. This is like saying "quick Barak quick." "Up" may also mean to maintain oneself and confirm oneself in the words which have been discussed. With this command, Barak was being called effectively to carry out the command of the Lord. There is a sense of urgency in Deborah's statement. "This is the day in which the LORD hath delivered Sisera into thine hand." The Hebrew reads thus; *qum! kiy tseh hayom asher naatan yhvah et cisraa bayadeeka*. The Hebrew word for "day" *yowm* (**yome**), is said to be derived from a primitive term meaning to be hot. Though it literally has to do with the warm hours of the day from sunrise to sunset, figuratively it signals a space of time conducive for a particular act or task. It can also mean that the plan had come of age.

There is a sense in which the phrasing reminds Barak of a prior divine promise. "Barak, do you remember what the Lord promised?" Deborah seems to be asking. It is as though Deborah is telling Barak that this day is the continuance of the victory already given him by the word of the Lord. In other words, at that moment his victory was being birthed into reality. Deborah also uses the phrase "in which the Lord hath delivered." The Lord's deliverance is referred to in the past tense. The word translated "delivered" here is *nathan* which usually means to give. In this context it could also mean several things. We could take it to mean appoint; God has appointed Barak and assigned him to avenge the suffering of the people. God has committed the enemy into the hands of Barak. One could also read it to mean granted a request. It was God who gave the enemy into the hands of Barak, the warrior in answer to the prayers of the people. The time had come when God would recompense Sisera and requite his army for their evil, and God would restore Israel and send her forth with victory. So when Deborah orders Barak "Up!" it is her reminder that the awesome power of God in operation was sufficient for him. Not only does she say that the Lord had delivered Sisera into the hand of Barak, Deborah poses a rhetorical question of faith: "Is not the Lord gone out before thee?" Just in case Barak was still struggling, he gets affirmation that the Lord had gone before him.

15 And the LORD discomfited Sisera, and all his chariots, and all his host, with the edge of the sword before Barak; so that Sisera lighted down off his chariot, and fled away on his feet.

The battle was a quick one, and the Lord did as He had promised. "Discomfited" means put in commotion or agitate greatly. In Hebrew, the word *hamam* (pronounced **hawman**) signifies a noisy movement meant to cause confusion to the hearer. God went to break their ranks and it was the Lord, not Barak, who discomfited the enemy. God was the One who threw the enemy into the tumultuous state that made them easy opponents for Israel to defeat. God did the major portion of the fighting with His supernatural power (see also Exodus 7:3, 13 and Joshua 10:10). God's power was highlighted even more by the repetitious mentioning of Sisera's vast army ("host") and all their chariots. Sisera realized, like so many other enemies before and since his time, that there indeed was ". . . nothing too hard for God" (Jeremiah 32:17). So, when Sisera saw the irresistible power of God destroy his forces, he took off running. We read ". . . Sisera lighted down off his chariot, and fled away on his feet." The word from the King James Version "lighted" is translated from the Hebrew *wayareed* taken from the root word *yarad*, (**yaw-rad'**) meaning to descend. Given the Hebrew play on words, this could also mean that he went downwards in terms of his ability to rule over the house of Israel. From a geographical viewpoint, he did descend to a lower region which was the valley of the two mountains where the war was fought. His aim may have been to flee to the border before the enemy could bring him down. This

oppressor of the people of God has just been cast down. Sisera's fall from power from his chariot and from the territory illustrates God's power. By God's commands, the Israelites "take him down." Not only did he come down, but he set out on foot.

22 And, behold, as Barak pursued Sisera, Jael came out to meet him, and said unto him, Come, and I will show thee the man whom thou seekest. And when he came into her tent, behold, Sisera lay dead, and the nail was in his temples.

Now, Barak got to see that everything God had promised through Deborah had come true, even down to the final details. Her words that ". . . the Lord shall sell Sisera into the hand of a woman" must have flashed through his mind. Again, Barak did not become inflamed with jealousy or resentment because he was seemingly upstaged by a woman. Instead, he must have felt both relieved that the enemy was vanquished and filled with awe and praise at the wondrous power of God.

DAILY BIBLE READINGS

M: Canaanites Oppress the Israelites
Judges 4:1-5
T: The Leadership of Deborah
Judges 4:4-10
W: Defeat of the Canaanites
Judges 4:11-16
T: Death of Sisera
Judges 4:17-24
F: The Song of Deborah
Judges 5:1-9
S: Praise for the Tribes
Judges 5:10-23
S: God's Enemies Will Perish
Judges 5:24-31

TEACHING TIPS

September 10
Bible Study Guide 2

1. Words You Should Know

A. Valor (Judges 6:12) Hebrew *Chayil*—Might, strength, power, able, valiant, virtuous. Mainly used to refer to strength provided by an army or wealth.

B. Miracles (v. 13) Hebrew *Pala*—To be extraordinary, wonderful, miraculous, or astonishing. The basic meaning is of something wonderful or of something that causes a wonderful thing to happen. Miracles give a clear-cut exhibition of God's capable care of Israel.

C. Midianite (v. 14) Hebrew *Midyan*—A descendant of Midian, who was a son of Abraham and his concubine Keturah (Genesis 25:1-2). The Midianites were counted among the people of the East (Judges 6:3, 33; 7:12); a general designation for the nomadic inhabitants of the Syrian and Arabian deserts.

2. Teacher Preparation

A. Prepare for today's lesson by reading the DAILY BIBLE READINGS throughout the week. Also examine the FOCAL VERSES and look up any confusing or difficult words in a Bible dictionary or concordance. Read through the lesson using the AT-A-GLANCE outline as your guide.

B. Materials needed: Bible, chalk or magic marker, and blackboard.

3. Starting the Lesson

A. Before students arrive, write the words GIDEON and ANGEL OF THE LORD on the blackboard.

B. Once students are seated, ask them to share specific characteristics which they are familiar with for each term.

C. Read the IN FOCUS story and open the class with prayer, using the LESSON AIM as the focus of the prayer.

4. Getting into the Lesson

A. Have a student read the BACKGROUND section of the lesson as well as THE PEOPLE, PLACES, AND TIMES.

B. Allow students a few minutes to silently read the IN DEPTH commentary, making specific notes on paper to be shared later with the class when they begin to answer the SEARCH THE SCRIPTURES questions.

C. Allow students to answer the DISCUSS THE MEANING questions. Have students list whether or not the answer is directly related to Gideon or to the angel of the Lord. Then ask students to explain their answers.

5. Relating the Lesson to Life

A. Give students a few minutes to brainstorm and come up with ideas for the LESSON IN OUR SOCIETY section.

B. Ask students to share any insights they may have gleaned from the lesson. Then ask how they can apply these truths to their lives today.

6. Arousing Action

A. Give students a few minutes to read and expound on the MAKE IT HAPPEN idea. Have them write down specific names of people they may be able to share with this week.

B. Have them commit to taking the lesson out of the classroom into the world.

C. Close the class with prayer.

WORSHIP GUIDE

For the Superintendent or Teacher
Theme: Gideon
Theme Song: "If You Can Use Me, Lord"
Scripture: Isaiah 6:1-9
Song: "Look What the Lord Has Done"
Meditation: Father, I thank You for Your promise of helping Your people in every situation. Help me never to doubt You or Your Word. In Jesus' name, Amen.

GIDEON

Bible Background • JUDGES 6—8
Printed Text • JUDGES 6:11-14; 7:1-3, 20-21
Devotional Reading • JOSHUA 1:1-9

LESSON AIM

By the end of the lesson, students will be able to summarize Gideon's challenge from the Lord, list at least two things that inspired Gideon to follow the Lord, and determine to follow the leading of the Lord in their lives.

KEEP IN MIND

". . . Go in this thy might, and thou shalt save Israel from the hand of the Midianites: have not I sent thee?" (Judges 6:14).

FOCAL VERSES

Judges 6:11 And there came an angel of the LORD, and sat under an oak which was in Ophrah, that pertained unto Joash the Abiezrite: and his son Gideon threshed wheat by the winepress, to hide it from the Midianites.

12 And the angel of the LORD appeared unto him, and said unto him, The LORD is with thee, thou mighty man of valour.

13 And Gideon said unto him, Oh my Lord, if the LORD be with us, why then is all this befallen us? and where be all his miracles which our fathers told us of, saying, Did not the LORD bring us up from Egypt? but now the LORD hath forsaken us, and delivered us into the hands of the Midianites.

14 And the LORD looked upon him, and said, Go in this thy might, and thou shalt save Israel from the hand of the Midianites: have not I sent thee?

7:1 Then Jerubbaal, who is Gideon, and all the people that were with him, rose up early, and pitched beside the well of Harod: so that the host of the Midianites were on the north side of them, by

LESSON OVERVIEW

LESSON AIM
KEEP IN MIND
FOCAL VERSES
IN FOCUS
THE PEOPLE, PLACES,
AND TIMES
BACKGROUND
AT-A-GLANCE
IN DEPTH
SEARCH THE SCRIPTURES
DISCUSS THE MEANING
LESSON IN OUR SOCIETY
MAKE IT HAPPEN
FOLLOW THE SPIRIT
REMEMBER YOUR THOUGHTS
MORE LIGHT ON THE TEXT
DAILY BIBLE READINGS

the hill of Moreh, in the valley.

2 And the LORD said unto Gideon, The people that are with thee are too many for me to give the Midianites into their hands, lest Israel vaunt themselves against me, saying, Mine own hand hath saved me.

3 Now therefore go to, proclaim in the ears of the people, saying, Whosoever is fearful and afraid, let him return and depart early from mount Gilead. And there returned on the people twenty and two thousand; and there remained ten thousand.

20 And the three companies blew the trumpets, and brake the pitchers, and held the lamps in their left hands, and the trumpets in their right hands to blow withal: and they cried, The sword of the LORD, and of Gideon.

21 And they stood every man in his place round about the camp: and all the host ran, and cried, and fled.

IN FOCUS

Gary Peters was the smallest man to ever play Division I basketball for Williams University. At 5 feet tall, many of the other players "towered" over Gary, trying their best to intimidate him. But Gary was a smart college basketball player. Not only did he use his short size and speed to his advantage, but he also became the most proficient point guard in the history of Williams U.

At first, Gary was reluctant and felt too inadequate to try out for the basketball team, convinced that he would not make it. However, before going to Williams, Gary's parents shared with him some important truths. "Never be reluctant to accept the challenges of life. While you may be short in size, God will give you creative and unusual ways of achieving success on the basketball court."

Now, as Gary stood on the podium next to David Stern, the commissioner of the National Basketball Association, after being selected as the first-round draft choice for the Houston Rockets, he remembered his parents' words. In spite of all the risks and challenges Gary faced at Williams University, he is now a professional basketball player. The first step to his achievement was overcoming all feelings of inadequacy and doubt.

Sometimes, we are faced with challenges that seem well beyond our abilities. We may feel reluctant and even inadequate to try. But we need to remember that as believers in the Lord Jesus Christ, God is on our side. In today's Bible lesson, we will be introduced to Gideon, a man who felt inadequate. But God had another idea.

THE PEOPLE, PLACES, AND TIMES

Abiezer. A son of Manasseh who received an inheritance in Canaan (Joshua 17:2) and who headed the clan of the Abiezerites to which Gideon belonged (Judges 6:11). The name also occurs as Iezer (Numbers 26:30).

(Harper's Bible Dictionary, Paul J. Achtemeier, San Francisco: Harper and Row Publishers, 1986 p. 4.)

Angel of the Lord. (or Angel of Yahweh) A figure appearing frequently in the Old Testament (Genesis 16:7-13; 22:11; Exodus 3:2; Numbers 22:22; Judges 13:3; Zechariah 1:11; 3:1, to cite only a few references) and also in the New Testament (Luke 2:9-15). References to this figure usually occur when something dramatic and meaningful is about to happen, generally with serious consequences either good or ill for God's people. The angel of the Lord seems to have been understood as being distinct from other angels, and in the earlier Old Testament literature it appears to be almost another designation for God. In most cases, however, the angel of the Lord served primarily as a messenger from God to the people to prepare the way for God's appearance and activity.

(The Harper Bible Dictionary, Paul J. Achtemeier, Editor, San Francisco: Harper and Row Publishers, 1986 p. 30)

BACKGROUND

Gideon is the fourth judge that God used to deliver the Children of Israel during their oppression in Canaan. Just to review, God's people lived a "treadmill" life while in the Promised Land. The Bible declares that they sinned against the Lord by practicing idolatry. Because Israel would not obey God, He delivered the people into the hands of their enemies. After the people suffered for a while, they would cry out to the Lord who would raise up a deliverer or judge. The judge would save the people from the hand of the enemy. Once Israel experienced peace, they would go right back to idolatry and the treadmill would start over again (see Judges 2:11-23).

After Deborah and Barak's victory against Sisera and Jabin (Judges 4:11—5:31), the people returned to their idolatrous ways. Thus, God allowed the Midianites, the Amalekites, and even "the children of the east" (Judges 6:3) to oppress Israel for seven years. Not only did the people flee from their land, but the Midianites also destroyed all of their crops and their livestock. For Israel, it seemed to be a hopeless situation. But God had promised to send a judge to help the people, and it was now time for the deliverer to be identified and get to work.

AT-A-GLANCE

1. The Angel of the Lord Visits Gideon (Judges 6:11-14)
2. The Lord Commissions Gideon (Judges 7:1-3)
3. The Lord Uses Gideon (vv. 20-21)

IN DEPTH

1. The Angel of the Lord Visits Gideon (Judges 6:11-14)

At the appointed time arranged by God, an

angel of the Lord appeared unto Gideon. Gideon was the son of Joash, the Abiezrite, and a descendant of the tribe of Manasseh (Joshua 17:1-2). The angel sat under an oak tree and watched as Gideon separated and beat the wheat near his father's winepress. Gideon must have been working hard and fast because he was trying desperately to finish the work so he could hide the wheat from the Midianites before they found it.

Joash lived in Ophrah, a town that belonged to the Abiezerite clan which was located near Bethel (Judges 6:15).

As Gideon continued working, the angel of the Lord finally made himself known to Gideon by approaching and speaking. Who was the angel? The Hebrew word is *malakh* and its root meaning is to dispatch someone as a deputy, a messenger or a herald. It is quite possible that the angel was a Christophany, the pre-incarnate appearance of Jesus Christ, because of the words that he spoke: "The LORD is with thee, thou mighty man of valor."

Gideon doesn't seem surprised to be talking with an angel. In fact, it seems as though Gideon releases his frustration on the angel. First, Gideon asks the same question that all believers have asked the Lord when trouble comes our way: "If God be with us, why then is all this befallen us?" How often have we felt the same way when things don't go our way? But we need to remember Jesus' words, "I am with you always even unto the end of the world" (Matthew 28:20). Satan would have us to believe that when calamity strikes, Jesus has taken a hike! But that is not true. Jesus also told us that He would send the Comforter who would be with us and in us (John 14:16-17). So it really doesn't matter what the devil says. Just because we FEEL like Jesus has left us doesn't mean it's true.

Secondly, Gideon asked the angel, "What happened to all the miracles which our father told us of, saying, did not the LORD bring us up from Egypt?" In essence, Gideon was reminding the angel of what he had been taught: that God is a miracle-worker. Contrary to what many people believe, God is still in the "miracle-working" business. Every day that we arise, we experience the miracle-working power of God. Every time someone is brought out of darkness into the marvelous light, God has worked a miracle. We must understand that God is supernatural and we are not. He is omnipotent, omniscient, and omnipresent. There is nothing too hard for God. While we may not witness miracles in our own lives, we shouldn't limit God based on our understanding of Him. Just as He parted the Red Sea and brought the Children of Israel through the wilderness, He is still bringing His children through the wilderness of life's situations today.

The third point that Gideon raised is similar to our response when we throw a "pity party" for ourselves: "But now the LORD hath forsaken us and delivered us into the hands of the Midianites" (v. 13). While it was true that the Lord allowed the Midianites to oppress Israel, it was not true that the Lord had forsaken His people. God sent His angel to visit Gideon!

Instead of looking down when we feel forsaken and all alone, we need to look up to heaven and realize that our strength and help comes from Almighty God who has promised to keep us even as He promised to keep Israel (Psalm 121:1-8).

Gideon was unprepared for the angel's next statement. As far as Gideon was concerned, if deliverance was to come for Israel, it would come at the hands of another servant, not his hands. However, God had another plan. Since it was Gideon who asked the questions and was concerned about the people, what better person to send but him? After Gideon had finished his "pity party," the angel gave him a specific charge. Gideon was to go, and through his determination and reliance on the Lord, he would be the one to deliver Israel out of the hands of the Midianites. Have you ever said, "God ought to do something about this or that problem?" Maybe God wants to use us to solve the problem. Maybe God wants to send us into the situation so that we become a catalyst for victory. Rather than complaining, we need to get involved. If we are not willing to be part of the solution, we may be part of the problem.

2. The Lord Commissions Gideon (Judges 7:1-3)

After Gideon was convinced that he was the one to save Israel (Judges 6:38-40), he mustered a large army of men and left Manasseh to travel to

Moreh near Jezreel. There, the Midianites were stationed on the northern portion of Moreh, and Gideon (who was also called Jerubbaal, which means "let Baal plead") and his men were on the southern section of the plain by the well of Harod, which was a strategic military location.

Gideon must have felt secure because of the strength and size of the army with him. But God wouldn't need that many people. With an army of 32,000 men, Israel would have surely bragged that their sheer strength and numbers was the determining factor in defeating the Midianites. However, no one would be able to receive credit for what God was about to do to Israel's enemy. Therefore, He told Gideon to give the people an ultimatum. Whoever was fearful and did not want to go to war against their oppressors was to leave the battlefield and go home. As a result 22,000 left, reducing Gideon's army to only 10,000 men, which God eventually pared down to 300 (vv. 4-8).

3. The Lord Uses Gideon (vv. 20-21)

Now that God had reduced the number of men in Gideon's army, He gave the judge specific plans regarding how they were to fight the Midianites. Though the Midianites had a large army, Gideon had received a promise from the Lord. He confidently told his men to arise because "The LORD hath delivered into your hands the host of Midian" (v. 15).

The Lord's plan was simple. Gideon was to divide the 300 men into three different companies and put a trumpet, an empty pitcher, and a lamp within the pitcher into each man's hand. They were to wait for Gideon's signal. At his command, the men were to place the trumpet in their right hand, break the pitcher and hold the lamps in their left hand, and blow the trumpet and cry with a loud shout, "The sword of the LORD and of Gideon" (v. 20). Once Israel did their thing, then the Lord did His. He caused the noise to so confuse the Midianites that they ran around the camp killing one another (vv. 21-22).

Gideon's victory didn't come because of his own ingenuity or greatness. Instead, he was willing to step out and do what God called him to do, no matter how difficult or inadequate he felt. Are we willing to do the same today?

SEARCH THE SCRIPTURES

1. What was Gideon doing when the angel of the Lord came to him? (Judges 6:11)

2. How did Gideon respond when the angel of the Lord spoke? (v. 13)

3. What charge did Gideon receive from the angel of the Lord? (v. 14)

4. Where did Gideon take his men to meet the Midianites? (Judges 7:1)

5. What specific instructions did the Lord give Gideon regarding his army? (vv. 2-3)

6. How did Gideon win the battle against Midian? (vv. 20-21)

DISCUSS THE MEANING

1. Does God still perform miracles today? Why or why not?

2. Are angels still used to convey God's message to His people today? Why or why not?

3. Why do you think that 22,000 men went home when Gideon gave them the opportunity to do so? Discuss.

4. Why would God allow Gideon and his small army of men to use only trumpets, pitchers, and lamps as weapons? Discuss.

LESSON IN OUR SOCIETY

Oppression comes in many forms. What can we learn from today's lesson and apply to our lives and community to help overcome or eliminate the turmoil and confusion we face every day? Brainstorm and share solutions that can be implemented this week.

MAKE IT HAPPEN

Do you feel overwhelmed by the challenges you face? Allow the Lord to speak to you through today's lesson. Instead of focusing on yourself, look for specific ways that you might be able to help someone else overcome life's challenges. Thank the Lord for the opportunities you will encounter and be prepared to give a report on next week.

FOLLOW THE SPIRIT

What God wants me to do:

_____

_____

REMEMBER YOUR THOUGHTS
Special insights you have learned:

_____

_____

MORE LIGHT ON THE TEXT
Judges 6:11-14; 7:1-3, 20-21

6:11 And there came an angel of the LORD, and sat under an oak which was in Ophrah, that pertained unto Joash the Abiezrite: and his son Gideon threshed wheat by the winepress, to hide it from the Midianites.

Many scholars consider an Old Testament reference to the "angel of the Lord" or "an angel of the Lord" to be an actual appearance by Christ himself. For Christ to have appeared on earth in human form prior to His birth in Bethlehem is not impossible. In Daniel 3:25, Nebuchadnezzar saw "four men" loose in the fire, rather than three. He went on to say that ". . . the form of the fourth is like the Son of God." In Judges 6:11 the "angel" who interacts with Gideon could arguably be an Old Testament appearance of Christ. It is certainly interesting to note that in verse 14, which follows, the Scripture indicates that it is God Himself who looks at and speaks to Gideon rather than merely one of God's created angelic beings. But, at the very least, the "angel" in this encounter clearly comes from God.

The Lord gave Gideon a divine commission while he was busy threshing wheat. Notice that Gideon was working at the time. This pattern of divine announcement was repeated when God notified the first humans of Christ's birth. The shepherds were also actively engaged in their work (Luke 2:8). Similarly, David was out working when Samuel came to anoint him as Israel's new king (1 Samuel 16:11). In Judges 6:11, we read that Gideon was busy doing that for which he was given responsibility. His diligence should be an example for all Christians. Even Jesus said, "I must work the works of him that sent me, while it is day: the night cometh when no man can work" (John 9:4). Every Christian must realize that God has given us specific work to do (Ephesians 2:10). Like Jesus, our "day" occurs during our lifetimes, because when our "night" (or death) comes, it will be too late to accomplish our assigned responsibilities.

Gideon was preparing wheat for food which was a basic necessity. His oppression was symbolized by the fact that even a simple, basic, and necessary function like this had to be done stealthily for fear that his enemy would come and take what belonged to him. He must have been fed up with having to sneak around to do a simple thing like prepare food for his family. God knew his heart and was ready to give him divine instructions. For Gideon, the time was right to do something about his people's situation.

For each believer and for the Body of Christ, a moment will come when our time is right as well. Instead of being idle, we must be constantly laboring to harvest souls into God's kingdom to fulfill the Great Commission (Matthew 28:19). As we answer God's call, follow His instructions, and get out there on our God-given mission, God will use us to point the way of salvation and to reverse the problems of drugs, gangs, crime, and poverty in our community. As we actively obey and follow God, like Gideon, the time will come when we can be used by God to improve the situation.

12 And the angel of the LORD appeared unto him, and said unto him, The LORD is with thee, thou mighty man of valour.

In a time of peril or when under oppression from our enemies, the best news a child of God can receive is that "the Lord is with thee." Whether the reassurance comes from the Holy Spirit within, while reading the Word, or from the lips of another believer, this truth reminds us that "all things are working together for (our) good" (Romans 8:28). When God is for us then no one can prevail against us (Romans 8:31). Our God is a loving Father who wants us to stay encouraged in the face of any troublesome circumstance. The same God who spoke to Gideon in verse 12 also encouraged Moses generations before (Exodus 3:12) and told Joshua that He was with him (Joshua 1:5, 9). Thousands of years later, our all-powerful, unchanging God knows each of us and everything we go through. He is the same God who promises "I am with you always, even unto the end of the world" (Matthew 28:20).

Without question, God is present during our troubling times. The question is whether He detects in us a spirit of might or valour. Apparently Gideon showed God such a spirit as he diligently threshed his wheat out of the possible sight of his enemies. The question concerning us could be stated something like, "Do we 'stand...and having done all...stand' as we should?" (Ephesians 6:11, 13). Or, do we "faint" under the weight of our afflictions? (2 Corinthians 4:16-18).

13 And Gideon said unto him, Oh my Lord, if the LORD be with us, why then is all this befallen us? and where be all his miracles which our fathers told us of, saying, Did not the LORD bring us up from Egypt? but now the LORD hath forsaken us, and delivered us into the hands of the Midianites.

Gideon was unaware that he was speaking with more than just another human being. He addresses the angel as "Lord" which in the Hebrew refers to a human master or owner. The title "LORD" refers to "Jehovah, the self-existent or Eternal One" in Hebrew. Gideon's questions reflect the confusion that many believers experience today concerning the presence of tribulation or suffering in life. Gideon's people were suffering at the hands of the Midianites because of Israel's own disobedience and idolatry (see Judges 6:1, 2). Those of us who are in Christ may also face tribulation because our spiritual enemies, led by Satan, are out to complete Satan's goal of killing us, stealing from us, and destroying us in every way imaginable (see John 10:10). Through sin, the Children of God brought upon themselves God's "rod of correction" (see Proverbs 22:15), and because of their disobedience God had to discipline them like a good parent disciplines a bad child. Although God disciplines His children (Hebrews 12:6-13), He never forsakes us, as Gideon claimed in verse 13. Through every situation both good and bad God has promised that He will never leave us nor forsake us (Hebrews 13:5).

In spite of the pagan idolatry that surrounded him, Gideon held on to the oral traditions of the truth about God which were handed down by his elders, i.e., ". . . which our fathers told us of." Similarly, today we should not allow our children to grow up without spiritual roots. Many of the children in the worst parts of urban America have never even set foot inside the foyer of a church, let alone received instruction in the ways of God. We, as "the church" under the leadership of Jesus Christ must take some of the responsibility. We must ask ourselves what kind of oral traditions we are passing down to *our* younger generations, if any. We must begin and continue to diligently teach children the Word of God.

14 And the LORD looked upon him, and said, Go in this thy might, and thou shalt save Israel from the hand of the Midianites: have I not sent thee?

Again, the use of the word "LORD" in this verse indicates that God Himself is the one who "looked upon him," or judged Gideon's heart. Notice that God does not get upset or "go off" in response to Gideon's little tirade. God is loving, understanding, and merciful. He knows where we are coming from, and He is gracious toward us when we are laboring under confusion.

As Gideon spoke and God "looked upon him," He saw the same kind of strength and fire inside of Gideon that He saw when He referred to Gideon earlier as a "mighty man of valour" (v. 12). At this point, He told Gideon to take that fiery spirit of his and vanquish the enemies of Israel. God's question, "have I not sent thee?" is really an affirmation that Gideon had all that he would ever need to be successful, for God had said He would be with Gideon (v. 12). Gideon had the most powerful ally in all the universe by his side. The name "Gideon" means to cut down or to destroy in Hebrew. Therefore, God's plan for Gideon to be used as His mighty instrument of vengeance was evident, even down to Gideon's very name.

Gideon's encounter is a clear example for believers today that God wants us to have faith in Him, and move forward to clean up the oppressive conditions which are destroying our community. The strong indignation, frustration, and disgust we feel upon seeing our neighbors hooked on drugs, engaged in senseless violence, and committing crimes needs to be redirected into an energetic effort to get them to turn their lives around by accepting and obeying Christ. Our anger toward a particular group of people whom we see as antagonists of equal opportunity must be converted into zeal for spreading God's truth that all men need to come to Christ.

2 Chronicles 7:14 says, "If my people, which are called by my name, shall humble themselves, and pray, and seek my face, and turn from their wicked ways; then will I hear from heaven, and will forgive their sin, and will heal their land." Even though that was written to Israel centuries ago, it serves as a good blueprint for us today. Just like with Gideon, God will clean up our community ("heal our land"), if we will quit being idle and relaxing comfortably behind church walls with our eternal salvation as our personal security blanket. God desires that we would get busy and become active and righteous leaders in our community, setting a Christlike example for all of our lost and unsaved neighbors to see. Then, just like with Gideon and the Midianites, our community would be freed from the oppressive influences which hold it captive. There simply is no other way.

7:1 Then Jerubbaal, who is Gideon, and all the people that were with him, rose up early, and pitched beside the well of Harod: so that the host of the Midianites were on the north side of them, by the hill of Moreh, in the valley.

Gideon's father, Joash, gave him the name "Jerubbaal," which means "let Baal plead for himself," after Gideon had torn down an altar to that false god and replaced it with one which Gideon dedicated to Jehovah (vv. 25-32). In Judges 7:1, we see that God does not do all the work for us just because He guarantees us a victory. What would happen to our children as adults if we did everything for them as they grew up? Would they even "grow up" without learning how to do things on their own? Can we grow into mature Christians who are capable of coping in a sin-sick world if God does every single thing for us? Or would God be crippling our spiritual development by doing so?

God expects us to do some things. That is our part in the battles of life. He gives us insight and wisdom to do those things which are most advantageous for our success. By accomplishing tasks under His guidance, we develop faith, patience, and confidence in Him (see James 1:2-5 and Philippians 4:13).

Gideon does three wise things which could serve his forces well in a military operation. First, he and his troops "rose up early." Getting a good headstart on the day could mean getting a headstart on the enemy. In something as serious and deadly as war, it is better to be prepared early than to be too late. Second, he situated himself near "the well of Harod." Thus, his troops would not have to worry about having a source of water. In battle during those ancient times and in that location of the world, water could be a seriously important commodity. Having a plentiful supply accessible to their needs was a plus. Finally, Gideon and his troops were stationed on higher ground than the Midianites who were "in the valley." Strategically, it is better to be in a position to roll (down) over your enemy than to fight an uphill battle.

We need to take a cue from Gideon and get a jump on the competition. We also should study God's Word and whatever we need to study in order to prepare ourselves for the trials and battles of life. For example, if we want to become nuclear physicists, we cannot refuse to take lots of science and math, then expect God to miraculously make our dream come true. God wants us to be in the best possible position to bring Him glory and achieve success. He will give guidance and wisdom to us (James 1:5). Our challenge is to take God's wisdom and to diligently apply it to our situations along the way. Our active obedience to God means we are going to have to do some work. The Bible also warns us against laziness, saying, "Slothfulness casteth into a deep sleep; and an idle soul shall suffer hunger" (Proverbs 19:15), and "By much slothfulness the building decayeth; and through idleness of the hands the house droppeth through" (Ecclesiastes 10:18).

2 And the LORD said unto Gideon, The people that are with thee are too many for me to give the Midianites into their hands, lest Israel vaunt themselves against me, saying, Mine own hand hath saved me.

God knew Israel inside and out. For centuries He had tried to get them to remain faithful to Him in their worship and to acknowledge all that He had done for them. But time and time again,

it was to no avail. In fact, Israel's oppression at the time of Gideon's commission from God was due to her latest lapse into spiritual unfaithfulness (Judges 6:1). Knowing their hearts, God knew that the Israelites would once again leave Him out of the equation for their success if He allowed them to gain victory over the Midianites in their own strength. God told Gideon that there were "too many" Israelites in his forces for God's purposes. If they won, their pride would cause them to "vaunt" themselves against God. In other words, the people would boast about themselves or embellish their own role in the victory. We struggle with this

same problem today. Pride is a human quality that exalts man's glory above God. God has repeatedly warned us of the consequences of pride, or a lack of humility, in His Word. For example, Proverbs 16:18, 19 teaches that "Pride goeth before destruction, and a haughty spirit before a fall. Better it is to be of an humble spirit with the lowly, than to divide the spoil with the proud." Proverbs 29:23 reveals that "A man's pride shall bring him low: but honor shall uphold the humble in spirit."

Unlike the Israelites at that time, wise believers today recognize that God deserves all the glory for every good and positive thing they experience.

The Bible says, "Every good gift and every perfect gift is from above, and cometh down from the Father of lights, with whom is no variableness, neither shadow of turning" (James 1:17). God alone is entitled to think highly of Himself, for "Thou art worthy, O Lord, to receive glory and honor and power: for thou hast created all things, and for thy pleasure they are and were created" (Revelation 4:11). It is foolish to usurp God's glory. A wise believer today will gratefully acknowledge that God is the author of the wonderful and magnificent occurrences of life.

3 Now therefore go to, proclaim in the ears of the people, saying, Whosoever is fearful and afraid, let him return and depart early from mount Gilead. And there returned of the people twenty and two thousand; and there remained ten thousand.

Gideon was from the tribe of Manasseh (Judges 6:15), and the forces he led were probably mainly from that region and tribe. Mount Gilead, where they were amassed near the enemy, was named after Gilead, who was an ancestor of many of the families of Manasseh living in the area (see Numbers 26:28-29; 32:33, 39-40). God commanded Gideon to proclaim to the crowd that the fainthearted could go home. This reduced the number of Israelite troops. The fewer the soldiers, the greater the glory that God would receive for the victory and the more clearly His undeniable power could be seen. Although God really could have wiped out the Midianites by His supernatural power alone, without the use of a single soldier, He chose to use a small band of men (v. 7) for His glory.

In response to God's command, Gideon issued a proclamation in keeping with the Mosaic Law concerning war as found in Deuteronomy 20:1-9. That law provided four grounds upon which a man could remove himself from service in war. The first three excused any man with either a new house, a new vineyard, or a new wife. If that man had not had a chance to enjoy one of those things yet, God did not want him to die in battle without the opportunity. The fourth ground was precisely the one offered by God on this occasion. Deuteronomy 20:8 states in part, ". . . What man is

there that is fearful and fainthearted? Let him go and return unto his house, lest his brethren's heart faint as well as his heart." God knew that cowardice in battle can become contagious. Similarly, to use Christian men and women in earthly battles today, God needs those who are unafraid. Three times in the Book of Joshua, chapter 1, God told Joshua to be "strong" and "courageous" (vv. 6-7, 9). Today, He tells Christians that He "hath not given us a spirit of fear; but of power, and of love, and of a sound mind" (2 Timothy 1:7). To be used by God, we must believe that He will make His Word come true. Then, we must faithfully move forward without fear of any enemy.

20 And the three companies blew the trumpets, and brake the pitchers, and held the lamps in their left hands, and the trumpets in their right hands to blow withal: and they cried, The sword of the LORD, and of Gideon.

God reduced the number of men that Gideon took with him down to 300 (v. 7). The unusual battle strategy of Gideon was inspired by God. It also made use of part of the information Gideon attained when he overheard a conversation among his enemies (v. 14). Gideon divided his men into three companies and surrounded the enemy camp (vv. 16, 19, 21). No blows were struck by Gideon or his men in order to achieve the objective. This was similar to God's unorthodox method of destroying the walls of the city of Jericho (Joshua 6:20).

Such feats of God are reminders for us that we should ". . . lean not unto (our) own understanding. (But rather) in all (our) ways acknowledge him, and he shall direct (our) paths" (Proverbs 3:5-6). Instead, we must always pray and seek God's guidance before embarking on projects or going against enemies. God's way is always superior to our way, for He alone is omniscient (allknowing) and omnipotent (all-powerful). God is all that and more. Therefore, His pattern for how we should proceed is flawless and guaranteed to succeed. We must take to heart God's admonition that ". . . (My) thoughts are not your thoughts, neither are your ways my ways, saith the LORD. For as the heavens are higher than the earth, so are my ways higher than your ways, and my thoughts than your thoughts" (Isaiah 55:8-9).

As they obeyed God's instructions, Gideon's army used the same words that Gideon heard spoken by the Midianites. It was clear that their enemies were already nervous and/or scared about the prospect of fighting against Gideon and Israel (vv. 13-15). So, Gideon instructed his men to shout, ". . . the sword of the Lord, and of Gideon," as they made their move. At least two very important things can be learned from this example. First, as was pointed out before, we need to make sure that we do whatever is necessary to get ourselves thoroughly prepared for our endeavors. Like the U.S. government, we need to do some "intelligence work" before embarking on our missions. The Bible places a high priority on God's people gaining the requisite knowledge for any undertaking. For example, we are told that, "A wise man will hear, and will increase learning; and a man of understanding shall attain unto wise counsel" (Proverbs 1:5). And Jesus put it this way, "For which of you, intending to build a tower, sitteth not down first, and counteth the cost, whether he have sufficient to finish it?" (Luke 14:28) Without a doubt, God can take us further if we have done our homework and found out the things we need to know about our mission beforehand.

Second, we need to make sure we always put God first. Gideon instructed his men to shout about God before they mentioned Gideon's name. He did so even though he had overheard that the enemy was afraid of him because he was the recipient of God's favor. We must also follow Gideon's example and put God first. This correct priority puts God in position to receive the honor and glory instead of us (Revelation 4:11). We must put God first because that is where He truly belongs. We would be nothing without Him (John 15:5).

21 And they stood every man in his place round about the camp: and all the host ran, and cried, and fled.

Gideon's battle strategy is one of the earliest and greatest examples of so-called "psychological warfare." His men made a lot of noise and flashed a lot of lights as they stood in their places. God's supernatural power was not aimed at the Midianites in a physical sense. Gideon's forces did not attack their enemies' natural bodies. God used 300 Israelites to attack thousands of Midianites in psychological warfare.

The Bible indicates that the mind is the true battlefield for the spiritual attacks that we as believers today experience on a regular basis. 2 Corinthians 10:4-5 says that satanic strongholds, vain imaginations, and ungodly thoughts are mental conditions which cause some of our greatest problems. These things must be pulled down, cast down, and brought into captivity to Christ if we are to be victorious in spiritual warfare. Our modern-day enemies, led by Satan, frequently seek to provoke fear, doubt, confusion, hopelessness, unbelief, and a host of other negative emotions and perceptions. The mind's capacity to entertain or maintain negative, ungodly, and compulsive thoughts can become a valuable resource for satanic purposes. Therefore, it is essential that we renew our minds (Romans 12:2) with the Word of God (Ephesians 5:26). Saturating our minds with God's Word and applying His Word in our lives will enable us to win the "psychological war" against Satan every time.

DAILY BIBLE READINGS

M: The Midianite Oppression
Judges 6:1-10
T: The Call of Gideon
Judges 6:11-24
W: Sign of the Fleece
Judges 6:36-40
T: Preparation for Battle
Judges 7:1-15
F: Defeat of the Midianites
Judges 7:16-25
S: Pursuit of the Midianites
Judges 8:4-21
S: Gideon's Latter Days
Judges 8:22-32

TEACHING TIPS

September 17
Bible Study Guide 3

1. Words You Should Know

A. Woman (Judges 16:4) Hebrew *Ishshah*—The basic meaning of the word is female and the opposite of a male. It also means a wife, a bride, and a woman.

B. Every one (v. 5) Hebrew *Ish*—The basic meaning is a man, a male, a husband, a possessor of manliness.

C. Nazarite (v. 17) Hebrew *Nazir*—It means a separate one, a dedicated one, a prince.

2. Teacher Preparation

A. Begin by reading the entire account of Samson's life (Judges 13—16). This will give you the resource you need to answer student's questions about this complicated figure.

B. Read the IN FOCUS and IN DEPTH commentary and prepare your personal comments.

C. Materials needed: Bible, paper, pencils, and a chalkboard or newsprint.

3. Starting the Lesson

A. Use the IN FOCUS section as a springboard to get the students into praying about the context of the lesson. Concentrate on the LESSON AIM as the focus of the prayer.

B. Write the words DELILAH and SAMSON on the board or newsprint. Ask several students to read the FOCAL VERSES, according to the AT-A-GLANCE outline.

C. Have one student read the BACKGROUND section of the lesson, making appropriate comments where necessary about the section.

4. Getting into the Lesson

A. After the students have read the IN DEPTH section of the lesson, use the SEARCH THE SCRIPTURES questions to review the highlights. Be sure to get students to comment on what they have read.

B. Refer to the words DELILAH and SAMSON on the board or newsprint. Ask several students which of the FOCAL VERSES have Samson as the focus and which have Delilah. Write the students' answers under the corresponding names.

C. Read THE PEOPLE, PLACES, AND TIMES section and discuss how this information relates to the lesson. Remind students that most of the Philistine's actions took place in Gaza.

5. Relating the Lesson to Life

Read the DISCUSS THE MEANING questions and allow time for students to share their responses. Encourage all students to give their reactions based on the truths uncovered in the lesson.

6. Arousing Action

A. Pass out 3" X 5" cards and ask each student to write the following: "As a result of today's lesson, I will commit to . . . ."

B. Have students complete the statement in silence. After a few minutes, ask for volunteers to share what they have written.

C. Close the class in prayer, thanking the Lord for the opportunity to study His Word today.

WORSHIP GUIDE

For the Superintendent or Teacher
Theme: Samson
Theme Song: "Work of Me, Lord"
Scripture: John 18:15-18
Song: "Give Me a Clean Heart"
Meditation: Lord, thank You for Your forgiveness when I sin. Help me always to walk in such a way that my life reflects Yours. In Jesus' name, Amen.

34

SAMSON

Bible Background • JUDGES 13-16
Printed Text • JUDGES 16:4-5, 17, 19-22, 28-30
Devotional Reading • PSALM 145:14-20

**SEP
17TH**

LESSON AIM

By the end of the lesson, students will be able to identify the source of Samson's defeat, understand why sinful behavior is unacceptable to God, and commit to eliminating willfully sinful behavior from their own lives.

KEEP IN MIND

". . . O Lord GOD remember me, I pray thee, and strengthen me, I pray thee, only this once . . . " (Judges 16:28).

FOCAL VERSES

Judges 16:4 And it came to pass afterward, that he loved a woman in the valley of Sorek, whose name was Delilah.

5 And the lords of the Philistines came up unto her, and said unto her, Entice him, and see wherein his great strength lieth, and by what means we may prevail against him, that we may bind him to affect him: and we will give thee every one of us eleven hundred pieces of silver.

16:17 That he told her all his heart, and said unto her, There hath not come a razor upon mine head; for I have been a Nazarite unto God from my mother's womb: if I be shaven, then my strength will go from me, and I shall become weak, and be like any other man.

16:19 And she made him sleep upon her knees; and she called for a man, and she caused him to shave off the seven locks of his head; and she began to afflict him, and his strength went from him.

20 And she said, The Philistines be upon thee, Samson. And he awoke out of his sleep, and said, I

LESSON OVERVIEW

LESSON AIM
KEEP IN MIND
FOCAL VERSES
IN FOCUS
THE PEOPLE, PLACES,
AND TIMES
BACKGROUND
AT-A-GLANCE
IN DEPTH
SEARCH THE SCRIPTURES
DISCUSS THE MEANING
LESSON IN OUR SOCIETY
MAKE IT HAPPEN
FOLLOW THE SPIRIT
REMEMBER YOUR THOUGHTS
MORE LIGHT ON THE TEXT
DAILY BIBLE READINGS

will go out as at other times before, and shake myself. And he wist not that the LORD was departed from him.

21 But the Philistines took him, and put out his eyes, and brought him down to Gaza, and bound him with fetters of brass; and he did grind in the prison house.

22 Howbeit the hair of his head began to grow again after he was shaven.

16:28 And Samson called unto the LORD, and said, O Lord GOD, remember me, I pray thee, and strengthen me, I pray thee, only this once, O God, that I may be at once avenged of the Philistines for my two eyes.

29 And Samson took hold of the two middle pillars upon which the house stood, and on which it was borne up, of the one with his right hand, and of the other with his left.

30 And Samson said, Let me die with the Philistines. And he bowed himself with all his might; and the house fell upon the lords, and upon all the people that were therein.

IN FOCUS

William was the pastor of one of the largest churches in Cleveland. Because of his ability to expound on the Word of God with such excitement, William's church grew by 100 members every two months, until he had an active congregation of over 2,000 members in just three years.

However, what many people in the congregation did not know was that Pastor William had a serious problem with lust. He started seeing one of the female members of the gospel choir. Then, he began calling the Sunday School Superintendent on an intimate basis. Because of his charisma, neither of the women reported Pastor William to the church board or the denomination's headquarters. During the time that Pastor William was philandering, the church continued to grow by leaps and bounds because he could "preach the Word."

Eventually, Pastor William was exposed by another woman in the church that he propositioned. The woman realized she would only be a hindrance to both the church and Pastor William if she did not speak out against his sin.

When the people found out about Pastor William's conduct, the church board called an emergency meeting. After a very close vote, Pastor William was asked to resign his position.

This man forfeited a promising future, left a wonderful church in shame, ruined his reputation, and lost his ministry, all because he could not control his lust. This lesson examines another man who lost his "ministry" because he could not control himself. His story is a sobering reminder for all of us.

THE PEOPLE, PLACES, AND TIMES

Gaza. A settlement about three miles from the Mediterranean coast, marking the southern border of Canaan. It was captured by Pharoah Thutmost III. It was part of the Philistine Pentapolis, the southernmost city in that league of five cities (Joshua 13:3; 1 Samuel 6:17; Jeremiah 25:20). The city was later taken by Tiglath-pileser III, king of Assyria. As part of the Philistine Pentapolis, Gaza played an important role in the Samson saga (Judges 14—16). It also flourished as a Roman city and remained a center for the Jewish community and the emerging Christian community throughout the Roman era (63 B.C.—A.D. 324) and continuing into the Byzantine period (324—1453).

(The Harper Bible Dictionary, Paul J. Achtemeier, editor, San Francisco: Harper and Row Publishers, 1986 pp. 333-334)

BACKGROUND

Samson is the thirteenth judge listed in the Book of Judges. His life is the epitome of Israel's time in the Promised Land: compromise and defeat.

Samson was born in Zorah during the time when Israel was in bondage to the Philistines for 40 years (Judges 13:1-2). Because of God's promise to His people (see Judges 2:16-18), the angel of the LORD appeared to Samson's parents and informed them that they would have a Nazarite child who would grow to be a deliverer for Israel (Judges 13:4-7).

According to Zodhiates, the word "Nazarite" is not to be confused with Nazarene. It means to be separated and, in the context of Samson, he was born to be separated unto the Lord. A Nazarite was called to let his hair grow until a specific time when he was to shave it. Then, the hair was to be used as a peace offering sacrifice (Numbers 6:2-21). Samson and Samuel are the two Nazarites mentioned in Scripture (see Judges 13:5; 1 Samuel 1:11, 28).

Samson was blessed by the Lord and the spirit of God moved on him many times in the camp of Dan. His strength and power exceeded that of an ordinary man, and Samson used that power to slaughter thousands of Philistines (Judges 14—15).

But there was another side to Samson that not only brought shame to his earthly parents, but also to his heavenly Father. Samson was a womanizer and that particular weakness brought about his downfall as we shall see in today's IN DEPTH study.

AT-A-GLANCE

1. Samson Is Deceived by Delilah (Judges 16:4-5, 17)
2. Samson Is Captured by the Philistines (vv. 19-22)
3. Samson Is Vindicated by God (vv. 28-30)

IN DEPTH

1. Samson Is Deceived by Delilah
(Judges 16:4-5, 17)

Samson's problem was similar to Solomon's. He

had an insatiable lust for women, especially foreign women. One of the women who caught his heart and his eyes was Delilah, who lived in the Sorek Valley. The Sorek Valley extended between Ashkelon and Gaza in southwestern Palestine. The Sorek Brook, which was part of the valley, runs westward and then northward into the Mediterranean Sea near Beer-shemesh.

Nothing significant is known about Delilah, except she was probably of Philistine descent and she was probably beautiful. One day, while Delilah was waiting for Samson to come see her, she was visited by the lords of the Philistines (v. 5). Why would they come to see Delilah? They were tired of Samson (see Judges 15:16-20). But the Philistines needed Delilah's help for their plan to succeed.

The Philistines wanted Delilah to use her feminine wiles on Samson so that he would reveal to her the source of his strength. Once Samson revealed his secret to Delilah, she would then be able to tell the Philistines how they could gain victory over him and put Samson to shame. If Delilah would follow the Philistines' plan, they would make her a rich woman. According to the Hebrew language, the word "lords" (v. 4) indicates that there may have been as many as five men who came to see Delilah. If that is true, Delilah would be paid a total of 5,500 pieces of silver (v. 5) for just a few days of "work."

The money must have been very enticing to Delilah because she devised a plan to deceive Samson. First, she tried the direct approach. She asked Samson, "tell me . . . wherein thy great strength lieth, and wherewith thou mightest be bound to afflict thee" (v. 6). Talk about boldness!

We must understand that Satan often uses those who are closest to us (see Matthew 16:21-23). That's why the Bible affirms that we must not be ignorant of Satan's devices (2 Corinthians 2:11). If the devil came to tempt Jesus, rest assured he will come to us for the same purpose to get us out of the will of God.

Samson must have recognized Delilah's tricks because he refused to tell her the truth even though she repeatedly asked him to tell her his secret (vv. 7-15). But Delilah wouldn't give up. She was thinking about the money she would get if she could get Samson to talk. So she pressed on him

day and night until he opened his heart to her. Because of her relentless pursuit, Samson's enemy learned the secret of his great strength, and his relationship with Delilah led to his own downfall.

Samson was a Nazarite from birth. His hair was not to be cut (Numbers 6:5) until a time appointed by God. Instead, it was to grow as instructed by the Lord. However, in Samson's case, if his hair was cut, he would lose his supernatural strength and the presence of God. It must be noted that Samson's strength was not in his hair, but in his covenant relationship with the Lord. Once Samson broke the covenant, he also lost the abiding presence of God in his life.

We must be careful that we don't rely on outward "things" as the source of our relationship with the Lord. While spiritual resources are vitally important, they cannot take the place of an intimate relationship with Jesus Christ.

2. Samson Is Captured by the Philistines (vv. 19-22)

Samson is a prime example of an old saying: "Loose lips sinks ships." The lust of the flesh, the lust of the eyes, and the pride of life (1 John 2:16b) caused Samson's life to change completely in a short period of time. Once he had shared his most intimate secret with Delilah, the second phase of her plan went into motion.

Delilah quickly called the lords of the Philistines, who also brought with them her "blood" money. Then Delilah got Samson to fall asleep on her lap. Perhaps she used her voice and her body to lead this "lamb to slaughter." Next, she had someone shave off Samson's hair. Finally, Delilah began to "afflict him" (v. 19) in order to see whether or not his strength was gone. Once she was assured that Samson was nothing more than a weakling, she woke him from his sleep to tell him that the Philistines had come to get him.

Samson was so deceived that he thought he could play in the enemy's camp and not be burned. Solomon gives us sound advice related to Samson's problem: "To keep thee from the evil woman, from flattery of the tongue of a strange woman. Lust not after her beauty in thine heart; neither let her take thee with her eyelids. For by means of a whorish woman a man is brought to a piece of bread: and the adulteress will hunt for the precious life. Can a man take fire in his bosom, and his clothes not be burned?" (Proverbs 6:24-27).

Once Samson stepped over the line, God departed from him. If we choose to live in sin, we cannot have an intimate relationship with God. Samson still believed that he could "shake" himself (v. 20) and everything would be all right. He didn't have a clue that the Lord had departed from him. When the Philistines came upon him, Samson probably tried to pick up a weapon or use his strength to overpower them. However, nothing worked. He had violated the Nazarite vow, his hair was cut, and God was gone. Now it was easy for the Philistines to bore out his eyes with a hot iron, bind Samson in chains, and drag this once proud man to the prison house in Gaza, in the southern part of Canaan.

The Bible does not indicate how long Samson remained in prison. But while he was there, his hair began to grow again, which may have been an indication that he was repentant and that the presence of the Lord was returning to his life. Once we repent, the Scriptures affirm that God is faithful to His people and is willing to give us another chance (1 John 1:9).

3. Samson Is Vindicated by God (vv. 28-30)

The Philistines threw a great party to celebrate Samson's capture. They not only called upon Dagon, who was a fish god, but they also brought Samson out of prison so they could make fun of him. Because Samson could not see, he had to be led around by a little boy. Samson asked the little boy to put him in between the pillars of the house where the Philistines were having their party.

What Samson did next is an important lesson for all believers. First, he called upon the name of the Lord. Samson finally recognized that God was the source of his strength. With all his foolish ways, Samson may have forgotten this truth. Now in defeat, Samson acknowledged his God. Second, Samson repented of his ways. By asking the Lord to "remember" him, Samson confessed that he was the source of his own problems. Third, Samson asked the Lord to grant him favor one more time so that he might be able to destroy the Philistines who were making fun of him and, by implication, God.

It is evident that Samson was a man of faith. After he prayed, he placed his hands on the support pillars of the house and began to push hard against them. Samson recognized that he was going to die along with the Philistines once the support beams gave way. But he felt good about his decision because he had made his peace with God.

As Samson pushed with all his might, God returned his strength to him one more time. The foundation of the house gave way and the people plunged to their death. In fact, the Bible says that Samson killed more people with this one act than in his entire lifetime.

While we commend Samson for his willingness to confess his sins and repent of his ways in his final hour, we must also recognize that Samson got into that position because he lived a compromising life and yielded to temptation. Let's commit our ways to the Lord so that we won't compromise when we are faced with temptation.

SEARCH THE SCRIPTURES

1. What was the name of the woman from the Sorek Valley who captured Samson's heart? (Judges 16:4)

2. What did the Philistine lords offer to Delilah to get her to go along with their plans? (v. 5)

3. How did Delilah get Samson to reveal his secret? (vv. 16-17)

4. What did the Philistines do to Samson once they caught him? (v. 21)

5. How did Samson vindicate himself? (vv. 28-30)

DISCUSS THE MEANING

1. How important is it for us to obey the Lord in every area of our lives? Discuss.

2. What is more important to the Lord, our spiritual abilities or our obedience?

3. What was Samson's greatest downfall?

4. Would it have been possible for Samson to kill the Philistines without dying? Why or why not?

LESSON IN OUR SOCIETY

Unfortunately, the African American community is full of "Samsons"—men who place their own pleasure above obedience to God. What can the church do to stop the numerous problems related to sexual immorality in our community which hurt all involved? Discuss.

MAKE IT HAPPEN

This week, examine your own life to see where you may have made some compromises that are displeasing to the Lord. Make a list and be honest with yourself and God. He already knows where you are. After you have completed the list, ask the Lord for help in overcoming any sinful habits or weaknesses you may have. Then, walk in faith believing that the Lord has given you victory.

FOLLOW THE SPIRIT

What God wants me to do:

_____

_____

REMEMBER YOUR THOUGHTS

Special insights you have learned:

_____

_____

MORE LIGHT ON THE TEXT
Judges 16:4-5, 17, 19-22, 28-30

16:4 And it came to pass afterward, that he loved a woman in the valley of Sorek, whose name was Delilah.

Verse 4 begins with the Hebrew word *wayahiy* which is translated in the King James Version "and it came to pass." The word can also mean "here is what came to befall" depending on the content of the narrative which is about to follow. Given the story of Samson, this introduction signals tragedy. It precedes the description of Samson's fall and signals that tragedy is about to occur. So the phrase "and it came to pass" is not just a casual phrase, especially from the point of view that any relationship between the Israelites and the Philistines would be considered as directly contravening the laws of God.

Note also the use of the word "afterwards" (Hebrew *acharey*). Even after everything that has happened, this is what Samson will do next. After all the attempts on his life, after all his confrontations with the Philistines, after his experience with

his fiancé, and with the leaders who used his love against him and his people—after all these things, "he (Samson) loved a woman." The Hebrew word *wayahab* contains the word *ahab* (pronounced **aw-hab'**) meaning affection or a sexual action. Samson became sexually involved with the enemy of his people. The tragedy of this situation is emphasized by the name of the woman, "Delilah." The name Delilah means languishing in Hebrew. The word "languishing" means becoming weak, dispirited, or sluggish in character. Delilah also comes from a Hebrew root word meaning to slacken or be feeble; figuratively, it means to be oppressed or brought low, dry up, and be emptied. In other words, by the very meaning of her name, Delilah symbolized that big trouble was ahead for this mighty man of God.

Samson had shown a propensity for looking upon the beauty of foreign women and lusting after them. In Judges 14:1-3, he argued with his parents to provide a Philistine woman for him. Then, in Judges 16:1-3, he kept company with a harlot and set himself up for an unsuccessful ambush by his enemies. Now he desired Delilah, who looked so good to him that her heritage and character traits seemed irrelevant.

Samson apparently wanted any woman that looked good to him, a problem that exists for many men. But today's Christian needs to be sensitive to God's warning about having a wandering eye. In Proverbs 5, we are told that strange women may look good on the surface but, like an iceberg in the ocean, there is much more underneath. The Bible says, "For the lips of a strange woman drop as a honeycomb, and her mouth is smoother than oil: but her end is bitter as wormwood, sharp as a two-edged sword. Her feet go down to death; her steps take hold on hell" (Proverbs 5:3-5).

5 And the lords of the Philistines came up unto her, and said unto her, Entice him, and see wherein his great strength lieth, and by what means we may prevail against him, that we may bind him to afflict him: and we will give thee every one of us eleven hundred pieces of silver.

In this verse we read "and the lords of the Philistines came upon her." It is interesting that the Hebrew does not use the word *adonai* or *rosh,* which indicates a place of high honor, but uses the Hebrew word *ceren* (**seh'-ren**) which means axle or wheels. That is, those Philistines who made the system turn came to Delilah. It could also mean that these men were peers. The word can also be translated *place*—indicating that these men bore authority. The fact that they came upon her (Hebrew *alah,* **aw-law'**) indicates the act of converging on someone as hyenas converge upon a carcass.

They came with a message which contained several points: First, they wanted her to entice Samson. The word "entice" is from the Hebrew word *pathah* pronounced **paw-thaw'** and suggests that they wanted her to open the door to Samson. They needed her to make room, figuratively, for them. The enticement was directed to Samson's mental and moral sensibility. To the Philistines he was a complex personality who needed to be made simple. There is a certain sinister tone to this phrase. It did not mean to lead one to love, but to deceive one through flattery. The purpose of this flattery was to discover the source of Samson's power. The Hebrew *uwraiy* translated "and see" comes from the word *ra'ah,* pronounced **raw-aw'**. They wanted her to have a direct experience of his power source. The use of the word also suggests that they were to be advised; Delilah was not only told to see how his power worked but to discern through experience the very source of his power. Samson's power was the target of this enticement; the result would be their ability to see his weakness and thus destroy him.

Samson's strength with God was the source of his physical strength. The Hebrew term which the King James Version translates "strength" is the word *yakol* (**yaw-kole'**), which means more than or fuller. Thus, she was to discover why he was able to so easily defeat them. But the word "strength" used here implies more than physical might; it includes moral underpinning. Even the Philistines knew that Samson's strength came from a source other than mere human ability. The question was: How was Samson able to attain his power? What gave him the ability to endure where others had failed? How could he overcome when others had crumbled? From whence came his power to prevail in circumstances that left others powerless?

Discovering the answers to these questions was Delilah's task. Her method? Her body. The Philistines' strategy was to use Delilah to entice Samson. The obejctive of the strategy was,"that we (Philistines) might prevail against him." To "prevail" here is Hebrew *'acar,* (**aw-sar'**) to yoke and to hitch as one would hitch an animal for plow. Then finally, they intended to "afflict him" (Judges 16:5.) The Hebrew `*anah,* (pronounced **aw-naw'**) conveys the idea of looking down on someone. The fact is that the Philistines already looked down on all of Israel and this was the one person they could not intimidate. They intended to depress literally and through his capture to abase. But here also is the sense that they wanted to deal harshly with him and defile him ritually so that he could no longer exercise the authority of his divine appointment. The idea here is to hurt him until he submitted himself in his weakened state to them.

They sought not so much to reveal Samson's weakness for women, as many interpret, but to discover his "ritual weakness." To get to his ritual weakness, they used his contravention of God's explicit command not to fraternize with the enemy. They immediately went to Delilah and struck a deal, which is reminiscent of the betrayal of Christ by Judas for "pieces of silver" (see Matthew 26:14-16), or what we now call "blood money." To accomplish their purpose they promised "to give" (Hebrew *nitan* which is a future form of the word *nathan*) Delilah something of value. The phrase "to give" is used to imply that they will appoint her to a place of prominence. They ascribe greatness to her. They will assign something special to her. There was a sense in which they were also promising to deliver her from any consequence that came as a result of this act. They were going to reward her for this production by giving her *me'yah* (pronounced **may-yaw**) or hundreds in term of increase; they were going to increase her wealth a hundred-fold.

It must be noted here that it was not only Samson's reputation that made him a mark for those who plotted to destroy him, but also the reputation of the woman he loved. In the highlighted verse, Samson's enemies wanted Delilah to uncover the source of his power and how he could be overcome so that they could "afflict" him or "deal harshly with him." In our own lives, we want to be of a "good report" so that human enemies will know of no weaknesses upon which they can prey (1 Timothy 3:7).

17 That he told her all his heart, and said unto her, There hath not come a razor upon mine head; for I have been a Nazarite unto God from my mother's womb: if I be shaven, then my strength will go from me, and I shall become weak, and be like any other man.

Samson finally gave in to Delilah and he told her "all his heart." In verse 16, we read that Samson's spirit was vexed. It is phrased as a "let-down." It's almost as though Samson might come to his senses. In this context, the phrase "he told her" carries the idea of "I can't believe he told her." Not only did Samson tell Delilah, but we read that he told her "all his heart." The Hebrew word *libow* translated "heart" suggests that he gave over his inner man. Samson's mind, will, heart, and under-standing were given over to the desire of Delilah. The use of the word "heart" may also point to the idolatrous nature of Samson's relationship. It was contrary to the law of the Most High to give over one's soul or heart to anything other than God. This Hebrew word implies not only the heart but also the source of knowledge. Samson's world, his knowledge—especially sacred knowledge—was power. Therefore, he had literally given over his power by giving over what he alone knew. We could also read this to mean that Samson gave over his conscience. He gave over his moral sense and char-acter. Samson revealed to Delilah the secret of his power and vulnerability. Obviously, this was not a wise thing to do. In verse 6, Delilah told him that she was seeking information which would lead to his downfall, and yet, Samson told her that secret which his enemies needed the most.

There are times in our lives when we need to keep our mouths shut. Or, situations may be such that we must be very guarded in what we say or reveal. Proverbs 13:3 says, "He that keepeth his mouth keepeth his life: but he that openeth wide his lips shall have destruction." If we have to say anything at all, we must be led by the wisdom of God in selecting the appropriate time. Nehemiah did just that concerning the rebuilding of the walls

of Jerusalem. He said, "And I arose in the night, I had some few men with me; neither told I any man what my God had put in my heart to do at Jerusalem. . . And the rulers knew not whither I went, or what I did; neither had I as yet told it to the Jews, nor to the priests, nor to the nobles, nor to the rulers . . ." (Nehemiah 2:12,16). If we must say something, let us become like Nehemiah and take a guarded approach.

We read further "and said unto her, There hath not come a razor upon mine head; for I have been a Nazarite unto God from my mother's womb." Here Samson does not just say "I have a secret that I will not tell you"; instead he explicitly ties his tremendous strength to the length of his hair. Unlike our Western world where rituals are often looked upon as mere appendages, this ritual of long hair is tied to God's promise to Samson and is the container of Samson's commitment to God. As one looks at his life, nothing else that Samson does diminishes his power, even his eating from a lion's carcass. The source of Samson's power was in this explicit promise of God which he reveals here to Delilah. Note the way in which Samson tailors his words. *Mowrah*, the Hebrew word for razor, points to the idea of that which brings death. Samson's hair represented life; thus the cutting of his hair symbolizes separation from God and hence death. It is interesting to note that in some African cul-tures the life of an individual is said to be in their head. Thus we have the idea of not letting some-one place their hand upon your head. In this case, Samson's head belongs to God. It symbolizes the Lordship of the God of Israel over Samson and also over the people whom he judged. It was also a divine protest against the lordship of foreign pow-ers over God's people. Samson adds that he has been a Nazarite (*Naziyr*) which means that he was dedicated to God. It is interesting that Samson does not say "I took a vow to be Nazarite" but "I have been a Nazarite from my mother's womb." The uniqueness of Samson's position is that he did not choose to be consecrated to God; God chose him for consecration.

Samson was aware of the link. He was able to understand that his strength came from God who worked in and through him. He apparently under-stood that his special relationship with God as a

Nazarite was the source of power for all he could do. Samson's ability to accomplish good works is predicated upon his relationship with God (see John 1:12). We can also be ". . . strengthened with all might, according to his glorious power" (Colossians 1:11). The Apostle Paul went on to say, "Whereunto I also labor, striving according to his working, which worketh in me mightily" (Colossians 1:29).

Samson's statement "If I be shaven, then my strength will go from me and I shall become weak, and be like any other man" is really both a commentary on human weakness without God, and a statement that describes his own immediate position. The word *galachtiy* translated "shaven" means to shave off or to become bald. This could be connected with the idea of death. But note also that this Hebrew word is connected to the word *wachaaliytiy* taken from the root *chalah* which means to make something weak or to become sick. Could it be that Samson connected breaking his covenant with God with becoming sick and, in his sickened state, becoming vulnerable to attacks from the enemy? Also, if Samson's hair symbolized his connection with God, the cutting of his hair would cause grief. In his grieved mental state, would he be so affected that he could not rouse himself to worship his God?

19 And she made him sleep upon her knees; and she called for a man, and she caused him to shave off the seven locks of his head; and she began to afflict him, and his strength went from him.

Note how the text reads, "And she made him sleep upon her knees." This phrase suggests that he may have remained asleep for long time. It also suggests that Samson was enticed to sleep. We know that Samson did not drink liquor and fall asleep because of his Nazarite status. As we would say, he was knocked out. But we do not know what caused this deep sleep that so incapacitated Samson ". . . she made him sleep upon her knees" clearly paints the picture that Samson felt totally safe and secure in his environment and situation. He was off-guard and lulled into a false sense of security by the very woman who orchestrated danger all around him. We read further "and she

called for a man" (*Watiqraa' laa'iysh*). The word *qara'* (**kaw-raw'**) used in *watiqara* is taken from a primitive root meaning to call out to another. Samson must have really been out for her to call out and still not be heard. In this case, she called forth those with whom she had previously had a conversation about the issue. The suggestion is that she invited him to come or that she mentioned who she had. It could also mean that she made a proclamation or public announcement for someone to come and cut Samson's hair. This was her second act. Her third act was to instruct the man to cut Samson's hair.

The writer does not just tell us that Samson's hair was cut, we are told that his "seven locks" were shaved. The use of the term *sheba`* is not just meant to convey a numerical significance, it also conveys the idea of sacred fullness. This term represents the infinite divine possibility represented by the partition of his hair. Note the term "lock" (Hebrew *machlaphah*, pronounced **makh-law-faw'**) refers to hair woven together and glided over each other. The next step Delilah took was to afflict Samson. The Hebrew word *chalal*, (**khaw-lal'**) implies that she began to inflict wounds on him. It could also mean that she began to profane or make him unclean. Remember that ritual purity was very important for the Nazarite.

We are not told exactly what she did, but this action began to break his spirit and create a wedge between Samson and his call. Again, this affliction is probably closer to a defilement that breaks covenant with the holiness of God. Delilah polluted him or made him become profane. The term also implies prostitution. Delilah prostituted his gift. There is also another interesting word used here, however ; note the English language does not seem to capture the second word. Two Hebrew words are used here: *Wataachel* and *le'anowtow*, translated as "afflict." The first term refers to pollution, the second word *le'anowtow* is rooted in the Hebrew *anah* (pronounced **aw-naw'**), which means that after ritually polluting him, Delilah began to look down on him. Now that he had become impure she could browbeat and abase him. His defilement now meant that she could force him to act according to her wishes. In his weakened spiritual state, Samson submitted himself. Why could Delilah do this to him? The next phrase tells us— "and his strength went from him" (*Wayaacar kochow mee`aalaayw anah*).

The term *kochow* is a form of the word *koach* (*ko'-akh*), which means to be firm and vigorous. Now Samson's vigor was gone. His capacity to be productive was gone. The phrase "was gone" with use of the word *suwr* (**soor**) makes it sound as though someone just reached out and literally turned off the fountain of his strength. He could not call his strength back. His force, as the Africans say, had declined. Something had departed from him. God withdrew and left him to himself.

20 And she said, The Philistines be upon thee, Samson. And he awoke out of his sleep, and said, I will go out as at other times before, and shake myself. And he wist not that the LORD was departed from him.

The verse begins with Delilah's statement "And she said, The Philistines be upon thee, Samson" (*Wato'mer Pᵃlishtiym `aaleykaa Shimshown*). This is more than just saying something. The Hebrew *watomer* translated "and she said" is taken from the root *'amar*, meaning to "say." It could also mean that she answered, but we know that Samson was not talking, so Delilah was not answering him. "And she said" could also mean that Delilah boasted. In order to certify that she was successful, she issued a challenge. The verse could read "and she challenged him, Samson the Philistines are upon thee." So far, every time she had issued this challenge, Samson arose and met the challenge.

The text then turns to the reaction of Samson. We read that first "he woke out of his sleep" (Hebrew *Wayiqats mishᵃnaatow*). The word "awake" here is more than just waking up from sleep, it means to become active. Hearing the names of his enemies, Samson became agile and sprang up, tasting a fight. The Hebrew language may indicate that he stopped being slack or languid and became active or lively. The passage continues with "and (he) said, I will go out as at other times before, and shake myself" (Hebrew *wayo'mer 'Eetsee' kᵃpa`am bᵃpa`am wᵃ'inaa`eer*). Note that the word *wayomer* speaks to the state of Samson's mind more than it does to his words. The context suggests that he said this in his heart. It was as though

he certified within himself that he was in control of the situation. Samson awoke and communed with himself. The Hebrew word for "go" is translated from *eetee* which is the future form of *yatsa'* (**yaw-tsaw'**) indicating that Samson intended to break out and bring forth in order to carry out a purpose. It can also mean that he sought to escape. He had always gotten away, so this time he thought "I will get away." The phrase "as at other times " is translated from the Hebrew *bapa'am from pa`am* (**pah`-am**), which indicates the putting of one foot in front of another in movement or dance. It also may indicate that he was going to do what he did before, once again or this time also. What was he going to do this time? He said "shake myself" (Hebrew wᵃ*'inaa`eer*, from the Hebrew *na`ar*) which suggests that he was about to rouse himself as a warrior. It could also mean that he intended to tumble about using his fighting skills. It suggests that he was going to gymnastically toss them up and down to escape his enemies. Finally, we read in this passage "And he wist not that the LORD was departed from him" or "he had not knowledge that the Lord had left him" (Hebrew *Wᵃhuw' lo' yaada` kiy Yahweh caar mee`aalaayw*). The sentence begins with *wahuw*, which speaks to the capacity for self-reflection. The next two words then tell us the problem with Samson—*lo yaada`* or "not knowing." That was the problem: "in himself he did not know." It is assumed that this is something Samson should have known because he was trained to understand the presence of God in his life. Could it be that everyone else knew that the Lord had left him, but Samson himself, the very candidate, of God's presence, did not know? The word *yaada`* (**yaw-dah'**) means to know, but it also suggests that Samson could not see what was happening to him. He had lost his sense of observation. It could also mean that he did not care. Another way to look at it is that Samson refused to acknowledge that the Lord had left him. Apparently, He did not realize that his hair had been cut when he was startled out of his slumber.

Our Heavenly Father loves us too much to let us think we can get away with sin. Just as any good earthly parent would, our Heavenly Father "chastens" or disciplines us when we are disobedient (see Hebrews 12:5-11). And, the justness of His nature requires that He appropriately deal with disobedience through corresponding punishment.

It is a sad commentary that Samson decided to spring into action without being aware that ". . . the LORD was departed from him." We should hope that we are always in such close, intimate contact with God that we will notice those times when we cause a disruption in our fellowship with Him (1 John 1:5-7).

God is longsuffering toward us (2 Peter 3:9), but He will also reach a point where He decides to let people go ahead and do their own thing. If we continue to push our gift of free will to the limit in the wrong direction, God has shown that He will let us go our own way. Israel's first king, Saul, learned that sad fact (see 1 Samuel 15:23, 28, 35). Furthermore, God "gave over" to their own lusts and desires all people who refused to reverence Him (Romans 1:18-32). So, we must never be foolish enough to "tempt" God (Matthew 4:7). His grace and mercy are too precious to be taken lightly. Nor can we presume that we can dictate to God what He can or should do. If we take license with the grace we have received (see Romans 6:15), then we are putting ourselves in the same unfortunate position as Samson. And, like Samson, we run the risk of being left alone to fend for ourselves.

21 But the Philistines took him, and put out his eyes, and brought him down to Gaza, and bound him with fetters of brass; and he did grind in the prison house.

The phrase "and the Philistines took him" (Hebrew *Wayo'ch*ᵉ*zuwhuw* *P*ᵃ*lishtiym*) suggests by the use of the Hebrew 'achaz (aw-khaz') that they seized him in such a way that it caused him to become frightened. Furthermore it suggests that they fastened him as one will fasten one's pet animal. That was the first act in the process of destroying Samson. Secondly, we read they "put out his eyes" (Hebrew *Way*ᵃ*naqruw 'et- `eeynaayw*). The phrase "put out" does not really bring out the cruelty evident in the use of the word *Wayanaqruw.* The word actually means that they plucked out or literally dug his eyes out from his head. This reveals the cruel ways the Philistines dealt with the people of God. They further made him a public spectacle. They "brought him down to Gaza," their religious headquarters at that time. The word *yarad* (**yaw-rad'**) is translated "brought" and is from a primitive root meaning to descend or go downwards. There is a certain play on the use of the word. It may mean that Samson was taken to a lower region. On the other hand, it could refer to being in the territory of the enemy. They made him fall. Then "they bound him with fetters of brass." This is the second time the Hebrew *'acar* (**aw-sar**) meaning yoke or hitch is used. This time Samson was probably tied to a chariot and dragged around the city.

We read further "and he did grind in the prison house," which in the Hebrew reads *Way*ᵉ*hiy Towcheen b*ᵃ*beeyt haa'*ᵃ*cuwriym.* They dragged him around the city and then took him we are told to the prison house. Every word in this verse points to the progression of bondage to which the Philistines subjected Samson. They were not satisfied to have plucked out his eyes. They shackled him, even in his blind state, with metal cuffs and then tied him to a chariot probably pulled by horses. As if that were not enough, they now incarcerate him. This was not just the normal process for punishment of a criminal; Samson's treatment reveals the deep pathological fear under which the Philistines labored. Note also that they "made him grind." The phrase *towcheen* is taken from the Hebrew *tachan* (**taw-khan'**) which means to grind meal. However, it can also mean to became a concubine. The phrase "made him grind" refers to how Samson got to this point. From the Philistines' perspective, he was now at their service.

22 Howbeit the hair of his head began to grow again after he was shaven.

The way this verse is written suggests that something new was coming into being. The use of the word "began" or *wayaachel* from the word *chalal* (**khaw-lal'**) suggests that something was going to be born. It is the same word used in reference to being wounded. But here it may refer to the fact that Samson's bondage was now being dissolved. Figuratively, Samson was about to profane the people and their god Dagon. He was about to have a breakthrough. There was going to be a break from his suffering. The word further implies the opening wedge of a window to release someone into freedom. Something was happening to Samson that would enable him to play the Philistines like a flute. The word is directed to the symbol of Samson's covenant relationship with God. This new beginning is signified by the Hebrew *se`ar* (pronounced **say-awr'** or **sa`ar, sah'-ar**), which really would be akin to the words "dreadlocks" so that hair could be tossed around. Another phrase to note is the *l*ª*tsameeach ka'ªsher gulaach* denoting the inherent ability of a seed to sprout from a dead state to a living state. It also shows here that Samson's time of suffering was over and now he was about to bring forth something positive. Interesting here is the use of the word *ka-asher* which means after. But here it is significant in that it is placed between the word "grow" and the Hebrew word *gulaach* which means shaven but can also mean death. Something that was dead is now coming alive in Samson. The broken covenant is being repaired. God was making Samson's strength grow again. This was symbolized by the growth of his hair.

28 And Samson called unto the LORD, and said, O Lord GOD, remember me, I pray thee, and strengthen me, I pray thee, only this once, O God, that I may be at once avenged of the Philistines for my two eyes.

Samson's hair may have begun to grow naturally, which in his case indicated that God was at work for him. But the evidence of a spiritual gift does not necessarily indicate that one is right with God. Samson's real trouble came not so much from what he did but from the focus and attitude of his heart. The simple phrase "he said to himself, I will go out as at other times and shake myself" indicated that Samson was addressing himself, as the source of his own power. However, in verse 28 for the first time we see Samson praying. The verse reads "And Samson called unto the LORD" (Hebrew *wayaqqraa shimshon el YAHWEH*) The word for "call" is the Hebrew word *qara'* (**kaw-raw'**). For the first time in a long time, Samson properly addresses God by name. Thus far he had depended on his "anointing," but now he asks for

God's power by calling on God's name. When he cared only about his own self-gratification, he never even mentioned God except as a side reference. By calling on God, it is implied that he made a pronouncement about God. By acknowledging that God is indeed God, Samson takes a second step to restore his relationship with God through prayer. Samson knew that the first and most important place to turn in time of trouble is to the Lord. Samson prayed, "O Lord GOD, remember me." The Hebrew *zakar* (**zaw-kar'**) translated "remember" means to mark someone or something for the purpose of recognition. Such remembrance implies that one will be mentioned since a person who has been forgotten is never mentioned. In several African cultures, when a person has committed an abomination the elders prohibit even the mention of the person's name until that person is forgotten from memory of the community. Remembrance is also an important part of reconciliation. Samson knew that if God remembered or was mindful of him, he stood a chance of being favored.

The second part of his prayer focuses on the strength that Samson had lost because he strayed from God. Samson prays, "strengthen me" (Hebrew *wachazaqniy na*). Note that the word from the Hebrew translated "strengthen" is the word *chazaq* (**khaw-zak'**). It could convey the idea of the Spirit of the Lord connecting Himself to someone. If we take the word to mean fasten upon, we could conclude that Samson desires to be seized by the same spirit of strength which seized him before. He was asking for a courageous spirit which comes from divine strengthening. The word "strengthen" can also mean to cure from sickness. Samson may have recognized his sickness; he knew now that he was without spiritual and physical health. The word "strengthen" can also mean to repair or to fortify. Samson asked for aid and confirmation from the Lord. He had been wishy-washy, but now he asks to remain constant. He is asking the God of his covenant to re-establish this covenant with him.

Finally, he prays to be avenged of the Philistines. Samson's motives are still self-centered. He does not ask like David to defeat the Philistines because they have blasphemed the name of the God of Israel, but asks for vengeance "for my two eyes." Note the Hebrew word *naqam (naw-kam')*, which denotes a deep grudge held against an enemy. The word means to punish. The ultimate goal in Samson's final prayer was not to glorify God, but to satisfy his anger and pride. But God reveals His mercy towards the children of men. Even though Samson's prayer seems to be for personal revenge, God answered it because Samson's action would bring glory to God. Samson knew that his effectiveness for God was at an end. His blindness doomed him to be at the Philistines' mercy for the remainder of his days. He would be avenged, and the world would know that the false god Dagon was just another "vain imagination" (Romans 1:21) compared to the one true God of Israel.

29 And Samson took hold of the two middle pillars upon which the house stood, and on which it was borne up, of the one with his right hand, and of the other with his left. 30 And Samson said, Let me die with the Philistines. And he bowed himself with all his might; and the house fell upon the lords, and upon all the people that were therein.

The spirit of Samson's last words is reminiscent of what the Apostle Paul said of himself in 2 Timothy 4:6, 7: "For I am now ready to be offered, and the time of my departure is at hand. I have fought a good fight, I have finished my course, I have kept the faith." What a marvelous attitude to have when a believer faces death.

Neither Samson nor Paul was afraid of death. Both men were mighty servants of God who had done wondrous works on His behalf. And, they had both suffered severely for their cause. Surely there was no thought that the lives which God had given them had been wasted. Such a track-record undoubtedly will bring peace to the hearts and minds of God's children. If that is the case, then we too can have satisfaction in knowing that ". . . to be absent from the body (is) to be present with the Lord" (2 Corinthians 5:8).

In Judges 16:29, we are told that Samson leaned on the pillars of the false god Dagon's house and brought it crashing down. Everybody was destroyed. The Philistine lords who had conspired to enslave Samson and all their pagan followers

were crushed by the mighty power of God working through His servant for the last time.

The toppling of that structure also illustrates how unstable and worthless a belief system is which does not have Jesus at the core. "For other foundation can no man lay than that is laid, which is Jesus Christ" (1 Corinthians 3:11). Every "faith" which is built upon any foundation other than Christ is worthless. Ultimately, none of them will support the weighty matters of life. However, with the church of Jesus Christ that is not so. As a matter of fact, the Bible says that ". . . the gates of hell shall not prevail against it" (Matthew 16:18). Jesus is our ". . . precious corner stone, a sure foundation" (Isaiah 28:16).

Samson may have made mistakes along the way, but in the end God gave him a chance for final redemption. Believers can be encouraged from the fact that Samson had faults like we do. Yet, God still uses imperfect people to accomplish His perfect will. In spite of Samson's human weaknesses, the Bible forever records a tribute to his greatness, saying, "So the dead which he slew at his death were more than they which he slew in his life." And we have assurance that the same God who loved Samson and who worked in and through him will also be gracious toward us (2 Corinthians 9:8; Ephesians 2:7).

DAILY BIBLE READINGS

M: Manoah Seeks Guidance
Judges 13:1-14
T: Manoah Offers a Sacrifice
Judges 13:15-25
W: Wedding Feast and Riddle
Judges 14:5-20
T: Samson Defeats the Philistines
Judges 15:9—16:3
F: Samson and Delilah
Judges 16:4-17
S: Samson's Capture
Judges 16:18-22
S: Samson's Death
Judges 16:23-31

TEACHING TIPS

September 24
Bible Study Guide 4

1. Words You Should Know

A. Lamp (1 Samuel 3:3) Hebrew *Nir*—A light, a lamp, prosperity, or instruction. It also refers to the small bowl-like objects which contained oil and a wick for providing light.

B. Servant (v. 9) Hebrew *Eved*—A laborer, a servant, a slave, a man in bonds, a subject, a worshiper. Often the term was used as a polite and humble reference to oneself; also often used when speaking to superiors.

C. Pray (1 Samuel 7:5) Hebrew *Palal*—To judge, decide, punish, think, and act as a mediator. To pray to God, make supplication, entreat, intervene, and intercede for someone or a group.

2. Teacher Preparation

A. Begin preparing for this lesson by making use of the DEVOTIONAL READING, the BIBLE BACKGROUND, and the DAILY BIBLE READINGS.

B. Study the FOCAL VERSES for this week's lesson. Be sure to look up any unfamiliar phrases in a Bible dictionary or commentary.

C. Read through the Bible study lesson and take notes from the Teaching Plan. Feel free to make necessary adjustments to fit your class.

3. Starting the Lesson

A. Before the students arrive for class, write the lesson title and the AT-A-GLANCE outline on the chalkboard or newsprint.

B. Have a student read the IN FOCUS section and discuss how Reginald and Cherilyn's situation is similar to Hannah's. Ask students: "How can our faith remain strong after a trying experience such as Hannah's and Daniel's family had ?"

C. Ask a student to lead the class in prayer, focusing on the LESSON AIM.

4. Getting into the Lesson

A. Have students read the BACKGROUND section of the lesson in silence. Then ask the students what they hope to learn from today's lesson.

B. After you have studied the lesson using the AT-A-GLANCE outline, have one or two students discuss what important points were gleaned from each section. Write their answers under the appropriate section on the newsprint or chalkboard.

C. Use the SEARCH THE SCRIPTURES questions to challenge students in their thinking.

5. Relating the Lesson to Life

A. Review and discuss the DISCUSS THE MEANING questions. Encourage all students to participate so that the lesson comes alive for each.

B. Read the LESSON IN OUR SOCIETY article and allow time for discussion. This will help students determine how they plan to apply the lesson where they "live."

6. Arousing Action

A. Give class members an opportunity to complete FOLLOW THE SPIRIT and REMEMBER YOUR THOUGHTS.

B. Close the class in prayer, thanking the Lord for His grace as well as thanking Him for each student's participation. Be sure to encourage them as they head off to worship service.

SEPT 24TH

WORSHIP GUIDE

For the Superintendent or Teacher
Theme: Samuel
Theme Song: "I'm a Soldier in the Army of the Lord"
Scripture: 2 Corinthians 4:1-7
Song: "Yes Lord"
Meditation: Thank You, Lord for hearing my prayer. Help me to respond to You at all times. In Jesus' name, Amen.

SAMUEL

Bible Background • 1 SAMUEL 3; 7:3-14
Printed Text • 1 SAMUEL 3:2-9, 19-20; 7:3-5, 12
Devotional Reading • LUKE 12:35-40

LESSON AIM

By the end of the lesson, students will be able to explain how God called Samuel, understand the importance of obeying God's Word and submitting to godly leadership, and commit to listening and responding to God's call on their lives.

KEEP IN MIND

"Speak; for thy servant heareth" (1 Samuel 3:10).

FOCAL VERSES

1 Samuel 3:2 And it came to pass at that time, when Eli was laid down in his place, and his eyes began to wax dim, that he could not see;

3 And ere the lamp of God went out in the temple of the LORD, where the ark of God was, and Samuel was laid down to sleep;

4 That the LORD called Samuel: and he answered, Here am I.

5 And he ran unto Eli, and said, Here am I; for thou calledst me. And he said, I called not; lie down again. And he went and lay down.

6 And the LORD called yet again, Samuel. And Samuel arose and went to Eli, and said, Here am I; for thou didst call me. And he answered, I called not, my son; lie down again.

7 Now Samuel did not yet know the LORD, neither was the word of the LORD yet revealed unto him.

8 And the LORD called Samuel again the third time. And he arose and went to Eli, and said, Here am I; for thou didst call me. And Eli perceived that the LORD had called the child.

LESSON OVERVIEW

LESSON AIM
KEEP IN MIND
FOCAL VERSES
IN FOCUS
THE PEOPLE, PLACES,
AND TIMES
BACKGROUND
AT-A-GLANCE
IN DEPTH
SEARCH THE SCRIPTURES
DISCUSS THE MEANING
LESSON IN OUR SOCIETY
MAKE IT HAPPEN
FOLLOW THE SPIRIT
REMEMBER YOUR THOUGHTS
MORE LIGHT ON THE TEXT
DAILY BIBLE READINGS

9 Therefore Eli said unto Samuel, Go, lie down: and it shall be, if he call thee, that thou shalt say, Speak, LORD; for thy servant heareth.

3:19 And Samuel grew, and the LORD was with him, and did let none of his words fall to the ground.

20 And all Israel from Dan even to Beersheba knew that Israel was established to be a prophet of the LORD.

1 Samuel 7:3 And Samuel spake unto all the house of Israel, saying, If ye do return unto the LORD with all your hearts, then put away the strange gods and Ashtaroth from among you, and prepare your hearts unto the LORD, and serve him only: and he will deliver you out of the hand of the Philistines.

4 Then the children of Israel did put away Baalim and Ashtaroth, and served the LORD only.

5 And Samuel said, Gather all Israel to Mizpeh, and I will pray for you unto the LORD.

7:12 Then Samuel took a stone, and set it between Mizpeh and Shen, and called the name of it Ebenezer, saying, Hitherto hath the LORD helped us.

IN FOCUS

Reginald and Cherilyn Daniels desperately wanted to be parents before Cherilyn's 30th birthday. They tried natural conception, artificial insemination, and in vitro fertilization, but nothing worked. Cherilyn's womb would not hold any of the seven fetuses, so they never developed to full term. Finally, the Daniels flew to Mayo Clinic in Minnesota to see a specialist who ran a series of tests to find out why Cherilyn's body rejected the babies before she gave birth.

After three months of consultations, examinations, and medications, the specialists had no answers for the Daniels. Cherilyn was physically fit and healthy enough to carry a baby to full term.

The Daniels returned home from Minnesota frustrated, angry, and saddened by their experience. So they prayed. "Lord, if you desire for us to be parents, we ask You to please intervene by performing a miracle on our behalf. In Jesus' name, Amen."

Reginald and Cherilyn called other Christian friends to pray for them and God truly answered their prayers! Today they have three healthy children, notwithstanding the initial diagnosis. This faithful couple experienced the joy of answered prayers. As a result, these parents feel that since they have received answers from the Lord, their children belong to God.

This week, we will examine the life of Samuel, another one of God's special children who became an intricate part of Israel's life in the Promised Land.

THE PEOPLE, PLACES, AND TIMES

Ashtaroth. A Caananite goddess, the wife of El according to Ugaritic tradition, but the consort of Baal in Palestine. It is thought that Ashtaroth and Baal were a "divine" couple, associated with fertility.

The cult of the goddess Ashtaroth and the use of the cultic object associated with her are persistently opposed in Israel's literature. Israel's faith did not permit the worship of gods other than Yahweh. The danger constantly existed that the exaltation of a form of idol worship modeled on the association of Baal and Ashtaroth would take root in Israel. This Canaanite divine couple lived with a sexual endowment. The Yahweh of the Bible, however, was not to be thought of as a sexual being.

(The Harper Bible Dictionary, Paul J. Achtemeier, Editor, 1986, San Francisco: Harper and Row Publishing Co., 1986 p. 75.)

BACKGROUND

Samuel is one of the key figures in the first of two books of the Bible which bear his name. He was the last of Israel's judges and also served as a prophet. In fact, Samuel was the transitional figure between the period of the judges and the beginning of Israel's monarchy.

Samuel's mother Hannah was not able to bear children by her husband Elkanah because the Lord had closed her womb (1 Samuel 1:5-6). But Hannah continued praying, believing the Lord would give her a baby, just as he had given children to Peninnah, Elkanah's other wife.

One day, while Hannah was in the temple praying, she made the Lord a promise. If God would let her conceive, Hannah would (1) give the child back to the Lord for the rest of his life; and (2) make her son a Nazarite (see 1 Samuel 1:11 and Numbers 6:2-21).

Eli, the priest of the temple, saw Hannah praying silently and thought she was drunk because she made no sound even though her lips were moving. However, Hannah assured the priest that she was not drunk. She was crying out in desperation to the Lord. Later, Hannah conceived and named her son Samuel, which means in Hebrew "asked of God" (1 Samuel 1:19-27). Hannah kept her promise and brought her child to the temple where he would be raised by Eli (v. 28).

God knew that Hophni and Phineas, Eli's sons, lived corrupt lives, sleeping with the women at the door of the tabernacle (1 Samuel 2:21). Because Eli failed to discipline his sons and allowed them to continue serving in the temple, God brought judg-

AT-A-GLANCE

1. Samuel Is Called by God
(1 Samuel 3:2-5)
2. Samuel Is Unsure of the Call
(vv. 6-9)
3. Samuel Walks in His Calling
(vv. 19-20)
4. Samuel's Calling Is Firmly Established
(1 Samuel 7:3-5, 12)

ment on Eli and his family. He would no longer be fit to serve Israel. Instead, God was grooming another who would eventually take Eli's place (1 Samuel 2:22-36).

IN DEPTH

1. Samuel Is Called by God (1 Samuel 3:2-5)

Samuel's apprenticeship in ministry began when he was young and during the time when God's Word to His people was scarce. Because Israel refused to obey the Lord and did what was right in their own eyes (Judges 21:25), there was no visionary leader who was ordained by God to speak into the lives of the people (1 Samuel 3:1).

The Bible does not say how long Samuel worked under Eli, but the prophetic word that was spoken by the man of God against Eli was coming true (see 1 Samuel 2:27-36). He was going blind and God was preparing to raise up Samuel as His prophet for Israel.

It is interesting to note that Samuel describes this time as when "the lamp of God went out in the temple of the LORD, where the ark of God was" (v. 3). One of the meanings for the word "lamp" is instructions and prosperity. The ark represents the manifest presence of God and the temple is where the Holy Spirit resides. As a result of Eli's refusal to discipline his sons, God's instructions, prosperity, and presence were leaving Eli and his family, never to return. We need to be careful that we don't allow sin to gain a tremendous foothold in our lives so that God's instruction and prosperity leave us!

Eli and Samuel were all alone in the temple. Both of them were sleeping soundly. Suddenly, Samuel heard the Lord call his name, but he did not know it was the Lord. Samuel must have heard a strong audible voice awaken him because he got up and ran directly to where Eli was sleeping, perhaps thinking that Eli wanted him to do some temple work. The old man must have been surprised to see Samuel standing at his bed when he awoke from sleep. In essence, Eli said, "What are you doing out of your room and in mine?"

Samuel was convinced that Eli had called him. However, Eli assured Samuel that he hadn't called him, that he should go back to sleep. Those may have been Eli's instructions, but God wasn't finished with Samuel.

2. Samuel Is Unsure of the Call (vv. 6-9)

Settled back in his room, Samuel was prepared to follow Eli's instructions: lie down and go to sleep. But God wanted Samuel's full attention. So, as Samuel probably pulled the covers over his head, God called his name again. This time, Samuel marched into Eli's room determined to find out why the old man had called him and said, "Here am I, for thou didst call me" (v. 6).

Eli rose slightly up from his bed and looked at the young boy, probably in frustration. "I didn't call you. Now go back to bed!"

Samuel went back to his room confused. Not only did he not yet know the voice of the Lord, but he had no intimate knowledge of God's Word (v. 7). All he knew was that someone had called his name. Since there was no one else in the temple besides him and Eli, Samuel concluded that it had to be Eli who spoke.

Samuel lay down on his bed again, but the Lord wasn't finished with him. The third time Samuel heard God's voice, he went to Eli's room. This time, Samuel wasn't leaving unto he got a satisfactory answer from Eli. Rather than arguing with the child, Eli finally got the message himself. He recognized that Samuel was hearing the voice of the Lord. So, the old man gave him specific instructions. If Samuel heard the voice again, rather than get up from his bed and run to Eli, he should simply say, "speak, LORD, for thy servant heareth" (v. 9). With those instructions, Samuel returned to his room for another encounter with "the voice."

Have you been unable to recognize the voice of the Lord in your life? Sometimes we are so busy that we don't take time to listen when the Lord speaks. It is vitally important that we train our spirits so that we are listening when God speaks to us.

3. Samuel Walks in His Calling (vv. 19-20)

Once Samuel spoke the words, "speak, LORD, for thy servant heareth" (v. 9), God gave him a message about His coming judgment against Eli and his sons. In essence, God confirmed to Samuel the word that the prophet had spoken earlier against Eli (vv. 10-18).

Because Samuel was obedient to speak the words of God to Eli, he increased in his understanding and knowledge and received tremendous favor from the Lord. In fact, Samuel became one of the greatest Old Testament prophets of God because he passed the test that the Lord had placed before him.

Has God given you specific instructions to speak to someone who may be out of His will? Don't let fear keep you from speaking. God may be testing you to see whether you will obey Him or seek to please others. We too can be used mightily of God if we are willing to pass the tests that He sets before us.

4. Samuel's Calling is Firmly Established (1 Samuel 7:3-5, 12)

The next time we see Samuel in Scripture is after the death of Eli and his crooked sons and the Philistines' capture of the Ark of the Covenant. Israel recognized that because they refused to follow the Lord, His glory had departed from them (1 Samuel 4:22). Now, as they mourned and lamented, Samuel is prepared to challenge and rebuke Israel about their lifestyle.

First, Samuel reminds them of the importance of putting away their foreign gods, Baalim and Ashtaroth, which were Canaanite fertility gods that the people worshiped, probably to restore their crop loss. Secondly, the prophet told the people to prepare their hearts unto the Lord. It is one thing to stop sinning and another to repent. Many believers will stop sinning, especially when they are caught in their sins. But God doesn't just want us to stop. He also wants us to forsake and turn away from our sins. That's what it means to repent.

Finally, Samuel challenged the people to become single-hearted in their devotion to the Lord. It is time for God's people to stop straddling the fence. We must be like Joshua: "and if it seem evil unto you to serve the LORD, choose you this day who ye will serve . . . but as for me and my house, we will serve the LORD (Joshua 24:15). Samuel assured the people that if they followed his counsel, the Lord would move on their behalf and deliver them from their enemy. Israel recognized that to gain God's help they had to follow God's prophet. So they ceased their idolatrous ways and committed themselves to serve the Lord God.

Convinced that the people meant business, Samuel gathered Israel at Mizpeh to offer up prayers of intercession on their behalf. Mizpeh was a border town between Judah and Israel and one of the cities that Samuel visited on his circuit judging Israel (1 Samuel 7:16-17). After Samuel prayed and the Lord answered, he built a memorial to remind Israel of God's intervention. The prophet took a stone and placed it between Mizpeh and Shen and called it Ebenezer, which in Hebrew means "the stone of help." Because of Samuel's intervention, Israel would never forget that the Lord had helped them.

SEARCH THE SCRIPTURES

1. What was Samuel doing when he heard the Lord's voice the first time? (1 Samuel 3:2-3)

2. Who did Samuel think was calling him? (vv. 5-6)

3. Why didn't Samuel recognize the voice of the Lord? (v. 7)

4. How did Eli tell Samuel to respond to the voice? (v. 9)

5. Where was Samuel established as a prophet to Israel? (vv. 19-20)

6. What did Samuel tell Israel they must do to please God? (1 Samuel 7:3-5)

DISCUSS THE MEANING

1. Why was Eli going blind?

2. Does God speak to us today as He did to Samuel? Why or why not?

3. Are there prophets of such magnitude as Samuel in our local churches? Discuss.

4. How was Samuel able to serve as both judge and prophet?

LESSON IN OUR SOCIETY

Are babies who are dedicated to the Lord from birth sometimes born to parents who live in impoverished conditions? What can we learn from today's lesson that can help us recognize those on whom God has placed His favor and blessing?

MAKE IT HAPPEN

This week, commit to spending at least 30 minutes a day listening to God's voice. You may have to turn off the television and radio and isolate yourself from others. Once you have trained your spirit to hear what He says to you, write it down in a journal so you can review it later. Then thank God for His presence in your life this week.

FOLLOW THE SPIRIT

What God wants me to do:

_____

_____

REMEMBER YOUR THOUGHTS

Special insights you have learned:

_____

_____

MORE LIGHT ON THE TEXT
1 Samuel 3:2-9, 19-20; 7:3-5, 12

3:2 And it came to pass at that time, when Eli was laid down in his place, and his eyes began to wax dim, that he could not see.

This verse begins "and it came to pass at that time" (Hebrew *Wayᵉhiy bayowm*), which could be translated "in those days." The word *yowm* (**yome**) could mean that it was hot, thus signifying the rise and set of the sun. Here it describes the character of an age. It can also convey the meaning "as life went on" through the perpetual movement of time. But in this passage of Scripture, the writer is about to speak to a particular season of one's life. As we read further, it becomes obvious this is the season of life "when Eli was laid down in his place."

The Hebrew phrase *hahuw' wᵉ-'Eeliy shokeeb bimqomow* places the emphasis on the words *shokeeb bimqomow* or "laid down in his place." This may suggest several things. First, that it was evening and Eli had gone to lie down. It could also suggest that Eli was cast down emotionally. Given what we learn about his children, the writer may have also used this word to cast a wide web over all that was happening to this man of God in the evening of his life. So, from a literal perspective, the phrase denotes the fact that he went to sleep after his work as priest. On the other hand, it could also symbolize the downcast spirit of a man of God whose children will not follow in his righteous ways. Second, the phrase "in his place" may suggest that, as was the custom of the priest, Eli slept in the tabernacle area during his time of service. "In his place" here would mean that he went to his normal place of rest.

The use of the word *bimqowmow* in the Hebrew from *maqowm* (**maw-kome'**) speaks to one's proper standing or ranking within a community. The word can mean a specific locality. However, figuratively it denotes a condition of the body or mind. It can symbolize the moral or mental outlook of a country or people in a home. So, in verse 2, Eli had stopped doing what he used to do and was now getting respite from his labor—either out of tiredness or from discouragement.

We read further that "his eyes began to wax dim, that he could not see" (Hebrew *wᵃ`eeynaayw heecheeluw keehowt lo' yuwkal lir'owt*). Eli had worked as a priest for quite awhile and was now either in retirement or ready to retire. Physically, he was deteriorating because "...his eyes began to wax dim, that he could not see." Spiritually, his failing eyesight may have been symbolic of the way he had overlooked or had been blind to the evil conduct of his two sons throughout the years (see 1 Samuel 2:22-25).

Eli had heard reports of how his sons led Israel astray (see v. 17), but apparently he had not taken any effective steps to curb their behavior and corrupting influence. At this point in Eli's life, he must have resigned himself to the fact that his life had run its course. As he lay down each night, he must have felt that he had come to the end of his road.

Unfortunately, many of our more senior Christians today allow themselves to feel that they are now too old to be of any use to God. They feel that they have little to offer toward the building of God's kingdom. So, they withdraw and become less active in the body of Christ (or the Church) to enter a kind of "spiritual retirement."

But that is a satanic deception. Nothing could be further from the truth. Every believer is important to the body of Christ (see 1 Corinthians 12:12-31). God knew that there would be members of every age when He first created the Church. He knew there would be very young Christians, middle-aged Christians, and very old Christians. Yet, His Word never indicates that a believer in Christ becomes obsolete.

On the contrary, God's Word places value on the fact that more senior believers have plenty to offer. God clearly has a role for our senior members. For example, God's Word describes them as

valued teachers, saying, "Let the elders that rule well be counted worthy of double honour, especially they who labour in the word and doctrine" (1 Timothy 5:17). The way they carry themselves and live their lives along their Christian journey is to be followed as a pattern by younger saints (see Titus 2:2-8).

3 And ere the lamp of God went out in the temple of the LORD, where the ark of God was, and Samuel was laid down to sleep;

Young Samuel was faithful to his role and his duties in the temple (see 1 Samuel 2:35; 3:1). Eli could not count on his own sons for righteous service in the temple, but Samuel was a different story. It must have done Eli good to see God provide such an industrious and obedient young man for temple service. Apparently, Samuel could be counted upon to be the last one to go to bed, ". . . ere the lamp of God went out in the temple."

Samuel's diligence is an example for today's church where there are many members who suffer from being lazy about the work of the Lord. There is an old and familiar saying in our churches that "eighty percent of the work is done by twenty percent of the people." And, we tend to receive that saying with little more than an Eli-type of nod and spiritual wink at such behavior. But God does not "wink" when we are spiritually trifling. God expects us to work on His program of building His kingdom within this corrupted world. God expects every believer to "bear fruit" (see John 15:5). Jesus said, "Every branch in me that beareth not fruit he (the Father) taketh away; and every branch that beareth fruit, he purgeth it, that it may bring forth more fruit" (John 15:2).

The Bible warns against idleness and laziness, or "slothfulness," saying, "Slothfulness casteth into a deep sleep; and an idle soul shall suffer hunger" (Proverbs 19:15). Further, "The soul of the sluggard desireth, and hath nothing" (Proverbs 13:4). And, "The hand of the diligent shall bear rule: but the slothful shall be under tribute" (Proverbs 12:24). The fact that young Samuel was the last person to go to bed at night, probably around midnight, is highly significant. His dedication to his work in the temple put him in a position to be greatly used and greatly blessed by God. If we are

wise, we will follow Samuel's lead. And, we will be greatly used by God and, accordingly, greatly blessed by Him as well.

4 That the LORD called Samuel: and he answered, Here am I.

Young Samuel's industry and dedication led to one of the highest spiritual blessings: a direct call from God by name. There were no prophets who proclaimed God's word at that time (v. 1). And, God chose not to employ the service of an angel. Rather, God Himself directly addressed the young man. Samuel's dedication to helping Eli in every way possible is evident by the way he quickly replied, "Here am I." Even though Samuel must have been tired and was finally in his bed, he thought he heard his elder's voice and did not hesitate to be available.

This attitude is quite a contrast to that of some of our modern-day youth. Today, some elders hear sighing or hissing sounds in response to their calls. It is a sound of exasperation, as though the elder is bothering, irritating, or imposing upon the youth. Or, oftentimes, there is no response at all to a perfectly audible call. So the elder has to repeat it . . . even louder. That "response" of silence is a disrespectful ignoring of the audible call because the youth does not want to be bothered. And, sometimes, the elder must repeat the call a couple of more times before hearing another exasperated response. At any rate, Samuel's rapid, "Here am I" is a good example for our youth to follow.

5 And he ran unto Eli, and said, Here am I; for thou calledst me. And he said, I called not; lie down again. And he went and lay down.

Again, the fact that Samuel "ran" to Eli is indicative of a good and compassionate servant's spirit within the boy. He did not know if the older man was sick, hungry, or whatever. But he was eager to do whatever he could. And, again, this attitude is one which we need to instill in all believers today.

6 And the LORD called yet again, Samuel. And Samuel arose and went to Eli, and said, Here am I; for thou didst call me. And he answered, I called not, my son; lie down again.

In verse 6, the sequence of events is repeated,

only this time Samuel goes straight to his master before verbally responding.

7 Now Samuel did not yet know the LORD, neither was the word of the LORD yet revealed unto him.

Samuel was dedicated by his mother for a life of service to God in the temple (see 1 Samuel 1:28). And, he had served in the temple since the time he was a child (see 1 Samuel 2:18). Yet, he still was not familiar with the person and presence of God. Samuel's state should make many Christians pause to ask serious personal questions at this point. For example, how well do we really know God for ourselves? Do we know when He is speaking to us? Is it through the Holy Spirit? Through other people? Through circumstances, or His Word? Do we know enough about Him to know His will and plan for our lives? Are we, in fact, living within that will and plan?

Many lifelong Christians are no more familiar with the person and presence of God than young Samuel appeared to be. Salvation is a wonderful thing. But God wants us to move beyond resting at the salvation stage. He wants us to progress to a true "relationship" with Him. One which is deep, intimate, and fulfilling.

Jesus said, "I come that they might have life, and that they might have it more abundantly" (John 10:10). That means that God considers our state in this life to be just as important to Him as our state in eternity (after death). We must "abide" in Jesus during this earthly life (see John 15:7) in order to experience the spiritually "abundant" life of which He speaks. And, to do this we must take every step to get to know Him and deepen our relationship with Him.

8 And the LORD called Samuel again the third time. And he arose and went to Eli, and said, Here am I; for thou didst call me. And Eli perceived that the LORD had called the child.

God called Samuel's name a third time. And, for the third time Samuel misdirected his response. This sequence is indicative of the fact that once our gracious Father has decided to call us to Himself, He will accomplish His purpose (see Romans 8:28-30). In our text, Eli finally real-ized that it was God who called Samuel. Eli understood that God was seeking to reveal Himself to Samuel and enter his life in a whole new way.

Many believers can testify that we did not come to Christ the first time we heard, or even understood, the Gospel message. Some of us rejected the call of God two, three, four and even more times. We continued on in our lives of sin and rebellion. Yet, God in His infinite mercy kept right on "calling." Just as He so patiently did with Samuel, God kept calling us until we responded to Him, and we owe Him the highest praise for His persistent pursuit of our souls.

9 Therefore Eli said unto Samuel, Go, lie down: and it shall be, if he call thee, that thou shalt say, Speak, LORD; for thy servant heareth.

It is conceivable that Eli could have let God's call to Samuel bother him since his own sons were such a severe disappointment. But Eli did not appear to get upset when he realized what God was doing. Eli immediately did what he could to help young Samuel in that situation.

The Bible condemns envy and jealousy in the lives of believers (see Romans 13:13; 1 Corinthians 3:3; Galatians 5:26; and James 3:14-16). Like Eli, we must not let such emotions overtake us or prevent us from serving God and helping other believers. What God does in the life of someone else is not our concern (see John 21:20-22). We have to concentrate on our own walk with the Lord.

Finally, in the highlighted verse, Eli did that which an older and more mature believer should do. He gave the younger person counsel and instruction. He told Samuel to say, "Speak, LORD; for thy servant heareth." Eli's instruction harbors good advice for people of all ages, throughout all the ages. We should always be attuned to hearing God's words above all others (see Isaiah 40:7-8 and Matthew 4:4). And, we must always see ourselves as servants, both of God and of men (see Matthew 23:11-12; Philippians 2:5-8).

3:19 And Samuel grew, and the LORD was with him, and did let none of his words fall to the ground. 20 And all Israel from Dan even to Beersheba knew that Samuel was established to be

a prophet of the LORD.

7:3 And Samuel spake unto all the house of Israel, saying, If ye do return unto the LORD with all your hearts, then put away the strange gods and Ashtaroth from among you, and prepare your hearts unto the LORD, and serve him only: and he will deliver you out of the hand of the Philistines.

With the rise of Samuel, Israel continues their roller-coaster relationship with God. They came to Samuel asking for help, but this time Samuel does not let them off so easily. He immediately let them know that they have left the Lord whom they now seek and were serving strange gods. His solution for the problem is highlighted by the use of the word *shuwb* (**shoob**), which means to turn back. Israel had indeed left God literally to worship other gods. They had turned away from God and now they wanted help from the very God whom they rejected. The word "turn" means to lie down. Israel had been fighting God; now they must lie down quietly. They were led into pain and sadness because of their wastefulness and now they must come back home again. They had forgotten what God meant to them. Samuel instructed them that in order to return to God they must first turn to God with their whole heart, and they must do so as a nation.

The use of the Hebrew word *cuwr* (**soor**) means they must turn off the voices of the other gods. The English translation reads "put away," but more importantly they must decline all help from these gods; they must shun these gods. These gods must now be seen as grievous entities. Whatever they may have planted for these other gods must be plucked away by God. Samuel says they must "prepare their hearts." The use of the Hebrew word *kuwn* (**koon**) suggests that Israel was bent over by the other gods and now they must stand erect. They must become direct in their dealings with God, exhibiting faithfulness in their worship. They must now intentionally serve God with all their heart.

4 Then the children of Israel did put away Baalim and Ashtaroth, and served the LORD only. 5 And Samuel said, Gather all Israel to Mizpeh, and I will pray for you unto the Lord.

In this passage we see that the Children of Israel followed the instruction of the Lord through Samuel and rebelled against the strange gods that led them into bondage. In verse 5 Samuel gives them one instruction to complete their conversion back to the Lord. They must *qabats* (**kaw-bats'**), or gather together for prayer to the God of their ancestors. Only then, Samuel insists, will he pray for them. The word *palal* (**paw-lal'**) used here to refer to prayer also refers to being a judge. The judges served as intercessors for the people. Therefore, Samuel is saying that he will not be their judge or leader until they decide to follow the Lord with all their hearts.

12 Then Samuel took a stone, and set it between Mizpeh and Shen, and called the name of it Ebenezer, saying, Hitherto hath the LORD helped us.

After Israel returned to the Lord and Samuel prayed for them, God answered their prayer and delivered them from the Philistines. Samuel then erected a memorial for the people to remember what God had done for them.

DAILY BIBLE READINGS

M: Samuel Listens for God's Call
1 Samuel 3:1-9
T: Samuel Hears God's Message
1 Samuel 3:10-14
W: Samuel Becomes God's Prophet
1 Samuel 3:15–4:1
T: Samuel Gathers Israel
1 Samuel 7:3-6
F: Defeat of the Philistines
1 Samuel 7:3-11
S: Samuel Judges Victorious Israel
1 Samuel 7:12-17
S: Always Be Watchful
Luke 12:35-40

TEACHING TIPS

October 1
Bible Study Guide 5

1. Words You Should Know

A. Goodly (1 Samuel 9:2) Hebrew *tov*—Good, beautiful, excellent and lovely. It may also refer to practical or economic benefit, happiness, or preference.

B. King (1 Samuel 10:19) Hebrew *Melekh*—A ruler, prince, or idol king. Officials at many levels were designated by this title. The approximate meaning of this root word is the same across many Semitic cognate languages.

2. Teacher Preparation

A. Begin preparing for the quarter by reading the GENERAL INTRODUCTION, the QUARTER AT-A-GLANCE, and the UNIT 1 INTRODUCTION.

B. Read 1 Samuel 9—10 and write down any points you may glean from your reading that would be helpful to share with students.

C. Now read and underline specific words in the FOCAL VERSES that you want to highlight in your teaching time.

D. Materials needed: Bible, pens or pencils, chalkboard or newsprint.

3. Starting the Lesson

A. After the students have settled in their seats, ask them to share any points they may have learned from last quarter's lessons.

B. Have a student read the IN FOCUS story and comment on how it relates to today's FOCAL VERSES.

C. Have a student lead the class in prayer, focusing on the KEEP IN MIND verse and the LESSON AIM in the prayer.

4. Getting into the Lesson

A. Have students silently read the FOCAL VERSES according to the AT-A-GLANCE outline and make appropriate comments as necessary.

B. Share the definition of "goodly" and "king" from the WORDS YOU SHOULD KNOW section in the *Teaching Tips* and allow students to discuss the meanings.

C. To help students understand the lesson in detail, read the BACKGROUND section and answer the SEARCH THE SCRIPTURES questions.

5. Relating the Lesson to Life

A. Have students answer the DISCUSS THE MEANING questions and develop ideas they may have regarding the LESSON IN OUR SOCIETY.

B. Ask students to read THE PEOPLE, PLACES, AND TIMES section. Encourage them to apply any points they may get from this section in their own lives.

6. Arousing Action

A. Remind students to write down any important points they learned in the FOLLOW THE SPIRIT and REMEMBER YOUR THOUGHTS sections.

B. Challenge students to read and meditate on the DAILY BIBLE READINGS throughout the week and write down any points they may learn in a journal.

C. Close the class with prayer and affirm your students as they leave for worship service today.

OCT 1ST

SAUL BECOMES KING

Bible Background • SAMUEL 9:1—10:27
Printed Text • 1 SAMUEL 9:1-2; 10:17-26
Devotional Reading • PSALM 119:1-8

LESSON AIM

By the end of the lesson, students should be able to explain how Saul became king, list some ways we try to usurp God's will for our lives, and commit to follow the Lord no matter how difficult or confusing His instructions may seem.

KEEP IN MIND

"And Samuel said to all the people, See ye him whom the LORD hath chosen, that there is none like him among all the people?" (1 Samuel 10:24)

FOCAL VERSES

1 Samuel 9:1 Now there was a man of Benjamin, whose name was Kish, the son of Abiel, the son of Zeror, the son of Bechorath, the son of Aphiah, a Benjamite, a mighty man of power.

2 And he had a son, whose name was Saul, a choice young man, and a goodly: and there was not among the children of Israel a goodlier person than he:

10:17 And Samuel called the people together unto the LORD to Mizpeh;

18 And said unto the children of Israel, Thus saith the LORD God of Israel, I brought up Israel out of Egypt, and delivered you out of the hand of the Egyptians, and out of the hand of all kingdoms, and of them that oppressed you:

19 And ye have this day rejected your God, who himself saved you out of all your adversities and your tribulations; and ye have said unto him, Nay, but set a king over us. Now therefore present yourselves before the LORD by your tribes, and by your thousands.

LESSON OVERVIEW

LESSON AIM
KEEP IN MIND
FOCAL VERSES
IN FOCUS
THE PEOPLE, PLACES,
AND TIMES
BACKGROUND
AT-A-GLANCE
IN DEPTH
SEARCH THE SCRIPTURES
DISCUSS THE MEANING
LESSON IN OUR SOCIETY
MAKE IT HAPPEN
FOLLOW THE SPIRIT
REMEMBER YOUR THOUGHTS
MORE LIGHT ON THE TEXT
DAILY BIBLE READINGS

20 And when Samuel had caused all the tribes of Israel to come near, the tribe of Benjamin was taken.

21 When he had caused the tribe of Benjamin to come near by their families, the family of Matri was taken, and Saul the son of Kish was taken: and when they sought him, he could not be found.

22 Therefore they inquired of the LORD further, if the man should yet come thither. And the LORD answered, Behold he hath hid himself among the stuff.

23 And they ran and fetched him thence: and when he stood among the people, he was higher than any of the people from his shoulders and upward.

24 And Samuel said to all the people, See ye him whom the LORD hath chosen, that there is none like him among all the people? And all the people shouted, and said, God save the king.

25 Then Samuel told the people the manner of the kingdom, and wrote it in a book, and laid it up before the LORD. And Samuel sent all the people away, every man to his house.

26 And Saul also went home to Gibeah; and there went with him a band of men, whose hearts God had touched.

IN FOCUS

Craig Bradshaw had been the incumbent mayor of Omaha for the past 15 years. Yet, his administration was never sensitive to the African American community. After a rash of drive-by shootings and a wave of senseless violence, many people were fed up with Mayor Bradshaw and demanded a change.

The groundswell for change came when George Peters, a young Black man who had graduated from Georgetown University's Law School, was convinced that he should run for mayor as a write-in candidate. Because Peters had the support of most of the Black churches in the city, not only did he run a clean campaign, but won the general election by an overwhelming percentage over Mayor Bradshaw.

When people are committed to change there is nothing they can't achieve when they come together. By combining social, economic, and political forces, people can make a difference in their future. Like the people of Omaha, Israel made a decision that affected their future; and we will see exactly how in today's Bible Study Guide.

THE PEOPLE, PLACES, AND TIMES

Gibeah. Gibeah is a Hebrew word meaning "hill" in contrast to "mountain." As a name, it is attached in Old Testament tradition to a site in Benjamin, the home of Saul and center for his career as king (1 Samuel 10:26). Under the modern name *Tell el Ful,* the site which is located about five miles north of Jerusalem, reveals a succession of occupations that, at least in part, corresponds with the Old Testament's account of Saul's residence. The earliest relevant level, destroyed by fire in the twelfth century B.C., provides the context for a more extensive and fortified construction from the Early Iron Age. The most important building from this level is an eleventh-century structure, a fortress with casemate wall and corner tower, perhaps the "rustic palace" of King Saul. Successive constructions suggest that some violent destruction occurred, with rebuilding of more modest quality. The site was finally abandoned.

(The Harper's Bible Dictionary, Paul J. Achtemeier, General Editor, San Francisco: Harper and Row Publishing Co., 1984 pp. 345-346).

BACKGROUND

The Book of 1 Samuel tells the story of Israel's transition from the period of the judges to the monarchy. Samuel, the last of the judges, is the key figure in the book for several reasons: (1) God

used him to anoint both kings: Saul and David; (2) as the spiritual overseer of Israel, Samuel played an important role in all phases of the nation's early life in the promised land; (3) as God's spokesman, Samuel was used mightily to challenge Israel to walk in the holiness of God despite the nations around them.

Samuel knew that the influence of the ungodly nations that surrounded Israel would affect their relationship with God since they were called to be a separated people.

However, like those nations, Israel wanted an earthly king who would represent them as head of state, and no amount of teaching from Samuel could convince them otherwise. Therefore, God instructed Samuel in the selection process of Israel's first king, whose name was Saul.

AT-A-GLANCE

1. Saul: A Good-Looking Man
(1 Samuel 9:1-2)
2. Samuel Identifies Saul
(1 Samuel 10:17-21)
3. Saul Is Named King Over Israel
(vv. 22-26)

IN DEPTH

1. Saul: A Good-Looking Man (1 Samuel 9:1-2)

Samuel begins by giving the genealogy of Saul, the man who would be king. Saul was the great, great, great grandson of Aphiah, the son of Kish, and a member of the tribe of Benjamin. Nothing extensively is known of Saul's immediate family, except that his father was a "mighty man of power." The Hebrew word that is used for "power" is *chayil* and one of its meanings is "wealthy and full of substance." So it is possible that Kish had a lot of money and property in Israel (see vv. 3-20).

Samuel goes on to describe Saul as "a choice young man and [a] goodly" which means he was very handsome. In fact, the Bible declares that there was not a more handsome man in all of Israel.

We must to be careful that we don't select people for leadership based on their looks or their bank accounts. We need God's knowledge and wisdom to make such selections, and it is vitally important that we seek Him when making leadership decisions.

2. Samuel Identifies Saul (1 Samuel 10:17-21)

The Lord had made it clear to Samuel that Saul would be Israel's first King (1 Samuel 9:15-17). Therefore, Samuel was instructed to bring the people together so he could share the news with them and introduce Israel to her new leader.

Samuel calls all of Israel to Mizpeh, one of the circuit cities where he ministered. Mizpeh is on the border of both Israel and Judah. Because of the importance of Samuel's announcement, it is possible he made his usual rounds, pricking the curiosity of the people so that they were eager to hear what he had to say as they arrived in Mizpeh.

Before Samuel introduced Saul, the prophet gives Israel a warning from God in the form of a brief history lesson. First, Samuel reminds the people that it was God who brought them out of Egyptian bondage and into Canaan in the midst of their enemies. No doubt, the people had heard how Moses led their fathers into the Promised Land and of Joshua's victories. But Samuel wanted the people to know that it was God who was in control of every situation that Israel faced.

We need to be careful that we don't exalt our accomplishments over God's ability and power. While Scripture affirms that God uses people to do His work (Ephesians 2:10; 4:11-13), we must keep in mind that without God we can do nothing!

The second point that Samuel makes is that by requesting a king and insisting on being like the other nations, Israel was rejecting the One who could help them the most for one who would ultimately fail Israel and God. No matter how the other nations fared under an earthly monarch, Israel's success was intimately tied to their allegiance and obedience to God. Because the people wanted to be like the other nations, that allegiance was being severed based on their own decision.

The Bible declares that believers are "a chosen generation, a royal priesthood, a holy nation [and] a peculiar people [who are called] to show forth the praises of [God] who hath called [us] out of darkness into His marvelous light" (1 Peter 2:9). We are not to be like "the Joneses" and others around us who don't have a personal relationship with Jesus Christ. No matter how successful or affluent they may be in the secular world, without Jesus in their lives, unbelievers are doomed to a Christless eternity.

The third instruction that Samuel gave the people was to line up by tribes so that he could begin to select the king. Though Samuel knew who would be chosen by divine wisdom, the prophet intended for the people to get involved in the process since it was their request that he (and God) was honoring.

Samuel had the people cast lots to select Benjamin as the tribe through whom the king would come. Next, Matri, the Benjamite family, also was selected by lot. Finally, the selection process was narrowed down to Saul, one of Kish's sons and a member of Matri's family.

Like the apostles who cast lots to discover who would replace Judas before the church began (see Acts 1:24-26), the Jews understood this procedure as a means by which God's will would be known to them in this decision. Once the lot fell on Saul, the people were ready to crown him king. However, there was one problem: Saul could not be found among the people!

3. Saul Is Named King Over Israel (vv. 22-26)

How could the people crown their king if he was nowhere in sight? Determined to be ruled by an earthly monarch, Israel did the only thing that would be sure to help them find Saul. They called on the Lord.

Human nature is strange. Israel had rejected the Lord's sovereignty for one of their own choosing. Yet, they sought the Lord's help to find the one who would replace Him in their lives. How often have we cried out to the Lord to get us out of a jam only to fall right back into the same hole He brought us from? Why do we reject the Lord's commands only to want His instructions and help when we suffer the consequences of that rejection? If we would stay on the right path at all times, we wouldn't have to cry out to the Lord in our desperate struggles.

Samuel shows how merciful the Lord is. Though the people had rejected Him, which was similar to a proverbial "slap in the face," the Lord helped them find their king. Perhaps the idea of being selected was too overwhelming for Saul. One day he had met the man of God, and the next day he became king over all of Israel. Whatever the reason, once Saul found out that he would be king, he hid himself among some baggage nearby. However, because God told the people where Saul was, it was easy for them to identify him, even if he was hiding.

Saul was very tall and good-looking; in fact, he was the most handsome man in the whole nation. As the people stood around admiring him, Samuel shouted out that Saul was indeed the king whom God had chosen for them. Elated and overjoyed at his stature, his demeanor, and even the "favor" that was on Saul, the people cried out in unison "God save the king" (v. 24).

The Book of Deuteronomy has specific instructions to Israel on the nature of an earthly monarchy. Samuel had already given the people God's Word about the kingdom (1 Samuel 8:10-18). Now it was time, not only for Samuel to reiterate the change that would take place in Israel with an earthly king, but also to write it down so that they would be reminded of their decision at a future date. Once Samuel had finished his task, he let the people go to their homes, and he instructed Saul to return to Gibeah with a band of soldiers whose main function was to protect the king at the instructions of the Lord.

Saul's rise to be king is a reminder of how important it is for believers to listen to the Lord rather than doing our own thing and going our own way. No matter how difficult and confusing God's instructions may appear to be, ultimately His will and way is the best for our lives.

SEARCH THE SCRIPTURES

1. What family was Saul from? (1 Samuel 9:1-2)

2. How was Saul described? (v. 2)

3. Why did Samuel call the people together in Mizpeh? (1 Samuel 10:17-19)

4. How was Saul selected to be king? (vv. 20-22)

5. Where was Saul when the people looked for him? (vv. 22)

6. What were Samuel's last words to the people? (v. 25)

DISCUSS THE MEANING

1. Why is it important that we listen to the Lord at all times?

2. What is the difference between being in God's perfect will and His permissive will?

3. Should we select people for leadership positions based on their gifts, their looks, or both? Why or why not?

4. Why do people reject God's counsel to follow their own? Discuss.

LESSON IN OUR SOCIETY

The African American community is often guilty of selecting leaders who are charismatic, but lack substance. What are the important principles we can learn from today's lesson that we can share with activists and others who have a vested interest in our communities? Write out a brief action plan to be shared with others in the class.

MAKE IT HAPPEN

This week, determine to follow the Lord's leading in your life not matter how unusual or unfamiliar it may be to you. Set aside at least 10 minutes every morning and evening in quiet meditation to hear God speak to you regarding His direction for your life. Write down in a journal any key words you may hear in order to reflect on them later this month.

FOLLOW THE SPIRIT

What God wants me to do:

_____

_____

REMEMBER YOUR THOUGHTS

Special insights you learned:

_____

_____

MORE LIGHT ON THE TEXT
1 Samuel 9:1-2; 10:17-26
   9:1 Now there was a man of Benjamin, whose

name was Kish, the son of Abiel, the son of Zeror, the son of Bechorath, the son of Aphiah, a Benjamite, a mighty man of power.

Benjamin, the smallest of the 12 tribes of Judah, gets its name from the youngest son of Jacob by Rachel. The name of the tribe of Benjamin is correctly interpreted as "the southerner" or "son of the south." The writer identifies Kish as a member of the tribe of Benjamin and establishes his genealogy through the identification of his ancestors: Abiel, Zeror, Bechorath, and Aphiah. It is through legends and oral traditions that include Aphiah that we find Kish, the Benjamite, to be a mighty man of power. He is described as a man of wealth who possesses servants and asses (1 Samuel 9:3), fields and oxen (1 Samuel 11:5). He is also a member of the Matrites clan (1 Samuel 10:20-24).

The beginning of this verse reads *Wayahiy- 'iysh mi-Binayaamiyn Uwshmow Qiysh* and is translated "There was a man of Benjamin named [or whose name was] Kish." This is a way of stating that this story is about a specific person. Some stories begin with "at that time" or "in those days." However, this one begins with a reference to a person, suggesting that the writer is about to narrate the pedigree of the one for whom the story is written.

The phrase "there was a man" if translated from *'iysh, eesh* would be stated as "one exists." However, the wording here implies more than just the existence of a human being. It is as though the writer is responding to a question about the existence of one who can perform a particular act. In this context, it could be construed as the response to Israel's inquiry for a king in 1 Samuel 8:6. Israel had asked, "Can we have a king like other nations?" The next logical question then would be, "Is there anyone who can be our king?" Hence the statement, "there was a man" becomes an answer to the people's query. In a communal people, the question often arises: "Who are his people?" Even today people in African cultures tend to begin the description of who they are by referencing their ancestry. It is often used as an adjunct to a more definite term (and in such cases frequently not expressed in translation). Here when the writer says "there was a man," he may really be saying there was a champion named Kish. This

word captured what it meant to be a man in Israel: a husband, a good father, and a friend. This man was from the tribe of *Binyamiyn* (**bin-yaw-mene'**), which is a combination of two words *ben* meaning son and *yamiyn* meaning right hand. "There was a man of the tribe of Benjamin, whose name was Kish" means he was already singled out as unique. The word translated "named" is the Hebrew is *Uwshmow* derived from the Hebrew word *shem* (pronounced **shame**) and refers to someone with a definite and conspicuous position, possibly meaning here that the person whose name appears has made a name for himself.

This man was named Kish (Hebrew *Qiysh*). Some have maintained that this name derives from the word for bow and that possibly his father was an archer. If it is related to the word *qowsh* (**koshe**), which means to bend, it may mean that this man Kish had something to do with archery. This man Kish was the son (Hebrew *ben*) or the bearer of the family name of *'Abiy'el* (pronounced **ab-ee-ale'**). His father's name in Hebrew means God of my father or God is father. Abiel was the son of *tserowr* (**tser-ore'**) meaning parcel or a package. His father was probably named from the occupation of packaging. Today in many African families, the naming of people based on their traditional occupation is still practiced.

The next ancestor of Kish is Bechorath (*Bekowrath* **bek-o-rath'**), whose name is probably Egyptian in origin. The name Aphiah (Hebrew *Apiyach*, pronounced **af-ee'-akh**) means to blow or breeze. Finally, the Scripture reads "a Benjamite, a mighty man of power" (Hebrew *Bin-yamiyniy gibowr chaayil.*) The question then arises, "Is the final phrase referring to Kish or to Aphiah?" It should refer to Kish, because he and his immediate descendants are the focus of this story. Thus we should read, "there was a man of renown, Kish . . . a Benjamite a mighty man of power." The word "might" comes from the Hebrew word *gibbowr* (pronounced **ghib-bore'**) and suggests that this man was a warrior, a champion of the people; he was among the chiefs of Israel. Another word attached to the word "mighty" is the word "power." It is taken from the Hebrew word *chayil* (**khah'-yil**) meaning that he had force or power because of the number of people under his leadership. In

African culture today, the idea of leading many people is to have power. We can therefore infer that Kish was also a man of means and resources. It also suggests that he was wealthy. The Hebraic idea of power also included virtue. Valor and strength must be undergirded with virtue and character.

2 And he had a son, whose name was Saul, a choice young man, and a goodly: and there was not among the children of Israel a goodlier person than he: from his shoulders and upward he was higher than any of the people.

The statement "And he had a son whose name was Saul" refers to Kish. "And he had a son" (Hebrew *Walow-haayaah been*) is a statement of accomplishment. The fact that no other child is mentioned may be a hint that this man searched for a son until he had Saul. Like his father before him, he had a son to carry on the family name. If the name Saul means "asked or requested for from the Lord," then the statement "he had a son" has more emotional meaning than appears at first glance. Remember that in the ancient world (as well as in African cultures today) a name defines a person's position and is a mark or memorial of one's uniqueness as a person. It is an embodiment of one's character. If the name Saul (Hebrew *Sha'uwl*) is connected with the word *wsha'al* which means to ask, it may either be that his parents asked for him or maybe God chose a person with that name to emphasize Israel's childish request for a king.

We read further that "he was a choice young man" (Hebrew *baachuwr waaTowb*). The writer now proceeds to describe Saul, and wants the reader to know that he was from a good family, as well as good-looking. From all appearances, he had the makings of a king. The phrase "choice young man" is taken from the Hebrew word *bachuwr* (pronounced **baw-khoor'**) and suggests that he was properly selected. It also suggests that Saul may have been collectively selected by his peers to be a leader. The next adjective is "goodly" from the Hebrew word *towb* (**tobe**) meaning good. In other words, he was all masculine, beautiful, and the best-looking man around. It also suggests that he was cheerful, at ease, and looked kind. We

read further "and there was not among the children of Israel a goodlier person than he" (Hebrew *Wa'eeyn 'iysh mibneey Yisraa'eel Towb mimenuw*). The writer makes a point of saying that there was no other man in Israel at that time who was as good looking as Saul. There was no other champion in Israel that would have won the consent of every one of his fellow kindred as being this handsome.

Next, we read a specific description of his physical features. First he was head, neck, and shoulders above all the people. The word *shekem* (**shek-em'**) translated shoulder could mean that his place of burden was higher than everyone else's. Another word used here is the Hebrew word *ma`al* (pronounced **mah'-al**) referring to the upper part of the body. However, as it is used here it means that he was above—from the top exceeding everyone. He was, in a physical sense, what they had envisioned a king to be. Note also the use of the word "higher." It is the Hebrew word *gaboahh* (**gaw-bo'-ah**), which may mean that he was more powerful; however, it can also mean arrogant. The Hebrew captures the idea that everything which may appear good has an underside. It could also mean that he was lofty and proud.

10:17 And Samuel called the people together unto the LORD to Mizpeh;

Samuel is the leader of all Israel who acts as a priest, judge, intercessor, and prophet of Yahweh. Samuel gathers the people at Mizpah, a city of Benjamin on the border between Judah and Israel, five miles north of Jerusalem. Many scholars identify Mizpah of Benjamin as a place where political and military decisions were made (1 Kings 15:22; 2 Kings 25:23). However, other sources claim it to be a place of prayer and worship for all Israel (Judges 20-21; 1 Samuel 7; 10:17-27).

We are told that "Samuel called the people together." The Hebrew word translated "called" is *tsa`aq* (**tsaw-ak'**) which forms the root word from which the phrase *Wayats`eeq* (meaning to shriek) is taken. Here it means that Samuel proclaimed an assembly. He sent out a cry across the land for the people to gather themselves. The word "people" is the Hebrew word `am. This was a call to the people as a congregated unit. It could also mean that

Samuel called all the troops together seeing that they were about to coronate a king, and he would need soldiers from the nation to work with him. But this gathering did not concern the king even though the purpose was to select a king. The gathering was unto the Lord. They gathered at Mizpeh. There were at least five places with this name in Palestine. It simply means a watchtower, meaning thus far Samuel had been the watchman of Israel.

18 And said unto the children of Israel, Thus saith the LORD God of Israel, I brought up Israel out of Egypt, and delivered you out of the hand of the Egyptians, and out of the hand of all kingdoms, and of them that oppressed you:

When Samuel summoned all the people of Israel he speaks for God among the people. First he reproves them for rejecting the governance of God through a prophet and desiring a king. He reminds them of what God has done for them; he reminds them of their happiness under the divine government of God, who brought them up out of Egypt, and delivered them from the kingdom that oppressed them. Samuel answered the people's action with a word from the Lord, challenging their action. He then proceeded to charge them with the sin of not recognizing what God had done for them. They had declared that God's government was not good enough and expressly demanded to be like the other nations around them. Now they must hear from the Lord.

Samuel begins with a prophetic word "thus says the Lord God of Israel" (Hebrew *Koh- aamar Yahweh 'Eloheey Yisraa'eel.*) Stated in a different way the word *koh* (**ko**) as translated here means "like this"; thus one can interpret this to say "God says it like this" or "what God says is this." It could also mean that Samuel is throwing the word to them; "here now is what God says." What does God say? "I brought up Israel"(Hebrew *Aanokiy he*ʿᵃ*leeytiy 'et-Yisraa'eel*) This could read "I myself brought Israel up." Just in case they had forgotten, it was not a king that brought them up from the bondage of Egypt. The word brought is from the Hebrew word ʿ*alah* (pronounced *aw-law'*) meaning that God caused them to ascend. God had made them higher than they were in Egypt; He caused them

to actively mount upward from the depths of despair. In numerous situations, literally and figuratively, they had seen God cause them to rise above their enemies. In their darkest hour God had been their break of day. In a sense this word means that God carried them up. He did not call them up, He reached down and carried them up. He has exalted them and caused them to excel. He has kept them from falling. The word also implies that God had given them increase. God had raised them, recovered them and restored them. This was not just an academic exercise. God names the place and time when He did all of this for them; it was in Egypt. The Hebrew name for Egypt is *Mitsrayim* (**mits-rah'-yim**) meaning a sense of limits, a besieged place, or a place of defense. Another translation is the word *matsowr* (**maw-tsore**), meaning a fortified place or strong tower, but some scholars say it means suffering. However, if the word *matsor* is derived from the Hebrew word *Mitsraim* it implies that Egypt was a place of enclosure. It was a place that limited Israel's ability to serve God. God says further that he snatched them away from the hand of all who oppressed them. The Hebrew word translated "delivered" is *natsal* (**naw-tsal'**) meaning that God always helped them escape the traps set for them by their enemies. God has preserved them. Samuel then says that it is God who delivered them from "out of the hand of all kingdoms, and of them that oppressed you."

The use of the word "hand" (*yawd*) indicates power or force. God delivered them not just from one oppressor but from "all" oppressors. Deliverance was whole and not partial. It was from any and every oppressor using all manner of methods. Some oppressors were rulers of "kingdoms" (Hebrew *mamlakah*, **mam-law-kaw'**) having dominion over vast areas. Others were just renegades with large estates seeking to rule someone. If their goal was to "oppress" (Hebrew *lachats*, **law-khats'**), that is, to press down God's people and to distress them, God was there to deliver them. In their affliction God stood with them and sent them help. Whoever sought to crush them by force had to face their God.

19 And ye have this day rejected your God, who

himself saved you out of all your adversities and your tribulations; and ye have said unto him, Nay, but set a king over us. Now therefore present yourselves before the LORD by your tribes, and by your thousands.

After telling Israel of all that the Lord God has done for them, Samuel likewise tells Israel of the offense they have put upon God in desiring a king to save them. Israel rejects God by demanding a king. Israel is greatly influenced by the surrounding nations and begin to conform to the accepted customs of the day. They want to imitate other nations by having a king to govern them. Often, following the crowd is not the right choice. Many adults seek to conform to widely accepted customs, even when they know their actions are wrong. It is possible that the writer of Matthew has these persons in mind when he writes, "Heaven can be entered only through the narrow gate! The highway to hell is broad, and its gate is wide enough for the multitude who choose its easy way. But the gateway to life is small, and the road is narrow, and only a few ever find it" (Matthew 7:13-14, LB).

God is not pleased with their requests, because He wants to be first and foremost in their lives. Yet, despite God's displeasure, He decides to grant them their desire. Samuel begins this section "and ye have this day"; it is almost as though Samuel is saying after all these things God has done for you, here you are today. Look at yourself Israel, tell me what you see. It is as though Samuel is the prosecutor of Israel. Here you are today rejecting that same God who has delivered you. "And ye have this day rejected your God"; the use of the word "this day" is powerful. The word "day" (Hebrew *yowm*, **yome**) suggests it was in the day-time. While this translation refers to a particular day, one could also translate this word to mean continually or daily. Thus Samuel could be referring to their continual rejection of God, or saying you daily reject God.

It could also be that Samuel is saying you are now rejecting God as at other times. This daily rejection of God as ruler did not just happen, it was a process. The word "reject" is taken from the Hebrew word *ma'ac* (pronounced *maw-as'*), meaning to spurn or to abhor someone or something.

Samuel is saying, "today you have cast away your God." The word used for God here is the Hebrew word *'Elohiym;* note that Samuel does not use the proper name for God. Could he be suggesting that Israel has treated the Lord as one of the pagan gods? Have they treated God as a thing of political expediency? The King James Version says, "who himself saved you out of all your adversities and your tribulations." In the undertone of this statement one can almost hear Samuel asking, "Do you know who you are rejecting? This God is the one who has saved you." The Hebrew word translated "saved" is *yasha`* (**yaw-shah'**); it is this God who has opened wide your prison doors and set you free. He is the one who has caused Israel to be safe. He is the one who gives you succor. It also means that God is the one who avenged and defended them. God has been their salvation from adversities and tribulations.

The two words "adversities" and "tribulation" in Hebrew are *ra`* meaning evil, natural, or moral, and *tsarah* (**tsaw-raw'**) meaning a tight place or trouble; often used to express rivalry between two women. In other words in misery God was their comfort; when they were vexed He soothed them; when wickedness overwhelmed them He allowed righteousness to flow. Samuel had just told them what God said and in the middle of this verse he states:… ye have said unto him, Nay, but set a king over us." By the use of the word "said" (Hebrew *amar,* **aw-mar'**) Samuel is saying not only have you "said" or "spoken out," but you have answered as well. God has said I will be your king, but you have said no. God will vouch for you but you have said "no." You have challenged God's rulership and thus charged God with injustice. Instead of looking at God's record with them and saying "yes" to God, they said "no" and demanded a substitute in the form of a king. Samuel tells us that they said, *"melek taasiym aleeynuw"* literally, "put a king over us."

The Hebrew word *suwm* (set) is a way of saying appoint someone. They were saying to God change things from the way they are and put someone else in charge. In their mind this someone in charge is a king. The Hebrew word for king is *melek* (**meh'-lek**). It can also be expressed as *malak* and means to ascend the throne, induct

into a secret group, or more importantly to take counsel. Thus from now on instead of seeking divine counsel and consulting God as they had under Samuel, they would seek the counsel of a human king. Samuel further instructs them to present themselves to the place of worship according to their tribes; he wants all the people in their place before the Lord. Here Samuel uses the Mosaic name for God, i.e. Lord. Maybe this was Samuel's last effort to discourage them from favoring a human king rather than the Divine rulership of Yahweh. But this was also probably to make sure everybody saw whom God would choose.

20 And when Samuel had caused all the tribes of Israel to come near, the tribe of Benjamin was taken.

Samuel uses the voting technique used in the ancient world of casting lots in the selection process of the king. The method is used to solve political and labor-related problems preventing all disputes and exceptions, thereby causing all contention to cease. Samuel knows whom God has chosen, and he has already anointed him. This is a method of confirmation. The writer makes a point to tell us that he caused them to come near. This suggests they were probably far away because they knew that they offended God with their request. The Hebrew word *qarab* (**kaw-rab'**) means to approach or to cause one to be brought near for whatever purpose. This was a call for them to join him in the presence of the Lord. As they came near, the rod of the tribe of Benjamin was taken. The Hebrew word *lakad* (**law-kad'**) seems suggest that the tribe of Benjamin was caught.

21 When he had caused the tribe of Benjamin to come near by their families, the family of Matri was taken, and Saul the son of Kish was taken: and when they sought him, he could not be found.

The lot fell on Saul, the son of Kish. He was selected out of the tribe of Benjamin, the family of Matri. Yet, Saul is not present. Perhaps he wanted to avoid responsibility or attention. The Hebrew word *shebet* (pronounced **shay'-bet**) means tribe, but can also mean a stick used for punishing. It may have come from the tribal staff which leaders of tribes carried (recall Judah's staff which he gave to Tamar). They were asked to approach and offer themselves in the presence of the Lord and their brethren. When they did a family was chosen. The Hebrew word for "family" is *mishpachah* (pronounced **mish-paw-khaw'**) representing a circle of relatives. We are then told that the family chosen was that of Matri, from the family of Saul, the son of Kish. But he was nowhere to be found. They "sought him" Hebrew *baqash* (**baw-kash**), that is to say they ran after him. They asked and begged him. They requested for him to take it but he was not there.

22 Therefore they inquired of the LORD further, if the man should yet come thither. And the LORD answered, Behold, he hath hid himself among the stuff.

After searching for Saul to no avail the people turned back to God for direction. Perhaps he withdrew hoping that in his absence, they would select someone else. Saul appears to refuse to accept responsibility. The Israelites believed that God had chosen Samuel by lot. Therefore, God must have approved Saul's appointment. So, they set out to search for him. They search and inquire for Saul, whose name in the Hebrew means "to inquire." The beginning of this verse shows the frustration of the people. Before he is even coronated he wearies the people and God. We read, "Therefore they inquired of the LORD further, if the man should yet come thither." A word used in this verse is the Hebrew word `owd ode which says that they continued to inquire of the Lord. They repeatedly beseeched the Lord. They questioned whether they should still choose him. The King James Version reads, "if the man should yet come hither?" Their question was should they still bring him up there to be their king. They seemed to not be quite sure that this man was the king they needed. In the later part of the verse the Lord answered them "he hath hid himself among the stuff." The Hebrew translation of the word "hid" is *chaba'* *(khaw-baw)* meaning to do something in secret. If we look carefully at the word "stuff" (Hebrew *keliy* pronounced **kel-ee'**) one could interpret this to mean he was hiding among the luggage or behind some sort of apparatus.

23 And they ran and fetched him thence: and when he stood among the people, he was higher than any of the people from his shoulders and upward.

When the people heard where he was they divided into search parties. They find Saul hiding among the carriages. Samuel presents him to the people, and they accept him because he stands taller than all the others. The Hebrew word for "ran" is the word ruwts (roots) and suggests they divided quickly and ran in haste. Again, we see the word "stood"(Hebrew *yatsab yaw-tsab*) meaning they wanted him to take his station i.e., they wanted him to stand in the middle.

24 And Samuel said to all the people, See ye him whom the LORD hath chosen, that there is none like him among all the people? And all the

people shouted, and said, God save the king.

Saul is proclaimed king of Israel. He is actually the people's king. God pleases the people by choosing a man who is outwardly pleasing. He is tall and has physical strength. Often in human affairs, it is the taller man who receives the promotion. Yet, when God makes a choice, God looks inwardly at the heart (1 Samuel 16:7). *The Matthew Henry Commentary* states that, "When God would please the people with a king he chose a comely man; but, when he would have one after his own heart, he should not be chosen by the outside. Men judge by the sight of the eyes, but God does not. The Lord looks on the heart . . . . " Samuel tells them that he is the one that God has chosen in response to their request. He uses the Hebrew word bachar (baw-khar') which is translated "chosen" meaning to try or appoint. Was this a trial king to see if they were ready? It is only by implication that the word also means to select or excellent. Samuel then proceeds to tell the people that there is none other like Saul in all the land. At this point we read that the people shouted. The Hebrew word ruwa` (pronounced roo-ah') means to make a shrieking noise which may split the ears. They blew horns and made a joyful noise. The King James Version reads, "God save the king." However, the original Hebrew translation of "save"—to make alive, to give or to promise life, to revive suggested by the use of the Hebrew word chayah (pronounced khaw-yaw') or "save," literally reads "may the king live" or "God revive the king." One can also read it as "God nourish and preserve the king."

25 Then Samuel told the people the manner of the kingdom, and wrote it in a book, and laid it up before the LORD. And Samuel sent all the people away, every man to his house.

Samuel settles his duties with the people. He is no longer politically or militarily responsible. Samuel tells them the state of affairs of the kingdom and explains the duties of the king. All this information is then recorded in a book. In this verse the writer uses the word "told" (Hebrew dabar daw-bar') to describe Samuel's last conversation with the people. This word means to arrange words so as to speak them correctly. He was speaking to subdue impetuousness. His was a declaration of kingdom rules; he was laying down for them the manner of the kingdom. The word used to describe these rules is "manner"—Hebrew mishpat (pronounced mish-pawt'). He has given them the verdict from their dialogue with God and is now making a judicial pronouncement. These divine laws were in the form of a formal decree concerning governing the people and their king. In the abstract sense this word manner means justice. Samuel was putting on paper the right manner in which to run the kingdom. Samuel dismisses the people, everyone to his own house.

26 And Saul also went home to Gibeah; and there went with him a band of men, whose hearts God had touched.

At Samuel's dismissal of the people, Saul returns to Gibeah, to his father's house, with a band of men. God touches the hearts of these men, and as a result, they go with Saul as his support.

DAILY BIBLE READINGS

M: Saul Searches for Man of God
1 Samuel 9:1—10:27

T: Samuel Recognizes Saul
1 Samuel 9:11-16

W: Saul Meets Samuel
1 Samuel 9:18-21

T: Saul Anointed King
1 Samuel 9:22-27

F: Samuel Directs Saul
1 Samuel 10:2-8

S: Saul Prophesies
1 Samuel 10:9-16

S: Saul Proclaimed King
1 Samuel 10:17-26

TEACHING TIPS

October 8
Bible Study Guide 6

1. Words You Should Know

A. Anointed (1 Samuel 16:13) Hebrew *mashach*—To rub with oil, to besmear, to consecrate. A very important part of Jewish ceremony.

B. Countenance (1 Samuel 16:7, 12) Hebrew *mar'eh*—The outward appearance, the face, or the part of a person visible to the eye.

2. Teacher Preparation

A. Familiarize yourself with the BIBLE BACKGROUND and DEVOTIONAL READING for the lesson.

B. Next, study the FOCAL VERSES, paying particular attention to the KEEP IN MIND verse.

C. Read the BIBLE STUDY GUIDE for today's lesson. Write down any questions you may have as you read the biblical content.

D. Materials needed: Pencils or pens, Bible, map of Israel and Judah.

3. Starting the Lesson

A. Before students arrive, write the AT-A-GLANCE outline on the chalkboard or newsprint along with the names SAMUEL and DAVID.

B. After the students arrive, assign three to read the FOCAL VERSES according to the AT-A-GLANCE outline. Be sure students have paper and pencils or pens to take notes.

C. Now assign several students to answer the SEARCH THE SCRIPTURES and DISCUSS THE MEANING questions later in the class time.

D. Have a student pray, using the LESSON AIM as the foundation of the prayer.

4. Getting into the Lesson

A. Have a student read the IN FOCUS story. Ask students to comment on how it relates to today's lesson.

B. Ask a volunteer to read the BIBLE BACKGROUND. Briefly review last week's lesson to see how it relates to today's lesson.

C. Direct students' attention to the names of SAMUEL and DAVID on the chalkboard or newsprint. Have students comment on how today's lesson relates to both men and write their comments under each name on the board.

D. After students have finished reading the IN DEPTH section, ask the students to give answers to the SEARCH THE SCRIPTURES and DISCUSS THE MEANING questions.

5. Relating the Lesson to Life

A. Have a student read the KEEP IN MIND verse.

B. Have students give brief comments on why God selected David. Also have them comment on whether or not David was qualified to be king.

C. Read the LESSON IN OUR SOCIETY assignment. Give students an opportunity to brainstorm ideas for implementation.

OCT 8TH

6. Arousing Action

A. Ask students to come up with a specific plan on how they intend to complete the MAKE IT HAPPEN assignment.

B. Remind students to read the DAILY BIBLE READINGS for the week which will help them grow in their walk with the Lord.

C. Close the class with prayer.

WORSHIP GUIDE -

For the Superintendent or Teacher
Theme: Saul Rejected and David Anointed
Theme Song: "I Say Yes, Lord"
Scripture: Psalm 23:1-6
Song: "I'll Go All The Way"
Meditational: Lord, help me to follow You no matter the cost. Keep me from rejecting or preferring others based on their looks. Help me to see and love others the way you see and love me. In Jesus' name, Amen.

SAUL REJECTED AND DAVID ANOINTED

Bible Background • 1 SAMUEL 15:10—16:13
Printed Text • 1 SAMUEL 16:1-7, 11-13
Devotional Reading • ISAIAH 55:6-11

LESSON AIM

By the end of the lesson, students should be able to explain why David was anointed to be king, affirm God's process of selecting leaders, and commit to obeying God's directions no matter the cost.

KEEP IN MIND

". . . The LORD seeth not as man seeth; for man looketh on the outward appearance, but the LORD looketh on the heart" (1 Samuel 16:7).

FOCAL VERSES

1 Samuel 16:1 And the LORD said unto Samuel, How long wilt thou mourn for Saul, seeing I have rejected him from reigning over Israel? Fill thine horn with oil, and go, I will send thee to Jesse the Bethlehemite: for I have provided me a king among his sons.

2 And Samuel said, How can I go? If Saul hear it, he will kill me. And the LORD said, Take a heifer with thee, and say I am come to sacrifice to the LORD.

3 And call Jesse to the sacrifice, and I will show thee what thou shalt do: and thou shalt anoint unto me him whom I name unto thee.

4 And Samuel did that which the LORD spake, and came to Bethlehem. And the elders of the town trembled at his coming, and said, Comest thou peaceably?

5 And he said, Peaceably: I am come to sacrifice unto the LORD: sanctify yourselves, and come with me to the sacrifice. And he sanctified Jesse and his sons, and called them to the sacrifice.

LESSON OVERVIEW

LESSON AIM
KEEP IN MIND
FOCAL VERSES
IN FOCUS
THE PEOPLE, PLACES,
AND TIMES
BACKGROUND
AT-A-GLANCE
IN DEPTH
SEARCH THE SCRIPTURES
DISCUSS THE MEANING
LESSON IN OUR SOCIETY
MAKE IT HAPPEN
FOLLOW THE SPIRIT
REMEMBER YOUR THOUGHTS
MORE LIGHT ON THE TEXT
DAILY BIBLE READINGS

6 And it came to pass, when they were come, that he looked on Eliab, and said, Surely the LORD'S anointed is before him.

7 But the LORD said unto Samuel, Look not on his countenance, or on the height of his stature; because I have refused him: for the LORD seeth not as man seeth; for man looketh on the outward appearance, but the LORD looketh on the heart.

16:11 And Samuel said unto Jesse, Are here all thy children? And he said, There remaineth yet the youngest, and, behold, he keepeth the sheep. And Samuel said unto Jesse, Send and fetch him: for we will not sit down till he come hither.

12 And he sent, and brought him in. Now he was ruddy, and withal of a beautiful countenance, and goodly to look to. And the LORD said, Arise, anoint him: for this is he.

13 Then Samuel took the horn of oil, and anointed him in the midst of his brethren: and the Spirit of the LORD came upon David from that day forward. So Samuel rose, and went to Ramah.

IN FOCUS

The Bradshaw administration was extremely nervous when they discovered that the African American community had selected one of their own to oppose the mayor in Omaha's general election. Having taken the Black vote for granted for years, Mayor Bradshaw knew that he would have to visit many of the black churches in the city if he expected to win another term as mayor.

However, this time the mayor's platitudes, one-liners, and broken promises did not win over the people. In the end, Mayor Bradshaw was ousted from office and young George Peters was voted in. When asked why the change occurred, many in the Black community stated that not only was it a rejection of the man, but also a rejection of his policies and the promise of good things to come with Mayor-elect Peters.

Sometimes change is important, especially when policies fail and people's lives are at stake. The idea of "out with the old and in with the new" should apply when corrupt leaders are more intent on following their own agenda rather than doing what is best for all. In today's Bible Study Guide, we will get a clear understanding of this principle when Saul is rejected and David is anointed as the new king of Israel.

THE PEOPLE, PLACES, AND TIMES

Bethlehem. The Hebrew word literally means "house of bread." Bethlehem was a small town of approximately 15,000 inhabitants, about five miles south of Jerusalem, but now forming part of the modern Jerusalem-Bethlehem conurbation. Perched 2,460 feet above sea level on the north-south ridge road along the central highlands, the city of Bethlehem faces westward to the fertile cultivated slopes around Beit Jala and eastward to the desolate wilderness of Judah.

Bethlehem was first mentioned in one of the Armana letters written to Egyptian pharaohs by local kings of Palestine and Syria prior to 1250 B.C. Prior to the period of the Israelite monarchy, Bethlehem was the home of the Levite who went to act as priest for a man named Micah in Ephraim (Judges 17:7-13) and of the unfortunate concubine, whose murder caused the tragic massacre of the people of Gibeah (Judges 19—20). Bethlehem also figures prominently in the story of Ruth, the great-grandmother of David (Ruth 1:2—4:11). Bethlehem was also the family home of King David and the place of his anointing by Samuel (1 Samuel 16:4-14).

After the division of the Hebrew kingdom into Israel and Judah following Solomon's death, Bethlehem was one of the 15 cities in Benjamin and Judah fortified by Rehoboam (2 Chronicles 11:5-12).

The great importance of Bethlehem for Christians throughout the centuries is that the Gospels record the birth of Jesus Christ as having taken place there in fulfillment of Bible prophecy (Micah 5:2).

Bethlehem was destroyed by the emperor Hadrian in the second century A.D.; but in about 325, after the empire had become Christian, Queen Helena, the mother of Constantine, promoted the building of the great church. Badly damaged during the Samaritan revolt of 521-528, the church was rebuilt in the sixth century in very much its present form by the emperor Justinian. It was spared during the savage Persian invasion of 614 because the soldiers saw the mosaic portrayal of the three Magi in Persian costume.

(The Harper Bible Dictionary, Paul J. Achtemeier, General Editor, San Francisco: Harper and Row Publishing Co., 1984, pp. 106-107.)

BACKGROUND

As Israel adjusted to life under the monarchy, it became increasingly clear that they were in God's permissive, and not His perfect will. What Samuel had prophesied began to take shape (see 1 Samuel 8:10-19). Not only did King Saul lack godly leadership, but he also sinned against God, making him unfit to lead Israel (see 1 Samuel 13:11-14).

The final strike against Saul was that he was more concerned about what the people thought of him than what God thought. After Saul failed to obey in a crucial and pivotal time in the life of

---

AT-A-GLANCE

1. Samuel Goes to Bethlehem on God's Instructions
(1 Samuel 16:1-4)
2. God Rejects Jesse's Older Sons
(vv. 5-7)
3. God Chooses David, Jesse's Youngest Son (vv. 11-13)

Israel and in his own life (see 1 Samuel 15:10-35), God made the decision to replace the king with a man who could be trusted to do His will no matter what.

IN DEPTH

1. Samuel Goes to Bethlehem on God's Instructions (1 Samuel 16:1-4)

Though King Saul had twice disobeyed God by refusing to follow Samuel's words as given to the prophet by God, it is clear from Scripture that Samuel deeply admired Saul. Once God rejected Saul from being king, Samuel returned to his home in Ramah to mourn (1 Samuel 15:34-35).

Perhaps Samuel mourned because he realized Saul's potential to be a great king was lost because the man would not follow instructions. Maybe the prophet mourned because he knew the effect that God's rejection of Saul would have on Israel. Whatever Samuel's reason for mourning, God had enough of hearing the prophet's gloom and doom. It was time for Samuel to be about the Father's work. There was still a nation of people to look after, God was still in control, and He had already chosen the next king for Israel. So, as Samuel continued mourning in Ramah, God visits him and gives the prophet specific instructions for his next assignment.

Samuel was told to go to Bethlehem, a city approximately 15 miles south of Ramah, with a horn full of oil to see a man named Jesse, the father of eight sons. Among the eight, Samuel would not only discover God's choice for Israel's next king, but would also be the one to anoint him, just as he had Saul. Samuel immediately protested at God's command since Bethlehem was not a part of Samuel's circuit (1 Samuel 8:16). The prophet reasoned that Saul would find out he was going to Bethlehem to anoint another king to replace him and would turn on Samuel and have him killed.

To relieve his fears, God told Samuel to take with him a sacrificial animal and invite Jesse and his sons to the sacrifice as they worshiped the Lord in the city. That way, if Saul found out Samuel was in Bethlehem, the king would conclude that the prophet was on an assignment from the Lord—which he was. Realizing the futility of arguing with

God, Samuel got himself together and made the journey to Bethlehem for the purpose of finding the man God had chosen to be Israel's next king.

When the prophet arrived in Bethlehem, the city fathers were surprised and shocked to see him. Because Samuel had shut himself in Ramah after Saul's rebellious actions, the elders were fearful that Samuel's arrival in town probably meant judgment and rebuke from the Lord. Therefore, they wanted to know whether or not Samuel's visit was a peaceful one.

When God gives us an assignment, we need to obey Him whether or not we are misunderstood by others. Our responsibility is to do what He has called us to do and let Him take care of the outcome and response of other people.

2. God Rejects Jesse's Older Sons (vv. 5-7)

Samuel lets the elders know that he had come to Bethlehem, not only in peace, but also to perform a sacrificial service unto the Lord. It was important for Samuel that these men attend the service, probably so they might be witnesses in case the king asked them the reason for Samuel's visit. Though Samuel was there to anoint Israel's next king, he understood God's requirement for sanctification. Therefore, the prophet told the elders to "sanctify themselves" (v. 5) before they came to the service. The Hebrew word for sanctify is *Qadash* and it means to make clean, to dedicate, to consecrate and to be holy before the Lord. Even today, God is calling His people to be holy and set apart for His service (1 Peter 1:15-16). Holiness is not a denominational label, but should be a way of life for all believers everywhere.

Samuel also invited Jesse and seven of his sons to join him in the service. The prophet made sure the eight men were sanctified before they came into the presence of the Lord. As the service progressed, Samuel looked at all of Jesse's sons with one purpose in mind. He had to anoint the man who would become king and he wanted to get it right. However, Samuel forgot that it wasn't his responsibility to choose the man, it was God's.

The first person Samuel saw was Eliab, the oldest of Jesse's sons. Scripture does not give us complete description of Eliab, but we can surmise that he was a tall, strong, and handsome man who greatly impressed Samuel (see vv. 6-7). Samuel probably thought "This isn't a hard job after all. The first son must be the one God has chosen. After all, look how handsome he is."

Samuel was about to call it a day when he suddenly heard the Lord speak to him. In essence, God said, "Hold on, Samuel. Eliab may be good-looking, strong and able, but I have not chosen him. In fact, I don't choose people based on fleshly qualifications. I choose people whose hearts are right before Me and are willing to follow My commands, no matter how good-looking or gifted they may-be."

So many churches are guilty of choosing leaders based on looks, financial contributions, political and social influences, or other characteristics that are not in line with God's Word. However, if we are to be faithful to God, we must only choose people for leadership positions whose hearts are perfect and in tune with God's calling.

3. God Chooses David, Jesse's Youngest Son (vv. 11-13)

Having been rebuked by God, Samuel wondered whether or not Israel's next king was among Jesse's seven sons who had come to the sacrifice. Had he truly heard from God? Was there another son nearby?

Jesse told the prophet that he did have a younger son, but he was out in the field taking care of the sheep. Since none of the other sons were chosen by God, Samuel concluded that whoever he was, the younger son must have been God's choice. Therefore, Samuel made it clear that no one would partake of the sacrificial meal until he had seen all of Jesse's sons.

When David arrived at the service, Samuel looked at him and noticed two things: (1) He was ruddy. The word literally means red or to show blood in the face. It is clear from this verse that David was not a white man; (2) like King Saul, he was a very handsome young man. Perhaps he was more handsome than all of his other brothers. Finally, because David was willing to be out in the field tending his father's sheep, God knew he could trust this young man with His "sheep."

To eliminate any doubts Samuel may have had about David, God spoke to the prophet and told him to get up and anoint David, who would be

Israel's next king. God wanted David's brothers to see him being anointed with the horn of oil for several reasons: (1) The Bible affirms that the last will be first. David's work in the field did not eliminate him from being chosen as God's man. We must learn that God can choose us for His work no matter where we are; (2) Only from the Davidic line would come the Messiah of the world. Thus, David's choice as king was not only to replace Saul, but also to fulfill biblical prophecy.

Once Samuel poured the oil on David's head, God's anointing came upon the young man for the rest of his life. Having successfully completed his assignment, Samuel returned to his home in Ramah.

SEARCH THE SCRIPTURES

1. What was the Lord's command to Samuel? (1 Samuel 16:1)

2. Why didn't Samuel want to obey the Lord? (v. 2)

3. When Samuel arrived in Bethlehem, how did the elders respond? (v. 4)

4. How did Samuel respond when he met Eliab, Jesse's oldest son? (v. 6)

5. Who did the Lord tell Samuel to anoint as Israel's next king? (vv. 12-13)

DISCUSS THE MEANING

1. How important is it for believers to follow God's Word even when we may not understand every detail?

2. What does it mean that the Lord looks on the heart of man? Discuss.

3. What is the significance of David being anointed with oil? Does anointing with oil have any significance for believers today?

4. Can we be chosen by God for a specific work without being in the right place and the right time? Discuss.

LESSON IN OUR SOCIETY

We live in a class-conscious society where people are chosen for success based on good looks, financial influence, or race. How can we help people who have been left out feel more accepted by our society regardless of their race, looks, or economic status? Explain.

MAKE IT HAPPEN

This week, ask the Lord to help you see people as He sees them. Perhaps spend a day or two at a homeless shelter or missions center, volunteering to help the less fortunate in our society. Report on your activities next week.

FOLLOW THE SPIRIT

What God wants me to do:

_____

_____

REMEMBER YOUR THOUGHTS

Special insights you learned:

_____

_____

MORE LIGHT ON THE TEXT

1 Samuel 16:1-7, 11-13

When Saul becomes the king of Israel, the prophet Samuel no longer serves in the public political arena. He now devotes his time solely to instructing and training the sons of prophets. Samuel knows that Saul had been rejected because of his disobedience to God. In this passage we learn that obedience to God is better than sacrifice; obedience to God is better than duty or works (1 Samuel 15:22). The passage speaks of the tendency of how we, as human beings, sometimes choose to please man instead of God. It was this course of action that led God to reject Saul as Israel's king. We also see Samuel, the man of God, as he mourns for Saul.

16:1 And the LORD said unto Samuel, How long wilt thou mourn for Saul, seeing I have rejected him from reigning over Israel? Fill thine horn with oil, and go, I will send thee to Jesse the Bethlehemite: for I have provided me a king among his sons.

This verse begins with the proper Hebrew name for God—*Yahweh*, derived from the Hebrew word *hayah* meaning "to be." Whenever this word is used it is meant to affirm the belief in the God of Israel as the Self-Existent Eternal One. This puts a clear distinction between the Lord and idols created by man or idols connected with nature (in Hebrew culture nature is a created organism and

as such is not self-existent.) It is this Self-Existent God who spoke to Samuel. The Hebrew word used here for "said" is *'amar,* (pronounced **aw-mar'**), and is used to distinguish God from idols which cannot speak or hear. This relates to the communicative nature of God; showing further that God is a being to whom one can call upon and receive an answer. Moreover, it speaks to the issue of God as One who considers action and who does not deal rashly with human beings. Note the play on Samuel's name—in Hebrew Samuel (*Shemuw'el*) means heard of God, to hear with intelligence, or with the intent of acting on what has been heard. God heard Samuel and answered him. But the response was in the form of a question, "How long will you mourn for Saul?" The word translated "how" is used here as a preposition and is the Hebrew word `ad. It could be translated "how much longer," "while you are. . ." or "until now." The word "mourn" in the Hebrew is *'abal* (pronounced **aw-bal'**) meaning to lament. Samuel seems to have cried for Saul so long that it took God to comfort him. We read further, "seeing that I have rejected him." We could interpret this as, you have been wailing until now because I have rejected him. The Hebrew word for reject is *ma'ac,* (**maw-as'**) indicating that God had spurned Saul. Indeed, God now abhors him and is casting him away. Saul's actions have caused God to look at him with contempt and disdain thereby causing God to loathe him. God not only rejects Saul but stops him from reigning over Israel. The Hebrew translation of the word "reigning" is *malak* (**maw-lak'**). When used in conjunction with the word "rejection" it means that Saul can no longer ascend the throne.

God instructs Samuel: "Fill thine horn with oil, and go, I will send thee to Jesse the Bethlehemite: for I have provided me a king among his sons." He was to consecrate oil and replenish the horn. The Hebrew word *qeren* (**keh'-ren**) suggests a horn, but it could also mean an elephant's ivory. The horn represented power; it was usually filled with oil. The Hebrew word *shemen* (**sheh'-men**) refers to liquid from the olive; it symbolized the richness of fruitfulness expected from the person being anointed. Samuel was to walk to Bethlehem. The word "send" (Hebrew *shalach* **shaw-lakh'**) suggests that he was to make an appointment; he is to stop whatever else he was doing to go there. He was to go to Jesse; whose name in Hebrew is *Yishay* meaning a man of God—to a place called *Beyth Lechem* (Bethlemite), the Hebrew word for house of bread. God tells Samuel "I have provided me a king." The word provide, or *ra'ah*, in Hebrew, means to see or to have a vision. God may be saying to Samuel that once he arrives at Bethlehem God will give him a vision of whom the king will be.

2 And Samuel said, How can I go? if Saul hear it, he will kill me. And the LORD said, Take a heifer with thee, and say, I am come to sacrifice to the LORD.

Samuel's apprehension concerning Saul is valid. Will Saul indeed kill him? This fear is possibly derived from the fact that he had informed Saul of his dethronement. From that moment on Saul grew more intolerant of the people around him.

Samuel is right to fear Saul's rage. Samuel asked God "How can I go?" The Hebrew translation reads, *Eglat†baaqaar tiqach b²yaadekaa.*" In actuality the phrase translates, "How do I go?" In other words, Samuel was asking for direction and a strategy for going to Bethlehem: "What is the best way to go so that I do not get killed?" The phrase can also be read "How do I carry myself?" It was a question dealing with his behavior. Immediately Samuel gave his reason for this question. "If Saul hear it, he shall kill me." If Saul hears that Samuel was gone, he would have witnesses against him and try him for treason. The word for kill is not the word used for accident or manslaughter; instead the Hebrew word harag (pronounced **haw-rag'**) is used here, meaning Saul will personally smite him with deadly intent. Saul was not beyond committing murder, even that of a prophet. There is also the implication that Saul would slaughter anyone connected with this. Here we see that God did not dismiss Samuel's fear. Rather the Lord gave Samuel a strategy to allay suspicion. God instructs Samuel to take a heifer with him as a sacrifice unto the Lord. This sacrifice was probably long overdue since Samuel was in mourning for Saul. Samuel would be asked why he was there. He is to say came to offer a sacrifice.

3 And call Jesse to the sacrifice, and I will shew thee what thou shalt do: and thou shalt anoint unto me him whom I name unto thee.

God's explicit instructions continue: Invite Jesse and his family to the sacrifice; wait for further instructions; anoint the one whom God names.

Those who go about doing God's work in God's way shall be directed step by step. Some adults prudently plan the best means of accomplishing their goals. Often, when God calls us to do something, we proceed without receiving the explicit instructions. Yet, God plans are not necessarily our plans. When God calls us for a purpose, He gives explicit instructions to accomplish His work. The word "call" *(Hebrew qara', kaw-raw')* as used here implies that Samuel would accost or encounter Jesse. He was to properly address Jesse by name, as he was going to be the father of the future king of Israel. This invitation was to be proclaimed and published. The Lord returns to his word, "I will shew thee what thou shalt do." Samuel would receive further revelation as he went. By using the word *yada`* (**yaw-dah'**) which the KJV translates as shew, the Lord is saying "you will know." Conversely, Samuel will gain understanding of God's intent when he gets there. It is only after he has received this revelation that he can anoint. The Hebrew word for anoint is mashach *(maw-shakh')* meaning to rub with oil and thus consecrate whomever or whatever has been rubbed. The implication is that the act of anointing is as though one is painting a portrait. It is from this word that the word Messiah is probably derived, signifying the emergence of a divine portrait of the anointed, thus meaning one who is in the portraiture of God. Not only will God show him the person to anoint, but He said that the person shall be named. Samuel may not like the person God chooses. He may not think him kingly material, but if he has been named by God the anointing oil must fall on him.

4 And Samuel did that which the LORD spake, and came to Bethlehem. And the elders of the town trembled at his coming, and said, Comest thou peaceably?

In this verse we see Samuel obeying God by going to Bethlehem. He takes the heifer to sacrifice. Samuel demonstrates obedience to God even though he feels uncomfortable. We must always obey God even if it makes us feel uncomfortable. Obedience is better than sacrifice (1 Samuel 15:22). God wants loyal actions, not lip service.

We read, "And Samuel did that which the LORD spake, and came to Bethlehem." The key word in this phrase is "did" (Hebrew asah awsaw'). Broadly translated "do" or "make" implies a sense of accomplishment, advancement of a cause, or the keeping of an appointment. This directly relates to Samuel's ability to follow the Lord's instruction. He had fulfilled the word of the Lord. Here is man who is industrious in his service to God, even when it may cost him his life.

The elders in Bethlehem are frightened by Samuel's visit, because often wherever he appears trouble follows. One reason the elders fear Samuel's visit is because of guilt. They know that God is displeased with them. They know that Saul

is displeased with Samuel, and if they entertain Samuel, Saul might turn his wrath on them. The elders realize that Saul will kill anyone who opposes him—guilt in turn causes fears. So they ask Samuel, "Do you come in peace?" The elders, (Hebrew zaqen, zaw-kane') or old people, the aged men and women who led the community, met Samuel at the other side of town. The word town, (Hebrew haa`iyr) meaning wall, suggests that they met him at the wall. Why they met him outside of town is clarified by the next phrase, "the town trembled." They were afraid. Actually, they were terrified. To describe their mood as they came to Samuel, the writer uses the word trembled (charad khaw-rad'), which means to shudder with terror. This word also means that they made haste or were anxious to meet with Samuel. But they were careful as they went to meet him. The next word liqraa'tow or "coming" is taken from the Hebrew qara' (kaw-raw') and suggests that they probably encountered him in a hostile manner. They did not want to be viewed as traitors to the kingdom since Samuel had fallen out with Saul. Hence their question, "Comest thou peaceably?" The word "peaceably" translated here as Shalowm (shaw-lome') means safe or well. In essence they were asking Samuel, "are you safe?" "Are you well?" They wanted to know did he come as a friend.

5 And he said, Peaceably: I am come to sacrifice unto the LORD: sanctify yourselves, and come with me to the sacrifice. And he sanctified Jesse and his sons, and called them to the sacrifice.

Samuel assures them that he comes in peace to perform a ritualistic sacrifice, not with a message of wrath against them. He comes not because he is fleeing from Saul, but with sacrifices of peace and reconciliation. Samuel invites Jesse and his household to attend the sacrifice. This is a pretext for Samuel's visit, but he keeps up the appearance. He orders them to "sanctify" themselves, that is, prepare their flesh to be purified. Hebrews 9:13 explains, "The blood of the goats and bulls and the ashes of the heifer sprinkled on those who are ceremonially unclean sanctify them so that they are outwardly clean." Samuel sanctifies Jesse and his son by praying with them and instructing them. God requires inward sanctification that comes from being washed in the blood of Jesus Christ. The word for "sanctify" is the Hebrew word qadash, *(kaw-dash')* which is the same as "make." It means to "make" holy, to consecrate or dedicate oneself to a task pertaining to divinity. This sanctification process is especially directed to the house of Jesse. Samuel, after dealing with the fear of the leaders of the town, now directs his attention to Jesse's family. He proclaims that Jesse and his family are the honored guests at this sacrifice.

6 And it came to pass, when they were come, that he looked on Eliab, and said, Surely the LORD's anointed is before him.

Elib was tall and physically strong. Because Samuel was aware of the appearance of the first king, he assumes that Eliab is the one to be anointed as Saul's successor. Sometimes people make choices based on past experiences and/or incorrect judgments. Samuel looks at Eliab's outer appearance; and because he looks like Saul, Samuel automatically jumps to his own conclusion and assumes that Eliab is God's choice.

A key phrase here is, "that he looked on Eliab." The name Eliab, **(el-ee-awb')** translated is God of my father. The word "looked" as it is used here is the Hebrew word *ra'ah* **(raw-aw')** inferring that Samuel's literal sight took over his visionary insight, and he approved of what he saw. The use of the word "surely," or *'ak,* **(ak)** in Hebrew, is similar to the English definition of the word "verily," which means in truth or in fact. By stating "surely the Lord" Samuel implies that God's choice is limited to Eliab only. Samuel calls him the Lord's anointed. The word for anointed here is direct translation of the word for Messiah. Therefore, this phrase literally says, "Look! The Lord's Messiah." The word *neged* **(neh'-ghed)** meaning before him; in front of someone, or counterpart of one who represents, such as a mate. Thus Samuel is saying "this one is the mate of the Lord's Messiah."

7 But the LORD said unto Samuel, Look not on his countenance, or on the height of his stature; because I have refused him: for the LORD seeth not as man seeth; for man looketh on the outward appearance, but the LORD looketh on the heart.

God quickly corrects Samuel's mistake. God responds that outward appearances do not matter to God. Some people are swayed by outward appearances, but God is not a respecter of persons. God does not care about a person's gender, ethnicity, age, weight, height, or status; God is concerned about a person's heart. Only what is in the heart matters to God. God knows the hearts of people and sees their thoughts and intents. God judges people by their hearts. Some people affirm that "it's what's inside a person" that matters. They know that there is more to a person than what meets the eye.

God's word to Samuel is a word of challenge. God tells Samuel to stop looking at the outward appearance. God tells Samuel that he has rejected Eliab. At this time Samuel is thoroughly confused because every nation wants a good-looking king. God takes the opportunity to give Samuel a lesson in theology. First, God does not look at things the same way humans do. How do human beings see? God says that human knowledge is based in physical sight. Humans beings have a truncated vision of reality. The Lord closes the conversation by stating how God sees. God sees beyond the physical appearance. God sees the heart.

11 And Samuel said unto Jesse, Are here all thy children? And he said, There remaineth yet the youngest, and, behold, he keepeth the sheep. And Samuel said unto Jesse, Send and fetch him: for we will not sit down till he come hither.

After all seven of Jesse's eldest sons are rejected, Samuel asks if they all are there and is told that the youngest son is keeping sheep. Notice that David is left alone in the fields even when there is a sacrifice going on in his father's house. Even David's father, who should know the character of his own children, did not suggest that David be brought home to participate in the sacrificial ceremony. Samuel, now frustrated with God's rejection of every eligible candidate, turned to Jesse. Samuel asks "Are here all your children?" The Hebrew term *tamam* (**taw-mam'**) translated "all" means complete. So we could read Samuel's question thus, "Does this complete the number of your children?" Jesse responds "Remaineth yet the youngest," in other words, there is one other, a little boy. In Hebrew the word *na`ar* (**nah'-ar**) refers to a boy from the age of infancy to adolescence. By implication this word can also mean a servant, and is probably derived from the custom of the younger serving the elders in African society. This servant heart may also be the reason that God chose David to represent the Messiah, the true servant of Yahweh. Jesse adds "behold, he keepeth the sheep." Samuel sends someone to fetch him and tells them we will not sit down to eat until he comes. This may have hinted to David's parents that he was the guest of honor.

12 And he sent, and brought him in. Now he was ruddy, and withal of a beautiful countenance, and goodly to look to. And the LORD said, Arise, anoint him: for this is he.

The youngest son does not have the appearance of height and physical strength. He is "ruddy," translated as a "redhead" or someone with a red complexion. Derived from the Hebrew word admoniy (ad-mo-nee') ruddy also means something from earth i.e., "adam" or earthen in color. When David appears Samuel is instructed by God to anoint him as the king. David was also beautiful, goodly and pleasant in his outward appearance. Samuel confirms and decrees him the new king.

Only God knows the beginning and the end; He sees what we cannot see. We must allow God to lead us in our decision-making efforts. Then, we must act in obedience to God's Word and His will.

13 Then Samuel took the horn of oil, and anointed him in the midst of his brethren: and the Spirit of the LORD came upon David from that day forward. So Samuel rose up, and went to Ramah.

Samuel anoints David, the youngest son of Jesse, on God's command in the presence of his brothers. In spite of David's youth, his lack of education, his lack of respect from his family, Samuel acquiesces in obedience to God, and takes the horn of oil and anoints David. The anointing of the oil signifies royal power and communication of God's gifts and graces. The Spirit of God comes mightily on David from this day forward. He finds himself growing inwardly wise, courageous, and concerned for the people. After the anointing of David we read that the Spirit of the Lord came upon him. The word *ruwach* (**roo'-akh**) means wind. Figuratively it means that life came upon David. The word *tsalach* (**tsaw-lakh'**) means to push forward. Therefore one could say, "from that day forward the Spirit of the Lord propelled David forward." His ascent to the throne is a gradual process.

Scholars estimate David's age to be 20 or 25; his trouble with Saul lasted either 10 or 15 years. Samuel returns to Ramah, and we don't read of him again until his death (1 Samuel 19:18). Matthew Henry's commentary tells us that "the best evidence of our being predestined to the kingdom of glory is our being sealed with the Spirit of promise, and our experience of a work of grace in our own heart." Often, when God calls us to a purpose, the manifestation does not occur instantly. This verse is the beginning of the Messianic promises to David. Jews recognized that the Messiah, the Christ, the Anointed One, would come from David's descendants. This was Samuel's final act as a prophet.

DAILY BIBLE READINGS

M: Attack Against the Amalekites
1 Samuel 15:1-9
T: A New Word
1 Samuel 15:10-16
W: The Confrontation
1 Samuel 15:17-23
T: God Rejects Saul as King
1 Samuel 15:24-29
F: Saul's Confession and Samuel's Departure
1 Samuel 15:30-35
S: Samuel Is Sent to Bethlehem
1 Samuel 16:1-5
S: David Is Anointed King
1 Samuel 16:6-13

TEACHING TIPS

October 15
Bible Study Guide 7

1. Words You Should Know

A. Uncircumcised (2 Samuel 1:20) Hebrew Arel—An unclean or unconsecrated person. A pagan or Gentile. Associated with a morally or spiritually unclean person.

B. Lovely (2 Samuel 1:23) Hebrew Ahav—A close tie of friendship or a strong emotional attachment to another. To be tender, to have compassion, and to be a friend.

2. Teacher Preparation

A. Begin preparing for today's lesson by reading the Scriptures identified for BACKGROUND and DEVOTIONAL READING, and the DAILY BIBLE READINGS.

B. Commit to spend at least 15 minutes a day in intercessory prayer for your students, church, pastor, and church leaders. Ask the Lord to make you sensitive to their needs and concerns.

C. Read the FOCAL VERSES, IN FOCUS, BACKGROUND and IN DEPTH sections of the lesson. Jot down any notes you may want to share with the class in the FOLLOW THE SPIRIT and REMEMBER YOUR THOUGHTS section of the lesson.

3. Starting the Lesson

A. When students arrive today, let them know how much you appreciate them and their contribution to the class.

B. Assign three students to read the IN DEPTH section of the lesson, according to the AT-A-GLANCE outline.

C. Conclude this section of the lesson by having a volunteer pray, thanking God for the opportunity to study His Word this week.

4. Getting into the Lesson

A. Have a student read the IN FOCUS story. Then ask students to identify its significance for today's lesson.

B. Have a student read the FOCAL VERSES. Then discuss the SEARCH THE SCRIPTURES questions so students can get a better understanding of today's lesson. Remind students of the closeness of David, King Saul, and Jonathan.

C. Have a student read THE PEOPLE, PLACES, AND TIMES section and relate it to today's lesson.

5. Relating the Lesson to Life

Review and answer the DISCUSS THE MEANING questions. Write the students' answers on the chalkboard or newsprint.

6. Arousing Action

A. Give students an opportunity to study and write out specific ideas for the LESSON IN OUR SOCIETY and MAKE IT HAPPEN assignments.

B. Remind students to be involved in the lives of others, and challenge them to see what a difference it will make in their lives as well.

C. Close the class with prayer, focusing on the LESSON AIM as the basis of the prayer. Don't forget to affirm your students as they leave today.

OCT 15TH

DAVID MOURNS SAUL AND JONATHAN

Bible Background • 1 SAMUEL 31:1; 2 SAMUEL 1:27; 1 CHRONICLES 10
Printed Text • 2 SAMUEL 1:17-20, 22-27
Devotional Reading • PSALM 77:1-9

LESSON AIM

By the end of the lesson, students will be able to identify David's reason for mourning Saul and Jonathan, list specific characteristics of David's mourning, and commit to helping someone who is mourning the loss of a friend or family member this week.

KEEP IN MIND

"The beauty of Israel is slain upon thy high places: how are the mighty fallen!" (2 Samuel 1:19).

FOCAL VERSES

2 Samuel 1:17 And David lamented with this lamentation over Saul and over Jonathan his son:

18 (Also he bade them teach the children of Judah the use of the bow: behold, it is written in the book of Jasher.)

19 The beauty of Israel is slain upon thy high places: how are the mighty fallen!

20 Tell it not in Gath, publish it not in the streets of Askelon; lest the daughters of the Philistines rejoice, lest the daughters of the uncircumcised triumph.

1:22 From the blood of the slain, from the fat of the mighty, the bow of Jonathan turned not back, and the sword of Saul returned not empty.

23 Saul and Jonathan were lovely and pleasant in their lives, and in their death they were not divided: they were swifter than eagles, they were stronger than lions.

24 Ye daughters of Israel, weep over Saul, who

LESSON OVERVIEW

LESSON AIM
KEEP IN MIND
FOCAL VERSES
IN FOCUS
THE PEOPLE, PLACES,
AND TIMES
BACKGROUND
AT-A-GLANCE
IN DEPTH
SEARCH THE SCRIPTURES
DISCUSS THE MEANING
LESSON IN OUR SOCIETY
MAKE IT HAPPEN
FOLLOW THE SPIRIT
REMEMBER YOUR THOUGHTS
MORE LIGHT ON THE TEXT
DAILY BIBLE READINGS

clothed you in scarlet, with other delights, who put on ornaments of gold upon your apparel.

25 How are the mighty fallen in the midst of the battle! O Jonathan, thou wast slain in thine high places.

26 I am distressed for thee, my brother Jonathan: very pleasant hast thou been unto me: thy love to me was wonderful, passing the love of women.

27 How are the mighty fallen, and the weapons of war perished!

IN FOCUS

Betty's friend Mildred suggested she call a company that would assist her in making final preparations for JoAnn's funeral. Betty hesitated, but Mildred insisted they were professional, courteous, and helpful in every area, even though their name was a little strange.

"Trust me, Betty. They've been in the business for over 30 years and they have hundreds of workers to choose from. They'll even send you a catalogue and background information to make your selection easier," said Mildred. Betty still wasn't sure. But she had to make all the arrangements in a couple of days, so she decided to call the number.

The telephone rang three times before a cheerful voice answered.

"Professional Mourners, Inc. No funeral or wedding is too large or small for us. We can mourn with the best of them. How can we help you?"

In some countries, mourning has become a big business. People will often go to funerals and weddings of others they don't know just to express their grief and sorrow. In fact, Jesus Christ has to evict some professional mourners before He would perform a miracle on behalf of a synagogue ruler (see Mark 5:35-43). However, in today's Bible Study Guide, we will get a glimpse of how the deaths of Jonathan and Saul greatly affected King David and Israel as David mourned their deaths.

THE PEOPLE, PLACES, AND TIMES

High Places. An elevated location used for religious rites and a common feature in the pagan religions of the small states surrounding Israel, such as Moab (Jeremiah 49:35). In the Old Testament, the use "high places" is associated with the Canaanite fertility religion and the worship of Baal (Jeremiah 19:5; 32:35), so it is generally condemned.

The rites practiced at the high places and the cultic objects found are typically Canaanite, including ritual prostitution (1 Kings 14:23-24; Ezekiel 16:16), child sacrifice (Jeremiah 7:31; 19:5; 32:35; Ezekiel 16:20), sacrifices and the burning of incense (1 Kings 22:32; 2 Kings 12:3), the stone pillar symbolizing Baal, and the wooden pole symbolizing the goddess Asherah (1 Kings 14:23; 2 Kings 17:10).

From the Old Testament denunciations, it is clear the high places had been a central part in popular religion and, before the Deuteronomic demand for their destruction and the centralization of worship at a single sanctuary, they were considered a legitimate feature of the worship of Yahweh. In 1 Samuel 9:12-24, Samuel sacrifices and presides at the attendant meal at the high place of Ramah, which was situated above the town, and in 1 Samuel 10:5, a band of prophets worshiped at the high place of Gibeath-elohim.

Cultic platforms, either circular or rectangular in shape, which were used for sacrifice, have been recognized as "high places" by archaeologists at several Palestinian sites during the period of Israelite occupation, among them Hazor and Arad; the one discovered at Dan was almost certainly built by Jeroboam (1 Kings 13:32).

(The Harper's Bible Dictionary, Paul J. Achetemeier, General Editor, San Francisco: Harper and Row Publishing Co., 1984, p. 391.)

BACKGROUND

In last week's lesson, David was anointed as Israel's future king because of Saul's inability to follow and obey the Lord. From the time David was anointed until the time he ascended to the throne, God prepared him for the task by serving King Saul.

First, David served as Saul's personal musician (1 Samuel 16:14-23). Next, God used David to defeat Goliath, Israel's enemy (1 Samuel 17:1-58). Third, David and Jonathan, Saul's son, became close friends (1 Samuel 18:1-8). Finally, David married the king's daughter (1 Samuel 18:17-30).

Saul continued serving as king, not understanding that he was in God's permissive will. So deceived was Saul that he called upon a spiritualist medium for answers regarding his ensuing battle with the Philistines. Because he had disobeyed God's Word, Saul was given a message through the medium that he and his son would die at the hand of Israel's enemy (1 Samuel 28:3-20). Indeed, the Bible affirms that Saul and Jonathan were killed in battle by the Philistines in Mount Gilboa (1 Samuel 31:1-13).

In the meantime, David had returned from fighting the Amalakites when he received word of Saul's and Jonathan's death (2 Samuel 2:1-16). David was deeply touched by the news and, as we shall see in the IN DEPTH, wrote a song to lament both the king and Jonathan.

AT-A-GLANCE

1. **David Is Saddened Over Saul's and Jonathan's Death**
(2 Samuel 1:17-20)
2. **David Affirms Saul's Contributions to Israel (vv. 22-24)**
3. **David Affirms Jonathan's Friendship (vv. 25-27)**

IN DEPTH

1. David Is Saddened Over Saul's and Jonathan's Death (2 Samuel 1:17-20)

David assumed that Saul and Jonathan would return from fighting the Philistines with a victory report. So when a young man came to David and told him that not only had the king and his son been killed in the battle, but that he had "speared" Saul to be sure of his death, even at the king's request, the Bible says that David did three things: (1) David mourned, wept, and fasted for Saul, Jonathan and Israel. The word "mourn" literally means to tear out one's hair, beat on one's breast, and wail with a loud voice. David was so affected by the loss of Saul and his friend Jonathan that he would not eat nor do anything while he mourned. (2) David had the young man who speared Saul killed. Even though he was acting on Saul's orders, as far as David was concerned, the young man should have refrained from killing Israel's king. (3) David wrote a song on behalf of Saul and Jonathan. The words "lament" and "lamentation" mean that David used a musical instrument and sang about the life of King Saul and Jonathan to the people.

Before David began singing, he commanded his warriors to teach the people how to use the bow and arrow. Perhaps David was preparing them to retaliate against the Philistines for their abominable act against Israel's king and his son. And David wanted his song to be published in the "book of Jasher" (v. 18). The word "Jasher" means that which is upright, righteous, and pleasing to God. Nothing is known about this book, except that the miracle of the sun standing still on behalf of Joshua is also recorded in it (Joshua 10:12-14). Zodhiates suggests that Jasher is a historical military book collecting all of the poetic songs of Israel's heroes.

Someone once stated that if we want to hide valuable information from people, write it in a book. The hypothesis is that most people don't read history or relevant information for their lives. However, it is important that we write down historical data to be passed on to generations for the posterity of our families and our race of people.

David begins his song by declaring a fact: Israel's king and representative of the nation had

been slain in battle at Mount Gilboa. The King James Version of the Bible uses the word "beauty" to describe Saul. However, the Hebrew literally reads "the prominent, splendorous or glorious one." However rotten and despicable King Saul had become in his latter years, one thing could not be denied: He was God's representative for Israel. And, no how many times Saul pursued David for the purpose of killing him, David would not criticize Saul or slander the king after his death. In fact, David affirmed that because Saul was God's representative, his death was a mighty blow for Israel.

David warned the people not to sing his song in Gath or Ashkelon, both Philistine strongholds. Gath was located about 30 miles northwest of Jerusalem and was the home of Goliath (1 Samuel 17:22). Ashkelon was situated on the coast of the Mediterranean Sea about 50 miles southwest of Jerusalem and was the place where Samson slew 30 men who could not answer his riddle (Judges 14:15-20). David did not want his enemies to gloat over Israel's loss.

2. David Affirms Saul's Contributions to Israel (vv. 22-24)

David continued his lamentation of Saul and Jonathan by reminding Israel of their courage and bravery. Against overwhelming odds and even an imposing death sentence, the king and his son had gone out to battle against the Philistines.

The Bible says that the Philistines "followed hard upon Saul and his son and . . . slew Jonathan, and Abinadab, and Melchishua, Saul's son. And the battle went sore against Saul . . ." (1 Samuel 31:2-3). Literally, the Philistines pursued Saul and his sons with all their might until they caught hold of them and punished the king. Yet, David honors Saul in song by affirming the king's bravery. For David, Saul and Jonathan "were lovely and pleasant in their lives" (v. 23). No matter how Saul tried to kill him, David would not criticize or bring the king's name down before the people. David highly respected Saul and the office he held. He was also very close to Jonathan so that their "souls were knit together" (1 Samuel 18:1).

David also acknowledged Saul's close ties with his own son Jonathan, despite the problems that later developed in their relationship because of Jonathan's support for David (1 Samuel 20:27-32). David likens their relationship and characteristics as "swifter than eagles [and] stronger than lions." In other words, they were men who were willing to fight for the nation.

Though David knew the character flaws of both Saul and Jonathan, he was determined not to "air their laundry" before the public. That's why God was able to put David in such a strategic position. We need to ask ourselves whether or not we can maintain a level of trust and integrity with our leaders, by not revealing their character flaws to others. Perhaps that is why some of us have not been elevated in the Body of Christ!

As David continues his song, he encourages Israel to cry over the loss of their king. Once again, despite Saul's many faults, he was God's king over the nation. As such, Saul's contributions to Israel included "clothing [them] in scarlet (and) with other delights . . . such as ornaments of gold upon them" (v. 24). In essence, Saul had brought prosperity to the nation and David wanted the people to remember it.

3. David Affirms Jonathan's Friendship (vv. 25-27)

Now David turns his attention to Jonathan. Having already acknowledged the strength and bravery of the king and Jonathan, David sings again, "how are the mighty fallen in the midst of the battle" (v. 25).

David had a special relationship and love for Jonathan. In fact, the Scriptures affirms twice that Jonathan loved David as his own soul (1 Samuel 18:1; 1 Samuel 20:17). David acknowledges that his friend also died in battle at Mount Gilboa (1 Samuel 31:1). In fact, David considered Jonathan not only a close friend, but also a "brother" (v. 26).

Jonathan was truly a friend to David in the sense that he relinquished his place as the heir of Israel's throne for the sake of David. Jonathan was willing to "cover" his friend to keep David from being harmed by Saul. Yes, Jonathan loved David so much that "his love even surpassed that of a woman's love for a man" (v. 26).

Some people want to use this passage to say that the Bible condones homosexual relationships.

But David's lament has nothing to do with homosexuality. He is simply stating a fact. He and Jonathan were very close friends who "agaped" one another. There was nothing perverted or amoral about their friendship. Their love for each other was pure and holy.

David closes his lamentation by reminding Israel again of the great loss they suffered in the passing of King Saul and Jonathan. Though the nation would survive and prosper with their next king, David did not want the people to forget Saul and Jonathan and the contributions that they made to the nation.

SEARCH THE SCRIPTURES

1. How did David react when he heard the news of Saul's and Jonathan's death? (2 Samuel 1:17-18)

2. Where did David want his song published? (v. 18)

3. Where didn't David want his song published? (v. 20)

4. How did David describe Saul and Jonathan? (vv. 23-24)

5. What was David's relationship with Jonathan? (v. 26)

DISCUSS THE MEANING

1. Why would David lament over Saul, a man who tried to kill him many times?

2. Why do you think David wanted his song published in Israel?

3. Is it permissible for men today to love one another as David and Jonathan did? Why or why not?

4. Should Christians mourn for family members and friends today when they know that eternal life awaits for all who trust in Jesus? Why or why not?

LESSON IN OUR SOCIETY

What happens to our communities when "heroic" figures die because of senseless violence or ravaging diseases? Write out a plan to share with people who may not know Jesus Christ on what they can do to bounce back from a devastating loss in the community. Perhaps students can work as a group on a specific action plan.

MAKE IT HAPPEN

This week, spend time in quiet reflection and mediation on how effective you can be in the lives of people who are suffering through trauma and grief. Ask the Lord to use you to touch someone's life with the love of Jesus Christ. Then thank God for His grace and mercy as He sends people your way.

FOLLOW THE SPIRIT

What God wants me to do:

_____

_____

REMEMBER YOUR THOUGHTS

Special insights you learned:

_____

_____

MORE LIGHT ON THE TEXT
2 Samuel 1:17-20, 22-27

In this text we begin to see the poetic originality of David as the composer of Israel. As an artist his is unparalleled in the ancient Hebrew Canon. But in the passage which we study today, we see David expressing himself, coming into his own as the poet laureate of Israel. What greater place to express the depth of one's creative ability as it relates to empathy for other human beings than in the midst of deep human loss. In this passage we meet the one whom God referred to as "the man after my own heart."

1:17 And David lamented with this lamentation over Saul and over Jonathan his son:

Here we see David as he writes a poem on the occasion of Saul and Jonathan's death. This is more than a poem, it is a poem set to music, representing a dirge. This is his method of grieving the dead which is common among ancient Africans at the death of great men and women. One may also do this at the death of a close friend. Today in many African cultures people still resort to singing their grief. David not only composes an elegy to express his sorrow, he impresses others to do the same. Thus he facilitated the healing of the nation at the death of the first king.

The Bible reads "And David lamented . . . "

(Hebrew *Wayaqoneen Daawid*). The phrase *Wayaqoneed* is rooted in the word *quwn* (pronounced **koonr**) meaning a wail for the dead, as is done in some parts of Africa. Typically among some African cultures when a father or mother dies a family member is seen singing a dirge (a slow mournful musical composition) accompanied by beating the breast or throwing the hands uncontrollably. This does not just mean to cry, but it is a display, or calling forth, of human emotions associated with the death and loss of a loved one. The practice was common among people of African descent. We see it in the mourning of Abraham for Sarah (Genesis 23:2). We see it in the mourning of Jacob for Joseph (Genesis 37:34-36). Often leaders were mourned for 30 days: Aaron (Numbers 20:29), Moses (Deuteronomy 34:8), and Samuel (1 Samuel 25:1). We would later see David repeat this same emotional intensity as he mourned Absalom (2 Samuel 19:4) and Abner (2 Samuel 3:31-32). Note that the word lament is used twice in this verse. This is a Hebraism in which the double use of a word is meant to show emotional intensity. Thus, as in the Ibgo culture instead of saying "he cried" we will say "he cried a cry" thereby guaranteeing one understands the intensity of emotion involved. Thus, the phrase "lamented . . . lamentation" is meant to have a double impact. The lament of David over Saul and Jonathan is the first example of funerary poetry we find in Scripture.

18 (Also he bade them teach the children of Judah the use of the bow: behold, it is written in the book of Jasher.)

This verse interrupts the flow of David's lamentation narrative. In this verse David orders that the Children of Judah be taught to use the bow. One might wonder what teaching the Children of Judah how to use the bow has to do with anything. In order to understand this one needs to know that the Philistines who killed Saul and Jonathan were experts in archery and had great skill in the use of the bow. We are not told where or what the book of Jasher is, but the writer does inform us that this method of teaching the bow is preserved in this book. David in the midst of his mourning still took the time to communicate with his people about their safety. The way this verse is phrased suggests that the Children of Judah were worried about their safety, given the power of the Philistines. David "bade" (Hebrew *wayomer la David*) suggests, with the use of the word *amar* (**aw-mar**), that at the root of this statement is the answer to Israel's cries. David challenged the leaders of Israel to teach God's people a way to protect themselves. It can also be construed that David, as commander-in-chief, commanded the officers to train them. There was always a fear that the Philistines were going to over take Israel. They were to consider what demand the death of their king at the hand of the enemy put upon them and they were to determine expressly which course of action to take. David made known his intent to them. David did not just cry by bidding them to teach a method of war, he was implicitly vowing to get even. In this word was a promise. He was publishing his anger and pain so the people will know where he stood. It must be remembered that at this time one was expected to avenge the death of a friend at the hand of an enemy. David claimed that Jonathan was closer to him than a brother; it was time for him to prove it. He knew that the people were watching to see how he responded. The implication here is that the Philistines were going to die in the same way they killed his friend.

Also of great importance in this verse is the word "teach." The Hebrew word *lamad* (**law-mad**) means to convince or to prod one through incentives to become diligent and thus gain expertise through instruction. They were not just to teach them any-and everything, they were to be specific. They were to teach them *qesheth* (pronounced **keh-sheth**) or bow, which may have meant literally how to bend the bow and how to shoot. Thus, we find not only the ability to shoot, but the technical ability to make a bow. While it is true that we do not know what the book of Jasher is, we may glean some meaning from the Hebrew word *yashar* (**yaw-shawr**), which in its translation may mean straight or the book of the just. This may be a book of knowing what is pleasing and upright.

19 The beauty of Israel is slain upon thy high places: how are the mighty fallen!

This verse begins David's poetic eulogy for his friend and his king. David said that Israel's beauty, not her glory, was slain with Saul and Jonathan. The choice of words is very informative. The glory of Israel is her God, not her king. One needs to remember that Saul was described as tall and handsome among the people. This may refer to the fact that most people chose a king that was good-looking. Even though Saul had done David a great injustice, David speaks regarding the only thing good he can say of Saul, and that was how he looked. David loved and respected Saul as the king and as his father-in-law. His love for Saul and respect for God would not allow him to speak evil of Saul now that he was gone. Therefore, he celebrates that which is praiseworthy in Saul: (1) his anointing by God; (2) that he is a mighty man of war; and (3) Saul and Jonathan were men of agreeable tempers.

Let us do an analysis of some key words. The word translated "beauty" is the Hebrew word *tsebiy* (**tseb-ee**); probably derived from the word *tsabah* which means prominence and splendor. The pronunciation of the word suggests that it probably grew out of the idea of washing something until it shines out of its true nature. This assumption can be made because of the translation of the word "slain," which in Hebrew is the word *chalal* (pronounced **khaw-lawl**). *Chalal* could either mean to pierce someone or something to death, or figuratively it refers to the pollution of that which was formerly clean and washed. It can also mean to profane that which was formerly sacred. Thus David's elegy speaks to the profanation of the anointing of God upon Saul and Jonathan by the uncircumcised. The beauty of Israel was profaned "upon the high places" (Hebrew *al- baamowteykaa*), meaning an elevation, referring to Mount Gilboah where Saul and Jonathan were slain. Figuratively, the high place can refer to the elevation of the king over the people. The beauty of Israel was indeed polluted in high places, not only in Saul's life but also in his death. The beauty of Israel was polluted by the shame of losing God's anointed to the unbeliever. The next phrase is a poetic exclamation "how are the mighty fallen" (Hebrew *Eeyk naaplu gibowriym*). It is not a question but an emphasis on the fact that the mighty have indeed fallen. The Hebrew word *eyk* (**ake**) used here can be the interrogative "how?" But here it is used "how." So, the verse should probably read "see how the mighty have fallen!" Another important point is that the word translated "mighty" is misleading, it is not the Hebrew word *gadal* or the word *ool*, which both refer to might, large and great. Here the Hebrew translation *gibbowr* (**ghib-bore**) is used instead. Though the implication refers to that of a warrior, it could also mean a tyrant. Thus David is referring to the tyranny of Saul in his later days of pursuing David and killing everyone in his path who supported David. It could also refer to the fact that the king was the champion of the people and his demise signaled the fall of the nation. The Hebrew word *naphal* (**maw-fal**) means to fall literally or figuratively. This word could also mean that one has been accepted or it can mean cast down or to die. We certainly know that David was not speaking of acceptance. If we look at David's experience with Saul it could mean that Saul has finally been judged, that he has been overthrown, overwhelmed, and has perished.

20 Tell it not in Gath, publish it not in the streets of Askelon; lest the daughters of the Philistines rejoice, lest the daughters of the uncircumcised triumph.

Interestingly this verse begins with David mentioning Gath. The phrase "tell it not in Gath," reminds us of the prominence of this city in the history of the Philistines. Why does David not want the deaths of Saul and Jonathan broadcast in Gath? One could assume that it is because David does not want the Philistines to be aware of and exult in their deaths. It is natural for people to celebrate victory over their enemies. David, of course, was deeply concerned for the honor of God. In 1 Samuel 17:4 we are told that Goliath, whom David defeated in battle, was from Gath. So when David says "tell it not in Gath" (Hebrew *Al-tagiyduba-Gat*) there is a real sense that the Philistines may feel that they have finally avenged the death of their champion. In fact the term *tagiyduw* derived from the Hebrew word *nagad* (**naw-gad**) means to front or to stand boldly in opposition. Thus David's concern may be that now the Philistines will be emboldened to attack them. So David was warning Israel not to announce that the king was dead as

this would only serve to invite their enemies to attack them. This is consistent with his instruction to teach the children of Judah how to use the bow. It may also mean that David was saying to the Philistines "do not get over confident." Israel was to remain silent, but the Philistines were not to declare a celebration in their major cities.

David also says "publish it not in the streets of Askelon." The Philistines were in the habit of parading their victims on the street and in their temples, as was done with Samson. Therefore, there may have been a real danger that Saul's and Jonathan's bodies could have been displayed as trophies on the streets. The Hebrew word translated publish is the word *basar* (**baw-sar**). Simply stated, it means do not be fresh in Askelon. Do not be full or cheerful. There is a certain tone of threat in this. David seems to be saying to the Philistines "do not think your troubles are over because you killed Saul, your troubles are just beginning with me." The word translated streets in the King James Version comes from the Hebrew word *chuwts* (**khoots**) and refers to a place separated by a wall. It refers to outdoors or the fields. But this may refer to the fact that in those days when people felt they were at peace they went outside the walls of the city to farm. Yes, it does refer to highway or street, but David was not at rest; he was a threat to the Philistines when they went outside the walls, implying that they would not be able to go outside the walls for fear of being attacked.

The Children of Israel must not make this news known so that the daughters of the Philistines can rejoice. The translation of "rejoice" in Hebrew is the word *Samach* (**saw-makh**) meaning to brighten up with glee. But much more than that, David did not want them to rejoice because they were daughters of the uncircumcised. Here he returns to the pollution of the beauty of Israel with which he began. Literally, the Hebrew word *arel* (**aw-rale**) refers to that which is exposed. By jumping for joy they would be polluting the glory and honor of the God of Israel.

22 From the blood of the slain, from the fat of the mighty, the bow of Jonathan turned not back, and the sword of Saul returned not empty.

Here we find warrior language. Every warrior is

expected to return from the battle. But this is not referring to the fact that Saul and Jonathan did not return from the battle, rather it refers to the fact that until now they have always returned with victory. As warriors in battle, they shed blood. The poetic eulogy is a two-edged sword referring to their exploits as warriors and to the fact that they suffered from what they inflicted on others. The use of the Hebrew word *chalal* refers to the ancient act of lancing one's opponent, or piercing him to death. This derives from the study of psychology where an enemy is always seen as something other than human.

In the next phrase "from the fat of the mighty" David is referring to the practice of taking the riches of the defeated. The Hebrew word *cheleb* (**kheh-leb**) could mean fat, but in this case means riches or the choicest part of the possession of the mighty who were defeated in war. The warriors usually took the best and finest for themselves. It was this practice that got Saul into trouble. The word *gibbowr* or mighty is used three times in this passage. Most of Israel's wars had been with her oppressors or those who sought to oppress her, therefore this word refers not just to warriors, but tyrannical warriors.

The statement "the bow of Jonathan turned not back" speaks of Jonathan's courage. The use of the Hebrew word *suwg* (pronounced, **soog**) means to retreat or turn back and suggests a certain tenacity of faith in Jonathan's life. Remember, to the Israelites turning back in battle was considered a lack of faith in God (see Psalm 106), But much more than mere courage from arrogance, the Hebrew understanding of courage was grounded in the nature of their God as ruler of the universe. Another Hebrew word to note here is *achowr* (aw-khore) or back; which could mean facing north or west—both of which for Israel signaled defeat or danger.

The final part of this verse refers to Saul, "and the sword of Saul returned not empty." Note that from this passage we can learn that Jonathan was an archer while Saul was a swordsman. The Hebrew word used here for sword is *chereb* (**kheh'-reb**) and refers to cutting instruments. When used by warriors it points to expertise in the use of weapons such as a knife, sword, or other sharp implement such as an axe or dagger.

The word "returned" or *shuwb* (**shoob**) points to the fact that Saul was not one to retreat. He was not just going to lie down and allow his enemies to rejoice over him. He always got his man, as the saying goes. The use of the Hebrew word *reyqam* (*ray-kawm*) or in English empty, points to the fact that Saul was not ineffectual in battle. David, in this verse, simply commemorates Saul and Jonathan as mighty warriors.

23 Saul and Jonathan were lovely and pleasant in their lives, and in their death they were not divided: they were swifter than eagles, they were stronger than lions.

In this verse David moves from life on the battle field to Saul and Jonathan's relationship with one another. To describe this relationship David used the Hebrew word *Ahab* (*aw-hab*) to describe the rootedness of the paternal love Saul held for Jonathan, and the affection Jonathan returned to his father. This verse suggests that Saul and Jonathan were friends. David was in the position to know this since he lived with Saul and Jonathan in the same house for several years as Saul's personal musician. He gives us further insight into the relationship by the use of the Hebrew word *na 'iym* (**naw-eembt**) from the people whom he led. The next word suggests that this relationship was alive, fresh and strong. It was an organic, living relationship not bound by mechanical rules but by mutual respect. Underneath this there is a suggestion that they maintained this relationship in spite of some problems that may have sprung up along the way. David closed the verse by pointing out that it was this closeness that led to their death together. The part of the verse which reads "and in their death they were not separated" should actually read "even in their death they were not separated." Not even the presence of death could separate them (Hebrew *parad*, **paw-rad'**), their bond did not break nor their ties to each other sever or sunder as a result of their pain.

David now turns back to their warrior character. They were "swifter than eagles." The Hebrew *qalal* (**kaw-lal**) translated "swift" suggests that they were light on their feet. But it can also mean that they despised danger and made movements in battle seem light and easy. The use of the Hebrew word *nesher* (**neh-sher**) meaning eagle, in the original usage would have been understood as connecting the cutting and piercing instruments already mentioned. Thus "swifter than eagles" complements the act of lacerating and piercing. The eagle is known for its swiftness and its sharp beak is now used in analogical complementary. Just in case one does not understand, David uses another metaphorical analogy: "stronger than a lion." The Hebrew word for strong is translated *gabar* (**gaw-bar**) and suggests that Saul and Jonathan were able to prevail over their enemies. It could also suggest that they were not afraid of the enemy and acted insolently. The Hebrew word *ariy* (**ar-ee**) translated lion in this verse contains within its meaning a sense of violence. The lion is not afraid of anything. It walks royally and pounces upon its prey without regard for size or strength. Again, all the words in this verse point to the violence of war.

24 Ye daughters of Israel, weep over Saul, who clothed you in scarlet, with other delights, who put on ornaments of gold upon your apparel.

In this stanza David acknowledged that Saul had brought prosperity to the people, and he called on them to mourn Saul's death. Saul enriched Israel with the spoils and booty of his conquests. But here he called upon the women of Israel to honor Saul for his courage. The women, just as the sons, were builders of the family name and ones whose relationships helped to cement the social structures protecting Israel from destruction. The quality or condition can usually be decided from the blessings that are bestowed upon the daughters of the land. This indeed was the way David and the men of his times thought. While the King James Version of the Bible uses daughters here, the word could be translated Children of Israel. Simply speaking, it could read, "offspring of Israel weep over Saul." The Hebrew *bakah*, (**baw-kaw**) translated weep, reminds one of the Igbo word *baakwah* which generally means to bemoan or to wail and complain. Usually it refers to a song of lament for a great loss. David tells them why they would go into lamentation. The answer is in the phrase "who clothed you in scarlet." The Hebrew word *labash* (**law-bash**) or wrap means to wrap clothing around as a web

found in Africa or in India, But not just any clothes, but crimson (Hebrew *shaniy* pronounced **shaw-nee**). This refers to material dyed in crimson or woven from dyed threads as is done today in many parts of Africa. Not only did Saul clothe them with delicate clothing which were booties of war, according to this passage he also lavished them "with other delights." The word delight comes from the Hebrew word `*eden* (**ay-den**) and means pleasure. He treated the people to delicate delights resulting in pleasure. In a sense, during Saul's reign the land of Israel was filled with "Eden's delight." We read further that Saul put gold upon the apparel of the people. The Hebrew word *adiy* (**ad-ee**) derived from the word *adah* suggests the putting on of finery. It could mean just outfit, but here it refers specifically to the things that are on or around the head, (i.e., the face, mouth, ears, nose) and all other such ornaments and trappings to enhance beauty. The word *zahab* (**zaw-hawb**) shows that Saul sought to make them shimmer from the gold.

25 How are the mighty fallen in the midst of the battle! O Jonathan, thou wast slain in thine high places.

David now moves from talking about Saul and Jonathan's exploits and their relationship to the people to his own personal feelings. Thus far his description of Saul has been aloof. Now this verse repeats the refrain "how are the mighty fallen in the midst of battle!" The "O" recalls the deep pathos usually expressed by prophesy or catastrophe. David uses it in this verse of his lamentation of Jonathan. He follows the refrain immediately with the name of Jonathan. David was very grateful to Jonathan, his sworn friend. David expressed his personal grief over the death of his friend. He curses the mountains of Gilboa because this is the place where Jonathan was slain. In his mourning he tells us his concern is that Jonathan's fall was in the midst of battle. Jonathan was in the center, in the middle. Could it be that Jonathan stood between his father and the warring horde? The Hebrew word *milchama* (**milkhaw-maw**) means engaging in war. David then tells us who fell in battle; it was *Yehownathan* (Jonathan) which means Jehovah gives. Jonathan who was a gift of God to his father, and to the nation, and to David, was pierced and polluted. This sacred gift of God has now been profaned by the infliction of a deadly wound. Note that he says Jonathan fell upon "high places." The use of the *bama* or high, though not clear, suggests that David held Jonathan in high esteem.

26 I am distressed for thee, my brother Jonathan: very pleasant hast thou been unto me: thy love to me was wonderful, passing the love of women.

Here David laments Jonathan as his particular friend. Jonathan's love to him was wonderful. They were true friends. Nothing is more distressing than to lose a true friend. Most adults value close friendships. The more we love, the more we grieve. The Hebrew word translated distressed is *tsarar* (**tsarar**) meaning to experience cramp. It is to suffer a deep affliction and to be besieged by pain. David is saying I feel like someone has bound me up. He felt like somebody has just shut up all his being and he was troubled and vexed. He calls Jonathan *aachiy* from the Hebrew word *ach* (**awkh**) meaning brother, but the word is used to describe a deep sense of relationship. Here it metaphorically describes the affinity that David felt for Jonathan. He then says "you were very pleasant to me." Recall, Jonathan could have been David's enemy because David was reaching for the throne. The use of the word *na`em* (**naw-ame**) means that David appreciated Jonathan's agreeable nature without which David would have died. David was saying what Jonathan did for him was a thing of beauty, and now he speaks of the love he shared with Jonathan. Keep in mind that David calls Jonathan his brother. Now he uses the Hebrew word *ahabah* (**a-hab-aw**) which speaks to that love. Because he is going to compare the love with the love of a young maiden he uses the feminine reference not suggesting sexuality, but to speak of how Jonathan distinguished himself by the love he showed. Jonathan's love for his father, his people and his friends had cost him his life in battle. But, it could also mean that Jonathan's love for David was difficult, although it was wonderful to have an accomplished friend who would rise up for him in hard times. To David, a fugitive, such love was wonderful, if not miraculous. To find a friend in the house of the friend who seeks your life was nothing short of a miracle. Such friendships are not often found among men of war and especially those who vie for the same position of power. Such stories are told of women who have fallen in love with someone considered the enemy. In that context, the same comparison can be seen here. It could mean that it was more than the love of many women, since the word *ishshah* (**ish-shaw**) is an irregular plural meaning one female of many women. In other words David was saying that there had been no one in his life who had shown him such care and concern as Jonathan did, not even his own family.

27 How are the mighty fallen, and the weapons of war perished!

This phrase is repeated three times (vv. 19, 25, 27). It is repeated in such a way that one can feel the ascendancy of the passion and emotion as one reads first "how are the mighty fallen!" (v. 19). Then proceed to read in verse 25 "how are the mighty fallen in the midst of battle." The final declaration in verse 27, we read: "How are the mighty fallen, and the weapons of war perished." In these three lines which finds their crescendo here in verse 27, David captures the grief of his people and their feelings of weakness.

DAILY BIBLE READINGS

M: The Battle of Mount Gilboa
1 Samuel 31:1-7

T: The Rescue of Saul's Body
1 Samuel 31:8-13

W: The Amalekite Messenger
2 Samuel 1:1-16

T: David's Lament
2 Samuel 1:17-27

F: Comfort in Times of Distress
Psalm 77:1-9

S: Death of Saul and His Sons
1 Chronicles 10:1-7

S: Burials and a Judgment Against Saul
1 Chronicles 10:8-14

TEACHING TIPS

October 22
Bible Study Guide 8

1. Words You Should Know

A. Blessed (2 Samuel 2:5) Hebrew *Barakh*—To bend the knee, to receive as well as invoke a blessing. There is a close association between kneeling and receiving a blessing.

B. Elders (2 Samuel 5:3) Hebrew *Zagen*—An important governing body that had influence in the life of Israel even during the time of the monarchy.

2. Teacher Preparation

A. To prepare for the lesson, read the BACKGROUND and DEVOTIONAL READING Scriptures. Imagine yourself as David. How would you have responded to the events as outlined in the Scriptures?

B. Take time to read the BIBLE STUDY GUIDE. Now answer the SEARCH THE SCRIPTURES and DISCUSS THE MEANING questions and write out the answers on 3 x 5 cards.

C. Materials needed: Bible, Bible map, and chalkboard or newsprint.

3. Starting the Lesson

A. Before students arrive, write out the SEARCH THE SCRIPTURES questions on 3 x 5 cards and tape one card under each seat in the class.

B. As students arrive have them take their seats. If they sit in assigned seats, you may want to change their seats for this lesson.

C. Have a student read the FOCAL VERSES. Now ask another student to read the KEEP IN MIND verse.

D. Have another student lead the class in prayer, focusing on the KEEP IN MIND verse as the foundation of prayer.

4. Getting into the Lesson

A. Ask a student to read the IN FOCUS story and discuss whether or not we should select leaders based on criteria other than race or personal preference.

B. Have a volunteer write the AT-A-GLANCE outline on the chalkboard or newsprint. Now ask for volunteers to read the BACKGROUND and IN DEPTH sections according to the AT-A-GLANCE outline.

C. Have a student read THE PEOPLE, PLACES, AND TIMES article. Locate Hebron on the Bible map that you brought to class so students will give a better understanding of its location.

5. Relating the Lesson to Life

A. Ask students to reach under their chairs, pull out the cards, and read the questions. Ask students to write their answers down on paper.

B. Next, have students read and answer the LESSON IN OUR SOCIETY. Remind students of the importance of taking the lesson out of the classroom where it will have an effect on other people.

6. Arousing Action

A. Ask students to read the MAKE IT HAPPEN assignment silently. Now ask whether or not they feel adequate to follow through on the assignment.

B. Challenge students to read and meditate on the DAILY BIBLE READINGS as they reflect on the lesson throughout the week.

C. Close the class with prayer, using the LESSON AIM as the foundation.

WORSHIP GUIDE

For the Superintendent or Teacher
Theme: **David Becomes King of All Israel**
Theme Song: "I'll Be a Sunbeam"
Scripture: Psalm 110:1-3
Song: "God Is in Control"
Meditation: God, help me to yield to Your voice as You thrust me out in leadership positions for Your glory. In Jesus' name, Amen.

DAVID BECOMES KING OF ALL ISRAEL

Bible Background • 2 SAMUEL 2—5; 1 Chronicles 11:1-3
Printed Text • 2 SAMUEL 2:1-7; 5:1-5
Devotional Reading • PSALM 78:67-72

LESSON AIM

By the end of the lesson, students should be able to clearly explain David's ascension to Israel's throne, list ways God selects leaders, and determine to be in a position to be selected as a leader for God's work.

KEEP IN MIND

". . . The LORD said to [David], Thou shalt feed my people Israel, and thou shalt be a captain over Israel" (2 Samuel 5:2).

FOCAL VERSES

2 Samuel 2:1 And it came to pass after this, that David inquired of the LORD, saying, Shall I go up into any of the cities of Judah? And the LORD said unto him, Go up. And David said, Whither shall I go up? And he said, Unto Hebron.

2 So David went up thither, and his two wives also, Ahinoam the Jezreelitess, and Abigail Nabal's wife the Carmelite.

3 And his men that were with him did David bring up, every man with his household: and they dwelt in the cities of Hebron.

4 And the men of Judah came, and there they anointed David king over the house of Judah. And they told David, saying, That the men of Jabesh-gilead were they that buried Saul.

5 And David sent messengers unto the men of Jabesh-gilead, and said unto them, Blessed be ye of the LORD, that ye have shewed this kindness unto your lord, even unto Saul, and have buried him.

LESSON OVERVIEW

LESSON AIM
KEEP IN MIND
FOCAL VERSES
IN FOCUS
THE PEOPLE, PLACES, AND TIMES
BACKGROUND
AT-A-GLANCE
IN DEPTH
SEARCH THE SCRIPTURES
DISCUSS THE MEANING
LESSON IN OUR SOCIETY
MAKE IT HAPPEN
FOLLOW THE SPIRIT
REMEMBER YOUR THOUGHTS
MORE LIGHT ON THE TEXT
DAILY BIBLE READINGS

6 And now the LORD shew kindness and truth unto you: and I also will requite you this kindness, because ye have done this thing.

7 Therefore now let your hands be strengthened, and be ye valiant: for your master Saul is dead, and also the house of Judah have anointed me king over them.

2 Samuel 5:1 Then came all the tribes of Israel to David unto Hebron, and spake, saying, Behold, we are thy bone and thy flesh.

2 Also in time past, when Saul was king over us, thou wast he that leddest out and broughtest in Israel: and the LORD said to thee, Thou shalt feed my people Israel, and thou shalt be a captain over Israel.

OCT 22ND

3 So all the elders of Israel came to the king to Hebron; and king David made a league with them in Hebron before the LORD: and they anointed David king over Israel.

4 David was thirty years old when he began to reign, and he reigned forty years.

5 In Hebron he reigned over Judah seven years and six months: and in Jerusalem he reigned thirty and three years over all Israel and Judah.

IN FOCUS

After a heated and sometimes violent campaign, John Bonner was elected as the first Black union foreman by the United Auto Workers at the Ford

Stamping Plant on Chicago's south side. The majority of the workers at the plant were white, so Bonner had a tough time winning over many of them who found it difficult to be represented by a Black man. However, Bonner made it clear that if he was elected, he wouldn't be just a "Black fore-man," but a leader for all the workers, regardless of race and gender.

Several of his opponents were convinced that because Bonner was Black, he wouldn't be able to negotiate a good deal for his constituents with the Ford Motor Company. But what his opponents failed to realize was that John Bonner had paid his dues in other Ford Plants around the country. In fact, everywhere he went, Bonner made working conditions for union members better because he cared for people who were committed to working hard and taking care of their families. "We've got to get away from picking people based solely on race or gender, and recognize that a union fore-man will stand up for everyone, no matter what his or her color may be," said Bonner.

Leadership is not an easy task. People select leaders based on many qualities. We must keep in mind that leaders are really servants for all people wherever their influence extends. If we remember these principles, we might be more selective of the leaders we choose.

This week, we will focus on how David became king of all Israel and his role in leading the nation after the death of Saul.

THE PEOPLE, PLACES, AND TIMES

Hebron. Hebron is the place where Abraham died, David reigned, and Absalom revolted. It is both one of the most biblically important and archaeologically disappointing sites in Palestine. Located about 19 miles south of Jerusalem in a generously watered valley high on the mountain-ous spine of Palestine (about 3,040 feet above sea level), Hebron has been almost continuously occupied since its founding in the middle of the fourteenth century B.C. The ancient city lay on the western side of the valley, but shifted some-what to the east after the Crusades. Today, it cen-ters upon the massive Haram el-Khalil, "the sacred precinct of the friend." This is the great mosque built over the traditional tomb of Abraham.

(Adapted from Bible Archaeology and Faith, Harry Thomas Frank, Nashville: 1971, Abingdon Press, pp. 127-128.)

BACKGROUND

In last week's lesson, David wrote a song of lamentation after he discovered that King Saul and Jonathan were killed in battle by the Philistines. Despite the troubles that he had with the king, David acknowledged Saul's contribu-tions to Israel as well as his place as king. David also lamented mightily over Jonathan who he dearly loved as a brother and friend.

It appears from Scripture that Saul and Jonathan's death had a tremendous effect on David. But it was time for him to get his act togeth-er and move on. God had plans for him and David needed to be of sound mind and spirit if he was to heed God's call on his life.

AT-A-GLANCE

1. David Is Told to Go to Judah
(2 Samuel 2:1-3)
2. David Is Anointed King over Judah
(vv. 4-7)
3. David Is Anointed King over Israel
(2 Samuel 5:1-5)

IN DEPTH

1. David Is Told to Go to Judah
(2 Samuel 2:1-3)

After David finished his lamentation of Saul and Jonathan and wrote it in the book of Jasher, he felt the need to move on to his next assign-ment. The Bible doesn't say why David sensed this need. Perhaps he knew he couldn't stay in Ziklag all his life weeping over two dead men. Or maybe he felt God's Holy Spirit tugging at his heart. Whatever the reason, David sought the Lord for clear directions on where he should go.

The word used in the King James Version of the Bible is "inquired" (v. 1) and it means to ask for specific information and to consult God for His direction and counsel. David realized that he was coming out of a traumatic time in his life and he didn't want to make a move until he heard clearly from God. We should be like that. When we are faced with making vital decisions for our future, it is imperative that we seek the Lord's permission and counsel before we move.

David sensed that he needed to go to Judah, although he wasn't sure where. But God knew that David's next assignment was in Hebron and it was important that David and his family move there as soon as possible.

Located about 25 miles southwest of Jerusalem, Hebron was the land that God gave to Abraham after he and his nephew Lot separated. From there, God affirmed His covenant with Abraham (Genesis 13:14-18). Hebron was also the place that was given to Caleb because of his unwavering faith in God (Joshua 14:13-15). Finally, Hebron was one of the places to which David sent treasure that he and his men won in their battle with the Amalekites (1 Samuel 30:1-31). Hebron would play a prominent role in David's life; and it was in Hebron, for a season, that God wanted him to reside.

David obeyed the Lord and took his two wives with him: Ahinoam, a Jezreelite, and Abigail, a Carmelite. Both Abigail and Ahinoam were married to David shortly after the death of Nabal, Abigail's former husband who had disrespected David in Carmel (1 Samuel 25:42-43). Jezreel was near the foot of Mount Gilboa where Saul and Jonathan died. Having lost his wives once before to the enemy (1 Samuel 30:5), David wasn't about to take that chance again. So, David gathered all of his belongings and moved from Ziklag, 20 miles northwest to Hebron, God's place for him.

However, David didn't move with his family alone. The 600 men who lived with David in Gath also moved with him to Hebron (1 Samuel 27:1-3). These were men who were loyal to David and had fought with him in the Philistine stronghold. They would be instrumental in David's kingdom and, therefore, needed to be in their rightful place when David ascended to the throne.

2. David Is Anointed King over Judah (vv. 4-7)

When David arrived in Hebron, he was readily received by the people. In fact, the Bible declares that it was the "men of Judah [who] came and . . .

anointed David king . . . of Judah" (v. 4). David had been anointed to be God's and Israel's next leader while he was in Bethlehem (1 Samuel 16:1-3). So, the people were actually confirming what had already been established by God.

Once David was anointed by the men of Judah, his first official act as king was to bless the men of Jabesh-gilead where the tribe of Benjamin lived. Jabesh-gilead was the first place that King Saul experienced victory for Israel (1 Samuel 11:1-15) and was located just east of the Jordan River. The men of Judah wanted the new king to know that it was those in Jabesh-gilead who took Saul's body and buried him shortly after his ugly defeat at the hands of the Philistines (1 Samuel 31:10-13). David was so touched at how they had cared for the king of Israel and Jonathan even in death that he sent his personal messengers to the city to tell the men of his indebtedness to them.

David's message affirmed that even though Saul was dead, David would not forget them for their kind act. As king of Judah, Jabesh-gilead would have the loyalty and protection of David even as they had it with Saul. David encouraged them to be strong and valiant. As long as he was king, Jabesh-gilead would have an important place in David's heart.

3. David Is Anointed King over Israel (2 Samuel 5:1-5)

David may have been satisfied with being king over the tribe of Judah, but God wasn't. God's intention and plan was for David to be king over all of Israel. Although Saul's son Ishbosheth ruled over the northern kingdom, that would not last long. God had already prepared David to be king over all the tribes. Once civil war broke out between Israel and Judah and Abner, Saul's right-hand man defected from Ishbosheth to join David; it was just a matter of time before things were set in motion for Israel to come and bow before David.

Eventually, Abner and Ishbosheth were both killed (see 2 Samuel 3:22—4:12), which left a vacuum of leadership in the northern tribes. The Bible affirms that once this vacuum was felt "all the tribes of Israel [came] to David [and said] behold we are thy bone and flesh" (v. 1).

How foolish we are to fight against the will and ways of God. We need to learn how to submit to God in every area of our lives so that we can experience all of the blessings He has in store for us. Unfortunately, many believers waste a lot of time and energy tying to avoid or subvert God's plan for their lives.

The men of Israel arrived in Hebron with a message for the king. In essence, they admitted that it was time for the war to cease because they understood that Israel and Judah were part of the same family—the seed of Abraham and sons of Jacob. The nations would not have survived an ongoing civil war.

The second reason they felt it necessary to cease the war against Judah was because they recognized David as a man with incredible leadership skills. They remembered when David and his men had been sent out by King Saul to fight against the Philistines and when he returned, the women shouted that David had killed ten thousands of Israel's enemies (1 Samuel 18:6-14). They also remembered how the king feared David because God's anointing was on him. And they remembered how David's office had been prophesied while he was just a shepherd boy in Bethlehem (1 Samuel 16:1). Just as David took care of his father's sheep, so too would he take care of God's sheep by being a commander, overseer, and head of all twelve tribes.

The elders of Israel came to Hebron as one to face David for the purpose of making "a league" with the king and the tribe of Judah before Almighty God (v. 3). The word "league" in Hebrew is *B'rith* which means a covenant, alliance of friendship, a treaty, and an obligation. In essence, the Israelites pledged their lives in service to David as king of both Judah and Israel with God's blessing on the covenant.

All of this took place 7 years after David ascended to the throne of Judah in Hebron at the age of 30. Therefore, David became king of the united nation at 37 years old, then he moved his kingdom to Jerusalem and ruled for an additional 33 years. In all, David served as king and spokesman for God to the nation of Israel for 40 years.

Leadership is not easy. However, we can be assured that if we are committed to God and sub-mitted to His divine call, we will be successful in the area where God has sent us to minister to His people.

SEARCH THE SCRIPTURES

1. Where did the Lord tell David to move? (2 Samuel 2:1)

2. Who did David take with him when he moved? (vv. 2-3)

3. What happened to David when he arrived in Hebron? (v. 4)

4. How did David treat the men of Jabesh-gilead? (vv. 5-7)

5. Who came to Hebron to see David? (2 Samuel 5:1-3)

6. What happened to David once the men of Israel came to see him? (vv. 3-5)

DISCUSS THE MEANING

1. Was David led by the Holy Spirit when he moved to Hebron or was he divinely appointed to live there? Discuss.

2. How should we select leadership in our nation?

3. How should we select leadership in the church?

4. Can leadership be effective in the Body of Christ without God's seal of approval? Why or why not?

5. What would have happened to the nation of Israel had they not yielded themselves to David?

LESSON IN OUR SOCIETY

How do we fill the apparent void of leadership in the African American communities in this country? Is the church a good place to look for leadership or should we depend on "grass roots" community organizations for our leaders? Discuss.

MAKE IT HAPPEN

This week, ask the Lord to give you opportunities in your church to use your God-given gifts of leadership. Perhaps taking some children on an outing or spending time with senior citizens would be a good place to start. Why not make an appointment with your pastor to discuss these and other needs in your church?

FOLLOW THE SPIRIT
What God wants me to do:

_____

_____

REMEMBER YOUR THOUGHTS
Special insights you have learned:

_____

_____

MORE LIGHT ON THE TEXT
2 Samuel 2:1-7; 5:1-5

2:1 And it came to pass after this, that David inquired of the LORD, saying, Shall I go up into any of the cities of Judah? And the LORD said unto him, Go up. And David said, Whither shall I go up? And he said, Unto Hebron.

After the death of King Saul, David knows that he is next in line to rule over Israel. But succession to the throne proceeds in a leisurely systematic manner. First, David seeks guidance from the Lord. God's word teaches us, "In all thy ways acknowledge him (the Lord), and he shall direct thy paths" (Proverbs 3:6). David knows that God has anointed him to be king over all of Israel. With this assurance of hope in God's promise, he does not hasten to the throne.

David demonstrates to you and me how we should react to God's calling. We must display the assurance in knowing that if God has called us for a purpose, God will use us in His time. *Matthew Henry's* Commentary says those who believe that they are summoned by God do not proceed in haste, but wait for God's time for the accomplishment of God's promise. David knew that the people needed time to grieve over their deceased king. David also demonstrates that we should pray to God always, that is, when things are good and when things are bad. The writer Paul tells us to "pray without ceasing" (1 Thessalonians 5:17).

Hebron means brotherhood (cf. v. 3, cities of Hebron, i.e., a federation of cities). It is now called El Khalil (the friend), a contraction for the city of the friend of God, viz., Abraham. It served as the center of the league of confederation of the clans of Judah and Caleb and those associated with them. It is approximately twenty miles south of Jerusalem, in the region famed in antiquity for its fertile vineyards. Hebron is the city where the priest resides, one of the cities of refuge. David takes his family with him to Hebron. God's placement of David in Hebron signifies that God is a sanctuary to David. This is why David is able to write, "God is our refuge and strength, a very present help in time of trouble" Psalm 46:1). David knows that God is a "present" help for those who depend upon Him. Zohhiates tells us "the phrase" 'very present' in the Hebrew emphasizes the speed, completeness, and might of the Lord's help." When God calls you and me for a purpose, God promises to be our refuge, a place where we can find security in times of uncertainty. We find here that David has received a respite from wandering as a result of the death of Saul. Here we see one of the reasons God spoke so tenderly of David. His first act is to enquire of the Lord. The Hebrew word *sha'al (shaw-al)* suggests that David was not just asking to go home but was requesting from the Lord the permission to return. He was not averse to asking counsel of the Lord. He consulted the Lord. He make known his desire. This is more than just asking; it is an earnest inquiry of one who is homesick. In the Hebrew it is as though he obtained leave. David's request was "Shall I go up to cities of Judah?" Just because Judah was his home did not mean that it was to be the location of his ministry to the Lord. But here he talks of going up. The Hebrew word alah *(aw-law)* translated "go up" means to ascend, or to mount. This will suggest that David was in the southern parts of Israel during his fugitive years. But it could also mean that he is asking if he could go at once to Judah or should he wait. In this question is embedded the request to bring up other questions. At other times this could mean war but in this context it does not mean war. Also here he could be asking will I be exalted in Judah.

This inquiry of the Lord is replete with concern for his future preservation and increase. Note the word for cities is the word *iyr* (pronounced **eer***),* a place guarded by watchmen. This suggests that David was probably still afraid that people may want to deliver him to his enemies. Note that he does not request to go back to other places in Israel but to his own tribe Yehuwdah. There is a play on words here. The word Judah means praise or celebration. Thus, we could say that he was asking God if he could go and celebrate with his people. The Lord's response was straightforward. But David does not stop there, he wants to know as in the Hebrew an (**awn**), the exact location. He was directed to Hebron. The significance should not be lost as it was the seat of association thus a friendly place. He could go where he can associate with his people and celebrate.

2 So David went up thither, and his two wives also, Ahinoam the Jezreelitess, and Abigail Nabal's wife the Carmelite.

After David receives directions from God, he obeys God's directions, the second step in his succession to the throne. It is not enough for you and me to hear God's directions. We must also act affirmatively on God's instructions. David takes his wives because they remained loyal to him during tumultuous days while fleeing from Saul. They were his companions; with him in tribulation. He rewards them during his days of triumph. David demonstrates how we should treat our spouses. Often, once we reach the top of the ladder of success, we forget those who helped boost us up the ladder. As a result, we leave or change our mate. This verse indicates that David went to the exact location that the Lord had selected for him. The text seems to suggest that he went first with his wives. It is interesting that it does not say he went up with his men of war. Going with a band of men may have signaled trouble, but going with his wives shows that he came in peace.

3 And his men that were with him did David bring up, every man with his household: and they dwelt in the cities of Hebron.

David takes his family and men with him to live in Hebron. He takes his friends and followers because they remained loyal to him during his time of wandering. Just as we are loyal to each other, God wants us to be loyal to Him. Like David's family and friends, those who remain faithful to the mission of Jesus Christ will receive a blessing on earth and in heaven.

It was unlike David to endanger the lives of the families of the men who followed him. The Hebrew word enowsh *(en-oshe)* properly means

mortal. It could also mean that he brought with him all fellows. Another meaning is that he brought up all husbands and their families, or he brought all those who had served in exile with him. The Hebrew word for house is bayith *(bah-yith)* which means family. They all dwelled in Hebron. The Hebrew word for dwell, yashab *(yaw-shab)* means to sit down. Understand that until now David has had no rest. He and his family and friends have been constantly on the move unable to sit still. This word suggests that he is now able to remain and to settle.

4 And the men of Judah came, and there they anointed David king over the house of Judah. And they told David, saying, That the men of Jabesh-gilead were they that buried Saul.

The people of Judah anointed David as their king. Judah is the largest of all the tribes, and they were accustomed to acting independently. This act of anointing David as king is an independent act. This is David's second anointing as king. Samuel, the prophet, performed the first in Bethlehem when David was around age 20 (1 Samuel 16:12-13). Here we see how David's rise to power is in succession. First God calls him, then man appoints him.

The second part of this verse deals with how the people of Jabesh-gilead buried Saul. They are indebted to Saul for saving them from the threat of Nahash the Ammorite. They remembered how Saul caused 300,000 Israelites to come to their aid, and to defeat the Ammorites (1 Samuel 11:1-15). So, they honor Saul as their deceased king by giving him a proper burial.

David did indeed return the celebration to his brethren. This consecration by the people of Judah may not have been the best thing—it will haunt David's children for times to come. Whenever there was a crisis the people saw David as King of Judah. As David was being consecrated king someone came to announce that Saul had been buried by the men of Jabesh-gilead. The Hebrew word for "told" is *wayagiduw* derived from the root word *nagad* meaning to boldly stand in front of someone. It seems the people who told David this news were not interested in announcing the burial of Saul. The people of Jabesh-gilead

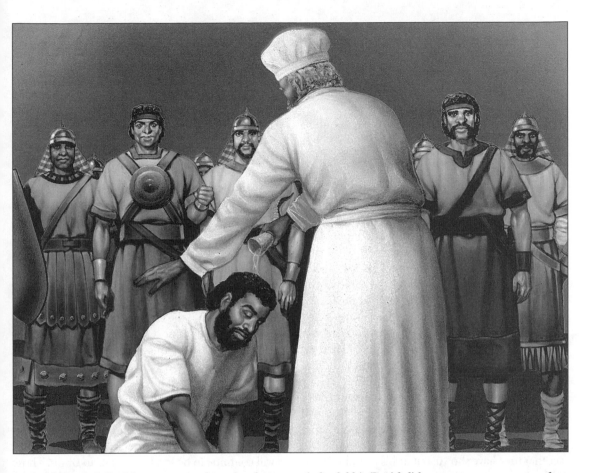

probably buried Saul in secret not knowing how David would react. The word as used here can also mean to expose, explain or denounce. Could it be that they were denouncing the people of Jabesh-gilead for burying Saul? This could be the case. For in many of the cultures of Africa a person who commits suicide is not buried.

5 And David sent messengers unto the men of Jabesh-gilead, and said unto them, Blessed be ye of the LORD, that ye have shewed this kindness unto your lord, even unto Saul, and have buried him.

David sends a message of blessing to the men of Jabesh-gilead because they have shown kindness to the Lord and to Saul by burying Saul. David commends them for their act of kindness showing respect for the dead. After all, Saul was their king anointed by God, and as king, he respected God. The word for "send" is the Hebrew word shalach

(sahw-lakh); David did not sent one messenger but many messengers. The word for messengers is the same as the Hebrew word for angels. The Hebrew word mal`ak (maw-awk) may mean that David sent prophets, priests, and respected teachers in Israel. His message was "blessed be ye of the Lord." The important word here is "blessed," (Hebrew barak), meaning bless or may it be beneficial to you from the Lord. The reader should know that this is the same word euphemism meaning to curse the king. When used in anger it can mean treason. Was David really blessing them or telling them that they had blasphemed by burying a man who committed suicide? David uses the word barak (blessing) and the word checed (mercy) together. The word checed (kheh-sed) means kindness. But by implication, though very seldom, it can be used to represent reproof. In Hebrew, depending on what is happening, when the word is used it can mean reproach or doing a wicked thing. Did they do a good thing in the eyes of David? Note that he calls Saul their lord.

6 And now the LORD shew kindness and truth unto you: and I also will requite you this kindness, because ye have done this thing.

David prays for God to bless them for their good deed. Not only does he want God to bless them, but he promises to reward them for their act of kindness. Good wishes are good things, but acts of kindness and gratitude are better.

God has blessed us and given us the ability to bless others. A tangible blessing is usually far better than words of encouragement. If a person is hungry, you would not say grace without giving them food to eat. Just as you and I know how to bless one another, God knows how to bless us. The Bible says that "If ye then, being evil, know how to give good gifts unto your children, how much more shall your Father which is in heaven give good things to them that ask him?" (Matthew 7:11) Therefore, God blesses you and me so that we may bless others.

David begins this passage with the word *attah* meaning this time. His request is that God will show them the same act of kindness and truth that they have shown. David himself will show them the act that they have shown. But in his promise David adds the word *emeth* (truth), which comes from the word *aman*, which is amen. As used here it connotes stability. David seems to be saying that as Saul has shown himself trustworthy to them, he will also show them that he is trustworthy.

7 Therefore now let your hands be strengthened, and be ye valiant: for your master Saul is dead, and also the house of Judah have anointed me king over them.

In this verse David continues his conversation with the people of Jabesh-gilead. After speaking to them about their action, he uses the word "now" (Hebrew *attah* meaning "this time"). The way the passage is phrased it is as though David is about to offer a challenge. The challenge is "let your hands be strengthened." The word translated "hand" is the Hebrew word *yad*, It indicates power or means of action. It can also be used to determine direction or a border. Could David have been saying

"strengthen your border"? Furthermore, this word may also be used to mean coast or dominion. In some forms it may be used to mean force. Could another interpretation be "strengthen your force"? The word strength is translated from the Hebrew word *chazaq* (**khaw-zak**) and means to repair or fortify. This suggests that David's intent was not so much to bless them, but to break the hold of Saul upon them. In fact, the word could mean "come out and play the man and I will show you. David adds another word, valiant, from the Hebrew word *chayil* (**khah-yil**), which means army. So we see that David is saying to them fortify yourselves with an army. The English translation, in my mind, fails to convey the intent of the passage. Take note how David tells them to "fortify themselves and raise an army." He then proceeds saying "your master Saul is dead." Note the phrase "your master," which is the equivalent to saying "see what your sister has done?" Given the fact that Saul was also David's master this way of stating it is meant not as a praise, but as a mockery. "Your master Saul is dead" could mean he has been destroyed. David follows this with another statement, "and the house of Judah has anointed me king over them." This whole passage reads like a threat to the people of Jabesh-gilead. David wanted to know if they will continue to be loyal to Saul or to David. Those who supported Saul, of course, saw the intent of this and it led to a long war between those loyal to Saul and those loyal to David.

5:1 Then came all the tribes of Israel to David unto Hebron, and spake, saying, Behold, we are thy bone and thy flesh.

In Chapter 5 we see David having subdued many of those loyal to Saul and he is now ready to rule all of Israel. After years of strife with Ish-bosheth and the northern tribes, the elders of all the tribes of Israel come to David in Hebron and ask him to be their king. They appeal to his kindred ties. So far he has been the king of Judah. However upon the death of Saul's son, Jonathan, we read "all the tribes of Israel." The Hebrew word *kol* (**kole**) suggests that they came to David as a whole. It may also be that enough of them came to him to assure his reign as king over the whole land They came with a message an official communique. The message began with the word *hen* (**hane**) a primitive particle meaning "lo!" It is as though they have been jarred from sleep. "Hey look here David, we are your brothers too." The word "bone" in Hebrew is *etsem* (**eh-tsem**). But it could also mean that they were reminding David they were part of what makes him strong. They were the structure that would help him build a kingdom. And they added, "we are thy flesh."

2 Also in time past, when Saul was king over us, thou wast he that leddest out and broughtest in Israel: and the LORD said to thee, Thou shalt feed my people Israel, and thou shalt be a captain over Israel.

They now reminded him that they have been watching him. His patience had not been lost on people. The people recognized David's good works when he was the leader of Saul's army. They suggest that in fact it was David who helped the nation come together and organized them in their gatherings. The phrase "in time past" is from one Hebrew word *ethmowl* (**eth-mole**) suggesting that this people were reminiscent of days gone by when David led the nation. They say that David *yatsa* (**yaw-tsaw**) appeared before them, brought them forth. In battle he helped them escape. But he also came with them when they needed him. Apparently there had been some prophecies about David. Here the people were saying that it was when he was going in and out before Saul that the Lord "said thou shalt feed my people Israel." As he had shepherded his father's sheep now he must also shepherd Israel. But they do not stop being fed by him, they also said that God had made him the captain of the people.

3 So all the elders of Israel came to the king to Hebron; and king David made a league with them in Hebron before the LORD: and they anointed David king over Israel.

Judah selected David as their king seven years prior. Now, the elders of Israel and David make a covenant, and David is anointed king over Israel. This is the inauguration of David as king over all of God's people. This is David's third anointing. David was anointed by Samuel in Bethlehem, by the people of Judah in Hebron, and by the

Israelites in Jerusalem. As king, David will be their judge in peace and captain in war; and they will obey him. David does something here that Saul never did; He makes a covenant with the people of Hebron. The Hebrew word for covenant is *beriyth* (**ber-eeth**) which means to cut. It really refers to the cutting of the flesh accompanied with an oath.

4 David was thirty years old when he began to reign, and he reigned forty years.

This verse merely tells us that he was "a son of thirty" when he began to rule over the people of God. The numerical importance of thirty can be seen in the life of Joseph, Moses, and Jesus. It was to David that the whole nation came as they sought for divine counsel. At the age of 30 he was inducted into royalty, and at age 30 the people came to take counsel from him.

5 In Hebron he reigned over Judah seven years and six months: and in Jerusalem he reigned thirty and three years over all Israel and Judah.

He rules the divided kingdom (Judah only) for 7 years. Then David rules the united kingdom, (Judah and Israel) for 33 years. Therefore, David is king for 40 years.

DAILY BIBLE READINGS

M: The Rival Kings
2 Samuel 2:1-11

T: Abner Defects to David
2 Samuel 3:6-21

W: The Plot Against Abner
2 Samuel 3:22-27

T: Joab Murders Abner
2 Samuel 3:27-39

F: The Death of Ishbaal
2 Samuel 4:1-12

S: David, King of Israel, Captures Jerusalem
2 Samuel 5:1-12

S: David Rules Israel From Jerusalem
1 Chronicles 11:1-9

TEACHING TIPS

October 29
Bible Study Guide 9

1. Words You Should Know

A. Ark (2 Samuel 7:2) Hebrew *Aron*—The sacred box which was kept in the Holy of Holies in the tabernacle and later in the temple. The word "ark" literally means a container.

B. Kingdom (v. 12) Hebrew *Mamiakhah*—The rule, dominion, realm, and sovereignty, specifically of God.

2. Teacher Preparation

A. Read 2 Samuel 5—7 which will help prepare you to make a smooth transition from last week's lesson to today's lesson.

B. Pray that your students will have a clear understanding of God's revelation to David regarding the house He would build.

C. Read the entire BIBLE STUDY GUIDE and answer all the questions in the SEARCH THE SCRIPTURES and DISCUSS THE MEANING sections.

D. Materials needed: Bible, 3 x 5 cards, chalkboard or newsprint.

3. Starting the Lesson

A. When students arrive, have them read the IN FOCUS story silently. Then ask them to discuss how important covenants are in our lives.

B. Next, write the KEEP IN MIND verse on the chalkboard or newsprint.

C. Have a student read the BIBLE BACK-GROUND Scriptures aloud to help prepare students to study the lesson.

D. Be sure to lead the class in prayer, focusing on the LESSON AIM.

4. Getting into the Lesson

A. Have students read the FOCAL VERSES and BACKGROUND to begin the lesson discussion.

B. Read the IN DEPTH section of the lesson according to the AT-A-GLANCE outline. Have students write down any questions they may have on the 3 x 5 cards to be shared later.

C. Assign several students to answer the SEARCH THE SCRIPTURES questions. Remind students that God is in control of every circumstance no matter what we face.

5. Relating the Lesson to Life

A. Assign students to read and answer the DISCUSS THE MEANING questions which will prompt them to apply the lesson to their lives.

B. Give students time to read and share ideas on how to implement the LESSON IN OUR SOCIETY exercise.

6. Arousing Action

A. Remind students to follow through on the MAKE IT HAPPEN exercise this week. Challenge them to write their answers in a journal so they can review it in the weeks ahead.

B. Be sure to have students read the DAILY BIBLE READINGS to strengthen and challenge their faith.

C. Ask a volunteer to close the class in prayer.

WORSHIP GUIDE

For the Superintendent or Teacher
Theme: God's Covenant with David
Theme Song: "Yes, Lord, I Believe"
Scripture: John 1:12-14
Song: "Jesus, You're the Center of My Joy"
Meditation: Heavenly Father, thank You for the covenant we have with You through Jesus Christ. Help us to stand firm in faith so we might confirm the promises You have already given us. In Jesus' name, Amen.

GOD'S COVENANT WITH DAVID

Bible Background • 2 SAMUEL 7; 1 CHRONICLES 17
Printed Text • 2 SAMUEL 7:1-13
Devotional Reading • 1 KINGS 8:15-21

LESSON AIM

By the end of the lesson, students should be able to explain God's covenant with David, list components of God's covenant with David, and be motivated to walk in covenant with God this week.

KEEP IN MIND

"And thine house and thy kingdom shall be established for ever before thee: thy throne shall be established for ever" (2 Samuel 7:16).

FOCAL VERSES

2 Samuel 7:1 And it came to pass, when the king sat in his house, and the LORD had given him rest round about from all his enemies;

2 That the king said unto Nathan the prophet, See now, I dwell in an house of cedar, but the ark of God dwelleth within curtains.

3 And Nathan said to the king, Go, do all that is in thine heart; for the LORD is with thee.

4 And it came to pass that night, that the word of the LORD came unto Nathan, saying,

5 Go and tell my servant David, Thus saith the LORD, Shalt thou build me an house for me to dwell in?

6 Whereas I have not dwelt in any house since the time that I brought up the children of Israel out of Egypt, even to this day, but have walked in a tent and in a tabernacle.

7 In all the places wherein I have walked with all the children of Israel spake I a word with any of the tribes of Israel, whom I commanded to feed my people Israel, saying, Why build ye not me a house of cedar?

LESSON OVERVIEW

LESSON AIM
KEEP IN MIND
FOCAL VERSES
IN FOCUS
THE PEOPLE, PLACES,
AND TIMES
BACKGROUND
AT-A-GLANCE
IN DEPTH
SEARCH THE SCRIPTURES
DISCUSS THE MEANING
LESSON IN OUR SOCIETY
MAKE IT HAPPEN
FOLLOW THE SPIRIT
REMEMBER YOUR THOUGHTS
MORE LIGHT ON THE TEXT
DAILY BIBLE READINGS

8 Now therefore so shalt thou say unto my servant David, Thus saith the LORD of hosts, I took thee from the sheepcote, from following the sheep, to be ruler over my people, over Israel:

9 And I was with thee whithersoever thou wentest, and have cut off all thine enemies out of thy sight, and have made thee a great name, like unto the name of the great men that are in the earth.

10 Moreover I will appoint a place for my people Israel, and will plant them, that they may dwell in a place of their own, and move no more; neither shall the children of wickedness afflict them any more, as beforetime,

11 And as since the time that I commanded judges to be over my people Israel, and have caused thee to rest from all thine enemies. Also the LORD telleth thee that he will make thee a house.

12 And when thy days be fulfilled, and thou shalt sleep with thy fathers, I will set up thy seed after thee, which shall proceed out of thy bowels, and I will establish his kingdom.

13 He shall build a house for my name, and I will stablish the throne of his kingdom for ever.

OCT 29TH

IN FOCUS

What is a covenant? One definition is: a formal agreement between two parties with each assuming a significant part of the agreement. Many years ago, people entered into marriages by covenant agreements. Today, most folk sign pre-nuptial agreements before going down the aisle.

Covenants are built and developed on trust. In fact, it is extremely difficult for covenant relationships to survive without it. As a result, we have divorces, broken families, and destroyed lives today, simply because people have broken covenants.

But praise the Lord, we serve a God who keeps covenant with His people. We can trust the Lord because He is true to His Word and will never let us down. We never have to sign a "pre-nuptial agreement" with the Lord before He becomes the Lord of our lives. In today's lesson, we will study why God's Word is sure and learn why He will not fail His people, no matter what.

THE PEOPLE, PLACES, AND TIMES

Nathan. The name Nathan means "gift of God." Nathan was a prophet in the court of David. Three significant events are recorded about him in Scripture: (1) In 2 Samuel 7 (and in 1 Chronicles 17), David consulted with Nathan on his intention to build a temple to house the ark of the covenant (vv. 1-13). After David committed adultery with Bathsheba and arranged Uriah's death, God sent Nathan to rebuke David (2 Samuel 12). (2) In 1 Kings 1, Nathan becomes the "king maker," setting the stage and directing the dialogue to convince David to crown Solomon as his successor (vv. 13-14). (3) Nathan is mentioned as the writer of part of the Book of Chronicles (1 Chronicles 29:29; 2 Chronicles 9:29) and partly attributes to his authority the musical role of the Levites in the temple (2 Chronicles 29:25).

(The Harper's Bible Dictionary, Paul J. Achtemeier, General Editor, San Francisco: Harper and Row Publishing Co., 1984, p. 688.)

BACKGROUND

In last week's lesson, David moved his family and soldiers to Hebron where he became king of Judah. After the civil war between Judah and Israel, the elders of the northern tribes came to David and submitted themselves to him. Thus, David became king of both Judah and Israel for 40 years.

It is clear that God was with Israel's new king, since David's first conquest as king over all Israel

was to capture Jerusalem and name it the City of David (2 Samuel 5:6-10). David goes on to defeat the Philistines with the blessings of the Lord (vv. 17-26).

The third act of King David was to return the Ark of the Covenant to Israel and settle it in Jerusalem. David was so excited when he brought the ark back to the nation, that he leaped and danced before all the people, which caused his wife Michal to despise him. Michal was the daughter of Saul who remained childless because she criticized the king.

On one occasion, while David sat in his house, the thought occurred to him to "bless" the Lord because of God's faithfulness to him.

AT-A-GLANCE

1. David Wants to Build A House for God
(2 Samuel 7:1-4)
2. God Responds to David's Request
(vv. 5-11)
3. God's Promise to David Will Stand
(vv. 12-13)

IN DEPTH

1. David Wants to Build A House for God (2 Samuel 7:1-4)

After subduing the Philistines (2 Samuel 5:17-25), and bringing the ark of God back to Israel (2 Samuel 6:1-23), King David had an opportunity to sit back and reflect on all that he had accomplished in a short period of time. While reflecting, David realized a significant point. The ark of God did not have a permanent place to reside in Israel as did the king.

The ark represented God's presence among His people. Thus, when David retrieved the ark from Obed-edom's house, he set it in the midst of the tabernacle behind a curtain (see 2 Samuel 6:17). According to Mosaic Law, the ark was to rest behind the curtain or veil which separated the holy and most holy places of the tabernacle (Exodus 26:33).

Though David had been given the responsibility to return the ark to Jerusalem, the king knew that the God He served deserved more than just a temporary structure as a place where the ark would reside. After all, God had prospered the king and had provided cedar wood for a house to be built for him (2 Kings 6:11-16). Shouldn't the king do more for His God?

Perhaps David felt guilty because of the apparent "inadequacy" between him and God. Or, maybe David felt the need to reciprocate to God what he had received. Whatever the reason, David confided in Nathan the prophet about his concern. Convinced that the king's heart was right, Nathan encouraged David to proceed with his plans, assuring him of God's presence and protection every step of the way.

The old song lets us know that we can't beat God giving, no matter how we try. God has blessed us with material resources and benefits, and we can give to Him by being generous to those less fortunate than we (Proverbs 19:17). Scripture declares two important principles that correlate with King David: (1) the king's heart is in God's hand who turns it wherever God wants the heart to go; and (2) we may have our own plan, but God is the One who searches and weighs the heart of people (see Proverbs 21:1-2).

Though David's request was noble and honorable, God never asked the king to build Him a house. To clarify that Nathan the prophet was speaking his own desire to please the king, rather than for Him, God came at night to Nathan in a vision and gave him a specific word to give to the king.

2. God Responds to David's Request (vv. 5-11)

The first word that God told Nathan to give to the king came in the form of a question. In essence, God wanted to know why did David want to build a house for Him. Next, God gave the king a history lesson that reflected both His character and His desire. God reminded David that He had carried the people from their place of bondage in Egypt to the Promised Land. In fact, the Scriptures declare that "the LORD went before [Israel] by day in a pillar of cloud, to lead them the way, and by night in a pillar of fire, to give them light; to go by day and night . . . before the people" (Exodus 13:21-22). In another instance, Moses affirmed that the "cloud of the LORD" lifted from the tabernacle of Moses when the Children of Israel went on their journey home. The cloud symbolized God's presence (Exodus 40:34-38). Never once did God ask or command the Children of Israel, or anyone else for that matter, to build Him a permanent dwelling place. Third, Nathan was told to remind the king of his own history. From all of Jesse's sons, God selected David who was feeding sheep to be His choice to replace Saul (1 Samuel 16:1-13) and to rule over both the reunited northern and southern kingdoms (2 Samuel 5:1-5). Finally, God told the king that He had been with him every step of the way, from the time when Saul made several attempts to take his life to David's victories over the Philistines.

Through everything that David experienced, from the time he was anointed until he was firmly established as king, God's desire and purpose was to make David's reign part of an everlasting kingdom. After all, it was through David's loins that the Messiah would be born to redeem the world. Thus, God made it clear that David would not build a house for Him (see 1 Chronicles 28:3). God did not want David to take credit for building Him a house. However, God promised that He would select the place for Israel to dwell and would plant them so they would never have to move again or be afflicted by their enemies (2 Samuel 7:10).

Where would God "plant" Israel? Through Jesus Christ, God's people would be in Him (see John 12:26; 15:5) so that the wicked one cannot touch us. Once we accept Jesus Christ as our personal Lord and Saviour, we have a covenant relationship and are assured of a permanent place with God (John 14:3).

We can never understand the mind of God. He reminds David that no human being can really build Him a house. God is the only One who builds "houses." God built an earthly tabernacle in the womb of Mary and dwelt among us full of grace and truth (John 1:14). Paul affirms that if our earthly "house" passes away, God Himself has already built for us an eternal "house" so that we can be with Him forever (2 Corinthians 5:1).

God's "houses" are more sure than any we can build for Him. It is clear from His Word and through the prophet Nathan that God had a higher, eternal plan for His people that was greater than King David could imagine.

3. God's Promise to David Will Stand (vv. 12-13)

The final word that God gave Nathan to convey to the king was that God's house would be permanent and last longer than David. Long after David

104

was dead and buried, two things would happen: (1) Solomon, David's son by Bathsheba and Israel's third king, would be responsible for building an enormous temple where Israel would worship (1 Kings 6:12); and (2) David's other "Son," Jesus Christ, would rule and reign over Israel forever (Luke 1:31-33; Acts 2:25-35).

Our God is eternal. His covenant will stand forever. We can be confident of our hope of salvation because Jesus Christ is the same today and forever (Hebrew 13:8). When we put our trust in Jesus as Saviour and Lord, we too are recipients of the New Covenant and are assured of a beautiful house where we will dwell with Him forever (John 14:3).

SEARCH THE SCRIPTURES

1. Where did the ark of God reside when King David returned it to Jerusalem? (2 Samuel 7:2)

2. What was God's response to David's desire? (v. 5)

3. Of What did God remind David? (vv. 8-10)

4. What did God promise the king? (vv. 10-11)

5. How would God fulfill His promise? (vv. 12-13)

DISCUSS THE MEANING

1. Why did David want to build a house for God?

2. Do you believe God was insulted by David's request? Why or why not?

3. What did God mean when He said that David's son would establish his kingdom?

4. Is it possible today to build a house which would please God? Why or why not?

5. Can we ever break God's covenant through our actions, words or deeds? Why or why not?

LESSON IN OUR SOCIETY

What can we learn from today's lesson that can help us reinforce covenant relationships in our families, communities, cities and nation? Make a commitment to help people who may not attend church to understand God's New Covenant and apply these truths in their lives.

MAKE IT HAPPEN

This week, focus on God's covenant to you as a believer in Jesus Christ. Remind yourself that God's promises are more sure than any problem or difficult circumstance we face. Spend time praising God for His Word, His promises, and His love for you. Report on your activities during next week's class time.

FOLLOW THE SPIRIT

What God wants me to do:

_____

_____

REMEMBER YOUR THOUGHTS

Special insights you have learned:

_____

_____

MORE LIGHT ON THE TEXT
2 Samuel 7:1-13

This passage deals with David's desire to build a house for God and God's response to David's proposal. God responded to David with a promise of perpetual kingship. This account in 2 Samuel is also repeated in 1 Chronicles 17. David thanks the Lord for this glorious promise in prayer, and praises the unmeasurable grace of God. He also prays for the fulfilment of this renewed promise of divine grace.

7:1 And it came to pass, when the king sat in his house, and the LORD had given him rest round about from all his enemies;

We read, "it came to pass, when the king sat in his house." What does it mean to say he "sat in the house?" The Hebrew for "sat" is *yashab* (**yaw-shab**) and primarily refers to sitting down. But specifically it is used to speak of judges. Here it anticipates the peace and quiet which the king is now experiencing. Until now David probably lived in a tent, and now he has a place where he can remain settled and established. The place of habitation signals a sense of security. Within the next phrase is an important Hebrew word *nuwach* (**noo-akh**) or rest. Note here that rest is a gift given to David from God. However, this rest was not merely from inner turmoil, but from external foes as well. The phrase "all around" is translated from the word *micaabiyb*. This word is rooted in the Hebrew word *cabiyb* (**saw-beeb,** which refers to a circle of neighbors. The environment was now friendly. Everyone who hated him was at peace with him.

2 That the king said unto Nathan the prophet, See now, I dwell in a house of cedar, but the ark of God dwelleth within curtains.

David's life demonstrates to you and me that in times of peace and rest, we should meditate on God's Word and think of doing His work.

David was concerned that the ark of God remained in a tent and therefore wanted to build a permanent structure to house it. David thought of building a temple to honor God. It seemed inappropriate for the king to live in a palace, while God's ark remained in a tent. David was grateful to God for his success. In spite of all his kingly glory, David sought to honor God. God resists the proud, but gives grace to those who are humble (James 4:16). Because every good gift comes from God, grateful souls can never do enough for God who has done everything for them. They cannot enjoy their comfortable accommodations while the church of God is in distress. When God blesses us, in gratitude we too should find ways to bless God.

David shares his revelation with the prophet, Nathan. He shares a reality. He lives in a cedar palace, yet, the ark of God dwells inside a curtain. But he does not tell Nathan of his real desire, that is, to construct a temple for God.

Everyone in leadership needs a prophetic presence to check their actions, whether it be good or bad. Which is what the Hebrew word *nabiy* (naw-bee) translated prophet means, someone who can check your actions. One thing that David seems to intuitively understand is that personal luxury cannot supersede the work of the Lord.

3 And Nathan said to the king, Go, do all that is in thine heart; for the LORD is with thee.

Nathan, the prophet, who often speaks for God, tells David to proceed with what is on his heart, for God is with him. Nathan speaks his heart and tells David to do what is in his heart. However, He does not know David's true intentions. Nathan's response is a prudent response given the fact that the king does not tell him what

he intends to do. Nathan literally tells David, "according to your heart." The word *yalak* (yaw-lak) translated here as "go" can mean literally or figuratively to walk. It can also be translated "go with your heart." David must let his action flow from the heart. Unlike us, who give credence to the head, for Nathan and David, the heart was the seat of thought. The word translated "heart" is *lebab* (lay-bawb). For the people of Israel in David's time and for the Egyptians, the heart was the most interior organ and held the power of life and death. So, for Nathan to say "go and do according to all that is in your heart" he may have been cautioning the king to make sure his motives were in the proper place, and that he had a good understanding of what he was proposing to do.

4 And it came to pass that night, that the word of the LORD came unto Nathan, saying,

Nathan had spoken well. However, what he said could be construed as tacit support for the king's project. God soon rectified the situation by revealing to Nathan what was the true desire of David's heart. The use of the word *layil* translated "night," is vital. What is interesting is not the fact that the word, as used here, means simply night. But some scholars think it is derived from the Hebrew word *luwl* which means to twist. Then it could mean that Nathan was restless as he went home. Figuratively, the word can mean adversity. Thus, Nathan may have suffered that evening and God would not let him rest until he heard what the Lord thought of David's proposal.

5 Go and tell my servant David, Thus saith the LORD, Shalt thou build me a house for me to dwell in?

God instructs Nathan to return to David and entrusts Nathan to deliver God's message to David. The revelatory message begins with a question to David that reveals his true intentions, "Shall you build me a temple to dwell in?" The message is given to dissuade David from building the temple. David's plan to build the temple is superseded by God. God knows the reasons behind David's desires. Yet, often our desires are not what God would have us to do. The task of building God's temple is not David's work. David is to enlarge the boundaries of Israel. Also, David is a great psalmist. God uses him to prepare the music for the temple.

Notice that God sends his message by the same person: (1) Nathan, the same person God uses to give David encouragement also gives discouragement. This is done to eliminate confusion; (2) God speaks to Nathan the same night in order to quickly eliminate the confusion. Because God's direct instruction cannot be misconstrued, as much as he wants to, David cannot build a house for God. This suggests that what was in his heart may not have been the building of a house for the Lord, though it was part of it.

6 Whereas I have not dwelt in any house since the time that I brought up the children of Israel out of Egypt, even to this day, but have walked in a tent and in a tabernacle.

God's message to David through Nathan continues. God reminds David that the ark has dwelled in a tent and in a tabernacle ever since Israel left Egypt. Jesus Christ was like a tabernacle; He was without a permanent home. The church of Christ should be like a tabernacle, in that it dwells in the hearts of men and women who take the Gospel (the Good News of salvation) into the world.

David misunderstands if he thinks that God needs a house to live in. God reminds him that this is not his priority. It is as though God is saying to David, "Certainly you do not think that when I saved Israel I did so in order for them to build Me a temple like the Gentiles do for their God, do you David?" The use of the word *kiy* (kee) suggests something like "assuredly, I did not ask them to build a house for me. Did I?" It is as though God is saying "doubtless, I asked for no such activity." God says emphatically, "you shall not build me a house," and proceeds to state "nevertheless for the sake of conversation, let me ask you this. Since the time I brought the children out of Egypt, even to this day, did I ask for a house?" The idea is that God has been open about what He demands from His people. The Lord may not be impressed with the idea of keeping His ark in areas away from the people. The use of the *ohel* (o-hel) suggests that God is saying

I have always been where I can be seen from a distance.

7 In all the places wherein I have walked with all the children of Israel spake I a word with any of the tribes of Israel, whom I commanded to feed my people Israel, saying, Why build ye not me a house of cedar?

In this verse God continues the interrogation of David. The question here is "did I tell any of the judges of Israel to build me a house of cedar?" The phrase "spake I a word" is translated from the Hebrew as *hadaabaar dibarity* and could be translated "did I make such arrangements?" Another way of stating this is "did I force them by a command to build me a house?" It must also be noted that this rebuke is also for Nathan who should have known better than to give David a false impression that this was what God wanted.

8 Now therefore so shalt thou say unto my servant David, Thus saith the LORD of hosts, I took thee from the sheepcote, from following the sheep, to be ruler over my people, over Israel:

God tells Nathan to remind David of how God changed him from a shepherd to a prince, and now the king of all Israel. David is reminded of the great things God had done for him. This is a powerful verse in that God reminds David that His choice of him has nothing to do with what he had accomplished lest David think that his building a house for God will give Him perpetuity. By the use of the word *tsaba* the verse also suggests that God called David to organize for war, not to build him a house.

9 And I was with thee whithersoever thou wentest, and have cut off all thine enemies out of thy sight, and have made thee a great name, like unto the name of the great men that are in the earth.

God reminds David of how He was with him wherever he went, and how it was God who cut off his enemies, and elevated him to greatness among the people. God gave David success over his enemies. God continues by reminding David that everything he has God has given to him. In a variety of situations God has walked with him and applied his strength on his behalf. It was God who had continually given growth. God allowed his enemies to fall and be destroyed. God says David has been given a great name. God has allowed him to make his mark.

10 Moreover I will appoint a place for my people Israel, and will plant them, that they may dwell in a place of their own, and move no more; neither shall the children of wickedness afflict them any more, as beforetime,

God promises to give Israel a permanent home where they will live in peace. God tells them that He will appoint, He is the one who calls Israel by name and is committed to Israel. God says He will cause Israel to stand. God will not let the enemy strike. Using the word *tachath* (takh-ath) translated afflict, God assures Israel that they will no longer be at the bottom, depressed by the hand of the oppressor. No longer will they be below, rather God will raise them up.

11 And as since the time that I commanded judges to be over my people Israel, and have caused thee to rest from all thine enemies. Also the LORD telleth thee that he will make thee a house.

In this verse God addresses David's major concern: his legacy. David wants to build God a house, but God promises to make David a house by blessing his family and posterity. God tells David what He will do for him. In this verse by using the word *asah* (aw-saw) God is saying that He will accomplish what David desires. God will advance David.

12 And when thy days be fulfilled, and thou shalt sleep with thy fathers, I will set up thy seed after thee, which shall proceed out of thy bowels, and I will establish his kingdom.

This verse contains really what David is looking for. Will he have the respect of posterity? Will he be remembered? The Bible indicates that David will die a peaceful death. God also promises David that his seed will succeed him on the throne. One of the greatest fears of ancient times was to die without a successor. There are three things inherent in this. First, it may mean that one dies young; second it could mean that one dies without an heir; and third one may have heirs but none of them is fit to carry on the spiritual legacy. God responds to all David's concerns. The word *mal'e* (maw-lay) suggests that God will fill him or cause him to be full. Even when he is dead and his body is ravished this fullness will continue to his heir. God says his seed (Hebrew *zera*, zeh-rah) figuratively means the fruit of his work or of his body or that which he has planted will experience establishment by God. Actually, the word used is the Hebrew word *kuwn* (koon); to stand straight. They will be as some say "set." It implies that God will prepare prosperity for his seed.

13 He shall build a house for my name, and I will establish the throne of his kingdom forever.

God reveals to David that his successor to the throne, his son, Solomon, would be the one to build the temple and his kingdom would be established forever. David is not allowed to build the temple because he is a man of war, but his son, Solomon, will be a man of peace. However, David is permitted to gather the materials that Solomon will need to construct the temple. This passage refers to the messianic reign. Here God moves from the temporal to the eternal by the use of the Hebrew word *owlam* (o-lawm) meaning eternity.

DAILY BIBLE READINGS

M: Nathan's Prophecy
2 Samuel 7:1-11
T: Nathan Reveals God's Word
1 Chronicles 17:1-10
W: God's Promise to David Through Nathan
2 Samuel 7:12-17
T: God Responds to David Through Nathan
1 Chronicles 17:11-15
F: David's Prayer
2 Samuel 7:18-29
S: David's Thanksgiving
1 Chronicles 17:16-27
S: God's Promise to David Fulfilled
1 Kings 8:15-21

TEACHING TIPS

November 5
Bible Study Guide 10

1. Words You Should Know

A. Uncleanness (2 Samuel 11:4) Hebrew *Tumah*—Impurity, pollution, and morally unclean. Also to be defiled.

B. Blaspheme (2 Samuel 12:14) Hebrew *Naats*—To revile, scorn, despise, reject, condemn, and deride. The idea of disdaining one who formerly received favorable attention and then rebelled.

2. Teacher Preparation

A. Begin by praying for each student in your class. Ask the Lord to help students overcome sin in their lives.

B. Read the Bible Study Guide for this week. Then answer the DISCUSS THE MEANING and SEARCH THE SCRIPTURES questions. Write down your answers on a legal tablet and bring it to class with you.

C. Read the BIBLE BACKGROUND and DEVOTIONAL READING Scriptures to become familiar with the overview of the lesson.

3. Starting the Lesson

A. As students arrive write the AT-A-GLANCE on the chalkboard or newsprint. Assign at least six students to read the lesson based on the AT-A-GLANCE.

B. Next, ask a student to pray for the success of the lesson, using the KEEP IN MIND verse as the foundation of the prayer.

C. Ask a student to read the FOCAL VERSES. Write down any ideas that may come to mind as the Scriptures are read.

D. Have a student read the IN FOCUS story and BACKGROUND section of the lesson.

4. Getting into the Lesson

A. Have students work in pairs as the lesson is read. Each pair will take a part of the lesson and write down specific ideas concerning David's downward spiral in his relationship with Uriah and Bathsheba.

B. Now have students answer the SEARCH THE SCRIPTURES questions. Write their answers on the chalkboard or newsprint.

C. Have all students read 2 Samuel 11:27 silently. Ask them why God was displeased with David and what he could have done to change that report.

5. Relating the Lesson to Life

A. Have students answer the DISCUSS THE MEANING questions. Challenge them to write their answers on paper to be studied this week.

B. Give students an opportunity to read and brainstorm ideas on the LESSON IN OUR SOCIETY. Have several students report on what they have developed for the week ahead.

C. Read THE PEOPLE, PLACES, AND TIMES section. Remind students that David did suffer mightily for a "one-night stand." Now ask students if they feel that what David did was worth the pain he endured.

6. Arousing Action

Have students commit to doing the MAKE IT HAPPEN assignment this week. Remind them that believers have a special relationship with Jesus Christ that must be maintained even in today's society.

DAVID AND BATHSHEBA

Bible Background • 2 SAMUEL 11:1—12:25
Printed Text • 2 SAMUEL 11:2-5, 14-18, 26-27; 12:13-15
Devotional Reading • NUMBERS 15:30-31

LESSON AIM

By the end of the lesson, students should be able to explain David's sin, understand the seriousness of sin, and commit to turning from known sin in their lives.

KEEP IN MIND

"Wherefore hast thou despised the commandment of the LORD, to do evil in His sight?" (2 Samuel 12:9)

FOCAL VERSES

2 Samuel 11:2 And it came to pass in an eveningtide, that David arose from off his bed, and walked upon the roof of the king's house: and from the roof he saw a woman washing herself; and the woman was very beautiful to look upon.

3 And David sent and inquired after the woman. And one said, Is not this Bathsheba, the daughter of Eliam, the wife of Uriah the Hittite?

4 And David send messengers, and took her; and she came in unto him, and he lay with her; for she was purified from her uncleanness: and she returned unto her house.

5 And the woman conceived, and sent and told David, and said, I am with child.

11:14 And it came to pass in the morning, that David wrote a letter to Joab, and sent it by the hand of Uriah.

15 And he wrote in the letter, saying, Set ye Uriah in the forefront of the hottest battle, and retire ye from him, that he may be smitten, and die.

16 And it came to pass, when Joab observed the city, that he assigned Uriah unto a place where he knew that valiant men were.

LESSON OVERVIEW

LESSON AIM
KEEP IN MIND
FOCAL VERSES
IN FOCUS
THE PEOPLE, PLACES,
AND TIMES
BACKGROUND
AT-A-GLANCE
IN DEPTH
SEARCH THE SCRIPTURES
DISCUSS THE MEANING
LESSON IN OUR SOCIETY
MAKE IT HAPPEN
FOLLOW THE SPIRIT
REMEMBER YOUR THOUGHTS
MORE LIGHT ON THE TEXT
DAILY BIBLE READINGS

17 And the men of the city went out, and fought with Joab: and there fell some of the people of the servants of David; and Uriah the Hittite died also.

18 Then Joab sent and told David all the things concerning the war;

11:26 And when the wife of Uriah heard that Uriah her husband was dead, she mourned for her husband.

27 And when the mourning was past, David sent and fetched her to his house, and she became his wife, and bare him a son. But the thing that David had done displeased the LORD.

2 Samuel 12:13 And David said unto Nathan, I have sinned against the LORD. And Nathan said unto David, The LORD also hath put away thy sin; thou shalt not die.

14 Howbeit, because by this deed thou hast given great occasion to the enemies of the LORD to blaspheme, the child also that is born unto thee shall surely die.

15 And Nathan departed unto his house. And the LORD struck the child that Uriah's wife bare unto David, and it was very sick.

IN FOCUS

Jacob Letterman was a successful attorney at one of the largest law firms in New York City. Jacob's clients and co-workers admired him because he was a hard working attorney and a man of integrity. Jacob was also a devoted Christian who served as a deacon in his local church.

In one of Jacob's cases, he was hired by a couple

to come to Washington, D.C. Jacob didn't know at the time that he got the case that he would be representing Kelly, his former high school sweetheart, and her husband Tom who were being sued for embezzlement. Jacob hesitated to take the case, but he consented, convinced that he was over any feelings he had for Kelly.

Jacob flew to Washington D.C. to meet the couple to prepare for their case. While at their home one evening, Tom received a business call which required him to leave Kelly and Jacob alone for a while. As Jacob sat quietly looking across the dinner table at Kelly, she responded with a smile. However, Jacob could see that she was hiding her frustration and fears. He took Kelly by the hand, and suddenly, she began weeping and sharing all the abuse and pain she had experienced as Tom's wife for ten years. Before Jacob realized it, he felt an emotional surge flowing through his body. He was still in love with Kelly and wanted to protect her from the pain she had suffered.

Moved by a great need to comfort her, Jacob took Kelly in his arms and began passionately kissing her. Within minutes, they were intimately involved and did not hear Tom return to the room. Shocked to find his wife in the arms of another man, Tom reached inside his desk and pulled out a gun and fired at both Jacob and Kelly.

What happens to people when they allow their emotions to get the best of them? Without thinking, they can resort to desperate measures that can destroy other people's lives as well as their own. This week, we will study how one man's moment of heated passion and sin affected the lives of several other people and the consequences that followed.

THE PEOPLE, PLACES, AND TIMES

David's Consequences. Nathan uses a parable to show David his own guilt and the consequences of his sin against the Lord (2 Samuel 12:1-14). As king of Israel, David had violated four of the ten commandments in one rash sin: thou shalt not kill (Exodus 20:13), thou shalt not steal (Exodus 20:15), thou shalt not commit adultery (Exodus 20:14), and thou shalt not covet thy neighbor's wife (Exodus 20:17). Although David's sins were not exposed for about a year, the Scripture affirms

that he truly repented of his sin (see Psalm 32:3-4; Psalm 51:1-19).

While David's repentance brought about forgiveness from God, it did not prevent him from suffering the consequences of his sin. God revealed that because of David's sin, the son born from his adulterous relationship would die (2 Samuel 12:14, 18), the sword would never depart from his house (v. 10), evil would come from his own family (2 Samuel 12:11; 2 Samuel 15—18), and his wives would be publicly shamed (2 Samuel 12:11; 16:22).

The important lesson to learn from David is that even the best of men can sin. Also, true repentance does bring forgiveness from God, but it does not eliminate the consequences of sin. (*The Hebrew-Greek Key Study Bible*, Spiros Zodhiates, General Editor, 1991, Nashville: AMG Publishers, p. 432.)

BACKGROUND

God made a covenant with David, Israel's second king, which would last unto eternity. Thus, David is firmly established as God's representative for both Israel and Judah. King David continues his conquest of the land with his victory over the Ammonites (2 Samuel 10). In his attempt to show kindness unto King Hanun, David sends his servants into Ammon. However, upon their arrival, the princes of the land convinced the king that David had sent his servants to "search the city, and to spy it out, and to overthrow it" (v. 3). Because Hanun had believed the false report, the king humiliated David's servants by shaving off half their beards and cutting off their garments in the middle, even to their buttocks.

David's initial act of kindness ended in a bloody war involving the Ammonites, the Syrians, the Israelites, and Abishai, the brother of Joab, David's servant. David assigned Joab, along with all the host of his mighty men, to the battle.

Joab laid out a strategic plan, which included himself and the choice men of Israel. Joab's army would attack the Syrians and Abishai's army would attack the Ammonites. They then agreed to come to the aid of one another, if need be. The Lord gave David and Israel the victory which caused all the people to ultimately be at peace with the

Israelites and become their servants. However, the Syrians feared Israel and they refused to help the Ammonites any longer.

Throughout all the battles that Israel faced, David remained in Jerusalem, rather than leading his army in battle. As a result, David made one of the greatest mistakes in his life.

IN DEPTH

1. David Falls from Grace (2 Samuel 11:2-5)

David's fall from grace began because he was out of the will of God. Rather than being in the heat of the battle, the king was still in Jerusalem (v. 1), feeling complacent and self-confident because of the victories he experienced over his enemies.

David had become a prosperous king for one reason: he had obeyed God and allowed the Holy Spirit to direct him. But because he was not leading his men into battle as he should, David was out of God's will. The king felt restless and couldn't sleep. Therefore, he arose from his bed and walked upon the roof of his house, possibly to view his kingdom and the magnificence of it all. The king did not expect to see in the next yard, a beautiful young woman taking a bath (v. 2).

David had an opportunity to go back into his house and forget about what he saw. However, because he was out of God's will, the king was "set up" by Satan and he pursued a course that would ultimately lead to God's judgment on his life. The Bible says that the "steps of a good man are ordered by God and He delighteth in His ways" (Psalm 37:23). David's steps were not being ordered by God and he dearly paid the price.

What happens to believers when we are out of God's will? Just like David, we become candidates for the devil's snares. We must be careful about what we see. We could possibly be setting in motion a strategic plan of the enemy that can alter the course of our lives as it did King David's.

Rather than going inside and praying for God to forgive him of sin, David inquired about this beautiful woman. Someone told the king that her name was Bathsheba and she was married to Uriah, the Hittite, one of David's soldiers who was out in the battle risking his life for the king and Israel.

Why didn't King David leave the matter alone? There are several possible answers: (1) David's arrogance prompted him to forget about the moral consequences of his actions; (2) As the king, David felt he was entitled to anything he wanted, including sexual favors from this lady; (3) David didn't believe anyone would find out about what he was thinking or about to do. Thus, the king pursued Bathsheba and had her come to his palace where he committed adultery (v. 4).

Once David's one-night affair had ended, the king was confident that no one would find out about it. But how wrong he was! God allowed Bathsheba to conceive to expose the king and his wicked ways (v. 5). The king had stepped over the line, believing that his position entitled him to violate God's commandments (see Exodus 20:14, 17). What David did not understand was that his position as king had tremendous effect on the whole nation. If he could get away with sin and a one-night stand, the spirit of adultery could have rippled throughout the whole nation bringing moral corruption to every fiber of Israel.

Leaders must be careful today. God has given us the indwelling power of His Holy Spirit which gives us the grace to obey Him in the midst of temptation. It is our choice whether or not we will yield to temptation or follow the Lord. If we yield to sin as David did, we can negatively affect the ministries and people we serve.

2. David Has Uriah Killed (vv. 14-18)

Once David realized that Bathsheba was pregnant, the king tried everything he knew to cover up his sin. First, he called for Uriah to come home, hoping that he would lay with Bathsheba. David figured that if he lay with his wife, Uriah would conclude that the child was his. But what David didn't consider was that Uriah was more loyal than the king. Rather than going down to his house to "find pleasure" with his wife during the heat of the battle, Uriah refused, which caused the king to lay out a strategic plan that ultimately included Uriah's death. Through all of his actions, David still had an opportunity to "turn himself in" and allow the Lord to deal with him. But Satan's "hooks" were so firmly in the king that he could not hear the "still small voice of the Lord" speak.

How did the king accomplish his diabolical task of murdering Uriah? David wrote a letter to Joab with specific instructions to have Uriah sent to the forefront of the "hottest battle." Then, Joab was to leave Uriah defenseless so that he would be killed by the enemy. Not only did the king commit "premeditated" murder, but he had the letter delivered to Joab by Uriah, who carried his own death sentence! The king must have seen something in Uriah's character to trust that he would not read the letter, but would give it directly to Joab. Unlike David, Uriah was faithful, full of integrity, and committed to Joab and the people of Israel.

Rather than standing up against the king, Joab followed David's instructions to the letter. He placed Uriah in the heat of the battle and "there fell some of the servants of David, and Uriah the Hittite" (v. 17). Why would Joab follow a plan that he knew would fail? Why would he sacrifice the life of one of his good men for the convenience of an arrogant king? Could it be that Joab feared David more than God? As believers, we will be faced with similar situations where we must decide to do what is right, even against the popular opinion of others. We may be criticized or ostracized by others, but the choice is ours!

3. David Takes Bathsheba As His Wife (vv. 26-27)

After the death of Uriah, Bathsheba received word that her husband had fallen in battle. The Bible says that "she mourned" for Uriah, which means she spent time crying and lamenting over her loss. Perhaps she mourned, not only for his death, but also because she knew she had betrayed

her husband while he was protecting Israel. However, once Bathsheba's mourning was completed, the king sent for her. David married Bathsheba, and she bore the son that he conceived on that dreadful night.

What would have happened had Bathsheba refused the king's advances? There are several possible scenarios: (1) her husband would still be alive; (2) the child in her womb would not have died; and (3) the king would have been spared the judgment of God in his family.

Often we are convinced that we can't make a difference in history. But we *can* make a difference if we are willing to stand for righteousness even in the face of overwhelming odds and "cry loud, and spare not." It may take courage and conviction on our part, but God will help us *if* we are willing to take a stand.

After David moved Bathsheba into his house, the king may have felt that everything was over. He was successful in getting the woman next door to sleep with him, he was successful in murdering her husband who refused to go along with his plans, and he was on his way to be a husband and father of a new child. What more could the king want? However, what David didn't foresee was that he would have to answer to God for his wickedness. The Bible makes it clear that "what he had done displeased the LORD."

4. David Is Judged for His Sin (2 Samuel 12:13-15)

Convinced that he was in "the driver's seat," the king was not prepared to hear Nathan the prophet confront him with his sin. Nathan was sent by God to give the king a parable. In the parable, Nathan makes it clear that the rich man who had stolen from the poor man was wrong. The prophet even used the parable to get the king to convict himself (2 Samuel 12:5-7).

Once David realized that the parable was about him and that he was being exposed for his wickedness, the king acknowledged his sin. Scripture affirms that we are to expose the works of darkness in the lives of others so that they may come to the knowledge of the truth (see Ephesians 5:11). It is not always easy to confront people about their sins. But if we love people and want to see them delivered from darkness, we will take the same steps as Nathan did, even if it makes us uncomfortable.

Once David acknowledged his sin (v. 13), Nathan assured the king that deliverance was his and that the Lord would not kill David (v. 13). But David still had to pay the price for his wicked deeds. As Israel's national leader, David was called to set the example for others to follow. However, his sin gave God's enemies a reason to blaspheme the name of the Lord. Therefore, there were consequences to the king's actions.

Not only would David's guilt be exposed before all the nation, but the child that David had secretly conceived died, and evil visited David's house for a long time (2 Samuel 13:7-14; 16:22). When Christian leaders compromise or disobey God's Word, not only do they cause other brothers and sisters in Christ to stumble, but they give the world a poor witness and the opportunity to mock the Lord.

David's affair with Bathsheba teaches us the dangers of sinning and how sin can result from living for the Lord in a haphazard way. Like David, we will be judged and may have to pay a high price for our sinful actions.

SEARCH THE SCRIPTURES

1. What happened when David stayed behind in Jerusalem? (2 Samuel 11:2)

2. What did David do after he found out that Bathsheba was a married woman? (v. 4)

3. By whom did David send a letter to Joab to make adjustments in his army? (vv. 14-18)

4. Who was displeased by the actions of the king? (v. 27)

5. What was the final outcome of David's sin? (2 Samuel 12:13-15)

DISCUSS THE MEANING

1. What can believers do to avoid spiritual failure in their lives? Discuss.

2. How important is it for believers to confront one another about their sin?

3. Should we be careful about what we view in this hour? Why or why not?

4. What important lesson can we learn from David's experience? Discuss.

LESSON IN OUR SOCIETY

Today, we may not be looking at naked women from our rooftops, but we are exposed to a barrage of wicked perversion from the media. As believers, we are warned to guard our eye and ear gates against anything that would turn us away from the Lord. What specific points in today's lesson can we teach to unbelievers and those around us so they will understand the serious implications of sin and perversion in our society? What points can we apply to guard our own lives?

MAKE IT HAPPEN

Make a decision to obey God's Word in the midst of a crooked and perverse society. Spend time reading the DAILY BIBLE READINGS and ask the Lord to show you areas in your life that are not submitted to Jesus Christ. Then, when you are faced with temptation to sin against the Lord, ask Him for the power to overcome. Report your activities to the class next week.

FOLLOW THE SPIRIT

What God wants me to do:

_____

_____

REMEMBER YOUR THOUGHTS

Special insights you have learned:

_____

_____

MORE LIGHT ON THE TEXT

2 Samuel 11:2-5, 14-18, 26-27; 12:13-15

11:2 And it came to pass in an eveningtide, that David arose from off his bed, and walked upon the roof of the king's house: and from the roof he saw a woman washing herself; and the woman was very beautiful to look upon.

One evening after King David had finished resting, he got up and went for a walk upon the palace roof. This roof was walled on every side to prevent the possibility of falling over its edge, but it was not covered. In the evening, as the heat of the day waned and the cool evening breezes blew, the roof provided an excellent place to meditate, view the city, or entertain special guests. This evening, King David strolled upon his roof and from that elevation was able to see a woman bathing herself. From that height, he could see clearly into the usually private bathroom of a nearby house. He saw a woman washing herself, and he did not turn away from her nakedness. The narrative describes her as very beautiful to look upon. One can imagine how King David, captivated by this woman's beautiful figure, watched every move she made until a strong desire for her had built up within him.

3 And David sent and inquired after the woman. And one said, Is not this Bathsheba, the daughter of Eliam, the wife of Uriah the Hittite?

It had been a private matter. No one knew what had transpired, but David's desire for her was so great that he sent messengers out to discover her identity and availability. Word came back to the king about her name, her lineage, and the name of her husband. It is unusual in the biblical narrative that a woman was identified both by her father and by her husband. This suggests that the father's identity is somehow important to the story. Her father Eliam was one of David's mighty men of valor. He was also the son of Ahithophel, who was once David's most trusted advisor. Her husband, Uriah the Hittite (from Asia Minor), was also one of King David's mighty men of valor. So this Bathsheba was associated with two men who had great loyalty to the king.

4 And David sent messengers, and took her; and she came in unto him, and he lay with her; for she was purified from her uncleanness: and she returned unto her house.

When David discovered that she was the wife and daughter of two of his warriors, who were away on a military campaign against the Ammonites, he sent messengers to bring her to him. There was no one home to protect her. David's desire had gotten the best of him. Who would defy the king? No one, especially not his own messengers, and not even the married woman. When she was brought to him, she entered into his bedchamber and he lay with her. Now David was aware that under Israelite law the penalty for adultery was death, but who

would put to death the head of state of any prospering nation for this act? It would simply be suppressed, kept quiet, or overlooked.

The uncleanness referred to her menstrual period, during which time a woman was considered ritually unclean. She could not participate in ritual acts until she was purified following this time of her cycle. In order to keep his activity under wraps, David sent her back to her home as soon as he finished with her.

5 And the woman conceived, and sent and told David, and said, I am with child.

That which is done in darkness shall come to light. Bathsheba was pregnant. Now the importance of her having a period becomes clearer. The fact that she had a regular menstrual period meant that her husband, who was away at war, could not have been the father of this child. David's little secret would be known. Bathsheba sent word directly to David to see what he would do about this mess.

11:14 And it came to pass in the morning, that David wrote a letter to Joab, and sent it by the hand of Uriah.

David tried everything he could think of to

keep his affair a secret. David had sent for Uriah the Hittite to return home at once. When Uriah arrived, David inquired about the war effort. But his true interest was in making sure that Uriah slept with his wife, so he would believe that he caused this pregnancy. David sent Uriah food from the king's own table, which was far better than the food Uriah had received in battle. David thought a full belly would ensure Uriah's desire to reunite with his wife. But instead of going home to be with his wife, Uriah slept with the king's body-guards. During wartime, soldiers were obliged to abstain from sexual relations (1 Samuel 21:6). When that failed, David tried to dull Uriah's sense of righteousness by getting him drunk. But even drunk, Uriah would not go to be with his wife. He was a dutiful soldier. David had to come up with an alternative plan. Since Uriah would not lay with his wife, David crafted a letter and sent Uriah back onto the battlefield with the letter.

15 And he wrote in the letter, saying, Set ye Uriah in the forefront of the hottest battle, and retire ye from him, that he may be smitten, and die.

Surely when Joab received this letter there must have been some momentary confusion. First the king sent for Uriah to return home from battle, then the king sent him back with a letter of execution. But the king had given an order, and who was Joab to question it? Joab could not possibly have guessed the motive of the king. He would never have become commander of the troops by questioning the king's orders.

16 And it came to pass, when Joab observed the city, that he assigned Uriah unto a place where he knew that valiant men were.

So Joab followed David's orders. Joab's intelligence reports informed him of the place that would be most heavily guarded by the best fighters. So he assigned Uriah to that location, increasing the likelihood of his death. If that alone did not work, then Joab would have pulled back his other warriors, leaving Uriah alone to fight outnumbered, as he was ordered to do.

17 And the men of the city went out, and fought

with Joab: and there fell some of the people of the servants of David; and Uriah the Hittite died also.

The warriors of Rabbah, the capital city of the Ammonites, went out to protect their city from Joab's troops. This was the stronghold, because the capital city is always heavily protected. So the army of David suffered losses, probably heavy losses judging from the tone of the report that Joab sent back to the king.

18 Then Joab sent and told David all the things concerning the war;

Joab sent word back to the king that this battle with the Ammonites was costly, but the mission to kill Uriah had been accomplished. This certainly was a costly way to cover up a sin. Many valiant men lost their lives to cover the king's sin. But with Bathsheba's husband dead, how did King David plan to conceal the fact of this pregnancy?

11:26 And when the wife of Uriah heard that Uriah her husband was dead, she mourned for her husband.

When Bathsheba was told of her husband's death, she must have been beside herself in grief. Her husband had just been home, but they did not get to spend any intimate time together. Furthermore, she was with child and was now a widow. How would she support the child? What would happen if the truth were discovered? Was her life also in jeopardy now?

27 And when the mourning was past, David sent and fetched her to his house, and she became his wife, and bare him a son. But the thing that David had done displeased the Lord.

When enough time had passsed to be publicly appropriate, David sent his messengers and once again brought Bathsheba to his palace. This time she became his wife. This act must have made David look generous to the people of Jerusalem. The king married the pregnant widow of one of his bravest soldiers, who had died serving the king. And she bore him a son. The secret was now safely covered up, or so David thought. But the Lord, Yahweh, was displeased by the act and by the cover-up.

Could Bathsheba have known of David's plan

to kill her husband? It is unclear from the text. She may have been completely in the dark about David's complicity in her husband's tragic death. If so, she could have married David thinking how unfortunate was Uriah's death, but that its timing helped cover their secret. Or she could have known that David was responsible for Uriah's death, and she dutifully mourned her husband for the sake of appearances before marrying David. However, her knowledge of David's plan would certainly have cast a shadow upon him as a husband and king in Bath-sheba's eyes. She would never have been able to love or respect him.

12:13 And David said unto Nathan, I have sinned against the Lord. Nathan then said to David, "Yahweh, for his part, forgives your sin; you are not to die."

Through the prophet Nathan, Yahweh brought David's secret to light. Nathan let David know that his deeds were known, and that the Lord was displeased. Moreover, he revealed David's punishment for these acts of disobedience and deceit. David's household would never be free from the sword (later, three of David's sons met violent deaths). Also, misfortune would arise from within David's own household, and David's wives would be taken by another man in broad daylight (not in secret). Upon this exposure of his sin and the pronouncement of punishment against his household, David became penitent and confessed his sin against Yahweh. He felt the weight of his sin and was truly remorseful. God mercifully forgave David of his sin of adultery and spared David's life. However, there were still consequences for his actions.

14 Howbeit, because by this deed thou hast given great occasion to the enemies of the LORD to blaspheme, the child also that is born unto thee shall surely die.

The name of the Lord, Yahweh, was to be exalted, not brought low or made a mockery of by God's enemies. If David had not impregnated Bathsheba, perhaps the punishment would not have been so severe. But the birth of this child would have raised serious questions. Surely the timing of the birth in relation to the marriage date would have been noticed. Surely the child's resemblance to David rather than to Uriah would have created much gossip among the people of Jerusalem. David, as the King of Israel, was supposed to set an example for his people and before the world of the benefits of keeping God's laws. His gross disobedience would send ripples of disbelief and dissent through the nation. Thus, the child would have to die, lest the other nations blaspheme the name of the god who allowed such a thing to occur. Would the great Yahweh, who had handed down laws for his people, allow the king to gain an heir by such treachery? Even Israel's faithful would have raised questions about Yahweh's laws and their administration. Could the king be blessed with a child for a crime deserving the most severe of punishments?

15 And Nathan departed unto his house. And the Lord struck the child that Uriah's wife bare unto David, and it was very sick.

After delivering the word of the Lord to David, there was nothing else for the prophet to do. So he returned to his home. The pronouncement could not be thwarted or altered. David himself had been forgiven but his sin had set things into motion which could not be revoked.

DAILY BIBLE READINGS

M: David and Bathsheba's Affair
2 Samuel 11:1-5

T: David's Plot
2 Samuel 11:6-13

W: Uriah's Murder and the Marriage
2 Samuel 11:14-27

T: The Prophet Nathan's Story
2 Samuel 12:1-6

F: The Judgment on David
2 Samuel 12:7-15

S: Death and Birth of David's Sons
2 Samuel 12:16-25

S: Atonement and Payment for Sins
Numbers 15:27-31

TEACHING TIPS

November 12
Bible Study Guide 11

1. Words You Should Know

A. Commandments (1 Kings 2:3) Hebrew *Mitswah* —A precept, a law, or an ordinance. The particular conditions of God's covenant with Israel.

B. Understanding (1 Kings 3:9) Hebrew *Shama*—To hear with attention and obedience; to give undivided listening attention; to perceive a message with understanding and clarity.

2. Teacher Preparation

A. Spend time in prayer, asking the Lord for wisdom, to teach today's lesson with clarity and purpose.

B. Read the DAILY BIBLE READINGS for the week. Ask the Lord to speak to you while you read. Then write down any ideas and thoughts that might come to you.

C. Read the Bible Study Guide for this lesson. Then answer the SEARCH THE SCRIPTURES and DISCUSS THE MEANING questions.

D. Materials needed: Bible, Old Testament map, and newsprint or chalkboard.

3. Starting the Lesson

A. Ask a student to volunteer to lead the class in prayer according to the KEEP IN MIND verse.

B. Have students give definitions for the following: (1) wisdom; (2) understanding; (3) precepts; (4) commandments; (5) judgments. Write their answers down and discuss them later in the class time.

C. Assign several students to read the following sections of the lesson aloud to the class: FOCAL VERSES, IN FOCUS, BACKGROUND, and IN DEPTH.

D. Then have students work in pairs for the remainder of the class time so that they can help each other get a better grasp on the lesson.

4. Getting into the Lesson

A. Have the students read the entire lesson in detail, according to the AT-A-GLANCE outline.

B. Now have students read and answer the SEARCH THE SCRIPTURES questions. Challenge students to put themselves in Solomon's shoes to gain better understanding of what he experienced.

C. Remind students to write some of their ideas in the REMEMBER YOUR THOUGHTS and FOLLOW THE SPIRIT sections of the lesson.

5. Relating the Lesson to Life

A. Have students work on the DISCUSS THE MEANING questions. Challenge them to be creative in their thinking.

B. Read THE PEOPLE, PLACES, AND TIMES section of the lesson. Then discuss what it means to be wise in the generation in which we live.

6. Arousing Action

A. Have students commit to doing the LESSON IN OUR SOCIETY and MAKE IT HAPPEN exercises for the week. Remind them of the importance of taking the lesson out into the world where they can make a difference.

B. Remind students to read the DAILY BIBLE READINGS for the week to encourage and strengthen their faith as they take the Gospel of Jesus Christ out to the world.

C. Close the class with prayer, and affirm your students as they go out for worship today.

WORSHIP GUIDE

For the Superintendent or Teacher
Theme: Solomon Succeeds David
Theme Song: "I'll Be A Witness"
Scripture: James 1:1-5
Song: "Father, Open My Eyes"
Meditation: Father, I realize I need your help to discern good from evil. Help me to walk in Your ways and teach me how to live for You. In Jesus' name, Amen.

118

SOLOMON SUCCEEDS DAVID

Bible Background • 1 KINGS 2:1-4; 3:1-15; 1 CHRONICLES 29:22-25; 2 CHRONICLES 1:1-13
Printed Text • 1 KINGS 2:1-4; 3:3-4, 5-10
Devotional Reading • PSALM 119:10-19

LESSON AIM

By the end of the lesson, students will be able to understand Solomon's succession to Israel's throne, explain why Solomon succeeded David to the throne, and commit to living a successful life before God.

KEEP IN MIND

"Give therefore thy servant an understanding heart to judge thy people, that I may discern between good and bad" (1 Kings 3:9).

FOCAL VERSES

1 Kings 2:1 Now the days of David drew nigh that he should die; and he charged Solomon his son, saying,

2 I go the way of all the earth: be thou strong therefore, and show thyself a man;

3 And keep the charge of the LORD thy God, to walk in his ways, to keep his statutes, and his commandments, and his judgments, and his testimonies, as it is written in the law of Moses, that thou mayest prosper in all that thou doest, and whithersoever thou turnest thyself:

4 That the LORD may continue his word which he spake concerning me, saying, If thy children take heed to their way, to walk before me in truth with all their heart and with all their soul, there shall not fail thee (said he) a man on the throne of Israel.

3:3 And Solomon loved the LORD, walking in the statutes of David his father: only he sacrificed and burnt incense in high places.

4 And the king went to Gibeon to sacrifice there;

LESSON OVERVIEW

LESSON AIM
KEEP IN MIND
FOCAL VERSES
IN FOCUS
THE PEOPLE, PLACES,
AND TIMES
BACKGROUND
AT-A-GLANCE
IN DEPTH
SEARCH THE SCRIPTURES
DISCUSS THE MEANING
LESSON IN OUR SOCIETY
MAKE IT HAPPEN
FOLLOW THE SPIRIT
REMEMBER YOUR THOUGHTS
MORE LIGHT ON THE TEXT
DAILY BIBLE READINGS

for that was the great high place:

5 In Gibeon the LORD appeared to Solomon in a dream by night: and God said, Ask what I shall give thee.

6 And Solomon said, Thou hast showed unto thy servant David my father great mercy, according as he walked before thee in truth, and in righteousness, and in uprightness of heart with thee; and thou hast kept for him this great kindness, that thou hast given him a son to sit on his throne, as it is this day.

7 And now, O LORD my God, thou hast made thy servant king instead of David my father: and I am but a little child: I know not how to go out or come in.

8 And thy servant is in the midst of thy great people which thou hast chosen, a great people, that cannot be numbered nor counted for multitude.

9 Give therefore thy servant an understanding heart to judge thy people, that I may discern between good and bad: for who is able to judge this thy so great a people?

10 And the speech pleased the LORD, that Solomon had asked this thing.

NOV 12TH

IN FOCUS

Theresa Carter was excited about her promotion from vice-president to president of her father's chain of successful restaurants. Sam, Theresa's father, had invested thousands of dollars and many years of hard work into the business. But his poor health had forced him to retire.

Sam felt that Theresa was well-qualified and capable of taking over the business. He knew that success was the result of hard work, love for and obedience to Jesus Christ, and concern for the customer. In fact, every decision that Sam made was "watered" with prayer and the results of his faithfulness to God was evident. Sam had opened his 300th restaurant just four months before he announced his retirement.

However, as the new head of the business, Theresa began spending more hours at the office, and she stopped attending mid-week Bible Study. She even missed several Sunday services every month. Within two years, Sam's prosperous business was in financial difficulty, many of the workers were laid off, and she had to close several restaurants.

Sam visited Theresa to find out what had happened. Theresa confided that she had put God on the "back burner" of her life, and she realized she was paying the consequences of her sin. Sam said, "Theresa, if you will put God first in every area of your life, I believe He will bring us out of this situation."

There is no way we can become successful in life without first submitting ourselves to God and allowing Him to direct every step of the way. The implications of disobeying the Lord can be enormous. This week, we will study David's words to his son Solomon, who was called to succeed David as the third king of Israel. David shares with Solomon the rewards of following the Lord.

THE PEOPLE, PLACES, AND TIMES

Wisdom. A term in the Hebrew Bible with many meanings, ranging from the technical skill of the artisan (Exodus 36:8) to the art of government (1 Kings 3:12, 28). It also designates simple cleverness (2 Samuel 14:2), especially the practical skill of coping with life (Proverbs 1:5; 11; 14), and the pursuit of a lifestyle of proper ethical conduct (Proverbs 2:9-11 and throughout). Wisdom is also seen as belonging properly to God (Job 28), associated with creation (Proverbs 8:22-31), and even identified with the Torah or the Law.

An outstanding trait of biblical wisdom is the personification of Lady Wisdom in chapters 1, 3, and 9 of the Book of Proverbs (see also Job 28).

She is described as originating from God and is associated with creation (Proverbs 3:19; 8:22-31). Wisdom theology is a theology of creation, for it was within the area of creation and human experience that the Hebrew sages operated.

(The Harper's Bible Dictionary, Paul J. Achtemeier, General Editor, San Francisco, Harper and Row Publishing Co., 1984 pp. 1135-36.)

BACKGROUND

Adonijah, David's fourth son, rebelled against the king and God in an attempt to succeed his father to the throne (1 Kings 1). Though God had appointed Solomon to be Israel's next king, Adonijah influenced Joab, the captain of the host and one of David's chief men, and Abiathar the priest to follow and assist him in his plot to be king.

When Nathan the prophet realized what Adonijah had planned, he told Bathsheba, Solomon's mother to go in to see the king and remind him of the promise that her son would be crowned as Israel's next king. Bathsheba did as Nathan instructed her. She told David all that Adonijah was doing in his attempt to become king: how he had slain oxen, fat cattle and sheep in abundance, and had called all the king's sons, with the exception of Solomon, to a feast to announce his coronation.

When King David realized the magnitude of the problem, he reaffirmed his promise to Bathsheba and Solomon. David also gave Zadok the priest and Nathan specific instructions to prepare Solomon to become king. Once Adonijah found out that King David had appointed Solomon to be Israel's next king, fear gripped his heart and all who had supported Adonijah fled, leaving him powerless and alone to face the new king. Stripped of his power and influence, Adonijah bowed himself before Solomon and recognized him as the rightful heir to Israel's throne.

In 1 Kings 2, King David is prepared to give Solomon final instructions on how to become a great king for the nation. These instructions can help New Testament believers today as we walk in obedience to Almighty God.

IN DEPTH

1. Solomon Is Encouraged to Be Faithful and Obedient (1 Kings 2:1-4)

David had reigned over Israel for 40 years, 7 in Hebron and 33 in Jerusalem (2 Samuel 5:5; 2 Chronicles 29:26-27). As the time of his death drew near, the king "charged" (v. 1) his son Solomon on how he should conduct himself as Israel's new king. The word "charged" means to make firm, establish, command, ordain, and to decree into the life of another. David had the responsibility to teach his son what to expect in his new "career" as Israel's next leader.

God had allowed David to live a long life. He had blessed the king with riches and honor. Like any father, David wanted these blessings to "flow down" to his son. However, in order for Solomon to experience all of the blessings that David enjoyed, the king instructed his son to "be (thou) strong therefore, and show thyself a man" (v. 2).

David understood by experience that it would take courage, determination, and strength to be a king. This was not a job for a "little boy." Therefore, Solomon's first priority was to have a right relationship with God (v. 3). On his death bed, David deposited spiritual truths into the life of his son. He wanted Solomon to know that if he obeyed the Lord, he would prosper in all that he did. However, if Solomon chose to disobey, he would ultimately fail as both a man and king.

David had learned these important truths the hard way (see 2 Samuel 12:1-14). He understood that disobedience and rebellion against God brings discipline and pain in one's life.

Thus, the king was determined to pass on to Solomon what he had learned.

Often, parents are able to share their experiences with their children to save them from calamity. A wise parent will not only share the good points, but also the mistakes they have made and the consequences of their actions with the hope that the child will listen and avoid the same pitfalls. David told Solomon about the importance of keeping "the charge of the LORD (thy) God, walking in His ways, and following to the letter His precepts, commandments, judgments, testimonies, and the laws of Moses (v. 3). In doing so, Solomon would not only have good success in his own life, but he would also bring prosperity to the nation. In addition, Solomon would walk and rule the kingdom as a godly man and would also fulfill the promise that God had given to David regarding his heir on the throne of Israel (see 2 Samuel 7:12-13). In essence, Solomon's obedience and faithfulness to God would facilitate the fulfillment of God's promise to his father David.

God's precepts, commands, judgments, and testimonies are found in the written pages of His Word. When we commit ourselves to following God's truths, we can be assured of His abiding presence and good success all the days of our lives (Joshua 1:8).

2. Solomon Sacrifices in High Places (1 Kings 3:3-4)

Shortly after the king's charge to Solomon, David died and Solomon consolidated his rule as Israel's new king. He was firmly in control of all Israel. Though the Bible affirms that Solomon "loved the LORD [and walked] in the statutes of David his father" (v. 3), the king made several mistakes early in his rule. First, Solomon married an Egyptian king's daughter (v. 1), which was forbidden by the Lord (Deuteronomy 7:1-3). This was a dangerous union because she would have the propensity to turn the king's heart away from serving God to follow after other gods (see 2 Corinthians 6:14-17).

Second, Solomon "sacrificed and burnt incense in high places" (v. 3). Before the temple was built, Israel often offered sacrifices to God on the hilltops of the country, as a central place for worship and sacrifice. However, many of these sites located in Canaan were former places of pagan worship. According to Old Testament law, offering sacrifices in such places was forbidden by God (see Leviticus 17:3-5; 18:3-5). Israel was commanded to destroy all Canaanite places of worship (Deuteronomy 7:1-5; 12:1-3). Though King Solomon "loved the LORD," he quickly forgot his father's admonitions and commands. The first place that Solomon went to sacrifice was at Gibeon, which was approximately six miles northwest of Jerusalem, and a former Canaanite stronghold (Joshua 9:7; 2 Samuel 21:1-2). Gibeon was also the place where Saul's seven sons were killed in an act of revenge, on the high place (2 Samuel 21:1-15). Before Solomon went too far, he needed a "wake-up call" to be reminded of the words that were spoken to him by his father.

We may be able to share words of wisdom about godly principles with our children, but it is more important for them to experience the Lord for themselves. Only then will our children understand the truths of Scripture and commit to applying them in their own lives.

3. Solomon Is Challenged to Ask for Wisdom (vv. 5-10)

While Solomon was still in Gibeon, the Lord came to him at night while he was sleeping. God was not interested in replacing the king since He had already made a commitment to both David and Solomon. Instead, God wanted to guide the king in the right direction so that he would not succumb to idolatry and paganism. So, God gave Solomon an invitation: "ask what I shall give thee" (v. 5).

Solomon had the opportunity to ask for anything his heart desired. Perhaps he realized the seriousness of his position or maybe Solomon understood the implication of God's "visit." Whatever the reason, the king recognized the need to commune with the Lord. First, Solomon reminds God of the mercy that He demonstrated to David who walked in righteousness and truth before the Lord. Solomon realized that he was in the position of king, not because of his good looks or his popularity, but because he was the "heir" to the throne, according to God's tender mercies demonstrated to David. Many people in

the body of Christ are in positions of leadership and authority because of the godly influences of parents and/or grandparents who have prayed us into the kingdom. We should never be so arrogant as to assume that we got there on our own accord.

Second, Solomon understood that even though David had spoken the words that propelled him to the throne, it was God alone who made him king. He also realized that being Israel's king was such an awesome task, that in comparison, he was like "a little child [that did not know] how to go out or to come in" (v. 8). In essence, Solomon admitted his immaturity. He understood that as the new king of Israel, he was in a place that he was unprepared to handle on his own. Here was God's representative to the nation still sacrificing at Canaanite strongholds, rather than leading the people in worship of the living God. Is there any wonder that Solomon felt like a child?

Finally, Solomon recognized that his position was a strategic one. He was not off in a corner somewhere, only to be seen by a few. As king, Solomon would be in "the midst of [God's] people" (v. 8). Every act that he performed and every word he spoke would be seen and heard by hundreds of thousands of people. Solomon understood exactly what the Lord meant when He told him to "ask" (v. 5). Having recognized the magnitude of the position and the strategic place he was in, Solomon's request was not based on fleshly desires. What the king wanted more than anything was "an understanding heart to judge [God's] people [so that he could] discern between good and bad" (v. 9).

Solomon needed godly counsel, spiritual understanding, pure motives, and a heart that was sold out to God so that when he made decisions that affected God's people, they would be based on God's wisdom and love for all Israel. Having heard the king's confession of weakness and his admission for help, the Lord was pleased not only with Solomon's choice, but also with the desires that the king had in his heart.

Christian leaders would do well to learn from Solomon. Rather than asking for big ministries, large cathedrals, huge budgets, or wonderful choirs, we should ask the Lord for His wisdom and counsel for every situation we face. If we lack wisdom, God promises to give it to us, if we would ask (James 1:5). This is the kind of prayer that pleases the Lord.

SEARCH THE SCRIPTURES

1. David charged Solomon to be_____ _____ and show _____ (1 Kings 2:2).

2. Solomon would prosper in all he did if he would do what? (v. 3)

3. How many burnt offerings did Solomon offer on the altar at Gibeon? (1 Kings 3:4)

4. What was Solomon's testimony about King David? (v. 6)

5. Why did Solomon ask God to give him an understanding heart? (v. 9)

DISCUSS THE MEANING

1. Why is it important for godly parents to instruct their children in the ways of the Lord? Discuss.

2. When we are faced with new challenges in our lives, why should we pray for God to give us an understanding heart?

3. Is it wrong for us to pray for riches and material possessions instead of wisdom and understanding? Why or why not?

LESSON IN OUR SOCIETY

Christian adults have a tremendous responsibility to the next generation to set godly principles and examples for our children to follow. By the Holy Spirit, we have been given the ability to be "channels" which deposit His truths in the lives of others. We are our brother's keeper, and we can make a difference in our community when we realize that we are here to help pass on God's legacy and love to other young people who may not know Jesus Christ. To whom will you pass on the spiritual principles that can make a difference?

MAKE IT HAPPEN

Pray for God to direct you to someone with whom you can share your faith. Be open and honest with people, not only sharing how God has blessed you, but also the mistakes you have made along the way. Help the person to understand how important it is to live for God, and

how to apply spiritual truths to their lives so that they may live victoriously for Jesus Christ. Be committed to share your experience with the class next week.

FOLLOW THE SPIRIT

What God wants me to do:

_____

_____

REMEMBER YOUR THOUGHTS

Special insights you learned:

_____

_____

MORE LIGHT ON THE TEXT
1 Kings 2:1-4; 3:3-4a, 5-10

2:1 Now the days of David drew nigh that he should die; and he charged Solomon his son, saying

David was now 70 years old (having ruled for 40 years) and was approaching death. His health was so frail that he could not even maintain his own body temperature, but had to be warmed by sharing the body heat of a young woman. His older sons had attempted to take the royal throne while David was still alive (just barely), believing it to be their right as elder-born sons. Even one Benjaminite had attempted to take the throne, but failed. However, it was for the king to choose who would succeed him. David had promised his wife Bathsheba that their son Solomon would receive the throne, though Solomon was the fourth son born to David. Bathsheba had to remind David of his promise, even as Adonijah was proclaiming his own kingship in the streets. With every ounce of strength he could muster, David gathered his wits and began the ritual of coronation, making Solomon king of Israel.

2 I go the way of all the earth: be thou strong therefore, and show thyself a man;

The "way of all the earth" is death. David was preparing his young son for the moment of his death. "Be strong . . . show thyself a man" were David's words to encourage this young man not to be overcome by his grief, and to gird himself up as he prepared to take on the responsibility of leadership of his people.

3 And keep the charge of the LORD thy God, to walk in his ways, to keep his statutes, and his commandments, and his judgements, and his testimonies, as it is written in the law of Moses, that thou mayest prosper in all that thou doest, and whithersoever thou turnest thyself:

The charge of the Lord was given to Moses and the Children of Israel, and to every leader and every generation thereafter. To "walk in his ways" means to be obedient to the things the Lord commanded. The commandments are the ten fundamental laws given to Moses (Exodus 20: 2-17), and the statutes refer to the host of elaborations found in the Book of the Covenant (Exodus 20:22-23:33) and in the Holiness Code (Leviticus 17-26). The judgments and the testimonies refer to the events attested to throughout the Pentateuch (first five books of the Bible) and how the law of God was administered therein.

Prosperity always followed the people when they were obedient to the ways of the Lord, and disaster followed their disobedience. No matter what goal one set out to accomplish; no matter what direction one took, success was sure to be obtained if the individual or group was within the will of God.

4 That the LORD may continue his word which he spake concerning me, saying, If thy children take heed to their way, to walk before me in truth with all their heart and with all their soul, there shall not fail thee (said he) a man on the throne of Israel.

David assured Solomon that if Solomon maintained his part of the covenant with God, then God would maintain His part of the covenant, as promised to David. The throne of Israel would always be held by a descendant of David. It would be a Davidic dynasty, but this promise was contingent on obedience. Saul had the throne taken from his family line, because of disobedience. The same could happen to David's family line.

3:3 And Solomon loved the Lord, walking in the statutes of David his father: only he sacrificed and burnt incense in high places.

Because Solomon loved Yahweh, he was obedient to the instructions of his father. However, there were many places of worship set upon hilltops to offer burnt offerings and incense to God. This was perceived as a problem at this point in Israel's history. Now that they had a centralized government, the need was felt to centralize the worship practices also. This could be accomplished by building a temple or house of worship for God. David was prevented from attempting such a building project, because his reign was characterized by warfare.

4 And the king went to Gibeon to sacrifice there; for that was the great high place:

Gibeon was located 26 1/4 miles northwest of Jerusalem. Just outside the city was a great hill, which caught the attention of many Israelite worshipers. Gibeon was significant as a worship center because King Saul had an encounter there with Yahweh. In addition, David had moved the Tabernacle of Moses and the Tent of Meeting to this location during his reign.

5 In Gibeon the LORD appeared to Solomon in a dream by night: and God said, Ask what I shall give thee.

While Solomon was in Gibeon, he had a dream or vision of God in the night. Such dreams were valued as significant and were not to be ignored. Kings underwent rituals of purification and fasting in order to put themselves in a state of spiritual openness to receive such revelations from God. In this way, the king would have direct knowledge from God as to how he should lead the people. He would not have to depend upon second-hand information from the priests or prophets, whose roles were valuable but could not substitute for the king's own relationship with God.

God asked Solomon an open-ended question, "What shall I give you?" Solomon's answer would indicate the character of his kingship and his manhood. There were no limits placed upon his request, thus the true nature of his heart would be revealed.

6 And Solomon said, Thou has showed unto thy servant David my father great mercy, according as he walked before thee in truth, and in righteousness, and in uprightness of heart with thee; and

thou hast kept for him this great kindness, that thou hast given him a son to sit on his throne, as it is this day.

Before Solomon answered God's question, he recounted what God had done for his father. God had showed great mercy to David, preserving his life, in spite of his sin with Bathsheba and the murder of Uriah. David's life was spared, and he was able to father another son with Bathsheba, namely Solomon. This act of recounting or remembering what God had done in the past is reminiscent of Moses' final speech to the Israelites. It demonstrates a heart of appreciation for God's loving kindness, but it also reminds both the speaker and listener of how they have gotten to the present moment. It demonstrates that the person is fully aware of what he or she is about to commit to.

7 And now, O LORD my God, thou hast made thy servant king instead of David my father: and I am but a little child: I know not how to go out or come in.

Next Solomon identified himself as a servant king of God. This is a statement of total humility. Solomon was chosen king by God, and not of his own design. In many ancient cultures, the son was obligated to kill his father in order to take his place as the king upon the throne. There was little room for co-regency or shared kingship. The actions of Adonijah were more typical of how a prince became king. However, since it was God's will, David was able to choose Solomon to replace him at the moment of death.

Solomon was a young man, who had several elder brothers, each one more prepared and ready to rule as king. But Solomon was chosen by God, just as his father had been. In his earnest sincerity, Solomon confessed his incompetence for the role of king. He did not know how to govern a nation; he knew he needed God's help.

8 And thy servant is in the midst of thy people which thou hast chosen, a great people, that cannot be numbered nor counted for multitude.

This statement is an acknowledgment of the fulfillment of the Abrahamic covenant (Genesis 15:1-6) that Abraham's descendants would be innumerable. Solomon recognized that Yahweh fulfilled promises, and thus he was prepared to trust Yahweh to fulfill the thing he was about to ask for.

9 Give therefore thy servant an understanding heart to judge thy people, that I may discern between good and bad: for who is able to judge this thy so great a people?

Solomon asked for understanding, the very thing he would need to be a competent king. He could have asked for riches, longevity, or that his enemies be slain, but instead he asked for something that would make him a better servant. This indicated that Solomon's character was not a selfish one, but he was truly oriented toward serving God and leading his people in the ways of God.

10 And the speech pleased the LORD, that Solomon had asked this thing.

Solomon had shown himself to be humble and obedient to God. Moreover, he put his trust in Yahweh and asked for a gift that would make him a better servant of God. The Lord, Yahweh, was very pleased by Solomon's request. His heart was indeed true.

DAILY BIBLE READINGS

M: David's Instruction to Solomon
1 Kings 2:1-9

T: Solomon's Prayer for Wisdom
1 Kings 3:1-9

W: God's Reply to Solomon's Prayer
1 Kings 3:10-15

T: David's Prayer for Solomon
1 Chronicles 29:10-19

F: The Crowning of Solomon
1 Chronicles 29:22-25

S: Solomon Sacrifices at Gibeon
2 Chronicles 1:1-6

S: Solomon's Vision and Request for Wisdom
2 Chronicles 1:7-13

TEACHING TIPS

November 19
Bible Study Guide 12

1. Words You Should Know

A. Altar (1 Kings 8:22) Hebrew *Mizbeach*—A place of sacrifice.

B. Perpetually (1 Kings 9:3) Hebrew *Yom*—A point and sphere of time, connected with the sovereignty of God.

2. Teacher Preparation

A. Begin by reading 1 Kings 6—9 as well as the BIBLE BACKGROUND and DEVOTIONAL READING.

B. Read Bible Study Guide 12 and answer the questions in the SEARCH THE SCRIPTURES and DISCUSS THE MEANING sections.

3. Starting the Lesson

A. Have a student pray, focusing on the LESSON AIM and the KEEP IN MIND verse as the foundation of the prayer.

B. Assign three students to read the lesson according to the AT-A-GLANCE outline.

C. Have students write down any key points that may come to them as a result of studying the lesson.

4. Getting into the Lesson

A. Ask two students to read the FOCAL VERSES and the BIBLE BACKGROUND Scriptures.

B. Have students comment on the IN FOCUS story. Remind them that structures are used to house ministries, just as our physical structures are used to house the real us.

C. Have students work in pairs to answer the SEARCH THE SCRIPTURES questions after the lesson has been completely read.

D. Assign a student to read and discuss briefly THE PEOPLE, PLACES, AND TIMES section of the lesson.

5. Relating the Lesson to Life

A. Focus on the DISCUSS THE MEANING questions. Challenge students to reflect on how this lesson impacts on their lives today.

B. Pass out the 3 x 5 cards with the KEEP IN MIND verse written on it. Have students discuss its implications for their lives.

C. Give them time to share their ideas about implementing the LESSON IN OUR SOCIETY assignment.

6. Arousing Action

A. Have students commit to doing the MAKE IT HAPPEN assignment for this week.

B. Remind students to read the DAILY BIBLE READINGS to reinforce the principles of today's lesson in their lives for the week.

C. Encourage students to write down any ideas or principles learned today in the FOLLOW THE SPIRIT and REMEMBER YOUR THOUGHTS sections of the lesson.

D. Close the class time with prayer, thanking God for allowing you to achieve the LESSON AIM.

WORSHIP GUIDE

For the Superintendent or Teacher
Theme: Solomon Builds the Temple
Theme Song: "I'm Working On a Building"
Scripture: Hebrews 3:1-6
Song: " Lord, Prepare Me to Be a Sanctuary"
Meditation: Father, thank You for allowing me to build a house for you. Help me to perfect every area of my house so that I may glorify You. In Jesus' name, Amen.

SOLOMON BUILDS THE TEMPLE

Bible Background • 1 KINGS 5:1-8; 6:1-22, 37-38; 8:4—9:5
Printed Text • 1 KINGS 6:37-38; 8:22, 27-30; 9:1-5
Devotional Reading • PSALM 84:1-4

LESSON AIM

By the end of the lesson, students should be able to identify with Solomon's determination to build God's temple; recount God's reaction when the temple was completed; and affirm the importance of building God's temple in our own lives.

KEEP IN MIND

"But will God indeed dwell on the earth? Behold, the heaven and heaven of heavens cannot contain thee; how much less this house that I have builded?" (1 Kings 8:27)

FOCAL VERSES

1 Kings 6:37 In the fourth year was the foundation of the house of the LORD laid, in the month Zif:

38 And in the eleventh year, in the month Bul, which is the eighth month, was the house finished throughout all the parts thereof, and according to all the fashion of it. So was he seven years in building it.

8:22 And Solomon stood before the altar of the LORD in the presence of all the congregation of Israel, and spread forth his hands toward heaven:

27 But will God indeed dwell on the earth? Behold, the heaven and heaven of heavens cannot contain thee; how much less this house that I have builded?

28 Yet have thou respect unto the prayer of thy servant, and to his supplication, O LORD my God, to hearken unto the cry and to the prayer, which thy servant prayeth before thee to day:

29 That thine eyes may be open toward this

LESSON OVERVIEW

LESSON AIM
KEEP IN MIND
FOCAL VERSES
IN FOCUS
THE PEOPLE, PLACES, AND TIMES
BACKGROUND
AT-A-GLANCE
IN DEPTH
SEARCH THE SCRIPTURES
DISCUSS THE MEANING
LESSON IN OUR SOCIETY
MAKE IT HAPPEN
FOLLOW THE SPIRIT
REMEMBER YOUR THOUGHTS
MORE LIGHT ON THE TEXT
DAILY BIBLE READINGS

house night and day, even toward the place of which thou hast said, My name shall be there: that thou mayest hearken unto the prayer which thy servant shall make toward this place.

30 And hearken thou to the supplication of thy servant, and of thy people Israel, when they shall pray toward this place: and hear thou in heaven thy dwelling place: and when thou hearest, forgive.

9:1 And it came to pass, when Solomon had finished the building of the house of the LORD, and the king's house, and all Solomon's desire which he was pleased to do,

2 That the LORD appeared to Solomon the second time, as he had appeared unto him at Gibeon.

3 And the LORD said unto him, I have heard thy prayer and thy supplication, that thou hast made before me: I have hallowed this house, which thou hast built, to put my name there for ever; and mine eyes and mine heart shall be there perpetually.

4 And if thou wilt walk before me, as David thy father walked, in integrity of heart, and in uprightness, to do according to all that I have commanded thee, and wilt keep my statutes and my judgments:

5 Then I will establish the throne of thy kingdom upon Israel for ever, as I promised to David thy father, saying, There shall not fail thee a man upon the throne of Israel.

NOV
19TH

IN FOCUS

After 27 years of ministry to the community, the

leaders of the Samaritan Evangelistic Center knew it was time for them to move out of their old facility. The walls were crumbling, the foundation was shifting, and the stairs had begun cracking. Plus, Samaritan Evangelistic Center was ministering to more people than they could possibly hold in the old building, which made the facility a fire hazard.

The executive committee of the center began looking for an existing structure in the community close to their present location. But after months of searching and talking with prospective realtors, the committee couldn't find a suitable building which would meet their needs and give them greater opportunities to expand their ministry to the poor and homeless. So, the committee decided to buy a parcel of land right next door to their present location and build a new facility from the ground up. Said executive director Brenda Charles, "Given the circumstance, it was the most feasible and logical thing to do."

Building projects are never easy to accomplish. Just ask a church or a para-church organization that has undertaken this enormous task. Not only are there finances to be raised, but also material to buy, construction crews to hire, and deadlines to meet in order to finish the goal in a timely manner. Any wrinkle in the schedule can hinder the process.

This week, we will examine Solomon's construction job as he commits to building the temple of God.

THE PEOPLE, PLACES, AND TIMES

Bul. (Hebrew, meaning produce.) A term designating the Old Canaanite name for the eighth month of the year, approximately October or November. After the exile, this month was called *Mark-heshvan* by the Hebrews.

Time. Like English, the Hebrew name for "month" is related to the word moon, *yereah*, or the new moon, *hodesh*. The lunar month had 30 days (Genesis 7:11; 8:3-4; Numbers 20:29; Deuteronomy 21:13). The new moon was a festival day (1 Samuel 20:5, 18, 24; 2 Kings 3:23; Isaiah 1:13-14), and important holidays such as Passover and the Feast of Tabernacles fell mid-month (Psalm 81:4).

Four apparently Canaanite names for months

are mentioned: *Abib* (Exodus 13:4); *Ziv* (1 Kings 6:1, 37), *Ethanim* (1 Kings 8:2), and Bul (1 Kings 6:38). Postexilic texts mention five Babylonian-derived names: *Nisan* (Nehemiah 6:15), *Chislev* (Nehemiah 1:1; Zechariah 7:1), *Tebeth* (Esther 2:16), *Shebat* (Zechariah 1:7), and *Adar* (Ezra 6:15; Esther 3:7, 13; 8:12; 9:1, 15, 17, 19, 21). These texts are the earliest evidence of the Jewish adoption of the 12 Babylonian names of the months.

Although 30 days are alluded to in the Bible as a month's duration, the lunar calendar averaged out to 29 ´ days a month. Since the calendar was also tied to the agricultural-seasonal year, it also had a solar element. The Hebrews apparently had two New Year dates, one at the spring equinox and one at the autumnal equinox (Exodus 12:2, 18; 23:16; 34:22). The tenth-century B.C. inscription known as the Gezer Calendar describes the months by their particular harvests and also commences in the fall.

The necessity of intercalating the lunar calendar of 354 days a year with the seasonal year resulted in the Babylonians adding a month every two or three years. This system was eventually adopted in Judaism, with 7 out of every 19 years including as an additional month a second *Adar.*

(The Harper's Bible Dictionary, Paul J. Achtemeier, Editor, San Francisco: Harper and Row Publishing Co., 1984, pp. 144, 1072-73.)

BACKGROUND

Solomon succeeded his father David as the third king of Israel. Solomon was the son that David fathered by Bathsheba. Once David understood he was dying (1 Kings 2:1-2), the king began teaching his son how to walk in the ways of God. As king, Solomon also began to bring consensus

AT-A-GLANCE

1. Solomon Completes the Temple
(1 Kings 6:37-38)
2. Solomon Prays over the Temple
(1 Kings 8:22, 27-30)
3. God Approves the Temple
(1 Kings 9:1-5)

to Israel (1 Kings 2:13-46), reached out to Egypt (1 Kings 3:1-2), and asked the Lord to give him wisdom whereby he could lead God's people (vv. 3-28). Shortly after Solomon assumed the throne, he began building God's temple which fulfilled the desire of his father's heart. Solomon had tremendous help and he received the needed materials to complete the job.

IN DEPTH

1. Solomon Completes the Temple (1 Kings 6:37-38)

The Bible says that King Solomon began building God's temple 480 years after Moses brought the Children of Israel out of Egypt. At the time of the building, the king had served Israel for three years (1 Kings 6:1). Reportedly, Solomon's temple was double in size to that of Moses' tabernacle (see Exodus 26) and far more splendiferous in appearance. Solomon did not spare any expense or materials in building God's house. Because of its magnitude, and what the temple represented, it took the king 7 years to complete the structure.

The significance of the number seven should not be overlooked since seven is the number of completion in biblical numerology. It took God seven days to finish creation (Genesis 2:1-3), and Jesus Christ rose from the grave on the third day. The resurrected Lamb has seven horns and seven eyes which are the seven Spirits of God (see Revelation 5:6). Solomon finished the temple in seven years signifying the completed work for Israel and a new or corporate relationship in worship of God by the people.

2. Solomon Prays over the Temple (1 Kings 8:22, 27-30)

Once King Solomon completed the temple, he did three things: (1) He furnished the temple with all the dedicated items (1 Kings 7:51); (2) He brought the ark of God into its permanent resting place (1 Kings 8:1-11); and (3) He offered up prayers and thanksgiving to God for the temple (vv. 22-53).

As Israel's national leader, Solomon knew the awesome responsibility of dedicating the temple and all that was within to God. God had given the king a tremendous opportunity and responsibility

to build His house. Therefore, Solomon did not take the task lightly. The king knew that if God's presence and power were not in the midst of the temple, all was in vain (see Psalm 127:1). So, Solomon invoked the Lord's divine presence, power, and protection by lifting up his hands and his voice toward heaven in prayer.

As believers in Jesus Christ we must understand the power of prayer. The effectual and fervent prayers of righteous people can accomplish many things (James 5:16). We can change cities and nations by the power of prayer since prayer is our direct link to God.

As Solomon prayed, he acknowledged one of the most important characteristics of God, which is His transcendency. Unlike human beings, God is beyond the time/space element of life. Therefore, despite the magnificent structure that was in Israel, the king understood that God could not be "chained" to the temple. If the heavens could not contain all of God, how did Israel expect for a building to contain Him?

Yet, despite God's transcendence, Solomon knew that God had given Him charge to build the temple which would bear God's name. There, he asked only that God would put His seal of approval upon it by: (a) hearing his prayers for the building (v. 28); and (b) allowing His Holy Spirit to dwell in the temple so that when the people gathered together to pray and confess their sins to Him, God would hear from heaven and forgive their sins (vv. 29-30).

Solomon teaches us the power of God's presence in our individual and corporate lives. No matter how magnificent our church structures may be, if God is not in them we worship in vain. And the only way that God's presence abides in our church structures is if He abides in us. Only as we yield ourselves to God can we feel His presence and power in a great way.

3. God Approves the Temple (1 Kings 9:1-5)

After King Solomon completed the temple, his own palace, and other building projects in Israel (1 Kings 7:1-14), God appeared to him a second time in a dream. God wanted the king to know that not only had He heard his prayer and supplication that was sent up to heaven during the cele-

bration and feasting by the people, but also that He had put His seal of approval upon all that Solomon had done. In essence, God told Solomon: "I like what I see because you were willing to praise and honor Me." Believers need to understand that God will take a little and make it much in our lives if we are willing to humble ourselves before Him in adoration and praise. God "hallowed" His own temple and put His name, eyes, and heart on it forever. Because of Solomon's faithfulness, God made the temple holy and called it His own. Believers are called "the temple of God" and His eyes are upon us (1 Corinthians 6:19). We needn't worry about our provisions or our earthly treasures because God is watching over us. Because God has given us His Holy Spirit, we can be confident that "no weapon formed against

us shall prosper" (Isaiah 54:17). God has our back!

God also made it clear the even though He had sanctified the temple for His glory, Solomon had a part to play to ensure God's perpetual presence remained. As God's "temple," Solomon had the responsibility of " walking before [God] as David [his] father walked" (v. 4) in integrity of heart. The word "integrity" in Hebrew means wholeness and perfection. Thus, Solomon was commanded to submit himself unto God and become a man committed to obeying the statutes, decrees, and laws of God. New Testament believers are commanded to do the same thing by the apostle Paul: "I beseech you therefore, brethren, by the mercies of God that you present your bodies a living sacrifice, holy, acceptable unto God, which is your reasonable service. And be not conformed to this world, but be ye transformed by the renewing of your mind, that ye may prove what is that good, and acceptable, and perfect will of God" (Romans 12:1-2). If Solomon obeyed God and committed his will to Him, God would not only establish Solomon's seed to sit on the throne of Israel forever, but the Davidic kingdom would become an everlasting kingdom throughout all eternity.

Though Solomon and his sons failed to obey God's law completely, we can rest assured that God's kingdom will never come to an end. Every day, Jesus Christ is building God's "holy temples" as people submit to Him and allow Him to be the Saviour of their lives.

SEARCH THE SCRIPTURES

1. How long did it take him to complete the temple? (1 Kings 6:38)

2. What did Solomon do after he finished building? (1 Kings 8:22, 27-30)

3. How did God respond to Solomon? (1 Kings 9:2-5)

4. What promise did God make to Solomon? (vv. 4-5)

DISCUSS THE MEANING

1. Why was it important for Solomon to build the temple?

2. How does this story relate to us as believers?

3. What should we do to ensure that our temples are correctly built?

4. Does God still visit us today as He did Solomon? Why or why not?

LESSON IN OUR SOCIETY

Many buildings in our urban communities are dilapidated and in need of repair. What can we do as a community of believers to make a difference in the neighborhoods where we live?

MAKE IT HAPPEN

This week, ask the Lord to "visit" you and give you an assessment of your temple. Does it need rebuilding or repairing? Let God speak, and then commit to follow and obey what He shares with you. Be sure to thank and praise the Lord for His chastening and correction in your life.

FOLLOW THE SPIRIT

What God wants me to do:

_____

_____

REMEMBER YOUR THOUGHTS

Special insights you learned:

_____

_____

MORE LIGHT ON THE TEXT
1 Kings 6:37-38; 8:22, 27-30; 9:1-5

6:37 In the fourth year was the foundation of the house of the LORD laid, in the month of Zif:

In the fourth year of Solomon's reign, the foundation for the house (temple) of the Lord was laid. This occurred in the spring of the year in the month of *Zif* (usually spelled *Ziv*). The name of the month was borrowed from the Babylonian calendar. The word means flowers, indicating the time when flowers began budding and blooming after the winter season. The Hebrews had at least two calendrical systems: one beginning in the spring, the other beginning in the fall. The former can be assumed in this case, because it would not be prudent to begin a massive building project in the fall and then have to stop because of winter conditions.

The term "house" is used to indicate a permanent structure, unlike the portable tent that the Israelites used in the days of their wandering.

38 And in the eleventh year, in the month of Bul, which is the eight month, was the house finished throughout all the parts thereof, and according to all the fashion of it. So was he seven years in the building of it.

By the fall of Solomon's eleventh year, the temple was completed. This included the structure of the building itself, and all the finely crafted furnishings and decorations within. It was actually seven and one-half years in the making, but for this chronologist it was important that it took less than eight years to build. The number seven was an important number in Israel's history, particularly in regard to the religious arena—seven days of creation, seven days of the week, the seventh day as a holy day, etc.

8:22 And Solomon stood before the altar of the LORD in the presence of all the congregation of Israel, and spread forth his hands toward heaven:

With the congregation of Israel gathered around the completed temple, Solomon officiated the dedication service. Solomon offered a prayer to the Lord, Yahweh, acting in the capacity of the High Priest. Solomon stood to offer the prayer because that was the customary position for prayer. The custom of kneeling for prayer came at a later period of Israel's history. The spreading of the hands toward heaven was also a customary act symbolizing the praise of God.

8:27 But will God indeed dwell on the earth? Behold, the heaven and heaven of heavens cannot contain thee; how much less this house that I have builded?

With great humility and recognition of Yahweh's magnanimity, Solomon poses these rhetorical questions. Will God indeed dwell on the earth? The dwelling place of the high gods of nearly all the cultures of the ancient near east was in heaven and not on earth. Would God bring himself down from that lofty abode to dwell on the earth among humans? Moreover, Solomon acknowledged that the highest part of heaven (heaven was conceived of in seven parts) could not contain Yahweh. So this little temple, as grand as it appeared to humans, could not possibly contain the fullness of God. It was an unworthy offering to God, therefore it had to be presented in the most humble attitude.

28 Yet have thou respect unto the prayer of thy servant, and to his supplication, O LORD my God, to hearken unto the cry and prayer, which thy servant prayeth before thee to day:

Solomon pleaded with God to listen to the prayer that he was about to lift up. Solomon's statement encompassed three types of prayer: intercessory prayer (*tepillah*), sincere pleas for mercy (*tehinnah*), and a cry of petition (*rinnah*). Solomon's prayer was on behalf of the entire nation gathered around the temple. He sought God's mercy because their best effort at building a dwelling for Yahweh was so unworthy of Yahweh's presence. Yet Solomon cried out for Yahweh to ful-

fill his promise to dwell among the people anyway.

29 That thine eyes may be open toward this house night and day, even toward the place of which thou hast said, My name shall be there: that thou mayest hearken unto the prayer which thy servant shall make toward this place.

The phrase "that thine eyes may be open" meant "keep watch; do not overlook the prayers and the praise that will be offered to You in this place." In as much as the temple could not contain the God of heaven, it would be enough that He simply keep a watchful eye upon people who gather in the temple. In Deuteronomy 12:5, Moses told the Israelites that God would choose a place to "put his name," and that it would be the dwelling of God. That location would be the place where all the tithes, offerings, and sacrifices should be brought. Solomon reminded Yahweh of that promise to "put his name" upon the temple and therefore dwell amongst the people.

When the Children of Israel were in Egypt, the Lord saw their oppression and misery and was moved to act on their behalf. Thus Solomon asked God to keep watch on the temple and be moved to respond to the people's requests.

30 And hearken thou unto the supplication of thy servant, and of thy people Israel, when they shall pray toward this place: and hear thou in heaven thy dwelling place: and when thou hearest, forgive.

In other words, "Listen to our pleas for your mercy when we pray in the direction of this temple." Solomon requested that God hear the prayers from wherever the people were, as long as they prayed in the direction of the temple. Thus the temple would serve as a focal point for those in faraway places. This would also cover the situation of captivity and deportation. If they simply turned back toward their homeland, it would be as good as being there.

9:1 And it came to pass, when Solomon had finished the building of the house of the LORD and the king's house, and all Solomon's desire which he was pleased to do,

Solomon had undertaken several massive building projects, because of the wealth of the land gained by his father's conquests, which Solomon expanded by diplomacy. Solomon built the temple, his palace, the House of the Forest of Lebanon, and a house for pharaoh's daughter (his wife) (1 Kings 7). But Solomon also built walls around the city of Jerusalem and other major cities, and built storage facilities in other cities throughout the kingdom. All this was possible, because Solomon ruled in a time of peace, whereas David was constantly fighting to protect the borders he battled to expand.

2 That the LORD appeared to Solomon the second time, as he had appeared unto him at Gibeon.

The first time God had appeared to Solomon at Gibeon was shortly after his coronation as king. Now after the completion and dedication of the temple, a second divine appearance occurred. Something significant was about to happen. The proximity of this appearance of God to the dedication of the temple, in which Solomon offers specific petitions for God's attention, suggests that this appearance was a direct response to those petitions.

3 And the LORD said unto him, I have heard thy prayer and thy supplication, that thou hast made before me: I have hallowed this house, which thou hast built, to put my name there for ever; and mine eyes and mine heart shall be there perpetually.

God acknowledged that Solomon's prayer and petitions had indeed been heard. Then God sanctified the dedicated temple, making it a holy place. Once sanctified, God fulfilled his promise to "put his name there forever," symbolizing God's presence. That "God's eyes would be there" meant that God would keep constant watch on the temple and its activities, as Solomon requested. That "God's heart would be there" meant that God would show mercy and kindness toward this people and their petitions.

4 And if thou wilt walk before me, as David thy father walked, in integrity of heart, and in uprightness, to do according to all that I have commanded thee, and wilt keep my statutes and my judgments:

God had fulfilled the promise that he made to David through his son Solomon. But the "forever" part of the fulfillment would depend upon Solomon's continued obedience. David was not perfect, but he did have integrity of heart and worshiped Yahweh alone. He never chased after other gods, because he had trusted in Yahweh since his youth; as a result, he was brought safely through many life-threatening circumstances. David worked diligently to be a godly king. Now it was Solomon's turn. He too would have to be obedient. When the king is not obedient, it is unlikely that the people will be obedient. But if the king lives with integrity and obedience to God, then the people will also.

5 Then I will establish the throne of thy kingdom upon Israel for ever, as I promised to David thy father, saying, 'There shall not fail thee a man upon the throne of Israel.

So it was made plain, if Solomon remained faithful and obedient, then God would continue to uphold his promise that the throne of kingship would remain in the family line of David. The promise was conditional, contingent upon the king's continued obedience.

DAILY BIBLE READINGS

M: Preparations for Building the Temple
1 Kings 5:1-12

T: Solomon Builds the Temple
1 Kings 6:1-13

W: The Interior of the Temple
1 Kings 6:14-22

T: Dedication of the Temple
1 Kings 8:1-13

F: Solomon's Prayer of Dedication
1 Kings 8:22-30

S: Rejoicing in the Sanctuary
Psalm 84

S: God Again Appears to Solomon
1 Kings 9:1-9

TEACHING TIPS

November 26
Bible Study Guide 13

1. Words You Should Know

A. Goddess (1 Kings 11:5) Hebrew *Elohim*—A singular word for god, and refers to a ruler or judge with divine connections.

B. Covenant (1 Kings 11:11) Hebrew *B'rith*—A treaty or alliance of friendship, accompanied by sacrifices, and a solemn oath by God which seals the relationship with promises of blessings for obedience and curses for disobedience.

2. Teacher Preparation

A. Before studying today's lesson, ask the Lord to help you identify any idolatrous ways in your life. Then, pray and repent so that you might be able to share divine truths with your students.

B. Read the Bible Study Guide for today. Then spend a few minutes answering the SEARCH THE SCRIPTURES and DISCUSS THE MEANING questions so you will be ready to help students incorporate the truths from today's lesson into their lives.

C. Materials needed: Bible, chalkboard or newsprint, Bible commentary or dictionary.

3. Starting the Lesson

A. Have students read the FOCAL VERSES according to the AT-A-GLANCE outline. Then give them an opportunity to discuss what they have read. Ask them to identify Solomon's biggest problem and what he could have done to avoid it.

B. Allow a student to lead the class in prayer, using the KEEP IN MIND verse as the basis of the prayer.

4. Getting into the Lesson

A. Read the IN FOCUS, BACKGROUND and IN DEPTH sections of today's lesson, paying particular attention to God's reaction to Solomon's life during the years he practiced idolatry.

B. Have students answer the SEARCH THE SCRIPTURES questions. Remind them that Solomon was human, just as we are, and prone to make mistakes, but he chose the life he lived of his own volition.

C. Read the DISCUSS THE MEANING questions to students and ask for volunteers to answer them.

5. Relating the Lesson to Life

A. Now have students look at the LESSON IN OUR SOCIETY exercise and identify the "strange gods" that exist in our community. Be sure students write the answers down on paper so they can take it with them to share with others.

B. Ask students to read the MAKE IT HAPPEN exercise. Have students make a commitment to follow through on the exercise so they will have a firm grasp on what the Lord is teaching them.

6. Arousing Action

A. Have students discuss what they have learned this quarter and how they plan to incorporate these truths in their lives.

B. Close the class in prayer, thanking God for revealing biblical truths throughout the quarter.

WORSHIP GUIDE

For the Superintendent or Teacher
Theme: Solomon's Mistakes
Theme Song: "Help Me, Lord to Walk with You"
Scripture: 2 Corinthians 6:12—7:1
Song: "I've Learned How to Be Holy"
Confessional: Lord, I am not always following You. At times, I do my own thing. However, I want to walk closely with You. Father, give me strength to live holily and righteously for You. In Jesus' name, Amen.

SOLOMON'S MISTAKES

Bible Background • 1 KINGS 11
Printed Text • 1 KINGS 11:1-13
Devotional Reading • NAHUM 1:2-8

LESSON AIM

By the end of the lesson, students should be able to identify some of Solomon's mistakes, affirm the importance of obeying the Lord, and commit to living holily so they won't make similar mistakes as Solomon.

KEEP IN MIND

"And the LORD was angry with Solomon, because his heart was turned from the LORD God of Israel . . . " (1 Kings 11:9).

FOCAL VERSES

1 Kings 11:1 But King Solomon loved many strange women, together with the daughter of Pharaoh, women of the Moabites, Ammonites, Edomites, Zidonians, and Hittites;

2 Of the nations concerning which the LORD said unto the children of Israel, Ye shall not go in to them, neither shall they come in unto you: for surely they will turn away your heart after their gods: Solomon clave unto these in love.

3 And he had seven hundred wives, princesses, and three hundred concubines: and his wives turned away his heart.

4 For it came to pass, when Solomon was old, that his wives turned away his heart after other gods: and his heart was not perfect with the LORD his God, as was the heart of David his father.

5 For Solomon went after Ashtoreth the goddess of the Zidonians, and after Milcom the abomination of the Am- monites.

LESSON OVERVIEW

LESSON AIM
KEEP IN MIND
FOCAL VERSES
IN FOCUS
THE PEOPLE, PLACES,
AND TIMES
BACKGROUND
AT-A-GLANCE
IN DEPTH
SEARCH THE SCRIPTURES
DISCUSS THE MEANING
LESSON IN OUR SOCIETY
MAKE IT HAPPEN
FOLLOW THE SPIRIT
REMEMBER YOUR THOUGHTS
MORE LIGHT ON THE TEXT
DAILY BIBLE READINGS

6 And Solomon did evil in the sight of the LORD, and went not fully after the LORD, as did David his father.

7 Then did Solomon build an high place for Chemosh, the abomination of Moab, in the hill that is before Jerusalem, and for Molech, the abomination of the children of Ammon.

8 And likewise did he for all his strange wives, which burnt incense and sacrificed unto their gods.

9 And the LORD was angry with Solomon, because his heart was turned from the LORD God of Israel, which had appeared unto him twice.

10 And had commanded him concerning this thing, that he should not go after other gods: but he kept not that which the LORD commanded.

11 Wherefore the LORD said unto Solomon, Forasmuch as this is done of thee, and thou hast not kept my covenant and my statutes, which I have commanded thee, I will surely rend the kingdom from thee, and will give it to thy servant.

12 Notwithstanding in thy days I will not do it for David thy father's sake: but I will rend it out of the hand of thy son.

13 Howbeit I will not rend away all the kingdom; but will give one tribe to thy son.

IN FOCUS

Pastor Winston sat silently outside the executive offices of his denominational

NOV 26TH

headquarters in Baltimore, awaiting the out-come of the meeting inside. Having been called there to answer questions about his conduct and character, Pastor Winston understood the impact that the meeting had on his future career as pastor of Shining Star Church. The denomination executives had weighed all the evidence they had received from the church in the past six months before calling him to appear before the committee, and Pastor Winston had no one but himself to blame. The deacons tried talking with the pastor about his relationship with some of the women in the church, but he refused to listen. They also questioned Pastor Winston about some of his sermons that could not be substantiated by the Bible. Finally, when Pastor Winston announced that he was getting a divorce from his wife to marry the executive assistant of the ministry, the deacons felt it was necessary to call the denomination executives. Said one deacon, "we really like Pastor Winston and the work he has done for the ministry. That's why it was extremely difficult to make the decision to report him to the denomination executives. But when he refused to listen to reason, we felt it was necessary for the good of the church and the people that he served to call the executives in Baltimore."

There is a price to pay for being a leader over people, especially in the ministry. Christian leaders must not only watch what they say, but also live exemplary lives so they cannot be accused of causing others to "stumble" in their walk with the Lord. In fact, Christian leaders can do harm to the cause of Christ when they fail to live right-eous before God and His "sheep."

This week's Bible Study Guide will help us understand this principle in detail when we examine the later years of King Solomon and the mistakes that he made in his walk with God.

THE PEOPLE, PLACES, AND TIMES

Moab. The Moabites were the descendants of Lot and were neighbors of the Amorites on the opposite side of the Arnon River (see Numbers 21:13). They possessed many great cities

(Numbers 21:28-30; 23:7; Isaiah 15:1), and were prosperous, arrogant, and idolatrous. They were mighty men of war (Isaiah 16:6). The Amorites deprived them of a large part of their territory (Numbers 21:26). The Moabites refused to let Israel pass through their country and were so greatly impressed and alarmed by the multitude of the Israelite army, that along with Midian, they sent Balaam to curse it (Numbers 22—24). Subsequently, Israel was enticed into idolatry and even intermarried with them. They were always hostile to Israel until King Saul subdued them (1 Samuel 14:47). Later they became tributary to David and succeeding Jewish kings (2 Samuel 8:2, 12; 2 Kings 3:4), but they finally joined Babylon against Judah (2 Kings 24:2). On several occasions, God pronounced judgments against Moab (Isaiah 15:1—16:14; Jeremiah 48:1-47; Amos 2:1-3). (The Hebrew Greek Key Study Bible, Edited by Spiros Zodhiates, Th.D., 1991, Nashville: AMG Publishing Co., pp. 29.)

BACKGROUND

Solomon was the wisest man who ever lived (see 1 Kings 3:12-13; Ecclesiastes 1:16). He was by far one of Israel's greatest kings and, because of his relationship with the Lord, Solomon built the temple and other projects with splendor. The king also accumulated riches beyond his wildest dreams because he was willing to obey the Lord and follow after Him with all his heart (1 Kings 3:13).

But something happened to Solomon that changed the course and destiny of his life. Perhaps his wealth got to him, or maybe he became so arrogant as a king that he failed to remember the promises of God as he moved up the "ladder of success." Whatever the reason, there was a turning point in the king's life where he stopped listening to God and began leaning on his own understanding (see Proverbs 3:5). As a result, Solomon fell out of favor with God and his kingdom went downhill from there. As we begin the IN DEPTH section of the lesson, we need to keep in mind that Solomon is an example for New Testament believers who choose to go their own way rather than listen to God.

IN DEPTH

1. Solomon Yields to His Fleshly Desires (1 Kings 11:1-3)

King Solomon became a man who believed his own "press." The Bible affirms that he "exceeded all the kings of the earth for riches and wisdom [and] all the earth sought to Solomon, to hear his wisdom, which God had put in his heart" (1 Kings 10:23-24). Solomon forgot two basic biblical principles: (1) "know ye that the LORD. . . is God: it is He that hath made us, and not we ourselves" (Psalm 100:3); and (2) "be not wise in your own conceits (Romans 12:16). Had Solomon practiced these two principles, he would not have succumbed to the idolatry which manifested itself in his life in a major way.

Solomon "loved many strange women" (v. 1). The Hebrew definition for "strange" literally means a foreigner or one who is outside the bounds of Israel. Though it is doubtless that Israel had many beautiful women whom the king could have had at any given time, the Bible says that Solomon loved women from Moab, Ammon, Edom, Zidon and Hittite which were all forbidden by God, in addition to the Egyptian wife that he had married (1 Kings 3:1-2). In doing so, Solomon broke at least two commandments that had been given to the people of Israel by God. First, God had forbidden Israel's kings to multiply wives to themselves because these women would have the propensity to turn the king's heart away from following God (Deuteronomy 17:17). Second, God commanded that Israel destroy the Canaanite culture and make no covenant with the people. He also instructed the people not to marry their sons or daughters because they would "turn away thy sons from following Me, that they may serve other gods." As a result, God's anger would "be kindled against [Israel], and destroy [them] suddenly" (Deuteronomy 7:3-4).

Both the Moabites and Ammonites were descendants of Lot's incestual relationships with his daughters (Genesis 19:30-37). The Edomites were the descendants of Esau, Isaac's oldest son after he married a Canaanite woman (Genesis 36:1-9). The Zidonians were also a part of the Philistine stronghold that oppressed Israel during the time of the judges (Judges 10:11-12), and the Hittites were from the land of Egypt that had been given to Abraham by God (Genesis 15:16-20). God had forbidden Israel to associate with all of these nations because He knew the strong influence they would have on the people. Yet, despite God's warning and command to Israel, King Solomon refused to listen because the Bible says he "clave unto these [women] in love" (v. 2).

How many foreign women did King Solomon allow to be a part of his life? The Scriptures record that he had 700 wives and princesses, plus 300 concubines. Every one of these women was instrumental in turning King Solomon's heart away from God and toward her way of life. Of course it is inconceivable for us today to imagine how the king kept each of these women satisfied. But the principle we can learn from this lesson is that we must be careful who we allow to become a part of our life. The Scriptures declare that we cannot be unequally yoked together with unbelievers (see 2 Corinthians 6:14). If we are not strong enough in our Christian walk, our association with unbelievers will be influential in bringing us down rather than enabling us to lift them up to walk with God.

2. Solomon Is Overcome with Idolatry (vv. 4-6)

Solmon's second grave sin took place in his old age. Instead of getting "wiser," Solomon allowed his wives' influence to lead him away from God and into idolatry so that "his heart was not perfect with the LORD. . . as was the heart of David his father" (v. 4). In essence, Solomon's heart became cold and callous. Every time he lay with one of his wives in sexual relations, he left a part of himself with her and received a part of her into his soul and spirit. As a result, Solomon lost the intimacy and love he had with God. Believers need to understand this principle. Every time we "sleep" with the enemy, we diminish our desire for righteousness and gain more of his ungodly characteristics in our lives. That's why we must "come out from among [individuals who are not pure before God] and be . . . separate . . . and touch not the unclean thing" (2 Corinthians 6:17). Had Solomon understood this principle, he would not have gone after Ashtoreth, the goddess of the Zidonians and Molech who was the god of the Ammonites (v. 5). Both of these idols were associated with sexual fertility and witchcraft, which God had forbidden His people to incorporate into their lives. Because Solomon was the king, it is doubtless that he influenced many in Israel to follow after his ways. Thus, in succumbing to idolatry, Solomon not only turned away from the Lord, but he was also instrumental in leading others down the same path. As a result of his actions, Solomon became evil in the sight of the Lord and lost the passion and desire for the Lord that his father David had (v. 6). We need to be careful that we don't allow this world's "treasures" to turn our hearts away from the Lord. We need the passionate pursuit of God if we expect to be effective for Jesus Christ in history's final hours.

3. Solomon Turns Away from God (vv. 7-10)

The third grave sin that Solomon committed was to build places of worship in Israel for the gods that he served, including Chemosh and Molech. The king built the altars in "hill" or high places of Jerusalem, which indicates that this was sacred ground that should have been reserved exclusively for the Lord. Not only did he build worship places for several of his wives, but the Bible indicates that Solomon built them for all of his wives. In essence, there were over 1,000 worship places for these pagan women to go where they could burn incense and sacrifice to their gods. Is there any wonder that God became increasingly angry with the king?

The word "angry" (v. 9) literally means to breathe out through the nostrils one's displeasure, and is used figuratively to express outrage by the act of breathing hard. God did not take Solomon's idolatry lightly. Having "visited" the king twice in his life to remind him of the importance of walking upright before Him (1 Kings 3:3-13 and 9:1-5), God was sure to come to Solomon to demand answers concerning his actions. By turning away from God to follow after these pagan women, Solomon had crossed a line that he would find difficult to return and it was time for the king to face the music.

4. God Judges Solomon (vv. 11-13)

Perhaps Solomon was in his palace, having spent time with his wives and admiring his accomplishments when the Lord came to him. Nevertheless, the king was not expecting a "visit" from God. Instead of asking Solomon what he had done, which would have given the king time to come up with a lame excuse, God went right to the heart of the matter. Simply put, Solomon was guilty of not keeping the Lord's covenant, which He had given to the king shortly after the death of his father. Solomon had refused to listen to God. He chose to go his own way by marrying women who turned his heart from the precepts of God to his own ideas. Thus, God promised that He would remove the kingdom from Solomon and give it to another.

Even though God had promised that Solomon would lose the kingdom, it would not happen while he sat on the throne. Instead, Solomon's son would suffer defeat and misery because of his father's disobedience. Just as in

David's time, civil war would resume in Israel and the northern and southern kingdoms would split. Yet, because of God's love and mercy for David, Solomon's seed would continue to reign over the tribe of Judah forever. It would be through Solomon that the Messiah would come to reign and rule forever.

Solomon teaches us the importance of following the Lord. If we listen to the Lord and heed His voice, we can avoid the mistakes and the pitfalls that ultimately plagued the last years of Solomon's life.

SEARCH THE SCRIPTURES

1. Who were the women that King Solomon loved? (1 Kings 11:1-2)

2. Why was God displeased with the king? (v. 2)

3. What did Solomon build for his wives? (vv. 7-8)

4. How did God deal with the king? (vv. 11-13)

5. What would be the final outcome of Solomon's disobedience? (v. 13)

DISCUSS THE MEANING

1. Why is God so concerned about His children's relationships with other people? Discuss.

2. Is it possible for us today to be influenced by men and women who are idolatrous just as Solomon was? Why or why not?

3. Do our negative actions affect our children? Discuss.

4. What are the important principles we can learn from Solomon that we should incorporate into our lives to help us overcome our own mistakes?

LESSON IN OUR SOCIETY

Today, our society is enamored with idolatry of every kind. We need to be careful that we don't fall into the same trap as King Solomon, who was given so much from God, yet turned his heart away to follow after strange gods. Identify the "strange gods" in our community. List why they are strange, and give specific suggestions we should incorporate into our lives to avoid the

consequences of involving ourselves in these things. Discuss how we can warn others of these consequences.

MAKE IT HAPPEN

This week, ask the Lord to help you identify those areas where you have failed to obey His word and His warning in your life. Write them down and commit to working on those areas so that they become less of a hindrance in your life. Report on your activities in next week's lesson.

FOLLOW THE SPIRIT

What God wants me to do:

_____

_____

REMEMBER YOUR THOUGHTS

Special insights you learned:

_____

_____

MORE LIGHT ON THE TEXT
1 Kings 11:1-13

11:1 But King Solomon loved many strange women, together with the daughter of Pharaoh, women of the Moabites, Ammonites, Edomites, Zidonians, and Hittites;

The term "strange women" referred to their status as foreigners, not of Israelite lineage. In an effort to secure his diplomatic and trade relations with the surrounding nations, King Solomon married princesses of each of the surrounding lands. This behavior was not uncommon. It was like insurance against war.

The virility of the king was viewed as a good omen for the nation. This idea was left over from the fertility cult practices of the region. That Solomon had so many wives was believed to be an indication of his strength and personal power.

2 Of the nations concerning which the LORD said unto the children of Israel, Ye shall not go in to them, neither shall they come unto you: for surely they will turn away your heart after their

139

gods: Solomon clave unto these in love.

With the exception of Egypt, the other nations listed in verse 1 were ones which Yahweh had instructed the Israelites to have no dealings with (Exodus 34). This commandment was given to avoid the danger of Israel forsaking its religious principles and its God to follow after those of the nations. Israel was numerically small by comparison, and its religious attempt at monotheism (the worship of one god) was relatively young. Such a religious practice, when attempted under the Pharaoh Akhenaton centuries before, nearly tore Egypt apart. Monotheism is difficult to maintain in an environment of polytheism (the worship of many gods). There was too great a tendency for Israel to fall into the more established pattern of worship, which the majority of persons in the region practiced. The names of the gods varied, but the religious structures looked very similar.

When Africans were brought to America during the slave trade, they were separated from their countrymen, separated from people of similar language, and separated from people of similar religious practices. Because they were outnumbered, oppressed, and stripped of most of their cultural foundations, it is easy to understand how many of them were able to adapt the religious practices of their oppressors. They understood a certain similarity of concepts and were able to continue their worship of god under anglicized names. Whether it was Catholic saints or Protestantism, the Africans identified the religious notions with their familiar traditional African deities.

The threat of syncretism is always present. The more exposure someone has to other religions and philosophies of religion, the more frequently he or she will pick out similarities and blend the ideas of different systems of thought. Often this is done without attempting to fully understand the ramifications of the greater philosophical and cultural foundation from which one borrows. For the past two decades, as Native American culture has been co-opted within the dominant culture, Native Americans continue to warn others of the dangers of imitating or stealing their ancient religious practices without understanding the greater picture of the philosophy of life and the meaning of the practice. Similarly Solomon found things that he liked in the cultic practices of these other religions, and grew to love them intensely. But he had given little thought to the consequences it would have upon his own religion.

3 And he had seven hundred wives, princesses, and three hundred concubines: and his wives turned away his heart.

Solomon was a virile man. With so many wives and secondary wives, it is a wonder that he had time to administer his kingdom. Solomon invested a lot in his sexuality, and allowed it to pull his focus away from his God and the covenant they had made. He grew to love the gods of his wives. These women were not evil or deceitful. They were probably saddened and homesick in Jerusalem. They were in a strange land with a strange god. Since Solomon loved them, he conceded to allow them to worship the gods of their cultures. This was an unwise and irresponsible decision on Solomon's part, for he had a covenant to uphold. Eventually, he let his heart be led away from his own God.

4 For it came to pass, when Solomon was old, that his wives turned away his heart after other gods: and his heart was not perfect with the LORD his God, as was the heart of David his father.

Often when physical strength diminishes with age, one's moral fortitude wanes as well. We make compromises on issues that we would have been unwilling to consider in our youth. We decide that we don't have the energy to resist the flow. Solomon, who had depended on God so closely in his youth, had finally turned his heart away from God. His heart was no longer perfect (shalem meaning whole, at peace) with God. He was no longer satisfied with God alone, but desired other gods. Of David's many faults, infi-

delity to God was not among them. David remained faithful to the God of his youth, but Solomon did not.

5 For Solomon went after Ashtoreth the goddess of the Zidonians, and after Milcom the abomination of the Ammonites.

Solomon began to worship the Canaanite goddess Ashtoreth (also known as Astarte, or Ishtar in Akkadian). She was the consort of Baal, the great storm and fertility god of the Canaanites. She was also known as a goddess of war.

Milcom was the chief god of the Ammonites, the descendants of Lot's son (Ben-Ammi), who was born of the incestuous relations Lot had with one of his daughters. Milcom was the Ammonite form of the Canaanite god, Baal. Thus Solomon had introduced the worship of this fertility cult into Israel. The term abomination (shiqqutz) means a very detestable thing. In religious terms, it meant something ritually unclean and abhorrent to God.

6 And Solomon did evil in the sight of the LORD, and went not fully after the LORD, as did David his father.

Solomon did not stay true to Yahweh, the God of his father. Solomon defied God's first commandment by worshiping false deities. Unlike his father David, Solomon did not love God with his whole heart and soul. Solomon credited these foreign gods for his virility and strength, rather than looking to his own God. As king, his worship of these gods was not a private matter, but gave national approval to such forbidden practices.

7 Then did Solomon build an high place for Chemosh, the abomination of Moab, in the hill that is before Jerusalem, and for Molech, the abomination of the children of Ammon.

Moab was another son of Lot born out of his incestuous relations with his other daughter. Chemosh was the chief god of the Moabites. The precise nature of this deity is not clear, but he appears in connection with war. After all that Yahweh had done for David in battle, would Solomon dare pay homage to another god of war? Solomon went so far as to build a place of worship upon a hill near the city of Jerusalem; perhaps it was not as grand as the one he built for Yahweh, but putting such worship on a par with the God of Israel was in defiance of the covenant.

Furthermore, he built a place for Molech, the Canaanite deity that occurs in the Bible in connection with child sacrifice by fire. This is a practice that Yahweh detested.

8 And likewise did he for all his strange wives, which burnt incense and sacrificed unto their gods.

Solomon had introduced numerous foreign religious practices and gods and goddesses into Israel, a nation that was supposed to be monotheistic. Yahweh is a jealous God who will not tolerate such syncretism. Yahweh was the God of abundance and of famine, the God of fertility and of barrenness, and the God of war and of peace. There was no need for all these separate false deities. Yahweh was the only God for Israel.

9 And the LORD was angry with Solomon, because his heart was turned away from the LORD God of Israel, which had appeared unto him twice,

Solomon had two direct encounters with God. His faith was not dependent upon hearsay, or a priest, or anything that might leave room for doubt. God had blessed Solomon with wisdom in his youth, and then his kingdom thrived in adulthood as he was given specific instructions for eternal success. And yet, in his old age, Solomon forsook God and led his people into disobedience.

10 And had commanded him concerning this thing, that he should not go after other gods: but

he kept not that which the Lord commanded.

When the Lord had appeared to Solomon the second time, after the dedication of the temple, the Lord warned Solomon to remain faithful and not follow other gods, lest the promise be revoked. But Solomon failed to observe those commandments throughout his lifetime. Yes, he was obedient for a while, but he was not obedient to the end. God requires a lifetime of obedience.

11 Wherefore the LORD said unto Solomon, Forasmuch as this is done of thee, and thou hast not kept my covenant and my statutes, which I have commanded thee, I will surely rend the kingdom from thee, and I will give it to thy servant.

Since Solomon failed to uphold his part of the covenant, God could not continue to grant His blessing unto Solomon, lest He appear to be a fool in the eyes of Israel and among the foreigners. For they would wonder, what God is Yahweh, who was once jealous and now allows so many others alongside Him? Saul and David had gone to battle with the Canaanite nations in the name of Yahweh, trying to root out all such worship practices. Now it appears that this same God is willing to share the hearts of His people with those same gods, and even share the high places of worship in His capital city! If Yahweh permitted this, it would have caused his name to be diminished. Thus, the promise of the enduring kingdom was forfeited by Solomon.

God's indignation with Solomon was indicated by the statement that the kingdom would be given to Solomon's servant. The initial promise was that the kingdom would remain in David's household perpetually, i.e. would pass from father to son perpetually. But for the kingdom to pass from Solomon to a servant not only broke the bloodline of the dynasty, but would also replace it by one deemed unworthy of such an office.

12 Notwithstanding in thy days I will not do it for David thy father's sake: but I will rend it out of the hand of thy son.

The kingdom would not be stripped from Solomon, because that would have made void the promise that God had made with David, his faithful servant. No, Solomon's actions would be counted against his own son. Just as Saul's disobedience caused God to raise up a new king from a different family line, so would a new king be sought because of Solomon's disobedience.

13 Howbeit I will not rend away all the kingdom; but will give one tribe to thy son . . .

Again, in deference to the fulfillment of the promise to David, Yahweh would allow one of the twelve tribes to be ruled over by Solomon's son. So the kingdom would be divided into the northern tribes of Israel (10), the southern tribe of Judah, and the lost tribe.

DAILY BIBLE READINGS

M: Acts of Solomon
1 Kings 9:10-25
T: Solomon's Idolatry
1 Kings 11:1-8
W: God's Judgment on Solomon
1 Kings 11:9-13
T: The Wrath of God
Nahum 1:2-8
F: Adversaries of Solomon
1 Kings 11:14-25
S: Jereboam's Rebellion Against Solomon
1 Kings 11:26-37
S: A Conditional Promise and Solomon's Death
1 Kings 11:38-43

INTRODUCTION TO DECEMBER 2000 QUARTER

Luke gives the world a well-organized narrative of the birth, ministry, death, and resurrection of Jesus. The thrust of the Gospel of Luke is fully evangelistic. To Luke, Jesus is God's salvation to all humanity. God's purpose in history was accomplished through the death and resurrection of the Christ. In this course, primary emphasis is given to passages that are distinctive to Luke. The early church fathers noted the emphases common to both Paul and Luke. Each emphasized the universality of salvation. Even Luke's parables focused on the response of individuals to God's grace, while Matthew's parables concerned the kingdom. Luke, like Paul, spoke often of faith, of repentance, of mercy, and of forgiveness.

Irenaeus held that Luke, Paul's companion, "put down in a book the Gospel preached by him," and Origen called Luke "the Gospel commended by Paul." If Mark was the "interpreter" of Peter, Tertullian wrote, Luke was the "illuminator" of the Apostle Paul. Augustine, saw the book as a clear articulation of the mind of God. It has always been argued that Luke was a Gentile but there is no evidence in the Gospel to show that he was a Gentile. We do know that he was Hellenistic, that is one educated in Greek thought and philosophy. But there is no doubt that Luke, like Paul's ministry, felt called to minister to the Gentiles, and particularly to the better educated Hellenists. In some of the most beautiful literary Greek language found in any ancient writing, Luke tells the story of Jesus, a true human being who is the Son of God. It is believed that Luke was a medical doctor probably from the city of Antioch where followers of Jesus were first called Christians. Luke may have been a member during the time Barnabas and Paul anointed disciples for missionary work. Luke's gospel displays linguistic elegance and finesse approximated only by the writers of the New Testament. Luke uses Greek words that does not appear anywhere else in the New Testament. Many of the stories which we find in Luke's gospel are not found in Matthew, Mark, or John. Luke's work calls us to acknowledge Jesus and His teaching. For your

information you may want to know that there are 15 parables found only in Luke and not in the other gospels. Luke's gospel is indeed Good News for the poor, the marginalized, and all who will come.

The Quarter at-a-Glance

GOOD NEWS OF JESUS: (The Gospel of Luke)

UNIT 1. A SAVIOUR IS BORN

Focus on John the Baptist and Mary and their roles in the fulfillment of God's promises to the Hebrew people and the world. Before Jesus was born and at His birth, He was recognized as a miracle of God's love. Form the beginning, Jesus was destined for the redemption of all humanity. The unit closes with Jesus being brought to the temple where He was presented to God.

LESSON 1: December 3
Preparing the Way
Luke 3:2-3, 7-18

The Biblical content of this lesson emphasizes the message of John the Baptist. The text tells us that after John the Baptizer received a message from God, he called the people to repent and be baptized for the forgiveness of their sins (vv. 2-3). We also read that John warned his hearers about the coming judgment and encouraged them to repent (vv. 7-8). In John's message we hear a warning not to trust in our line of descent. The people of Israel are warned not to trust mainly in the fact that they are descendants of Abraham; because God would judge their lives by the quality of their deeds, not by their ethnic heritage (vv. 8-9). As we study the text we shall see John's response to the crowd. When the crowds responding to John's message asked what they should do, he declared that they should share with the needy and deal honestly and justly with others (vv. 10-14). This text does not tell us of John's message but it give us insight into the people. The people were filled with expectation and asked if John might be the Messiah (v. 15). In this text John directs their expectation away from himself to someone greater. John's message to them was to contrast his baptism by water with the baptism of the Messiah Who was coming to baptize with the Holy Spirit and fire (vv. 16-17).

In this lesson the life concerns focus on the spiritual and emotional problems we encounter when we are faced with rapid change in society. The lesson directs us to the fact that in such times human beings seek connection with something that is permanent, established, and trustworthy. Though in the present we may be living in trouble times, this lesson calls us to look to the future with great optimism rather than apprehension, because like these people we expect the coming of the Messiah. This lesson also warns us against the tendency to live for the moment and failure to consider any accountability beyond the present. We are also warned from the words of John the Baptist of our tendency to display sensitivity to hypocrisy and self-righteousness in others and yet remain blinded to our own sickness.

LESSON 2: December 10
Responding to God
Luke 1:26-38

The biblical text for this lesson deals with the narrative of how God sent the angel Gabriel to Nazareth to visit Mary, a virgin who was engaged to Joseph, a descendent of David (vv. 26-27). We read how naturally Mary was very perplexed by the greeting of the angel and the statement that she was favored by God (vv. 28-29). The text also states that the angel told Mary not to be frightened for she was favored by God and would become pregnant with a Son whom she would name Jesus (vv. 30-31). In this text the angel of the Lord promised Mary that her son would be called "The Son of the Most High" and that God would make Him ruler over the house of Jacob forever (vv. 32-33). When Mary asked how she, a virgin, would become a mother of the promised King, the angel explained that she would conceive the child by the Holy Spirit (vv. 34-35). After the angel told Mary the impossible news that her relative Elizabeth was pregnant through the power of God, Mary accepted the special honor

and responsibility of becoming the mother of the Messiah (vv. 36-38).

The topic of this lesson is "Responding to God." Life in Christ is a life of obedience. We are often perplexed by unusual and unexpected experiences and happenings. In many cases our response to the unexplainable is fear and apprehension. Thus we find that deep inside we long for a future when problems and troubles will disappear. In our word today as in the word of Mary we struggle with what cannot be explained scientifically or rationally. But this lesson calls us to believe in the miraculous and that God can do anything. Like Mary we are being called within the body of this lesson to readily accept the challenge of Divine favor and resulting assignments that come with such blessings.

LESSON 3: December 17
Praising God
Luke 1:39-55

The Biblical text from which today's lesson is taken narrates Mary's visit to her relative Elizabeth, who lived in a town in the hill country (vv. 39-40). We hear that when Mary greeted Elizabeth, the child in Elizabeth's womb leaped (vv. 41-44). Here in this text we also see the Holy Spirit at work. We see within the text how filled with the Holy Spirit, Elizabeth responded by exclaiming that Mary was blessed among women and that the child she carried in her womb was like-wise blessed (vv. 41-45). This encounter results in Mary's praise and magnification of the God who looks with favor on the lowly (vv. 46-49). In Mary's praise we see how Mary praised God for what He has done in the life of Israel to establish justice, show mercy, and impart blessing (vv. 50-53). Mary acknowledged that the Lord had kept the promise to Abraham by sending the Messiah (vv. 54-55).

The topic for today's lesson is "Praising God." This lesson speaks of human response in a time of anticipation. Anxiety is a common response in times such as this. But in such times this lesson calls us to understand God's promises and know that God intends to keep them. In times of anxious anticipation we can find reasons for gratitude even in the most difficult circumstances. Hopefully through this lesson we can appreciate and celebrate the benefits we receive from families and heritage. For they are a sign of God's faithfulness.

Instead of being skeptical about things that lie outside our experience, this lesson calls us to trust in the truthfulness of things that God has promised, even though they may seem unreasonable to them.

LESSON 4: December 24
A Saviour is Born
Luke 2:4-20

The Biblical text for today's lesson contains several emphases. First it speaks to the fact that Joseph and Mary went from Nazareth to Bethlehem to be registered (vv. 4-5). It also tells us what happened during that journey. While in Bethlehem, Mary gave birth to a Son, whom she laid in a manger because there was no place for them in the inn (vv. 6-7). We also read of heaven's response. We are told that an angel appeared to the shepherds and told them that the Messiah had been born in Bethlehem (vv. 8-12). The text also tells us that a multitude of the heavenly hosts also appeared and praised God (vv. 13-14). We also read of the earthly response to this blessed event. First we see the response of the shepherds they went to Bethlehem; found Joseph, Mary, and the Baby; and reported what the angel had told them (vv. 15-18). We also see the parental response: Mary treasured and reflected on the words of God's fulfilled promise, and the shepherds spread the news of all they had been told (vv. 19-20).

The topic for this lesson is "A Saviour Is Born." As in the days of Mary and Joseph many of us today are frustrated by government restrictions, regulations, and requirements. As in those days, too, the birth of a child is a significant family experience that contains both anxiety and hope, apprehension as well as joyous anticipation. The birth of our Lord embodied all of these emotions for the people of Israel. As we work daily may we have significant religious encounters through our work as the shepherds did on the day of the Lord's birth. The birth of Christ answers our longing for peace. Hopefully this lesson will lead you into personal reflection as a way to gain perspective on God's will for your lives, to plan for the future, and to evaluate values, priorities, and meaning.

LESSON 5: December 31
Presented in the Temple
Luke 2:25-38

The Biblical content of this lesson is based on the text concerning the representation of Jesus in the temple. Here find Mary and Joseph as they follow the law of Moses. They took Jesus to the temple in Jerusalem to present him to the Lord (vv. 22-24). We also see the state of personal piety in the house of Israel. The text tells us that there was a righteous and devout man named Simeon who had been told by the Holy Spirit that he would see the Messiah before his death (vv. 25-26) guided by the Spirit, Simeon went to the temple where he took the child Jesus in his arms and praised God for this Child who would bring God's salvation to all people (27-32). When Jesus' parents expressed amazement at what was being said about Him, Simeon told Mary that Jesus' destiny would include conflict and pain (vv. 33-35). The text also points us to another devout Israelite, Anna, a devout and aged prophetess who worshiped in the temple night and day. She praised God and spoke of the Child as the fulfillment of Israel's hope for redemption (vv. 36-38).

The topic of this lesson is "Presenting in the Temple." The lesson teaches us not to discount rituals. Rituals can play an important part in the religious experience of many adults and their families. This lesson, through the example of Jesus calls us to give affirmation to children which enhances their self-esteem and engenders hope for their future. As with Simeon and Anna may we demonstrate the patience required to see long-term goals fulfilled. Here we see that not only can children bring happiness to their parents, they also can bring great sorrow. May we learn to discern the will of God and to maintain our devotion until the Messiah comes.

UNIT 2. MISSION AND MINISTRY

Unit 2 covers the major portion of the gospel of Luke. At Nazareth, Jesus made public His calling to introduce the Kingdom of God. On several occasions, Jesus spoke to his disciples and would-be followers of the cost of discipleship. He told a parable about being lost and found; in another parable He contrasted earthly wealth and the riches of God's kingdom.

LESSON 6: January 7
Jesus in Nazareth
Luke 4:16-26, 28-30

The Biblical text for today's lesson deals with one of Jesus' visits to the temple. We read that Jesus went to the synagogue in Nazareth on the Sabbath day as was His custom (v. 16). When Jesus read the Scripture, He read Isaiah's prophecy of the Messiah's mission (vv. 17-19). Jesus then told the people that this Scripture had been fulfilled that day in their hearing (vv. 20-21). After speaking well of Jesus, the listeners asked if He were the son of Joseph, a local carpenter. Jesus responded that no prophet is accepted in his home town (vv. 22-24). Jesus angered by the people pointing to examples from Israel's history of God's sending prophets to those outside the nation (vv. 25-26, 28). As a result of this encounter we read that the people tried to kill Jesus, but He passed through the midst of them and went on His way (vv. 29-30).

This lesson teaches us how to discover our mission in life. One of life's major concerns is the experience of rejection. Another is that of dealing with change. Many adults cannot accept that others have changed. This refusal to accept the change wrought by God in the life of another may derive from the simple fact that many of us tend to have low expectations for those with whom we are familiar. Often, those with this low expectation of others are surprised when they accomplish great things. This lesson also examines our tendency to be happy as long as we are told what we want to hear. The final point of this lesson is to show that Jesus knew His mission. We are then called in this lesson to recognize that God has a personal mission in life for us.

LESSON 7: January 14
The Cost of Discipleship
Luke 9:57-62; 14:25-33

The Biblical content for this lesson is taken from the text that deals with the definition of discipleship. On the way to Jerusalem, Jesus defined the cost of discipleship in response to several people who indicated an interest in following Him. A person offered to follow Jesus wherever He went, and Jesus responded that He had nowhere to lay His head (vv. 57-58). Jesus told other people that in order to follow Him, they must make a radical commitment to the kingdom of God (vv. 59-62; 14:25-26) Jesus said that you cannot be His disciple without accepting the cost (v. 27). He used two parables to illustrate the importance of counting the cost of being His disciple (vv. 28-32). Jesus taught that following Him means giving up everything (v. 33).

The topic for this lesson is "The Cost of Discipleship." It is true that most of us want to have the comfort of a home. Our familial relationships are important and they force us to struggle with priorities. When God is left out of the equation these priorities will have to be reconsidered. This lesson teaches us that discipleship involves re-prioritization in light of the call of God. It also teaches us that becoming disciples result in difficulties that will require our perseverance. Hopefully as you study this lesson you will examine the many commitments that may distract you from Divine priorities. Finally, as you study this lesson you will gain insight into the meaning of sacrifice for the cause of Christ.

LESSON 8: January 21
Lost and Found
Luke 15:1-22, 11-24

In the text for today's lesson we see Jesus being criticized for welcoming and eating with tax collectors and sinners (vv. 1-2) In response to the criticism , Jesus told a parable about a father whose younger son demanded and received the share of his father's property that would belong to him (vv. 11-12). In this story Jesus tells us how the younger son realized how foolish he had been and decided to return home to ask his father to treat him as a hired hand (vv. 15-20) Instead of treating the son as he requested, the father saw the son from a distance, ran to meet him, rejoiced over his return, and welcomed him back as his son (vv. 20-22). In the final part of the narrative we are led to a feast planned by the father to celebrate his lost son who was now found (vv. 23-24).

"Lost and Found" is the topic of today's lesson. It calls us to examine the fact that at some points in our lives we have felt lost. We then go on to try new adventures which leads us to the experiential negativity which is often the consequence of wrong decisions. But as we find in this lesson God wants to restore us. For each one of us when restoration occurs we need to celebrate. It is natural to celebrate when relationships are restored. But in this lesson we also deal with the fact that some of us find it hard to forgive and thus we push back the possibility of restoration. While it is true that many of us are reluctant to admit our mistakes, this lesson teaches us to admit our shortcomings and to turn to the one who is able to restore us to fellowship, even Jesus Christ.

LESSON 9: January 28
Threat of Riches
Luke 16:1-13

The parable of the wise steward is well known to Bible students. It raises questions for the serious Bible student. This is the text that grounds our lesson for today. Jesus told a parable of a rich man who decided to fire his dishonest manager (vv. 1-2). The manager reduced the debts of those who owed his master so they would take care of him (vv. 3-7). The steward's master commended his shrewdness in preparation for the future (v. 8). Jesus commented that His disciples could learn from the manager's shrewdness in preparing for their futures (v. 9). Jesus said that if the disciples could not be trusted with the things of this world, they could not be trusted with true riches (vv. 10-12). In concluding the parable Jesus warned that nobody can serve God and wealth (v. 13).

Today's topic is "Threat of Riches." The future is a serious life concern to both adults and youth. One of the concerns we have of the future is how to manage money. The truth is that some of us have mismanaged money given to us by God. For some of us self-indulgence and the lack of discipline to stay on track with our goals has resulted in artificial poverty. Instead of giving as we ought we struggle with stewardship. As with the man in the text many of us fear the possibility of unemployment. Some see wealth and financial security as primary sources of the meaning of life.

UNIT 3. CROSS AND RESURRECTION

Unit 3 includes Jesus' foretelling of His death and resurrection. It also describes Jesus' encounter with Zacchaeus, which indicated the personal nature of God's salvation. With his disciples, He celebrated Passover as One determined to be the servant of all. Unjustly condemned to crucifixion, Jesus showed concern for two criminals—as all three of them faced death. Raised to new life, Jesus appeared to His disciples and empowered them to be his witnesses to all nations.

LESSON 10: February 4
Going to Jerusalem
Luke 18:31-34; 19:1-10

In this text Jesus explained that the journey to Jerusalem was a fulfillment of prophecy (v. 31) Jesus described the trials and death he had to face, but the hearers did not understand His meaning (vv. 32-34). En route to Jerusalem, Jesus passed through Jericho where He encountered a tax collector, Zacchaeus, who climbed a tree to see Jesus (vv. 1-4). The crowd grumbled when Jesus asked Zacchaeus for a personal visit at his house (vv. 5-7). When Zacchaeus repented and promised to repair the damage he had caused others, Jesus reclaimed him and proclaimed salvation for him and his house (vv. 8-9). Jesus said that the Son of Man came to seek and save the lost (v. 10).

How can we reclaim the lost? This chapter is a lesson on reclaiming the lost. Life concerns of this lesson deal with the thought that many of us experience prejudice because of our roles in life. It also points to the fact that personal history and culture are significant influences in the lives of adults. The lesson also deals with the experience of guilt which some of us feel when we are made aware of our wrong-doing. The lesson also points us to the fact that repentance and forgiveness usually results in the experience of much joy. This lesson also calls us to learn to forgive ourselves. Hopefully as you study, you will move to repentance. If you have already moved to repentance, prayerfully others will experience Love and acceptance from you and move to repentance for their sins.

LESSON 11: February 11
One Who Serves
Luke 22:14-30

In this text, Jesus told the disciples how eagerly He wanted to observe the Passover with them prior to His suffering (vv. 14-16). At the Passover meal, Jesus gave His disciples bread and wine and told them that the bread and wine were His body and the new covenant sealed in His blood (vv. 17-20). Jesus instructed his disciples to partake of the meal in remembrance of him (v. 19). Jesus told the disciples that one of them sitting at the table were going to betray him (vv. 21-23). When a dispute arose among the disciples about who was to be regarded as the greatest, Jesus told them that the leader must become like one who serves (vv. 24-27) Jesus affirmed His disciples for their support and assigned them present and future rewards in the kingdom (vv. 28-30).

This lesson points us to Jesus' way of greatness. One of life's concern has to do with how we measure ourselves. This text tells us that sharing together is often spiritually rewarding for many and can be one of the ways in which true greatness may be measured. Sharing with the people of God can help us gain new insights and build strong bonds. Knowing that many of us are confused about the way to achieve true greatness, Jesus tells us that greatness comes from serving. It is true that some people find serving others highly rewarding. But also we must remember as we teach this lesson that some people whose lives have been demeaned by being servants do not find the image of service appealing. Nonetheless, we must all serve someone if we seek to be great in the kingdom of God.

LESSON 12: February 18
Dying on a Cross
Luke 23:33-49

Biblical textual emphasis is taken from the story of the crucifixion of the Lord. In the text we learn that Jesus was crucified between two criminals (v. 33). We watch Him as He prayed for the forgiveness of those who crucified Him (v. 34). The text also shows us that as Jesus died, some soldiers mocked Him and gambled for His clothing, some leaders scoffed at Him, and one of the criminals taunted Him (vv. 34-39). When the other criminal responded that Jesus was innocent and pleaded for mercy, Jesus assured him that he would be with Him in paradise (vv. 40-43). As Jesus died, He asked the Father to receive his spirit; a centurion then praised God and declared that Jesus was an innocent man (vv. 44-47). The women and all who saw Jesus die were deeply affected (vv. 48-49).

This lesson answers the question how does one fulfill one's mission in life. The title "Dying on a Cross" speaks to the life concerns for accomplishing something worthwhile that is part of all of us. Death can be a fearful and dreaded event, espe-

cially if one does not feel that they have accomplished what they set out to accomplish. The death of Jesus let's us know that we may not be ready for death but we may prepare for death by living in the will of God. The death of Jesus is the supreme act of self-giving on the part of the Lord. His death answers our search for the meaning of life. Jesus laid down His life for our salvation. Though His suffering and death were not necessary for Himself, it was necessary for our lives. Hopefully through this lesson those of us who know the Lord will rejoice that He was willing to give His life for us. Those who do not know Him will reach out and receive His sacrifice for their own salvation.

LESSON 13: February 25
Witnesses to the Resurrection
Luke 24:33-49

In this text the disciples related to one another their first-hand encounters with the risen Saviour (vv. 33-35). When Jesus appeared in their midst, the disciples were afraid because they thought He was a ghost (vv. 36-37). Calming their fears and doubts, Jesus invited the disciples to touch Him; and He ate first to prove His real human form (vv. 38-43). Jesus opened the believers' minds to understand the prophecies regarding His death and resurrection (vv. 44-45). Interpreting the Scripture to them concerning Himself, Jesus commanded the disciples to witness for Him in all nations (vv. 46-48). Jesus instructed them to stay in the city, and He would send them the gift of the Holy Spirit which the Father had promised (v. 49).

"Witnesses to the Resurrection" that is what this lesson is meant to communicate. In a words where many are skeptical of experiences that do not seem to have a logical, rational explanation, we are called to bear witness to the reality of faith based on the God becoming a human being, dying, resurrecting, ascending, and coming again from the heavens. But the truth is that many people's lives are affected dramatically by meaningful spiritual experiences each day. This lesson also shows us that we can influence others by building relationships of trust. Hopefully as you study this lesson you will feel led to share with others experiences that have changed your life.

THE GOAL OF CHRISTIAN EDUCATION

Rev. Donald Bean Jr., B.S., M. Div.

What is the goal of Christian Education? The answer to this question has eluded the minds of scholars, Christian educators, and lay persons for many years. Yet, defining the goal or goals of Christian Education is critical for the Church community and the wider community so that those gifted and called to function in this area of ministry will do so with a strong sense of boundaries, direction, and purpose. Defining the goal of Christian Education communicates clearly and informs indisputably the expectations for all participants in the process of Christian Education.

What is the goal of Christian Education? The answer is as complex and convoluted as the simplicity of the question. Before proceeding with haste to answer, consider the question itself for a moment. The question posed is not the same as 'what is the task of Christian Education?' for a task and a goal are completely different. According to *Webster's New World Dictionary*, a task is "a piece of work assigned to an individual" and a goal is "an object or an end that one strives to attain." The task is a means to an end. The goal is the end accomplished by various means. Said another way, there is an end or terminal result in Christian Education. What is it? There is an outcome or emerging product in Christian Education. What is it?

Let us explore this question further. Primarily, the question suggests that a singular goal of Christian Education exists. Is there more than one goal for Christian Education? If so, what are the other possibilities or considerations? Secondarily, the question specifically and judiciously deliberates education that is Christian. This differentiation glaringly reveals that non-Christian or secular educational processes do exist! Since this is true, how then do we distinguish "Christian Education" from secular education? If Christian Education processes are both distinct and different from non-Christian processes, are the methods utilized in both interchangeable? Are secular educational processes of value in Christian environments? Conversely, are Christian educational processes of value in secular environments? Are then the goals of Christian Education different from secular or non-Christian education? All of these questions strongly point us to one summary question—*What is the goal to Christian Education?*

The Apostle Paul was a mastermind of the goal concept. Paul said, writing to the Church at Philippi, "but this one thing I do . . . I press toward the mark for the prize of the high calling of God in Christ Jesus," (from Philippians 3:13-14). The Apostle Paul was not overly concerned about fulfilling multitudinous goals. He focused on one goal. Just as Paul defined his goal, so too must the Church define her goal for Christian Education so that those called and gifted to serve in this capacity will know what is expected. Christian Education must have a terminal goal in order to be effective. Often, in the game of chess, a player must begin at the end of the board and move backwards in order to move forward. Using this strategy, let us examine the terminal or end goal of Christian Education? Another Pauline concept found in Ephesians 4:11-16 depicts this end. The Apostle Paul says here, "that he gave some, apostles, and some, prophets; and some, evangelists; and some, pastors and teachers; for the perfecting of the saints, for the work of the ministry, for the edifying of the body of Christ: until we all come in the unity of the faith, and of the knowledge of the Son of God, unto a perfect man, unto the measure of the stature of the fullness of Christ . . . ." These few verses depict the goal of Christian Education.

Described in one word, this author ascertains that the goal of Christian Education is discipleship! Discipleship is a process of spiritual formation where believers become effective followers of Christ, transformed, and nurtured into the image of Christ. Discipleship is more than cognitive training. Discipleship does not entail simply the transmission of religious information because one can be religious without being Christian, (i.e. Hindu, Buddhist, Islamic, even Satanism). Again, one can be religious and not Christian. Rather, discipleship is character formation. Discipleship is the process of spiritual formation whereby we help believers in Christ become effective followers of Christ. Christian Discipleship is a process of spiritual formation designed to help believers in Christ become transformed into the image of Christ. The end goal of the discipleship process is that the believer achieve Ephesians 4:13 which says, "until we all come in the unity of the faith, and of the knowledge of the Son of God, into a perfect man, unto the measure of the stature of the fullness of Christ." The NIV translation helps us understand the four distinct segments of this verse:

1. Until we all reach unity in the faith (this represents understanding or why)

2. Until we all reach knowledge of the Son of God (this represents knowledge or what)

3. Until we all become mature (this represents attitude or who)

4. Until we attain to the whole measure of the fullness of Christ (this represents skill or how)

Now we have a personified image of the goal of Christian Education. We have identified Ephesians 4:13 as the "mark of the prize of the high calling of God." Working backwards fur-

ther, we must ask another question, why? Why choose discipleship as the goal of Christian Education? There certainly could be other goals.

The foundation for discipleship as the goal of Christian Education rests confidently and solely upon the words that Jesus issued to the disciples prior to His ascension in the great commission found in Matthew 28:18-20 which says, "Therefore go and make disciples of all nations, baptizing in the name of the Father and of the Son and of the Holy Spirit, and teaching them to obey everything I have commanded you. And surely I am with you always, to the very end of the age" (NIV translation). The words of Christ give us great peace and solace, but they also give us direction and instruction. This command of Christ is what drives us to make disciples. The command to make disciples is the task to be filled by the individuals; discipleship is the goal or object that we strive to attain. In this case the task of making disciples is a means to an end. The goal of discipleship is accomplished by various means of making disciples.

What has happened to making disciples in the Church? The Church has done a premiere job with teaching, preaching, and worship. Yet, various questions still remain about the effectiveness and practical relevance of its work. How have we done in the process of making disciples? The challenge for Christian Education in the Church in the 21st century is not space, land, worship, or even Church growth. The challenge is attaining and sustaining quality growth through discipleship. How will we help believers achieve practical personal growth and maturity? How will Church provide a strong Christian foundation and doctrinal orientation? How will we create Christian identity and foster personal and corporate worship? How will we promote service in the Body of Christ? How will the Church provide practical training for persons who function in youth, Christian Education, music, counseling, administration, lay leadership, and other diaconal ministries? The answer is found in the goal of Christian Education—Discipleship!

POINT OF VIEW

The African Roots of Christianity

Melvin E. Banks, Litt.D.
A. Okechukwu Ogbonnaya, Ph.D.

Africa's contribution to Christianity has been ignored at worst and at best marginalized. No longer can we ignore the contribution of Africans to the development of Christian thought. Many of our ideas in the Christian faith have African roots. For example, revered fathers of the church such as Tertulliam, Origen, Anthony, Anthanasius, and Augustine were African. Such saintly mothers of the faith as Perpertua, Felicitas and Augustine's mother, Monica, were African women who contributed to the depth of Christian thought. So it is fitting to speak of African roots and to examine Christian thought from an African perspective.

When we speak of African roots we are defining Africa not merely as the area from the River of Africa southward. Rather we refer to the land which extends from South Africa into Mesopotamia—present day Iraq and Iran. The tendency to isolate Mesopotamia as though it were not a part of Africa is of recent origin. Ancient peoples recognized the cultural and geographical "connectedness" of these peoples.

The location of the Garden of Eden is today more likely identified with East Africa along the Nile River because the oldest remains of human life have been found in the area near Tanzania. In the past Mesopotamia was the best choice because of the two identifiable rivers mentioned in Genesis 2, the Hiddekel and Euphrates Rivers.

It is now believed that humankind migrated from East Africa northward along the Nile into the area known as Mesopotamia, then further north, east, and west. This migration from Africa into Mesopotamia is bolstered by the findings of Sir Henry Rawlinson, a noted Assyriologist. He concluded that the Sumerian culture, the earliest to exist in Mesopotamia, was brought to the area by people who came from Africa. His conclusion confirms the biblical indication that Cush, whose name means "black," was the father of Nimrod. Nimrod built Asshur which is in Mesopotamia. It is the conclusion of many scholars that the Hamitic and Semitic people of this area were people of color. This conclusions is based upon geography, anthropology, and archeology.

From this Land of the Chaldeans (Mesopotamia) Abraham departed around 2,000 B.C. and migrated into the land of Canaan (Genesis 12:5). When he arrived in this land he lived among other descendants of Ham through Canaan: the Sidonians, Hittites, Jebusites, Amorites, Girgasites, Hivites, Arkites, Sinites, Arvadites, Zemarites, and Hamathites (Genesis 10:15-18). The name "Ham" means "black" or "swarthy." It follows that the Canaanites, Ham's children, were people of color.

Abraham fathered Isaac, Isaac fathered Jacob and Esau, Jacob fathered 12 sons who migrated to Egypt around 1800 B.C. When they arrived in Egypt they lived among people who were black. The name "Egypt" is a Greek word which means "black." Europeans have attempted to show that the name refers only to the black soil found in the area. Other scholars have shown that the name referred to the people as well as the soil. Prior to the arrival of Greeks into that area around 332 B.C., the people called themselves "Kemet."

While in Egypt, the Israelites learned much from the people among whom they lived for some 400 years. They absorbed Egyptian customs and culture, as well as learned and benefited from Egyptian education and skills. When they left the country a "mixed multitude" went with them. Bishop Alfred Dunston in his seminal work, *The Black Man in the Old Testament and Its World*, has demonstrated that this "mixed multitude" had to have been Egyptians who left with the Israelites.

When they arrived back into the land of Canaan the people of color were still there. God empowered the Israelites to break the backs of the Canaanites militarily, but they did not wipe them out. Instead they lived among, intermarried with them, and worshiped their idols (See Judges 1–3; Ezra 9).

The presence of Europeans in Egypt and Palestine did not occur until Alexander invaded Egypt in 332 B.C. When this conqueror arrived in Egypt, he was so impressed with the knowledge of Egyptians that he built the city of Alexandria where housed untold thousands of books and scrolls. African scholars have demonstrated that much of the knowledge which Greeks disseminated to the rest of the world as though it were their own, was in fact, learned from ancient Egyptians. The Romans conquered the Mediterranean world during the first century B.C. and remained there until the time of Christ. They maintained military control of the Egyptian/Mesopotamia corridor, but the complexion of the bulk of the people did not change significantly.

As the Gospel traveled out from Jerusalem, Judea, Samaria, were many Jews of black hues dwelt, and the utmost parts of the earth (Acts 1:8), it reached into Africa through African Jews. Those gathered at Jerusalem for Pentecost when the Holy Spirit arrived were from many countries with known African populations, including Medes, Mesopotamia, Egypt, Libya, and Cyrene.

The Ethiopian eunuch (Acts 8) was the first known recorded African to embrace the faith although eunuchs could not be proselytes, there were many Jews who were eunuchs. The church at Antioch embraced mixed leadership including Simeon known as "the Black Man" (Niger). See Acts 13:1. As the Gospel reach Asia and Europe it found there Africans who had migrated into these areas. One scholarly suggestion is that the Gospel of Mark was written for the believers who lived in Cyrene where the population was Black Jewish people.

This discussion of the presence of Africans in the biblical records is not intended to elevate Blacks above the presence of other racial groups. Indeed, in God's economy all primary racial groups have had a part in his plan to communicate the Gospel to the entire world. The purpose is to show that Blacks have been included, not excluded as many scholars and Bible commentators have attempted to do.

GOOD NEWS OF JESUS

Georgia Kurko, Ph.D.

If you were the "most excellent Theophilus" to whom the writer of this letter addressed his Gospel, you would have most likely appreciated the first four verses of the Book of Luke. As this Gospel begins with a classic Greek formulaic introduction that explains the writer's procedure for gathering information and his intended purpose in writing, Theophilus could begin reading at once. The recipient knew, as does the modern reader, the end of the story and would probably accept the classification of this letter as "good news." To a reader unfamiliar with Luke's ending—or to one who stops reading after Jesus' crucifixion—titling this book "good news" would appear inappropriate. After all, the main character is put to death in the twenty-third chapter.

To stop reading this Gospel at that point would surely cause the reader to campaign for a new theme for this book—perhaps "bad news" or "sad news." But thanks be to God! The story continues in chapter twenty-four, with an ending that details Jesus' resurrection and which makes even the classification "good news" seem inadequate in describing this turn of events.

"Good news" is perhaps an understatement. "Good news" may accurately describe the uncomplicated content of a report from the laboratory personnel who have completed testing one's blood; "good news" may be assigned to a portion of the daily newspaper that details a report of how an ordinary citizen went to extraordinary means to help a neighbor escape danger. But does "good news" accurately describe the outcome of God's gift to humankind in sending His Son to earth on a mission involving that Son's arrest, trial, and crucifixion? It was a mission so essential to establishing the foundation upon which Christians base their salvation? Perhaps the Gospel message should be renamed "best news!"

Whether "good news" or "best news," the effect upon the person who has access to such news flash-es is usually significant. Such data is not generally kept to oneself. The very nature of the Christian community is that, unlike the world's emphasis on negativity, believers share what God has done, is doing, and has promised to do in the future among themselves and with unbelievers. Such a testimonial response to "good news" is the norm for Christians. The author of the Gospel of Luke is reacting in typical Christian fashion by communicating the content of the account to his audience, Theophilus.

Who is that author? To an unbeliever or to a skeptic, questions about Luke's authorship cannot be satisfactorily answered. Nowhere within the verses of the book does the author's name appear. While most scholars believe that the author, Luke, was a Gentile and a physician, a minority wrestle with issues relating to Luke's identity. Some question whether Theophilus was an individual (the name means "one who loves God") or a term used to refer to a group of people who loved God. Still others analyze Luke in comparison to the other synoptic Gospels and struggle with identification of sources which may have been used by all as they wrote their accounts, reducing the miracle of inspiration to a more mechanical process.

These issues and many others would be of utmost importance had this letter been received in today's postal delivery or discovered in the hope chest of someone's great-great-great-grandmother. Respectable scholarship demands careful attention to a writer's background, credentials, and motive. Biographies of celebrities exist in abundance in today's world and authors' credibility and level of eyewitness interaction seem to be closely related. Christians who accept the Scriptures as the inspired and infallible Word of God, however, are free to relegate such issues to a secondary level of inquiry and to focus on the content and message of the Gospel of Luke. Luke's account, because of its inclusion in the Bible, is of course deemed credible and authentic.

What is Luke's message? William Barclay, accepting the traditional viewpoint that Luke, a Gentile physician, authored the book, introducing his commentary on the Gospel by writing, "It has been said that a minister sees men at their best; a lawyer sees men at their worst; and a doctor sees men as they are. Luke saw men and loved them all."[1] Surely, a central tenet of the "best news" is that Jesus came to offer salvation to all, both Jew and Gentile. Luke's Gospel emphasizes the universality of salvation, as well as historicity, prayer, praise, and the special role women played in Jesus' life and ministry[2] (xiv-xvii).

Luke's careful investigation and his orderly account of the life of Jesus Christ from His birth through His ascension was intended to provide Theophilus with a reinforcement of the things he had been taught. This describes the Gospel's value to the Christian who has been a believer for many years. To a new believer, this Gospel account can work in reverse, laying a foundation upon which further reading and study can be built. No matter what their background, the Book of Luke gives readers a biography of Jesus Christ, God's Son, Who offers salvation to all. What news could be better?

As you read through the chapters of Luke, perhaps you can record the verses that convey "good news." The eighty verses of chapter 1 contain plenty of facts that should show up on your list: the author has written an orderly account of Jesus' life, a barren wife gives birth to one who will serve as a prophet as he prepares the way for the Lord, an angel announces that God's Son is to be born, a man struck dumb for his unbelief gets his voice back and uses it to praise God and to prophesy, and so on and so on. Your list will be a long one; through its compilation you will begin to see that Luke's message is one of hope and awe, and that even the "sad" and "bad" news of Jesus' arrest, trial and crucifixion are essential parts of the "good" and "best" news of His resurrection and ascension. Jesus' biography not only contains "good news" but it is "good news!"

When your list of "good news" flashes is complete, meditate upon this: why did God provide for us not one, not two, not three, but four Gospels? Why four books in a library of sixty-six that provide basic information about the incarnation of the Trinity? Duplication? Repetition? Redundancy? Not at all! Our Heavenly Father has provided four different accounts, four different Gospels. As Barclay wrote,

"Mark is the simplest and the most straightforward of the Gospels. It has been well said that its characteristic is realism . . . Matthew was a Jew writing for Jews and he saw in Jesus the Messiah . . . the One whom all the prophets had predicted . . . John is the theological gospel . . . the gospel where the philosopher can find themes to think about for a lifetime and to solve only in eternity . . . Luke saw in Jesus the sacrifice for all the world. In Luke above all the barriers are broken down and Jesus is for Jew and Gentile, saint and sinner alike. He is the Savior of the world"[3] (xiv).

Taken together, as a unit, the Gospels provide a complete account of Jesus' earthly life, a life poured out and spent upon humanity, a life synonymous with "good news" for all people. And so one reads, meditates upon, and digests Luke's Gospel, a process that consumes a few hours, a few years, one's entire lifetime. In the midst of this process, may we be committed now and in the future to the careful investigation of Jesus' life that Luke conducted, to the recording of an orderly account of Jesus' life within our hearts and minds, and to the conveying of that account to those around us like Theophilus in order that the things we have been learned may be shared with others. This final step—one that ends only when our earthly existence ends—is the use to which the "good news," the "best news," is to be put. The Gospel is to be shared. The author of Luke shared with Theophilus, and, in so doing, shared with us.

Do Christians have the right to share the Gospel? Should our unique viewpoints regarding salvation and the authority of Jesus Christ be presented to those who hold other beliefs? In Unit 3, as the latter part of the Gospel of Luke is studied, the focus will be on Jesus' ascension and on the work of the Holy Spirit to empower the disciples to bear witness to His suffering, death, and resurrection and to preach repentance and forgiveness in His name to all nations. As modern-day disciples, we are not only given the right to share the Gospel but the responsibility—and the privilege—to do so. May we continue to pass along the Gospel, using the content of the Book of Luke as the basis for our sharing, in Jesus' name.

[1] *The Gospel of Luke, by William Barclay. The Westminster Press, Philadelphia. February 1956 reprint, second edition.*
[2] *Ibid*
[3] *Ibid*

Charles Harrison Mason
(1866-1961)

Charles Harrison Mason was a charismatic religious leader and founder of the Church of God in Christ, one of the largest black Pentecostal denominations.

Born in 1866 to former slaves, Jerry and Eliza Mason, Charles lived with his family in Shelby County, Tennessee, where they were poor tenant farmers. As a child, Charles was struck with yellow fever, which claimed the life of his father. After his illness, Charles was converted to evangelical Christianity and baptized by his brother who was a Baptist preacher.

Charles attended Arkansas Bible College in 1882 for three months. He found, however, that he was more educated by the spirituality of former slaves. He was a natural leader. He began to preach doctrines associated with the Holiness Movement, a movement that supported the notion that once a person accepted Jesus Christ, that person would move toward a second state of perfect love—sanctification—brought on by spiritual baptism. Because of this, Charles was expelled from the Baptist church for heresy. As a result, in 1895 in an abandoned cotton gin building in Mississippi, Charles Mason, along with Charles Jones, founded the Church of Christ.

Founding a new church was not easy, as Charles would soon learn. His church was attacked by white racists. The publicity from the attack, however, brought new members to the small, fledgling, church. In 1897, the name of the church was changed to the Church of God in Christ (COGIC). Charles said that God had given him the name of the church one day on a street in Little Rock, Arkansas.

Charles believed strongly in increasing his knowledge and spirituality by attending revivals. In 1907, he attended the Azusa Street Revival in Los Angeles. The Azusa Street Revival marked the beginning of the Pentecostal movement. Theologically based on Acts chapter 2, where Christ's disciples were baptized by the Holy Spirit at the gathering of Pentecost, Pentecostalism supports the belief of Divine presence in worship services. This is characterized by glossolalia, or speaking in tongues, holy dancing, singing, and testimony services.

Pentecostalism spread rapidly across Mississippi and throughout the world, as did the Church of God in Christ. Although his church was criticized, under Charles Mason, what began small, with about ten congregations, grew to millions in a short period of years. Today, the Church of God in Christ has nearly five million members.

TEACHING TIPS

December 3
Bible Study Guide 1

1. Words You Should Know

A. Esaias (v. 4)—Isaiah, the prophet.
B. Viper (v. 7)—a poisonous snake.
C. Publicans (v. 12)—tax collectors.
D. Latchet (v. 16)—sandal strap.
E. Purge (v. 17)—to cleanse or purify.

2. Teacher Preparation

A. Read the background Scripture to gain information on John the Baptist. Study other passages that describe the person and physical appearance of John the Baptist.

3. Starting the Lesson

A. If possible, ask someone to draw a picture of the way John the Baptist might have looked. Ask class members if the message of a man dressed like John the Baptist would be received today?

B. Read today's IN FOCUS story about Jim Jones and The People's Temple cult. Talk about the dangers of being dependent on a personality and not the Gospel message. Ask what are some things believers can do to prevent being drawn into viewing a charismatic personality as a godlike figure.

4. Getting Into the Lesson

A. Consider some well-known evangelists or preachers who have had a great impact on the lives of others as well as the "keys" to their effectiveness.

B. Spend time talking about the spiritual condition of those who heard John's message. Why were they open to listening? Why did they submit to baptism? Ask what does it mean to be prepared for Christ's return?

C. Discuss why persons like John, who point others to Christ no matter what, are more effective preachers than those who concern themselves with pleasing others?

5. Relating the Lesson to Life

A. Review the concept of Truth as described in today's THE PEOPLE, PLACES, AND TIMES arti-cle. Discuss the effect of the Roman Empire on the Jews. What kinds of tensions existed between Jewish religious leaders and Roman authorities. Recall how they conspired to kill Jesus, even though the two groups were adversaries.

B. Give students an opportunity to answer the questions in SEARCH THE SCRIPTURES.

C. Today's DISCUSS THE MEANING questions ask why a repentant heart is generally a more compassionate heart. Discuss our need for repentance and how it affects the nature of our relationship to God.

D. What responsibility do charismatic personalities have to those who may be weak in the faith and who focus more on a particular religious personality rather than Christ. How will God hold those accountable who have misused the trust placed in them by weaker Christians? How will God hold the weaker Christians accountable for their actions?

6. Arousing Action

A. John preached about the need for preparation. Talk about what every human being needs to do in order to prepare for the return of Christ. Ask members if they feel the call to tell others to prepare is a gift given to some or a command given to all believers. Ask them to support their beliefs using the Bible.

WORSHIP GUIDE

For the Superintendent or Teacher
Theme: Preparing the Way
Theme Song: Go Tell It on the Mountain
Scripture: Isaiah 40:1-5
Song: More About Jesus
Meditation: Lord, help me to remember that I live to fulfill Your calling. Help me to discern Your voice so that I am not distracted by my human frailties.

PREPARING THE WAY

Bible Background • LUKE 1:5-25; 3:1-18
Printed Text • LUKE 3:2-3, 7-18
Devotional Reading • ISAIAH 40:1-5

DEC 3RD

LESSON AIM

After studying today's lesson, students should understand the central purpose of the ministry of John the Baptist and how he drew the people's attention to their need for repentance and preparation for the coming Messiah.

KEEP IN MIND

"As it is written in the book of the words of Esaias the prophet, saying, The voice of one crying in the wilderness, Prepare ye the way of the Lord, make his paths straight" (Luke 3:4).

FOCAL VERSES

Luke 3:2 The word of God came unto John the son of Zacharias in the wilderness.

3 And he came into all the country about Jordan, preaching the baptism of repentance for the remission of sins;

3:7 Then said he to the multitude that came forth to be baptized of him, O generation of vipers, who hath warned you to flee from the wrath to come?

8 Bring forth therefore fruits worthy of repentance, and begin not to say within yourselves, We have Abraham to our father: for I say unto you, That God is able of these stones to raise up children unto Abraham.

9 And now also the axe is laid unto the root of the trees: every tree therefore which bringeth not forth good fruit is hewn down, and cast into the fire.

10 And the people asked him, saying, What shall

LESSON OVERVIEW

LESSON AIM
KEEP IN MIND
FOCAL VERSES
IN FOCUS
THE PEOPLE, PLACES, AND TIMES
BACKGROUND
AT-A-GLANCE
IN DEPTH
SEARCH THE SCRIPTURES
DISCUSS THE MEANING
LESSON IN OUR SOCIETY
MAKE IT HAPPEN
FOLLOW THE SPIRIT
REMEMBER YOUR THOUGHTS
MORE LIGHT ON THE TEXT
DAILY BIBLE READINGS

we do then?

11 He answereth and saith unto them, He that hath two coats, let him impart to him that hath none; and he that hath meat, let him do likewise.

12 Then came also publicans to be baptized, and said unto him, Master, what shall we do?

13 And he said unto them, Exact no more than that which is appointed you.

14 And the soldiers likewise demanded of him, saying, And what shall we do? And he said unto them, Do violence to no man, neither accuse any falsely; and be content with your wages.

15 And as the people were in expectation, and all men mused in their hearts of John, whether he were the Christ, or not;

16 John answered, saying unto them all, I indeed baptize you with water; but one mightier than I cometh, the latchet of whose shoes I am not worthy to unloose: he shall baptize you with the Holy Ghost and with fire:

17 Whose fan is in his hand, and he will thoroughly purge his floor, and will gather the wheat into his garner; but the chaff he will burn with fire unquenchable.

18 And many other things in his exhortation preached he unto the people.

IN FOCUS

In the fall of 1998, many cable and commercial channels showed documentaries and movies depicting the life of the Rev. Jim Jones and The

People's Temple, marking the 20th anniversary of the mass suicide which took place at Jonestown, Guyana, in South America.

When his ministry began in Indianapolis, Indiana, he appeared to be a humble servant of the Lord, willing to take an unpopular stand for the equal treatment of all human beings. He soon gained a loyal following. Understandably, his following included a huge number of African Americans. Over the years, however, the purpose of his mission and ministry became perverted and grossly distorted. The People's Temple grew from a small body of believers into a religious cult in the truest sense of its meaning.

In a movie which depicted his life and ministry, one can see how the focus of Jones's ministry moved from Jesus Christ to himself. Whenever we displace Christ to uplift, glorify or worship another human being, we are headed for certain destruction.

When John the Baptist began his ministry of preaching and baptism, the opportunity arose for him to displace Christ and glorify himself. He was a charismatic preacher who had the ability to mesmerize the crowds he addressed. But John would not allow Satan to use him in that way.

Even today Christians, especially those who are in the public eye, must keep the message focused on the One who will return, not on any human personality.

THE PEOPLE, PLACES, AND TIMES

The Roman Empire. Considering its vast size, the Roman Empire's bureaucracy and military were relatively small. The system of rule was effective for over 1,000 years, but that largely depended on the compliance of the kingdoms that were part of the Empire. Kingdoms that cooperated and complied with Rome were given leniency. By giving them some degree of autonomy, Rome was able to concentrate its limited military force on troubled areas. Rebellions against the Empire were savagely crushed, thus creating a strong and effective deterrent to thoughts of revolution and an incentive to remain loyal to the Roman Empire.

Information from The Word in Life Study Bible, Nashville: Thomas Nelson, Inc., 1993, 1996, p. 1772.

Tetrarch. A political position in the early Roman Empire. The tetrarch determined the size of the territory ruled and the degree of dependence on Roman authority. Over time, the position became less powerful. After the death of Herod the Great, his kingdom was divided among his three sons.

Based on information from Holman Bible Dictionary, Trent Butler, general editor, Nashville: Broadman & Holman Publishers, 1991, pp. 1335-1336.

Baptism. The background of Christian baptism has its roots in Judaism. The Qumran sect, which produced the now famous Dead Sea Scrolls, attempted to cleanse Judaism. They placed great emphasis on purity and purification rites. These rites generally involved some form of immersion under water.

Around the time of Jesus, Judaism began to place a great deal of emphasis on ritual washings designed to provide cleansing from impurity. It was also around this time that Jews began to baptize Gentile converts to Judaism.

In the New Testament, baptism is for those who believe in Jesus Christ. True baptism occurs when a person trusts and accepts Christ as personal Lord and Saviour and obeys the command to be baptized in water.

Based on information from Holman Bible Dictionary, Trent Butler, general editor, Nashville: Broadman & Holman Publishers, 1991, pp. 149-152.

BACKGROUND

The introduction to Jesus' ministry in the third chapter of Luke is the first information we are given about Him since His parents found Him in the Temple listening to the teachers when He was twelve years old.

To set the tone for Jesus' public ministry, Luke briefly described the political climate which reigned at the time. Herod was tetrarch of Galilee in those days.

Then, having set the political climate, Luke described the religious context which influenced the region. Caiaphas, son-in-law of Annas, was high priest during Jesus' public ministry. Scholars assume, however, that Annas still held some influence and power during those days.

It was into this world that John the Baptist

began to preach a message of repentance. John was called to be a spokesman for the truth that has been given from On High.

He kept himself apart from the daily distractions of others and devoted himself to prayer and meditation. When he came out among the crowds to deliver his message, those who heard him were magnetized by his words.

John was careful not to draw attention to himself, a temptation that would compromise lesser men. He kept his attention focused on his mission—to announce the coming of the Messiah.

AT-A-GLANCE

1. John the Baptist (Luke 3:2-3)
2. Preaching Repentance (Luke 3:7-14)
3. The One to Come (Luke 3:15-17)

IN DEPTH

1. John the Baptist (Luke 3:2-3)

John, son of Zechariah and Elizabeth, was clear about his mission—to prepare the way for Jesus. He helped the people understand their need for a Saviour and called for their repentance in light of His coming.

John received his call in the wilderness. He took heed of the call and went into the region around the Jordan to fulfill that call.

Scholars are not certain of the origin of John's baptism. It is believed his practice may be connected to the baptism of proselytes (converts to Judaism), except that he was calling for Jews to submit to his baptism. Still, it can be argued that John's baptism was considered unique from other religious sects who also performed the rite. He became known as "the baptizer" (Mark 1:4), a name which probably would not have been attached to him if his baptism had been identified with other baptisms. As John preached, many of those who heard him identified with his message and were baptized. He immersed them in the Jordan River.

The word baptism is taken from the Greek word *baptisma*, meaning "to dip" or "to immerse."

John's message *was the baptism of repentance for the remission of sins*. He called for them to be baptized as a way to demonstrate their desire to separate from their old way of life and to prepare their hearts for the coming of the Messiah.

2. Preaching Repentance (Luke 3:7-14)

Instead of preaching to the Pharisees and Sadducees (as in Matthew 3:7), Luke records John's preaching being directed to the multitudes. He referred to them as a generation of vipers. A viper is a poisonous snake. The people were living unaware of their depraved state. Their religion was both insincere and superficial. The crowds were drawn to hear John's message, but their hearts were not ready. The Jews had long awaited a Messiah, but their expectations for a ruler were much different from the King and the kingdom that John announced.

The Jews relied on their heritage as the children of Abraham for their salvation. John warned that genealogy cannot change one's attitude toward God. They were arrogant about their biological relationship to Abraham. They believed that Abraham immunized them from the penalty of sin and guaranteed their status as children of Yahweh. John told them they needed to bear the fruits of repentance.

John illustrated his warning by comparing them to trees and vineyards which are hewn down and cast into the fire because they cannot produce good fruit. By their arrogance they were cutting themselves off from God's election and promise. God has no room for the unrepentant. God the Creator can raise up new *children* of Abraham from stones.

John's illustration struck the arrogant hearts of the people. They asked him, "What shall we do then?"

John called upon them to demonstrate evidence of genuine repentance before baptizing them. The first thing they could do as a mark of repentance would be to share their food and clothing with the poor. Generally, the Jews looked upon the poor with disdain. When persons have repented and live in the knowledge of God's grace and all that He has done for us, we have compassion for those who are less fortunate.

John's preaching was so powerful that even *publicans* came to be baptized! The publicans, or tax collectors, mentioned in the New Testament were mainly minor revenue agents. Many of them were known to be corrupt. The Jews held tax collectors in particular contempt because they were agents of a hated foreign power in their land. The publicans made themselves wealthy by robbing their fellow countrymen.

The repentance of the publicans who heard John the Baptist was evidenced by the fact that they asked, "What shall we do?" John advised them concerning how they ought to handle their responsibility with honor.

The soldiers John addressed are believed to have been Jews who were recruited to assist local tax collectors. In fact, their use of the person pronoun when they asked "And what shall we do?" indicates that they identified themselves with the tax collectors.

Just as he had advised the publicans, John advised them not to use their position to take advantage of others to boost their personal income.

3. The One to Come (Luke 3:15-17)

Because of John's power and charisma, the people began to wonder if John himself was the promised Messiah. The intensity of his preaching kindled their messianic expectations. The phrase "whether he were the Christ or not" indicates the tentative nature of their question. John did not possess any of the characteristics of the prophesied Messiah. He was not from David's genealogical line, nor did he perform any of the miraculous deeds expected from the Messiah. Apparently some people in those days believed the Messiah would not reveal his presence among the people because of their sins. Therefore, some probably suspected that John was this hidden Messiah.

John plainly rejected any notion that he was the promised One. This was John's first direct mention of Jesus. There would be one mightier than he who would come to save the people. There was no comparison between John the Baptist and the One to come, the latchet of whose shoes he was not worthy to unloose. According to the Talmud, one of the duties of a slave was to take off his mas-

ter's shoes. Basically, John did not view himself to be worthy to even take off the shoes of the Messiah.

John knew the limitations of what he had to offer the people. His baptism was with water, a mere symbol. His ministry was to prepare the people for the great One to come. When the Christ came, however, "he shall baptize you with the Holy Ghost and with fire."

John the Baptist continued by describing the Messiah's power by comparing it to the threshing process used to harvest wheat. The "fan" referred to a wooden fork-like shovel that lifted the grain in the air so that the wind could separate it. The heavier grain, the wheat, would fall to the floor, while the wind carried away the lighter and useless chaff. When the threshing was complete, the farmers destroyed the chaff by setting it on fire. God's judgment would much like the threshing of wheat—it would separate the genuine Israelites from those who were false and useless. His fire would be unquenchable—meaning that His judgment is inescapable and unavoidable.

SEARCH THE SCRIPTURES

1. Where did John the Baptist receive the word of God? (v. 2)

2. What message did John preach? (v. 3)

3. Who did John address with his message? (v. 7)

4. What claim did the Jews make concerning their status? (v. 8)

5. What analogy did John use to help the people understand what would happen to those who were worthless to the Lord? (v. 9)

6. What did the publicans and the soldiers ask John? (vv. 12, 14)

7. What did John admonish both groups to do? (vv. 13, 14)

8. What did the people begin to wonder about John? (v. 15)

9. How did John respond to them? (v. 16)

10. What farming procedure did John use to demonstrate the Lord's righteousness? (v. 17)

DISCUSS THE MEANING

1. Luke tells us that John the Baptist received his call in the wilderness. Was that perhaps a place

of solitude where John could better discern the voice of the Lord calling to Him? Do we all need to have times in the wilderness? If so, how can this serve to strengthen our faith?

2. Think about the threshing process used to separate wheat from chaff. If the Lord came and performed a threshing process in your church today, would you make the cut? Would you fall to the floor with the valuable grain, or would you blow away like the useless chaff?

3. Why is repentance often evidenced by such things as giving to the poor and sharing with those who have fallen on difficult times?

LESSON IN OUR SOCIETY

Because of the availability of electronic media, many religious "celebrities" have been made. Some have been shown to have feet of clay. Others have accumulated a loyal following of believers. Those who have been given the gift of charisma must use it carefully, especially church leaders. Far more people than most of us would like to admit are babes in the faith. They are prone to confuse the message with the messenger. John the Baptist preached about the coming of the Messiah and the need to prepare for His coming through repentance. Today we have the opportunity to preach of His return, and the need to prepare so the we will be ready when He comes.

All that we do is for His sake. No matter how dynamic the preacher or motivational speaker, or how prolific the religious writer, or how gifted the Christian musician or vocal artist, if there was no Christ, there would be no message. Not only is He the Reason for the Season, He is the Reason for all that we do.

MAKE IT HAPPEN

John the Baptist preached the need for repentance in preparation for Jesus' arrival. But what about His return? Are you ready for His return? What if He came back today?

Make a list of the things you have done and continue to do to prepare for His return. How do you incorporate these things into your daily living?

Do you ever talk to others about the need to prepare for His return? If not, why not?

FOLLOW THE SPIRIT

What God wants me to do:

_____

_____

REMEMBER YOUR THOUGHTS

Special insights you learned:

_____

_____

MORE LIGHT ON THE TEXT
Luke 3:2, 3:7-18

Luke begins chapter three of this historical narrative by providing the exact date the events took place—the beginning of John's ministry. Luke's introduction here and provision of the date with precision conforms to the Palestinian Jewish characteristics in style, language, and setting; it also reflects the opening words of Old Testament prophets (Isaiah 1:1; 6:1; Jeremiah 1:1-3; Hosea 1:1; Amos 1:1).

3:2 The word of God came unto John the son of Zacharias in the wilderness. 3 And he came into all the country about Jordan, preaching the baptism of repentance for the remission of sins;

Here Luke uses the Old Testament formula of the prophetic call "the word of God came" (Genesis 15:1; 1 Samuel 15:10; 2 Samuel 7:4; 24:11; 1 Kings 6:11, etc.) to introduce us to John, usually known as "the Baptist"—the last and the greatest of the prophets (Matthew 11:11). Luke identifies this John as "the son of Zacharias," probably to separate him from other people with the same name. The name "John," *Ioannes*, was a common Jewish name and it means "Jehovah (Yahweh) is a gracious giver." It is also consistent with the Jewish custom whereby people are identified by attaching their names either to their parents, family, or ancestral names. Luke tells his reader that John is the same one whom he had introduced in chapter 1 (vv. 5-25, 57-66, 80), whose story he interrupted to tell the story of the birth of Christ (chapter 2).

Luke continues his story about this John from where he left it (1:80). It is, therefore, no surprise when Luke says that "the word of God came to John in the "wilderness" where he had gone

his father (1:11), or in a dream or vision, or by an audible voice as with Jesus (v. 22)—Luke is silent. It seems unimportant for him to put it in writing. What seems more important to Luke here is that when "the day of his shewing unto Israel" (1:80) came (i.e., the appointed day for the beginning of his ministry), John received a full commission and instruction from God. The content and nature of the commission is to be inferred from verses 4-6.

Having received God's order, John started his preaching and baptism ministry along the coastal countries and cities of the Jordan River. The wilderness was a large, rocky, dry and barren piece of land through which the Jordan River took its course. It is in the same region that Elisha asked Namaan to go and wash to be clean (2 Kings 5). Since John has the ministry of baptism for repentance, it is natural that he went where there was enough water

(1:80). The "word" here, *rhema* (**hray'-mah**) means an utterance, speech, a pronouncement, or declaration of one's mind. Here the declaration is from God. That means, in a simple term, that God spoke to John as He had to the prophets that preceded him in the Old Testament. The significance of the desert is not clear, but some think that it held memories of the wilderness wandering of the post-Exodus Israel. It was believed that the deserts were inhabited by demons and it was alleged that John had a demon (Matthew 11:18). However, John received the spoken word of God while he was in the wilderness. How he received the word from God—whether it was through an angel like (Luke 3:3) for baptism. John preached the baptism of "repentance" (*metanoia*, pronounced **met-an'-oy-ah,** i.e, a change of mind or heart of something one has done, or of a purpose one has formed). It is a sorrowful reversal of unpopular decisions, usually bad ones, which, in this case, is sin. The basic idea is from the Hebrew *sub* ("turn," from sin to God.) The noun form, *metanoia* (repentance), is used also in 3:8; 5:32; 15:7 and 24:47. The verb form is *metanoeo* and appears in 10:13; 11:32; 13:3, 5; 15:7, 10; 16:30 and 17:3-4. The purpose of the baptism of repentance is for the "remission of sins" of those who are being baptized. Remission, *aphesis,* has the idea of release from bondage or imprisonment, or forgiveness, or pardon, from the penalty of "sins," *hamartia* (**ham-ar-tee'-ah**). *Hamartia* is generally defined as missing the mark, to err, or to wander from the path of uprightness and honor. It also refers to wandering away from the precepts of God's law, or to violate the divine law. The forgiveness of sins is the result of the repentance expressed through the act of baptism.

In verses 4-6, John declares the purpose of his ministry, and that is to prepare the way of the Lord. Here he quotes the prophecy of Isaiah (40:3-5) as the pattern of his ministry, and implicitly claims to be the fulfillment of that prophecy.

7 Then said he to the multitude that came forth to be baptized of him, O generation of vipers, who hath warned you to flee from the wrath to come?

As he preached the repentance message, a "multitude" *ochlos* (**okh'los**) responded and came forward to be baptized. The word *ochlos* means a throng of people flocked together in a place without order. It is often used for the common people, as opposed to the rulers and leading men. It refers to an assorted group of people (a mixed group), instead of *laos* used in verse 18, which refers to a people group, tribe or nation, all those who are of the same stock and language. Luke does not specify the makeup of this group. Matthew (3:7) says that the group's makeup included the Pharisees and Sadduccees, while John (1:19, 24) says that it was made up of priests and Levites sent from Jerusalem by the Jews. Mark says, "And there went out unto him all the land of Judaea, and they of Jerusalem, and were all baptized of him in the river of Jordan, confessing their sins" (Mark 1:5). This confirms that the group was mixed, probably with both religious leaders, such as priests and Levites, Pharisees and Sadduccees who perhaps came to confront John, and the ordinary people who came just to hear him. Luke says they came to be baptized by John. It is possible that they came to hear John, and those who were convinced and convicted by John's teaching repented and were baptized.

John's address to this crowd was with caustic language, indeed insulting language, similar to his predecessors in the Old Testament. Luke's record (vv. 7-9) is identical with Matthew's account (3:7-10). According to Luke, John's address was directed to the whole crowd, while Matthew says it was directed specifically to the Pharisees and Sadduccees who came "to his baptism." John addresses them as "generation of vipers," i.e., offsprings of "vipers." Vipers, or the Greek word *echidna* (pronounced **ekh'-id-nah**), are very thin poisonous snakes (asps or adders), about 4 inches in length. They usually lurk under stones, in the sand of the desert, or in the crack of old walls waiting for their prey. They are very deadly, and aggressive, little creatures. It is used figuratively for a person regarded as cunning, malicious or treacherous. John's question here—"Who hath warned you to flee from the wrath to come?"— suggests that although their coming to be baptized was a proper thing to do, their motives were in question. Hence, he called them "vipers" (cf. also Old Testament usage Isaiah 59:5; Job 20:16). Jesus himself would use the same designation later for the Pharisees (Matthew 23:33). "Wrath" (*orge*) means indignation or agitation of the soul, or violent emotion, or anger. Here it refers to the anger exhibited in punishment, hence it used for punishments inflicted by magistrates or judges. Here John refers to the eternal punishment which awaits those who walk not according to Lord's precepts. John's question here seems rhetorical in nature and tends to reveal the inner feeling of the people. The people seem to know the consequence of their sin, and probably are pricked in their conscience. Hence, they come to be baptized. The idea here, John seems to say, is "it is time you repented by changing your ways to avoid the coming punishment."

8 Bring forth therefore fruits worthy of repentance, and begin not to say within yourselves, We have Abraham to our father: for I say unto you, That God is able of these stones to raise up children unto Abraham. 9 And now also the axe is laid unto the root of the trees: every tree therefore which bringeth not forth good fruit is hewn down, and cast into the fire.

Using the agricultural metaphor, John calls for genuine repentance, rather than mere pretense, or outward show. He calls on them to "bring forth," i.e., to bear "fruits worthy of repentance," instead of assuming or claiming a special privilege of being the sons of Abraham. A true repentance, John seems to say, is based on the fruit each one bears, or the type of life one lives, or the attitude one exhibits outwardly, rather than on ancestral background. The Jews, especially the Pharisees, thought that being descendants of Abraham was a license for entry into the kingdom of God. John refutes this claim. He says that being a descendant of Abraham is unimportant because God can "raise" (*egeiro*) i.e., bring to life stone, or create children out stones for Abraham. Replying to the Pharisees' complaint about the multitude's loud praise, Jesus told them if the people "should hold their peace" God would cause the stones to cry out in praise of him (19:40). The theme of the children of Abraham is also dealt with in the following passages by Jesus (John 8:31-41) and Paul (Romans 4:12-17; Galatians 3:6-9).

The Bible uses fruit metaphors frequently to describe the type of life expected of all who profess to be children of God. Jesus speaks later in this book of those who bear fruit which is consistent with their lives (6:43-45). He gives a parable about cutting down of a barren tree (13:6-9), and this reflects the judgment that awaits those who do not live according to what they profess. John presents the same imagery for judgment here (v. 9). He says, "The axe is laid unto the root of the trees," ready to chop down and burn any tree that does not "bear good fruit." The laying of the "axe" on the foot of the trees signifies the immediacy of the judgment. Some believe that this was a prediction about the destruction of the nation of Israel. Like a fruitless tree, Israel would be destroyed if it did not start to bear good fruits. The proponents of this theory believe that this prophecy was fulfilled in A. D. 70 under Nero.

10 And the people asked him, saying, What shall we do then? 11 He answereth and saith unto them, He that hath two coats, let him impart to him that hath none; and he that hath meat, let him do likewise.

John's prophetic pronouncement of judgment evokes some responses from the crowd (v. 10), then from the publicans or tax collectors (v. 12),

and from the soldiers as well (v. 14). Each of these groups asks the same question, "What shall we do?" John's response to the crowd stresses the need for community, social justice, and the showing of mercy. It was practical. He says that those who have "two coats" and those who have "meat" (food) should learn to share with those without. This is the principle of community living. This does not in any way contradict Paul's teaching (1 Timothy 5:8), neither does it encourage strict communal life as practiced in the Qumran, nor is the idea here communism. Rather it stresses the need for bearing one another's burden (Galatians 6:2; Philippians 2:4), and bearing the fruit of righteousness similar to Paul's teaching (Galatians 5:22-23). John mentions two of the essential life's necessities: covering and food. "Coat," also translated "tunic," is the Greek *chiton* (**khee-tone'**), an undergarment, like a vest usually worn next to the skin under a longer robe. It was customary for people to take extra *chiton* for warmth or a change of clothes (cf. 9:3). It seems that since people came from different places (some from far places) to the riverbank to hear John, they must have come with food knowing it was going to be a long day. John probably noticed that some in the crowd had extra coats and food, while others did not have any undercoat or food. Hence, he used the present situation to teach an eternal truth. The crowd, therefore was to practice generosity and show compassion, the works of love, rather than the works of the law. This is consistent with the teachings of both Christ and Paul.

12 Then came also publicans to be baptized, and said unto him, Master, what shall we do? 13 And he said unto them, Exact no more than that which is appointed you.

The next group that inquired from John what to do in response to his teaching was the "publicans," *telones*, also known as tax collectors. They were the most despised and hated class because of the nature of their job. They operated under an unpopular system, the Roman Empire (cf., 5:27; 15:1), and they often carried out their duties with harshness, greed, and deception. They made their gain by extorting from the people more than they were required from their Roman masters. They were detested by both the Jews and other nations and were seen as sinners by the Pharisees (cf. Luke 5:30; 9:10-11; Mark 2:15-16). Because of this, they were alienated from the Jewish community. In his reply to their question, "What shall we do?" John told them to reform their behavior. They should not collect more than what is required by the law.

14 And the soldiers likewise demanded of him, saying, And what shall we do? And he said unto them, Do violence to no man, neither accuse any falsely; and be content with your wages.

The soldiers here were probably Jewish, not Roman, assigned to the internal affairs of the people. They, like the tax collectors, probably used unnecessary force and perhaps illegally extracted belongings from the people. To them, John gives a three-fold instruction. The first two are negative instructions and the third is positive. Firstly, they should not treat people with violence, or terrify people with their office. "Do violence (*diaseio*) to no man" means that they should stop extorting money and other property from the people. Secondly, the soldiers should stop accusing people falsely or wrongfully. This contradicts the principles of the second great commandment (Luke 10:27). Thirdly, John advises them to "be content with your wages." That means they should be satisfied with their official wages rather than misuse their offices and forcefully extract money from people by false accusation and intimidation. This advice of contentment probably goes for the tax collectors as well. We notice that, although John showed social concern, he did not advocate overthrowing the system, rather he called for a reform of the abuses and a change in the practices of those concerned—it was a call for individual reform.

15 And as the people were in expectation, and all men mused in their hearts of John, whether he were the Christ, or not;

John's teaching held people in suspense. The authority with which he taught, coupled with the wisdom with which he answered their questions, prompted the people to wonder within their hearts whether he was the long expected Messiah or not. John the Apostle relates the popular opinion concerning John the Baptist in detail (John 1:19-25). There the people confronted John with the question. Here John, through the power of the Holy Spirit, knew what they were thinking and debating about in their hearts. In layman's words, John "read" their minds. The word "muse" used here is the Greek *dialogizomai* (**dee-al-og-id'-zom-ahee**) which means to deliberate, to dispute, or to reason. His answer to their query was clear and multiple.

16 John answered, saying unto them all, I indeed baptize you with water; but one mightier than I cometh, the latchet of whose shoes I am not worthy to unloose: he shall baptize you with the Holy Ghost and with fire: 17 Whose fan is in his hand, and he will throughly purge his floor, and will gather the wheat into his garner; but the chaff he will burn with fire unquenchable.

He told them that he was not the Messiah; indeed, he was much less than the Christ in a number of ways. While John baptized with water, the coming Messiah "will baptize with the Holy Ghost and with fire," because He will be greater ("mightier") than John. He was so great that John felt too unworthy to loosen the "latchet" of his shoes. "Latchet" is the Greek word *himas,* i.e., the strap of his shoes or the thongs by which sandals were fastened to the feet. To untie shoes was a lowly job for a lowly servant. Even so, John felt inadequate to perform even this task for the Messiah (cf., John 3:30).

In his answer, John spelled out the difference between his type of baptism, and that of Christ. John's baptism was with water, a baptism of repentance in preparation for the coming Messiah. The Messiah will baptize "with the Holy Ghost and with fire," not in the sense of two separate baptisms, but a single event. The Holy Spirit will have the effect of fire on those who receive him. The significance of this fire is clear: it is for purging and cleansing rather than for judgment. Fire is also associated in the Bible as an emblem of the Holy Spirit for zeal and as refining agent (Isaiah 4:3-4; Psalm 104:4; Malachi 3:1-4; Acts 2:3). Therefore, in spite of what the people thought of him, John accepted his secondary position, and affirmed the superior position of the Messiah. While John performed the ceremonial and ritualistic cleansing with water, the One coming will purge peoples' hearts with the fire of the Holy Spirit.

Using the agricultural imagery once more, John goes on to explain further the ministry of this coming Messiah in terms of judgment of the sinner and preservation of the righteous. He likened the Messiah as a grain farmer which, in the time of John and Christ, was the common occupation of the Jewish world. Many African countries thrive in local farming, and many still use the same method today as was used in the time of John the Baptist. Grain, or wheat, was the common staple food. The grain is said to be threshed in the open air by being trampled under the feet of the oxen (Deuteronomy 25:4), or other types of instruments (Isaiah 28:27). Most African countries do this by pounding the grain (wheat or rice) in a "mortar" with "pistol." To separate the husks from the main grain, a fan or a wooden pitchfork was used to blow it. Africans use wide, round, and almost flat baskets specially made for this. A quantity of the grain with the husk is put in the basket, and the farmer will throw the grain up against the wind. The wind blows the chaff away, while the grain falls back into the basket. As it was in the time of John, the grain is sometimes sifted after the winnowing (Luke 22:31). Usually the grain is gathered and stored, while the chaff is burned with fire. This metaphor is used a number of times to picture the judgment (Job 21:17-20; Psalm 1:4; Isaiah 29:5; 41:16).

With this metaphor, John describes the work of Christ as the judge whose job is twofold, preserving the righteous and punishing the sinner. The raw grain represents humanity as a whole, both the good and the bad. As the farmer, Christ sifts the people, separating them. The good are preserved unto everlasting life, while the bad are reserved for everlasting punishment. Just as the unfruitful tree is cut down and cast into fire (v. 9), and the chaff burned with fire (v. 17), the unrighteous will be cast into an everlasting fire, described here as the "unquenchable" *asbestos* (**as'-bes-tos**). It means that the fire, called Hell, or Hades, burns with perpetuity. This is eternal punishment—"the wrath to come" (v. 7). Hence,

John warns them and calls on them to repent and be baptized.

18 And many other things in his exhortation preached he unto the people.

Luke summarizes John's ministry by saying that John not only warned (exhorted) the people, but "preached" the good news to the people. This is made clear from the use of the word "preached," *euaggelizo* (pronounced, **yoo-ang-ghel-id'-zo**), from which we derive our English verb "to evangelize," or the noun, evangelism. It means to announce good news, to declare glad (good) tidings. It is used in the Old Testament of any kind of good news, of the joyful tidings of God's kindness, and of the messianic blessings in particular (cf., Isaiah 9:6-7). In the New Testament, it is used especially of the glad tidings of the coming kingdom of God, and of the salvation to be obtained through Christ. Announcing the birth of Christ to the shepherds, the angel of the Lord said to them: Fear not: for, behold, I bring you good tidings (*euaggelizo*) of great joy, which shall be to all people (Luke 2:10).

DAILY° BIBLE READINGS

M: The Prophecy of John's Birth
Luke 1:5-17

T: Too Good to Be True
Luke 1:18-25

W: John the Baptist's Birth
Luke 1:57-66

T: Prophetic Words of Hope
Isaiah 40:1-5

F: John's Proclamation
Luke 3:1-6

S: Baptism, Repentance, and Change
Luke 3:7-14

S: The Truth Hurts
Luke 3:15-20

TEACHING TIPS

December 10
Bible Study Guide 2

1. Words You Should Know

A. Gabriel (v. 26)—an angel of the Lord, God's messenger.

B. Espoused (v. 27)—betrothed or engaged to be wed.

C. Salutation (v. 29)—greeting.

D. Barren (v. 36)—unable to conceive a child.

E. Cousin (v. 36)—other translations refer to Elizabeth as a relative of Mary. Their exact form of kinship is not known.

2. Teacher Preparation

Read the entire first chapter of Luke. Pay careful attention to Zacharias's annunciation (vv. 11-25). Compare the response of Zacharias, an aging priest, to that of Mary, a teenager with little religious experience. Think about why age and religious experience are not necessarily indicators of one's spiritual readiness.

3. Starting the Lesson

A. Have students make a mental profile of young Mary. Imagine what her upbringing may have been like as a young Hebrew girl which shaped her in such a way. Why did God choose her? Why wasn't a woman of a higher social standing chosen?

B. Read today's IN FOCUS story about young Jerome. Opportunities come to us after we have demonstrated ourselves through hard work and commitment. Talk about the fact that people often observe our behavior even when we are unaware. Consider the merits of being spiritually ready for opportunities that arise.

4. Getting Into the Lesson

Make a list of the differences in the way that Zacharias and Mary responded to the message of Gabriel. In what ways were their responses similar? How did Gabriel deal differently with Zacharias and why?

5. Relating the Lesson to Life

A. Review the concepts described in today's THE PEOPLE, PLACES, AND TIMES. Discuss how our concept of engagement in modern society is different from biblical times. Talk about how different marriages might be today if engagement was viewed in the same way today that it was years ago.

B. Give students an opportunity to answer the questions in SEARCH THE SCRIPTURES.

C. The LESSON IN OUR SOCIETY contrasts human knowledge based on our life in the information age versus living in a simpler time as Mary did. Discuss how human knowledge can often interfere with faith.

6. Arousing Action

A. Think about the principle characters who played a role in the birth of Jesus. Ask members to think about how God uses others in our lives to bring His will into fruition. Ask them to think about how God has used others to enable them to do God's will.

B. Give class members an opportunity to complete FOLLOW THE SPIRIT and REMEMBER YOUR THOUGHTS.

WORSHIP GUIDE

For the Superintendent or Teacher
Theme: Responding to God
Theme Song: Angels We Have Heard on High
Scripture: Matthew 1:18-25
Song: Angels, from the Realms of Glory
Meditation: May I have the willingness to submit myself to Your leading and Your will. I pray that I will move beyond my fears to answer Your voice when You call unto me.

RESPONDING TO GOD

Bible Background • LUKE 1:26-38
Printed Text • LUKE 1:26-38
Devotional Reading • MATTHEW 1:18-25

LESSON AIM

After studying today's lesson, students should understand the events which led to Mary's understanding that she would be the mother of the Messiah. Students will also understand the importance of the qualities of humility and submission among God's servants.

KEEP IN MIND

"And Mary said, Behold the handmaid of the Lord; be it unto me according to thy word. And the angel departed from her" (Luke 1:38).

FOCAL VERSES

Luke 1:26 And in the sixth month the angel Gabriel was sent from God unto a city of Galilee, named Nazareth,

27 To a virgin espoused to a man whose name was Joseph, of the house of David; and the virgin's name was Mary.

28 And the angel came in unto her, and said, Hail, thou that art highly favoured, the Lord is with thee: blessed art thou among women.

29 And when she saw him, she was troubled at his saying, and cast in her mind what manner of salutation this should be.

30 And the angel said unto her, Fear not, Mary: for thou hast found favour with God.

31 And, behold, thou shalt conceive in thy womb, and bring forth a son, and shalt call his name JESUS.

32 He shall be great, and shall be called the Son of the Highest: and the Lord God shall give unto him the throne of his father David:

LESSON OVERVIEW

LESSON AIM
KEEP IN MIND
FOCAL VERSES
IN FOCUS
THE PEOPLE, PLACES,
AND TIMES
BACKGROUND
AT-A-GLANCE
IN DEPTH
SEARCH THE SCRIPTURES
DISCUSS THE MEANING
LESSON IN OUR SOCIETY
MAKE IT HAPPEN
FOLLOW THE SPIRIT
REMEMBER YOUR THOUGHTS
MORE LIGHT ON THE TEXT
DAILY BIBLE READINGS

33 And he shall reign over the house of Jacob for ever; and of his kingdom there shall be no end.

34 Then said Mary unto the angel, How shall this be, seeing I know not a man?

35 And the angel answered and said unto her, The Holy Ghost shall come upon thee, and the power of the Highest shall overshadow thee: therefore also that holy thing which shall be born of thee shall be called the Son of God.

36 And, behold, thy cousin Elisabeth, she hath also conceived a son in her old age: and this is the sixth month with her, who was called barren.

37 For with God nothing shall be impossible.

38 And Mary said, Behold the handmaid of the Lord; be it unto me according to thy word. And the angel departed from her.

IN FOCUS

Jerome couldn't wait to get home and talk to his family! He had just been offered a fantastic opportunity to enter a training program at work. He'd never applied for it because he assumed the program was open only to college graduates.

When Ms. Vernon, the general manager, had her secretary call him to set up an appointment to see her in her office, he was a little afraid. "Uh-oh, " he first thought, "what did I do wrong?"

Much to his surprise, Ms. Vernon greeted him warmly. "I know a summons from the boss is a little scary," she said. "But I think I have some news that will excite you."

Her words were so complimentary, Jerome just knew something bad was going to come out of her mouth soon. He tried to relax as he listened to her words. He was afraid that he was about to be transferred to another facility.

Much to his surprise, Ms. Vernon offered him a chance to enter the training program, which is where the higher paying jobs were. "I want other employees to know that we look at dedication and hard work, not just education. You've demonstrated a high level of commitment to your job, and you have a good attitude about your work. A lot of other young employees who, like you, don't have a degree are going to be looking at you to see whether you can make it through," she explained.

"All I can do is give it my best shot," Jerome told her. "I'll work as hard as it takes to succeed at this— even harder if I have to!"

THE PEOPLE, PLACES, AND TIMES

Espoused. When couples were engaged to be married during biblical times, the relationship was as binding as marriage. In the Old Testament, espousal is nearly synonymous with marriage. To be promised to another and marriage itself were based on moral and spiritual principles for the home and for society at large. Under the Law of Moses, anyone who violated this principle by committing an act such as fornication, rape, or incest, was stoned to death. Later the Jewish legal system allowed for divorce.

Joseph and Mary set the model for espousal in the New Testament. Matthew records that when Joseph was informed about Mary's condition, he planned to divorce her quietly, being a kind and just man. Under Hebrew law, Joseph would have been well within his legal right to do away with her. Mary, herself, could have been stoned for being pregnant by someone other than her espoused husband.

Based on information from Holman Bible Dictionary, Trent Butler, general editor, Nashville: Broadman & Holman Publishers, 1991, pp. 176-177.

Nazareth. The name of a city meaning "branch." Nazareth only gained prominence after the birth of Jesus. Located in lower Galilee, it lies halfway between the Sea of Galilee and the Mediterranean Sea. In Jesus' day, Nazareth was a small village, having only one spring to supply fresh water to residents. Today that spring is known as Mary's well.

Nazareth did not have a good reputation in Jesus' day, as reflected in Nathanael's question, "Can there any good thing come out of Nazareth?" (John 1:46). Jesus was rejected by His townspeople and was thrown out of the synagogue there (Luke 4:16-30; Matthew 13:54-58; Mark 6:1-6).

The early church was also looked upon with disdain, being referred to as a sect of the Nazarenes (Acts 24:5). Part of the reason for Nazareth's lack of respect was likely due to the unpolished dialect of its inhabitants, a lack of culture, and possibly some immorality.

Modern Nazareth has about 20,000 residents, most of whom are Moslems and Christians.

Based on information from Holman Bible Dictionary, Trent Butler, general editor, Nashville: Broadman & Holman Publishers, 1991, pp. 1010-1011.

BACKGROUND

Christianity faced important challenges in its early history. Luke's Gospel, in part, is designed to counter certain false claims about Jesus. Followers of John the Baptist were teaching that John was the Messiah and was superior to Jesus of Nazareth, whom he had baptized. Luke details the roles of John the Baptist and Jesus of Nazareth in such a way that there is no confusion. He makes it clear that each held an important role in God's plan of salvation for humanity. Nevertheless, Jesus is the Messiah and, therefore, superior to John.

Also important to Luke was to affirm that Jesus was Israel's long-awaited Messiah, King and Deliverer. He was the fulfillment of God's promise to His people to send a Saviour.

The first part of Luke's Gospel is devoted to divinely orchestrated events which lead to the birth of the Messiah. Previous verses in chapter one tell how the angel Gabriel spoke to Zacharias and told him that his wife was going to bear him a son who became known as John the Baptist. In the sixth month of Elizabeth's pregnancy, Gabriel appeared to her relative, Mary.

IN DEPTH

1. A Visit from the Angel (Luke 1:26-30)

Luke tells his account of Jesus' birth from Mary's perspective, in contrast to Matthew's account, which focuses on Joseph.

When the angel Gabriel appeared to Mary, she was probably no more than about 15 years old. Perhaps the Lord chose such a young woman because she still held a level of childlike faith which enabled her to accept Gabriel's announcement without a great deal of questioning.

Luke alone records that Mary was a virgin. Other Gospel accounts do not take this fact into consideration. But this information fits into Luke's overall purpose for writing his Gospel. By establishing Mary's virginity, Luke affirmed Jesus' uniqueness—that He was both divine and human. He was not like ordinary men. God alone was responsible for His birth.

The virgin birth account also affirmed that Jesus was born of a human mother, countering some claims that He only appeared to be human. Those who believed that Jesus was not human also did not believe that His suffering on the cross was a real occurrence.

By paralleling the annunciation of Mary to that of Zacharias, Luke was able to establish Jesus' superiority over John. At the same time, he was able to show that John and Jesus were not members of opposing movements. Rather, there was unity between them, just as there is unity between the prophecies of the Old Testament and the coming of Jesus as Messiah. Luke's mention of a city of Galilee, named Nazareth, further indicates that Luke's message was directed to a Gentile audience who were unfamiliar with Palestinian geography.

Luke described Mary in such a way as to elevate two ideas. First, the fact that Mary was still a virgin. Second, that she was espoused, or engaged, to Joseph. Engagement in those days was a much more serious affair than it has become in contemporary times. According to the type of engagement Joseph and Mary had, she was already considered his legal wife. However, a period of time normally elapsed between the espousal and the actual celebration of the marriage, when the couple would begin to live together.

Gabriel addressed Mary as "thou that are highly favoured," indicating that the Lord had a special purpose for her. Before Gabriel even told her the wonderful news, he assured her that "the Lord is with thee."

Understandably, the sight of Gabriel and the words he was saying was a lot for a young woman to absorb. Mary was troubled. She was trying to figure out what Gabriel was talking about. Often the call of God strikes fear in our hearts as it comes. In His presence, any task He would have for us seems too great for our unworthiness. In the presence of His fullness, we are made fully aware of our inadequacies. No matter what the calling, we fear that we are not sufficient to fill it. As much as being afraid, Mary was probably overwhelmed. Picture an angel bringing accolades and a divine message!

Sensing Mary's fear, Gabriel assured her not to be afraid. She was not in trouble with the Lord. On the contrary, she had found favor with God.

2. Important Instructions (Luke 1:31-35)

Mary probably never could have imagined what the Lord had in store for her. She was about to conceive a child in her womb and bring forth a son. Gabriel even told her what the son's name would be—Jesus. The name Jesus is the Greek equivalent of the Hebrew word "Joshua," meaning "the Lord is salvation." The boy to whom Mary would give birth would bring salvation to the world.

Mary's son would be great. Undoubtedly, every mother believes she has given birth to a wonderful living being. Gabriel wanted Mary to understand the full extent of what she was about to experience. He would be called many names, including Son of the Highest.

The promised Messiah was also to be from the lineage of David, which accounts for the mention of Joseph. God fulfilled His promise to David through His own Son and David's descendant Jesus. His birth was the fulfillment of the Old Testament teaching concerning the righteous reign of God. David reigned on a throne in Jerusalem for only a few years. Jesus reigns forever in the hearts of those who believe.

The Jews rested their hope in the Messiah's Davidic lineage, even though their hope was for an earthly kingdom and a politically powerful king. Gabriel's words recall the predictions of 2 Samuel 7:13-16 and Isaiah 9:6-7. Israel's long awaited king would be born to a family of humble means in an unfamiliar city. His birth was without great human fanfare.

Knowing herself to be a virgin, Mary naturally questioned how she could conceive a child. She wondered how she might have a child seeing she did not know a man? Gabriel affirmed his message by explaining that Mary's Son would come out of supernatural conception. The Holy Ghost would come upon Mary. The child would be holy; He would be the Son of God. What actually took place was creation, rather than conception. Through the intervention of the Holy Ghost, Mary became the mother of God's Son.

3. All Things Are Possible (Luke 1:36-38)

Much to Mary's own surprise, God chose her to accomplish His purpose. Perhaps because she was younger, Mary did not ask Gabriel to authenticate his message, as did Zacharias. Nevertheless, she was told of Elizabeth's pregnancy so she would know that with God nothing shall be impossible. The angel Gabriel was full of miraculous news. The same God who had allowed Elizabeth to conceive in her old age held the power to create life in Mary's womb. Elizabeth had never given birth and was considered barren. She and Zacharias had long given up hope for having a child of their own. God keeps His promises to His people no matter how difficult the circumstances may seem.

In spite of her surprise, bewilderment, confusion, and any other emotions she experienced, Mary gave herself in humble submission to God's will. The Lord was able to use her because she was willing to accept whatever consequences would follow as a result of doing God's will. She was willing to accept shame and ridicule in order for God

to use her. For her obedience, Mary became mother of the world's Saviour. She affirmed her humble status by referring to herself as the handmaid of the Lord. Mary put herself in the hands of the God whom she both trusted and served.

SEARCH THE SCRIPTURES

1. When did Gabriel appear to Mary? (v. 26)
2. How does Luke introduce Mary? (v. 27)
3. How did Gabriel greet Mary? (v. 28)
4. How did Mary react to Gabriel's words? (v. 29)
5. What message did Gabriel have for Mary? (vv. 30-33)
6. What was Mary's reaction to what Gabriel told her? (v. 34)
7. What explanation did Gabriel give as to how Mary would conceive her Son? (v. 35)
8. What incident did Gabriel cite as affirmation of what was about to happen to Mary? (v. 36)
9. How did Gabriel explain Elizabeth's circumstances? (v. 37)
10. How did Mary respond to the great call God had extended to her? (v. 38)

DISCUSS THE MEANING

1. Gabriel referred to Mary as "highly favoured" and "blessed . . . among women." God's blessings do not always come as we expect them. Although Mary is celebrated throughout the Christian faith as the mother of our Lord, consider what she endured during her life. How can Mary's life of submission to the will of God help us to understand our own call to do God's will?

2. Mary was very young when Gabriel told her about God's plans for her life. How might an older woman have reacted to such news?

3. Did Mary have a choice in what was about to happen to her? Could she have refused to be the mother of the Messiah.

LESSON IN OUR SOCIETY

Living in the "information age" is beneficial to our existence on earth. But how beneficial is it to our faith? We are exposed to more knowledge than any society before us. Often our children know more by the time they are ten than we knew in our twenties.

Mary's question to Gabriel, "How can this be?" made sense. Still she willingly submitted herself to the will of God. In this information, high-tech age, we must be careful that we do not have so much knowledge and technical understanding that we lose our ability to see the wonder and mystery of God's handiwork. When we look at our lives in terms of logic, reason, and intellect, we leave little room for faith.

MAKE IT HAPPEN

None of us ever has any idea of the full extent of our faith journey when we answer God's call. Although Mary was told she would give birth to the Messiah, she could not conceive of the full meaning of being the mother of Jesus. How has your own life twisted and turned as you have allowed yourself to be shaped and molded in God's will? How different is your life in God's will than it would have been if you had followed only your own plans for your life?

FOLLOW THE SPIRIT

What God wants me to do:

_____

_____

REMEMBER YOUR THOUGHTS

Special insights you learned:

_____

_____

MORE LIGHT ON THE TEXT
Luke 1:26-38

Luke, the physician, begins the book that bears his name by stating the purpose of his writing, and to whom he is writing the "Gospel," in a preface (1:1-4). He begins with the story of the birth of John the Baptist, beginning with the angel's announcement to Zacharias, John's father, Zacharias' encounter with the angel, the conception of John by Elizabeth until her fifth month of pregnancy (1:5-25). Luke then turns our attention to the historical narration of the announcement by the angel Gabriel, of the conception and consequent incarnation of Christ to Mary, and Mary's reaction to this unusual news (vv. 26-38).

1:26 And in the sixth month the angel Gabriel was sent from God unto a city of Galilee, named Nazareth,

Luke begins this section of the story by referring back to the story about the birth of the John. "In the sixth month" points to the Elizabeth's pregnancy with John (v. 24) and links it with the announcement of the birth of Christ. It has been six months since the angel Gabriel announced to Zacharias about the birth of his son. Elizabeth is now six months pregnant, and the Lord sends Gabriel out again to the city of Nazareth in Galilee. His mission is to announce the birth of yet another Son. Gabriel, which means man of God, is one of the chief angels. He is sent to a "virgin," *parthenos* (**par-then'-os**), which means a young girl, a marriageable maiden.

Two Hebrew words, *betula* and `*alma,* are translated virgin in the Old Testament. *Betula* comes from a root meaning "to separate" and it is commonly used for women (and men) who have never had sexual intercourse. It is also figuratively used of nations, e.g., the virgin of Israel (Jeremiah 18:13; 31:4, 21; Amos 5:2) the virgin daughter of Zion (Isaiah 37:22), etc. The second Hebrew word, `*alma,* is derived from a root meaning "to be sexually mature." It refers to a woman of marriageable age who has not yet borne children, though she may be married. It is used seven times and is translated "virgin" (Genesis 24:43; etc.), "maid" (Exodus 2:8; Proverbs 30:19), and "damsels" (Psalm 68:25). Therefore, the use of the Greek word *parthenos* here refers to a pure virgin who has never known a man in an intimate way, one who has never experienced a marriage relationship. As we shall see later, in Mary's case it is clearly stated that she has never known a man (v. 34). There are therefore no grounds to question or deny the virgin birth of Christ.

27 To a virgin espoused to a man whose name was Joseph, of the house of David; and the virgin's name was Mary.

The angel Gabriel is sent "to a virgin espoused to a man whose name was Joseph." The word translated "espoused" is the Greek word *mnesteuo* (**mnace-tyoo'-o**) which means to be promised in marriage or to be betrothed, or to give a souvenir (engagement present), i.e. betroth. It simply means to be engaged as signified by the giving of a diamond ring. Betrothing someone in the Jewish custom was the most important part of marriage. It was as legal as the actual marriage; and it cannot be broken off except by a bill of divorce. In the Bible the betrothed woman was regarded as a wife and was under an obligation to be faithful (Genesis 29 21; Deuteronomy 22:22-24; Matthew 1:18, 20), and the man was regarded as the husband (Joel 1:8; Matthew 1:19). Although both were regarded as husband and wife, they did not engage in any marital relationship (sexually) until the actual marriage took place according to the custom. It is said that the girls were usually espoused at the age of puberty, i.e., in their teens. Usually the parents of the man or woman chose the wife or husband for their son or daughter as in the case of Hagar and Ishmael (Genesis 21:21) and Judah for Er (Genesis 38:6). In other cases the man did the choosing and his parents did the negotiating, e.g., Shechem (Genesis 34:4, 8) and Samson (Judges 14:2).

This Jewish custom is comparable with most African marriages, where not only do the parents arrange or negotiate for their sons or daughters' marriages, they also arrange for their betrothal at infancy. For example, in most communities in the Igbo land of Nigeria, before the coming of the "white man," families marry for their children, or betroth for their children, at birth. When a boy is born to a family, the father starts planning for his wife to be. He looks for a family where a girl is born, especially in a good family, preferably among family friends. He places a token or a souvenir (engagement present) into the drinking container or cup of the newborn girl. This signifies a promise of marriage between the two. This act is usually binding and honored by the two families. The children are introduced to each other at very young age and told they have been betrothed to marry. Although they are regarded as husband and wife, they cannot engage in any marital affair until they are of marriageable age and were married. They are to keep themselves pure and reserved for each other. The girl lives with her parents until after the actual marriage ceremonies are completed. She then goes and lives with the man. This is the idea expressed here by Luke.

The angel goes to the village of Nazareth, and approaches a virgin engaged to a named Joseph.

The virgin's name is Mary. Luke refers to Joseph as "of the house of David," and Matthew's genealogical account traces Mary's lineage also to King David. This is in fulfillment of the messianic prophecy (v. 32; cf. Psalm 132:11, 17; Isaiah 9:6, 7; 16:5) that the Messiah will be from the lineage of David.

28 And the angel came in unto her, and said, Hail, thou that art highly favoured, the Lord is with thee: blessed art thou among women.

The angel comes to Mary and greets her, "Hail, thou art highly favoured." Hail here is the Greek *chairo* (**khah'-ee-ro**) a common form of greeting, which can be used in various ways and occasions. It can be used as salutation on meeting, or parting from, someone. It is often translated rejoice, be glad, joy, or simply greetings, and farewell. It also means to be "cheerful." It is used to wish someone well and often appeared at the beginning of ancient letters, especially Hellenistic letters. The angel adds three more clauses to the greeting. The first one is "thou art highly favoured," i.e., Greek *charitoo* (**khar-ee-to'-o**), which is to say, "You are endued with special honor or grace," that is, to be encompassed with divine grace or favor. The verb *charitoo* is derived from the noun *charis*, which means grace, usually interpreted as "unmerited favour" from God. *Charis*, "grace" (with *eirene*, "peace") was a form of Jewish greeting, and was used also in ancient letter writings, both at the opening and closing of letters. Paul often used both Hellenistic and Jewish forms of greetings in most of his epistles (cf., Ephesians 1:6; Philippians 1:2). Here the angel also combines the two, probably to reflect both the Jewish and the contemporary Grecian culture of the time.

The second clause the angel adds in the greeting is "the Lord is with you." Mary was not only endued or encompassed with divine grace or God's favor, the angel assures her of the Lord's presence with her. This is reminiscent of the angel's address to Gideon assuring him of God's help and encouragement in the special assignment he was about to receive from God (Judges 6:12).

Finally, the angel adds, "Blessed art thou among women." Doubtless, having been highly favored and having the Lord with her translates into being specially blessed of God. The idea here is that among all women, Mary was the most blessed of them all. The word translated "blessed" is the Greek word *eulogeo*, pronounced **yoo-log-eh'-o** (to eulogize, or eulogy), i.e., to praise, to speak well of, or to invoke a benediction upon someone. It also has the idea of making happy or to bestow blessings. Here, because she has been highly favored of God and because of what God is going to accomplish through her, Mary would either be the most well spoken of among all women, or the most blessed in terms of being happy among all women, or both. However, the angel declares her as the most honored (and most privileged) of all women.

29 And when she saw him, she was troubled at his saying, and cast in her mind what manner of salutation this should be. 30 And the angel said unto her, Fear not, Mary: for thou hast found favour with God.

The angel's greeting "troubled" Mary, and she wondered what type of greeting this was. The word "troubled" is a translation *diatarasso*, pronounced **dee-at-ar-as'-so**, which is to disturb wholly or to be greatly agitated or alarmed. That means she was gripped with fear. Earlier in this chapter (v. 12) we read that when Zacharias saw the angel "he was troubled," *tarasso*, which has the same meaning with *diatarasso* but in a lighter sense. Both of these have the idea of having inner commotion, taking away the calmness of mind, to be disturbed. Unlike Zacharias, Mary was more perplexed at the angel's greeting rather than the angel's appearance (cf., v. 12 and v. 29). She "cast in her mind," i.e., *dialogizomai* (**dee-al-og-id'-zom-ahee**), simply means that she pondered it in her mind the type of greeting it was. She was more afraid, highly agitated, and frightened than surprised at the "strange" greeting. Hence the angel calms her down, and tells her not to "fear" and assures her that she has found favor with God. The Lord said to Isaac, "I am the God of Abraham thy father: fear not, for I am with thee, and will bless thee, and multiply thy seed for my servant Abraham's sake" (Genesis 26:24).

31 And, behold, thou shalt conceive in thy womb, and bring forth a son, and shalt call his name JESUS.

The angel goes on to explain why and how she

has found favor with God, that she has been chosen by God to bear a son whose name would be called Jesus. Legend has it that because of the prophecy of the Old Testament concerning the virgin birth of the Saviour, all young Jewish girls kept themselves "holy"; each anticipated being the agent of the prophecy's fulfillment. Now Mary is the agent through whom God would fulfill His divine plan, hence she is the "highly (most) favored" among women. The angel tells her that she would "conceive," *sullambano* (**sool-lam-ban'-o**), that is, she would take in, or she would be pregnant and bear a son. Notice the wording here is identical with the virgin birth passage of Isaiah (7:14), and reminiscent of the Lord's assurance to Hagar (Genesis 16:11). She would "bring forth (*tikto*, i.e., she would bear) a son and would call his name Jesus." The name Jesus (*Iesous*, **ee-ay-sooce'**) is the Greek equivalent of the Hebrew "Joshua" (*Yehoshua*), which means Saviour or Yahweh is Salvation. It is the earthly name of God's Son; it describes the purpose of his birth, to deliver or save the people of God from their sins (Matthew 1:21). Hence, the name also means deliverer.

The name "Jesus," or its Hebrew equivalent "Joshua" (Jehoshua), was common among the Jews. Many parents are said to have given this name to their sons as the expression of their yearning that their son might be the promised Messiah, or that their son would be a great leader like Joshua of the Old Testament. This practice is common among Africans. In many cases, African names usually reflect the parents' wishes for the children. For example, the Igbo might name a son Eze, which means "king"; it is an expression of their wish for that child to grow to be great, famous, or even to be a king. However, the name of "Jesus" to be born of the Virgin Mary was a direct command from God, and it described distinctly the purpose of Christ as the real "Redeemer," the one to fulfill the long expected One of Israel.

32 He shall be great, and shall be called the Son of the Highest: and the Lord God shall give unto him the throne of his father David: 33 And he shall reign over the house of Jacob for ever; and of his kingdom there shall be no end.

Angel Gabriel continues to describe to Mary the

type of child to be born of her. "He shall be great," the angel says. To Zacharias, the angel said that his son "will be great in the sight of God" (v. 15), but to Mary, he says her Son will be great without any qualification. Is there any significance to the difference in the two sayings? Both John and Jesus would be great, but Jesus was to be the greater (John 3:27-30; Matthew 11:11). The word translated "great" here is *megas,* and it speaks of eminent in ability, virtue, authority, and power. It has the idea of a thing or a person highly esteemed for excellence, and for preeminence. Christ's greatness is also inferred from the fact that He "shall be called the Son of the Highest" (vv. 33, 35, 76) in the sphere of His divinity, while in His humanity "the Lord God shall give unto him the throne of his father David." The man with unclean spirit called Him Son of the most high God (Mark 5:7). Of the 11 times the phrase "Most High" appears in the New Testament, it is used seven times in Luke (vv. 32, 35, 76; 2:14; 6:35; 8:28; 19:38). The statement "the Lord God shall give unto him the throne of his father David" is a confirmation of the Old Testament prophecy to David (2 Samuel 7:16; Isaiah 9:6-7;). It also implies that Mary was a descendant of David. Since there is mention of Joseph here, and the child would be born without the help of a husband, Mary had to be a descendant of David for the child to belong to the lineage of David. His reign shall be forever over the "house of Jacob," and his kingdom shall have no end. His rule over the "house of Jacob" seems to be a spiritual one and it will be eternal, endless. The "kingdom," or *basileia* (**bas-il-i'-ah**), does not indicate a territorial rule, but a spiritual reign over the hearts of men.

34 Then said Mary unto the angel, How shall this be, seeing I know not a man?

Still overwhelmed with the angel's announcement, Mary asks the angel, "How shall this be, seeing I know not a man?" We should note the difference between Mary's question and Zacharias' (v. 18). Mary's language here indicates a surprise (not doubt) and a desire for more information, rather than a request for proof or a sign, whereas Zacharias' words "Whereby shall I know this? for I am an old man, and my wife well stricken in years," show a doubting man that needs a sign to prove the

truth of what has been spoken. Mary only wants to know how the saying is going to be fulfilled when she says, "I know not" (*ginosko* pronounced **ghin-oce'-ok**) "a man." The verb *ginosko* is used here in the same sense as the Hebrew verb *yada* in Genesis (4:1; 19:8, etc.). It means to have an intimate or sexual relationship. Mary's reaction and her question confirm the Jewish custom as described above; it also indicates that the announcement has an immediate or imminent undertone to its fulfillment. It is not what would happen after the customary Jewish marriage ceremony, but before it. This is how Mary understood it. Hence her question, "How shall this be, seeing I know not a man?"

35 And the angel answered and said unto her, The Holy Ghost shall come upon thee, and the power of the Highest shall overshadow thee: therefore also that holy thing which shall be born of thee shall be called the Son of God.

The angel's reply is one of the most profound statements in the Bible and it has shaped the Christian doctrine of incarnation, the virgin birth, and the doctrine of the trinity. In it contains the holiest mysteries of all time, a mystery that has never been, or ever will be, unfolded. Here the creative power of God through the Holy Spirit is made manifest in the birth of the Son of God. The angel said to Mary that the Holy Ghost (Spirit) "shall come" (*eperchomai,* **ep-er'-khom-ahee**) upon her. That means the Holy Spirit would descend upon her. The Greek is also translated to "overcome" and is used of sleep, of disease, of calamities, or of an enemy attacking. Here, as in Acts of the Apostles (1:8), the word is used of the Holy Spirit descending and operating in a person. We can sense the overpowering force of the Holy Spirit coming upon her as on the day of the Pentecost. The Holy Spirit will come upon (and overpower) her and the power (presence) of the Highest (i.e., Most High) will "overshadow" her. "Overshadow," *episkiazo* (**ep-ee-skee-ad'-zo**), has the idea of casting a shade upon a thing, i.e., to envelope or engulf. That means she would be saturated with the presence of the Almighty just like the cloud which filled the tabernacle symbolizing the glory and presence of the Lord (Exodus 40:34; Numbers 9:15). The angel further told Mary that He who would be born of her would be "holy" and "shall be called the Son of God." The use of the conjunction "therefore" indicates the result of this supernatural phenomenon, i.e., the conception, the "thing" to be born, would be holy, and consequently He will be called the Son of God. It is important to point out here, as Geldenhuys also noted, that the angel "does not say that through His conception by the Holy Ghost Jesus will become the Son of God." (Norval Geldenhuys, *Commentary on the Gospel of Luke*, Grand Rapids, Wm. B. Eerdmans Pub. Co., 1979, p. 77). He is the Son of God. Here we see the dual nature of Christ: His divine and human nature. As the Son of God He is human "born of a woman" (Galatians 4:4) in order that He might identify with mankind whom He came to save. As deity He is holy and only someone free from the taint of sin would be able to redeem people from their sins. It takes a holy One to reconcile man to God. These qualities are found in Christ. His deity and humanity both are reconciled to accomplish God's purpose.

36 And, behold, thy cousin Elisabeth, she hath also conceived a son in her old age: and this is the sixth month with her, who was called barren. 37 For with God nothing shall be impossible.

In order to further confirm the accuracy of this announcement and strengthen her faith, the angel informs Mary that Her cousin Elisabeth, who is already advanced in age, has also conceived a son. She is already six months pregnant, the angel tells her, which seems to dispel any doubt and further assures Mary of the truthfulness of God's word. The phrase "who was called barren" further strengthens the miraculous tendency of the pregnancy. Here the angel says, "Even (*kai*) your cousin, Elisabeth, the one who is now very old and beyond the age of bearing, and one who has been deemed by all as barren, unable to have kids, she is now pregnant, and already is six months into her pregnancy." This is totally the work of God. "For with God nothing shall be impossible," the angel concludes. This phrase refers both to Mary and Elisabeth, and tends to assure Mary that if God could make an old woman have a child like her cousin Elisabeth, God is able to do whatever He purposes to do. Jesus told His disciples "With men this is impossible; but with God all things are possible" (Matthew 19:26; Luke

18:27), an echo of the Lord's rhetorical question to Sarah on a similar occasion (cf., also Job 42:2; Jeremiah 32:17). It also emphasizes the omnipotence and faithfulness of God (Isaiah 55:11)

38 And Mary said, Behold the handmaid of the Lord; be it unto me according to thy word. And the angel departed from her.

After being told of the "impracticable" news of her relative's pregnancy through the working power of the Almighty, Mary surrenders herself completely to the will and plan of God for her life, and accepts the special honor and responsibility as announced by the angel. She does this in a solemn and simple way, "Behold the handmaid of the Lord; be it unto me according to thy word." The language here "behold," *idou* (**id-oo'**), which is interpreted as look, see, or lo, means, here am I." Likewise "handmaid," (*doule*, the female form of *doulos* slave) signifies a voluntary submission to God, a response to the task ahead. As we learn from the rest of the Gospels and from Simeon's prophecy (2:34-35) in particular, to be the mother of Jesus Christ, God's Son, was not an easy task. Indeed Mary's heart was "pierced with the sword" when her Son began to suffer for the rest of mankind.

DAILY BIBLE READINGS

M: The Birth of Jesus Foretold
Luke 1:26-33
T: Mary Says Yes to God
Luke 1:34-38
W: The Joy of God's Presence
Psalm 16
T: The Lord Helps Me
Psalm 121
F: The Miraculous Conception
Matthew 1:18-25
S: The Genealogy of Jesus the Messiah
Matthew 1:1-17
S: The Mercies of God
Lamentations 3:22-26

TEACHING TIPS

December 17
Bible Study Guide 3

1. Words You Should Know

A. Magnificat—Mary's song of praise; the first word of Mary's song in the Latin Vulgate scriptural text.

B. Salutation (v. 41)—a greeting.

2. Teacher Preparation

Read today's lesson text and the Old Testament verses on which Mary based her words of praise: Deuteronomy 10:21; Psalm 103:17 and Psalm 111:9. Review material concerning the promised Messiah, including the prophecies of Isaiah. Think about how Mary, even from the beginning, understood that this child was not for her and Joseph alone. Though she did not understand the full scope of His ministry and purpose, she understood that His purpose and calling included those who were suffering and oppressed.

3. Starting the Lesson

A. Tell the class to imagine the thoughts that went through Mary's head as she traveled the 80 or so miles to visit her older relative. Talk about how comforting Elisabeth's words of praise must have been to this young girl and served as a confirmation of the angel's message.

B. Read today's IN FOCUS story about Karen. Discuss how the consequences of life often "throw us for a loop." Ask members to share how the Lord has used their adverse or unexpected circumstances to bless them with something great.

4. Getting Into the Lesson

A. Compare Mary's song of praise with other songs of praise, such as Hannah's Song (1 Samuel 2:1-10), Moses' Song (Exodus 15:1-18) and Miriam's Song (Exodus 15:21). Talk about how the Lord made a way for each of them to come through a difficult situation. When all of them realized what the Lord had brought them through, they were moved to praise Him.

B. Talk with class members about the Hebrews'

expectation concerning a Messiah and how Mary's Song affirms the fulfillment of God's promise through her.

5. Relating the Lesson to Life

A. Review THE PEOPLE, PLACES, AND TIMES article. Talk about the person Elisabeth. She may have wondered for years why she had not conceived yet, still she remained faithful to the Lord. Compare how we desire things of the Lord yet we must wait in faith.

B. Give students an opportunity to answer the questions in SEARCH THE SCRIPTURES.

C. The LESSON IN OUR SOCIETY addresses how blessings often come through unexpected circumstances in life. Discuss the importance of leaving ourselves open to God's leading.

6. Arousing Action

Give each member a pencil and paper. Ask each of them to create a short song of praise, recalling a time when God moved in their lives in a mighty way. If some members have difficulty doing so, ask them to find a hymn which in some way parallels the way God has moved in their own life.

WORSHIP GUIDE

For the Superintendent or Teacher
Theme: Praising God
Theme Song: Angels We Have Heard on High
Scripture: Psalm 34:1-3
Song: Angels, from the Realms of Glory
Meditation: I thank God for all the blessings that have been manifested in my life. I will even thank God for the difficult times as I have often received the greatest blessings in and through times of trouble.

PRAISING GOD

Bible Background • LUKE 1:39-56
Printed Text • LUKE 1:39-55
Devotional Reading • PSALM 34:1-3

LESSON AIM

After studying today's lesson, students should have a greater understanding of the relationship between Mary and Elisabeth. Class members will also learn about the Old Testament foundation for Mary's song of praise.

KEEP IN MIND

"And Mary said, My soul doth magnify the Lord, And my spirit hath rejoiced in God my Saviour. For he hath regarded the low estate of his handmaiden: for, behold, from henceforth all generations shall call me blessed" (Luke 1:46-48).

FOCAL VERSES

Luke 1:39 And Mary arose in those days, and went into the hill country with haste, into a city of Judah;

40 And entered into the house of Zacharias, and saluted Elisabeth.

41 And it came to pass that, when Elisabeth heard the salutation of Mary, the babe leaped in her womb; and Elisabeth was filled with the Holy Ghost:

42 And she spake out with a loud voice, and said, Blessed art thou among women, and blessed is the fruit of thy womb.

43 And whence is this to me, that the mother of my Lord should come to me?

44 For, lo, as soon as the voice of thy salutation sounded in mine ears, the babe leaped in my womb for joy.

45 And blessed is she that believed: for there

LESSON OVERVIEW

LESSON AIM
KEEP IN MIND
FOCAL VERSES
IN FOCUS
THE PEOPLE, PLACES,
AND TIMES
BACKGROUND
AT-A-GLANCE
IN DEPTH
SEARCH THE SCRIPTURES
DISCUSS THE MEANING
LESSON IN OUR SOCIETY
MAKE IT HAPPEN
FOLLOW THE SPIRIT
REMEMBER YOUR THOUGHTS
MORE LIGHT ON THE TEXT
DAILY BIBLE READINGS

shall be a performance of those things which were told her from the Lord.

46 And Mary said, My soul doth magnify the Lord,

47 And my spirit hath rejoiced in God my Saviour.

48 For he hath regarded the low estate of his handmaiden: for, behold, from henceforth all generations shall call me blessed.

49 For he that is mighty hath done to me great things; and holy is his name.

50 And his mercy is on them that fear him from generation to generation.

51 He hath shown strength with his arm; he hath scattered the proud in the imagination of their hearts.

52 He hath put down the mighty from their seats, and exalted them of low degree.

53 He hath filled the hungry with good things; and the rich he hath sent empty away.

54 He hath helped his servant Israel, in remembrance of his mercy;

55 As he spake to our fathers, to Abraham, and to his seed for ever.

IN FOCUS

"Why did this have to happen to me?" Karen asked with tears stinging down her face. "It wasn't supposed to be this way!" She sank into her favorite chair to try and figure out what had happened to her today.

As the first African-American to be promoted to vice-president of her company, Karen had made her family and a lot of other people proud. She

180

always received high praise on her performance evaluations. They said they were letting her go because the company was "reorganizing" and "changing its vision."

Inwardly, Karen knew she was let go because she'd continued to push for a minority recruitment program at the company. Other than herself, a person was hard-pressed to find other black and minority faces.

Just as she pondered whether to take legal action against the company, her husband, James opened the front door. "What's wrong?" he asked as soon as he took one look at her.

Karen told James the shocking news. "What should I do?" she asked the man who had supported her through so many career decisions.

"Well," James replied, "it's not something we planned, but surely something good can come out of it."

"Good?" Karen said sarcastically. "What good could possibly come out of a mess like this?"

James smiled and answered, "You know how you've been talking about moving back home and using your law degree to help poor and struggling women go after the dead-beat dads?" Karen nodded as he continued. "Well, it might just be that the Lord is telling you it's time to move on and start doing what you really want to do."

For the first time since she'd gotten the bad news, Karen began to look hopeful. Even though she had "made it big" in the corporate world, she never truly felt that God blessed her to earn a law degree just so she could make lots of money at a big company. A small law firm in her hometown had always been her dream. James was self-employed and could basically do his job from anywhere in the country.

THE PEOPLE, PLACES, AND TIMES

Elisabeth. Her name means "my God is good fortune" or "my God has sworn an oath." The mother of John the Baptist, the forerunner of Christ, was a descendant of Aaron, the daughter of a priestly family, and wife of Zacharias the priest. Both she and her husband were uplifted as examples of piety and devotion to God. They were righteous in the eyes of the Lord (Luke 1:6). In spite of their faithfulness, Elisabeth remained barren in her old age. Infertility was viewed as a punishment from God, yet this couple was faithful and true to the Lord. In His mercy, God chose to remove the social and religious stigma of childlessness. Although she and Mary, mother of Jesus, were relatives, the versions other than the King James do not specify the extent of their kinship. Elisabeth was equally joyous over the anticipated birth of the Messiah, inspiring Mary to create a song of praise.

Based on information from Holman Bible Dictionary, Trent Butler, general editor, Nashville: Broadman & Holman Publishers, 1991, p. 413. Additional information from All the Women of the Bible, by Edith Deen, San Francisco: Harper & Row Publishers, 1988, pp. 168-170.

Hill Country of Judah. This region was located along a desert tract west of the Dead Sea, possibly near Ain Karem, located four miles north of Jerusalem. The home of Elisabeth and Zacharias was probably within walking distance of the Temple in Jerusalem where Zacharias carried out his priestly duties. The hill country named throughout the Bible is generally characterized by elevated land, lower than a mountain or with lower peaks than the mountain region.

Based on information from Holman Bible Dictionary, Trent Butler, general editor, Nashville: Broadman & Holman Publishers, 1991, p. 648. Additional information from All the Women of the Bible, by Edith Deen, San Francisco: Harper & Row Publishers, 1988, pp. 168-170.

BACKGROUND

Two women whose lives probably seemed very different were now joined together, both figuring prominently in the most spectacular event known to all of humanity. One woman, Elisabeth, was older and well past the normal childbearing years. Her relative, Mary, was propelled into motherhood somewhat sooner than she had anticipated. Both women were joyous over the events that were taking place around them. Both were pleased that God had somehow seen fit to use them as part of His divine plan.

Motherhood did not fit conveniently into the lifestyle of either woman at the time she conceived. Nevertheless, each woman yielded themselves to the will of God.

After Gabriel left Mary, she decided to pay a visit to Elisabeth. Now that Elisabeth was in the final months of pregnancy, perhaps Mary decided to help her older relative to prepare for the coming of her baby. Surely Mary was calmed by being in the presence of another woman who had experienced a rather miraculous conception at the hand of the Lord. Mary probably was able to learn some things about married life as she observed the actions of an older woman who had been married for many years.

IN DEPTH

1. Mary's Visit to Elisabeth (Luke 1:39-45)

Mary's visit to Elisabeth brings together the two events which have taken place up to now in Luke. The visit gives readers more insight into the relationship between the two women's sons.

Mary probably couldn't wait to visit Elisabeth. She probably wanted to talk with someone who wouldn't think she was going insane. Although Joseph had been made privy to the sequence of events, there was no one who could understand Mary's predicament like another woman. Mary probably also wanted to verify the sign that Gabriel had given to her also.

Mary went to visit Elisabeth's home, located in the hill country of Judah. By most accounts, Mary traveled about 80 miles to visit Elisabeth, a long journey for a young woman to travel alone.

The purpose of Mary's visit is diverted as soon as Elisabeth hears her voice. At the sound of the Mary's voice, the baby Elisabeth was carrying leaped in her womb, and Elisabeth was filled with the Holy Ghost. The verb translated leaped, denotes a movement motivated by joy. The attention was now placed on Mary, the mother of the world's Saviour. This part of Luke's story points out the superiority of Mary's child over Elisabeth's. Elisabeth herself blesses Mary, the mother of her Lord. Once again it is affirmed that Mary is blessed among women. John the Baptist's mother, like her son would do later, proclaimed her unworthiness to be honored by

such an event.

Elisabeth explained how she came to know of Mary's status as the mother of the Messiah. She shared with Mary what had happened in her womb. Apparently, Mary had already conceived. As forerunner to the Christ, John the Baptist gave testimony to the coming Messiah even before he was born. The angel Gabriel had already predicted that his son would be filled with the Holy Ghost even while he was still in his mother's womb (v. 15).

Elisabeth was in awe of the grace that God extended to her, allowing her to have a role in the great plan of salvation. God owed her nothing, yet through His grace, had given her much. Elisabeth explained why she called Mary blessed and praised her for her obedience. Faithfulness to God's call always lends itself to His blessings.

2. Mary's Song (vv. 46-55)

Mary's response to Elisabeth was a song of praise known as the Magnificat. Although the song has to do with Mary, it also has to do with her Son. She did not rejoice in what she might do, rather she rejoiced in what might be done by the One she now carried in her womb. Mary began her song by saying, "My soul doth magnify the Lord." The word magnify means to praise God by declaring His greatness.

Mary's spirit rejoiced in God as her Saviour. Even though she was a young woman, she recognized God's redemptive work. Not only was He sending a Saviour, born to her from a miraculous virgin birth, but God Himself is that Saviour. She praised God for his faithfulness.

Her words are a fabric of words woven together from strands of the Old Testament. In the first part of the Magnificat, verses 46b-50, Mary expressed her joy and praise for personal blessings. Her words can easily be compared with Deuteronomy 10:21, Psalm 103:17, and Psalm 111:9. God Almighty had looked upon a young woman of no particular acclaim. Her use of the word henceforth, meaning "from now on," reveals Mary's understanding that things would never be the same again. This poor unknown Hebrew girl would now be honored above all women.

Mary listed many of the attributes of God in

her song. She praised God as a mighty God who had done great things for her. Holy is the name of the God who bestowed such blessings upon her. God extends His mercy to them that fear Him, to them who look upon Him with reverence and respect. Here the word mercy expresses the Old Testament understanding of God's loyal, gracious and faithful love.

In her song of praise, Mary praised God that, through Jesus, Israel would receive help, and the promises made to Abraham would be fulfilled. Mary's Son was the hope around which the Old Testament was focused.

Part two of Mary's song of praise relates the significance of Jesus' birth to all of Israel. Verses 51-53 represent a turnaround in the end days, when those who have abused the power given to them will be judged, and those who have been persecuted will be exalted. What God had done for Mary, God would also do for Israel. Mary awaited the day when God's people would be oppressed no longer, but instead would be blessed by the Lord. By describing God's strength with His arm, Mary was describing in a figurative manner God's power and His actions as Saviour of His people.

In her praise, Mary spoke prophetically of the blessings that would be bestowed under the reign of her Son. He would fill the hungry with good things, but the rich He would send away empty. The proud, mighty, and the rich represent those who use their position and authority to exploit and oppress others. Conversely, the hungry and those of low degree are those who have put their trust in God and wait confidently for Him to bring deliverance. The Messiah would be the divine challenge to the unjust powers of society. God will overthrow the oppressors and deliver the oppressed. This passage clearly refers to the genesis of the long-awaited messianic age during which Israel would be redeemed and restored to her former glory.

The concept of Israel as God's servant appears frequently in the Book of Isaiah (Isaiah 41:8-9; 44:1-2, 21; 48:20; 49:3). God's activity in Mary's life was rooted in promises he had made centuries before.

SEARCH THE SCRIPTURES

1. Where did Mary go after Gabriel appeared to her? (vv. 39-40)

2. What happened when Elisabeth heard Mary's voice? (v. 41)

3. What blessing did Elisabeth utter when she saw Mary? (v. 42)

4. What blessing did Elisabeth proclaim for Mary's faithfulness? (v. 45)

5. What words did Mary utter in response to Elisabeth's greeting? (vv. 46-47)

6. Why did Mary praise the Lord? (v. 48)

7. What other thing did Mary say God had done for her? (v. 49)

8. What attributes of God did Mary recite? (vv. 50-55)

DISCUSS THE MEANING

1. In what ways did Elisabeth possibly serve to uplift and strengthen young Mary for the journey ahead? How did the association of the two women possibly benefit each of them, especially in light of the fact that the two women were in different seasons of life?

2. Is it possible that Mary would not have offered such words of praise at that point in her life if she had not been strengthened by the praise and testimony of Elisabeth?

3. Was the primary purpose of Mary's visit to Elisabeth for verification of the angel Gabriel's announcement or was it more for spiritual and emotional support?

LESSON IN OUR SOCIETY

Most people in our society have been indoctrinated with the notion of planning for the future. But sometimes life throws us a series of twists and turns which are far from what we planned for ourselves. Just when we have comfortably placed ourselves on the fast track, God shifts our direction. When our lives are off track, we should not view it as failure. Sometimes God causes us to "derail" from the fast track so we can be redirected toward His will.

Neither Elisabeth nor Mary planned for what happened to them. Because they willingly received it, both received great blessings. As we plan for our futures, our plans must remain open to God's hand of movement to guide and direct us in the right way.

MAKE IT HAPPEN

Perhaps the most terrible thing that could happen to a betrothed girl is to be pregnant by someone other than her intended. Think of something in your life that you considered terrible at the time—perhaps the worst thing that ever happened to you. After you have considered the event and its outcome, think about how God managed to bestow blessings upon you as you yielded yourself to Him, allowing Him to move in your life. In retrospect, what blessings do you believe came out of that experience?

FOLLOW THE SPIRIT

What God wants me to do:

_____

_____

REMEMBER YOUR THOUGHTS

Special insights you learned:

_____

_____

MORE LIGHT ON THE TEXT
Luke 1:39-55

In the last section, we are left with the young virgin, Mary, who was overwhelmed by two strange announcements. First, that she would be the mother of the Saviour, and second that her old cousin, Elisabeth, who had passed the age of childbearing, was already six months pregnant. With this latter surprising announcement, Mary rushes to visit her cousin.

1:39 And Mary arose in those days, and went into the hill country with haste, into a city of Judah; 40 And entered into the house of Zacharias, and saluted Elisabeth.

Luke's use of the clause "and Mary arose in those days" seems to indicate that she took her journey immediately after the angel's visitation, probably one or two days later. That Mary took the trip fairly soon is apparent from the fact the angel Gabriel told her that Elisabeth was already six months pregnant (v. 36), and that Mary remained

with Elisabeth for three months (v. 56). Mary returned home just before the birth of John (v. 57). The next clause "and went into the hill country with haste" also adds to the urgency and immediacy of the journey. The word "haste," *spoude* (**spoo-day'**), indicates a "speedy" dispatch and makes it clearer that she traveled immediately, it adds excitement and a wonderous undertone to the story.

The suggestion by some commentators that Mary went to Elisabeth because Joseph was about to put her away privately, or that she was being shunned by the inhabitants of Nazareth, is baseless since her pregnancy was not evident before her travel. Moreover, Joseph and Mary had not started living together. The events recorded by Matthew (1:18-25) took place after her return from Elisabeth. By now Mary was three months pregnant and it showed.

However, with excitement mixed with wonder and anxiety, Mary took the journey to see this miracle, which had been told her by the angel. She traveled from Nazareth in the north to a city in Judea. Some have suggested that the distance from Nazareth to Elisabeth and Zacharias' home was about 70 miles, and others suggest the journey took Mary between three and five days. This information, and the name of the city, do not seem to matter so much for Luke here. Hence, the silence. What is important to Luke here is what took place as Mary enters the house of Zacharias and greets Elisabeth.

41 And it came to pass that, when Elisabeth heard the salutation of Mary, the babe leaped in her womb; and Elisabeth was filled with the Holy Ghost:

The Greek word, *ginomai* (**ghin'-om-ahee**), translated "it came to pass," has a number of renderings in English, including "it happened." The underlying idea here is "as soon as," "just as," or "immediately" Elisabeth heard Mary's greeting some strange thing happened in her womb. That strange thing is the child in her womb "leaped," *skirtao*, i.e., to jump. The word appears only two other times in the New Testament (v. 44 and 6:23) and is associated with joy. One can argue that it is natural for babies to make movements in the womb during the sixth month of pregnancy. Indeed Elisabeth must have been experiencing such movements before now. However, she was able to differentiate this from other movements. This was an extraordinary one. The child, stirred by the power of the Holy Spirit, purposely revealed to Elisabeth the fulfillment of God's blessing and the prophesy of the Messiah. The leaping of the child is the result of the "filling of the Holy Spirit" and not the other way around. Both events definitely happened simultaneously. The angel told Zacharias that the child born to Elisabeth would be filled with the Holy Spirit from his mother's womb (v. 15). Elisabeth is also filled with the Holy Spirit in the same way that the Spirit of God filled some people in the Old Testament as they prophesied, e.g., King Saul (1 Samuel 11:6), Saul's messengers (1 Samuel 19:20), and David (2 Samuel 23:2). This filling of the Holy Spirit is for specific purposes and is temporary. It differs from the outpouring and the filling of the Holy Spirit, which started at Pentecost (Acts 2). Here the Holy Spirit uses Elisabeth to confirm to Mary the prediction of the angel to her.

42 And she spake out with a loud voice, and said, Blessed art thou among women, and blessed is the fruit of thy womb.

Filled with the Holy Spirit, Elisabeth responded with great excitement and exclaimed that Mary has been blessed among women, and the child she was carrying was equally blessed. That she "spoke out with a loud voice" underlies the excitement. The statement "blessed art thou among women" echoes the angelic blessing from Gabriel (v. 28), and means that Mary is the most blessed of all women (see discussion of v. 28 in the December 10 commentary). The child born of her is also blessed, which also echoes the pronouncement of the angel concerning Jesus (vv. 32-33). Elisabeth's declaration through the power of the Holy Spirit of blessings to both Mary and "the fruit of (her) womb" confirms to Mary that what God has spoken will surely happen (Isaiah 55:11). It also increases her faith and trust in God as the angel told her, "With God nothing is impossible." The added lesson is that God uses different agents to speak to us: the Holy Spirit, angels, and humans.

43 And whence is this to me, that the mother of my Lord should come to me? 44 For, lo, as soon as the voice of thy salutation sounded in mine ears, the babe leaped in my womb for joy.

The Holy Spirit also revealed to Elisabeth that this child born of Mary was the promised Messiah, hence she calls him "Lord." She is overwhelmed with excitement and joy, and she expresses her amazement by rhetorically asking, "Why should this happen to me (my own words), that the mother of my Lord should come to me?" Here Elisabeth recognizes that it was a special privilege to be visited by Mary, the mother of the Redeemer of Israel. She also recognizes that Mary has been conferred with a greater honor than her, and she is happy with her. The tone of her question is that of wonder, humility, and excitement. Elisabeth shows no sign of jealousy whatsoever. Her excitement was so apparent that Mary herself must have wondered what was happening, hence the explanation of verse 44 of the strange thing that happened within her womb.

45 And blessed is she that believed: for there shall be a performance of those things which were told her from the Lord.

Elisabeth praises Mary for her faith. This statement here shows that Elisabeth is aware of God's prediction and promise to Mary. How she knew this is not told to us. It could be argued that Mary had told Elisabeth of how the angel had visited and of the promises of God to her. This is the natural way to think about it. However, the supernatural way is that the Holy Spirit, as continuation of His work, probably revealed it to her. The word "blessed" is the Greek *makarios,* pronounced (**mak-ar'-ee-os**), which can also be rendered happy, or fortunate, and it is used to pronounce blessing upon one. Here Elisabeth pronounces blessing on Mary because of Mary's faith in accepting the word of God. The same idea is expressed in Psalm 1 (vv. 1-2). Why is Mary happy? What does Elisabeth mean by the statement? We can look at this in three possible ways. The first way is to follow the New International Version translation, i.e., that she is blessed because she believed that which God had promised her will be accomplished. The second way is to follow King James Version rendering, i.e., that she is blessed because of the assurance that what God has promised He will definitely accomplish. Here is the premise for faith, and an urge to trust in God's faithfulness. He does not fail. Mary believed, so she is, and will be, happy. Finally, she is happy and blessed because she does not have to go through the same fate as Zacharias who doubted God and became dumb as a sign of his faithlessness (v. 20). Any of these three or a combination of all three could be possible interpretation of Elisabeth's pronouncement of blessing on Mary.

Verses 46 to 55 constitute what is generally known as the Magnificat or Mary's song. Although some early scholars have attributed the Magnificat to Elisabeth, its content definitely fits Mary's situation and sequence of events, rather than that of Elisabeth. It is not within the scope of our study here to discuss the pros and cons regarding the singer of this song (see *Commentary on the Gospel of Luke,* Norval Geldenhuys, Grand Rapids, Wm. B. Eerdman Publishing Co., 1979, p. 87, no. 1). We will accept the biblical assertion that Mary sang the hymn, and focus our attention on its content.

After Elisabeth had explained what happened when heard Mary's greeting, how blessed Mary was, Mary praised God for what He has done. The song can be divided into three strophes (stanzas). The first strophe, verses 46-49, speaks of God's grace or favor on Mary. The second strophe, verses 50-53, talks about what God has done in the life of the people of Israel. The third strophe, verses 54-55, is about God's faithfulness in keeping His promise to Abraham by sending the Messiah.

46 And Mary said, My soul doth magnify the Lord, 47 And my spirit hath rejoiced in God my Saviour.

We first notice that Mary praises the Lord after

Elisabeth, by the Holy Spirit, has revealed to her the mind of God concerning her, confirming what the angel had told her earlier. Overwhelmed with joy and gratitude, and in acceptance of the promise of God, Mary reacts spontaneously and glorifies God. The statement "My soul doth magnify the Lord, and my spirit hath rejoiced in God my Saviour" indicates a total involvement of the whole of self (emotional and spiritual) in the praise of God. The use of both "soul" and "spirit" underlies this fact. The word "soul" is a translation of the Greek, *psuche* (**psoo-khay'**), which generally means breath, or life. It is the center of and makes up of the whole being. The soul is the seat of feelings, emotion, desire, and affection. The word "magnify," *megaluno* (pronounced **meg-al-oo'-no**), is to make great, to extol or to esteem highly. "Spirit," *pneuma* (**pnyoo'-mah**), oftentimes is synonymous with soul, and speaks of the rational, or mental, disposition—the core of the inner being. Mary employs the totality of her being (the soul and spirit) to glorify God in grateful worship of God her "Saviour."

48 For he hath regarded the low estate of his handmaiden: for, behold, from henceforth all generations shall call me blessed. 49 For he that is mighty hath done to me great things; and holy is his name.

In verses 48-49, Mary gives the reason for her rejoicing and gratitude—God "hath regarded the low estate of his handmaiden." This means that God had looked upon her with respect, that God had shown favor to her who was otherwise insignificant. Mary calls herself God's "handmaiden," *doule*, which means female slave. This is the lowest position one can get in Jewish custom. Women and slaves were regarded as the lowest class in the Jewish community of the day. They were relegated to the background, to the place of dishonor. To be both (woman and slave) makes her place even worse; the society has no regard for her. In contrast, God has regard for her. He has looked upon her with favor, and has given her a place of honor. The magnitude and extent of her elevation is brought to bear in the person who made it possible, the "mighty" and the "holy" (v. 49).

Here Mary brings out what systematic theologians call the immutable (i.e., unchangeable) and the incommunicable attributes of God—His omnipotence and holiness. Here we see God, who is so mighty and holy on one hand, is able to look upon and have regard for Mary who, on the other hand, is of the lowest class. Her low estate is not only because of her person, but also her heritage—Nazareth. Nazareth was one of the most insignificant and despised villages in Galilee (when the Apostle Philip told Nathanael, "We have found him, of whom Moses in the law, and the prophets, did write, Jesus of Nazareth, the son of Joseph," Nathanael replied, "Can there any good thing come out of Nazareth?" (John 1:45-46). In spite of these seeming "disadvantages," God is able to exalt and honor Mary. She has been tremendously blessed of God, she says. For "all (every) generations shall call me blessed," i.e., every generation will acknowledge her as one

blessed and most fortunate woman among of all women (cf. vv. 28, 42).

We have seen that the first strophe deals with God's blessing to Mary. She now turns to sing about what God has done in the life of the people of Israel (vv. 50-53).

50 And his mercy is on them that fear him from generation to generation.

The conjunction "and" (*kai*) and the possessive pronoun "his" (*autou* from *autos*) connect us to the previous subject and refer us to God respectively. Here Mary brings to bear the merciful attribute of God, His consistency, and His faithfulness. Here she celebrates God's mercy on all those who "fear" (*phobeo*) Him, i.e., those who venerate or reverence him. The fear of God is verifiable by the people's obedience and keeping God's law. God's mercy is accorded specifically to the people of Israel in keeping with God's promises, which started with Abraham (Genesis 17:7; 18:18; 22:17). This mercy is demonstrated in the display of God's strength and power (vv. 51-53).

51 He hath shewed strength with his arm; he hath scattered the proud in the imagination of their hearts. 52 He hath put down the mighty from their seats, and exalted them of low degree. 53 He hath filled the hungry with good things; and the rich he hath sent empty away.

Here are two pairs of contrasting parallels, which are the direct results of God's mighty act in the coming of the Messiah. This one act results in the reversal of the human principles of living or thought. By His show of strength, God has completely altered the human view of life in general. The "proud," *huperephanos* (**hoop-er-ay'-fan-os**), the haughty, or those who exalt themselves, are scattered. The verb "scattered," *diaskorpizo* (**dee-as-kor-pid'-zo**), is figuratively used here and has either a military or an agricultural idea in view. In its military sense the strong, proud army, which relies in its own strength without God, is brought to nothing and is driven and dispersed by a stronger force. In its agricultural sense, scatter refers to the winnowing process, where the chaff is separated from the wheat and is blown away (or abroad in the air) by the wind.

Not only are the proud scattered, like chaff, or put in disarray, like an egoistic army, God has also "put down the mighty from their seats." Here the mighty are synonymous with the proud. They are the "powers that be," the oppressors of the poor, the self-exalted who look down on and tyrannize others. The mighty are deprived of their self-exalted positions, while those who are truly humble ("them of low degree"), the insignificant, are exalted.

The next pair of parallelism starts with the insignificant, "the hungry," which is synonymous with "them of low degree," and associated with poverty. The hungry here describes those who realize their need for God and aspire for spiritual food, those who "fear Him" (v. 50); they are fed, i.e., "filled with good things," and are shown mercy (v.50). On the contrary, those who are "rich," the proud, those who are self-sufficient without God, He sends "away empty." This is revolutionary indeed; it describes the purpose of Christ's coming into the word, i.e. to change the human view and principles of living. Christ spells out this principle in his Sermon on the Mount, generally known as the "Beatitudes" (esp. Matthew 5:3-6), and teaches the same to his disciples (Matthew 23:12; Luke 11:1-4; 18:14). Here Mary insinuates God's transformation of society, whereby the proud and powerful are brought low, while the lowly are brought up. Not only do Mary and Elisabeth represent the humble who have been exalted, but Nazareth as well signifies the revolutionary aspect of God's act through the coming of the Messiah.

Historically, the Old Testament is full of examples of the "proud" and "mighty" whom God, by His infinite power and design brought down: Pharaoh (Exodus 15:1-11); Haman (Esther 6:6-14); Nebuchadnezzar (Daniel 4:24-37), etc. The scriptures include "all proud" and haughty people (Psalm 33:10; 1 Peter 5:5; James 4:6). Likewise there are abundant examples of the humble exalted by God: Joseph (Genesis 41:16); David (1 Samuel 18; 2 Samuel 7); Mordecai (Esther 6:6-14); Daniel (Daniel 1:8-21), etc. The Bible includes all the humble (James 4:6; 1 Peter 5:3-6; cf., Matthew 23:12). Do we have examples of either of these two groups in our society today? If so, give examples.

54 He hath helped his servant Israel, in remembrance of his mercy; 55 As he spake to our fathers, to Abraham, and to his seed for ever.

The third strophe of Mary's hymn reveals God's faithfulness in fulfilling His promises to Abraham by sending the Messiah. Here Mary celebrates God's mercy to Israel. Just as He promised Abraham and his descendants, God has kept His promise in keeping His word to Israel, and helping them partake in this promise, not forgetting His promise but remembering His mercy. This act of mercy is an old promise (covenant) God made to Abraham and to all his generation after him. It is a living covenant to all mankind that is fulfilled in the incarnation of Jesus Christ—the Son of God.

Through this hymn of praise, Mary reveals the excellent nature of God: His divine power and authority over all things both spiritual and human (vv. 49, 51); His holiness (v. 49); His mercy and justice (v. 50); and His faithfulness and trustworthiness in fulfilling His promises (vv. 54-55). Through the incarnation of Christ we realize the omnipotence, holiness, mercy and justice, and faithfulness of God.

DAILY BIBLE READINGS

M: Gratitude
Psalm 34:1-4

T: It Is Good to Give Thanks
Psalm 92:1-4

W: Mary Visits Elizabeth
Luke 1:39-45

T: Mary's Song of Praise
Luke 1:46-56

F: Sing to the Lord
Psalm 96

S: Bless the Lord
Psalm 103:1-5; 19-22

S: Daniel's Prayer and Praise
Daniel 2:17-23

TEACHING TIPS

December 24
Bible Study Guide 4

1. Words You Should Know

A. Espoused (v. 5)—betrothed, engaged.

B. Swaddling Clothes (vv. 7, 12)—strips of cloth used for newborns to keep their arms and legs straight, and to wrap bodies for burial.

C. Manger (vv. 7, 12, 16)—a feeding trough for animals.

D. City of David (v. 11)—Bethlehem.

2. Teacher Preparation

Find passages in the Bible that address the concept of shepherding. Think about how Jesus' birth was first announced to the shepherds and that He later referred to Himself as the Good Shepherd. Compare how shepherds care for and protect their sheep and how Jesus cares for and protects those who believe in Him.

3. Starting the Lesson

A. Tell the class to consider the times in their lives when God has led them away from danger and into the safety of His arms.

Have a volunteer read the IN FOCUS story. Discuss the following implications: unlike the couple in the story, Mary and Joseph had a little baby whom they knew was destined for greatness. Still, just how that greatness would be manifested was not explained to them.

In the same way, Sheila and Ronald, and couples like them all over this country, can look back with rejoicing at how, by the grace of God, their child is on the right path to doing great things in life.

4. Getting Into the Lesson

Many might have thought that unlearned men like shepherds could not adequately comprehend the message of the angel. God's message of salvation is not a "heavy" theological treatise. It is good news for the downtrodden and oppressed.

Although we cannot fully understand God's mystery, Christians sometimes complicate the Gospel beyond what is necessary. In fact, the Gospel can be made so complex that nonbelievers cannot seem to find an opening through which to enter. Discuss this phenomena and how we can effectively make the Gospel known to those who yet do not know Christ.

DEC 24TH

5. Relating the Lesson to Life

The LESSON IN OUR SOCIETY recalls how the Saviour's birth occurred on a quiet night, without much human acknowledgment. Point out that often we miss the glory of the Lord because we are looking for it to come in ways other than what we expect.

6. Arousing Action

A. Write the following occupations on small sheets of paper: butcher, writer, professor, mechanic, accountant, homemaker, fast-food worker. Give each class member three or four of the occupations. Ask them to imagine being at a gathering with these persons. What would they talk to them about? Remind them that Christ brings together people from all walks of life and gives our lives new meaning through Him.

B. Close the class with prayer.

WORSHIP GUIDE

For the Superintendent or Teacher
Theme: Away in a Manger
Theme Song: Angels We Have Heard on High
Scripture: Matthew 16:13-16
Song: Joy to the World!
Meditation: God has already given me the gift of salvation. May I seek to spread the Good News with the same fervor and excitement as the shepherds did on that first Christmas day.

A SAVIOUR IS BORN

Bible Background • LUKE 2:1-20
Printed Text • LUKE 2:4-20
Devotional Reading • MATTHEW 16:13-16

LESSON AIM

After studying today's lesson, students will know about the events which surrounded the birth of our Saviour and how God chose to bring His Son into the world in obscurity.

KEEP IN MIND

"For unto you is born this day in the city of David a Saviour, which is Christ the Lord" (Luke 2:11).

FOCAL VERSES

Luke 2:4 And Joseph also went up from Galilee, out of the city of Nazareth, into Judaea, unto the city of David, which is called Bethlehem; (because he was of the house and lineage of David:)

5 To be taxed with Mary his espoused wife, being great with child.

6 And so it was that, while they were there, the days were accomplished that she should be delivered.

7 And she brought forth her firstborn son, and wrapped him in swaddling clothes, and laid him in a manger; because there was no room for them in the inn.

8 And there were in the same country shepherds abiding in the field, keeping watch over their flock by night.

9 And, lo, the angel of the Lord came upon them, and the glory of the Lord shone round about them: and they were sore afraid.

10 And the angel said unto them, Fear not: for, behold, I bring you good tidings of great joy, which shall be to all people.

LESSON OVERVIEW

LESSON AIM
KEEP IN MIND
FOCAL VERSES
IN FOCUS
THE PEOPLE, PLACES,
AND TIMES
BACKGROUND
AT-A-GLANCE
IN DEPTH
SEARCH THE SCRIPTURES
DISCUSS THE MEANING
LESSON IN OUR SOCIETY
MAKE IT HAPPEN
FOLLOW THE SPIRIT
REMEMBER YOUR THOUGHTS
MORE LIGHT ON THE TEXT
DAILY BIBLE READINGS

11 For unto you is born this day in the city of David a Saviour, which is Christ the Lord.

12 And this shall be a sign unto you; Ye shall find the babe wrapped in swaddling clothes, lying in a manger.

13 And suddenly there was with the angel a multitude of the heavenly host praising God, and saying,

14 Glory to God in the highest, and on earth peace, good will toward men.

15 And it came to pass, as the angels were gone away from them into heaven, the shepherds said one to another, Let us now go even unto Bethlehem, and see this thing which is come to pass, which the Lord hath made known unto us.

16 And they came with haste, and found Mary, and Joseph, and the babe lying in a manger.

17 And when they had seen it, they made known abroad the saying which was told them concerning this child.

18 And all they that heard it wondered at those things which were told them by the shepherds.

19 But Mary kept all these things, and pondered them in her heart.

20 And the shepherds returned, glorifying and praising God for all the things that they had heard and seen, as it was told unto them.

IN FOCUS

Sheila and Ronald sat across from each other at the dining room table, a mountain of papers between them. Their son, RJ had just finished showing them the stack of information he had compiled about colleges, tuition, scholarships and financial aid packages.

"Did you think we would ever see this day?" Sheila asked her husband. "I remember how young and broke we were when RJ was born—not much older than he is now."

"Yeah," Ronald agreed. "We were so young we didn't have sense enough to know how tough things could be raising a child. All I remember thinking was, 'This is my son—mine—well, ours.'"

"No," Sheila laughed. "You had it right. I think you think you had that boy all by yourself!" Then she turned serious for a moment. "I remember asking the Lord to help us take care of him properly."

"Well," Ron replied. "That's one prayer that's definitely been answered. Through thick and thin, the Lord has seen us through."

THE PEOPLE, PLACES, AND TIMES

Shepherd. The title given to one who is employed to tend sheep. Shepherding was the primary occupation of Israelites during the days of Abraham, Rachel, Jacob, and Moses. As farming began to produce greater yields, shepherding became less popular, later being assigned to younger sons, hired hands, and slaves. The farmers of Egypt held shepherds in great disdain.

The first shepherd recorded in the Bible is Abel, son of Adam and Eve (Genesis 4:2). Shepherds protected their sheep at night, either in the open (Luke 2:8) or in sheepfolds (Zephaniah 2:6) where sheep were counted as they entered the gate. Shepherds took care of their sheep, even carrying weak lambs in their arms.

Because of their role of caretaking, the word shepherd was later applied not only to those who tended sheep, but also to kings and to God Himself. Jesus referred to himself as the Good Shepherd, who knew His sheep and would lay down His life for them.

The Latin word "pastor" means shepherd.

Based on information from Holman Bible Dictionary, Trent Butler, general editor, Nashville: Broadman & Holman Publishers, 1991, p. 1263.

Heavenly Hosts. The word "host" is primarily a military term most often associated with battle or war. The most frequent use of the word is to designate a group of men organized for war. The Hebrew word often refers to a human army.

A heavenly host is the army at God's command, composed of either heavenly bodies (e.g., sun, moon, stars) or angelic beings. Psalm 33:6 reveals that God created this host by His breath. The term heavenly hosts evolved because celestial bodies were thought to be organized in the same way as military bodies on earth. The sun, moon, and stars began to be looked upon as the host of God (Genesis 2:1).

Based on information from Holman Bible Dictionary, Trent Butler, general editor, Nashville: Broadman & Holman Publishers, 1991, pp. 671-672.

BACKGROUND

Luke told the story of Mary and Joseph's journey to Bethlehem to explain why they were there and how Jesus' birth there was a fulfillment of Old Testament prophecy. He continued to describe the political climate of the day, giving the names of various political leaders, including Caesar Augustus.

In those days, Roman influence extended all across the region of the Mediterranean, across the British Isles and eastward into Asia. Under the rule of Augustus, great nephew of Julius Caesar, the name "Rome" was the epitome of wealth, power, and authority. He came to power after the murder of his uncle, being named his adopted son and heir.

During biblical times, censuses had major political implications, as they do today. But for many in those days, registration was a tool of exploitation and oppression, especially in those places where government was maintained without the people's consent. Such was the case with Israel and the

AT-A-GLANCE

1. A Baby Is Born in Bethlehem
(Luke 2:1-7)
2. The Shepherds Told (Luke 2:8-14)
3. The First Visitors (Luke 2:15-20)

Roman government. It was into this political climate that the Messiah was born.

IN DEPTH

1. A Baby Is Born in Bethlehem (Luke 2:1-7)

God used many people to fulfill the events that had been prophesied, including the birth of the Messiah in Bethlehem (Micah 5:2). Caesar Augustus determined that the entire Roman Empire would be taxed. His rule extended to a Nazarene couple who began making the journey back to the husband's ancestral home. The Roman government, in an effort to obtain the cooperation of Jews who were hostile to the very notion of a census, may have required the "ancestral home clause" in order to give the census a nationalistic appeal.

Because Joseph was from the lineage of David, he was required to return to Bethlehem. The little town was known as the City of David because of its ties to the former king of Israel. It was in Bethlehem that the prophet Samuel anointed David king of Israel. The city held a special place in David's heart. Bethlehem was located about 90 miles from Nazareth, likely a three-day journey for the couple.

Mary is referred to as Joseph's espoused wife. However, the fact that Mary made the journey with him may suggest that they were already married, though the marriage was not yet consummated. At the time of their arrival in Bethlehem, she was in an advanced state of pregnancy, being great with child.

With the advent of modern technology, some births are planned to occur at a specific time for medical reasons. But in its natural occurrence, the birth of a child cannot be predicted, it sometimes occurs at a time that is inconvenient to the parents. Possibly the physical strain of the journey to Bethlehem caused Mary to go into labor.

At His birth, Jesus was wrapped in swaddling clothes, which were strips of cloth used to wrap both newborns and the deceased. The cloths were wrapped around the baby to keep its arms and legs straight.

Luke is careful to note that Jesus is Mary's first-born son, giving further proof of her virginity by making it known that any other children came afterward.

The manger which served as Jesus' crib is generally believed to be an animal feeding trough located in a stable or a cave which served as a stable. Joseph and Mary found themselves in such primitive surroundings because there was no room for them at the inn. The inn referred to in the text was, scholars believe, most likely a large room in a private home or a space in a public hall, not a large building with individual rooms.

The words no room at the inn have been popularly attached to a number of meanings. Generally the phrase is used in connection with the ironies of life that appear to be divinely inspired. In Bethlehem a divine King is born, but His earthly parents could not secure him access in a simple hotel room upon His birth. Although he was denied accommodations, His death and resurrection would insure there would be room for everyone who desired to have a home in eternity.

It is likely that finances played a great role in determining who could get a room and who could not. In any case, they were not people of high social standing. No one knew that this young woman carried within her womb the Christ child. God had willed that His Son be born in the most humble surroundings so that He was understood to be the Saviour of all, not simply the rich or the politically connected.

2. The Shepherds Told (Luke 2:8-14)

Jesus' birth announcement was not engraved on fancy stationery. He did not receive a welcome full of pomp and circumstance. Instead, His birth was announced by angelic messengers to a lowly group of shepherds.

Why shepherds? It carried forth the message that the gospel was meant for the downtrodden and despised. These men were not highly regarded. The lifestyle their occupation required made it impossible for them to meet the requirements for religious cleanliness.

Because they were in the field, keeping watch over their flock by night, the time was probably between April and November, the time when sheep could be kept in the field. While they were faithfully tending their sheep, the angel of the Lord came, bringing them a message of hope and redemption. At the appearance of the angel, the glory of the Lord was all around them, causing them to be afraid. They were, after all, simple unlearned men. Their nights were generally uneventful, except for an occasional incident with the flock. The sight of the glory of the Lord shining all around was an awesome sight—a frightening sight.

The angel assured them there was no need to be afraid. The message was one of great joy, which shall be to all people. What message could an angel of the Lord possibly have for a group of lowly shepherds? Why wasn't the angel at Herod's palace. Why not at Augustus Caesar's throne. Why not to the chief priest or one of the rabbis? The divine message of great joy was first given to shepherds abiding in the field.

The message for these humble men, and all like them, was a Saviour was born, which was Christ the Lord. Jesus' three titles, Saviour, Christ, Lord, are the essence of His work and authority. In ancient times, a saviour was one who was able to deliver persons from human misery, disease or danger. Rulers in both the Greek and Roman were called saviours. The title was also given to Greek gods. The fact that Jesus was proclaimed a Saviour in this environment affirmed that He was a Deliverer for whom all people longed. He was the One who could do for them what no ruler or god could accomplish.

The word Christ means anointed, referring to Jesus' position as the Messiah. Lord was the title given to rulers. Jesus would rule the earth as no other could do. The Saviour who has been born is the Messiah whom God had promised to Israel. When the shepherds ventured to the city of David, they would find Him wrapped in swaddling clothes, lying in a manger. Shepherds would not have felt comfortable walking up to a king's palace. They would have been considered ritually unclean, and therefore unworthy to entire the space of holy men. But they could safely enter a stable. They were comfortable around animals. They journeyed to see the Saviour of the people.

Suddenly, there was not just one angel, but a host of heavenly beings. God's entourage of angels burst forth with praise, saying, "Glory to God in the highest, and on earth peace, good will toward men." The last phrase is believed to be more prop-

erly interpreted as "good will among those who please God." Peace is possible among those who are of God's good pleasure, even in the midst of the most difficult circumstances. Through every trial and tribulation, those who please God do not rely on outward circumstances for peace. Rather, it is the peace that passes all understanding.

3. The First Visitors (Luke 2:15-20)

Having witnessed such a spectacular sight, the shepherds were not about to go back to their work as though nothing had happened. Instead they were moved to go to Bethlehem and see this thing that has happened.

Obedient to the instructions given to them, the shepherds made the journey to Bethlehem where they discovered the baby whom the angel had described. Mary and Joseph must have wondered how the men happened upon them and how they knew about the baby's identity. The shepherds shared with them all that the angel had said.

Apparently there were others in the stable who heard the shepherds' testimony. All those who heard their amazing story wondered at those things which were told them.

The shepherds' words must have caused Mary to review her own encounter with Gabriel and all that he had told her. These things she pondered in her heart.

Since the shepherds were laborers, they could not afford to tarry at the birth site. They had to return to work. When they left, however, they were glorifying and praising God for their experience. They knew they had been made privy to a great honor, one that had not been bestowed upon royalty or religious hierarchy. They were moved to worship God for His goodness. When we reflect upon the things God has done for us, our only response can be to praise the One who makes all things possible.

SEARCH THE SCRIPTURES

1. Why did Joseph and Mary go to Bethlehem? (v. 4)

2. What happened after they arrived there? (v. 6)

3. How was Jesus clothed after He was born? (v. 7)

4. Where were the shepherds? (v. 8)

5. What was the shepherds' response to the angel's presence? (v. 9)

6. How did the angel seek to comfort the shepherds? (v. 10)

7. What good news did the angel bring? (v. 11)

8. How would the shepherds know the babe? (v. 12)

9. What words of praise did the heavenly host offer? (v. 14)

10. What did the shepherds do after the angels left them? (vv. 15-16)

11. What did the shepherds say to Joseph, Mary and the others? (vv. 17-18)

12. What was the shepherds' response to all they had experienced? (v. 20)

DISCUSS THE MEANING

1. Why are there so many ironies surrounding the birth of our Saviour? Why was He born in a stable, to a poor young couple? Why was His birth announced to shepherds? Why did Jesus' birth seem, to many, like just another baby being born?

2. How do you imagine the lives of the shepherds were changed by their angelic encounter and by their visit to the newborn King?

3. Is the angel's message, "Glory to God in the highest, and on earth peace, good will toward men" understood today in the same way it was when the shepherds first heard these words?

LESSON IN OUR SOCIETY

Our lives are so bombarded by things that are glittery attention-getters that the subtleties of life often pass us by. The Saviour of the world was born on a quiet night. There were no fireworks around him. There was no processional of kings, queens, and heads of state. There was no fancy layette nor engraved diapers for the Messiah. The most powerful and meaningful event in the world was missed by most of the world.

What are we missing today because we seek the profound in places that are not quiet and simple? How many blessings have we overlooked because we are too busy trying to be "connected" with the "right people?" How many times has Jesus been in our midst, yet we missed Him because we were looking beyond His presence for bells and whistles

instead of the still soft voice?

MAKE IT HAPPEN

The shepherds were not learned men in the traditional sense. Their job was considered menial and left them as religious outcasts. Yet the Lord chose them to receive the first birth announcement. Although they were nobodies, they followed the Lord's command.

What thing have you not done out of fear that you are not educated enough, important enough, or socially connected enough to fulfill the task? What would happen if you took your eyes off yourself and put them on the Lord instead?

FOLLOW THE SPIRIT

What God wants me to do:

_____

_____

REMEMBER YOUR THOUGHTS

Special insights you learned:

_____

_____

MORE LIGHT ON THE TEXT
Luke 2:4-20

Luke introduces us to the chronological historical events leading to the birth of Jesus—the long expected Messiah (Luke 2:1-3). It was during the reign of Caesar Augustus, the emperor of Rome. According to this account, the emperor had issued a decree that all the inhabitants of the empire should be taxed, each in his or her province. The intent of this historicity probably is to give the reason why Mary and Joseph had to go to Bethlehem. The account of Christ's birth is simple and straightforward.

2:4 And Joseph also went up from Galilee, out of the city of Nazareth, into Judaea, unto the city of David, which is called Bethlehem; (because he was of the house and lineage of David:)

Since Joseph is an offspring of David, he leaves Nazareth with Mary, now very pregnant, and travels to Bethlehem to be taxed. Why would Joseph have to travel to Bethlehem to register? Why not register in his native land Nazareth? There are two obvious reasons, one implicit and the other explicit.

The explicit reason why Joseph traveled to Bethlehem is because "he was of the house and lineage of David" (Matthew 1:6, 16), therefore the need to return to his ancestral village to be taxed. From biblical accounts, we learn that David was brought up in Bethlehem (1 Samuel 20:6; cf., Ruth 1:1, 19ff.; 4:13ff.). Bethlehem, which means the house of bread, is about five miles south of Jerusalem in Judea. It is also called the "city of David" (or Zion, cf., 2 Samuel 5:7-9; 6:10-16), probably a suburb of Jerusalem.

According to Jewish custom and tradition (which is very similar to the Africans), ancestral ties are strong; they are never broken, wherever one is born, or resides. For example, Africans never make any place home, other than their own native place of birth. One can reside in a foreign land as long as one wants, but one would still regard one's ancestral place of birth as home. Although I have been here from Africa for over 17 years, and my children were born here, we still regard Africa as our home. My children understand that they are Africans. As such, I am obligated to the development of my ancestral village. When one leaves one's village to work elsewhere, one does not break ties with those at home. In the light of this example, we can understand why Joseph had to leave his village, Nazareth of Galilee, to go to Bethlehem of Judaea to be registered.

The implicit reason why Joseph traveled to Bethlehem is because it was a fulfillment of the Old Testament prophecy, which said that the Saviour would be born in Bethlehem of Judaea, an insignificant city (Micah 5:2; cf., Matthew 2:6). Luke's historical narrative, which is absent from Matthew's account of the nativity of Christ, points to the fact that God is faithful to His word, and that He works out His purpose providentially. Why Mary had to go along with Joseph to Bethlehem has many scholars speculating. One reason that is often suggested is that Joseph took her along to protect her from further embarrassment, to support her. Whatever the reason, one thing is certain. God works through cultures and through circumstances. Here God providentially worked

through the Jewish culture (the need to return to Bethlehem) and through the political setting of the Roman Empire (the order to be registered or taxed) in order to fulfill His promise that the "Child" would be born in Bethlehem, the city of David.

5 To be taxed with Mary his espoused wife, being great with child. 6 And so it was, that, while they were there, the days were accomplished that she should be delivered.

Luke tells us that Joseph goes with his espoused wife, which means that they were still engaged according to the custom, and were practically husband and wife, but still without the usual marital or sexual intimacy. Joseph has obeyed the angel and fulfilled his contract to marry Mary. Hence, he has the responsibility to take care of her. We remember that Mary was about three months pregnant when she left Elisabeth just before the birth of John (1:56-57). The phrase "being great with child," though generally translated "she was pregnant," seems to suggest that her pregnancy had reached an advanced stage—probably the last trimester of her pregnancy. This assumption is confirmed in verse (six).

While they are in Bethlehem, Mary delivers "her firstborn son," wraps him in "swaddling clothes," and lays "him in a manger." Luke does not say how long they have been in Bethlehem before the birth. Probably as soon as they get there, or a few days later, she begins labor. The clause "the days were accomplished that she should be delivered" simply means she reached her time to deliver. It also means the time was according to God's own timetable.

7 And she brought forth her firstborn son, and wrapped him in swaddling clothes, and laid him in a manger; because there was no room for them in the inn.

"Her firstborn son," prototokos (**pro-tot-ok'-os**), indicates that Jesus was not Mary's only child. She had other children (Matthew 13:55-56). Nevertheless, after His birth His mother "wrapped him in swaddling clothes," sparganoo (**spar-gan-o'-o**). It is said that swaddling clothes were bandages tightly wrapped around a newborn according to the Oriental custom. The splendor and the cost of these bands indicated the rank of the child. The rich used costly scarves or fine shawls to wrap their children, while the poor used common clothes. Babies were wrapped so that they looked like mummies, with no sign of their arms or legs. Their heads were wrapped with only their eyes visible. This custom is referred to when God challenged Job (Job 38:9) and when Ezekiel reminded Israel of their abominations against God, "And as for thy nativity, in the day thou wast born thy navel was not cut, neither wast thou washed in water to supple thee; thou wast not salted at all, nor swaddled" (Ezekiel 16:4).

The newborn baby is laid on a manger rather than in a crib, Luke says, "because there was no room for them in the inn." The Greek word translated "inn" here, kataluma (**kat-al'-oo-mah**), does not refer to a place of public accommodation like the one where the good Samaritan took the wounded man (10:34). It is the same word that is later translated as guest-chamber, a private home with an "upper room" where Christ and His disciples celebrate the Passover (22:11-12). It is common for such homes to have barns for domestic animals. Manger, phatne (**fat'-nay**), is a stall, or an eating trough, where food is placed for animals. This is the only available space for the Son of God, because all the "hotel," or "inns" are over-booked because of the number of people that have gathered in Bethlehem. It can be argued that Joseph could not secure a proper place for the birth of their Son because they arrive late due to the long journey, or perhaps it took longer because of Mary's pregnancy. However, the main reason I would suggest is God's providence. It establishes the humanity and servitude of Christ, which Luke tries to emphasize throughout his book (9:58). It establishes at the outset the type of reign God purposed for Him.

8 And there were in the same country shepherds abiding in the field, keeping watch over their flock by night. 9 And, lo, the angel of the Lord came upon them, and the glory of the Lord shone round about them: and they were sore afraid.

In the following few verses, Luke details the strange events that happened after the birth of Christ—the angelic announcement of the birth. He informs his reader about shepherds living in the same country (or region), who were keeping their flock at night. The angel came to announce the birth of Christ. The fact that the shepherds were grazing their herd in the field by night, contradicts the assumption that Christ was born in December. Shepherds never kept flocks outside during the winter months because of the cold. It was customary to send flocks out after the Passover until the first rain in October or November. The actual month and year of Christ's birth is impossible to prove. Throughout the centuries different Christian sects have given hundreds of suggestions for the date of His birth, to no avail. However, we do not need to speculate. One thing is certain, and that is He was born of a virgin in Bethlehem of Judea according to Scriptures. That suffices.

As the shepherds watch their flock that night, the angel suddenly appears to them. The glory of the Lord shines around them. The "glory" doxa (**dox'-ah**) is used here as in the Old Testament. It always symbolizes the presence of God (Exodus 24:16; 1 Kings 8:10; Isaiah 6:1-6). It describes the radiating splendor and majesty of God's presence. The glory of God, or God's presence, is always seen or felt in different forms. To the Israelites in the wilderness it was seen as a pillar of cloud and fire. To Moses, it was seen as a burning bush. To the worshipers of the tabernacle and the temple, it was felt as the radiance of His glory. This same radiance would appear to Peter, James, and John on the Mount of Transfiguration. This phenomenon is often associated with the appearance of an angel. Here a bright light represents the glory, as described by the phrase "shone round about them." The reaction of the shepherds is consistent with Zacharias and Mary's reaction when Gabriel visited them (1:12, 29). Probably Moses had the same reaction when he encountered the burning bush (Exodus 3:2ff.). They are all overwhelmed by fear and wonder because of the strange supernatural happening. "They were sore afraid" underlies this fact.

10 And the angel said unto them, Fear not: for, behold, I bring you good tidings of great joy,

which shall be to all people. 11 For unto you is
born this day in the city of David a Saviour,
which is Christ the Lord.

Here again the reassuring words of the angel,
"Fear not" (cf., 1:13, 30), are echoed. The angel
tells them not to fear and gives them the reason
why they need not fear. He is bearing "good tidings (news) of great joy, which shall be to all people." The noun "good tidings," *euaggelizomai,* is
from the verb *euaggelizo,* pronounced **yoo-ang-
ghel-id'-zo**, which means to announce, to declare
good news. The English verb "evangelize" is a
transliteration of the Greek and can mean to
preach, especially the Gospel. Hence, evangelism
is the act of preaching, and evangelists are those
who preach or proclaim the Good News of the
Gospel. *Euaggelizomai* referred to any type of
happy news in the Old Testament, but in the New

Testament it is used for the Gospel of salvation,
which is through Christ's redemptive sacrifice.
The angel qualifies the Good News that he
announces to the shepherds. It is "good tidings of
great (*megas*) joy (*chara*)." The great news is not
only for all people, but also it will bring joy to all
people. The word "all people" (*pas laos*) has the
idea of all people groups everywhere. Therefore,
this Gospel is for people (all nationalities) and is
intended by God to bring joy to all people universally. What is the good news? The angel
announces that the long expected Messiah, the
hope of Israel, the Saviour, is born "this day in the
city of David." Notice how the angel describes this
newborn babe that is born.

First, He is a "Saviour," *soter* (**so-tare'**), which
means a deliverer, a preserver. It was a name given
by the ancients to deities, to princes, kings, and to

men who had brought deliverance to their country. It is used repeatedly of both God and His Christ, the medium of God's salvation to men.

Secondly, He is Christ. The word "Christ," a direct transliteration of the Greek, *Christos* (**khristos'**), which means anointed (the anointed one), an equivalent of the Hebrew Messiah, which is an epithet of Jesus. In Jewish thought, the Messiah would be the king of the Jews, a political leader who would defeat their enemies and bring in a golden era of peace and prosperity. In Christian thought, the term Messiah refers to Jesus' role as a spiritual deliverer, setting His people free from sin and death. (*Nelson's Illustrated Bible Dictionary, general editor, Herbert Lockyer. New York: Guidepost, 1986.*)

In Old Testament times, anointing with oil was part of the ritual of commissioning a person for a special task. Thus, the phrase "anointed one" was applied to the person in such cases. Messiah is used more than 30 times to describe kings (2 Samuel 1:14, 16), priests (Leviticus 4:3, 5, 16), and the patriarchs (Psalm 105:15). The Persian King Cyrus was referred as a messiah (Isaiah 45:1). The word is also used concerning King David, who became the model of the messianic king who would come at the end of the age (2 Samuel 22:51; Psalm 2:2). During the time of Daniel, 6th century B. C. the word Messiah was used as an actual title of the future king (Daniel 9:25-26). Even later, as the Jewish people struggled against their political enemies, the Messiah came to be thought of as a political, military ruler. Non-Christians Jews still do not accept Jesus as the Messiah and are still waiting for one. However, the angel announces to the shepherds that the cause of the strange event, which they have observed is the birth of the Christ—the long anticipated Messiah of Israel. Later on Andrew meets Jesus and tells Simon (Peter) his brother, "We have found the Messiah, which is, being interpreted, the Christ" (John 1:41). The woman at the well said to Jesus, "I know that the Messiah cometh, which is called Christ: when he is come, he will tell us all things" (John 4:25).

Thirdly, He is the "Lord." The word is a translation of the Greek, *kurios* (pronounced **koo'-ree-os**), meaning master. It signifies ownership, one

with supreme authority over another, or a group of people. It is a title of honor expressive of respect and reverence by a servant to his/her master. It was used in reference to princes, chiefs, and the Roman emperor. In the African context, servants, students, or apprentices, call their owners, teachers, or instructors "master" as sign of respect, never their names. The Igbo call their master *Nna anyi ukwu* (our big father or "dad") or *Oga*. To them the owner, the teacher, or instructor, has the same responsibility and care over them as their real father during the time they are under them. As such they have the obligation to respect them as they respect their birth father or mother. "Lord" is often used in the New Testament for God and the Messiah—the Christ. Here the angel's designation of the newborn babe as the Lord identifies him as the possessor and supreme owner of all creation. Later in the Bible, the apostle Peter declares that "God hath made . . . Jesus . . . both Lord and Christ" (Acts 2:36). While "Messiah," or Christ (the Anointed One), refers to Jesus' humanity, *Kurios*, "Lord" refers to His deity as the Supreme Being and Lord.

Who were the shepherds? Why did the angel announce the news first to the shepherds? What are the implications of announcing the birth of the Christ to the shepherds first? The Bible is silent about who the shepherds were. However, they probably were pious religious Jews who, like many others, have been praying and waiting for the promised Messiah and Deliverer.

There seems to be a number of reasons and theological implications for the role of the shepherds in the events of that night. The main reason is probably for the purpose of identification. Shepherding in the Jewish tradition was a lowly occupation usually reserved for slaves. Therefore, the announcement was to identify Christ's humility with the shepherds (cf., Philippians 2:7-8). The announcement also identified His mission—caring and protecting. In both the Old and New Testaments, and from the very meaning of the Greek *poimen* (**poy-mane'**), "shepherds," or pastor, symbolize those who care for God's people. Christ later identifies himself in John's Gospel as the "Good Shepherd" (John 10:2, 11, 12, 14, 16). The Psalmist writes, "The Lord is my shepherd" (Psalm

23:1). A number of passages in both Testaments identify the Lord as the Shepherd of His people (Isaiah 40:11; Jeremiah 23:1-4; Hebrews 13:20; 1 Peter 2:25; 5:2).

Shepherds were not only considered poor at the time of Jesus, they were considered untrustworthy. Their work, like the tax collectors, made them ceremonially unclean. Therefore, the implication is that the Gospel came first to the social outcasts of Jesus' day. This accounts for the recurring emphasis in Luke of Jesus' identification with both the poor and the societal outcasts of His day. He ate with "sinners" (Luke 7:37-39; 19:7). He said that the "Son of man" did not have a place to lay His head (Luke 9:58; cf., Matthew 8:20). He declared that He was commissioned to preach and care for the poor, the sick, and the less privileged in the society (Luke 4:18-19). Even at death He was buried in a borrowed grave (Matthew 27:57ff.).

12 And this shall be a sign unto you; Ye shall find the babe wrapped in swaddling clothes, lying in a manger. 13 And suddenly there was with the angel a multitude of the heavenly host praising God, and saying, 14 Glory to God in the highest, and on earth peace, good will toward men.

After the announcement, the angel does not instruct the shepherds to go and see the Child. He assumes they would. However, he does inform them how they would recognize Him. They would find Him, rather than being surrounded by grandeur and glory, wrapped in swaddling clothes and lying in a manger. This information is necessary because there are probably other children born in Bethlehem on this same day, but none would be lying in a manger. As the angel announces the news to the shepherds, he is suddenly joined by "a multitude of the heavenly host praising God." The word "host" or Greek *stratia* means an army of celestial beings or angels. "Multitude," *plethos* (**play'-thos**), quantifies the number of these angels that appear before the shepherds as a great or large number. They are probably too many to count, hence Luke uses the adjective *plethos* "multitude," to describe them. The host is described as

"heavenly," which means they are from heaven. The heavenly host fills the air with praises to God singing, "Glory to God in the highest, and on earth peace, good will toward men." What does this host of angels mean by the song? What message do they convey through this chorus?

By the phrase "glory to God in the highest," the angels seem to declare the purpose of the birth of the newborn Child. First, His birth brings the highest degree of glory to God. Here the angels foresee the ultimate purpose of Christ on earth, i.e., to glorify God through His death and resurrection. Someone has said that creation glorifies God, but not so much as redemption. Second, Christ's birth ushers in peace on earth. This peace does not mean tranquillity in the cosmos, but peace between a holy God and sinful man—peace made possible by and purchased through the redemptive blood of Christ. It is the peace that is offered freely to all who come to Him through faith. This peace is the perfect peace that starts inwardly, radiates outwardly; it affects others, making it possible for people to live peaceably with one another. Isaiah said centuries before that He shall be called "the Prince of Peace" (Isaiah 9:6). Thirdly, the birth of Christ reveals God's "good will" for man. Right from creation, God has never willed otherwise. His desires for man has always been for their good or well being, and He seeks to convince man of that desire. We can see this through the creation narrative (Genesis 2:8). The Psalmist says, "The LORD God is a sun and shield . . . no good thing will he withhold from them that walk uprightly" (Psalm 84:11). The Lord through Jeremiah assured Israel of His desire for them, "For I know the thoughts that I think toward you, saith the LORD, thoughts of peace, and not of evil, to give you an expected end" (Jeremiah 29:11). God's wish for mankind is to "have all men saved" (1 Timothy 2:4). Peter writes, "The Lord is not . . . willing that any should perish, but that all should come to repentance" (2 Peter 3:9). Here the angels proclaim the wish of God for mankind.

15 And it came to pass, as the angels were gone away from them into heaven, the shepherds said one to another, Let us now go even unto Bethlehem, and see this thing which is come to

pass, which the Lord hath made known unto us. 16 And they came with haste, and found Mary, and Joseph, and the babe lying in a manger.

After these spectacular and supernatural happenings, the shepherds decide to go to Bethlehem to see for themselves what the angels had told them. They never questioned or doubted the story, but went rather to see this strange event which the Lord has revealed to them through the angels. The clause "which the Lord hath made known unto us" confirms the fact that they accepted the message of the angels as truth and from God. Hence, they hurried with excitement into Bethlehem to visit the newborn Child. They find not only what the angel has told them concerning the Child (v. 12), but they also saw Mary and Joseph with the Baby in the manger. What happened to their flocks, whether the shepherds left them by themselves under the protection of God, or under the care of some other people, the Bible does not tell us. How they found the right manger, the Bible does not say. However, the verb used here, "found" (*aneurisko*, pronounced **an-yoo-ris'-ok**), seems to show that they searched before they found the Child.

17 And when they had seen it, they made known abroad the saying which was told them concerning this child. 18 And all they that heard it wondered at those things which were told them by the shepherds. 19 But Mary kept all these things, and pondered them in her heart.

The shepherds were the first to hear the Good News of the birth of the Saviour; they were also the first to proclaim it to others. Their message was simple; they declared what the angels told them concerning the child, and what they had seen. Their message left the listeners with wonder and marvel. However, "Mary kept all these things, and pondered them in her heart." "All these things" include the story the shepherds told—the appearance of the angel and the heavenly host. This story adds to the chain of miraculous events regarding the Christ, which began with the initial visit of Gabriel announcing to Mary that she would be the mother of the Messiah. The word "kept" is the Greek *suntereo* (**soon-tay-reh'-o**), i.e., to preserve, to conserve something of great importance.

Hence, it is translated as "treasured" by New American Standard and New International Version. Mary preserved the words of the shepherds in her heart with all the strange things that had been taking place, and she meditated upon them as future events unfold.

20 And the shepherds returned, glorifying and praising God for all the things that they had heard and seen, as it was told unto them.

After visiting the newborn, and finding the child as the angels had told them, the shepherds return, glorifying and praising God. The object of their joyful praise is obvious—the long expected Messiah is born and they have been witnesses. The birth of a Redeemer brings joy and peace to those who accept Him. Here the shepherds accepted the good tidings. Therefore, they praised and worshiped the Lord, and proclaimed to others the wonders of God's dealing with mankind. Like the shepherds, we are called to declare the birth of the Saviour and its purpose to the world. Christ was born to bring peace and redemption to the world. This event occurred over two thousand years ago, but it is still relevant to us today, as it was then. He came that we might have peace, He suffered that we might be healed, and He died that we might live. That is the message of Christmas.

DAILY BIBLE READINGS

M: The Future King
Isaiah 9:1-7
T: The Ruler from Bethlehem
Micah 5:2-5
W: The Birth of Jesus
Luke 2:1-7
T: The Ancestors of Jesus
Luke 3:23-38
F: The Shepherds and the Angels
Luke 2:8-14
S: The Adoration of the Shepherds
Luke 2:15-20
S: Sons and Daughters, Not Slaves
Galatians 4:1-7

TEACHING TIPS

December 31
Bible Study Guide 5

1. Words You Should Know

A. Consolation of Israel (v. 25)—a name used primarily by rabbis concerning the coming of the promised Messiah.

B. Custom of the law (v. 27)—a practice which was outlined in the Laws of Moses, but which was now practiced primarily out of custom, not legal requirement.

2. Teacher Preparation

Read today's lesson text. Find other passages in the Bible which highlight faithful servants of the Lord. Think about what it means to be a "faithful servant" of the Lord. Pause and think of someone you consider to be a faithful servant. What behaviors/attitudes has that person portrayed?

3. Starting the Lesson

A. Read today's IN FOCUS story about Marlon and his fond memories of Deacon. Talk about the special contribution that older adults often make in the lives of younger people. Ask class members how they can help to inspire younger people to give them a sense of confidence and hope concerning the future.

4. Getting Into the Lesson

As you move into today's lesson, discuss the joyous feeling that results from living in the fulfillment of God's promises. Every class member probably has experienced a long-awaited promise or goal being fulfilled. Talk about how God keeps His promises to us. Discuss some of the biblical promises of God which have been and are still being fulfilled.

5. Relating the Lesson to Life

A. Review the concepts described in today's THE PEOPLE, PLACES, AND TIMES article. Talk about the ritual of purification, which was a central part of the Jewish worship experience many years ago. Could it help some Christians today to get in touch with the understanding that they have been forgiven for their sins and that through Christ they are made pure.

B. Give students an opportunity to answer the questions in SEARCH THE SCRIPTURES.

C. Today's DISCUSS THE MEANING focuses on Simeon's description of Jesus and on Mary and Joseph's obedience to the rituals of their faith. Talk about the hope for all of humanity that is implied in Simeon's words, "light to lighten the Gentiles" and "the glory of Israel."

D. The LESSON IN OUR SOCIETY deals with the Western tendency to revere youth and devalue the aging process. Talk about the value of wisdom, which helps to balance the untamed vigor of youth.

DEC 31ST

6. Arousing Action

A. Think about the obedience of Joseph and Mary and the obedience of Simeon. List some of the characteristics they possessed which clearly demonstrate their devotion to God and their commitment to serve Him no matter what. After you have developed a profile for each person, list the ways that God blessed each of these faithful servants.

B. Close the class with prayer.

WORSHIP GUIDE

For the Superintendent or Teacher
Theme: Presented in the Temple
Theme Song: I Am Thine, O Lord
Scripture: Isaiah 52:7-10
Song: It's Wonderful to Live for Jesus
Meditation: I pray that I may be a faithful servant and a shining example of God's love. May I open myself to allow His great works to be evidenced through my daily living.

PRESENTED IN THE TEMPLE

Bible Background • LUKE 2:21-40
Printed Text • LUKE 2:25-38
Devotional Reading • ISAIAH 52:7-10

LESSON AIM

After studying today's lesson, students will learn that Jesus' earthly parents exposed Him to the rituals and tenants of their faith; they will be reminded that God keeps His promises; they will recognize the benefits of having elderly persons around them; and they will know the importance of being faithful to God through all circumstances.

KEEP IN MIND

"For mine eyes have seen thy salvation, Which thou hast prepared before the face of all people; A light to lighten the Gentiles, and the glory of thy people Israel" (Luke 2:30-32).

LESSON OVERVIEW

LESSON AIM
KEEP IN MIND
FOCAL VERSES
IN FOCUS
THE PEOPLE, PLACES,
AND TIMES
BACKGROUND
AT-A-GLANCE
IN DEPTH
SEARCH THE SCRIPTURES
DISCUSS THE MEANING
LESSON IN OUR SOCIETY
MAKE IT HAPPEN
FOLLOW THE SPIRIT
REMEMBER YOUR THOUGHTS
MORE LIGHT ON THE TEXT
DAILY BIBLE READINGS

FOCAL VERSES

Luke 2:25 And, behold, there was a man in Jerusalem, whose name was Simeon; and the same man was just and devout, waiting for the consolation of Israel: and the Holy Ghost was upon him.

26 And it was revealed unto him by the Holy Ghost, that he should not see death, before he had seen the Lord's Christ.

27 And he came by the Spirit into the temple: and when the parents brought in the child Jesus, to do for him after the custom of the law,

28 Then took he him up in his arms, and blessed God, and said,

29 Lord, now lettest thou thy servant depart in peace, according to thy word:

30 For mine eyes have seen thy salvation,

31 Which thou hast prepared before the face of all people;

32 A light to lighten the Gentiles, and the glory of thy people Israel.

33 And Joseph and his mother marveled at those things which were spoken of him.

34 And Simeon blessed them, and said unto Mary his mother, Behold, this child is set for the fall and rising again of many in Israel; and for a sign which shall be spoken against;

35 (Yea, a sword shall pierce through thy own soul also,) that the thoughts of many hearts may be revealed.

36 And there was one Anna, a prophetess, the daughter of Phanuel, of the tribe of Ahser: she was of a great age, and had lived with an husband seven years from her virginity;

37 And she was a widow of about fourscore and four years, which departed not from the temple, but served God with fastings and prayers night and day.

38 And she coming in that instant gave thanks likewise unto the Lord, and spake of him to all them that looked for redemption in Jerusalem.

IN FOCUS

Marlon stood in front of the steel grey casket and looked at the remains of the man he sometimes thought would live forever. The Lord had finally called old Deacon Crawford home. To most of the people at church, he was known simply as "Deacon." He was everything a deacon should be.

When Marlon stood at a crossroad during his adolescent years, it was Deacon who helped to direct him down the right path. "I expect great things outta you, boy," Deacon always said to him. In fact, he'd said it to Marlon just a couple of weeks ago. "Deacon expected great things from me when it seemed that no one else did," Marlon reflected.

As he made his way to a pew, Marlon looked around the church and saw so many others who, like himself, had it not been for Deacon, might be in a different place entirely. He remembered the times when Deacon privately pressed a $10 or $20 bill in his hands to give him a little spending money in college. He remembered the Bible Deacon gave him—the first Bible that belonged to Marlon alone.

Marlon often wondered whether Deacon had actually seen visions of his future or whether he just said positive things to Marlon to build up his self-esteem. As he sat down, Marlon began to ask the Lord if he might be able to inspire at least one kid who is like he used to be and help him or her along—just like Deacon helped him.

THE PEOPLE, PLACES, AND TIMES

Sacrifice. Offerings were an important part of Jewish life during ancient times. The system of sacrifice among Hebrews apparently was not organized until after the Exodus.

Many of the sacrifices that were made as part of Israel's worship were burned on an altar made from accacia wood with a copper overlay (Exodus 27). The animals that were used for burnt offerings were generally young bulls, lambs, goats, turtledoves, or pigeons. The type of animal offered often depended on the offerer's financial ability. The animal had to be a perfect physical specimen.

The person making a sacrifice did so to atone for some sin and restore his or her relationship with God. That person would lay a hand on the animal to symbolize that the animal was taking the person's place and then it was killed. The priest collected the blood of the dead animal and sprinkled it around the altar and the sanctuary. The offerer cut and skinned the animal. The priest would then arrange the various animal parts on the altar and the entire carcass was burned. The only part which was kept was the hide, which was given to the priest (Leviticus 7:8).

Offerings generally fell into certain categories: burnt (animal) offering; grain offering (from the harvest of the land); peace (animal in which only certain internal organs were burned); sin (animal blood) offering; guilt (restitution of violated property) offering.

When Jesus turned over the tables at the temple, it was because the business of sacrifice had been allowed to overshadow the spiritual intent of the offerings. Paul declared that Christ is our supreme, once-and-for-all sacrifice, making physical sacrifice unnecessary.

When the temple in Jerusalem was destroyed (A.D. 70), the system of sacrifice as a part of Jewish worship ended. Although sacrifice was an acceptable component of worship in early Christianity, the Church began to separate itself from Judiasm entirely, ending the practice of physical sacrifice among Christians.

Based on information from Holman Bible Dictionary, Trent Butler, general editor, Nashville: Broadman & Holman Publishers, 1991, pp. 1218- 1221.

Purification. The Jewish rituals of purification were observed in order to make persons free of some flaw or uncleanness which would otherwise bar them from having contact with holy objects or places.

Purification qualified a person for participation in worship, a pivotal activity in the life of ancient Israel. Impurity was a serious matter. The purification process usually began with a waiting period which began once the cause of the impurity ceased. The waiting period could be as little as one day for lesser conditions.

Purification also required a cleansing agent, such as water, blood, or fire. The most common element used was water, which was used to wash the clothes and bathe the body of the unpure person (Leviticus 14). Blood was used to purify the altar and the holy place (Leviticus 16:14-19) and was mixed with other ingredients for cleansing from leprosy (Leviticus 14) and contact with the dead (Numbers 19).

The final element of purification was sacrifice which generally was a lamb and a pigeon or turtledoves. One bird was for a sin offering and the other for a burnt offering. The poor were allowed to offer less valuable animals for sacrifice.

In the New Testament, Christ's sacrifice brings purification. He cleansed as part of the work of the high priest. His blood cleanses believers from sin (1 John 1:7).

Based on information from Holman Bible Dictionary, Trent Butler, general editor, Nashville: Broadman & Holman Publishers, 1991, pp. 1154-1155.

BACKGROUND

Mary and Joseph were faithful Jews who adhered to the requirements of the Law. They had Jesus circumcised on the same day that he was named, as John the Baptist's parents had done (1:59). They followed the angel's instructions and named the child Jesus.

According to the Law of Moses, a new mother was to undergo a ceremony of purification to make her ceremonially clean after childbirth. The ceremony was to take place 40 days after the birth. The mother was to bring a lamb or two pigeons to the ceremony as an offering. Since Mary and Joseph chose to offer pigeons, they may not have been able to afford a lamb.

They made the five-mile journey to Jerusalem from Bethlehem and made their offering. It was not mandatory for the ceremony to be held in Jerusalem, but it was appropriate. While they were there, they encountered an old man named Simeon, a devoted man of faith who had been waiting for the promised Messiah.

AT-A-GLANCE

1. Simeon's Witness (Luke 2:25-27)
2. Simeon's Praise (Luke 2:28-32)
3. Simeon's Prediction to Mary (Luke 2:33-35)

IN DEPTH

1. Simeon's Witness (Luke 2:25-27)

Joseph and Mary's encounter with Simeon did not happen by accident. The old man who took Jesus up in his arms had been anticipating the day for many years. Like all His other promises, God fulfilled His promise to Simeon by allowing him to be in the temple at just the right moment. He was able to gaze upon the consolation of Israel—the Messiah. The phrase, consolation of Israel, was commonly used by rabbis, meaning "the fulfillment of Jewish messianic hopes."

Like Zacharias and Elisabeth, Simeon was devout in morality and faith. He fulfilled the law in every possible way. The Holy Ghost was upon him. The Holy Ghost had revealed to him that he should not see death until he had laid eyes on the Messiah. Many people desire to accomplish things before they die. Some desire wealth, some desire fame or recognition for an achievement, others desire to experience love and have a family, still others wish to see the world before they die. Simeon wanted none of these things. He wanted something far greater than material goods or fame. Simeon's desire was to witness the fulfillment of God's promise for His people.

The Spirit led Simeon to the temple on the day that Joseph and Mary brought Jesus there. In addition to the law requiring purification of the mother, there was also a law requiring the redemption of the firstborn child (Exodus 13:2, 12-16). Since God had spared the firstborn of Israel during the tenth plague (Exodus 12:12-13), henceforth He required that Israel's firstborn be dedicated to Him. Later the Lord allowed the tribe of Levi to become a substitute for the firstborn (Numbers 3:11-13).

The fact that Joseph and Mary observed this ritual at the time of Jesus' birth symbolized their commitment to the Lord. The redemption price for male children was set in Numbers 18:16 at five shekels. This requirement was to be fulfilled when the child was a month old. Apparently, Joseph and Mary fulfilled the two requirements at the same time.

Exactly where they met in the Temple is not known. Since Mary was present, they were probably in the Court of Gentiles or the Court of Women. It must have been the most magnificent feeling Simon had ever known, to hold the baby Jesus in his arms. Simeon identified Jesus as the embodiment of God's salvation.

2. Simeon's Praise (Luke 2:28-32)

Seeing the promise of the Lord as a living being and holding the Babe of promise in his arms moved Simeon to sing a song of praise. This song is now known as the "Nunc Dimittis," which are the first two words of the Latin translation.

Simeon was now ready to die, having witnessed the fulfillment of God's promise. Now Simeon could depart in peace, knowing that the salvation of his people had come to earth. He called himself God's servant, literally slave. He was faithful to God's Word and to the law of Judiasm.

His song contained not only praise, but a prophetic aspect as well. By recognizing that Jesus was the fulfillment of God's promise, Simeon then took on the attitude that would have been fitting for all of Israel. While Jesus was yet a babe in his arms, the Jewish prophet foresaw that salvation was intended for all of humanity. This old man, facing the last days of his life, saw hope in a baby who was just a few days old. Not only was Jesus the glory of Israel, He is the light of the Gentiles, too. Even today, Christians try to place Jesus in narrow confines, trying to determine where He does and does not belong. Two-thousand years ago, Simeon prophesied that Jesus was sufficient for all—Jew and Gentile alike. The Gospel is not reserved for a select few, as some would have it.

Simeon and those who lived during Jesus' day had the privilege of seeing salvation in the flesh. Today we see salvation through the eyes of faith as we invite others to join us. Even though He is no longer with us in the flesh, we too can marvel at the hope that lies in Him, just as Simeon did that day in the temple.

3. Simeon's Prediction to Mary (Luke 2:33-35)

Understandably Joseph and Mary were amazed at what was said about Jesus. The message of the angel and been confirmed by yet another person. Simeon blessed the young couple and then focused his attention on Mary.

Simeon prophesied concerning the great and powerful effect Mary's Son would have upon the world. He would be destined for the fall and rising again of many in Israel. The presence of her Son would introduce a crisis to the nation, dividing them. Those who reject Him will fall, but those who receive Him will be lifted up. The Messiah will do away with the proud and lift up the downtrodden and oppressed.

But the destiny of Mary's Son would not be

without consequences to Mary herself. She would, to some extent, share in His suffering. The things that would be done to Him would be like a sword piercing through her own soul. In later verses, the Gospels make little or no reference to Joseph, leading scholars to conclude that he must have died before the start of Jesus' public ministry. Therefore, the pain to be beared would be Mary's alone.

Mary and Joseph probably spent countless hours thinking about the responsibility that lay before them. They had received much encouragement from many people. The little baby who was totally dependent on them at that moment had the future of the world in His hands.

They might have begun to wonder if they would have such encounters everywhere they went. It had begun on the first night their Son was born. Even while fulfilling their religious duties, they could not escape prophecies concerning their Son.

Simeon's prophecies may have seemed all the more powerful because they were from the mouth of an elderly man. His reputation as a godly man had probably preceded him. The young couple must have had a whirlwind of mixed emotions as they heard the various words spoken about their Son. Thankfully, they were people who trusted in God for their lives. They would have to continue to trust in Him to lead and guide them as they raised and nurtured the Baby who already held the name Saviour.

SEARCH THE SCRIPTURES

1. How does Luke describe Simeon? (v. 25)
2. What had the Holy Ghost revealed to him? (v. 26)
3. Why did Simeon go to the temple that day? (v. 27)
4. Why were Mary and Joseph at the temple? (v. 27)
5. What did Simeon do when he saw Baby Jesus? (v. 28)
6. What praise did Simeon offer upon seeing the Messiah? (vv. 29-32)
7. What words did Simeon say to indicate that Jesus was the Saviour for all people? (v. 32)
8. What did Simeon offer to Joseph and Mary? (v. 34)

9. What did Simeon tell Mary about her Baby's purpose in life? (v. 34)

10. What painful prophecy did Simeon give Mary concerning her own fate? (v. 35)

DISCUSS THE MEANING

1. What did Simeon mean when he described Jesus as the "light to lighten the Gentiles?" In what way is Jesus "the glory of thy people Israel?"

2. Mary and Joseph continued to observe all of the Jewish laws and rituals, even though they had been blessed with the charge of raising the Messiah into manhood. How might this fact have affected the way they viewed their participation in the rites of their faith?

LESSON IN OUR SOCIETY

Western culture tends to place a high value on youth and on that which is new. The words of Simeon were even more valuable because of his age and the devotion he had demonstrated to the Lord over the years. Many African American churches have gained attention for their ability to attract boomers, buppies and Generation Xers. It is an accomplishment worthy of attention. In their pursuit of the young, educated, and powerful, some churches overlook a valuable resource that is missing from their congregations—senior adult members. Their presence often serves as a healthy balance to the "go-getter" attitude of younger generations. It is their wisdom which helps to guide the paths of young minds, setting them on the right path to be the leaders of the future.

MAKE IT HAPPEN

Think of two or three older persons who helped to shape your faith and understanding of what it means to be a Christian. Then examine your own life and faith journey. Give an honest assessment of whether or not you have lived your life in a way that gives you the spiritual authority to address younger generations? Through his life of devotion, Simeon left a legacy to those who are committed to faithful living. What legacy can you leave to future generations?

FOLLOW THE SPIRIT

What God wants me to do:

_____

_____

REMEMBER YOUR THOUGHTS

Special insights you learned:

_____

_____

MORE LIGHT ON THE TEXT
Luke 2:25-38

Luke 2:21-38 is a narrative of the purification ceremony of Mary and Jesus according to the Jewish custom. Here contains an extraordinary event, which is unique to Jesus—the confirmation of the mission of Christ through prophecy. In verses 21-24, Luke introduces us to the general process of the ceremony, and in verses 25-38, he gives us in detail what happened at the ceremony—the prophecies of Simeon and Anna.

2:25 And, behold, there was a man in Jerusalem, whose name was Simeon; and the same man was just and devout, waiting for the consolation of Israel: and the Holy Ghost was upon him. 26 And it was revealed unto him by the Holy Ghost, that he should not see death, before he had seen the Lord's Christ.

Here Luke introduces us to a man whom he describes as "just and devout," a man "waiting for the consolation of Israel." This man is filled with the Holy Spirit and lived in Jerusalem. His name is Simeon. We know nothing about Simeon before the birth of Christ. However, he must be one of the devout Judaizers who were expecting the coming of the Messiah. What is unique about Simeon?

At the time of the birth of Christ, it is believed that religion in Israel was at its lowest ebb. Yet in the midst of the religious vacuum is a man Luke describes as "just and devout," a man on whom "the Holy Ghost (Spirit) was upon." The word "just" is equivalent to righteous and is a translation of the Greek *dikaios* (**dik'-ah-yos**). This means that he was an upright, or virtuous man, who not only observed the divine law, but also conformed to the will of God. Hence he is described as "devout" (Greek *eulabes*), a pious man, one who is devoted to, and revered, God (see 1:6; cf. Philippians 3:6). Simeon was among the few pious men who were expecting the coming of the Lord Jesus, which Luke termed here as the "consolation of Israel." The noun "consolation," *paraklesis* (pronounced **par-ak'-lay-sis**), which means comfort, exhortation, or encouragement, describes the coming ministry of Christ. *Paraklesis* is a noun derivation of the Greek verb *parakaleo* (**par-ak-al-eh'-o**), to call near, to comfort, entreat, or to exhort. The Holy Spirit is frequently described as the Comforter (*parkletos*) especially in John's Gospel (John 14:16, 26; 15:26; 16:7). Here the coming of Christ was to be a comfort for the people of Israel, who at this time were under the rule of the Roman Empire. Israel had been promised a Deliverer and a Counselor, one who would restore to Israel the Davidic kingdom (Isaiah 9:6-7). The word "waiting" is a translation of the Greek *prosdechomai* (pronounced **pros-dekh'-om-ahee**), which means to wait or to expect patiently with confidence. Simeon was waiting expectantly and patiently for the fulfillment of the Lord's promise of the Messiah to Israel. His confidence probably lies in his relationship with God and in his trust to the God of Israel who is faithful to keeping His promises. Moreover, the Holy Spirit has assured him that he would not die until he saw the Lord's Christ (Messiah). The word "revealed" used here is the Greek *chrematizo* (**khray-mat-id'-zo**), which is interpreted in various ways in the New Testament, e.g., to be warned (Matthew 2:12, 22; Hebrews 11:7); admonished (Hebrews 8:5); or be spoken to (Hebrews 12:25). It is often used for divine communication. Here Simeon had been instructed through the Holy Spirit that he would see the Messiah in his own lifetime.

Luke does not seem to think it necessary to tell us the background of this man, whether or not he was a priest. All we know about him is that he was a just, devout man, who was waiting for the fulfillment of the Lord's promise, a man full of the Holy Spirit. It is therefore only an assumption by some interpreters who labeled him a priest. There is nothing in Scripture to verify that assumption. I believe if he were a priest, Luke would have told us in his narrative as in the case of Zacharias (cf., 1:5).

Another unfounded assumption regarding Simeon is the notion by scholars and preachers that he was an old man. Here again, unlike the prophetess Anna whose age has been hinted at (vv. 36-38), Luke does not tell us how old Simeon was. His prayer in verse 29 does not in any way suggest that he was an old man, neither does it imply that he died soon after seeing the Messiah. It should be noted that both young and old in the Jewish were equally waiting and devoting their lives for the coming of the Messiah.

27 And he came by the Spirit into the temple: and when the parents brought in the child Jesus, to do for him after the custom of the law, 28 Then took he him up in his arms, and blessed God, and said,

As a devout Jew, it was not out place for Simeon to go into the temple at certain times for prayer. Indeed, it was a requirement for Jewish religious worshipers to routinely go into the temple to pray. Simeon, therefore, must have formed the habit of going to the temple to pray. However, on this special occasion "he came by the Spirit into the temple" and met with Mary and Joseph with Jesus as they came to fulfill their Jewish rites. The language here seems to indicate that the meeting was neither prearranged, nor was it a coincidence. Rather it was divinely planned—a providential timing. He came "by" *en* (in) the Spirit means that he was led by Holy Spirit into the temple in order to fulfill the promise of verse 26. Here is one of the functions of the Holy Spirit—leading God's people.

While Simeon was in the temple, Mary and Joseph brought their son Jesus to perform the Jewish ritual according their customary law. Through divine revelation, Simeon was informed who this child was; He was the long awaited Messiah. Hence, Simeon takes Jesus "up in his arms" and blesses God. Taking children up in the arms was common practice in the Jewish tradition (Matthew 19:13-15; Mark 10:13-16; Luke 18:15-16). The word "blessed" is the Greek word *eulogeo* (**yoo-log-eh'-o**), which means to praise, or to speak well of, which is a direct transliteration of the English word eulogy or to eulogize. During funerals, people are often called upon to bring a eulogy of friends or relatives who have passed on. When we speak well of, or praise, people for what they have done for others, or achieved in life, we eulogize them. Here Simeon is praising God, which includes a thanksgiving for God's faithfulness in fulfilling His promise not only to Israel, but also to him.

29 Lord, now lettest thou thy servant depart in peace, according to thy word: 30 For mine eyes have seen thy salvation,

Simeon begins his eulogy to God by expressing his gratitude to God for allowing him see the Messiah—the Saviour—in fulfillment of His promise (v. 26). The underlying tone here is satisfaction of a task accomplished—joyful relief. The praise, or song, begins with the Greek word *nun* ("now"), which indicates that the Messiah has indeed arrived. "Now" that the Messiah has finally arrived, Simeon seems to say, the Lord should dismiss or release him. The verb *apoluo* (pronounced **ap-ol-oo'-o**) with its various renderings, to free fully, i.e., (literally) relieve, release, or dismiss, underlies this fact. Hence, the Latin title "Nunc Dimmittis" ("Now dismiss"). Figuratively used here, *apoluo* means "allow to die."

The underlying thought here, as described by Norval Geldenhuys, is of a slave instructed by his master to watch through a long, dark night on a high hill for the rising of a special star, and then to announce it. After wearisome hours of watching, he at last sees the star rising in its brightness. "He announces it and is then discharged from keeping watch any longer" (*Commentary on the Gospel of Luke*, Grand Rapids, Wm. B. Eerdmans Pub. Co., 1979, p. 119). With Jesus in his arms, Simeon has seen the promised "Star out of Jacob" (Numbers 24:17), the "Sun of righteousness" (Malachi 4:2). He has now beheld the redemption of God in the person of Christ Jesus. Now the watch is over. He is now to be discharged according to God's word. Note the contrast between God the "Lord" and Simeon "the servant." The word "peace," *eirene*, used here has the sense of tranquillity or rest and contentment. After seeing the God's promised "salvation," Simeon is ready to depart peacefully into God's presence. Simeon does not say that he has seen the Messiah (although it is implied), but that his "eyes have seen" God's "salvation" personified and embodied in Christ Jesus—the Messiah. To see Jesus is to see salvation, a theme Luke repeatedly emphasizes in his book (1:69, 71, 77; 19:9).

31 Which thou hast prepared before the face of all people; 32 A light to lighten the Gentiles, and the glory of thy people Israel.

Contrary to the expectation and belief of the Jewish religion, i.e., the Messiah was to come only for the people of Israel, the salvation is universal in scope. The phrase "before the face (or in the sight) of all people" supports this fact. God's plan of salvation is not only made available to the few pious people, or to the nation of Israel only, but to all people of the earth because His love is universal (John 3:16). Verse 31 echoes the prophecy of Isaiah (52:10) and the psalmist's song which says in part that "all the ends of the earth shall see (or have seen) the salvation of our God" (Psalm 98:3).

There are dual functions of this salvation. First, it will dissipate as light to the spiritual darkness which has enveloped the Gentiles for centuries. The darkness represents ignorance, sin, and misery; it is a symbol of death and disobedience. In place of the darkness, the redemption will bring light—a symbol of life, growth, knowledge, and obedience—to the nations. Second, the salvation will bring glory to the nation of Israel. That means, the nations will realize the glorious special privilege Israel has enjoyed in its relationship with God through the ages, a privilege now consummated and perfected in the birth and person of Christ Jesus. Here we see the same light (Isaiah 42:6; 49:6) which brings revelation to the Gentiles—those who sit in darkness and in the shadow of death (Luke 1:78-79)—also brings salvation through the remission of sins to Israel, God's people (1:77).

33 And Joseph and his mother marveled at those things which were spoken of him. 34 And Simeon blessed them, and said unto Mary his mother, Behold, this child is set for the fall and rising again of many in Israel; and for a sign which shall be spoken against;

Mary and Joseph knew through the announcement of the angel Gabriel (1:26-38 and Matthew 1:20), that their child was the Christ—the expected Messiah. This destiny was confirmed by the supernatural conception, by the words of Elisabeth (1:41:45), and by the words of the shepherds (2:15-19). Still they could not fully comprehend the significance of it all. They were amazed and overwhelmed at the words of Simeon. The word "marveled" used here is not expressing doubt, but excitement, as we learn from the Greek equivalent *thaumazo* (pronounced **thou-mad'-zo**). It means to admire, to have in admiration, or to wonder.

After that, Simeon blessed them, Jesus and His parents. Simeon then addressed Mary, as if all that has been said about Christ was not enough. He predicts the effect the birth of Christ will have on the nation of Israel, and how this will affect Mary his mother. It is important to notice that Luke tells us that Simeon, after addressing and blessing Mary and Joseph, now addresses Mary alone. The reason is clear. Joseph did not father Jesus in the natural sense of the word. Indeed, it is safe to say that Jesus had no earthly father (only an earthly mother), since his conception was supernatural. Hence, He is called the Son of God. Joseph, at best, can be described as a "step father." It is apparent that Simeon is aware of this unique situation. Instead of addressing Joseph, or both parents, Simeon speaks directly to Mary. It should be noted that, apart from here, in verse 42, and in the genealogy of Christ (3:23), there is no further mention of Joseph as the father of Jesus, or any other reference of Joseph in that connection in the rest of Luke.

Luke uses the emphatic Greek word *idou* (**id-oo'**), translated "behold" here, which also means see, look, listen. It is used often to call someone's attention to important information. Simeon informs Mary that the "Child is set for the fall and rising of many in Israel." What does this statement mean? Simply stated, the presence of Christ will either be a curse for those who reject Him or a blessing for those who accept Him. The prophet Isaiah says, concerning the Messiah, "He shall be for a sanctuary; but for a stone of stumbling and for a rock of offence to both the houses of Israel, for a gin and for a snare to the inhabitants of Jerusalem. And many among them shall stumble, and fall, and be broken, and be snared, and be taken" (Isaiah 8:14-15; cf., Matthew 21:42-44; Acts 4:11; Romans 9:33; 1 Corinthians 1:23). Simeon says that Jesus, on the one hand, will be a stone on which some will trip and fall and perish; on the other hand, He will be "a stepping stone" on which others will be enabled to arise and be saved.

Not only that. Christ will also be a means by which those who have fallen will be able rise "again." The word "again" appears only in the King James Version. The idea here is that He will be the means of salvation for sinners, or those who formerly reject him and later repent. They would rise again into new life and their relationship with God would be restored. The conversion of Saul, who formerly persecuted the church, was nothing short of rising again from the dead. The phrase also speaks of those who fall because of him "rising again," referring to the resurrection of the saints—the raising of the dead in Christ into eternal life. Either one is theologically sound. However, there is no neutrality, Simeon seems to point out. Either He is rejected, which results in a downfall, or He is received, which results in a rising again.

Simeon adds that the Child is also set "for a sign, which shall be spoken against." This has been fulfilled and is being fulfilled constantly through the ages. The birth, death, and the person of Christ have been the basis for untold controversies among many throughout the generations. During His life on earth and afterwards, Christ has been the object of hostility among unbelievers. He was rejected to the point of crucifixion. From the beginning many rejected and persecuted Him, and many have spoken against Him, which is also the rejection of God's salvation.

35 (Yea, a sword shall pierce through thy own soul also,) that the thoughts of many hearts may be revealed.

By the statement "a sword shall pierce through thy own soul also," Simeon foretells the anguish which Mary shall experience because of the Christ. It will be a heart-piercing sorrow—as sharp and painful as the sword. It describes the extreme anguish which Mary will undergo seeing her Son suffer. This was fulfilled at the Cross when she stood and watched her son die. Through Christ, His life, death, and resurrection, "the thoughts of many hearts will be revealed." The Gospel brings light in the inner being of all humanity and exposes their character and attitude towards God and His Christ. Here Christ is to carry out the mission, which Jeremiah lamented in His prophecy, "The heart is deceitful above all things, and desperately wicked: who can know it? I the LORD search the heart, I try the reins, even to give every man according to his ways, and according to the fruit of his doings" (Jeremiah 17:9-10). The Gospel of John describes Jesus as a light that shines in the darkness (1:5) and gives light to everyone in the world (1:9). Later in the same Gospel, Jesus calls Himself the "light of the world" (8:12; 9:5; 12:35ff.).

36 And there was one Anna, a prophetess, the daughter of Phanuel, of the tribe of Ahser: she was of a great age, and had lived with an husband seven years from her virginity; 37 And she was a widow of about fourscore and four years, which departed not from the temple, but served God with fastings and prayers night and day. 38 And she coming in that instant gave thanks likewise unto the Lord, and spake of him to all them that looked for redemption in Jerusalem.

In verses 36-38, Luke introduces us to another devout woman, who had also been waiting for the long promised Messiah, and who had the special privilege to see Christ at His dedication. Her name was Anna, a prophetess. She was from the tribe of Asher, one of the ten tribes of Israel, usually known as the lost tribes. Luke further describes her as of a great age. This means that she was very old. Luke does not tell us the exact age. She was married for only seven years when her husband died, and for 84 years she was a widow and dedicated her life serving the Lord. Luke says that she never departed from the temple but worshiped God by fasting and prayers night and day.

The word "served" is *latreuo*, pronounced **lat-ryoo'-o,** which means to render service, to minister, or to worship, whether of priests, or laity, especially in public worship. The word is also used in the performance of both sacred and secular services like hired labor. Another bit of information we have about Anna is that she never departed from the temple. The suggestion here is that she was constantly in the temple worshiping God through fasting and praying, and probably doing other manual jobs necessary for the keeping of the temple. It does not mean that she lived in the temple, as the statement seems to convey. Indeed, the next statement (v. 38a) supports this fact. She, like Simeon, came into the temple providentially—"in that instant"—just at that same moment, as

Jesus and His parents were in the temple. She also gave thanks to God for allowing her to see the Messiah in her lifetime. Like the shepherds (v. 17), and the Samaritan woman (John 4), Anna could not keep the Good News about the Messiah to herself, but she "spake of him to all them that looked for redemption in Jerusalem." That means she declared to others in Jerusalem who, like her, had been waiting prayerfully for the Messiah—the redemption of Israel.

The dedication of Christ in the temple is the sole fulfillment of the prophecy of Malachi which says, "Behold, I will send my messenger, and he shall prepare the way before me: and the Lord, whom ye seek, shall suddenly come to his temple, even the messenger of the covenant, whom ye delight in: behold, he shall come, saith the LORD of hosts (3:1). While the people expected a mighty, strong warrior, the Redeemer came suddenly into the temple as an infant in the arms of His mother, a poor woman, and her husband. The only witnesses were a man and an old woman. No wonder He was and is being rejected by many in Israel. Others are still praying and waiting for the Messiah. Are you still waiting?

DAILY BIBLE READINGS

M: The Consecration of the Firstborn
Exodus 13:11-16
T: According to the Law
Luke 2:21-24
W: Our Love for God
Deuteronomy 6:1-9
T: Adoration and Prophecy of Simeon
Luke 2:25-35
F: The Good News of Peace
Isaiah 52:3-10
S: Adoration of Anna
Luke 2:36-38
S: Honor Widows Who Hope in God
1 Timothy 5:3-8

TEACHING TIPS

January 7
Bible Study Guide 6

1. Words You Should Know

A. Esaias (v. 17)—Isaiah, the prophet.

B. Minister (v. 20)—an assistant to the ruler of the local synagogue.

C. Elias (v. 26)—Elijah, the prophet.

D. Eliseus (v. 27)—Elisha, the prophet.

E. Brow of the Hill (v. 29)—edge of the hill.

2. Teacher Preparation

Read the lesson text and the prophecy as it appears in Isaiah 61. Think about how that promise is being fulfilled through followers of Jesus. Prepare a list of the kinds of miracles Jesus performed throughout the Gospels and present the ways He is still doing so.

3. Starting the Lesson

Have a volunteer read the IN FOCUS story about Eloise and her experience with Sister Grimes. Discuss how people sometimes want to believe the worst about others. Talk about the ways we can guard against getting discouraged when others refuse to support our changes for the better. What should we do when we are criticized? To whom should we look for approval?

4. Getting Into the Lesson

Help the class consider what happened to the Messiah and understand that His experience in Nazareth was not unique. Many people have experienced receiving "no honor" from hometown folk. Even though they sought to kill Him, they could not succeed because God had other plans for Him.

Point out the importance of keeping our eyes and hearts fixed on the Lord and whether or not He is pleased with our doings. Human praise and acceptance is fickle and changes like the wind. Therefore, it is unreliable as a means of judging whether or not our actions are pleasing to God.

5. Relating the Lesson to Life

A. Review the concepts described in today's THE PEOPLE, PLACES, AND TIMES article. Discuss the role of the synagogue in the Jewish community, both from a religious and social perspective. Also discuss how Jesus often met with confrontation in the synagogues. Although He went faithfully and participated in worship, He often upset the Jewish rulers giving women and outcasts a place of significance in God's realm.

B. Give students an opportunity to answer the questions in SEARCH THE SCRIPTURES.

C. The LESSON IN OUR SOCIETY focuses on spiritual growth and the ways we can be hindered. Discuss God's ability to create great results from meager beginnings.

6. Arousing Action

A. Ask members to think of someone who is trying to turn his or her life around and needs encouragement. What could happen if no one comes forward to offer support to that person?

JAN 7TH

B. Remind members that negative thought and criticism abounds. It is important for believers to act out the love of Christ, demonstrating Jesus' mission as He proclaimed it in Luke 4:18-19.

C. Give class members an opportunity to complete FOLLOW THE SPIRIT and REMEMBER YOUR THOUGHTS.

WORSHIP GUIDE

For the Superintendent or Teacher
Theme: Jesus in Nazareth
Theme Song: Just a Little Talk with Jesus
Scripture: Isaiah 61
Song: The Name of Jesus
Meditation: It is my hope and desire to always focus on pleasing God. As I go about the business of fulfilling God's call to me, I will remember that some people will not believe in what I am doing. It is during those times that I must remember that I am accountable to God alone for my actions.

JESUS IN NAZARETH

Bible Background • LUKE 4:14-30
Printed Text • LUKE 4:16-26, 28-30
Devotional Reading • ISAIAH 61

LESSON AIM

After studying today's lesson, students will gain insight into the nature and scope of Jesus' sense of call and revisit the early days of Jesus' ministry.

KEEP IN MIND

"The Spirit of the Lord is upon me, because he hath anointed me to preach the gospel to the poor; he hath sent me to heal the brokenhearted, to preach deliverance to the captives, and recovering of sight to the blind, to set at liberty them that are bruised, To preach the acceptable year of the Lord" (Luke 4:18-19).

FOCAL VERSES

Luke 4:16 And he came to Nazareth, where he had been brought up: and, as his custom was, he went into the synagogue on the sabbath day, and stood up to read.

17 And there was delivered unto him the book of the prophet Esaias. And when he had opened the book, he found the place where it was written,

18 The Spirit of the Lord is upon me, because he hath anointed me to preach the gospel to the poor; he hath sent me to heal the brokenhearted, to preach deliverance to the captives, and recovering of sight to the blind, to set at liberty them that are bruised,

19 To preach the acceptable year of the Lord.

20 And he closed the book, and he gave it again to the minister, and sat down. And the eyes of all them that were in the synagogue were fastened on him.

21 And he began to say unto them, This day is

LESSON OVERVIEW

LESSON AIM
KEEP IN MIND
FOCAL VERSES
IN FOCUS
THE PEOPLE, PLACES,
AND TIMES
BACKGROUND
AT-A-GLANCE
IN DEPTH
SEARCH THE SCRIPTURES
DISCUSS THE MEANING
LESSON IN OUR SOCIETY
MAKE IT HAPPEN
FOLLOW THE SPIRIT
REMEMBER YOUR THOUGHTS
MORE LIGHT ON THE TEXT
DAILY BIBLE READINGS

this scripture fulfilled in your ears.

22 And all bore him witness, and wondered at the gracious words which proceeded out of his mouth. And they said, Is not this Joseph's son?

23 And he said unto them, Ye will surely say unto me this proverb, Physician, heal thyself: whatsoever we have heard done in Capernaum, do also here in thy country.

24 And he said, Verily I say unto you, No prophet is accepted in his own country.

25 But I tell you of a truth, many widows were in Israel in the days of Elias, when the heaven was shut up three years and six months, when great famine was throughout all the land;

26 But unto none of them was Elias sent, save unto Sarepta, a city of Sidon, unto a woman that was a widow.

28 And all they in the synagogue, when they heard these things, were filled with wrath,

29 And rose up, and thrust him out of the city, and led him unto the brow of the hill whereon their city was built, that they might cast him down headlong.

30 But he passing through the midst of them went his way,

IN FOCUS

Eloise was so heartbroken she didn't know if she would ever walk through the doors of that church again. The ministry she had started to help teenage girls in the church stay focused and in school was really doing well. That is, until Sister Grimes came and insulted her. To make matters worse, she did it in front of the kids!

Just when it seemed that things were going so well, out of nowhere Sister Grimes walked up to her and said, "I don't know what kind of role model you're supposed to be. Humph! I remember when you left town to have that baby and you were just 16 yourself!"

It made Eloise sad that, even after thirty years, people were still wanting to believe such a vicious lie about her. She was so shocked by Sister Grimes' words that she didn't even bother to correct her.

The words hurt, even after three decades had passed. To this day, only a few people know that she had to go away because she had been diagnosed with leukemia. He doctors found a way for her to receive treatment at a special children's hospital that her parents could never have afforded.

For whatever reason, her parents didn't want anyone outside the family to know about her illness. They didn't even tell the school why she moved to another city. Thinking back on it, Eloise still believes that telling everyone about the leukemia couldn't have been worse than enduring the lies about her being pregnant

THE PEOPLE, PLACES, AND TIMES

Synagogue. The local meeting place and assembly hall for Jews during the days of the New Testament writings. This type of synagogue had its origin in the time after Solomon's Temple was destroyed and many of the Hebrews were sent into exile. It became necessary to develop local centers of worship and instruction. Even after their return from exile and the Jerusalem Temple was rebuilt, these local centers of worship continued.

Most communities of size had at least one synagogue and some had several. Jewish sources hold that a synagogue was to be built wherever there were ten or more Jewish men. The primary meeting was held on the Sabbath. The usual worship service consisted of the recitation of the *Shema* (Deuteronomy 6:4-9), prayers, Scripture readings from the Law and from the Prophets, a sermon, and a benediction.

Local elders were given the responsibility for oversight of the synagogue. Often they appointed a ruler, a layman, who cared for the building and selected those who participated in the worship service. The ruler was assisted by an attendant.

Based on information from Holman Bible Dictionary, Trent Butler, general editor, Nashville: Broadman & Holman Publishers, 1991, pp. 1311-1312.

Jesus in the Synagogues. Jesus, on many occasions, encountered opposition and conflict in the synagogues. The incident at Nazareth is just one example. Early in His ministry He encountered opposition in the synagogue at Capernaum because He healed a man there (Mark 1:21-28; Luke 4:31-37). The ruler of one synagogue was angered because Jesus healed a woman on the Sabbath (Luke 13:10-16). Jesus' statement that He was the fulfillment of the Isaiah prophecy angered those who heard him in the synagogue at Nazareth. His preaching and teaching often evoked negative reactions (Matthew 13:54-58; Mark 6:1-6).

Jesus issued a stern warning against those who paraded their righteousness in the synagogue, calling them hypocrites. As opposition to Him grew, He warned His disciples of a time in the future when they, too, would be persecuted in the synagogues (Matthew 10:17; 23:34; Mark 13:9; Luke 12:11; 21:12).

Based on information from Holman Bible Dictionary Trent Butler, general editor, Nashville: Broadman & Holman Publishers, 1991, pp. 1312-1313.

BACKGROUND

At the age of about 30, Jesus began his public ministry. He had already submitted Himself to baptism to demonstrate His faithfulness and obedience, even though He was without sin.

Following His baptism, the Holy Ghost led him into the wilderness, where He endured forty days and nights of fasting and isolation. This was a period of physical weakness, but spiritual strength. Three times Satan tried to tempt Jesus, offering Him lures that might appeal to His humanness. By the power of the Holy Ghost, Jesus endured this period and refused the devil's temptations.

The power of the Holy Ghost which had given Jesus the victory over Satan in the wilderness led Him to Galilee. There He was able to teach in the synagogues and He was well received, gaining popularity among the people there. Jesus must have been encouraged by His reception. He was glorified by all those around Him.

The accolades Jesus received in Galilee did not represent the true glory of Jesus, which was to come. Still, Jesus' ministry began with Him being glorified and it ended with Him being glorified.

AT-A-GLANCE

1. Prophecy Fulfilled in Jesus
(Luke 4:16-21)
2. Hometown Boy Rejected
(vv. 22-26)
3. Move to Kill Jesus
(vv. 28-30)

IN DEPTH
1. Prophecy Fulfilled in Jesus (Luke 4:16-21)

From His glorious reception at Galilee, Jesus' first stop on His preaching circuit was His hometown, Nazareth. He sought to bring the Good News to His own people first. Perhaps they felt no close identity with Him. The phrase "where he had been brought up" gives the impression that Jesus had not been in Nazareth for a while prior to this visit.

Jesus had been raised by devout Jewish parents who reared Him up to participate in the tenets of His faith. Therefore, as His custom was, He went to the synagogue on the Sabbath day. It was normal and usual for Him to participate in worship.

During the synagogue service, the first Scriptural reading was from the Torah. These readings followed a schedule of 155 specific lessons which were designed to allow completion of the entire Pentateuch in three years. In both Palestine and Babylon, the verses were read from the Hebrew text. This was followed by an Aramaic translation, the familiar language of the Middle East. The reading from the Torah was followed by a reading from the prophets. Scholars are uncertain as to how the reading from the prophets was

chosen. Perhaps the particular reading was left to the discretion of the man reading. Anyone could be invited to read the Scripture lesson for the synagogue services. The reading was followed by a sermon if a competent teacher was present.

It is possible that Jesus Himself chose the particular passage to be read after He was given "the book of the prophet Esaias" (Isaiah), as indicated by the phrase, "he found the place where it was written." The reading from Isaiah reflects back to Jesus' baptism, where He was anointed for His ministry. The nature of His ministry is given in this prophecy by Isaiah. His purpose was to bring Good News to the poor, the brokenhearted, the captives, the blind, and the bruised. The Gospel is Good News to those whose hope lies in Almighty God to act on their behalf. Jesus identified Himself with the social, religious, and economic outcasts of His day. The acceptable year of the Lord had been launched in the person and ministry of Jesus.

When He finished reading, Jesus handed the book over to the minister, one who served as an assistant to the head of the synagogue (a role somewhat similar to that of a deacon in the early church). After His reading, the congregation was still. All eyes were fastened on Him. Jesus broke through the silence with a simple, yet powerful declaration, "This day is this scripture fulfilled in your ears." There He was, standing before them. Jesus of Nazareth was the Messiah of God's promise.

2. Hometown Boy Rejected (vv. 22-26)

Initially, those who heard His words responded favorably to Him. They wondered at the gracious words He had just spoken. Still, they were confused about His identity. They could not move beyond the fact that He was Joseph's son. How could a carpenter's son declare Himself to be the Son of God?

Apparently He knew their thoughts, that they were saying to Him, "Physician, heal thyself." Some Bible scholars interpret His statement as reflecting future deeds rather than something that has already taken place. Nevertheless, the message is clear. Jesus was being challenged to do for those in His hometown what He had done for those in neighboring towns. He will have to substantiate His words with action. Since He claimed Himself to be the Messiah, He should be able to perform miracles that one might expect from the Son of God.

No prophet is accepted in his own country. Luke categorizes Jesus' rejection as being the same as the rejection experienced by the Old Testament prophets. Jesus refused to give in to the people's demands for a sign. He cited two incidences from the Old Testament to justify His refusal.

Jesus reminded them that both Elias (Elijah) and Eliseus (Elisha), great prophets of Israel, performed great works for those outside of Israel that they could not accomplish for their own people. Both prophets experienced great need among their people. Elias (Elijah) witnessed the hunger of widows during a period of great famine in the land, but the Lord sent him to a widow in Sarepta. Eliseus (Elisha) was surrounded by lepers in Israel, but only Naaman was cleansed.

3. Move to Kill Jesus (vv. 28-30)

When the people heard Jesus' words, they were filled with wrath. Very early in Jesus' ministry, people began to display a desire to mold Him into the kind of Messiah they thought He should be instead of accepting Him as God's perfect gift. Even today, many people attempt to mold Jesus according to their own expectations.

The people of Nazareth were so enraged that they sought to kill Jesus. Perhaps they were so angry because Jesus had told them the truth and it hit home. Nothing angers like the truth! They managed to take Him out of the city where they led him to the brow of a hill. Although the city itself is built on a slope, the supposed site of the brow is a precipice that ranges from 80 to 300 feet high located southeast of Nazareth. They attempted to throw Jesus off this hill.

Of course, their attempt was not successful. It was not time for Jesus' ministry to end. Luke credits their failure to divine intervention as Jesus was able to pass through the midst of them and went His way. He was immune to the results of mob violence.

SEARCH THE SCRIPTURES

1. What did Jesus do once He arrived at Nazareth? (v. 16)

2. What did He do once He arrived at His destination there? (v. 16)

3. From what book of prophecy did Jesus read? (v. 17)

4. What responsibilities had Jesus been given because the Spirit of the Lord was upon Him? (vv. 18-19)

5. What did Jesus do when He had finished reading? (v. 20)

6. How did the people react to what Jesus had read? (v. 20)

7. What words did Jesus speak to break the silence? (v. 21)

8. What was the people's initial reaction to Jesus' statement? (v. 22)

9. What question did they ask about His background? (v. 22)

10. How did Jesus respond to their question? (vv. 23-24)

11. What examples did Jesus cite for His refusal to show them a sign? (vv. 25-27)

12. How did the people respond to Jesus' explanation? (v. 28)

13. What did the people plot to do to Jesus? (v. 29)

14. How did Jesus escape? (v. 30)

DISCUSS THE MEANING

1. What was it so difficult for the people to belief that Jesus was indeed the Messiah who had been prophesied in the Old Testament? Do you think the people were totally unjustified in requesting a sign? Would they have believed Jesus even if they had been given a sign?

2. Why were the people so enraged by the example Jesus gave them concerning Elisha and Elijah.? Why were they so angry that they wanted to kill Jesus?

LESSON IN OUR SOCIETY

It is often difficult for us to allow someone to grow as God intends. As soon as a person makes a step toward correcting negative behavior with positive behavior, he or she is often ridiculed by others. Instead of support, the one seeking the strength to make a life change often receives criticism for daring to be different. Perhaps that is because many peoples' vision of God is too small. Sometimes people find it difficult to believe that, through the power of the Holy Spirit, ordinary people can, and do, grow into extraordinary persons.

The people at Nazareth would not allow Jesus to move beyond their image of Him as a carpenter's son. They missed out on a great blessing because of their limited sight. We, too, can miss out on great things if we attempt to limit people according to our own narrow visions.

MAKE IT HAPPEN

Is there something you wish to change in your life but are afraid to because you fear the criticism or ridicule of others? It may be something as inconsequential as changing your hair color. Or it might be as serious as eliminating a bad habit or fulfilling a call that God extended to you long ago. Write down the barriers that inhibit your ability to make a change for the better in your life. Ask yourself, "What is the worse thing that could happen if I go ahead and _____?" Then, ask God for the strength and guidance to help you take that leap.

FOLLOW THE SPIRIT

What God wants me to do:

_____

_____

REMEMBER YOUR THOUGHTS

Special insights you learned:

_____

_____

MORE LIGHT ON THE TEXT
Luke 4:16-26, 28-30

Jesus has been baptized (3:21ff.) and is led to the wilderness (desert place) by the Spirit where the devil tempted Him for forty days (4:1-13). Having overcome all the temptations of the devil, and filled with the power of the Holy Spirit, Jesus returns to the region of Galilee where He officially begins his ministry (cf., Matthew 4:12; Mark 1:14). He is now about 30 years old (3:23).

According to the Jewish law this is the age priests begin their duties (Numbers 4:23; 1 Chronicles 23:3). From the context, Jesus has been teaching in other cities in this region (e.g., Caparnaum, see v. 23), especially in their synagogues, before He goes to his own hometown, Nazareth. His fame has spread all over the place because of the miracles and the authority with which he taught them (vv. 14-15; Mark 1:21-28; 3:32ff.).

4:16 And he came to Nazareth, where he had been brought up: and, as his custom was, he went into the synagogue on the sabbath day, and stood up for to read.

Continuing his itinerary in the Galilee region, Jesus comes into Nazareth, his hometown. Nazareth (watchtower) was a town on the lower part of Galilee where Jesus spent His boyhood years (Matthew 2:23). Nazareth was a small, but beautifully secluded, town nestled in the southernmost hills of the Lebanon Mountain range. It was situated in the territory belonging to Zebulun. The origin of the city is unknown and probably was insignificant in importance. It is never mentioned in the Old Testament.

It is said that Nazareth lay close to the important trade routes of Palestine and overlooked the Plain of Esdraelon, through which caravans passed as they traveled from Gilead to the south and west. North of the city was the main road from Ptolemais to the Decapolis, through which the Roman legions frequently traveled. This fact probably accounts for the origin of the name Nazareth in the Aramaic, meaning "watchtower."

However, geographically, Nazareth itself was situated in a valley about 366 meters (1,200 feet) above sea level overlooking the Esdraelon Valley. To the north and east were steep hills, while on the west the hills rose to an impressive 488 meters (1,600 feet). The city, therefore, was somewhat isolated from nearby traffic. This apparent isolation as a frontier town on the southern border of Zebulun contributed to the fact that Nazareth was regarded as a less important part of the national and religious life of Israel. Coupled with its seclusion Nazareth had a bad reputation both morally and religiously. It is also believed that Nazareth had a certain crude dialect in the Galilean. All this seems to make Nazareth notorious, and probably prompted Nathanael, when he first learned of Jesus of Nazareth, to ask, "Can anything good come out of Nazareth?" (John 1:46). The city became known in the New Testament because of Christ.

At Nazareth Jesus went into the synagogue on the Sabbath day, a habit He has formed from childhood (Luke 2:41-50). He grew up in the city and in the synagogue, He was therefore a familiar face. He also was familiar with the worship rituals. It was customary during a synagogue service on the Sabbath for seven people to read from the scriptures: a priest, a Levite, and five ordinary Jews. It was not therefore strange that Christ is handed the Scripture to read. Of course, He must have done that many times before.

17 And there was delivered unto him the book of the prophet Esaias. And when he had opened the book, he found the place where it was written,

As we have already noted, the reading of Scripture formed an integral part of the temple or synagogue worship. Indeed Scripture reading remains the most important part of worship in the Jewish religion even today. Before and during Jesus' time the Jewish people read the Scripture systematically. They read from the Law and from the Prophets.

Jesus is then handed the book of the prophet "Esaias" (Isaiah). In the Hebrew scrolls, the prophetic books were in single volumes (except the 12 Minor Prophets). Jesus opens the book to the prophetic passage, which summarizes His earthly mission. Whether Jesus looked for a passage He wished to read, or that He just opened the book and His eye fell upon the particular passage, or that it was the passage assigned for that Sabbath day, we do not know. Most likely Jesus was reading from the assigned lesson from the Prophet for the day. Jesus would probably comply with, and adapt to, the set routine of the synagogue rather than disrupt it.

18 The Spirit of the Lord is upon me, because he hath anointed me to preach the gospel to the poor; he hath sent me to heal the brokenhearted, to preach deliverance to the captives, and recov-

ering of sight to the blind, to set at liberty them that are bruised, 19 To preach the acceptable year of the Lord.

He reads from Isaiah 61:1-2 and includes a single phrase from 58:6. He probably read in Hebrew and translated into Aramaic, the common spoken language at the time. He reads, "The Spirit of the Lord is upon me," which means that He is filled with the power of the Holy Spirit. As we see in verse 21 Jesus identifies Himself as the subject of Isaiah's prophecy. Here He says that He has the Holy Spirit for a specific ministry. We should note that He has the Holy Spirit because He has been "anointed." This seems to indicate that the filling, or the possession, of the Holy Spirit is consequent to the anointing. The word "anointed" here translates the Greek, *chrio* (pronounced **khree'-o**), which means to consecrate, ordain, or to set apart, a person for a particular service.

In the Old Testament persons or things were anointed, symbolized by the pouring of oil to signify holiness and separation unto God, e.g., the tabernacle and its furniture (Exodus 30:22ff.), priests (Exodus 28:41), kings (Judges 9:8; 2 Samuel 2:4; 1 Kings 1:34), and prophets (1 Kings 19:16). The anointing also symbolized authority, appointment, and equipping for a special function or service to God. It was usually associated with the outpouring of the Spirit of God (1 Samuel 10:1, 9; 16:13; Isaiah 61:1). The anointing was always regarded as an act of God, and it was sometimes used to mean the bestowal of divine favor (Psalm 23:5; 92:10). The same idea is also carried over into the New Testament (Acts 10:38; 1 John 2:20, 27) and generally refers to the anointing of the Holy Spirit. As we see in this passage and other places in the New Testament, anointing is also frequently related to healing. In Mark 16:18 the disciples of Jesus anointed the sick, and James instructed the elder to anoint the sick with oil for healing purposes (James 5:14).

Here the writer declares that Jesus has been consecrated as evidenced by the power of the Holy Spirit for a two-fold ministry—to preach and to heal. He is called "to preach the gospel," i.e., Greek *euaggelizo* (pronounced **yoo-ang-ghel-id'-zo**), that is, to announce good news, or glad tidings, to the "poor" (Greek *ptochos* i.e., the poor, the

This includes those who are broken in mind and soul, or psychologically sick (Acts 10:38). He will bring comfort and hope to the destitute in heart. This is the work of the Holy Spirit, which Christ promised His disciples before He ascended, and which is demonstrated repeatedly in the Gospels. The anointing is also for the "recovering of sight to the blind" body, spirit, and soul for those in darkness (Matthew 4:16; Luke 1:79; 2:32; John 1:4-9; 9:32, 33; Acts 26:18). Jesus is also sent to liberate those "that are bruised," *therauo*, shattered, or completely crushed in life. This speaks of the oppressed and broken (Isaiah 58:6-14; cf., Mark 5:1-20; Luke 13:16). Although this passage refers to the immediate situation of Israel's captivity, the reality is to be fulfilled in the future of Christ's ministry.

20 And he closed the book, and he gave it again to the minister, sat down. And the eyes of all them that were in the synagogue were fastened on him. 21 And he began to say unto them, This day is this scripture fulfilled in your ears.

Luke now resumes his narrative. After reading the lesson for the day, Jesus "closed the book," which might be better rendered rolled or folded together the parchment (*ptusso*), then handed it back to the minister, and sat down, and was about to start a sermon. It was customary in the Jewish religious tradition that after the reading from the Scripture, the reader sits down to preach a sermon on the passage (2:46; 5:3; Matthew 5:1; 13:1-2; 15:29; 24:3). As He sat down to preach, all the people in the synagogue focused their attention on Him. Jesus explained to them the Scripture. We do not have the full content of Jesus' teaching, but only a summary of the main theme of Christ words: "This day is this scripture fulfilled in your ears."

Here Jesus declares to them that the words

destitute, or the needy). This probably includes the physically and spiritually poor. He is called to preach "deliverance to the captive," those who were bound and imprisoned in sin, sickness, and death (Acts 10:38; Ephesians 4:8-10; Hebrews 2:14-15). He is also sent to "preach" (proclaim to all) "the acceptable year of the Lord." The year of the Lord is typified by the year of Jubilee when liberty was proclaimed to all people on the Day of Atonement as instituted by God (Leviticus 25:8-13, 28). The atonement of Christ is fully embraced when the poor, the sick, the sinful, and the helpless are restored to prosperity, health, holiness, power, and dominion over Satan and receive membership and communion in the family of God.

The second function of the anointing is for healing. Here is meant both spiritual and physical healing. Jesus is sent "to heal the brokenhearted."

which He has read to them have finally been fulfilled in their presence. In essence that He, Jesus, is the One anointed by God, endued with the Holy Spirit, spoken of in the Old Testament to proclaim the Good News of salvation, deliverance, and to heal all manner of diseases. He was sent to proclaim the "acceptable year of the Lord,"—the Messianic age and the year of Jubilee, an age ushered in by His presence, a period in which God has planned to grant salvation to all people.

22 And all bore him witness, and wondered at the gracious words which proceeded out of his mouth. And they said, Is not this Joseph's son?

At first, the people's reaction was that of wonder and excitement, as the following words suggest, "witness," "wondered," and "gracious." All have a positive connotation. To "witness," *martureo* (pronounced **mar-too-reh'-o**), simply means to give an honorable report of what one saw or heard. It has also the idea to affirm a truth or bear testimony. To "wonder," *thaumazo* (**thou-mad'-zo**), means to admire, marvel, or to have in admiration. Jesus spoke with such grace and authority that the people marveled at His words. His words and His claim were so startling and amazing to them that they began to question within themselves, "Is not this Joseph's son?" Although they had known Him, they had never heard such words from Him in the 30 years He had lived among them. Moreover, they reflected on Jesus' background and family—He was only the son of Joseph, an ordinary person. How could He make such a claim? This was the turning point. They changed from an attitude of awe and wonder to doubt, skepticism, and prejudice. They must have thought, "How can Jesus, whose father, Joseph, is poor, be the One anointed to preach to the poor?" Jesus endured such prejudice repeatedly as recorded in the Scriptures (cf., Mark 6:3; John 1:46; 7:52).

23 And he said unto them, Ye will surely say unto me this proverb, Physician, heal thyself: whatsoever we have heard done in Capernaum, do also here in thy country. 24 And he said, Verily I say unto you, No prophet is accepted in his own country.

Jesus observes their skeptical attitude and says to them "Ye will surely say unto me this proverb, Physician, heal thyself." The origin of the proverb is not given; however, it seems to be a common saying, understood by everyone. It sounds also like a prophetic saying fulfilled at His Crucifixion (23:39). The people also want Jesus to perform the same miracles He had done at Capernaum, one of the cities of Galilee. This probably would prove to them the genuineness of His claim as God's anointed. The Gospels of Matthew and Mark have records of Christ's successful ministry in the Capernaum (Matthew 4:13; Mark 1:21-28). Earlier in this chapter (vv. 14-15), Luke himself records Christ's extensive and successful ministry in Galilee, including His work at Capernaum. The saying reminds us of Satan's demands of Jesus for miraculous feats before His public ministry. Here Jesus expresses either the reply He expects the people to make in response to His message, or what He knows they are individually thinking. Like the wilderness encounter with the devil, Jesus refused their demands.

Jesus continues by telling them an important fact, which is probably another common saying among the people, namely that a prophet is never accepted in his own country. Jesus introduces this fact with the common formula, "Verily I say unto you" (*amen lego hymin*), often used to introduce a solemn assertion. This is used six times in Luke, but more frequently in Matthew and Mark. The saying simply means that people who have achieved some fame or honor in life are never acknowledged at home. No one is popular in his own hometown. This also anticipates the rejection Jesus would face in His earthly ministry (especially among the Jews), like the prophets who were also rejected by their own people.

25 But I tell you of a truth, many widows were in Israel in the days of Elias, when the heaven was shut up three years and six months, when great famine was throughout all the land; 26 But unto none of them was Elias sent, save unto Sarepta, a city of Sidon, unto a woman that was a widow.

With a similar formula as in verse 24, "I tell you the truth," Jesus gives examples of two Old Testament prophets, Elijah (v. 26) and Elisha (v.

27), who ministered to Gentiles when they were rejected by the house of Israel. The formula means "I assure you" and calls for close attention to the importance of the fact to be stated. Note that He does not say that the prophets ministered to the Gentiles because they were rejected; however, it could be implied by the context. His rejection by the people should not be a surprise. Why are people not generally popular in their own home? Why was Christ not popular in Nazareth? Why could He not perform miracles in Nazareth as He did in other cities?

Although Jesus is discussing the rejection of His ministry by His own people, He is also introducing another dimension of God's divine plan of reaching all nations with the Good News. The mention of the widow (poor and destitute) from Zeraphath, and Naaman (the honorable and strong warrior) from Syria attest to this fact. It also signifies the scope of God's salvation to all types of people—both rich and poor. In addition, it defines and supports Christ's claim that He is anointed to preach the Good News to the poor and to heal those who are both physically and spiritually sick (vv. 18-20). Here Jesus redefines God's the plan of salvation. Contrary to the belief that salvation (deliverance by the Messiah) was for the Jews alone, the example of sending the prophets to the Gentiles indicates that salvation is for anyone whose heart is open to receive it. God does not discriminate by race, statute, or gender. Salvation is for all.

By this response and the examples from the Old Testament, Jesus tells His audience implicitly that unless they, the people of Nazareth (indeed the Jewish people as a whole), accept Him as the promised Messiah, He would turn to the heathens who are willing to receive Him.

28 And all they in the synagogue, when they heard these things, were filled with wrath, 29 And rose up, and thrust him out of the city, and led him unto the brow of the hill whereon their city was built, that they might cast him down headlong. 30 But he passing through the midst of them went his way,

Jesus' answer infuriated all the people in the synagogue. The word "wrath," *thumos* (**thoo-mos'**),

is described as fierce indignation, or a forceful, vindictive anger. Such fierce anger is usually associated with, or often results into, hatred and bitterness. Here "all" the people, with no exception, are angered at His words. They take Him out of the synagogue, and out of the city to a hilltop to throw Him from the cliff. They "thrust him out of the city" means that they drag him from the synagogue to the outskirts of the city. They bring Him to the mountain peak around Nazareth, and are about to "cast (throw) Him down headlong," but He walks through them and goes His own way. We are not told how He actually did this. In any case, He departs from them unharmed without any further incident. He spiritually disarms them by the power of the Spirit. He goes up to Capernaum and continues His teaching. It is significant that they looked for a miracle, and He demonstrated the same, though not on their own terms, but on His own. He walked away because it was not yet time for Him to lay down His life. Hence, He foiled their wicked plan through His divine power. Jesus says that He lays down his own life voluntarily; no one takes it away from Him (John 10:17ff.; 15:13).

DAILY BIBLE READINGS

M: Tempted As We Are
Luke 4:1-13
T: A Mission to the People
Luke 4:14-21
W: The Good News of Deliverance
Isaiah 61
T: His Own Received Him Not
Luke 4:22-30
F: The Healing of Naaman
2 Kings 5:1-14
S: The Rejection of Jesus
Matthew 13:54-58
S: Whoever Does the Will of God
Mark 3:31-35

TEACHING TIPS

1. Words You Should Know

A. Plough (9:62)—plow.

B. Lest haply (14:29)—otherwise.

C. Ambassage (14:32)—a delegation.

2. Teacher Preparation

Read today's lesson text. Think about those who walked away from Jesus' demands for discipleship versus those who stayed. Were those who stayed more committed than those who walked away, or were they more interested in being associated with someone who had a promising future?

3. Starting the Lesson

A. All Christians have the desire to follow Jesus, but all Christians also fall short of His demands. Ask members to think about the times and ways in which they have "walked away" from the demands of discipleship. What caused them to walk away? Fear? Rebellion? Anger? Lack of Courage? Confusion? Emphasize how Satan uses each of these tools and more to block God's people from staying on the path of righteousness.

B. Read today's IN FOCUS story about Paul's decision to become a deacon. Discuss how Christians place service to the Lord in a lesser role, although not necessarily intentionally. Talk about ways that other life pursuits can distract our attention away from the Lord. How can we be made aware of the right course of action when we are facing a crossroad?

4. Getting Into the Lesson

Talk about the very real difficulty many Christians face in putting Christ first. In your discussion, be sure that members recognize that the call to discipleship does not mean neglect of one's family. Many times, people associate discipleship solely with church attendance and church work. Part of Christian accountability includes how we care for those who have been placed in our care.

5. Relating the Lesson to Life

A. Today's DISCUSS THE MEANING calls for members to interpret the meaning behind Jesus' response to the three men. Discuss how every believer has weaknesses, although different, that sometimes hinder us from following Him. Talk about Jesus' motive for dismissing the three potential disciples.

B. The LESSON IN OUR SOCIETY focuses on the sacrifices that are required of a disciple. Some disciples of Christ have been called upon to give more than others. Dr. Martin Luther King, Jr. was just such as disciple. He answered the high call of discipleship and gave his life for his friends.

6. Arousing Action

Ask each member to think of five people whom they consider to be good Christian disciples. Then ask them to name the characteristics, qualities, and traits that make them so. Give them an opportunity to discuss whether those characteristics, qualities, and traits can be possessed by every believer. Ask them to choose one characteristic, quality, or trait that each person possesses and commit themselves to adopt them as a part of their own daily Christian living.

JAN 14TH

WORSHIP GUIDE

For the Superintendent or Teacher
Theme: The Cost of Discipleship
Theme Song: I Surrender All
Scripture: Matthew 10:34-39
Song: It's Wonderful to Live for Jesus
Meditation: My desire is to be a true
disciple, one who follows in the
footsteps of the Master Teacher. I will
read my Bible and pray daily, so
that I may continuously learn more
about His precious ways.

THE COST OF DISCIPLESHIP

Bible Background • LUKE 9:18-25, 57-62; 14:25-33
Printed Text • LUKE 9:57-62; 14:25-33
Devotional Reading • MATTHEW 10:34-39

LESSON AIM

After studying today's lesson, students will learn what Jesus expects of His disciples, what it means to follow Him, and the cost of following Him.

KEEP IN MIND

"And whosoever doth not bear his cross, and come after me, cannot be my disciple" (Luke 14:27).

FOCAL VERSES

Luke 9:57 And it came to pass that, as they went in the way, a certain man said unto him, Lord, I will follow thee whithersoever thou goest.

58 And Jesus said unto him, Foxes have holes, and birds of the air have nests; but the Son of man hath not where to lay his head.

59 And he said unto another, Follow me. But he said, Lord, suffer me first to go and bury my father.

60 Jesus said unto him, Let the dead bury their dead: but go thou and preach the kingdom of God.

61 And another also said, Lord, I will follow thee; but let me first go bid them farewell, which are at home at my house.

62 And Jesus said unto him, No man, having put his hand to the plough, and looking back, is fit for the kingdom of God.

14:25 And there went great multitudes with him: and he turned, and said unto them,

26 If any man come to me, and hate not his father, and mother, and wife, and children, and brethren, and sisters, yea, and his own life also, he cannot be my disciple.

27 And whosoever doth not bear his cross, and

LESSON OVERVIEW

LESSON AIM
KEEP IN MIND
FOCAL VERSES
IN FOCUS
THE PEOPLE, PLACES,
AND TIMES
BACKGROUND
AT-A-GLANCE
IN DEPTH
SEARCH THE SCRIPTURES
DISCUSS THE MEANING
LESSON IN OUR SOCIETY
MAKE IT HAPPEN
FOLLOW THE SPIRIT
REMEMBER YOUR THOUGHTS
MORE LIGHT ON THE TEXT
DAILY BIBLE READINGS

come after me, cannot be my disciple.

28 For which of you, intending to build a tower, sitteth not down first, and counteth the cost, whether he has sufficient to finish it?

29 Lest haply, after he hath laid the foundation, and is not able to finish it, all that behold it begin to mock him,

30 Saying, This man began to build, and was not able to finish.

31 Or what king, going to make war against another king, sitteth not down first, and consulteth whether he be able with ten thousand to meet him that cometh against him with twenty thousand?

32 Or else, while the other is yet a great way off, he sendeth an ambassage, and desireth conditions of peace.

33 So likewise, whosoever he be of you that forsaketh not all that he hath, he cannot be my disciple.

IN FOCUS

Paul was honored that Pastor Watson had approached him about becoming a deacon. He asked his pastor to give him a little while to pray over a decision. Pastor Watson agreed and told Paul that he would pray about the matter, too.

A couple of days after their conversation, Paul decided to pick up the phone and call his daddy, himself a deacon for nearly 30 years now. "I just don't know, Daddy," Paul said. "I mean, I'm in the running for that new position that's opening up at

222

the end of the year. I don't want to ruin my chances to get it if my time is taken up with my responsibilities as a deacon. Maybe I'll just pass it up right now and wait until a few years down the road."

Always calm and full of wisdom, his father replied, "Son, if you're going to make the commitment, you should be prepared to give yourself to the task." He continued, "Paul, you have to choose according to your own conscience and what you believe God is calling you to do. But you've got to decide what's really important in this life."

THE PEOPLE, PLACES, AND TIMES

Sons. Each of the men who considered following Jesus in today's lesson were Jewish sons.

During ancient times, sons were particularly important as they were considered second to the father in importance to the family. Sons were trained in the traditions of the community and in the meaning of wisdom.

Central to the Jewish household was the oldest male relative who was viewed as the father or master of the household and the ultimate authority. All those who belonged to him and claimed allegiance to him were considered part of the household.

Based on information from Holman Bible Dictionary, Trent Butler, general editor, Nashville: Broadman & Holman Publishers, 1991, pp. 475-476.

Disciple. This term comes from a Latin root word meaning "learner" or "pupil."

In ancient Greece, the word "disciple" generally referred to someone who adhered to a particular teacher, or school, or religion/philosophy. It was the disciple's responsibility to learn, study, and share with others the sayings and teachings of the master.

In Judaism, a disciple was one who was committed to the interpretations of Scripture and religious tradition given to him by the master or rabbi. The disciple would become more and more devoted to the teacher and his teachings. The instructional process was extensive, involving a definite meeting time, and such educational tools as question and answer, instruction, repetition, and memorization. Over time the disciple would

then pass on those teachings and traditions to others.

In the New Testament, 233 of the 261 occurrences of the word "disciple" are found in the Gospels, with the remaining 28 found in the Book of Acts. The Gospels often refer to Jesus as Teacher or Rabbi. Therefore, it can be assumed that Jesus employed traditional rabbinical teaching techniques to instruct His disciples. Yet, those who heard Him recognized that He was different because He spoke with authority.

The Gospels use the term disciple to refer to many others besides the Twelve. The verb "follow" came to be a somewhat technical term that Jesus used to call His disciples, who became known as "followers." This larger group of followers included men and women from all walks of life. Although Jesus held particular appeal to social and religious outcasts, He also attracted people of wealth and religious influence.

Based on information from Holman Bible Dictionary, Trent Butler, general editor, Nashville: Broadman & Holman Publishers, 1991, pp. 365-366.

BACKGROUND

Today's Scripture lesson includes a portion of Luke which directs every aspect of Jesus' ministry toward the Cross. Jesus' destiny is now revealed. There is now no doubt that the climax of Jesus' ministry will happen in Jerusalem. Jesus knew what the end would be. He set out to prepare His disciples for what is to come. Luke explains to his readers that Jesus will be rejected and executed. From this point on, no matter what Jesus does, everything builds up to Jerusalem and the Cross.

In the passage which precedes today's lesson text, Jesus had begun to teach His followers about the true nature of discipleship. Believers are to win others to Christ by offering the benefits of salvation over the threat of destruction. Christianity

AT-A-GLANCE

1. The Demands of Discipleship
(Luke 9:57-62)
2. Terms of Discipleship (Luke 14: 25-33)

is about discipleship; it is not a popularity contest.

IN DEPTH

1. The Demands of Discipleship (Luke 9:57-62)

Even though Jesus was a controversial figure, He enjoyed much popularity because of His teaching and healing abilities. Many people wanted to be near Him. They wanted to be connected with this Man on the move. But if they were to join Him, Jesus wanted His followers to be clear in their minds that their choice was not the path of human glory. Following Jesus did not mean a life of fame, fortune, and luxury. Those who chose to follow Him would have to be willing to pay a price.

Not everyone received Jesus' message so readily, however. The "sons of thunder," James and John, did not take the Samaritans' rejection of Jesus lightly (Luke 9:51-56). They wanted to use the power and authority that had been given to them for their mission to make the Samaritans suffer for their failure to respond positively to His message, just as the prophet Elijah had done (2 Kings 1:9-16).

Jesus began to help them understand their own purpose by explaining the nature of His own purpose. He did not come to destroy the lives of those He encountered. Rather His purpose was to save them. Jesus exhibited patience toward those who were not yet ready to receive Him. He was, in fact, more stern with those who wanted to follow Him, especially those who anticipated some earthly fame or a chance to be associated with a rising political power.

No doubt many wanted to follow Him because they wanted to be part of a powerful political movement. Not knowing what it meant to be His disciple, some made broad declarations of loyalty, such as the man who came to him claiming, "I will follow thee whithersoever thou goest." The man probably was sincere in his pledge of dedication of Jesus. Possibly Jesus could sense that the man did not really know what he was committing himself to.

The man probably thought that although Jesus roamed the countryside with a few followers, one day His journey would lead to earthly power and glory. The man had no inkling of the true power and glory the Messiah would receive after He had completed His task on earth. Jesus' path to power and glory came by way of Gethsemane and Golgotha.

Emotional enthusiasm was not the most important criteria for Jesus as decisions made solely on emotions tend to wane, especially during difficult times. What Jesus desired most was disciples who were committed to follow Him even to the Cross. Following Jesus meant sharing in His experience, which meant no permanent home or family life, and no worldly possessions or acclaim. Ultimately discipleship meant sharing in His rejection and suffering.

The second man was willing to follow Jesus, but only after he has taken care of some other obligations. The man's request, "Suffer me first to go and bury my father," was a plea to put off discipleship until his father had passed away.

Some people erroneously interpret Jesus' reply, "Let the dead bury their dead," to mean that Jesus callously would not allow the man to go to his father's funeral (as though the man was already deceased). In Jesus' day, sons were expected to care for their fathers in old age and provide them with an honorable burial. Therefore, to ask a son to cast this obligation aside was a bold and shocking demand!

Jesus was referring to those who are spiritually dead because they have not responded to the demands of the kingdom. Discipleship cannot take second place to any other commitment or obligation. Ministry to the living God is more important that ministering to the dead.

The third man who came to Jesus wanted an opportunity first to go back to his family and bid them farewell. Perhaps the man's family dominated his life. Possibly they would have talked him out of casting aside everything to follow Jesus. It is in the nature of parents to be concerned about the well-being of their children. Perhaps they were concerned that Jesus would never "amount to anything" in human terms and did not want their son to associate with Him.

In each instance, Jesus was able to determine the man's stumbling block and challenge him on that ground. The first man was most concerned about material security. The second man placed earthly tradition before the kingdom. Finally, the third man was bound by relationships deemed more important than his relationship to Christ. Family relationships are important. God gave us the family to promote stability and provide a means of support and loving care. But no relationship can be more important than our relationship to Him. Jesus calls us to place discipleship before all of these things. Half-hearted discipleship prevents one from being used to the fullest for the kingdom.

2. Terms of Discipleship (Luke 14:25-33)

As Jesus' popularity grew, great multitudes began to follow Him. Even though many, however, had wrongly interpreted His mission and destiny. They could not foresee something as horrifying as His humiliation and suffering as He died on the Cross. Therefore, Jesus found it necessary to clarify what it means to follow Him. Anyone who chose to follow Him had to have the rest of their in the proper perspective.

Jesus taught that those who wanted to follow Him must hate his father, mother, wife, children, brothers, and sisters, even his own life. When Jesus used the word hate, it did not mean He expected His disciples to harbor emotional or mental disdain for family or self. Rather, Jesus expected everything, and everyone, to fall behind on one's commitment to Him. The Gospel of Matthew (10:37) states Jesus' demand in terms of anyone who loves father and mother more than Him, or who loves son or daughter is not worthy of Him. Jesus demands first place in the lives of His followers.

Having lived under Roman rule, the Jews were well familiar with the gruesome image of death by crucifixion. It was not an image that was unfamiliar to them. Whoever does not bear his cross, whoever is not willing to follow Jesus, to endure suffering, cannot be His disciple. For those who were looking for a reward, Jesus made it clear that following Him involved pain and suffering.

He then appealed to those listening from a very practical stance. A person who was planning to build a tower would not simply take bricks and mortar and start building. First, that person would sit down and count the cost in order to make sure that he had sufficient supplies to finish it. Being a

disciple, then, was not a superficial undertaking. There was a cost, and each person considering discipleship needed to first sit down and determine whether he or she was willing to pay that price.

The person who begins such an undertaking without first determining the cost runs the risk of not being able to complete the task. Then there is always the possibility of ridicule from those who watch the person begin a project he or she could not complete.

Jesus then gave another example. A king who was about to go to war against another king would first sit down to determine whether he, having an army of ten thousand, could realistically defeat a king with an army of twenty thousand. Once a sensible king realizes the nature of the consequences, he will send an ambassador to make peace. Once again, Jesus was urging those who followed Him to take careful account of their decision.

Those who are weak or feebly committed do not make good disciples. There are times when the odds may seem to be against Christ and His cause. His disciples must decide whether or not they are willing to take a stand for Him even when it seems like an impossible undertaking. The demands of Christianity are great. Therefore, every believer must count the cost before undertaking the mission.

SEARCH THE SCRIPTURES

1. What did the first man Jesus encountered pledge to Him? (Luke 9:57).

2. How did Jesus respond to Him? (v. 58)

3. What did the second man Jesus encountered propose to Him? (v. 59)

4. How did Jesus respond to the man's request? (v. 60)

5. What did the third man Jesus encountered want to do before going off to follow Him? (v. 61)

6. How did Jesus let the man know that following Him takes precedence over all other relationships? (v. 62)

7. What did Jesus teach concerning discipleship and family relationships? (Luke 14:26)

8. What graphic description did Jesus use to let His followers know the nature of discipleship? (v. 27)

9. What practical example did Jesus use to help

them understand that they needed to calculate the cost of discipleship? (v. 28)

10. What would happen to the person who began a great endeavor, only to leave it unfinished? (vv. 29-30)

11. What was the second illustration Jesus gave concerning the cost of discipleship? (vv. 31-32)

12. Who did Jesus exclude from discipleship? (v. 33)

DISCUSS THE MEANING

1. Why do you think Jesus responded to the three men with responses that could be interpreted as harsh or lacking in compassion? What message was he trying to give? Why would such a demand be particularly difficult for a Jewish son? For what reason did Jesus challenge these long-held traditions?

2. Was Jesus trying to "weed out" those who were simply following Him because it was a fad or because He had popular appeal at the moment? Do you believe the great multitudes at that point took seriously His demands for discipleship?

LESSON IN OUR SOCIETY

Most Christians will never know the cost of discipleship as Jesus explained it to the multitudes. Rarely are believers in the United States truly persecuted for their beliefs. Some have counted up the cost and have taken another step forward, enduring hardship, persecution, pain, and suffering.

When Dr. Martin Luther King, Jr. counted the cost of following Jesus, given the call that had been extended to him, King took a great leap forward. He put discipleship before family, before the acceptance of many of his peers, and even before the entire nation. He gave his life for his friends. Jesus said, "Greater love hath no man than this" (John 15:13). Few people will ever know what it means to take such a stand and to pay such a price for the cause of Christ.

MAKE IT HAPPEN

How can you, as a contemporary Christian, count the cost of discipleship you must pay in light of the standard Jesus set forth in Luke 14:26-33?

FOLLOW THE SPIRIT

What God wants me to do:

_____

_____

REMEMBER YOUR THOUGHTS

Special insights you learned:

_____

_____

MORE LIGHT ON THE TEXT
Luke 9:57-62; 14:25-33

One of the major themes in the Gospel of Luke is discipleship and its cost. In today's lesson, Jesus spells out to His disciples what is involved in being a disciple or follower of Christ. His time of departure is fast approaching, Jesus and His disciples going are towards Jerusalem. He sends His disciple ahead to go and make ready for one of the Jewish feasts, perhaps the Passover. They are rejected at a village in Samaria. Angry because of this treatment, James and John ask that they be permitted to call down fire to consume the villagers. Jesus calls their attention to the real purpose of His mission on earth—"not . . . to destroy men's lives, but to save them" (v. 56). They continue their journey toward Jerusalem.

9:57 And it came to pass that, as they went in the way, a certain man said unto him, Lord, I will follow thee whithersoever thou goest. 58 And Jesus said unto him, Foxes have holes, and birds of the air have nests; but the Son of man hath not where to lay his head.

According to Luke, as they continue their journey, a certain man approaches Jesus and tells Him that he will follow Jesus wherever He is going. Luke does not give us the man's name or who he was. However, in Matthew the "certain man" is called a "certain scribe" (Matthew 8:19). Also, according to Matthew's account (Matthew 8:18-22), Jesus and His disciples were journeying from Capernaum across the Sea of Galilee. If Luke and Matthew are narrating the same story then we are dealing with a scribe. Scribes are almost hopeless to reach at the time of Christ because of their ties with the Jewish ruling class. However this man pledges to follow the Master all the way, probably not knowing fully the cost of following Christ.

The man uses the Greek word *akoloutheo*, pronounced (**ak-ol-oo-theh'-o**), translated simply "follow," to accompany as a disciple, or to join as an attendant. The language here is clearly terminology for discipleship. The man, therefore, knows what he wanted. Jesus' reply is in accord to His previous definition of discipleship in verse 23. Here Jesus defines the cost of discipleship. He tells the man that foxes and birds have homes where they retire after the day's toil for rest, but that He, the "Son of Man," does not even have a place to "lay His head." Jesus is neither complaining of His busy schedule, nor of His constant movement from place due to rejection (cf., vv. 52-56), nor is He moaning because He has nothing. Rather Jesus lays bare to the man the reality of His life of extreme sacrifice in order to call the man's attention to the implication of what he (the man) is requesting. It is a life of hardship and unrest. Such knowledge would help the man to make the right decision—whether to go ahead with his desire or withdraw his request. Here the cost of discipleship includes lack of pleasure, privation, and restlessness.

What Jesus intends to communicate to the man is that discipleship, or following Christ, is not easy—it is full of all types of hardships. In discipleship there are numerous obstacles and forces to contend with: the world, the flesh, and the devil. There will be all types of persecution, slander, hatred, and hunger. Christ does not want anyone enlisted into His army without counting the cost, and neither does He want anyone enlisted under false pretenses. This is not meant to discourage the man, or any person for that matter, who wants to join the Christ's army. Rather Christ wants the man, or anyone who wants to follow, to be aware of what he is getting himself into, and to search himself very well before committing himself.

59 And he said unto another, Follow me. But he said, Lord, suffer me first to go and bury my father. 60 Jesus said unto him, Let the dead bury their dead: but go thou and preach the kingdom of God.

In the preceding case, the man volunteers to follow Christ, but in the following case (vv. 59-60),

Jesus invites the person to follow him. Using the same Greek word translated here "follow me," Jesus invites the man to be his disciple. The man's answer is both remarkable and reasonable. He says, "Lord, suffer (*epitrepo*, i.e., allow, or permit) me first to go and bury my father." Looking at it with human rationale, there is nothing wrong with taking care of one's family duties, especially one's parents, which includes arranging funerals. The following questions arise. Does this mean that the man's father is already dead, and he wants to go and bury him? Or does he have some family obligations, such as an old or sick father that he would like to take care of before he decides to follow Christ? Why did Jesus ask him to follow Him?

The man's request, as suggested by some interpreters, does not necessarily mean that his father is already dead. If so, he would have been home helping in the funeral preparation. A second alternative is probably the case. He probably means that his father is getting old or is sick. He, therefore, would like to take care of that family obligation until after his death and burial, then he can commit himself to following the Lord constantly. This request sounds fair and reasonable, and judging from the previous case, he seems to know what it takes to be a follower of Christ.

Even more remarkable is Christ's answer to him, "Let the dead bury their dead: but go thou and preach the kingdom of God." By this, Jesus is saying that doing the work of the kingdom is of greater importance than any family obligation. "The dead" who are to perform the funeral duties are those who are spiritually dead those who do not follow Jesus. The call to follow Christ is of prime importance that demands immediate and urgent attention. Why? There are many spiritually dead people who will be able to take care of the domestic affairs, such as burying those who are physically dead. However, there are only few workers for God's kingdom (10:2; Matthew 9:37). Hence, Christ's demand is for a radical transfer of loyalty as we shall see later in this study (14:25-27).

61 And another also said, Lord, I will follow thee; but let me first go bid them farewell, which are at home at my house. 62 And Jesus said unto him, No man, having put his hand to the plough,

and looking back, is fit for the kingdom of God.

Jesus addresses the case of yet another who offers to follow Him but with conditions. The person desires to be Christ's disciple, but wants to bid farewell to his family first. Jesus replies to him with a metaphor. Using an analogy of a farmer, Jesus says to him, "No man, having put his hand to the plough, and looking back, is fit for the kingdom of God." Just as plowing requires a total and undivided attention of the worker to avoid crooked or sloppy work, those who desire to be part of God's kingdom must not allow any distractions in their service to their high calling. Indeed, the work of the kingdom does not accept half-hearted devotion, but a complete dedication and an absolute faithfulness to the task. These are fundamental requisites for following Christ.

We should observe that in these three cases, Jesus never rejected any of the men, but called their attention to the demands and costs of being His followers. He does not condemn personal or family responsibility, but says that personal and family responsibilities should not take priority over the things of God. Indeed, Levi did what the third man desired to do (5:27-29). He gave a farewell party to his family and relatives in honor of Christ and to introduce them to Jesus. Christ attended. Such is not this man's intention.

14:25 And there went great multitudes with him: and he turned, and said unto them, 26 If any man come to me, and hate not his father, and mother, and wife, and children, and brethren, and sisters, yea, and his own life also, he cannot be my disciple. 27 And whosoever doth not bear his cross, and come after me, cannot be my disciple.

On another occasion, Jesus reiterated the same fact that following the ways of the Lord demands a radical transfer of loyalty and a sincere consideration of the cost. In this instance, Jesus is being followed by a "great multitude" (big crowd of people) after a banquet at the house of a Pharisee. Seeing the crowd following, He tells them what it takes to be a true follower or disciple of Him. This involves denial of family—father, mother, wife and children, brothers, and sisters. Jesus uses a strong idiomatic expression to drive home the magnitude of one's devotion and obedience to God and

Christ. One must love God more than anything and anyone else. That means God must be first in every relationship. Therefore, the word "hate" is not used in its literal meaning. It does not mean that one has to be an enemy to one's family in order to be a true follower of Christ. Rather it speaks to the degree of loyalty between loved ones and God. When the two clash, one has to treat their loved ones as if they hated them. Following God demands complete and unconditional allegiance.

To stress further the magnitude of this dedication to Christ, Jesus makes an even more radical pronouncement, i.e., one has to hate "his own life" if one desires to be Christ's disciple. Indeed, unless one is prepared to carry one's own cross "and follow me," Christ emphasizes, one "cannot be my disciple." The "cross," metaphorically used here, is a translation of the Greek word *stauros,* (pronounced **stow-ros'**), and symbolizes suffering and death. The cross was a well-known instrument of a most cruel and shameful mode of punishment which the Greeks and Romans borrowed from the Phoenicians. This method of punishment was reserved mainly for the worst and guiltiest criminals, particularly the lowest slaves, robbers, and insurrectionists. Occasionally, in the Roman provinces, some upright and peaceable men also were hung on a cross at the arbitrary pleasure of the governors.

To carry one's own cross, therefore, means that one must be willing to suffer, even the most cruel and shameful death of the cross, for the sake of Christ in order to be a true follower of Christ. Bearing, or taking up, the cross, therefore, means the voluntary acceptance of all types suffering, persecution, and martyrdom during the course of following Christ. The New Testament contains numerous examples of people who suffered and died following Christ (Acts 5:17ff.; 7:57-60; 12:1-6; etc.).

28 For which of you, intending to build a tower, sitteth not down first, and counteth the cost, whether he has sufficient to finish it? 29 Lest haply, after he hath laid the foundation, and is not able to finish it, all that behold it begin to mock him, 30 Saying, This man began to build, and was

not able to finish. **31 Or what king, going to make war against another king, sitteth not down first, and consulteth whether he be able with ten thousand to meet him that cometh against him with twenty thousand? 32 Or else, while the other is yet a great way off, he sendeth an ambassage, and desireth conditions of peace.**

Jesus uses two parables in verses 28-32 to illustrate how important it is that all prospective disciples should think it through, realizing fully what it would cost them, both in their relationship with their family and their own life, before they resolve to follow Christ. In the first parable, Jesus applies the metaphor of a builder or building contractor. Here He says that before one undertakes a building project, one has to sit down and do a thorough estimate of its cost, check how much material he has to see whether he has enough for the project. The second parable tells how essential it is for a king planning a war against another king to make a good and thorough estimate of his strength,

both in personnel and material, to see whether he would be able to face the coming enemy. These two parables have one basic interpretation. Before one commits oneself to something of great importance, as wars and buildings, one should make sure whether one will be able to complete the undertaking. With these illustrations, Jesus teaches that following Him requires not just a reckless and hasty decision, but a thorough and conscious commitment with a realistic estimate of the ultimate cost to one's personal pleasure and life. Therefore, to be a true disciple of Christ, one must be prepared to pay the full price the denial of oneself for Christ's sake. Following Christ demands total obedience to the point of rejecting family, friends, and possessions.

33 So likewise, whosoever he be of you that forsaketh not all that he hath, he cannot be my disciple.

Here Christ declares the indispensable requirements for discipleship. With the use of the adverb "likewise," (*houto*) which means in like manner, or in the same way, Jesus gives the interpretation of the parable and stresses the cost of discipleship that has pervaded His teaching. The crucial requirement here is whoever desires to follow Christ must "forsake . . . all that he has." What does Christ mean to forsake all? Does it mean that a Christian should not have any personal possessions? Does it mean that one has to dispose all one's belongings in order to be a true follower of Christ?

The key word here is "forsake," a translation of the Greek *apotassomai* (pronounced **ap-ot-as'-som-ahee**), and it has a number of renderings. When it is used for persons, it literally means to say *adieu*, or good-bye (to bid farewell), to someone. It also means to separate or to withdraw oneself from another to take leave of. It is also translated to send away, from which we have the word "apostles"—(sent out ones). When used for things, it means to renounce, or to give up something, especially something very important. In the case of the rich young ruler (18:22), Jesus says that he ought to sell all that he has and distribute it the poor. Here Jesus says that a true disciple must relinquish all his possessions (not only material things, but also dear ones), his desire, his plans, and yes, his own life.

Practically speaking, this does not mean that one must sell all they possesses, or give away all the money, or desert family. It does not mean that one has to become a hermit or a beggar, rather one must give Christ full control over one's life ones own being, possessions, time, plans, desires, and aspirations. It means that one must place at Christ's disposal his all, so much so that, though still in possession of his goods, he serves the Lord with them. Sometimes it can mean that one must desert his worldly pleasures and possessions, and his family, to take up a missionary work in a distant land for the sake of Christ and His kingdom.

A note of warning needs to be made at this point. Many people have erred in the interpretation and appropriation of Christ's teaching here, especially verses 25-26. Many have literally hated their families, denounced friends and relatives, have avoided family responsibilities (selling all

their possessions and leaving their families destitute), and indeed have neglected their own physical well-being in the name of following Christ. This is not what Christ teaches here, as we have already stressed. That contradicts Christ's teaching about love, as clearly shown in all the Gospels, especially in John's Gospel. It could be argued that the first disciples (apostles) abandoned all things and followed Christ, but they did not literally abandon their family responsibilities, or denounce their family members. The disciples maintained a relationship with their immediate families, e.g., when Simon Peter's mother in-law was healed (Mark 1:30-31), or when James and John maintained such good relationship with their mother that she advocated on their behalf asking that they be seated next to Christ (Matthew 20:20-21). However, in many cases, following Christ, that is, becoming a Christian, may cost one a relationship with others—family and friends. To be a true follower of Christ demands inward freedom from worldliness, covetousness, and selfish desires, and a devotion to Christ. Following Christ demands that one count the cost before taking the plunge!

DAILY BIBLE READINGS

M: On the Master's Mission
Luke 9:1-9

T: Hospitality Refused
Luke 9:51-56

W: The Christ and His Suffering
Luke 9:18-27

T: The Would-Be Followers of Jesus
Luke 9:57-62

F: Warnings and Encouragements
Luke 12:4-12

S: Guilt By Association
Luke 22:54-62

S: The Cost of Being a Disciple
Luke 14:25-33

TEACHING TIPS

January 21
Bible Study Guide 8

1. Words You Should Know

A. **Publicans** (v. 1)—tax collectors

B. **Swine** (v. 15)—pigs

2. Teacher Preparation

Recall a time in your life when you thought you knew what was best and rebelled against an authority figure. Then think about a time when you rebelled against God's command. What caused you to wake up and realize that you had allowed yourself to stray far from God. Consider why it is so difficult for us to trust that God knows best and follow His Word?

3. Starting the Lesson

A. When we choose to depart from God and indulge in rebellious behavior, we often find that there are many who are willing to join us in our sinful endeavors. Think about a time when you encountered "fair weather" friends who abandoned you when things got tough. Ask the class to recall how it feels to know that God welcomes us back with open arms and rejoices over us.

B. Read today's IN FOCUS story about Darnell and Kelley. Talk about concrete ways that a church can help prodigal members' return to the fold and celebrate their return, rather than gossip about them. Discuss the fact that such persons generally repent on their own. When they have made the decision to return to the Lord, they are in need of love, support, and encouragement.

4. Getting Into the Lesson

As you guide class members through today's lesson, help them to recall the days of their youth, when they were young and naive about the ways of the world. Spend some time talking about spiritual immaturity and how we can be deceived into thinking that we know better than God.

5. Relating the Lesson to Life

A. Today's DISCUSS THE MEANING addresses human nature concerning forgiveness and repentance. Talk about ways that our Christian witness may be positively affected if we conduct ourselves according to the lesson Jesus taught in this parable.

B. The LESSON IN OUR SOCIETY focuses on the attitude Christians should have concerning those who have strayed from the faith, yet repented. Talk about the assertion that, "The Christian army is the only army that shoots its wounded." Discuss ways that we can avoid such behaviors.

6. Arousing Action

A. Ask members to think of someone they know who is has recently committed or recommitted his or her life to Christ. What events or circumstances caused the person to turn to the Lord? Talk about ministry possibilities for your church that can serve to help those who have turned or returned to walk in the Lord's way. Compare the benefits of showing forgiveness and compassion to others versus acting toward others with judgment and resentment. Which set of behaviors will yield the greatest results for God's kingdom?

JAN 21ST

B. Give class members and opportunity to complete FOLLOW THE SPIRIT and REMEMBER YOUR THOUGHTS.

WORSHIP GUIDE

For the Superintendent or Teacher

Theme: Lost and Found

Theme Song: Just a Little Talk with Jesus

Scripture: Ephesians 1:15 2:2

Song: Come to Jesus

Meditation: My desire is to be a true disciple—one who follows in the footsteps of the Master Teacher.

I will read my Bible and pray daily, so that I may continuously learn more about His precious ways.

LOST AND FOUND

Bible Background • LUKE 15
Printed Text • LUKE 15:1-2, 11-24
Devotional Reading • EPHESIANS 1:15—2:2

LESSON AIM

After studying today's lesson, students will gain insight into the nature of the kingdom of God and how the Lord looks upon those who are apart from Him.

KEEP IN MIND

"For this my son was dead, and is alive again; he was lost, and is found. And they began to be merry" (Luke 15:24).

FOCAL VERSES

Luke 15:1 Then drew near unto him all the publicans and sinners for to hear him.

2 And the Pharisees and scribes murmured, saying, This man receiveth sinners, and eateth with them.

11 And he said, A certain man had two sons:

12 And the younger of them said to his father, Father, give me the portion of goods that falleth to me. And he divided unto them his living.

13 And not many days after the younger son gathered all together, and took his journey into a far country, and there wasted his substance with riotous living.

14 And when he had spent all, there arose a mighty famine in that land; and he began to be in want.

15 And he went and joined himself to a citizen of that country; and he sent him into his fields to feed swine.

16 And he would fain have filled his belly with the husks that the swine did eat: and no man gave unto him.

17 And when he came to himself, he said, How

LESSON OVERVIEW

LESSON AIM
KEEP IN MIND
FOCAL VERSES
IN FOCUS
THE PEOPLE, PLACES,
AND TIMES
BACKGROUND
AT-A-GLANCE
IN DEPTH
SEARCH THE SCRIPTURES
DISCUSS THE MEANING
LESSON IN OUR SOCIETY
MAKE IT HAPPEN
FOLLOW THE SPIRIT
REMEMBER YOUR THOUGHTS
MORE LIGHT ON THE TEXT
DAILY BIBLE READINGS

many hired servants of my father's have bread enough and to spare, and I perish with hunger!

18 I will arise and go to my father, and will say unto him, Father, I have sinned against heaven, and before thee,

19 And am no more worthy to be called thy son: make me as one of thy hired servants.

20 And he arose, and came to his father. But when he was yet a great way off, his father saw him, and had compassion, and ran, and fell on his neck, and kissed him.

21 And the son said unto him, Father, I have sinned against heaven, and in thy sight, and am no more worthy to be called thy son.

22 But the father said to his servants, Bring forth the best robe, and put it on him; and put a ring on his hand, and shoes on his feet:

23 And bring hither the fatted calf, and kill it; and let us eat, and be merry:

24 For this my son was dead, and is alive again; he was lost, and is found. And they began to be merry.

IN FOCUS

Darnell and Kelley had been away from church for a while. The business venture they had tried was not exactly the kind of thing they were proud to get up in church and talk about. But the money was promising, and they decided it was worth a shot.

Once they got into their new business, they soon discovered it called for them to regularly associate with people who were amoral. Some were just downright sleazy! When Darnell got into a fight with a guy who was trying to come on to Kelley, they decided it was time for them to pull away and get back to the values they were raised with.

"People are gonna be buzzing," Kelley said as they were getting dressed for church. "I just don't know if I can go back over there and face those folks. You know how judgmental they can be, Darnell. They all know the kind of business we owned!"

Darnell didn't answer Kelley. He just kept getting dressed.

They purposely got to church a little late to cut down on the number of people who might say something to them before the service began. Much to their surprise, all they got was warm smiles.

After the sermon, Darnell motioned for Kelley to come down the aisle with him so that they could rededicate their lives. She followed, but was still a little concerned about what Reverend Collier's reaction to them coming back might be. However, as soon as they walked up to him, Reverend Collier hugged them both tightly and said, "Praise the Lord!"

THE PEOPLE, PLACES, AND TIMES

Fatted Animals. In ancient times, a young animal was set aside to be fed for slaughter. In the Old Testament, the fatted, or choice, animals were sometimes associated with prosperity (Genesis 41:2, 18; Ezekiel 34:3, 16, 20) or was used as a general reference to the strongest or choicest among the flock.

Fattened cattle were part of the menu for banquets and feasts, such as wedding celebrations.

In the New Testament, James (5:5) associates the fatted animal with a day of slaughter.

Based on information from Holman Bible Dictionary, Trent Butler, general editor, Nashville: Broadman & Holman Publishers, 1991, p. 480.

Inheritance. In the ancient Hebrew tradition, the possessions of the father were passed on to his sons. Daughters could receive the father's inheritance only in the absence of sons. Before this ruling from the Lord came into effect (Numbers 27:1-11), a man who had no sons left his inheri-

tance to his brothers, to his father's brothers, or to his male next-of-kin. The Hebrew interpretation of inheritance did not necessitate death before the disposition of property.

Traditionally, the eldest son was to receive a double portion (Deuteronomy 21:17) of the father's inheritance, although this rule was not absolute. Reuben lost his place of prominence because of incest with Bilhah (Genesis 35:22; 49:3-4; 1 Chronicles 5:1), and Esau relinquished his birthright to Jacob (Genesis 25:29-34).

Based on information from Holman Bible Dictionary, Trent Butler, general editor, Nashville: Broadman & Holman Publishers, 1991, p. 696.

BACKGROUND

As Jesus continued His journey toward Jerusalem, He was met with those who were drawn to Him and those who rejected Him. Those who criticized Him generally were those who had a stake in the oppressive system which benefitted them while it held others down.

The Jewish religious hierarchy probably thought Jesus was a bright, young man who had gone off in the wrong direction to promote His own cause. Instead of investing Himself in the traditions and practices of His religion, He regularly challenged them, much to their discomfort. They probably wanted someone of His giftedness to be one of them, but He would have none of it. Others were probably jealous of His power and charisma. Even those who did not accept Him as Messiah were trying to mold Him into who they thought He should be.

AT-A-GLANCE

1. The Pharisees and Scribes Disapprove
(Luke 15:1-2)
2. The Prodigal Son (vv. 11-24)

IN DEPTH

1. The Pharisees and Scribes Disapprove (Luke 15:1-2)

The Pharisees and Scribes criticized Jesus for His open fraternization with publicans and sinners. Jesus socialized with those whom Israel rejected. His free association with them threatened the very foundation on which the pious stood.

Publicans, or tax collectors, and sinners were considered to be unclean. The publicans had given themselves over to be used by the Roman government to collect taxes from their own oppressed compatriots. Sinners were those who failed to adhere strictly to the Law. By contrast, the Pharisees and Scribes considered themselves to be among the most holy.

Through His association with these transgressors of the Law, Jesus was contaminating Himself. It was bad enough that He associated with them at all. To make matters worse, He ate with them as well. Sharing a meal together indicated that Jesus had chosen them as friends. The English word "companion" is derived from the word *com-panis,* meaning "with bread." Jesus was clearly not a sinner, yet He chose to ignore the boundaries that had been established by religious and social convention. Jesus chose to associate with the outcasts over acceptable church folk!

In response to their indignation, Jesus told three parables designed to address the biases of the Jewish leaders. He wanted to teach them that no one was hopeless in the eyes of God. Even those considered godless were capable of redemption. In fact, those most difficult to redeem are the persons who fail to recognize their need for it!

Jesus did not wait until the downtrodden came to Him; He went to where they were and reached out to them. As the Pharisees sucked in their breath and pulled their robes tightly around them to avoid contamination, Jesus freely associated with them. A physician cannot heal a wound if he isolates himself in another room. Jesus went to those who needed Him and received them with open arms of love.

2. The Prodigal Son (vv. 11-24)

Prior to telling the story of the wayward son, often referred to as the prodigal Son, Jesus told two other parables. The first was about the value of even one lost sheep to the shepherd. The shepherd steps away from 99 sheep that are secured to find the one that has gone astray. When the lost sheep is found, the shepherd rejoices.

In the second story, Jesus told the parable of the Lost Coin. Jesus used this story to explain that every soul is valuable to the kingdom, no matter how many may already be present.

Finally, Jesus told the story of the lost son, something far more valuable than a coin, or even a sheep. When this story is interpreted in terms of the kingdom, those who are supposed to be in the right may be less pleasing to God than the penitent one who has gone astray.

The story of the Prodigal Son is a vivid representation of the point Jesus was trying to make with the Pharisees. In this story, the younger of a man's two sons came to his father requesting his inheritance.

According to Jewish Law, the younger son was to be allotted one-third of the estate following the death of his father. Knowing it was within his father's power to abdicate his wealth prior to his death, this young man didn't want to wait any longer. Once the son accepted his portion of the inheritance, he had no further claim on his father's estate or the family possessions. The very nature of the son's request indicates that the younger son possessed a rebellious spirit which could only be quenched through a hard life lesson.

Instead of being a dutiful son, one who honored his father and his mother according to the fifth commandment (Exodus 20:12), this young man went away into a far country. He showed no concern for the welfare of his father in old age. He was driven solely by selfish desires. He left Palestine and went into a Gentile region.

The son was not wrong for requesting his share of the inheritance. His transgression was in cutting himself off from his father's love and protection, assuming he could take care of his own needs. Through his actions, the son denounced his status as son.

This is also the condition of sinners whom Jesus has called to repentance. They have no claim to the inheritance of eternal life because they are not a part of His family. Many people search elsewhere for salvation, just as the prodigal went elsewhere seeking what he thought would make him happy.

Because he cut himself off from his father, the

prodigal now had to rely on his own resources. He had squandered his inheritance quickly. He gave no thought to planning for his future and disposed of all he had through riotous living. He did not anticipate that a day of trouble would come in the form of a mighty famine. Fear and panic likely prevailed as everyone was probably having a hard time during the period of famine. The prodigal made no provisions for his future and had cut himself off from the only one who cared to help him.

All he had left now was his own thoughts and the time to assess how and why he had ventured down the wrong path. He left home seeking the thrills that he thought life had to offer. Instead, he found the hard truths of life when away from the safety and security of his father's home. Having no money and probably no friends gave him an opportunity to think about the self-centered choices he had made.

Things got so bad that he was forced to take the most disgusting form of employment a Jew could undertake—feeding swine. Leviticus 11:8 reveals the Jewish attitude toward swine: "Of their flesh shall ye not eat, and their carcass shall ye not touch; they are unclean to you." Swine were not even to be touched by Jews. The young man had left his loving Jewish home where there was love and abundance only to descend into the worst kind of job, working for a Gentile boss.

He got so hungry that he would gladly have eaten the animal's feed, the pods of the carob trees, eaten only by animals and the very poorest humans. He had hit bottom! Then the prodigal came to himself. It was as though he was able to step outside of himself and see the sorry state he was in. He remembered that he was the son of a wealthy father who had servants and bread enough to spare. He had no need to beg because the father who loved him was wealthy.

At this point, the parable of the prodigal distinguishes itself from the story of the Lost Sheep and the Lost Coin. Those objects which were lost had to be found at the initiative of someone. In the case of the prodigal, he could not be found until he desired to be found. He now understood all that he had given up when he renounced his sonship by taking his inheritance and going far away from his father.

Now that he was aware of his transgression and his helpless state, he was ready to be found. He decided to return to the land of his father. The prodigal still used the term father, although he recognized that he is no longer worthy to be called son. The prodigal's penitence and humility is demonstrated by his willingness to go home and be a servant in his father's house. He was ready to acknowledge his wrongdoing.

Here it is important to recognize that before the son had an opportunity to make his confession, the father had compassion on him; he hugged and kissed him. The prodigal repented and was fully prepared to take whatever the father was willing to give. But the father received his long lost son with joy and open arms.

While the prodigal needed to confess his sinfulness and his unworthiness, the father was more interested in rejoicing over the fact that his son had come home. His return was a cause for celebration. Looking at the prodigal's father as our heavenly Father, all believers can know that once we are prepared to come to Him in humility and repentance, He joyously receives us. In fact, He cannot wait for the opportunity to lavish His love on His wandering children who have returned to Him.

God wants the best for us, just as the prodigal's father wanted the best for his son, stripping off the rags he had worn and exchanging them for a robe worthy of his son. The fatted calf was killed to be eaten as the homecoming celebration. It was time to be merry because the son who was dead is alive again.

By telling this parable, Jesus invited the religious men of the day to discard their resentments of the lowly and to join the celebration with Jesus and the other prodigals who had come home to the Father. Later in the parable, the resentment of the older brother parallels the resentment of the Pharisees, but God loves them all equally, the wayward and the devoted.

SEARCH THE SCRIPTURES

1. What kind of people were drawn to Jesus? (v. 1)

2. Why were the Pharisees and scribes critical of Jesus? (v. 2)

3. What did the younger son desire from his father? (v. 12)

4. What did the son do once he received his portion? (v. 13)

5. What unforeseen circumstance worsened the son's plight? (v. 14)

6. How did the son provide for himself once his money was gone? (v. 15)

7. What did the son realize once he came to himself? (v. 17)

8. What did the son say to indicate he had repented for his misdeeds? (vv. 18-19)

9. How did his father receive him? (v. 20)

10. What did the father do to celebrate his son's return ? (vv. 22-24)

DISCUSS THE MEANING

1. Why do some Christians find it so difficult to receive those who come to the Lord when God obviously rejoices in their return to Him?

2. Do you think the father was able to recognize his son's penitent spirit by the simple fact that he had returned home?

3. Why is it that sometimes people must endure hard experiences in order to recognize the blessings that have always been available to them?

LESSON IN OUR SOCIETY

Jesus repeatedly gave illustrations of how God rejoices over finding those who had been lost. Yet, within the Christian community, we often behave punitively toward those who have strayed, even though the persons have confessed and repented. This is not the model we have been given.

A well-known Christian leader has said, "The Christian army is the only army that shoots its wounded." The example we have been given is not to beat down those who have fallen and are trying to pick themselves up. We should provide every opportunity to help those who have strayed from the path of righteousness and desire to return to it. When we encounter such persons, we should hold before us the image of our heavenly Father rejoicing and celebrating, just as the prodigal's father rejoiced over his lost son's return.

MAKE IT HAPPEN

Do you know of someone who desires to return

to the active Christian community but is reluctant for fear of how he or she will be received?

What are some positive steps that Christians can take to help rejoice at such a person's return to the fold? What protective measures can be taken by the Church and fellow Christians to provide an environment to help strengthen a person so that he or she will not readily or hastily fall back into old patterns of sinful behavior?

FOLLOW THE SPIRIT

What God wants me to do:

_____

_____

REMEMBER YOUR THOUGHTS

Special insights you learned:

_____

_____

MORE LIGHT ON THE TEXT
Luke 15:1-2; 11-24

We read in 14:25 that a "great multitude" followed Jesus as He and His disciples went towards Jerusalem. The crowd probably was a mixture of all types of people—publicans, sinners, Pharisees, and scribes—and He taught them.

15:1 Then drew near unto him all the publicans and sinners for to hear him. 2 And the Pharisees and scribes murmured, saying, This man receiveth sinners, and eateth with them.

With the use of the particle *de* (**deh**) translated here as "then" (King James Version, "now" in New International Version and New American Standard), Luke connects us to the preceding narrative. Its use here serves as transition and indicates a continuation of the story. The statement that all the publicans and sinners drew near to hear Jesus shows that He paid attention to them, or associated with them, to the dismay of the Pharisees and scribes. Hence their criticism of Him (v. 2). The Pharisees and scribes, ignorant of the purpose and mission of Christ on earth, "murmured" against Jesus, complaining that he received sinners and ate with them. In answer to their objection, Jesus gives three successive parables to illustrate the purpose of His mission on earth, i.e., "the Son of man is come to seek and to save that which was lost" (Luke 19:10; Matthew 18:11).

The noun "sinners" is a translation of the Greek *hamartolos* (pronounced **ham-ar-to-los'**), and refers to people associated with bad or wicked deeds. It was used specifically for people stained with certain vices or crimes. The non-Jewish, or the heathen, were regarded as sinners. The word *hamartolos* is derived from the verb *hamartano*, which generally means to miss the mark. It has the idea of missing or wandering from the path of uprightness and honor, to do or go wrong. According to the Jewish standard, a sinner is one who wanders away from or violates the law of God.

The "publicans," *telones* (**tel-o'-nace**), often translated as tax collectors, were the people employed by the Romans to collect revenues. Among the Romans, tax collectors were a highly respected class, but detested by the Jews and other nations. They were hated both because of the nature of employment and because of the harshness, greed, and deception, with which they carried out their duty.

The publicans were charged by the Roman authorities to collect custom duties and taxes and send them to Rome. These publicans were generally local natives of the province in which they were stationed. They were known for overcharging (Luke 3:13) and bringing false charges against the populace in the hope of extorting hush money (19:8). Because they were forcibly subjected to the Roman rule, the Jews strongly resented paying tribute to the Romans. The publicans were, therefore, regarded as traitors, or apostates, and defiled because of their frequent contacts with the heathen and their willingness to be tools of the oppressor. The publicans were practically ostracized from the Jewish community, but they became some of the earliest disciples of John the Baptist and Jesus (Matthew 9:9-11; Mark 2:14-15; Luke 5:27-30). The position of Zaccheus, as a "chief tax-gatherer" (Luke 19:2, Greek *architelones*), implies a gradation of some kind among the publicans. This probably means that he had other tax collectors under him who sent their collection him and he forwarded them to Rome. To the Jewish people, the publicans were

sinners. To the Pharisees and scribes, tax collectors and sinners were synonymous.

The Pharisees and scribes' charge against Jesus here, "This man receiveth sinners, and eateth with them," implies that while on his way to Jerusalem with the crowd, Christ had time to sit at dinner with some other people. This, therefore, was another instance in which Jesus dined with "sinners" (cf., 5:27ff.; 19:1ff.; Matthew 9:9ff.; Mark 2:14-17). In these references, the Pharisees and scribes referred to the publicans and sinners separately, but referred to both as sinners here. The word "receiveth," *prosdechomai* (**pros-dekh'-om-ahee**), means to accept or to welcome. Why did they murmur against Him? The answer is twofold. Christ has established Himself through His teaching and miracles as One from God and thus holy and righteous. For the Pharisees and scribes, it was improper for the righteous to mingle, or have any dealing, with sinners, much less accept them and eat with them. However, they never accepted, or acknowledged, the authenticity of Christ's work and teaching as divine. Therefore, Christ's acceptance of "sinners" confirms their skepticism about Him, His claims, and His work.

With the three parables that follow the parable of the lost sheep (vv. 3-7), the parable of the lost coin (vv. 8-10), and the one generally known as the parable of the prodigal son, (vv. 11-24), Jesus answers the Pharisees and scribes. He exposes their ignorance of, and at the same time, redefines the true purpose of religion and His mission as He had previously done (5:32).

11 And he said, A certain man had two sons: 12 And the younger of them said to his father, Father, give me the portion of goods that falleth to me. And he divided unto them his living. 13 And not many days after the younger son gathered all together, and took his journey into a far country, and there wasted his substance with riotous living.

As if the two previous parables (vv. 3-10) are not enough to fully illustrate His point, Jesus proceeds to tell them a story which has become one of the greatest illustrations of man's relationship with God the Father. Here Christ illustrates the sinful nature of man, how man by his act has wandered away from God, and how God, through His loving

African countries), at the death of the father, the children would share his inheritance among themselves. For example, among the Igbo of Nigeria, the eldest of the children would inherit one-half of the property and the other half shared among the rest of the children. If there are only two children, the eldest will have two-thirds of the inheritance. However, among the Jewish people the eldest gets two-thirds, or a double portion of the inheritance (Deuteronomy 21:17), while the rest share the remaining portion among them. This knowledge will help us understand the implication of the younger child's request of the father, and the gravity of his sin. Asking his father, "Give me the portion of goods that falleth to me" is irregular and out of place in the Jewish custom. It shows disrespect for the father and, by implication, amounts to treating father as if he were already dead. Neither Jewish nor Roman law permitted the father to arbitrarily make disposal of his estate.

compassion, seeks to save man from his sin. It further illustrates God's attitude to repentant sinners who come to Him. It also illustrates the difference between God's concern and the attitude of the murmuring religious people over the salvation of a lost soul.

The setting of this story is typical of a Jewish household where the children can live off their family's inheritance during their father's lifetime, while the estate remains under his control until his death. According to the Jewish custom, and consistent with that of many countries (especially

The young man asks his father to give him his own portion of his father's estate. His father complies. He divides his estate between his two sons. The younger son takes off after a few days to "a far country" with his booty. There he "wasted his substance with riotous living." The word "wasted" used here is the Greek *diaskorpizo*, (**dee-as-kor-pid'-zo**), which means to disperse or scatter abroad. It also means to separate, as in to winnow grain (wheat) in order to separate the chaff. Figuratively used, it means to squander. Therefore, the young man squanders his possession with "riotous" (Greek *asotos*) or loose lifestyle. The word *asotos* is found only here in the New Testament. Its noun form, *asotia*, is found three times and translated as excess (Ephesians 5:18) and riot (Titus 1:6; 1 Peter 4:4). The clause "wasted his substance with riotous living" therefore gives a picture of a young man, overwhelmed with so much wealth who does not know how to control himself. He lives extravagantly.

14 And when he had spent all, there arose a mighty famine in that land; and he began to be in want. 15 And he went and joined himself to a citizen of that country; and he sent him into his fields to feed swine. 16 And he would fain have filled his belly with the husks that the swine did eat: and no man gave unto him.

After he has "spent all" (*dapanao*, **dap-an-ah'-o**), i.e., wasted or squandered all, he finds himself starving. He becomes destitute in a foreign land. His situation is made worse because of "a mighty (great) famine" that fell on that land. He is left without help, including those who helped him waste his riches. No one seems to care about him. The situation becomes so desperate that he accepts the most humiliating and repulsive type of work taking care of the swine of one of the citizens of that country. To this Jewish audience, indeed to many other nations, tending to swine is a most repugnant and degrading employment, because to them pigs are unclean animals.

Among the Egyptians swine tenders were cut off from the society. They were not allowed to marry even from the "lowest class" in the society, and they could not worship the gods. In Jewish society swine tenders would be treated as lepers. Jesus made use of this fact to show how desperate the young man was, to what depths of misery which his riotous living had brought him. This illustrates the depravity and misery of sinners in their lust and sin.

His deplorable situation is heightened by the fact that not only does he accept this most humiliating job, feeding the pigs, he lusts after their food, as described by the clause "He would fain have filled his belly with the husks that the swine

did eat." The word "fain" is the Greek *epithumeo* (pronounced **ep-ee-thoo-meh'-o**), which is to desire, to lust after, or to covet. It is used of those who desire or seek things forbidden. This word and the clause "and no man gave unto him" suggests that he is in the field as a slave, feeding swine without food or pay. It also implies he is not even allowed to eat of the swine's food, just as sugar slaves were forbidden to eat sugar canes else they would be beaten. How much lower could he go?

17 And when he came to himself, he said, How many hired servants of my father's have bread enough and to spare, and I perish with hunger! 18 I will arise and go to my father, and will say unto him, Father, I have sinned against heaven, and before thee, 19 And am no more worthy to be called thy son: make me as one of thy hired servants.

The turning point of the story comes when his condition brings him to his senses and he realizes that if he continues in it that would be his end. Disillusioned by his desperate condition, he acknowledges how foolishly he has acted by deserting his family, and plans a way to return home. "And when he came to himself" is a figurative way of saying that when he came to his senses. Talking to himself (or thinking aloud) and out of frustration and disgusted with himself, he exclaims, "How many hired, servants of my father's have bread enough and to spare, and I perish with hunger!" He compares his present unpleasant and shameful condition to the condition of his father's "hired servants," or *misthios* (**mis'-thee-os**). They are paid servants, and they have "enough and to spare" while he is not even allowed to eat from the pigs' pen. The phrase "enough and to spare" is a translation of the Greek *perisseuo* (**per-is-syoo'-o**), which means superfluous, to have excess. They have more than enough while he suffers in penury.

The thought of this spurs him to a decision. Instead of continuing in this unenviable and despicable situation, he decides to return home and plead for the lowest place in his father's household. He rehearses how he is going to plead with his father. From this plea, we see a sense of remorse, repentance, faith, and action working together. He feels sorry for his action and repents. He has faith that his father would not reject his confession nor his plea. Hence, he says that he would "arise and go to" his father and would confess to him saying, "I have sinned against heaven, and before thee." He realizes that his sin is both vertical (against heaven) and horizontal (against man) in nature. That means he admits that he has sinned against God and his father. This stresses the fact that all sin, no matter to whom it is against, is sin against God, for all sin is disobedience of God's law. His remorsefulness and genuine repentance is demonstrated in the fact that he sees his unworthiness to be a son. He acknowledges that sin separates man from man; it breaks relationships, not among human beings, but between man and God. The broken relationship between man and God can only be restored by receiving Christ and believing in Him (John 1:12). In his plea for mercy, the prodigal son would plead to be accepted as a hired servant. The once rich self-sufficient arrogant "brat," who demanded his portion of the father's estate, is now pleading and willing to take the lowest place and to obey his father's commands.

20 And he arose, and came to his father. But when he was yet a great way off, his father saw him, and had compassion, and ran, and fell on his neck, and kissed him.

After his resolve to return home and rehearsing how he would approach his father, the prodigal son acts. He begins his journey home. As he gets near, his father sees him while he is still afar off, runs to him, embraces, and kisses him. The word "fell" translates the Greek verb *epipipto* (**ep-ee-pip'-to**), which means to seize, embrace, to press or fall upon, someone. Used metaphorically, it means to take possession of one. It is used, for example, of the Holy Spirit in His inspiration and impulse. The word translated "kissed" here is *kataphileo* (**kat-af-ee-leh'-o**), which literally means to kiss repeatedly or to kiss tenderly.

There are a few important facts to be noted here about the father. Although his son deserted the home, his father's love for him never wavered. He never ceased to hope and look out for the return of his lost son. That is why he is able to recognize him afar off. Driven by loving "compassion" (*splagchnizomai,* **splangkh-nid'-zom-ahee**), literally to be moved to one's bowels (bowels were thought to be the seat of love and emotion), he runs immediately to meet him, affectionately hugging and kissing him. This clearly demonstrates God's inexplicable love for the repentant sinner. He always yearns, and lovingly awaits, for the return of the wayward. Not only does He forgive the sinner, but meets him halfway, and embraces him in His loving grace. God, in His infinite mercy and grace, and even before the sinner shows remorse for his sins, seeks and welcomes with open arms the sinner through the redeeming work of Christ through the power of the Holy Spirit. This is made clearer in the Christ's utterance in John 3:16. It is also illustrated by Paul in Romans 5:8, "God commendeth his love toward us in that, while we were yet sinners, Christ died for us." It is only God's grace and love, and the work of the Holy Spirit, that the sinner is brought back and accepted by God.

21 And the son said unto him, Father, I have sinned against heaven, and in thy sight, and am no more worthy to be called thy son.

Overwhelmed by such an undeserved reception and touched by his father's unconditional love and compassion, the prodigal son probably feels stronger the magnitude of his sin. He confesses, "Father, I have sinned against heaven, and in thy sight, and am no more worthy to be called thy son." The personal experience of God's unreserved love makes one realize fully the sinfulness of one's sins and his absolute unworthiness before God. This realization, which is the work of the Holy Spirit, is what compels one to repent and confess one's sin, just as the son does here.

22 But the father said to his servants, Bring forth the best robe, and put it on him; and put a ring on his hand, and shoes on his feet:

Verses 22-24 further demonstrate the magnitude of the father's love for his son. Before his son can complete his plea for forgiveness, the father interjects and does not allow his son to finish his well-rehearsed speech. The father orders servants to prepare a feast. It is important to understand the degree of the father's acceptance of the prodigal son—it is total. This is seen in the father's detailed instructions to the servants.

He tells the servants to put on his son the best robe, a ring on his finger and shoes on his feet. The items are significant because each shows that the father fully accepts him back as son and gives him back a place of honor. Robes in the Jewish tradition were long fitting clothes usually worn by kings, priests, and persons of rank and authority. It was a mark of dignity. Rings were worn as a badge of office, e.g., "Pharaoh took off his ring from his hand, and put it upon Joseph's hand, and arrayed him in vestures of fine linen, and put a gold chain about his neck" (Genesis 41:42). Rings were also given as tokens of authority and as a seal to a covenant (Esther 3:10, 12; 8:2-10). Shoes or sandals were a common form of attire in the Jewish custom. However, captives had their shoes removed as a sign of captivity, and their shoes were restored when they were liberated, which signifies freedom (Isaiah 20:2).

23 And bring hither the fatted calf, and kill it; and let us eat, and be merry: 24 For this my son was dead, and is alive again; he was lost, and is found. And they began to be merry.

The father also orders the servants to fetch the "fatted calf, and kill it" for a feast. Fatted, or fattened, calves were usually kept for special occasions, such as sacrifices and important ceremonies. The father declares a feast to celebrate the return of his lost and found son. Luke uses two sets of metaphors to describe the former life of the prodigal son before (in the far country) and after his return. While away from home he was "dead" and "lost." When he returned he became "alive again" and "is found." These figures of speech describe succinctly the sinner's position before and after he returns to the Lord through Christ. Like the father of the prodigal son, our heavenly Father is no longer concerned about our past life the moment we return to

Him. He does not reproach, punish, or humiliate the sinner who turns to Him with sincere and heartfelt repentance. He fully restores the repentant sinner to the position of "sonship" with all its privileges, rather than accepting him in a hired servant or slave position.

Through this parable, Christ points out God's loving compassion for sinners, His concern for their return, and the joyful celebration that follows when a sinner returns to the Lord.

Like the parables of the lost sheep (vv. 4-7) and the lost coin (vv. 8-10), this parable describes the joy that fills heaven when a sinner returns to the Lord. There is indeed joy in heaven among the angels and saints. There is, as well, an unspeakable joy and peace that floods the heart of the returnee—joy that cannot be fully described.

DAILY BIBLE READINGS

M: Lost Sheep and Lost Coin
Luke 15:1-10
T: The Lost Son
Luke 15:11-16
W: Repentance, Return, and Rejoicing
Luke 15:17-24
T: A Plea for Pardon
Psalm 51
F: No One Cares for Me
Psalm 142
S: Your Sins Are Forgiven
Mark 2:1-12
S: The Elder Brother
Luke 15:25-32

TEACHING TIPS

January 28
Bible Study Guide 9

1. Words You Should Know

A. Steward (v .1)— manager.
B. Measures (vv. 6, 7)—a standard of capacity.
C. Mammon (v. 9)—money, riches.

2. Teacher Preparation

Look in a newspaper or magazine to find an article dealing with someone who either committed a crime or some other outrageous act for money or something of monetary value. Spend some time discussing why money is often at the root of many of the wrongs that happen in life.

3. Starting the Lesson

A. Who suffers when Christians, especially Christian leaders, demonstrate through their behavior that they are more concerned about getting money than about spreading the Gospel? What does that say to nonbelievers about Christianity? Open the topic for discussion among class members.

B. Read today's IN FOCUS story about Luther promoting young Michelle to a position of higher authority in his company. Discuss the rewards of faithful stewardship. In particular, talk about the internal and spiritual rewards one receives by being a good steward.

4. Getting Into the Lesson

Open a discussion about the Christian's motivation for stewardship. Focus on stewardship as a way of life, not a series of activities that one does. Be sure to emphasize that good stewardship includes more than money. Good stewardship has to do with putting the blessings we receive in proper perspective, having no other thing come before our relationship to God.

5. Relating the Lesson to Life

A. Review the concepts described in today's THE PEOPLE, PLACES, AND TIMES article. Discuss the definition of mammon as generally being associated with having an evil influence. Talk about how Jesus used parables to teach His disciples biblical truths.

C. Today's DISCUSS THE MEANING calls for members think about the mindset of the just steward's lord and Jesus' purpose for telling the story.

D. The LESSON IN OUR SOCIETY deals with the topic of "honor among thieves." Members should be led to think about the fact that those who are involved in unethical and illegal behavior often exhibit virtue toward one another than do Christians. Discuss how believers can best honor one another, in turn, giving honor to our God.

6. Arousing Action

Ask the class to think about persons whom they know at some point placed money and lifestyle above the Lord but was later converted and began to serve God. Talk about factors that caused them to turn their lives around. Then talk about ways the class can relate this experience to others whom they know need a closer relationship with God.

WORSHIP GUIDE

For the Superintendent or Teacher
Theme: Threat of Riches
Theme Song: It Pays to Serve Jesus
Scripture: Luke 12:15-21
Song: My Faith Looks Up to Thee
Meditation: May I always put God first in my life and not put my trust in the things of this earth—things that rust, or that moths destroy, or that thieves steal. I cannot serve two masters at the same time. This day, I choose to serve Jesus.

THREAT OF RICHES

Bible Background • LUKE 16
Printed Text • LUKE 16:1-13
Devotional Reading • LUKE 12:15-21

LESSON AIM

After studying today's lesson, members will learn what Jesus counts as faithful stewardship. They will be reminded of Jesus' teaching that believers can have only one master and what it means to put Him first.

KEEP IN MIND

"No servant can serve two masters: for either he will hate the one, and love the other; or else he will hold to the one, and despise the other. Ye cannot serve God and mammon" (Luke 16:13).

FOCAL VERSES

Luke 16:1 And he said also unto his disciples, There was a certain rich man, which had a steward; and the same was accused unto him that he had wasted his goods.

2 And he called him, and said unto him, How is it that I hear this of thee? give an account of thy stewardship; for thou mayest be no longer steward.

3 Then the steward said within himself, What shall I do? for my lord taketh away from me the stewardship: I cannot dig; to beg I am ashamed.

4 I am resolved what to do, that, when I am put out of the stewardship, they may receive me into their houses.

5 So he called every one of his lord's debtors unto him, and said unto the first, How much owest thou unto my lord?

6 And he said, An hundred measures of oil. And he said unto him, Take thy bill, and sit down quickly, and write fifty.

7 Then said he to another, And how much owest

LESSON OVERVIEW

LESSON AIM
KEEP IN MIND
FOCAL VERSES
IN FOCUS
THE PEOPLE, PLACES,
AND TIMES
BACKGROUND
AT-A-GLANCE
IN DEPTH
SEARCH THE SCRIPTURES
DISCUSS THE MEANING
LESSON IN OUR SOCIETY
MAKE IT HAPPEN
FOLLOW THE SPIRIT
REMEMBER YOUR THOUGHTS
MORE LIGHT ON THE TEXT
DAILY BIBLE READINGS

thou? And he said, An hundred measures of wheat. And he said unto him, Take thy bill, and write fourscore.

8 And the lord commended the unjust steward, because he had done wisely: for the children of this world are in their generation wiser than the children of light.

9 And I say unto you, Make to yourselves friends of the mammon of unrighteousness; that, when ye fail, they may receive you into everlasting habitations.

10 He that is faithful in that which is least is faithful also in much: and he that is unjust in the least is unjust also in much.

11 If therefore ye have not been faithful in the unrighteous mammon, who will commit to your trust the true riches?

JAN 28TH

12 And if ye have not been faithful in that which is another man's, who shall give you that which is your own?

13 No servant can serve two masters: for either he will hate the one, and love the other; or else he will hold to the one, and despise the other. Ye cannot serve God and mammon.

IN FOCUS

Luther was sure that he would be criticized for making someone as young as Michelle the new manager of operations. But in his heart, he knew she was the most qualified person for the job.

Over the years, he had seen other employees at his manufacturing plant try to figure out ways to take as much from him as they could. When

Michelle came to the department, she was always suggesting ways to cut waste and improve efficiency. Through all of that she quietly endured the criticisms of her coworkers.

"Well," Luther thought as he looked out on the production floor, "I have to reward loyalty and commitment. Besides, Melva's been on me about taking some time off from this place. I feel better leaving Michelle to run the place than some of those others who have only tried to use me for what they could get."

THE PEOPLE, PLACES, AND TIMES

Mammon. Found only in the New Testament and used only by Jesus, the word is the Greek form of an Aramaic or Syriac word meaning "money," "riches," "property," "worldly goods," or "profit." Mammon was generally used as a pronoun for riches as an evil spirit or god. From about A.D. 1500, it has been used to describe the evil influence that wealth has upon human beings.

Based on information from Holman Bible Dictionary, Trent Butler, general editor, Nashville: Broadman & Holman Publishers, 1991, p. 914.

Parables. Although this art of telling parables was perfected by Jesus, their origin goes back to the Old Testament and other sources of a secular nature. Parables were recognized as a literary form prior to Jesus' day in the rhetorical writings of the Greeks. The famous Greek writer Homer used 189 parables in *The Illiad* and 39 in *The Odyssey.*

In the Old Testament, the broader term *mashal* is used, referring to all illustrations that contain a comparison. A *mashal* can be a proverb (1 Samuel 10:12), a taunt (Micah 2:4), a riddle (Psalm 78:2), an allegory (Ezekiel 24:3-4), or a parable.

Parables were often told as a means to provide a picture of life, specifically life in God's kingdom. Jesus' parables could be either prophetic or pastoral. They could be either harsh or soothing. Jesus' parables were also evangelistic in that they sought to evoke a life-changing decision from the hearers. They were intended to awaken the faith of those who had fallen asleep.

Many of Jesus' parables grew out of conflict as He answered His critics. As Jesus wove His story,

His words became pictures. Jesus interpreted His ministry and its role in the salvation of humanity through parables. Jesus' stories sometimes got Him into trouble as He made veiled claims to His status while exposing the hypocrisy of the religious hierarchy.

Based on information from Holman Bible Dictionary, Trent Butler, general editor, Nashville: Broadman & Holman Publishers, 1991, pp. 1071-1073.

BACKGROUND

In the previous parables, Jesus' focus was on the Pharisees and scribes. He now turned His attention to the disciples, yet the Pharisees were still in the picture.

Chapter 16 is devoted entirely to the right attitude toward the use of wealth. What Jesus continually pointed out was that service to the Master, not mammon, is most important in life. This value goes against human nature, but it wins favor with God.

Jesus had concern for those who worked hard to secure their earthly future, yet had done nothing to prepare for eternity. He did not teach that wealth was bad, nor did He teach that the poor would automatically go to heaven and the rich would be condemned. Instead Jesus issued a warning to all those who live this life as though there is nothing more. Jesus' concern was for the attitude and outlook of the wealthy, nor for their wealth itself.

Material abundance can blind people to what is important in life. Jesus taught there is nothing more important that God.

AT-A-GLANCE

1. A Shrewd Employee (Luke 16:1-9)
2. Using Wealth Rightly (vv. 16:10-13)

IN DEPTH

1. A Shrewd Employee (Luke 16:1-9)

As with His other parables, Jesus used a practical illustration with which His hearers could identify. In this story, Jesus told of a man who was about to lose his job for dishonesty. This parable differs from others in that the principal character is an unsavory sort.

The challenge of this parable, therefore, is to discern the point Jesus was trying to make. Was he praising the man for his dishonest ways? Hardly! The behavior of the main character is not to be emulated or admired. By telling the story, Jesus reflected on the fact that people often go to extremes to secure favorable treatment when they are in financial or legal trouble. They may bend or even break the law to do so. Yet their conduct reflects a certain amount of wisdom in having practical concern for oneself. He desires that people devote as much concern to eternal security as they do to earthly security.

In Jesus' day, a steward was one who served as administrator, or manager, over his employer's business affairs. His responsibilities were great in that he was in charge of property which did not belong to him. Every person on this earth, no matter how rich or poor, is the holder of property which does not belong to him or her. We are all stewards of the blessings God has given us. Everything we have has been entrusted to us by the One who created it. We are responsible to Him for the proper usage of it.

Through some unknown means, the rich man discovered that his steward was guilty of mismanagement and ordered him to give an account of his stewardship. The steward did not deny, or attempt to defend, the accusation so his guilt is not in question. We are not made privy to the nature of his offense, yet it was sufficient for dismissal from his employ. He had probably found some means to cheat his boss in order to feather his own nest. The employer ordered him to turn over all records before his services were terminated.

Following the confrontation with his employer, the man adopts a plan of action befitting one who has been caught in wrongdoing. He envisioned the financial crisis which was about to befall him. He appeared to have two options to dig or to beg. Neither option was desirable, so the man devised a plan to insure some financial stability for himself upon losing his job. With time running out, the steward devised a plan to take advantage of his authority while he still held some. He decided to position himself so that his lord's debtors would be obligated to him. Then, he reasoned, when he himself was in a time of need, he could turn to those debtors for aid. The debtors were probably merchants who had received merchandise from the rich man and had not yet settled their accounts with him.

The debts which had been incurred were substantial. One measure of oil amounted to eight or nine gallons. Therefore, the first man's debt was reduced by about 438 gallons. A measure of wheat amounted to 10 or 12 bushels, reducing the second man's debt by as much as 220 bushels.

When the lord discovered what the unjust steward had done, he commended his employee, claiming he had done wisely. The lord praised his worker because he was a shrewd businessman who would appreciate such an action, even though it was at his own expense.

Jesus did not tell the story to praise dishonesty and deceit. Yet He reflected on the fact that the children of this world are, in their generation, wiser than the children of light. Jesus wants His followers to be wise stewards. The children of this world were giving more attention to their affairs than were the children of light. Although the steward was unscrupulous, he was clever. The children of light should emulate that cleverness for godly ends.

Some believers tend to become too "otherworldly," in that they do not allow the Lord to make full use of them while on earth. The unjust steward was a realist. He faced the facts which lay squarely before him. He calculated the situation without emotion or sentimentality.

This child of the world was willing to do whatever was necessary to insure his survival. By contrast, the children of light rarely exhibit the same passion and willingness to do whatever is necessary to secure their place in eternity.

Jesus cautioned those who heard Him: "Make to yourselves friends of the mammon of unrighteousness. Wealth in and of itself is amoral—capable of being used for good or evil depending on the one in possession of it. Disciples can use their material means to help those whom the Lord came to set free. Our use of material wealth is to be tempered by the fact that we know its limitations in that it is a temporary state. Money cannot buy our way into heaven. Yet our use of the resources we have been given lend insight into our relationship with God.

2. Using Wealth Rightly (Luke 16:10-13)

At the close of this parable, but prior to beginning the next parable of this chapter, Jesus issued a collection of sayings about wealth. The character and actions of a godly steward stand in stark contrast to that of the unjust steward. One who is entrusted with God's riches is expected to be faithful, no matter whether the steward has been given little or much. Likewise, the person who is unjust over the least amount is also unjust over much.

Jesus gave insight into the nature of one who can be trusted. A trustworthy servant exhibits the same degree of faithfulness whether that servant is given a little or a lot. The little here refers to material goods for which we are held responsible in this life. When we have been given charge of unrighteous mammon, it will determine our ability to be entrusted with true riches, which are the rewards God bestows on faithful servants in the life beyond. Therefore, an individual's earthly stewardship may be thought of as the proving ground where the true nature of his or her character is revealed.

All the things we possess in this world belong to another, that being God Himself. Everything that we possess is retained on a temporary basis. As the old saying goes, "You can't take it with you." The world has not been given to humanity to do with as we please. Instead, God expects faithfulness in all things. We cannot put anything before Him. We must love Him more than we love the things He gives us.

Our earthly possessions come from God and they will always belong to Him. These things are simply on loan to us while we live. If we approach our understanding of material possessions in any other way, we will have a divided mind and a divided loyalty. We cannot truly serve God if we believe that our security and hope lies in the things we accumulate instead of on God who gives them to us.

Jesus used the strong and definitive word "can-

not" to determine that one cannot serve two masters. He did not teach that we should not, nor that we ought not. We simply cannot serve God and mammon. It is an impossibility to give total allegiance and service to two potentially opposing masters. Mammon must always come under service to God. One of the masters will become more important than the other. The servant will either hold to the one and despise the other. As a result, one master will be loved more than the other.

This torn loyalty that comes from attempting to serve two masters may exhibit itself in a time of crisis or decision-making. One master will demand that the servant choose sides. To choose mammon is to choose against God, because God will not take second place in our lives. To chose God means that mammon may still have a reasonable place in our lives. Material wealth can often be used to lend aid to those in need, providing an opportunity for believers to demonstrate God's love.

SEARCH THE SCRIPTURES

1. What was the rich man's steward accused of doing? (v. 1)

2. What did the man say to his steward about the matter? (v. 2)

3. What was the steward's response to his lord's decision? (v. 3)

4. What provisions did the unjust steward make for his future state of unemployment? (v. 4)

5. How did the steward implement his plan? (vv. 5-7)

6. How did the lord react when he discovered what the unjust steward had done? (v. 8)

7. What words did Jesus offer immediately after telling the parable? (v. 9)

8. What did Jesus say about faithful stewardship? (v. 10-11)

9. What did Jesus observe about those who could not be entrusted with earthly riches? (v. 12)

10. What happens when a person attempts to serve two masters? (v. 13)

DISCUSS THE MEANING

1. Why did the lord commend his unjust steward for his actions once he had been fired?

2. Why do some Christians invest more time

and thought in planning for their retirement than they do in planning for spending eternity with the Lord?

3. Why do you believe Jesus chose the story of such an unsavory character to illustrate the need for stewardship and preparation?

LESSON IN OUR SOCIETY

The phrase "honor among thieves" is popular because of its irony. Sadly, sometimes those outside the Christian community are greater examples of courage and virtue, albeit for the wrong reasons.

The crooked steward was willing to do anything necessary to secure his future once his job was gone. Many people would empathize with his behavior even though they might not agree with his actions. By nature, human beings take action to secure their own survival.

Somehow, when it comes to matters of salvation and eternity, there are too many people who are willing to leave their destiny to "fate" or some other means. How different our world might be if people worked as hard to secure their eternal home as they do to secure resources for retirement in their old age.

MAKE IT HAPPEN

Draw a line down the center of a sheet of paper. On the left side, write down the steps you have taken to insure your earthly security, including higher education, or some other skill development training, retirement plans, savings, insurance policies and so forth.

On the right side of the page, write down what you have done to secure your home on high. Have you accepted Jesus as Lord and Saviour? Do you follow His teachings and His ways? Are you faithful over the resources you have been given? Have you tried to lead others to accept Jesus? Answer these questions to determine your strengths and weaknesses in the area of preparing for eternity.

FOLLOW THE SPIRIT

What God wants me to do:

_____

_____

REMEMBER YOUR THOUGHTS

Special insights you learned:

_____

_____

MORE LIGHT ON THE TEXT
Luke 16:1-13

Jesus has just concluded addressing the Pharisees and scribes (and the crowd), teaching them through three parables—the lost sheep, the lost coin, and the lost and found son (chapter 15). He turns to His disciples and tells them another parable teaching them the importance of wisdom, how faithfulness to little things could mean faithfulness in bigger things (16:1-12). He emphasizes to them that one can only be a true servant to one master at one time; one cannot serve God and mammon and be faithful to both (v. 13).

16:1 And he said also unto his disciples, There was a certain rich man, which had a steward; and the same was accused unto him that he had wasted his goods. 2 And he called him, and said unto him, How is it that I hear this of thee? give an account of thy stewardship; for thou mayest be no longer steward.

After he had finished telling about Christ's encounter with the Pharisees and scribes, Luke now directs our attention to Christ and His disciples. With the use of two conjunctions *de*, translated "and" (KJV) here, but better rendered "now" (NAS), and *kai* "also," Luke seems to indicate an abrupt change of focus from the Pharisees and scribes to the disciples. Luke, however, does not explain why the abrupt change or what prompted the parable. He simple tells the parable. Before we venture into this parable, it is important to acknowledge the difficulty in its interpretation. Scholars have battled through the years to reach a consensus in the correct interpretation of this parable, but they have failed. Therefore, our interpretation will be open to debate.

In His usual manner, Jesus tells the story to His disciples in order to teach them. He speaks about a certain rich man and his steward. The steward is accused of wasting his master's goods. On hearing the accusation the rich man calls the steward and asks him to give account of his stewardship (that is to hand over his work) because he is soon to be fired from his job. The word translated "steward" here is the Greek noun *oikonomos* (pronounced **oy-kon-om'-os**), which literally means a house-distributor (i.e., manager), or overseer.

Stewards were also called house agents, or superintendents, who were given the task of managing or overseeing the household affairs of their master. Such affairs included the management of farms or landed estate, taking and keeping records of receipts and expenditures, assigning tasks to servants, and training of the heirs who are not yet of age. Stewardship is a position of honor and trust. Eliezer was Abraham's steward (Genesis 15:2; 24:2), and Joseph, as the prime minister in Egypt, had stewards to which he entrusted the affairs of his kingdom (Genesis 43:19). In a larger sense, stewards can be regarded as superintendents, finance ministers, or treasurers of cities, states, or countries. Metaphorically, the apostles and other Christian teachers, bishops, and overseers are stewards of the Word of God.

The steward in this parable is accused of "wasting" his master's goods. Whether the accusation is well-founded or not, we are not told. The word "accused" (Greek *diaballo,* **dee-ab-al'-lo**) implies malice, to slander in order to defame (not necessarily falsehood). The word "wasted" used here is the same Greek word *diaskorpizo* (**dee-as-kor-pid'-zo**) used in the story of the prodigal son (Luke 15:13) when the younger son "wasted his substance with riotous living" in a foreign land (see last Sunday's lesson). Literally, it means to disperse or scatter abroad. It also means to separate, especially to winnow grain to separate the chaff. As we have learned in a previous study, the grain is thrown up into the air so that it may be separated from the chaff as the wind blows away the chaff. In the case of the prodigal son, "wasted" is used figuratively, and it means to squander. Here, we suggest that the steward was accused, or suspected of, mismanaging his master's goods— probably meaning squander—carrying over the same thought from the previous story. However, Luke does not tell us how he wasted the goods.

3 Then the steward said within himself, What shall I do? for my lord taketh away from me the stewardship: I cannot dig; to beg I am ashamed. 4 I am resolved what to do, that, when I am put out of the stewardship, they may receive me into their houses.

Realizing that he is in danger of being dismissed and soon to be out of job, he conceives a plan for his future. He examines himself—his weaknesses and strengths. Realizing his inability to do manual jobs that require physical energy and his pride to condescend to begging, he comes up with another plan to secure his future after the job is taken away from him. The phrase "to beg I am ashamed" has two possible meanings. Firstly, it could mean that he is ashamed to beg for food or help from other people. Secondly, it could mean he is so proud that he could not go to his master and plead his case or ask for forgiveness. Luke does not tell us the true meaning of the phrase. However, realizing his weakness, the steward comes up with a plan.

The plan is to make friends with his master's debtors, or tenants, by altering their debts to their benefit (reducing what owe) so that they can return the favor by accepting him into their houses after he has been put out his job. As we can see from the two examples which follow, the debts are cut from one fifth to one half. The rest of the debtors, no doubt, are cut on the same basis.

5 So he called every one of his lord's debtors unto him, and said unto the first, How much owest thou unto my lord? 6 And he said, An hundred measures of oil. And he said unto him, Take thy bill, and sit down quickly, and write fifty. 7 Then said he to another, And how much owest thou? And he said, An hundred measures of wheat. And he said unto him, Take thy bill, and write fourscore.

He goes to his master's debtors, one after the other, and alters their debts accordingly. To the first, who owed a hundred measures of oil, he asks him to change his bill to fifty measures. The Greek for "measure" here is *batos* (or Hebrew, *bath*), which is a Jewish measure for liquid, and it is equivalent to eight gallons. One hundred measures would, therefore, be about 800 gallons owed by the debtor. The steward urges the debtor to change it to 50 *batos* (i.e., 400 gallons of oil). To the second debtor he asks him to reduce the 100 measures of wheat he owed to fourscore, (i.e., 80). Here "measure" is the Greek *koros,* (or Hebrew *corus* or *cor,* a Jewish dry measure for wheat, meal). One *koros* is equivalent to 10 bushels (about 350 liters). The steward, therefore, asks the second debtor to alter his agreement from 1000 bushels of wheat to 800 bushels. He would go to his master with the new figures with the hope that it would not be discovered. Thus, the debtors would be obligated to him and support him in the scheme.

8 And the lord commended the unjust steward, because he had done wisely: for the children of this world are in their generation wiser than the children of light.

The owner probably is informed of the steward's scheme of making a provision for his future by treating the debtors kindly for his own gain. Since the steward has talked to the debtors individually and has destroyed the old bills, the master has no proof or witnesses to challenge the steward. He cannot prove that the new bills are not the original ones. All he can do is to acknowledge the steward's shrewdness and commend him for his cleverness. It ought to be noted clearly that "the lord" here does not refer, to God or to Christ, but to the master of the steward. The master "commended," *paineo* (**ep-ahee-neh'-o**), i.e., applauded or praised, the steward "because he had done wisely." The commendation is not because of the steward's dishonest act, but rather the wisdom behind the act, that is, planning for his future. It is not the rightness or wrongness of the act, or even the means used that the master has applauded. It is the "worldly wisdom" the steward has applied.

The object of the parable is to direct our attention to the wise manner in which worldly people conduct themselves in order to achieve their goals. The Lord contrasts this worldly shrewdness with the unwise manner in which members of the kingdom of light conduct themselves towards others. Rather than acting in such away as to attract others to themselves, those of the light seem to repulse others through their unfriendly attitudes. The Pharisees and scribes, for example, repel the "publicans" and "sinners" by their self-righteous attitude rather than attract them. They look down on others, rejecting, and condemning them, rather than accepting them in order to gain their attention and trust.

Although critics of the New Testament and of Christ have used this verse, indeed, this parable, to attack and condemn Christianity of an ethical flaw. They argue that Christ, in this parable, condoned and promoted fraud by commending the steward. This suggestion definitely contradicts the teachings of Christ, who constantly throughout Scripture condemns any suggestion of fraud. Christ Himself calls the steward "unjust" (v. 8), and there is no reason to suggest that His audience would misinterpret Him of commending the steward and his dishonest methods. As we have noted already, the commendation was from the "lord" (or the master) to his unjust steward, not from the Lord Jesus Christ. It is an unjustifiable lack of knowledge coupled with an ignorance of the Scriptures for anyone to launch an attack against Christ's ethical standards and against the New Testament based on this one parable.

9 And I say unto you, Make to yourselves friends of the mammon of unrighteousness; that, when ye fail, they may receive you into everlasting habitations.

In this verse, Jesus gives the moral of the parable to teach the disciples how to appropriate worldly riches in order to gain life everlasting. Again, to insinuate that riches gained by unjust means is sanctioned by Christ, or God, and that such riches can gain one a place in heaven is a distortion of the words and teachings of Christ here and elsewhere in the Bible. Indeed, it contradicts His thought in verses 10-13, and other Scriptures both in the Old and New Testaments which teach that any riches gained by dishonest means should be restored to the rightful owner (Exodus 22:1-4; Leviticus 6:2-5; Proverbs 6:30-31). Zacchaeus promised to "restore fourfold" to anyone whom he had falsely taken from (Luke 19:8).

What then does Jesus mean in verse 9? Its understanding lies in the interpretation of two phrases, "mammon of righteousness" and "when ye fail." I suggest that Christ's use of the first phrase is figurative to describe riches. The word "mammon" (Greek *mammonas*) means treasure or riches as it is contrasted with the true riches (v. 11). Here Christ calls it unrighteous riches, which probably refers to worldly treasures (or possessions) or to the monetary system, because they give people false hope and false security when people apply their minds to them. In 1 Timothy (6:9-10, 17), Paul writes about the falsity of riches, a consequence of trusting in money rather than in the living God who richly gives us all things to enjoy.

Earthly possessions are called the "mammon of unrighteousness," not because they are, in and of themselves, evil, but because of people's sinful attitude in the accumulation of wealth, which most often involves injustice. Christ never condemned riches, but rather man's evil attitude toward riches. He warns that putting riches (mammon) as a master above, or on an equal basis with, God is evil, because no man can serve (or love) God and money at the same time (v. 13; Matthew 6:24). It, therefore, follows that while worldly treasures are rightly labeled as the "mammon of righteousness," Jesus urges His disciples to view and use worldly riches differently from how the world views and uses them. They should use them in an appropriate manner which will bring blessing and honor to God and to mankind, not with the selfish and covetous motives which the world and the unjust steward use.

An appropriate use of possessions will be to the disciples' credit in the everlasting habitation, i.e., after death—"when ye fail." So the phrase "when you fail" refers to physical death, passing from mortality into immortality. Thus "fail," (Greek *ekleipo* (**ek-li'-po**), means to cease, to quit, and to eclipse (i.e., the sun or moon). By implication the word also means to die, or cease to exist. "They" probably refers to the triune God, or to those who receive just men into the eternal abode, habitation (Greek *skene*, **skay-nay'**) or home. In verse 22 Jesus explains that angels carry the soul of the righteous to "Abraham's bosom," the Jewish expression for paradise. Christ seems to be saying that if the disciples use their worldly possessions

wisely and unselfishly, helping others, they will gain for themselves an everlasting home. They will lay up for themselves treasures in heaven "where neither moth nor rust doth corrupt, and where thieves do not break through nor steal" (Matthew 6:20). The idea here is that all earthly treasures are God's, and they should be used faithfully to honor Him. By so doing, Jesus points out that the disciples, indeed the children of light, will have learned from the unjust steward and his shrewdness in preparing for the future. This idea will be explained further in the next four verses where Jesus teaches the importance of faithfulness in the little things entrusted to us by others. Such faithfulness in earthly things determines whether one can be trusted with heavenly things, which are much bigger and more valuable.

10 He that is faithful in that which is least is faithful also in much: and he that is unjust in the least is unjust also in much. 11 If therefore ye have not been faithful in the unrighteous mammon, who will commit to your trust the true riches? 12 And if ye have not been faithful in that which is another man's, who shall give you that which is your own?

Jesus teaches whoever is faithful in that which is least will also be faithful in that which is much. Likewise, whoever is unjust (i.e. not faithful) in that which is least will also be unjust in that which is much. The word "faithful" is the Greek *pistos*, which means trusty, or trustworthiness. It is used of persons who show themselves faithful in the transaction of business, the execution of commands, or the discharge of official duties—ones that can be trusted. The word "unjust," *adikos*, is used here in opposition to faithful (*pistos*), and it has the idea of dishonesty. It is used to describe persons who are deceitful, who deal fraudulently with others—ones who cannot be trusted.

We notice the general statement in verse 10 and the application in verses 11 and 12, from general to particular. In verse 10, Jesus tells the disciples the general view of things concerning trust and faithfulness, and in verses 11 and 12 He applies it to the disciples, urging them to use their earthly treasures faithfully and wisely. Here Christ compares earthly possessions with the heavenly treasures, worldly gifts with spiritual gifts. Jesus says that if one is unfaithful or false in the acquisition, and use, of worldly possessions and gifts entrusted to him (which are "the least" things, i.e., smallest value), how can one be entrusted with eternal goods and "true riches" (which are of highest value)? The adjective "true" used here is the Greek *alethinos*, pronounced **al-ay-thee-nos'**, which has the idea of real as opposed to fake. It is the opposite of fictitious, counterfeit, or imaginary, and contrasts reality with unreality. Here the "mammon of unrighteousness" is the counterfeit of the eternal riches, which are stored up in the "everlasting habitations" for the faithful.

Verse 12 teaches the truth that one's attitude towards other people's property (how we look after people's things) determines one's attitude towards one's own property (how we take care of our own things). That reminds me of an elementary school proverb which goes, "Little thing is a little thing, but faithfulness in a little thing, is a great thing."

It should be noted that this group of concluding sayings, verses 10-13, attached to the parable, can be linked to other teachings of Christ in other passages in Luke. These passages deal with the question of accountability and attitude to wealth. For example, verse 10 can be linked to the teaching of 12:43-48; verse 11 can be linked to 12:21,33; and verse 12 can be linked to the parable of the nobleman and his servants (19:11-27).

13 No servant can serve two masters: for either he will hate the one, and love the other; or else he will hold to the one, and despise the other. Ye cannot serve God and mammon.

Verse 13 concludes Christ's address to His disciples before He turns again to address the Pharisees (v. 14ff.). It should be noted that verse 13 is also found in Matthew (6:24), in the so-called "Sermon on the Mount." Here Jesus states the incompatibility of worldly riches and God. The verse deals with our attitude toward wealth and riches—i.e., greedy pursuit of riches—enslaving ourselves to earthly possessions. The verse also addresses the erroneous notion that riches, the accumulation of money, and the enjoyment of earthly treasures are the end, and the main object, of living. The statement seems harsh. It does not give room so that one can use one's wealth to serve God. Rather it states that one cannot enslave oneself to two masters at the same time—one would either love money and hate God, or one would "love" God and "hate" riches. The use of "love" and "hate" is relative. It is explained in the use of the clause "hold (devoted) to the one, and despise the other." Naturally speaking, it is almost impossible to serve two people with equal devotion. It does not matter how "religious" one is, or how sincere one would like to be, there is a tendency to prefer one master above the other. When we make wealth the dominant purpose of life, or when we use our wealth wrongly or selfishly, despising others who, who do not have, we enslave ourselves to it. We, therefore, cannot serve God effectively. However, Christ's teaching here does not negate the acquisition of wealth, but the stress is on its wrongful use and attitude. Our attitude to, and our use of, earthly possessions should not in any way affect, interfere, or tarnish our love, devotion, and service to God the Creator of all things. We should look at our worldly possessions as God's; we are only caretakers. As such we should endeavor to use them to honor and worship Him.

DAILY BIBLE READINGS

M: The Dishonest Manager
Luke 16:1-8

T: Faithful Stewardship
Luke 16:10-13

W: Give to God
Deuteronomy 14:22-26

T: The Law and God's Kingdom
Luke 16:14-18

F: Rich Man, Poor Man
Luke 16:19-26

S: Warnings About Riches
Luke 16:27-31

S: Respect the Great King
Psalm 24

TEACHING TIPS

February 4
Bible Study Guide 10

1. Words You Should Know

A. Entreated (18:32)—flogged; beaten.

B. Publican (19:2)—a tax collector.

2. Teacher Preparation

Before class begins, make a list of persons who have occupations that are considered sinful to believers. Think about how Christians generally respond to such persons. Prepare to discuss how Christians should respond to them if our intent is to spread the Good News and offer them hope in Jesus Christ.

3. Starting the Lesson

A. Open the discussion. Remind members that Christians often point to particular occupations as sinful, especially those which are carnal in nature. Discuss the fact that many people, like Zaccheus, commit corrupt acts through their occupations which harm people. Their actions may not be criminal, but would not be pleasing to Christ. Many of these persons are active in the church and community. How can the Christian community minister to such persons in order to help them see that their actions are also wrong?

4. Getting into the Lesson

As you begin the lesson, remind the class that Jesus called for righteousness. A previous lesson focused on Jesus' high call for discipleship. Yet, in spite of His high demands, He continuously showed unconditional love, mercy, and kindness to those who were in darkness. Ask students to keep in mind that the only people Jesus ever called sinners and vipers were the religious people of His day, not those who were lost.

5. Relating the Lesson to Life

A. Review the concepts described in today's THE PEOPLE, PLACES, AND TIMES article. Discuss the meaning of Jesus being the Son of Man. Also talk about the position of chief and why these men were so despised by the Jews.

B. Give students an opportunity to answer the questions in SEARCH THE SCRIPTURES.

C. Today's DISCUSS THE MEANING focuses on the meaning of Jesus' encounter with Zaccheus. Discuss how Zaccheus made a total and complete change in his life because He received Jesus' love and mercy, not harsh treatment and condemnation.

D. The LESSON IN OUR SOCIETY deals with the proper Christian attitude toward those who have strayed from the path of righteousness. Discuss how believers can serve to either help or hinder those who are lost and need help to bring them into a right relationship with God.

6. Arousing Action

Ask members to think of someone they know (either personally or through media accounts) who is currently being condemned by others for some unrighteous act or deed that the person committed. How many Christians are condemning that person? How many have regarded the person with unconditional love compassion? Members should make a commitment to demonstrate God's love to people they know who are under condemnation.

WORSHIP GUIDE

For the Superintendent or Teacher
Theme: Going to Jerusalem
Theme Song: Love Lifted Me
Scripture: Matthew 10:34-39
Song: Have Thine Own Way, Lord
Meditation: I pray that I always may have the mercy, compassion and mercy toward others that Jesus has shown to me. Help me to see those who have strayed as the object of God's love, not of human wrath.

252

GOING TO JERUSALEM

Bible Background • LUKE 18:15—19:10
Printed Text • LUKE 18:31-34; 19:1-10
Devotional Reading • MATTHEW 10:34-39

LESSON AIM

After studying today's lesson, members will understand more about the significance of Jesus' encounter with Zaccheus. They will also recognize how Jesus' actions demonstrated that He had come to save all humanity, not just the children of Abraham.

KEEP IN MIND

"For the Son of man is come to seek and to save that which was lost" (Luke 19:10).

FOCAL VERSES

Luke 18:31 Then he took unto him the twelve, and said unto them, Behold, we go up to Jerusalem, and all things that are written by the prophets concerning the Son of man shall be accomplished.

32 For he shall be delivered unto the Gentiles, and shall be mocked, and spitefully entreated, and spit on:

33 And they shall scourge him, and put him to death: and the third day he shall rise again.

34 And they understood none of these things: and this saying was hid from them, neither knew they the things which were spoken.

19:1 And Jesus entered and passed through Jericho.

2 And, behold, there was a man named Zacchaeus, which was the chief among the publicans, and he was rich.

3 And he sought to see Jesus who he was; and could not for the press, because he was little of stature.

4 And he ran before, and climbed up into a

LESSON OVERVIEW

LESSON AIM
KEEP IN MIND
FOCAL VERSES
IN FOCUS
THE PEOPLE, PLACES, AND TIMES
BACKGROUND
AT-A-GLANCE
IN DEPTH
SEARCH THE SCRIPTURES
DISCUSS THE MEANING
LESSON IN OUR SOCIETY
MAKE IT HAPPEN
FOLLOW THE SPIRIT
REMEMBER YOUR THOUGHTS
MORE LIGHT ON THE TEXT
DAILY BIBLE READINGS

sycamore tree to see him: for he was to pass that way.

5 And when Jesus came to the place, he looked up, and saw him, and said unto him, Zacchaeus, make haste, and come down; for today I must abide at thy house.

6 And he made haste, and came down, and received him joyfully.

7 And when they saw it, they all murmured saying, That he was gone to be guest with a man that is a sinner.

8 And Zacchaeus stood, and said unto the Lord; Behold, Lord, the half of my goods I give to the poor; and if I have taken anything from any man by false accusation, I restore him fourfold.

9 And Jesus said unto him, This day is salvation come to this house, forsomuch as he also is a son of Abraham.

10 For the Son of man is come to seek and to save that which was lost.

IN FOCUS

Larry couldn't believe he was actually sitting in church listening to one of the most famous preachers around. "I knew who this dude was even when I didn't go to church!" he thought. Although Larry had gotten to the church early, he'd purposely sat in the back. He didn't want to be an embarrassment to his church. All those days of hard living on the streets had left him pretty beaten down.

As he mentally assessed his appearance—teeth missing, a scar over his left eye, and second-hand clothes—Larry decided that he would do everyone

FEB
4TH

a service simply by sitting where he would hardly be noticed. The people at the church treated him decently enough; however, he could tell that some people wished he wasn't there.

Larry thought he was safely hidden in the back when the minister began to call some people forward for a time of prayer and blessing. Suddenly, he called out to Larry. "Come down, my brother," the preacher invited him. "The Spirit is leading me to reach out to you. The Lord has a blessing in store for you, brother!"

THE PEOPLE, PLACES, AND TIMES

Son of Man. With the exception of the books of Daniel and Ezekiel, the term is used as a synonym for the word "man" or "humanity" throughout the Old Testament.

In the New Testament, the term is a designation for Jesus as God in the flesh and the agent of divine judgment. Mostly the term is connected with references to Jesus suffering, death, and resurrection.

Based on information from Holman Bible Dictionary, Trent Butler, general editor, Nashville: Broadman & Holman Publishers, 1991, pp. 1291-1293.

Chief Publican (Tax Collector). A position which probably paid extremely well. Little is known about the position, but it can be assumed that the chief publican was the head of a district with a number of subordinate collectors being responsible to him.

Although personal and property taxes were collected by the Roman government, taxes on goods were farmed out to independent collectors. This system gave rise to numerous opportunities for exploitation. By virtue of the fact that he held the position, Zaccheus was probably guilty of many of the evils which were associated with his profession.

Based on information from The Broadman Bible Commentary, Clifton J. Allen, general editor, Nashville: Broadman Press, 1970, p. 146.

BACKGROUND

Although the number of Jesus' disciples grew, the Twelve constituted his inner circle of followers and friends. He taught many things to the multitudes, but He revealed special things to His disciples. The disciples still did not understand the nature of His mission, however. His references to Jerusalem or to death or to suffering were not fully comprehended by the Twelve.

Ministering with Jesus must have been exciting! The Twelve watched as He performed miracles. They were probably mildly amused at the way their Teacher engaged in verbal battle with the Jewish hierarchy, always coming out on top. They traveled from town to town, meeting new people, and helping those who had been refused help through religious channels and whose only hope lay in Him. Their ministry must have made this band of ordinary men feel special. They were a part of something big, although they did not have full knowledge of just what that something was.

Today's lesson text offers another illustration of Jesus embracing one who has been cast aside by religion. Every so often, Jesus pulled His band of Twelve away from the crowds to deal with them on a particular issue. They were about to enter into Jerusalem. The fact that they were going there was not by accident or coincidence. The journey to Jerusalem, and the people they encountered there, were very much a part of Jesus' destiny.

AT-A-GLANCE

1. Jesus Speaks on His Destiny
(Luke 18:31-34)
2. Zacchaeus' Conversion
(Luke 19:1-10)

IN DEPTH

1. Jesus Speaks on His Destiny (Luke 18:31-34)

His disciples did not understand the depth and full meaning of His words, but still Jesus took the time to explain His journey to them. Traveling from town to town, healing people, and meeting interesting folk must have been heady stuff for the Twelve. They could not imagine the full-blown scale of rejection that awaited

described by Jesus here. The prophets did, however, acknowledge two images which would play a role in the redemption story.

First, the Suffering Servant of Isaiah was sent to suffer by God. He was not just someone in misery, He was God's Servant sent to suffer—like Jesus did on the Cross.

The second image was that of the King-Messiah in the Psalms and other writings. As the sovereign ruler, He is to rule with glory after His resurrection. In this way, Jesus was the fulfillment of all the prophets declared concerning the suffering and glory of God's servant.

Jesus compatriots would play a crucial role in this redemption story by handing Him over to the (Gentile) Roman authorities in the person of Pilate and the soldier who would actually carry out the crucifixion order.

While the Jews would conspire to bring about Jesus' death, it was the Gentiles who actually accomplished

Jesus in Jerusalem. In the midst of their present popularity, Jesus did not want them to lose their focus from His mission. Here Jesus reminded them for the third time of their destination and the meaning of their journey. Earlier He had revealed something of the nature of their destiny (Luke 9:22, 44). Even with their lack of understanding, Jesus explained that Jerusalem was to be the place of rejection and death.

The Old Testament prophets had written that suffering was an essential precursor to glory. What the men of old had written would be accomplished. None of the prophecies gave a detailed account of a death such as that

it. Despite their plots and plans, it is God who has the final word. At the end of this horrific series of events, the Son of man would rise again. The victory belongs to God! The final outcome is in His hands.

The disciples could not make the connection between suffering and glory. As far as they knew, the two conditions arose from entirely different circumstances.

2. Zacchaeus' Conversion (Luke 19:1-10)

There would be many stops to make before the climax of events at Jerusalem occurred. One stop on that journey to Jerusalem included a dramatic encounter with a little man named Zacchaeus.

Before Jesus arrived at Jericho, He encountered a blind man just outside who called out to Him for help. When others in the crowd tried to silence him, he cried out all the more loudly. Perhaps they felt a blind beggar was not worthy to deter someone as important as Jesus. But the man was determined that nothing would stop him from obtaining the healing that the Son of David had to offer (v. 39). By stopping to take care of the man's needs, Jesus demonstrated His concern for the needs of all people. Just after He had healed a blind beggar, Jesus moved on to provide healing for one who had a different kind of hurt. Zacchaeus was an outcast among the Jews because of his occupation. His position as chief among the publicans had made him a rich man. Perhaps he wanted to see Jesus merely out of curiosity. After all, a celebrity of sorts had come to town. He may have felt an emptiness in his life and somehow felt that Jesus held the answer. Possibly word had circulated that Jesus had compassion on those who were outcasts, and Zaccheus wanted to know if it was true. For whatever reason, Zaccheus wanted a look at the man called Jesus of Nazareth. He wanted to see the man he had heard so much about.

Zaccheus was not alone in his desire to see the great Teacher. A great crowd had gathered around Him. The gathering was so intense that Zaccheus could not make his way through the crowd. Complicating matters was the fact that Zaccheus was short. The fact that he was despised among the people probably didn't help his chances of getting to the front of the crowd. Zaccheus positioned himself to be ready when the Master came by.

Determined to see Jesus for himself, Zaccheus climbed up into a sycamore tree that was near where Jesus would pass. We can never know what Zaccheus expected to happen. Perhaps he would have been satisfied with merely a glimpse of Jesus. No matter what his plans were for the outcome of his encounter with Jesus, the Teacher took the encounter into a different direction.

As He did many times, Jesus diverted His attention away from the pressing masses to call out to one person in need. The Lord called out to Zaccheus and commanded him to make haste and come down from the tree. Jesus had made plans for Himself and Zaccheus, "For I must abide at thy house." Though the invitation surely surprised him, Zaccheus quickly came down from the tree and over to the Master. While holy men criticized and challenged Jesus, Zaccheus, a sinner, received him joyfully. Imagine Jesus inviting Himself into the home of one of the Pharisees or the Chief Priest! They had no joy for Him.

Those who heard Jesus were aghast! Some were probably jealous that Jesus had chosen Zaccheus rather than themselves. The opportunity to entertain Jesus was probably one of the few times the tax collector was able to use his wealth for something that brought joy to him. What gave him greater joy, however, was the fact that a Man like Jesus saw fit to come into his home and abide with him.

While Jesus made his way to Zaccheus' house, the crowd grumbled that "he was gone to be guest with a man that is a sinner." Neither Jesus nor Zaccheus were deterred by the criticism around them.

The event made such an impact on Zaccheus that he repented and wanted to make right the wrong that he had done to others. First, he offered to give half of his goods to the poor. Second, if he had cheated anyone out of anything, he was willing to pay back fourfold. Jewish law only required that a man give back twenty percent more as restitution. Zaccheus was willing to do much, much more than the law required.

Jesus neither criticized, nor condemned, Zaccheus for his occupation. As a result of his encounter with the Lord, he willingly repented; he wanted to make restitution for all he had done wrong. Obviously his decision pleased Jesus. He announced, "This day is salvation come to this house." Zaccheus' actions were even greater cause for celebration because he was also a son of Abraham.

So many of the Jews who criticized Jesus were

unwilling to take the courageous step that this sinner had. Jesus proclaimed that salvation did not come only to those who had rigidly adhered to Pharisaic laws. One who was condemned for not observing the law became willing to do far more than the law required of him. Faithfulness cannot come only through adherence to laws written in black and white. Our faithfulness must be rooted in something far greater—our belief in, and acceptance of, Jesus Christ as Lord and Saviour. By coming to Zaccheus' house that day, Jesus demonstrated that salvation was open to anyone, Jew or Gentile, who had repented and committed themself to righteous living.

Jesus' ministry and His purpose was not what the people who followed Him, or even those who opposed Him, expected. He took the time to deal with outcasts, sinners, and those who were considered unworthy to associate with righteous men. In verse 10, Jesus again contradicted popular thought by announcing the true purpose of His mission, which was devoid of political consequences. His purpose was to seek and to save that which was lost.

SEARCH THE SCRIPTURES

1. What did Jesus reveal to the Twelve concerning His destiny? (18:31)

2. What things, specifically, did He foretell would happen to Him? (vv. 32-33)

3. How did the Twelve react to what Jesus told them? (v. 34)

4. Who was making plans to see Jesus in Jericho? (19:2)

5. What stopped Zaccheus from being able to get a glimpse of Jesus? (v. 3)

6. What did he do so that he could see Jesus? (v. 4)

7. What did Jesus call out to Zaccheus? (v. 5)

8. How did Zaccheus respond to Jesus' invitation? (v. 6)

9. What did the people say about Jesus? (v. 7)

10. What did Zaccheus decide to do after his encounter with Jesus? (v. 8)

11. What did Jesus say in response to Zaccheus' announcement? (v. 9)

12. What did Jesus reveal about His purpose for coming to earth? (v. 10)

DISCUSS THE MEANING

1. Why did the Lord invite Himself to Zaccheus' house instead of some of the other Jews?

2. Of what significance is it that Zaccheus planned early and positioned himself to be able to see the Master when He came by? What do Zaccheus' actions say to other believers.

3. Why did Zaccheus decide to change his ways, even though Jesus issued no judgment, or condemnation, of him? In fact, Jesus extended Himself to Zaccheus when others would have nothing to do with him.

LESSON IN OUR SOCIETY

All people make mistakes. Everyone, at one time or another, goes down a wayward path out of greed, ignorance, or some other human desire. Some people are walking down that wayward path simply because no one has ever shown them another way.

Jesus showed Zaccheus a "more excellent way," while other Jews scorned and condemned him.

Christians are often guilty of making harsh judgments against those who are living sinfully. More people might come to Christ if we only showed them the same love that He does, instead of offering disapproving looks and scornful glances. People who are without Christ need love and mercy, not guilt and condemnation.

MAKE IT HAPPEN

Think about what feelings might a person like Zaccheus might have about himself. He was wealthy, but he was greatly despised by those who knew him. Even though many people are financially well-off, they might be living in poverty in other areas of life.

Don't think just about those who arouse only minor feelings of disapproval. Think of those persons who make you angry every time you consider the fact that they are making lots of money doing the things that they do.

Then, instead of focusing on how you feel about them, make of list of the feelings such people might have about themselves. Then, having made yourself aware of those feelings, determine how you might best minister to such as person to expose them to the Good News available to them through Jesus Christ.

FOLLOW THE SPIRIT

What God wants me to do:

_____

_____

REMEMBER YOUR THOUGHTS

Special insights you learned:

_____

_____

MORE LIGHT ON THE TEXT
Luke 18:31-34; 19:1-10

18:31 Then he took unto him the twelve, and said unto them, Behold, we go up to Jerusalem, and all things that are written by the prophets concerning the Son of man shall be accomplished.

The first thing that Jesus did was to bring the His disciples unto Himself. None of us can truly hear what the Lord has to say to us unless we first come to Him. We all must be obedient to the call of God on our lives. Once we are in the presence of the Lord, He can begin to speak to us and we can begin to hear. When the disciples came to Jesus, He made a very powerful statement. He informed them that everything that the prophets had said concerning Him was going to be fulfilled, and they would be eyewitnesses to these world changing events. Having spent the last three years being taught by Jesus and reading the writings of the Old Testament prophets, the disciples should have understood what it was that Jesus was really saying to them.

32 For he shall be delivered unto the Gentiles, and shall be mocked, and spitefully entreated, and spit on:

The promised Messiah, as the prophets had foretold, was about to be arrested in order to free us, to be humiliated in order to give us worth, and to be tortured so that we could be comforted.

Jesus was trying to prepare the disciples for what was about to happen. Never does our Lord allow any of the attacks of the enemy to come upon His children without first giving them preparation and warning.

33 And they shall scourge him, and put him to death: and the third day he shall rise again.

Imagine how the disciples must have felt as they listened to the same Jesus whom they had seen raise several people from the dead. Now He is telling them that He, too, is going to die. How puzzling it must have been to hear Jesus who, at the grave of His friend Lazarus, claimed to be the resurrection. Here He is telling them that He is going to be killed. However, in the same breath, He is also telling them He was going to rise from the dead.

34 And they understood none of these things: and this saying was hid from them, neither knew they the things which were spoken.

It was not until after Jesus' resurrection that the disciples understood many of the things that Jesus said to them. The same is often true in our lives; the Lord tells us something, or we learn something from the Word of God, but we don't fully understand until we experience what was said. Nevertheless, our Lord always gives us advanced preparation, and warning, in order to insure our victory over the enemy.

19:1 And Jesus entered and passed through Jericho. 2 And, behold, there was a man named Zacchaeus, which was the chief among the publicans, and he was rich.

The name Zacchaeus is a Greek form of the Hebrew name meaning innocent. How ironic, because Zacchaeus was a corrupt tax collector who had become wealthy by overtaxing his own people the Jews. He was considered a sell-out, a traitor, an Uncle Tom. But the Lord Jesus Christ came to redeem him and declare him innocent.

3 And he sought to see Jesus who he was; and could not for the press, because he was little of stature.

Not only did Zacchaeus want to see Jesus with his eyes, but he sought to find out who Jesus really was. In other words, he was seeking Jesus with his whole heart, and he would not let anything, or anyone, stop him from seeing the Saviour.

4 And he ran before, and climbed up into a sycamore tree to see him: for he was to pass that way.

Zacchaeus was not concerned what others thought about him as he began his search for Jesus. As wealthy as he was, he was willing to run ahead of everyone, and climb a tree in order to see Jesus for himself.

5 And when Jesus came to the place, he looked up, and saw him, and said unto him, Zacchaeus, make haste, and come down; for today I must abide at thy house.

Zacchaeus was considered to be an unethical employee of the oppressive Roman government. He was despised by his own race because he cheated them out of their hard-earned money.

Yet, of all the many people who came to see Him, Jesus spoke to Zacchaeus personally and invited Himself to his home.

6 And he made haste, and came down, and received him joyfully.

If only we would respond to the call of God in our lives as Zacchaeus did. If only we would make haste, and come down from our lofty positions, and humbly receive Jesus into our homes. Our lives, and the lives of our family members, would be blessed beyond measure.

7 And when they saw it, they all murmured saying, That he was gone to be guest with a man that is a sinner.

Isn't it sad when people can't stand to see God bless you? When the Lord delivers you, some will not only get mad, but they will also murmur against God for delivering a sinner.

8 And Zacchaeus stood, and said unto the Lord; Behold, Lord, the half of my goods I give to the poor; and if I have taken anything from any man by false accusation, I restore him fourfold.

This is a true sign of repentance. Zacchaeus was willing to give back four times the amount of everything that he had taken illegally. He was also willing to give half of all that he owned to the poor.

Many of us are not willing to give the Lord one tenth of what He has blessed us with.

9 And Jesus said unto him, This day is salvation come to this house, forsomuch as he also is a son of Abraham.

How wonderful it is when the Lord Jesus Himself declares that salvation has come to your house. We must all examine our homes to see if everything that we do in them, and everyone who lives in them, manifest the salvation of the Lord Jesus Christ.

10 For the Son of man is come to seek and to save that which was lost.

Each of us must allow the Saviour of the world into our hearts and into our homes that He might seek and save that which is lost. Regardless of what we have done, or who we have hurt, the Lord Jesus Christ is not ashamed to come right where we live and speak to our hearts and save our souls. Let us respond to His call immediately, as Zacchaeus did, and humbly receive the salvation, deliverance, and fellowship of the Lord Jesus Christ.

DAILY BIBLE READINGS

M: The Coming of the Kingdom
Luke 17:20-30
T: Keep on Praying
Luke 18:1-8
W: The Pharisee and the Tax Collector
Luke 18:9-14
T: The Rich Ruler
Luke 18:18-30
F: One Way to Discipleship
Mark 10:17-31
S: Join the Procession
Luke 18:31-43
S: Jesus and Zacchaeus
Luke 19:1-10

TEACHING TIPS

February 11
Bible Study Guide 11

1. Words You Should Know

A. Benefactors (v. 25)—a title of honor bestowed for service to the people.

B. Synoptic Gospels—the three Gospels which closely parallel: Matthew, Mark, and Luke.

2. Teacher Preparation

Before the session begins, choose several famous persons who are considered great either in the political, athletic, entertainment, religious, civic, or academic area. Ask members why these persons are considered to be great. Ask if they personally feel that these persons are great. Why or why not?

3. Starting the Lesson

A. Using a chalkboard or a large sheet of paper, ask the class to help you develop a list of criteria for greatness, according to human standards. Guide this activity carefully so that the class will avoid talking about Jesus' definition of greatness at this point. Keep the discussion focused on human greatness.

B. Read today's IN FOCUS story about Earlene's dilemma. Spend time discussing how people vie for power and recognition, even in the church. Talk about how such attitudes hinder the work of Christ.

4. Getting Into the Lesson

A. As you discuss today's lesson, help members to understand that because of human nature, most people would have done as the disciples did, arguing over who would hold the position closest to Jesus. Remind them that the disciples were still hoping Jesus would establish an earthly kingdom. The disciples probably thought there was going to be a "showdown," rather than a crucifixion. They could not imagine Jesus' victory coming in the way that it did.

5. Relating the Lesson to Life

A. Review the concepts described in today's THE PEOPLE, PLACES, AND TIMES article. Take time to profile Judas Iscariot. Ask members to imagine what kind of man he might have been.

B. Today's DISCUSS THE MEANING asks members to think about the lack of humility that seems to strike many leaders. Guide the class in thinking about why Jesus did not reveal Judas specifically as His betrayer.

C. The LESSON IN OUR SOCIETY addresses greatness through service and how it may be manifested in contemporary times. Ask members: How do we as Christians demonstrate humility in such as way that people do not interpret it as weakness?

6. Arousing Action

A. Prior to the class session, write the names of several Christian "heroes" on separate sheets of construction paper. The persons may be local people or they may be famous. Tape the names on the wall. Create a banner from a computer, or tape several sheets of paper together that reads, "Great Wall of Christ." Discuss how, through their servanthood, each person deserves to be considered as having achieved greatness in Christ.

B. Ask members to find a Bible personality (other than Jesus) whom they believe came under Jesus' definition of greatness as much as any human can and give their reasons for choosing that particular individual.

WORSHIP GUIDE

For the Superintendent or Teacher
Theme: One Who Serves
Theme Song: Lord, I Want to Be a Christian
Scripture: Mark 10:35-45
Song: Let Others See Jesus in You
Meditation: I will only concern myself with greatness in the eyes of Christ. I pray that when my life's journey is over, the Master will look to me and say, "Well done, My good and faithful servant."

ONE WHO SERVES

Bible Background • LUKE 22:1-30
Printed Text • LUKE 22:14-30
Devotional Reading • MARK 10:35-45

LESSON AIM

After studying today's lesson, members will learn what Jesus commanded concerning service and the believer's path to true reward.

KEEP IN MIND

"But ye shall not be so: but he that is greatest among you, let him be as the younger; and he that is chief, as he that doth serve" (Luke 22:26).

FOCAL VERSES

Luke 22:14 And when the hour was come, he sat down, and the twelve apostles with him.

15 And he said unto them, With desire I have desired to eat this passover with you before I suffer:

16 For I say unto you, I will not any more eat thereof, until it be fulfilled in the kingdom of God.

17 And he took the cup, and gave thanks, and said, Take this, and divide it among yourselves:

18 For I say unto you, I will not drink of the fruit of the vine, until the kingdom of God shall come.

19 And he took bread, and gave thanks, and brake it, and gave unto them, saying, This is my body which is given for you: this do in remembrance of me.

20 Likewise also the cup after supper, saying, This cup is the new testament in my blood, which is shed for you.

21 But, behold, the hand of him that betrayeth me is with me on the table.

22 And truly the Son of man goeth, as it was determined: but woe unto that man by whom he is betrayed!

LESSON OVERVIEW

LESSON AIM
KEEP IN MIND
FOCAL VERSES
IN FOCUS
THE PEOPLE, PLACES, AND TIMES
BACKGROUND
AT-A-GLANCE
IN DEPTH
SEARCH THE SCRIPTURES
DISCUSS THE MEANING
LESSON IN OUR SOCIETY
MAKE IT HAPPEN
FOLLOW THE SPIRIT
REMEMBER YOUR THOUGHTS
MORE LIGHT ON THE TEXT
DAILY BIBLE READINGS

23 And they began to inquire among themselves, which of them it was that should do this thing.

24 And there was also a strife among them, which of them should be accounted the greatest.

25 And he said unto them, The kings of the Gentiles exercise lordship over them; and they that exercise authority upon them are called benefactors.

26 But ye shall not be so: but he that is greatest among you, let him be as the younger; and he that is chief, as he that doth serve.

27 For whether is greater, he that sitteth at meat, or he that serveth? is not he that sitteth at meat? but I am among you as he that serveth.

28 Ye are they which have continued with me in my temptations.

29 And I appoint unto you a kingdom, as my Father hath appointed unto me;

30 That ye may eat and drink at my table in my kingdom, and sit on thrones judging the twelve tribes of Israel.

IN FOCUS

FEB 11TH

Earlene just couldn't understand why things always turned out this way. "Why can't people just be satisfied serving the Lord?" she wondered.

She was greatly discouraged over the fact that so many people were trying to get credit for initiating the "It's All Good" program for youth. Now that the ministry was getting local and national attention,

261

people were coming out of the woodwork trying to take credit for the ministry! Everybody wanted to be interviewed by the television crew. People Earlene had never even seen before were hanging around the IAG office acting like they were running the show.

By the time she talked to her mother about the situation, Earlene was ready to burst into tears. Her mother always had the gift of giving comfort and wisdom. The wise matriarch told her, "You know, honey, all that really matters is that the young people have a program that is really doing some good. The good Lord knows who did what. Don't you worry about it none. You just do what's right and the Lord will bless your faithfulness, baby."

Earlene left her mother's house feeling a great sense of peace. She had to admit that perhaps she was suffering from the same desire for recognition that she was criticizing the others for. "Mama's right," she thought. "The thing that is really important is already being done."

THE PEOPLE, PLACES, AND TIMES

Passover. Passover and the Feast of Unleavened Bread was the first of three great Hebrew festivals. Passover is the annual observance of the Israelite slaves from bondage in Egypt. God sent His angel to destroy the firstborn sons of the Egyptians in order to soften Pharaoh's hardened heart and to convince him to release Israel from bondage.

In preparation for the arrival of the angel of death, Hebrew families were instructed to sacrifice a lamb and spread its blood over the doorpost of those homes. The blood was a sign to God's angel that he should "pass over" that house, leaving those inside unharmed.

Passover was observed on the fourteenth day of the first month, known as *Abib,* which is currently March/April on our calendar. The Passover service begins in the evening as it was on the evening of that day long ago when Israel left Egypt in haste. Unleavened bread is used in the celebration as a reminder to the people that there had been no time for the Hebrew slaves to leaven their bread (make it rise). The yeast-free bread and the bitter herbs they ate constituted their last meal as slaves in Egypt.

Based on information gathered from The Word in Life Study Bible, Nashville: Thomas Nelson, Inc, 1993, 1996, p. 1837.

Judas Iscariot. A Greek transliteration of the Hebrew name Judah, which means "Praise Yahweh." The name was very common during the time of Jesus, not only because it was the Greek name of Judah, but because it had also been made popular by the Jewish hero Judas Maccabaeus, who led the nation in their fight for independence from Syria in 166 B.C.

The name Judas is used to designate seven different men in the New Testament, most of them merely in passing. He may have hailed from Kerioth, a Judean town.

Judas Iscariot will forever be known as the man who betrayed Jesus. His name means "Judah from Kerioth," a town in the tribe of Judah.

Based on information from Holman Bible Dictionary, Trent Butler, general editor, Nashville: Broadman & Holman Publishers, 1991, pp. 821-822.

BACKGROUND

Jesus had already made preparation for the final fellowship meal He would share with the men He had taught and come to regard as friends. This was a time for Him to share his final thoughts with them.

The meal came at the time of Passover, a great time of celebration for the Jewish community. Jesus had sent Peter and John ahead of the rest to secure the necessary items for the meal. A location for the meal had already been secured (22:10-12) in the upper room of a house in Jerusalem.

In Jesus' day, during Passover large numbers of people gathered in Jerusalem to observe the annual celebration. Therefore, an unusually large crowd was present to participate in the events surrounding Jesus' entry into the city, His arrest, trial and crucifixion.

AT-A-GLANCE

1. The Elements of Communion
(Luke 22:14-23)
2. Who Is Greatest? (vv. 24-27)
3. Jesus Predicts Peter's Denial (vv. 28-30)

During that last meal together, Jesus spoke with them about His impending death. But He also spoke with confidence of a reunion that would occur around a banquet table in the kingdom of God.

IN DEPTH

1. The Communion Elements (Luke 22:14-23)

As he did with the birth account, Luke gave more attention to the Last Supper than the other Synoptic Gospels. Jesus used the Passover occasion as an opportunity to instruct the Twelve on what was about to happen.

The translation "he sat" is more accurately translated as "he reclined at the table." Many popular religious drawings and portraits depict Jesus and the Twelve sitting at a table eating the meal, particularly Leonardo da Vinci's *Last Supper*. In Palestine, however, the custom was for guests to recline at the Passover meal.

Jesus' opening words to them indicated two things. First, this would be their last encounter together before His time of suffering. Second, the Last Supper is linked to the great banquet Jesus will share with His disciples in the kingdom to come.

Jesus then took a cup and began what we now observe as the ritual of the Last Supper. In the usual observance of the Passover meal, each person had his or her own cup. At the meal with Jesus, the disciples all drank from Jesus' cup. This action pointed to the unity of their fellowship with Jesus, but it also served as a reminder to the disciples that they are all called to drink from His cup. Jesus vowed not to drink from the cup again "until the kingdom of God shall come."

At this point Jesus took some bread and spoke, "This is my body which is given for you." Scholars have long debated the meaning of the verb "is" here. Many feel a more accurate translation would be "this means my body." Still the question may be asked, "How does the bread represent the body of Christ?"

According to Paul, the body of Christ is not the bread, rather, it is the people who partake of the bread (1 Corinthians 11:27-29).

Luke arranged the sequence of events in a different manner than John. Luke places the meal first and the conversation afterward. In John's Gospel, Judas was gone by the time the meal was shared. Luke does not mention Judas' departure at all. Additionally, Luke mentions the presence of two cups while the other Gospels mention only one. The Passover meal had four courses and four cups. Therefore, the Gospel writers summarized all the events of the meal.

This new fellowship meal that Jesus instituted serves not only as a memorial of His death, it is a unity meal. It is both a proclamation and a symbol of the believers' anticipation of the time when Jesus will return and all of God's promises will be fulfilled. The cup represents the new covenant, which is sealed with his blood (note that some translations, such as Revised Standard Version, omit verses 19b-20).

Jesus then turned His attention to "him that betrayeth me." The Lord Jesus had to be betrayed in order that the prophecy could be fulfilled. It concerned the disciples deeply that the one who would betray the Master was sitting among those in His innermost circle. He did not reveal the identity of the one who betrayed Him, but He did say, "Woe unto that man by whom Jesus is betrayed." That Jesus would suffer and die was a great part of His mission, His ministry, and His destiny. He willingly went to the Cross out of obedience to His Father. Still that did not excuse Judas' decision to hand Him over to the Jews, nor does it diminish his guilt or the responsibility for his actions.

After Jesus made the announcement that the traitor sat among them, they all began to examine themselves to find out "which of them it was that should do this thing." It seems they all began to doubt themselves, as if each man somehow knew he was capable of such an act.

2. Who Is Greatest? (vv. 24-27)

The disciples' argument probably began over accusations concerning the identity of the traitor. From that the disagreement probably escalated into who loved Jesus most, who was most loyal to Him, then to who would be His right-hand man when He came into His kingdom.

So in the midst of Jesus' struggle, the disciples were arguing among themselves, wondering who

was the greatest. They were judging themselves and their circumstances in the same way that the Gentiles did, expecting a similar structure of hierarchy.

The term "benefactor" was a title commonly used to acknowledge Gentile rulers. The disciples were looking for honor and recognition as defined by humans, no doubt expecting to have some power and authority over others once their Teacher took the throne.

Instead of affirming their shallow, limited notions of greatness, Jesus defined greatness according to a new standard, a standard much more difficult to achieve. Jesus said, "He that is greatest, let him be as the younger." As for the one who would be chief, let him serve. In Jesus' day, the youngest member of the family was the least important member. They had to perform the most menial tasks and could expect the smallest reward.

One who chooses to be greatest, therefore, should be the one who is willing to do the most for the least amount of recognition. That is how Jesus defined greatness. Additionally, the one who

would be chief should be given to serve others. Instead of jockeying to get ahead of others in the human race, believers in Jesus Christ are to position themselves to serve others.

Jesus then asked the disciples which person is greater, the one who sits at the table or the one who serves? As human beings count greatness, the one who sits at the table is greater than the one doing the serving. Not so with Christ! In the kingdom, the one who serves is the greatest, and Jesus showed Himself as the prime example.

Those who serve as leaders in the church should not seek exaltation. Rather leaders should seek opportunities for service. The greatest leaders this world has known have been men and women who sought to serve others, not glorify themselves.

3. Jesus Predicts Peter's Denial (vv. 28-30)

Jesus recognized that the Twelve had been present and had suffered with Him during Him ministry. With the exception of Judas, they had been faithful to Him since the beginning. He had spent a great deal of time teaching them and training them.

After He acknowledged their steadfastness, He then handed over to them a kingdom "as my Father hath appointed unto me." Jesus passed His kingdom authority to the apostles who were charged to continue spreading the Good News. That authority was much like the authority that the Father had bestowed upon Him.

Jesus made a promise to His disciples. First, He promised that they would share in the fellowship of His kingdom as they would eat and drink at His table. Second, they would share in His rule because He would appoint them to sit on thrones judging the twelve tribes of Israel.

Because their expectations were limited to the earthly realm, the disciples probably still could not fully appreciate what Jesus had bestowed upon them. Many times believers are so busy looking to God to answer prayer according to our limited understanding that we cannot appreciate the greater blessing He sometimes gives.

SEARCH THE SCRIPTURES

1. What did Jesus want to do with the disciples before His time of suffering began? (v. 15)

2. When would Jesus eat another fellowship meal with them? (v. 16)

3. What did Jesus do with the cup? (v. 17)

4. When would Jesus again drink of the fruit of the vine? (v. 18)

5. What did Jesus say concerning the bread? (v. 19)

6. What did the cup represent? (v. 20)

7. What did Jesus say concerning the one who would betray Him? (v. 21)

8. How did the disciples react when they heard that one of them would betray Him? (v. 23)

9. What did the disciples argue about? (v. 24)

10. How did Jesus describe those who strive to be the greatest? (vv. 26-27)

11. What was Jesus' first promise to the disciples who had been with Him through all His temptations? (vv. 28-29)

12. What was Jesus' second promise to them? (v. 30)

DISCUSS THE MEANING

1. Jesus called for humility within those who desire to be leaders, yet it seems that many people who are assertive enough to be leaders often lack that humility. Do such people tend to learn humility as a spiritual lesson?

2. Why do you think Jesus left the name of His betrayer nameless? Why do you think all of the disciples began to question themselves, wondering if he was the one who would betray their Teacher?

3. Why did Jesus go through this time of sharing His fate with the disciples, even though they did not fully understand the purpose of what He was doing?

LESSON IN OUR SOCIETY

The Lord expects His leaders to be humble. Yet often, people regard humility as weakness and arrogance as power and authority. Some leaders have the ability to exert both humility and authority at the same time.

It must always be remembered, however, that the greatest person is the one who leads through service, not the one who acquires the greater amount of media attention, fame, church members, or material possessions. A person who is not willing to serve is not one who will be concerned with the needs of his/her followers. When the resurrected Christ addressed Peter, His instructions were to "feed my sheep."

Believers must look to Jesus' criteria for greatness as we prayerfully look for leaders to serve in our churches and to lead our people according to His way. In order to do this human definitions of greatness must be cast aside so that we may then view the situation through spiritual eyes.

MAKE IT HAPPEN

Is it wrong to desire greatness? How can the one who desires to do his/her best and do great things be distinguished from one who is only concerned with achieving greatness? How can you assess yourself to determine whether you are seeking to be the best you can be, or whether you are concerned about achieving greatness as human beings count greatness?

FOLLOW THE SPIRIT

What God wants me to do:

_____

REMEMBER YOUR THOUGHTS
Special insights you learned:

_____

_____

MORE LIGHT ON THE TEXT
Luke 22:14-30
22:14 And when the hour was come, he sat down, and the twelve apostles with him. 15 And he said unto them, With desire I have desired to eat this passover with you before I suffer:
The phrase "with desire I have desired" simply means, _I have had an intense desire._ Therefore, Jesus was telling His disciples that this particular Passover had a special significance for several reasons. One reason was that Jesus was about to fulfill the true meaning of Passover through His death, burial, and resurrection. Jesus knew that He was about to suffer great pain, rejection, humiliation and suffering, and He wanted to spend His final moments, and celebrate this Passover, with those who had become His closest friends, students and brothers in the ministry.

16 For I say unto you, I will not any more eat thereof, until it be fulfilled in the kingdom of God.
Jesus also knew that He would not celebrate Passover with His disciples until we all celebrate it together in the kingdom of God. What a wonderful thought, being in the presence of Jesus and all the saints of God—past, present, and future—all worshiping and singing praises to God and celebrating the Passover in remembrance of the work of our Lord and Saviour Jesus Christ.

17 And he took the cup, and gave thanks, and said, Take this, and divide it among yourselves:
What humility, what a demonstration of love. Jesus was the one who was about to be tortured and killed, yet He wanted to serve those for whom he was going to suffer; including the one who would betray Him and the one who would deny Him. Jesus took the cup realizing that it was a symbol of His own blood that would be shed, and He thanked God for it. Jesus told the disciples to

divide the cup among themselves meaning that His blood was available to everyone who would believe and receive His atonement. Jesus was thankful for the opportunity to bring salvation to the world even though it meant that He would have to die a cruel and undeserved death.

18 For I say unto you, I will not drink of the fruit of the vine, until the kingdom of God shall come.
The joyful expectation of the kingdom of God coming to earth gave Jesus the strength and the willingness to endure such pain and suffering. He knew that He was the door through which the Kingdom of God would come.

19 And he took bread, and gave thanks, and brake it, and gave unto them, saying, This is my body which is given for you: this do in remembrance of me.
Again we see this marvelous demonstration of love and humiliation as Jesus takes the bread realizing that it symbolized His own body. He breaks it and gives thanks to God. Jesus knew that His brokenness would bring our wholeness, His pain would bring our peace, and by His stripes we would be healed. All that Jesus asked was that we would celebrate the Passover in remembrance of Him.

20 Likewise also the cup after supper, saying, This cup is the new testament in my blood, which is shed for you.
Jesus was letting the disciples know that He was the sacrificial lamb that had to be slain in order to establish a new and better covenant built upon better promises than the old covenant. And this new covenant was being established on their behalf and ours.

21 But, behold, the hand of him that betrayeth me is with me on the table.
Although Judas was one of the disciples of Jesus, Jesus knew that Judas was going to betray Him. Now it was time for Judas to be exposed, and it was time for Judas to do what he was destined to do—betray the Son of God.

22 And truly the Son of man goeth, as it was

determined: but woe unto that man by whom he is betrayed!

The Greek word for "woe" is *ouai* and is an interjection used in denunciation. Jesus was denouncing Judas for his role in betraying Him. Judas was a tool of Satan and was being used to destroy Jesus and all that He was sent to accomplish. Jesus would soon die for the sins of the whole world, but because Judas did not accept the atonement that Jesus provided, (in fact, he worked against it), he was therefore denounced by Jesus.

23 And they began to inquire among themselves, which of them it was that should do this thing.

Jesus had said that the hand of His betrayer was on the table. The other disciples were also at the same table. At some point their hands too were on the table. Therefore each of the disciples began to question who among them would do such a horrible thing to their leader.

24 And there was also a strife among them, which of them should be accounted the greatest.

What a contrast! First, the disciples are asking themselves who is the lowest, the traitor, the one who would betray the Son of God. Now they are trying to determine who among them is the greatest.

25 And he said unto them, The kings of the Gentiles exercise lordship over them; and they that exercise authority upon them are called benefactors. 26 But ye shall not be so: but he that is greatest among you, let him be as the younger; and he that is chief, as he that doth serve.

Jesus is telling the disciples that their concern should be not on their greatness among others but on their service to others.

27 For whether is greater, he that sitteth at meat, or he that serveth? is not he that sitteth at meat? but I am among you as he that serveth.

The disciples were focusing on themselves, but Jesus was demonstrating to them how the greatest is the one who serves. Truly Jesus Christ is the Servant King.

28 Ye are they which have continued with me in my temptations.

In this verse we hear Jesus expressing His appreciation to His disciples for their continued loyalty and devotion to Him even in times of great opposition and danger. Faith can only be measured in times of trial, and the disciples had been tried, tested, and found true and loyal to their leader.

29 And I appoint unto you a kingdom, as my Father hath appointed unto me;

As Jesus was true and loyal to His Father, and rewarded for His loyalty, so too the disciples would be rewarded for their loyalty to Jesus. Jesus was bestowing unto them a kingdom.

30 That ye may eat and drink at my table in my kingdom, and sit on thrones judging the twelve tribes of Israel.

What an honor! The disciples hear from Jesus Himself that they would eat and drink at His table in His kingdom. Furthermore, they will sit on thrones and judge the twelve tribes of Israel.

Our Lord is true to His promises, and very generous when He rewards, and He promises eternal rewards to all who serve Him.

DAILY BIBLE READINGS

M: The Plot to Kill Jesus
Luke 22:1-6

T: The Preparation of the Passover
Luke 22:7-13

W: The Feast of Unleavened Bread
Exodus 12:14-20

T: The Institution of the Lord's Supper
Luke 22:14-23

F: Jesus Foretells His Betrayer
John 13:18-30

S: The Dispute About Greatness
Luke 22:24-30

S: The Request of James and John
Mark 10:35-45

TEACHING TIPS

February 18
Bible Study Guide 12

1. Words You Should Know

A. Raiment (v. 34)—clothing.

B. Superscription (v. 38)—a sign which was posted above the criminal's head on the cross.

C. Malefactors (v. 39)—criminals.

2. Teacher Preparation

Find a newspaper or magazine article, or write down the details of a story which tells of a sacrifice one person made on behalf of another person or organization. Share the story with the class. Allow members to share other acts of sacrificial giving.

3. Starting the Lesson

A. Using a chalkboard or a large sheet of paper, write the word SACRIFICE. Ask class members to think of the most painful sacrifice they have ever made on behalf of someone else. Enlist volunteers to share their experience. Remind them that no matter what sacrifices we make, it will never compare to Jesus' sacrifice on the cross.

B. Read today's IN FOCUS story about Chester coping with his father's impending death. Coping with the death of a loved one is painful enough. However, when the person we love has not accepted Jesus as Lord and Saviour, we do not have the assurance of seeing them again in eternity.

4. Getting Into the Lesson

As you discuss today's lesson, think about the fact that Jesus was still concerned with others, even as He hung on the Cross, suffering excruciating pain and humiliation. He offered the promise of life in paradise to the thief who asked. Point out that Jesus is always willing and ready to receive us, no matter what our need, if we but ask Him.

5. Relating the Lesson to Life

A. Review the concepts described in today's THE PEOPLE, PLACES, AND TIMES article. Discuss the particulars of crucifixion as a form of capital punishment. If you have other resources

available to you about the origin the practice of crucifixion, bring it to the class. Think of how Jesus endured this heinous act, knowing that He was the Son of God.

B. Today's DISCUSS THE MEANING questions deal with the dynamics associated with the Crucifixion. Pay particular attention to the question dealing with the criminal's concern. Talk about how some people are overly concerned with this life while others may be overly concerned with the afterlife. Stress the importance of balance, securing our heavenly goal, yet taking care of pertinent matters on this earth.

C. The LESSON IN OUR SOCIETY focuses on our willingness to endure the trials and sufferings of this life in faith. Ask a member to share a difficult time he or she had that required absolute faith in God to bring resolution.

6. Arousing Action

Ask members to name some people whom they feel have truly suffered for the sake of the kingdom. What was the outcome of their suffering? Remind class members that many people endure suffering, and some may blame God, or godliness, for their self-induced suffering. Help members understand that suffering for the sake of the kingdom is redemptive in its outcome.

WORSHIP GUIDE

For the Superintendent or Teacher
Theme: One Who Serves
Theme Song: The Old Rugged Cross
Scripture: Luke 23:50-56
Song: Take My Life and Let It Be
Meditation: I submit myself to the will of my God, trusting in Him to strengthen me through times of trial and tribulation.

DYING ON A CROSS

Bible Background • LUKE 23:13-49
Printed Text • LUKE 23:33-49
Devotional Reading • LUKE 23:50-56

LESSON AIM

After studying today's lesson, members will study the events which took place as Jesus hung on the cross to die. Members will also recognize ways that they may fulfill the mission God has for them, just as Jesus did.

KEEP IN MIND

"And when Jesus had cried with a loud voice, he said, Father, into thy hands I commend my spirit: and having said thus, he gave up the ghost" (Luke 23:46).

FOCAL VERSES

Luke 23:33 And when they were come to the place, which is called Calvary, there they crucified him, and the malefactors, one on the right hand, and the other on the left.

34 Then said Jesus, Father, forgive them; for they know not what they do. And they parted his raiment, and cast lots.

35 And the people stood beholding. And the rulers also with them derided him, saying, He saved others; let him save himself, if he be Christ, the chosen of God.

36 And the soldiers also mocked him, coming to him, and offering him vinegar,

37 And saying, If thou be the king of the Jews, save thyself.

38 And a superscription also was written over him in letters of Greek, and Latin, and Hebrew, THIS IS THE KING OF THE JEWS.

39 And one of the malefactors which were hanged railed on him, saying, If thou be Christ, save thyself and us.

40 But the other answering rebuked him, saying, Dost not thou fear God, seeing thou art in the same condemnation?

41 And we indeed justly; for we receive the due reward of our deeds: but this man hath done nothing amiss.

42 And he said unto Jesus, Lord, remember me when thou comest into thy kingdom.

43 And Jesus said unto him, Verily I say unto thee, Today shalt thou be with me in paradise.

44 And it was about the sixth hour, and there was a darkness over all the earth until the ninth hour.

45 And the sun was darkened, and the veil of the temple was rent in the midst.

46 And when Jesus had cried with a loud voice, he said, Father, into thy hands I commend my spirit: and having said thus, he gave up the ghost.

47 Now when the centurion saw what was done, he glorified God, saying, Certainly this was a righteous man.

48 And all the people that came together to that sight, beholding the things which were done, smote their breasts, and returned.

49 And all his acquaintance, and the women that followed him from Galilee, stood afar off, beholding these things.

LESSON OVERVIEW

LESSON AIM
KEEP IN MIND
FOCAL VERSES
IN FOCUS
THE PEOPLE, PLACES, AND TIMES
BACKGROUND
AT-A-GLANCE
IN DEPTH
SEARCH THE SCRIPTURES
DISCUSS THE MEANING
LESSON IN OUR SOCIETY
MAKE IT HAPPEN
FOLLOW THE SPIRIT
REMEMBER YOUR THOUGHTS
MORE LIGHT ON THE TEXT
DAILY BIBLE READINGS

FEB 18TH

IN FOCUS

Chester had sat in the chair of his father's hospital room so many times that he knew how many stripes were on the wallpaper! A couple of days ago, the doctor had told him and his wife, Shirley, that his father would not live very much longer. There was a time when that news would have been even more frightening to them than it was at the moment they heard it.

Just five years ago, Chester's dad had given his life to Jesus and confessed Him as Lord and Saviour. Even though the man he'd called "Pop" was lying in a hospital bed near death, Chester had a tremendous sense of peace.

Just then, Chester's concentration was broken by a soft touch on his shoulder. Shirley had quietly entered the room and laid her hand on his shoulder. She smiled as he looked up at her.

"You know, Baby," he said to her. "I'm not worried about Pop anymore. I'm gonna miss him, but I feel better knowing that I'll see him again in heaven one day. There was a time when I never thought I'd be able to say that."

THE PEOPLE, PLACES, AND TIMES

Crucifixion. The most painful and dehumanizing form of capital punishment in the ancient world. Initially, the cross was a pointed wooden stake used to build a wall or to erect some type of fortification around a town.

The Assyrians and the Persians began to use the stakes to display the head of captured enemies or those of particularly heinous criminals. Later, crucifixion became a form of capital punishment. Enemies of the state were impaled on the stake itself.

At first, the Greeks and Romans reserved such punishment for slaves, believing it was too barbaric for freeborn persons or citizens. Eventually, the Romans used crucifixion as a crime deterrent. By the time of Jesus' execution, crucifixion was a common occurrence.

Crucifixion was a gruesome process. During Jesus' time, the person to be crucified was first scourged, or beaten with a whip made of pieces of metal or bone attached to the end. Some were simply flogged until blood was drawn. This was done primarily to hasten death, not to be cruel. After the beating, the condemned was forced to carry his crossbeam to the execution site in order to signal to him that his life was already over and

to lessen his will to live.

At the crucifixion site, the criminal was nailed or tied to the crossbeam (nails were used when a hasty death was desired). The nails were driven in the victim's wrist rather than the palm as the smaller bones in the hand could not support the weight of the body. The body and crossbeam were then affixed to an upright pole. Pins, or a small wooden block, was placed halfway up to provide a seat for the body so that the nails would not tear open the wounds (or the ropes would not force the arms from their sockets).

The final step involved nailing, or tying, the feet to the post. Death generally occurred due to a the loss of blood and coronary failure. Many victims, especially those who were tied, could endure days of excruciating pain. Executions were done in public places where the body was allowed to rot for days and where scavengers would eat the corpse's flesh.

Based on information from Holman Bible Dictionary, Trent Butler, general editor, Nashville: Broadman & Holman Publishers, 1991, pp. 319-320.

BACKGROUND

Although Jesus' fate occurred according to prophecy, it seemed as though a chaotic series of events was unfolding. Jesus had endured a hasty arrest, trial, and sentencing. He was condemned to die. All of His disciples had abandoned Him. Just as He had foretold, Judas betrayed Him and Peter denied Him.

The crowds that shouted and cheered His praises just a few days earlier now shouted words of condemnation. It seemed that no one was willing to stand up for Him. The soldiers mocked Him and beat Him. Pilate was more concerned about the political consequences of his decision than he was about administering justice.

History has judged Pontius Pilate harshly, but

AT-A-GLANCE

1. Jesus' Execution (Luke 23:33-38)
2. A Thief Repents? (vv. 39-43)
3. Death on the Cross (vv. 44-49)

he was, in actuality, a reluctant participant in this gross miscarriage of justice. Pilate even tried to offer a way out so that Jesus could be released from His sentence. But instead the people chose Barabbas, a man guilty of the very same crime for which Jesus had been wrongly convicted.

IN DEPTH

1. Jesus' Execution (Luke 23:33-38)

Jesus was accompanied to the execution grounds by two malefactors, one hung to His right and the other on the left. The Son of God hung on the cross between two criminals who had been sentenced to death.

In the midst of this traumatic experience, Jesus prayed for those who were against them saying, "Father, forgive them; for they know not what they do." Even as He prayed for them, their desire to humiliate Him knew no bounds. The soldiers tore his robe and cast lots over it.

At Jesus' feet, the soldiers gambled over His clothing, and the people stood by watching as the rulers derided Him. Perhaps those who scoffed at Him were being used as instruments of Satan to torment Him. Knowing that He had all power, He would not come down from the cross. Their limited thinking would not allow them to understand why Jesus chose to remain nailed to that cross. In their human thinking, one who had the power to alleviate His suffering would use it. Since Jesus was still suffering, in their minds, He had no power.

Still their words must have cut deep as Jesus willingly remained nailed to the cross: "He saved others; let him save himself." Their words were mocking, for they probably did not believe He was able to do it. They jeered, "If he be Christ, the chosen of God, He could save Himself from death on the cross." The chosen of God would certainly possess such power. Surely God Himself would not allow His chosen to suffer in such a way.

Their understanding of God was based upon their own understanding. They could not understand the idea that God would send His Son into the world to suffer and die. Nor could they comprehend the Son of God willingly choosing to suffer. In their minds, the fact that He would not come down from the cross was sufficient proof that Jesus of Nazareth was not the Messiah promised of God.

The cynicism of the crowd only grew stronger and bolder. The soldiers also began to participate in the humiliating free-for-all. As Jesus hung on the cross, He lost bodily fluids. He was thirsty. The soldiers offered Him vinegar and mocked Him by saying, "If thou be the king of the Jews, save thyself."

Above each condemned man's cross hung a description of the nature of his crime. The accusation was written on a placard and either affixed to the cross or hung around the condemned man's neck. Jesus' superscription was written above His cross in Greek, Latin, and Hebrew, "THIS IS THE KING OF THE JEWS." This was done so that all would know the nature of the victim's crime. Jesus was convicted of sedition, or being a rebel against Rome. Ironically, He was killed for being exactly who He is!

2. A Thief Repents (vv. 39-43)

The account of the exchange with the thief is only recorded in Luke. While Mark states that the men who were crucified with Jesus were against Him (Mark 15:32b), Luke describes how one of the men perceived Jesus' identity.

The first malefactor who spoke to Jesus could not understand why He did not save Himself and them. If a person had been condemned to crucifixion, surely the best person to be crucified with was the One who had the power of God. The first thief was not interested in worshiping Jesus, nor was he interested in salvation. All he wanted was to be rescued from death on the cross!

The second malefactor was more reverent. He rebuked the other thief saying, "Dost not thou fear God?" He further explained to the first malefactor that they were rightly being punished for their misdeeds. Jesus, however, had done nothing wrong.

The penitent malefactor then turned to Jesus and asked, "Lord, remember me when thou comest into thy kingdom." Perhaps the man did not fully understand the nature of what he asked; perhaps he did. Yet he keenly discerned that Jesus held more power than was apparent at Golgotha.

The thief knew that the man hanging beside him was different. He had something to offer beyond what was to be had in this world. Whatever Jesus was able to offer, the man wanted it for himself.

Jesus was ready to receive the man upon his request. As the two hung dying, Jesus promised, "Today shalt thou be with me in paradise." The first thief was concerned only with this life. He wanted Jesus to save him to resume life on earth. The second thief also desired the salvation that he knew only the Messiah would offer. Yet the salvation he desired was for eternity. The first thief tried to dictate to Jesus the type of salvation he should have. By contrast, the second thief placed himself in Jesus' hands, accepting that whatever He had to offer was sufficient.

Jesus' assurance to the man was not to be redeemed at a future time. His promise was to be fulfilled immediately. That very day, Jesus promised, "shalt thou be with me in paradise." The penitent thief received far more from the Messiah than what he requested!

3. Death on the Cross (vv. 44-49)

As His time of death drew near, certain unnatural disturbances occurred. Luke records two significant signs. First, there was a darkness all over the earth. At around noon, the entire earth became dark. The period of darkness lasted for three hours until the ninth hour. This period of darkness emphasized the significance of Jesus' death. Since Passover falls on the full moon, an eclipse of the sun was not possible.

Second, the veil of the temple was rent. The curtain which was torn apart separated the Holy of Holies from the rest of the sanctuary. Only the high priest was able to enter the Holy of Holies, and he was allowed to do so only once a year. At that time, the high priest would enter the presence of God to offer a substitionary sacrifice for the sins of the people. The opening of the curtain at His death signaled that, through Christ, all believers have direct access to God. The torn curtain may also be interpreted as a sign of judgment against the temple, which was destroyed in A.D. 70.

Having done all that He was sent here to do, Jesus spoke a prayer of faithfulness and trust,

"Father into thy hands I commend my spirit." The task was done. Having spoken those words, Jesus gave up the ghost. Unlike Mark (15:34), Luke omits Jesus' cry of despair taken from Psalm 22:1. As Luke records the death of Christ, He did not falter in His confidence that His Father was with Him. Jesus willingly gave up His life. He did not surrender to death out of defeat. He surrendered to death out of victory.

Death, however, came quickly to Jesus. It was not unusual for men to hang on the cross for days as death slowly crept in.

Upon his death, a centurion received a revelation and glorified God. The Roman officer knew that Jesus was a righteous man. At the centurion's statement, all of the Roman officials assigned to Palestine who were at the crucifixion site that day agreed that an innocent man had been executed. All those who had once cheered and jeered now smote their breasts and went home.

The Galileans who followed Jesus stood afar off, watching the crucifixion events unfold. The women Luke mentions here are the same women referenced in 8:2, 23:55 and 24:10. By mentioning them here, Luke established them as witnesses to Jesus death, burial, and resurrection. The women had actually seen Him die. They saw Him taken to the tomb. That is how they knew where to go in search of His body after the Sabbath was over.

SEARH THE SCRIPTURES

1. Where did the crucifixion take place? (v. 33)

2. Who was crucified along with Jesus? (v. 33)

3. What did Jesus pray for those around Him? (v. 34)

4. What did the people say in an effort to ridicule Jesus? (v. 35)

5. How did the Roman soldiers mock Jesus? (vv. 36-37)

6. What did they hang over Jesus' cross to indicate the nature of His crime? (v. 38)

7. What did the first criminal want Jesus to do? (v. 39)

8. How did the second criminal react to the first criminal's request? (vv. 40-41)

9. What did the second criminal ask Jesus and what did Jesus promise him in response? (vv. 42-43)

10. What two things happened to signal the

importance of Jesus' death? (vv. 44-45)

11. What did Jesus say just before He died? (v. 46)

12. What comment did the centurion make concerning Jesus' death? (v. 47)

DISCUSS THE MEANING

1. Why did the very persons who once praised Jesus turn around and taunt Him at His crucifixion?

2. Why do you think the first criminal was only concerned with saving himself from death on the cross while the other was concerned about his destiny after death?

LESSON IN OUR SOCIETY

So often we utter the words "Jesus suffered and died" that they lose their impact. Jesus' willingness to endure and His concern for those around Him even in the midst of His suffering is our model for handling the circumstances of life.

Our faith does not demand that we be crucified, but we are bound to fact unpleasant circumstances in life. How we respond to those circumstances is important. We may choose to respond with anger and self-pity, or we may choose to respond as Christ did, always looking to the Father in faith with unending love for those we encounter.

MAKE IT HAPPEN

Jesus told His disciples that those who would be His followers had to take up their crosses and follow Him. What is your Cross? Jesus willingly accepted His Cross. Have you willingly accepted yours or do you feel as though it was forced upon you? How you perceive your Cross will greatly affect how you carry it.

FOLLOW THE SPIRIT

What God wants me to do:

_____

_____

REMEMBER YOUR THOUGHTS

Special insights you learned:

_____

_____

MORE LIGHT ON THE TEXT
Luke 23:33-49

33 And when they were come to the place, which is called Calvary, there they crucified him, and the malefactors, one on the right hand, and the other on the left.

The name Calvary is from the Latin *Calvaria,* which is taken from the Aramaic word *Golgotha* which means "skull" or "a place of a skull." The Greek equivalent is *Kranion* which is where we get the word cranium. This place received this name probably because of the fact that the hill itself looked like a skull. Here it was that the most honest man who ever lived was punished between two guilty thieves. As it was prophesied, Jesus was numbered with the transgressors.

34 Then said Jesus, Father, forgive them; for they know not what they do. And they parted his raiment, and cast lots.

What a merciful Saviour. Jesus asked the Father to forgive His executioners as He was being crucified. Jesus knew that they did not know the truth concerning who He was and what it was that He was doing. This was also a fulfilment of the prophesy in Psalms 22:18 which says, "They part my garments among them, and cast lots upon my vesture."

35 And the people stood beholding. And the rulers also with them derided him, saying, He saved others; let him save himself, if he be Christ, the chosen of God.

Jesus knew what His purpose was and He was determined to fulfill it regardless of the ridicule and cruelty of others. He was not moved by the position or titles of those who scorned Him. Jesus was determined to obey the Father no matter what anyone else thought, said, or did. We can learn a valuable lesson from this. They wanted Jesus to save Himself, but they did not realize that His refusal to obey them was paving the way for their salvation.

36 And the soldiers also mocked him, coming to him, and offering him vinegar,

This vinegar they offered to Jesus was actually mixed with gall. This was a drugged wine. This is significant because we see our Saviour refusing to take drugs, and we see Him paying the penalty for all drug abusers. This makes it possible for them to receive salvation and deliverance.

37 And saying, If thou be the king of the Jews, save thyself.

They wanted Jesus to prove His kingship and power by saving Himself, but Jesus was proving His kingship and power by not saving Himself. He was submitting Himself to their torture at the cost of His life in order to conquer death, hell, and the grave.

38 And a superscription also was written over him in letters of Greek, and Latin, and Hebrew, THIS IS THE KING OF THE JEWS.

What a shameful sight to see the Creator of the universe being humiliated in such a cruel and painful manner. Yet what a glorious demonstration of the love He has for us, even when we think, speak, and act shamefully.

39 And one of the malefactors which were hanged railed on him, saying, If thou be Christ, save thyself and us.

Jesus was being scornfully urged and tempted to save Himself first by the people, then by the rulers, then by the soldiers and now by one of the thieves. Jesus knew that if He saved Himself we would perish. Therefore, He refused to yield to them so that we would live.

40 But the other answering rebuked him, saying, Dost not thou fear God, seeing thou art in the same condemnation?

There was at least one person present who did not reject Jesus. One of the thieves rebuked the other for a lack of reverence to God and for a lack of remorse for his crime.

41 And we indeed justly; for we receive the due reward of our deeds: but this man hath done nothing amiss.

Now we hear the confession of this second thief. He admits that he was deserving of the punishment that he was receiving. He also realized Jesus had done no wrong and that He was being punished for crimes He did not commit.

42 And he said unto Jesus, Lord, remember me when thou comest into thy kingdom.

Romans 10:9-10 says, "If thou shalt confess with thy mouth the Lord Jesus, and shalt believe in thine heart that God hath raised him from the dead, thou shalt be saved. For with the heart man believeth unto righteousness; and with the mouth confession is made unto salvation."

In Luke 23:42 we see how salvation worked in the life of this thief. He called Jesus Lord. He believed that Jesus would not go to an eternal grave, but instead He would be going to His kingdom.

43 And Jesus said unto him, Verily I say unto thee, Today shalt thou be with me in paradise.

What peace this must have brought to the heart and mind of this repentant criminal to know that he would immediately go from a cross of torture to paradise with Jesus Himself.

44 And it was about the sixth hour, and there was a darkness over all the earth until the ninth hour.

The sixth hour would be 12:00 noon (the time when the sun was at it's brightest) but on this day the sun was not shining at all. There was darkness all over the earth. Creation itself was a witness to the magnitude of this event.

45 And the sun was darkened, and the veil of the temple was rent in the midst.

Not only was the sun darkened, but the veil of the temple was torn from top to bottom, symbolizing that we now have free access to the throne of God.

46 And when Jesus had cried with a loud voice, he said, Father, into thy hands I commend my spirit: and having said thus, he gave up the ghost.

Jesus left with a shout, and He will return with a shout. In 1Thessolonians 4:16-18 we read, "For the Lord himself shall descend from heaven with a shout, with the voice of the archangel, and with the trump of God: and the dead in Christ shall rise first: Then we which are alive and remain shall be caught up together with them in the clouds, to meet the Lord in the air: and so shall we ever be with the Lord Wherefore comfort one another with these words."

47 Now when the centurion saw what was done, he glorified God, saying, Certainly this was a righteous man.

Even the soldier who was in charge of the crucifixion realized that Jesus was a righteous man. There was so much life in Jesus's death that His righteousness was apparent. Surely the centurion

had never witnessed such a death where even the sun paid respect to the one dying.

48 And all the people that came together to that sight, beholding the things which were done, smote their breasts, and returned.

After witnessing the things that occurred at the Cross, the very people who had shouted "crucify him," and those who mocked and blasphemed Him, and those who beat Him, are now leaving the scene of the crucifixion. They beat themselves in remorse and misery.

49 And all his acquaintance, and the women that followed him from Galilee, stood afar off, beholding these things.

Those who were the closest friends and relatives of Jesus watched these events from a distance. We too often see and hear others denouncing and misrepresenting our Lord. Instead of coming to His defense we keep our mouths shut and keep our distance for fear of how we may be perceived.

DAILY BIBLE READINGS

M: Jesus Before Pilate and Herod
Luke 23:1-12
T: Jesus Sentenced to Death
Luke 23:13-25
W: Pilate Sentences Jesus to Death
Mark 15:6-15
T: The Crucifixion of Jesus
Luke 23:26-38
F: The Two Crucified Criminals
Luke 23:39-43
S: Jesus' Death on the Cross
Luke 23:44-49
S: The Burial of Jesus
Luke 23:50-56

TEACHING TIPS

February 25
Bible Study Guide 13

1. Words You Should Know

A. **The eleven** (v. 33)—the twelve disciples, minus Judas.

B. **Behooved** (v. 46)—necessary.

C. **Tarry** (v. 49)—to remain.

2. Teacher Preparation

Look in a Bible dictionary or commentary to obtain more information about the resurrection of Jesus Christ. Ask a class member to share the feelings he/she experienced concerning the death of a loved one. Ask if they often long to see that person again. Ask them to imagine how the disciples must have felt at the sight of Jesus after they had seen Him die on the Cross.

3. Starting the Lesson

A. Read today's IN FOCUS story about Mildred's experience with Lena and her sister-in-law. Ask members to share memories of things that have happened to them that seemed too good to be true. The disciples had difficulty believing in Jesus' resurrection because they believed it was a physical impossibility, but they also thought Jesus' return was simply too good to be true.

4. Getting Into the Lesson

Have class members consider the combination of both joy and fear that the disciples experienced upon seeing their Teacher. Since they had never fully understood the nature of Jesus' messiahship, they could not understand His bodily resurrection. This was a powerful event to witness. Jesus wanted them to stop at nothing to tell others about it and the hope that the message brings.

5. Relating the Lesson to Life

A. Review the concepts described in today's THE PEOPLE, PLACES, AND TIMES article. Discuss the significance of Emmaus and how it has become a symbol of having an encounter with the Lord. Also, discuss the bodily resurrection of Jesus

Christ. Talk about the significance of Easter as a day of celebration in the Christian community.

B. Give students an opportunity to answer the questions in SEARCH THE SCRIPTURES.

C. Today's DISCUSS THE MEANING questions address how Jesus helped His disciples to understand that His bodily resurrection was real and that all these things were prophesied.

D. The LESSON IN OUR SOCIETY highlights the role of a believer in Jesus Christ. Talk about ways your church witnesses to others and ways that additional witnessing efforts may be a part of the church's ministry.

6. Arousing Action

A. Use this time as an opportunity to allow members to give testimony to the goodness of the Lord. Allow them to praise and exalt the Lord for what He has done in their lives. Allow the Holy Spirit to use the class as an opportunity to help some who may be reticent to witness about His goodness.

B. Look in the New Testament for models of Christian witnessing. Ask each member to choose one Bible personality who will serve as a role model for him/her concerning how believers should witness to others.

WORSHIP GUIDE

For the Superintendent or Teacher
Theme: Witnesses to the Resurrection
Theme Song: He Arose
Scripture: Matthew 28:16-20
Song: I Love to Tell the Story
Meditation: I am a witness to all of the marvelous things Christ has done for me. May I eagerly desire to tell others the Good News about how Jesus has moved in my life and offered me the gift of salvation.

WITNESSES TO THE RESURRECTION

Bible Background • LUKE 24:13-49
Printed Text • LUKE 24:33-49
Devotional Reading • MATTHEW 28:16-20

LESSON AIM

After studying today's lesson, members will discover how the resurrected Lord revealed Himself to His disciples and commissioned them to spread the Good News.

KEEP IN MIND

"And that repentance and remission of sins should be preached in his name among all nations, beginning at Jerusalem. And ye are witnesses of these things" (Luke 24:47-48).

FOCAL VERSES

Luke 24:33 And they rose up the same hour, and returned to Jerusalem, and found the eleven gathered together, and them that were with them,

34 Saying, The Lord is risen indeed, and hath appeared to Simon.

35 And they told what things were done in the way, and how he was known of them in the breaking of bread.

36 And as they thus spake, Jesus himself stood in the midst of them, and saith unto them, Peace be unto you.

37 But they were terrified and affrighted, and supposed that they had seen a spirit.

38 And he said unto them, Why are ye troubled? and why do thoughts arise in your hearts?

39 Behold my hands and my feet, that it is I myself: handle me, and see; for a spirit hath not flesh and bones, as ye see me have.

40 And when he had thus spoken, he showed them his hands and his feet.

LESSON OVERVIEW

LESSON AIM
KEEP IN MIND
FOCAL VERSES
IN FOCUS
THE PEOPLE, PLACES, AND TIMES
BACKGROUND
AT-A-GLANCE
IN DEPTH
SEARCH THE SCRIPTURES
DISCUSS THE MEANING
LESSON IN OUR SOCIETY
MAKE IT HAPPEN
FOLLOW THE SPIRIT
REMEMBER YOUR THOUGHTS
MORE LIGHT ON THE TEXT
DAILY BIBLE READINGS

41 And while they yet believed not for joy, and wondered, he said unto them, Have ye here any meat?

42 And they gave him a piece of a broiled fish, and an honeycomb.

43 And he took it, and did eat before them.

44 And he said unto them, These are the words which I spake unto you, while I was yet with you, that all things must be fulfilled, which were written in the law of Moses, and in the prophets, and in the psalms, concerning me.

45 Then opened he their understanding, that they might understand the scriptures,

46 And said unto them, Thus it is written, and thus it behooved Christ to suffer, and to rise from the dead the third day:

47 And that repentance and remission of sins should be preached in his name among all nations, beginning at Jerusalem.

48 And ye are witnesses of these things.

49 And, behold, I send the promise of my Father upon you: but tarry ye in the city of Jerusalem, until ye be endued with power from on high.

IN FOCUS

Mildred just refused to believe that her favorite gospel singer was the sister-in-law of Lena Andrews. After all, Lena had never said anything about it. Then rumors began to circulate that, not only did Lena have a famous sister-in-law, but that she was coming to visit Lena and her husband very soon.

FEB 25TH

277

Mildred was reluctant to say anything to Lena about it. Lena was a very private person, but with a heart of gold. So Mildred decided not to say anything, but she kept hearing those rumors!

Just a few days after Mildred decided not to push the matter, her telephone rang and Lena was on the other end. "Mildred," Lena said, "Leon and I are having some people over for dinner on Friday night, and we want you and Walter to come if you can."

"Oh, we'd love to!" Mildred exclaimed. "But, if you don't mind," she couldn't resist inquiring. "What's the occasion?"

"Leon's sister is coming to town to conduct some business, and I thought you might like to meet her."

"Who is Leon's sister?" Mildred inquired further. She was both surprised and satisfied when Lena called out the name of the woman whose voice she loved to hear!

THE PEOPLE, PLACES, AND TIMES

Emmaus. The name of a village meaning "hot baths." Emmaus was located about seven miles from Jerusalem. Bible scholars are not certain of the exact location of Emmaus, but as many as four sites have been proposed as the location.

Based on information from Holman Bible Dictionary, Trent Butler, general editor, Nashville: Broadman & Holman Publishers, 1991, p. 417.

Resurrection. The real, bodily appearance of Jesus Christ after He was crucified and buried. The resurrection provided sure and certain hope for believers. The Greek word for resurrection, *anastasis*, literally means "to stand again."

Based on information from Holman Bible Dictionary, Trent Butler, general editor, Nashville: Broadman & Holman Publishers, 1991, p. 1179.

Easter. With the exception of Sunday worship, Easter is the oldest Christian festival. The exact date for the institution of Easter has been debated. The particulars which make up the celebration of Easter were developed over the years.

Since the passion and resurrection of Christ occurred at the time of the Jewish Passover, the first Jewish Christians probably transformed their Passover observation into a celebration of the central events of their new faith.

In the early centuries, the annual Resurrection observance was called the *pascha*, the Greek word for Passover, and focused on Christ as the paschal Lamb.

The celebration of Easter was probably well-established in most churches by A.D. 100. The earliest Easter observance probably consisted of a vigil beginning on Saturday evening, ending on Sunday morning, and included the remembrance of Christ's crucifixion. By the year A.D. 200, the climax of the vigil was the baptism of new Christians and the celebration of the Lord's Supper. By the next century, most churches had begun dividing the original Easter observance, devoting Good Friday to the crucifixion and Sunday to the Resurrection.

Based on information from Holman Bible Dictionary, Trent Butler, general editor, Nashville: Broadman & Holman Publishers, 1991, p. 386.

BACKGROUND

Luke's resurrection account offers two episodes with Jesus encountering His disciples in or near Jerusalem.

First, the women who followed Him had gone to the tomb seeking His body so that they could adequately embalm the body with spices. Instead of a dead body, the women found an empty tomb. After the angels had spoken, the women remembered the words Jesus had told them. Three of the women present are named Mary Magdalene, Mary, mother of James the younger and Joses, and Joanna.

Second, the women went to where the apostles were hiding and told of their remarkable encounter with the angels guarding the entrance

---

AT-A-GLANCE

1. **Emmaus Road Encounter**
   (Luke 24:33-35)
2. **Proof of Jesus' Resurrection**
   (vv. 36-43)
3. **The Scriptures Interpreted**
   (vv. 44-49)

of the tomb. But the men did not believe them. Perhaps they thought the women were so consumed with grief that they imagined the incident in order to comfort themselves. It took a personal appearance from Jesus to convince them that the resurrection was indeed true.

IN DEPTH

1. Emmaus Road Encounter (Luke 24:33-35)

All that consumed the disciples, and probably everyone else in Jerusalem in the days following Jesus' crucifixion, was the event itself and probably how it would impact all of them. Two of His followers, Cleopas and another disciple, were walking on the road to Emmaus; they were discussing the series of events. They were caught up in their conversation when a stranger came up to them and asked what they were talking about (their eyes were blocked from recognizing Jesus). The men were surprised that the stranger didn't know what was going on, as it was the talk of Jerusalem.

As they walked along the road, the two men must have felt a sense of kinship with the man who walked along with them. They invited Him to stay with them. The man ate with them. When He took the bread and blessed and broke it, they recognized Him as Jesus. At that moment He disappeared.

The men had apparently planned on spending the night in Emmaus. After their eyes were opened to what they had just witnessed, they received a burst of energy. Instead of remaining there, they returned to Jerusalem, having realized they were in the presence of the resurrected Lord. They went to where the eleven were gathered, along with a few others. When they arrived, they told those present that the women's story was true. The Lord is risen indeed!

Their story corroborated what Peter and the women had already revealed. It was probably becoming more and more real to them. Their Teacher had come back to life! They were probably frightened, confused, and excited all at the same time.

2. Proof of Jesus' Resurrection (vv. 36-43)

Just as those who gathered were comparing notes and going over all of the events, Jesus Himself stood in the midst of them. Now there was no more room for doubt. All those gathered in the room were witnesses to the resurrected Christ. It really was Him! The women had not made up a tale to comfort themselves. The two disciples had not been suffering from exhaustion or hallucinations on the road to Emmaus. Peter had not imagined that the stone was rolled away from the tomb and that there was no body.

Luke used this passage to acknowledge the fact that the same person who stood before those gathered in that room was the same person who had suffered and died on the cross just three days earlier. The figure before them was, indeed, Jesus of Nazareth.

Terrified and affrighted by the presence of the being, the disciples thought that the figure was an apparition. After Jesus' death, some Gnostic dogma circulated which denied any relationship between Christ, who is pure spirit, and the flesh, which is basically evil. The appearance of Jesus here points out the Gnostic thinking as being in error.

But the disciples were afraid. Sensing their disposition, Jesus asked, "Why are ye troubled? and why do thoughts arise in your hearts?" He did not want His followers to be afraid out of superstition or ignorance. In their defense, however, they thought He was dead. Therefore, seeing Him appear before them was frightening. The disciples also may have been frightened because the prospect of their Teacher being back among them was just too good to be true.

Not only that, they were vindicated in their belief. Everyone in and around Jerusalem had seen Him hanging on the cross until death came to Him. Both the Roman and the Jewish officials had shunned Him. Most people would have nothing to do with Him. As far as they were concerned, Jesus of Nazareth was just another pretender who gathered the confidence of those who believed in Him and followed Him. Jesus had died on the cross at Calvary just like any other man would have died.

The Jewish officials must have wondered what kind of Messiah did He claim to be? He hadn't fought against His jailers or His accusers. He did not use His power to free Himself from the cross.

He just died out there like anybody else who had been crucified.

But His presence among them now changed all of that! It could now be proven that death could not hold Him in the grave. He was alive again—resurrected from the dead.

As always, Jesus handled His followers with gentleness and love. He calmly helped them to understand that there was no need for fear. He invited them to look at His hands and His feet so that they could know for certain that it was indeed Him. He reminded them that a spirit does not have flesh and bones as He did.

Jesus showed them His hands and His feet. Still they did not believe that He was real, that He was not a spirit. After all, He had been dead for three days. There were people present who had actually watched Him die. Their thinking was so limited that they assumed God's power to be limited as well.

To further convince them that He was more than spirit, Jesus asked for something to eat. Of course, a spirit has no need for food. Therefore, by asking for something to eat, Jesus helped them to understand that He was more than spirit. This passage also may have been included by Luke in order to further counter claims from the Gnostics that Jesus was never a real human being, only a spirit. Jesus took the fish and did eat before them. Something as simple as eating a piece of fish served as confirmation that what seemed impossible had actually taken place.

3. The Scriptures Interpreted (vv. 44-49)

While He was with them before, Jesus had explained the Scriptures to His disciples, but they did not understand. He then set about to give them the proper perspective for understanding Scripture. Jesus told the disciples that all the things "which were written in the law of Moses, and in the prophets, and in the psalms, concerning me."

At that point, Jesus opened their understanding, so they could understand the Scriptures. Jesus explained to the eleven apostles how the entire Old Testament related to Him, to His life, and His purpose. Everything that had been prophesied about Jesus had been fulfilled. Prophecy had

revealed that the Christ would suffer and rise from the dead on the third day. Not only did the Scriptures prophesy the death and resurrection of the Messiah, but the Scriptures decreed that the redemptive message is to be offered to all nations. The repentance and remission of sins should be preached in the name of the Messiah and the starting place was Jerusalem.

Because of their presence there with Jesus, the disciples were made witnesses to the fact that messianic prophecy had been fulfilled in Jesus Christ. They were to go out among others and tell others of the marvelous things they had witnessed. They were to spread the Good News throughout Jerusalem and beyond.

The faithful ones who had accompanied Jesus from Galilee, watched Him die. Now they were standing in His presence and received a promise through Jesus from the Father. This promise is referenced from Luke 2:28-33 and from Jeremiah (31:31-33). Jesus further instructed them to remain in the city until they had been endued with power from on high.

Jesus has given believers the privilege and the responsibility of spreading the Good News about forgiveness and eternal life to all who will hear. Since Pentecost, all believers have been baptized in the Holy Spirit, giving them the resources and gifts needed for God's purpose.

SEARCH THE SCRIPTURES

1. Where did the two disciples go once they left Emmaus? (v. 33)

2. What did the disciples say to those who were gathered? (v. 34)

3. What did Jesus say to those who were gathered? (v. 36)

4. How did those gathered react to Jesus' appearance? (v. 37)

5. How did Jesus respond to their fear? (vv. 38-39)

6. What did Jesus do to help them know His resurrection was real? (v. 40)

7. What did the disciples give Jesus to eat? (v. 42)

8. What prophecies did Jesus speak about? (v. 44)

9. What did the prophecies reveal about the

mission and purpose of the Christ? (vv. 46-48)

10. How long were the disciples to wait in Jerusalem? (v. 49)

DISCUSS THE MEANING

1. Why did Jesus choose that particular time to reveal Himself to His followers?

2. How did eating food serve to convince the disciples that Jesus resurrection was a bodily resurrection, not just a spiritual representation?

3. What testimony about Jesus could those present give to nonbelievers?

4. What is the significance of Jerusalem being the starting place for spreading the Good News?

LESSON IN OUR SOCIETY

Jesus told His followers to tell what they had witnessed so that it would encourage others. Believers today are still called upon to be witnesses. We did not witness His death and resurrection, but we are witnesses to His love, His power, and His saving grace.

Very often Christians are confused about what it means to spread the Good News. Simply put, spreading the Good News means telling others what He has done for you. But many people remain silent because they are afraid to reveal the details of their deliverance.

There are many believers whose powerful testimonies could serve as encouragement to those who do not know Christ. Sadly, fellow Christians often make it difficult for others to be honest about their past and the things they did before having an encounter with Christ. Jesus specifically taught that no one has the right or the authority to judge another. If our attitudes about the former transgressions of others were less judgmental, there would probably be many more people willing to give testimony to "how I got over."

MAKE IT HAPPEN

Have you thought about what you might say if a nonbeliever approached you and asked, "What has Jesus done for you? Why do you serve Him?"

Use a pencil and a sheet of paper to write down a brief testimony that you would give to help someone know why you chose to accept Jesus Christ as your Lord and Saviour.

FOLLOW THE SPIRIT

What God wants me to do:

_____

_____

_____

REMEMBER YOUR THOUGHTS

Special insights you learned:

_____

_____

MORE LIGHT ON THE TEXT

Luke 24:33-49

24:33 And they rose up the same hour, and returned to Jerusalem, and found the eleven gathered together, and them that were with them,

As soon as the two who walked and talked with the stranger on the Emmaus road realized that the stranger was Jesus Himself they immediately went to Jerusalem to inform the other disciples. How excited they must have been having seen for themselves the risen Saviour.

34 Saying, The Lord is risen indeed, and hath appeared to Simon.

When they found the nine disciples, the two disciples shared the Good News that the Lord Jesus has risen in deed. To verify their story they also informed them that He had appeared to Peter as well.

35 And they told what things were done in the way, and how he was known of them in the breaking of bread.

They shared with the other disciples all the things which happened as they walked and talked with Jesus, and how they recognized Him by the way He broke the bread. There must have been a great deal of meaning and emotion in the heart and mind of Jesus as He broke the bread. I think it is safe to believe that He remembered how His body had been broken as He broke the bread, and how a victorious healing was made available to all who believed and received Him as Lord and Saviour.

36 And as they thus spake, Jesus himself stood in the midst of them, and saith unto them, Peace

a state of shock and unbelief.

39 Behold my hands and my feet, that it is I myself: handle me, and see; for a spirit hath not flesh and bones, as ye see me have.

Jesus tried to calm them down. He wanted to assure them that He was not a ghost, and He sets out to prove to them that He has risen. He invites them to examine Him. He showed them His nail scarred hands; He showed them His wounded feet. He even allows them to handle his flesh and feel His bones.

40 And when he had thus spoken, he showed them his hands and his feet.

Still they did not believe. How often Jesus reveals Himself to us in ways that we should understand, yet we remain in unbelief.

41 And while they yet believed not for joy, and wondered, he said unto them, Have ye here any meat?

The disciples thought this was too good to be true, they were overwhelmed. Our Lord always gives confirmation to His word and to His will. The disciples still did not believe that He had risen. Jesus continued to provide them with proof. He asked them for food because a spirit can not digest food. Jesus was determined to gain the belief of the disciples that He was risen.

42 And they gave him a piece of a broiled fish, and an honeycomb. 43 And he took it, and did eat before them.

The disciples wanted to be absolutely sure that this was Jesus. Therefore they continued to test Him to see if it was truly Him. They gave Him a piece of fish and a honeycomb. Jesus ate the food in front of them. The fact that Jesus was able to eat physical food was proof that His physical body had returned to life.

44 And he said unto them, These are the words

be unto you.

While they were in the process of testifying, Jesus appeared in the midst of them. This must have really brought joy and fear to them. Suddenly out of nowhere there Jesus was standing in their midst. Realizing that this was almost too much for them to bear, Jesus spoke to them, "Peace be unto you."

37 But they were terrified and affrighted, and supposed that they had seen a spirit.

How would you have responded? Imagine having watched the awful events surrounding the crucifixion, witnessing Jesus's death and burial, seeing His body bruised, beaten beyond recognition. All of a sudden there He is standing in front of you in His glorified body. How would you have responded? What would you have thought?

38 And he said unto them, Why are ye troubled? and why do thoughts arise in your hearts?

The disciples thought that they had seen a ghost. Their minds, emotions, and nerves were in which I spake unto you, while I was yet with you, that all things must be fulfilled, which were written in the law of Moses, and in the prophets, and in the psalms, concerning me.

The law of Moses, the prophets, and the Psalms contained many lessons that Jesus taught His disciples during His earthly ministry. Jesus was now reminding the disciples of those lessons and reinforcing the fact that He was the fulfillment of them. Indeed, they were witnessing many of them with their own eyes.

45 Then opened he their understanding, that they might understand the scriptures,

How refreshing it is when our Lord gives revelation and illumination to His Word that we might understand the Scriptures. It is through asking that we receive; it is through seeking that we find , and it is through knocking that the doors of understanding are opened to us.

46 And said unto them, Thus it is written, and thus it behoved Christ to suffer, and to rise from the dead the third day:

Again the Lord Jesus confirms His Word by quoting what the Scriptures have already said. It is vitally important that we know and understand the Scriptures in order to know what the Lord is doing in this season. We, too, are His disciples and we are to carry on the work of His ministry as He gives instruction.

47 And that repentance and remission of sins should be preached in his name among all nations, beginning at Jerusalem.

Here Jesus reminds His disciples of their mission to preach repentance and remission of sins in His name among all nations, beginning at Jerusalem. In other words we are to be witnesses first at home and then we are to be witnesses away from home to people of all nationalities. Too often we are only concerned about those who think like us, look like us, and those who talk just like us. Yet we have been commanded and commissioned to go into even hostile areas as the Holy Spirit leads us and share the Gospel to this dying world.

48 And ye are witnesses of these things.

Jesus proves to the disciples that they have witnessed things that were foretold in Scripture. This should give the disciples the courage to continue doing the work of the Lord under any circumstances. We, too, are witnessing many things in our lifetime that were prophesied in the Holy Scriptures concerning the end times and should be encouraged to continue to do the work of the ministry as the Holy Spirit leads us.

49 And, behold, I send the promise of my Father upon you: but tarry ye in the city of Jerusalem, until ye be endued with power from on high.

The disciples were commanded to wait for the Holy Spirit before they went anywhere or did anything. Nothing can be done for the Lord without the aid of the Holy Spirit. Jesus, as always, has been true to His promise, for He has sent the promise of the Father from on high. We are to go forth in the power of the Holy Spirit. Nothing is impossible for us because the Holy Spirit is God, and He is available to us all. Hallelujah!

DAILY BIBLE READINGS

M: The Sign of Jonah
Matthew 12:38-42
T: The Resurrection of Jesus
Mark 16:1-8
W: The Walk to Emmaus
Luke 24:13-27
T: Recognizing Jesus and Testifying of Him
Luke 24:28-35
F: Jesus Appears to His Disciples
Luke 24:36-49
S: Reassurance
John 20:19-23
S: The Commissioning of the Disciples
Matthew 28:16-20

INTRODUCTION TO MARCH 2001 QUARTER

The Acts of the Apostles describes the dynamic and life-transforming spread of the Gospel that resulted in the growth of the church during the first century. Acts recounts the power of the Holy Spirit in the lives of the followers of the risen Christ, many of whom were persecuted for their faith. This quarter focuses on the beginnings of the church in Jerusalem, the church's witness in Judea and Samaria, and early efforts to spread the Gospel in the Greco-Roman world.

The Quarter at-a-Glance

CONTINUING JESUS' WORK

UNIT 1. BEGINNING IN JERUSALEM

Unit 1 deals with the Holy Spirit as God's continuing presence among the followers of Jesus. First came the promise of the Spirit and then, at Pentecost, the powerful manifestation of the Spirit. Through the gift of the Spirit, the apostles were confident and obedient in their witness and ministry.

LESSON 1: March 4
The Promise of the Spirit's Power
Acts 1:3-14

The Biblical text from which this lesson is taken emphasizes the post-resurrection appearances of our Lord Jesus Christ. Jesus appeared to and taught the apostles many times in the 40 days following His death. (v. 3) Jesus ordered the apostles to wait in Jerusalem for the "promise of the Father" and baptism of the Holy Spirit. (vv. 4-5) In response to the apostles' question about the coming of the Kingdom, Jesus told the apostles that the Holy Spirit would empower them to witness to the world. (vv. 6-8) After Jesus ascended, angels told the apostles that He would return the same way. (9-11) The apostles returned to Jerusalem, where they, certain women, and Jesus' brothers devoted themselves to prayer. (vv. 12-14)

The concern of the lesson is meant to help us understand that desirable outcomes may require waiting. The lesson deals with the difficulty we have waiting for future events to unfold. The lesson addresses our questions about spiritual power and its uses; they are answered by Jesus' action as He encounters His followers after the resurrection. By studying the life of our Lord, we are taught not to lose sight of the objectives of Jesus' life on earth.

LESSON 2: March 11
The Holy Spirit Comes in Power
Acts 2:1-4, 37-47

The Biblical content of this lesson deals with the reception of power. In the text we read that the believers were gathered together on the Day of Pentecost when suddenly there came a noise like a strong wind. (vv. 1-2) We read that tongues of fire touched each person, and they were filled with the Holy Spirit and began talking in many languages. (vv. 3-4) Here we see Peter, who a short while ago had been paralyzed with fear, exhort the people to repent and be baptized in the name of Jesus Christ for the forgiveness of sin. (vv. 37-40) Through the power of the Holy Spirit 3000 people responded and were baptized and spent time with the apostles—learning, breaking bread, and praying. (vv. 41-42) As we continue in the text, we notice that all who believed devoted their time, efforts, and possessions to meeting people's needs. (vv. 43-45) As the believers met daily to fellowship, worship, and praise God, they had the goodwill of the people; and others continued to be added to their number. (vv. 46-47)

Many of life's concerns are intrinsically connected with the power to live fully. One of the ways we can receive the power to live fully is to have had profound religious experiences. The Holy Spirit empowers us as we seek spiritual insight and growth. Because many of us are attracted to exhibitions of spiritual phenomena, the presence and power of the Holy Spirit becomes a way to effectively witness. This lesson teaches us that we can have power to overcome our guilt. It teaches us that we can undo the stranglehold of past actions upon us and move forward in the power of the Lord.

LESSON 3: March 18
The Holy Spirit Works With Power
Acts 3:1-10; 4:1-4, 13

The Biblical content of this lesson is taken from a Scriptural text narrating the healing of the lame man at the gate of Beautiful. The text tells us that as Peter and John were going to the Temple for prayer, a man who was lame was being carried in to lie by the gate and beg for alms. (3:1-2) When the man asked Peter for alms, Peter said they had no money but healed the man in the name of Christ. (vv. 3-8) When the people saw the man who had been lame walking and praising God, they were filled with wonder and amazement. (vv. 9-10) As a result of this miracle and the message highlighting Jesus as the source of the healing, Peter and John were arrested in the Temple for teaching that in Jesus there is the resurrection of the dead. (4:1-3) Following this miracle about 5,000 people who heard Peter and John teaching believed the Word. (v. 4) The authorities, amazed by the boldness of such ordinary men as Peter and John, recognized them as companions of Jesus. (v. 13)

The Christian life is a life of service. There are various ways in which one can provide service: physically, spiritually, and emotionally. This lesson tells us that we ought to be involved in meeting the needs of others. The text calls us, as the church, to offer hope and services to the poor, infirmed, and marginalized members of society. The text teaches us that the greatest thing we have to offer is not material, but the spiritual principle embodied in the name of Jesus. We must care for others who are unable to do so because of their circumstances. This is the call of Jesus upon the life of the believer. Our active empowerment of the weak may bring us trouble, but we must follow the example of these apostles; who in spite of the consequences to them, stopped to care about someone else.

LESSON 4: March 25
Obedient to the Spirit
Acts 5:27-32, 33-36, 38-42

Within the text for this lesson, we study how the religious authorities told the apostles not to teach in Jesus' name because they had filled Jerusalem with their teaching. (vv. 27-28) To this injunction Peter and the others say they would obey God rather than human authority. (v. 29) Peter testified before the authorities about how God had raised Jesus from the dead and exalted Him as Saviour. (vv. 30-32) One of the authorities, Gamaliel, advised his colleagues not to take action against the apostles but to wait and see if God was with them. (vv. 33-36, 38-39) Moved by Gamaliel's argument, the authorities had the apostles beaten, commanded them to stop witnessing about Jesus, and let them go. (vv. 39-40) The apostles rejoiced in their suffering on behalf of the Gospel and continued to witness to Christ at every opportunity.

This lesson teaches us that we must be willing to suffer for our beliefs. It calls us to consider questions regarding ultimate authority. Who is the ultimate authoritative reference for our action? We are, through the pages of this lesson, to remain steadfast even in the face of opposition because of our faith in God. For those of us who will be quick to persecute others because they disagree with us, this lesson teaches the importance of caution when decisions are being made. From this lesson we also learn that we are not called merely to have a vested interest maintaining the status quo, but to manifest the transformation of Jesus' message. For those us who wish we had more courage regarding our convictions, this lesson is meant to help us stand for God.

UNIT 2. WITNESSING IN JUDEA AND SAMARIA

Witnessing in Judea and Samaria traces the movement of the church as the Spirit led Christ's disciples to share the gospel beyond Jerusalem. Additional leadership was chosen and empowered. Believers such as Philip began to touch the lives of non-Jews. The Easter session highlights the witness of women who followed Jesus and the beginning of Paul's far-reaching ministry. Finally, Peter learned that Gentiles were to hear the Good News and receive the Spirit.

LESSON 5: April 1
Empowered to Serve
Acts 6:1-8; 7:55-8:1

The text for this lesson deals with the issue of service. We note within the text that as the numbers of believers increased, the Greeks complained that their widows were being neglected. (6:1) To solve the problem, the twelve asked the believers to choose seven men to distribute food so the apostles would be free to continue praying and preaching. (vv. 2-4) The believers chose seven men, including Stephen and Philip, who were full of faith and of the Holy Spirit to distribute food to the widows. (vv. 5-6) As the word of God continued to spread, the number of disciples, including priests, increased greatly. (v. 7) The passage selects Stephen from among the group for special comment. We read that Stephen did great wonders and signs, which led the leaders to bring him before the council where he was accused and convicted of blasphemy. (6:8; 7:55-57) The people dragged Stephen outside the city and stoned him to death, and Saul approved. (7:58-8:1)

The basic content for today's lesson is "Called to Serve and Forgive." One of life's concern is how to respond when people betray you. This lesson not only teaches us the value of community and fellowship, but it also shows us that we can be discriminated against because of our racial or cultural differences. The lesson points out the difficulty many of us have in sharing in the success and good fortune of others. We do not know if the fact that Stephen was a Hellenistic Jew led to his death, but we do know that hatred was the cause. As Christians, we ought to believe that the continuing presence of hate groups within our society does not serve the purpose of the gospel. Like Stephen, we must be willing to serve at the point of reconciliation. Men and women of good will must take a stand for truth, fairness, and justice. The lesson leads us to forgive those who deliberately hurt us, even when it seems difficult.

LESSON 6: April 8
Witnessing Beyond Jerusalem
Acts 8:4-8, 26-35

The content and emphasis of this lesson shows how because of persecution, many believers fled Jerusalem, preaching Christ where ever they went. (v. 4) We see Philip as he went to Samaria, preaching Christ and demonstrating the power of the Holy Spirit. (vv. 5-8) Having been led to the south by an angel of the Lord, Philip encountered a high-ranking African from Ethiopia, an official who had been to Jerusalem to worship. (vv. 26-27) The Spirit directed Philip to join the Ethiopian, who was reading from the prophet Isaiah. (vv. 28-29) At the Ethiopian's invitation, Philip explained the Scriptural text, telling the man the Good News about Jesus. (30-35)

While it is true that many of us are reluctant to socialize with people outside our group, this lesson teaches us the importance of reaching beyond our immediate group for the sake of the Gospel. We *must* share the Good News.

This sharing may result in our being persecuted for our beliefs, but we cannot falter from our obligation. We must strive to be inclusive in our ministry though sometimes we are more effective with a particular group of people than with others. Hopefully, as you study this lesson, you will seek to understand the social and political persecution of persons for their religious beliefs in other parts of the world and make them a regular part of your daily prayer.

LESSON 7: April 15
Proclaiming the Risen Lord
Luke 24:1-10; Acts 9:19-20, 26-28, 31

The Biblical text for this lesson is taken from the what scholars call the Luke-Act narrative. In the Gospel portion we read of how the women who went to prepare Jesus' body found it missing from the tomb. (24:1-3) We read how they saw two men in dazzling clothes announce that Jesus had risen, and they reminded the women that Jesus had foretold what would happen. (vv. 4-7) The women reported to the disciples what had happened. (vv. 8-10) From Acts the text tells of the experience of Paul, who at that time was still named Saul. We see here that while spending several days with the disciples in Damascus, Saul proclaimed Jesus as the Son of God. (Acts 9:19-20) While the disciples in Jerusalem were afraid of Saul, Barnabas affirmed Saul's conversion and Saul was accepted. (vv. 26-28) During the peaceful period that followed, the churches were built up and increased in numbers. (v. 31)

Today's lesson addresses the difficulty many have believing in something they cannot comprehend. But the truth is that many of us long for a message of hope which cannot be given to us through our natural senses. Yet this lesson shows our concerns about the mysteries surrounding death and the afterlife. This lesson calls us to see that the experience of profound transformations in our lives is possible for us as it was for Saul because Jesus got up. It is the very experience of the resurrection principle that makes us capable of sharing our faith experience with others in a variety of ways. In fact, if we have met Jesus on the resurrection way, we will feel compelled to share our faith experience with others.

LESSON 8: April 22
Gentiles Receive the Spirit
Acts 10:30-39, 44-48

The Biblical content of this lesson is taken from the encounter between Peter an Cornelius. Here Cornelius explained to Peter that he had sent for Peter in response to a vision. (vv. 30-33) After some hesitation Peter declared that God shows no partiality, but accepts all people who revere Him and do what is right. (vv. 34-35) Peter preached the Good News of Christ to the people gathered with Cornelius. (vv. 36-39) While Peter was preaching, the Holy Spirit came upon the people who heard him. (v. 44) The members of the house of Israel who believed in Jesus saw the Gentiles had received the Holy Spirit and were amazed. (vv. 45-46) Peter commanded that the Gentile converts be baptized. (vv. 47-48)

What this lesson teaches us is that we must try not to exclude others from various religious, social, and community groups. The lesson also shows us that it is possible for outsiders to change their minds about basic values and beliefs. It also shows that some believers hold prejudices that are barriers to communication. Here we are called to listen to the voice of the Lord and heed the revelations that God gives.

UNIT 3. SPREADING THE GOSPEL INTO ALL THE WORLD

Unit 3 begins with the development of the church at Antioch and its outreach through Barnabas and Saul. At Antioch of Syria, the mission to Gentiles became international. A conference in Jerusalem found the apostles affirming the work among Gentiles and prescribing guidelines for non-Jewish converts. Roots were established in Macedonia when the Spirit led Paul and his companions to Philippi. Later, facing trial and prison, Paul maintained humility and brotherly concern for the Ephesians.

LESSON 9: April 29
The Church in Antioch
Acts 11:19-30; 13:1-3

The content of this lesson deals with how believers who fled from persecution preached to Jews living outside Judea. (vv.11:19) One of the first places they gathered was Antioch. In Antioch believers from Cyprus and Cyrene preached to Greeks, many of whom believed in the Gospel. (vv. 20-21) When

the news of these Greek believers reached Jerusalem, the church sent Barnabas to Antioch. (v. 22) Barnabas rejoiced to see the gospel spread to the Greeks and enlisted Saul to help him in the work in Antioch, where believers were first called "Christians." (vv. 23-26) Agabus predicted a famine, and the Christians in Antioch sent an offering to the church in Jerusalem. (vv. 27-30) Here Barnabas and Paul were called by the Holy Spirit and sent out by the church in Antioch as missionaries. (13:1-3)

Paul, like most of us when bad things happen, withdrew from contact with others. But it also speaks to our willingness to respond creatively to adversity. Here we also see that future leaders can be influenced by the convictions of others. This lesson also teaches that we can find strength in working cooperatively with others as Paul and Barnabas did. This lesson tells us that we ought to take initiative in sharing our resources with people who have greater needs, especially those who seek to minister the gospel. We are thus empowered through participation in community.

LESSON 10: May 6
Mission to Gentiles
Acts 13:14-15, 42-52

The Biblical content of this lesson focuses on how the synagogue officials in Antioch in Pisdia invited Barnabas and Paul to speak to the sabbath assembly about Jesus. (vv. 14-15) Paul and Barnabas spoke to the Jews and converts to Judaism who followed the two out of the synagogue, urging them to continue in the grace of God. (vv. 42-43) On the next sabbath almost the whole city gathered to hear the word of the Lord. (v. 44) When jealousy caused the unconverted Jews to contradict what Paul said, Paul and Barnabas declared boldly that the Lord had commanded the Jewish people to bring salvation to the ends of the earth. (vv. 45-47) Upon hearing this, many Gentiles became believers and the word of the Lord spread throughout the region, but the unconverted Jews stirred up persecution against Paul and Barnabas and drove them away. (vv. 48-50) Paul and Barnabas left in protest and went to Iconium, where they were filled with joy and with the Holy Spirit.

In this lesson, we learn how to open doors to new ideas without resistance. We are taught that as we are emboldened by the Spirit of God, we can take advantage of opportunities made available to us by our God. One of the reasons for continual resistence to a prophetic call to new ideas is because we become jealous when others come into what we view as our arenas of influence. This combined with the difficulty of handling rejection may make us resistant to doors being opened by God. But this lesson teaches us that we need to hear Good News which comes to us from new voices.

LESSON 11: May 13
The Jerusalem Conference
Acts 15:1-2, 6-15, 19-20

From this passage we learn certain individuals taught that Gentiles must become Jews and be circumcised in order to receive salvation (v. 1) This, of course, caused confusion among the people. Paul, Barnabas, and other believers at Antioch were appointed to confer with the apostles and elders at Jerusalem about the question of circumcision. (v. 2) As a response to this issue, Peter testified at the conference to his experiences in preaching to Gentiles. (vv. 6-11) After Barnabas and Paul told of the signs and wonders that God had done through them among the Gentiles, the leaders reconsidered their previous position.(v. 12) Based on Peter's report and its consistency with prophecies, James announced his decision that circumcision should not be required of Gentile believers before accepting them into the church. (vv. 13-15, 19) James also proposed that Gentile believers should be admonished to keep certain other precepts. (v. 20)

In this lesson we deal with what one must do in order to truly belong to the Church. However, the lesson also calls us to confront issues on which adults within the church disagree. This lesson also teaches us that it is acceptable to consult recognized authorities when seeking an answer to serious disputes.

LESSON 12: May 20
Reaching into Macedonia
Acts 16:9-15, 27-33

The Biblical content of this lesson comes from the story of Paul's call to Macedonia. In obedience to a vision Paul received, he and his companions traveled into Macedonia, stopping first at Philippi. (vv. 9-12) On the Sabbath, Paul and his friends went to a place of prayer by the river and spoke to a group of women. (v. 13) Lydia, one of the women at the place of prayer, listened eagerly to Paul, received baptism along with her household, and welcomed the missionaries into her home. (vv.14-15) While imprisoned at Philippi, Paul and Silas prevented their jailer from committing suicide and proclaimed the gospel to him and his family. (vv. 27-32) The jailer treated Paul and Silas in a kingly fashion, and he and his entire family were baptized. (v. 33)

In this lesson we see how God provided for Paul in a new place. We see how the power of the Lord was revealed in the deliverance of Paul and Silas from the jailhouse. We learn what it means to have compassion for others. This further teaches us that salvation must lead to hospitality from time to time. Here we learn that in times of discouragement and fear, God is near. We are taught that even in the midst of curtailment of our freedom we must pursue the preaching of the gospel. Hopefully, through this lesson you will learn to face adversity with renewed determination to succeed. It is also hoped that if you do not know the Lord, like the Phillipian jailer, you and your household shall be saved.

LESSON 13: May 27
Serving With Humility
Acts 20:18-32

This text deals with Paul's departure from Ephesus. In leaving, Paul reminded the elders in Ephesus of the trials he had endured in preaching the gospel to both Jews and Greeks. (vv. 18-21) Though Paul expected additional persecution, he longed only to finish the ministry he had been given. (vv. 22-24) In his final farewell, Paul admonished the elders to live up to their calling as overseers of the church. (vv. 25-28) Paul warned of false teachers, even within the church, who would threaten to lead the believers astray. (vv. 29-31) Paul then commended the elders to God, reminding them of the power of God's grace. (32)

The lesson deals with how we can serve with faith and confidence. It teaches us that in this struggle of faith we must persevere in the face of difficulty. We must be willing to suffer for what we see as a just cause of Christ the Lord. It is only in this way, like Paul, we can hope to leave a worthwhile legacy. This lesson also calls us to see hope for the future beyond the charismatic leaders who may have guided us.

"EDUCATING AFRICAN AMERICAN YOUNG WOMEN"

Rev. Carol McIlwain Edwards

To educate African-American young women is a formidable task, but it is our obligation and our pleasure. Their education must include some of their history; who God is; who they are; something about their enemy, Satan; how to defeat his devices; and their purpose in life. Let us define our terms. **Educating** is providing knowledge or training, teaching, stimulating or developing mental moral growth. **African-American** is a term describing individuals of African and American descent. The **Young** are defined as persons in the age group between childhood and maturity. **Women** are adult female human beings.

African-American young women must be taught extensively to know that God has preserved our race throughout history in spite of the historic deprivation and discrimination in this society. They can no longer tolerate or internalize the limited view others have of them. It has been found that the Garden of Eden was on the continent of Africa, from whence they came.

They must learn that the Lord preserved us when we were stolen from our families in Africa and sold into slavery. Our God kept us throughout the horrible journey of the middle passage in ships to America and other ports, through enslavement and the abolition of slavery, to this present age. **Only the strong survive!** Satan is still trying to destroy us today through sexual impurity (fornication, adultery, and homosexuality); communication problems between males and females (often unequally yoked); divorce; teen pregnancy; child, wife and husband abuse;

drug and alcohol addiction; guns and a myriad of acts of violence. We have survived by the grace of God, through faith and the prayers of our ancestors. As slaves, the reason we wanted to learn to read was to read The Holy Bible. Somehow we have lost our first love, God. He wants us to return to Him so we can spend eternity with Him. God does not want any of us to perish (John 3:16)! He created us to please Him and to accomplish a specific purpose in life (Revelation 4:11 and Ephesians 1:4-5).

There are unquestionable differences between Africans and Americans. Africans take the village approach to life which includes love, nurturing, support, caring and sharing for each other. Americans derived their customs from Europe. They are separatists, isolating themselves and operating best in a highly competitive, aggressive environment where they strive to gain and maintain a dominant position. Our African-American young women must be educated to know these differences in order to adapt, operate and change the dominant environment. And they must learn to capitalize on the strength of their African-American heritage. Love and nurturing truly comes from the Lord. God is love. David tells the Lord in Psalm 18:35 "... and thy gentleness hath made me great."

When our young women learn about the dual society in which they live, they can recognize the advantage of knowing and drawing from both African and American values and apply appropriate strategies as the situation requires. The Word of God states in John 10:16 "Behold, I send you forth as sheep in the midst of wolves: be ye therefore wise as serpents, and harmless as doves."

African-American young women must be taught *first* that God loves them with an everlasting love, and that they must seek Him *first* in all things. He also wants them to love Him with all their heart, and with all their soul, and with all their mind, and with all their strength"(Mark 12:30). The heavenly Father tells us in 1 Corinthians 2:9, "But is written, Eye hath not seen, nor ear heard, neither have entered into the heart of man, the things which God hath prepared for them that love him." Before they can expect these things, they must first seek God!

Our young women must be taught that God is God the Father, God the Son and God the Holy Spirit, and that they are also three-part beings (they are spirit, they have a soul and they live in a body); that God is love and that He is their loving Heavenly Father. The Hebrew name for Father is "Abba Father," translated, "Father God," The Lord lets us know in the Scriptures that our earthly fathers and mothers can fail us. Parents are human and are subject to error, but our Heavenly Father will not fail us (Psalm 27:10 "When my father and my mother forsake me, then the Lord will take me up."). When African-American young women allow themselves to experience God's love, they will recognize real love when they see it in others. This helps them have a positive image of a father. They will not have to look for love in all the wrong places. God is their source of everything (Philippians 4:19 "But my God shall supply all your need according to his riches in glory by Christ Jesus.").

Our young women must be taught that God created them in His image. God shows us that He has a special place in His heart for women, especially in the way He made them. As we know, in Genesis 2:7 God formed man (Adam) from the dust of the earth. The Hebrew word for formed is *yatsar*, which means "to mold like a potter or squeeze into shape." When God made woman (Eve), He skillfully formed her and carefully molded (Hebrew - *bannah*) her from Adam's rib. God did not make Eve from Adam's foot to trample on her, but from his rib—near his heart to be his equal, to walk beside him and not behind him. God blessed Adam and Eve and told them both in Genesis 1:28 to be fruitful, and to multiply, and to replenish the earth, and subdue it: and have dominion.

Let us look in The Word of God to see how young women are to be educated. In 1 Timothy 5:14 Paul tells Timothy, " I will therefore that the younger women marry, bear children, guide the house, given none occasion to the adversary to speak reproachfully." This will keep African-American young women from having idle minds. The same instruction the Lord gave to Adam and Eve applies to us today (Genesis 1:28). Because African-American women are studying the Word of God, their lives will be meaningful. Titus 2:3-5 reads, "The aged (wise and seasoned women of the Word of God) women likewise, that they be in behavior as becometh holiness, not false accusers, not given to much wine, teachers of good things; that they may teach the young women to be sober, to love their husbands, to love their children. To be discreet, chaste, keepers at home, good, obedient to their own husbands (only if they are following Christ). While on the subject of marriage, Proverbs 22:24, reads " Make no friendship with an angry man; and with a furious man thou shalt not go."

Our African-American young women must be taught that there will be occasions where individuals (wolves in sheep's clothing) will try to deceive them using the Word of God for their own advantage. Young women must be taught to discern good from evil through the study of the God's Word. If an individual does not exhibit the fruit of the Spirit and give honor to God's Word, they will know not to follow that person.

Our African-American young women should also know that Satan is their *only enemy* and that they are the target of Satan primarily because they are bearers of children. The Lord says in John 16:33, "These things I have spoken unto you, that in me ye might have peace. In the world ye shall have tribulation: but be of good cheer; I have overcome the world." This means they, too, can overcome the world. The primary reason Satan hates them is because he knows that women of the Word of God will train up their children in the way they should go: and when they are old, they will not depart from it

(Proverbs 22:6). Satan wants them to fail so that our generations will end up in hell with him.

Satan started his attack on women in Genesis chapter 3. He tempted Eve to eat of the tree of knowledge of good and evil. Adam was to dress and protect the Garden of Eden, which included the tree of knowledge of good and evil, and to protect Eve. After Satan deceived Eve, God put enmity between Satan and Eve; Satan understands the seed of woman will crush his head. Therefore, Satan has persecuted women in child-bearing for they are his enemy. He knew the Seed that was to come would be his greatest enemy. Through the virgin birth, God sent a Savior, Jesus Christ, and through faith in Him salvation is available to all who believe. Another illustration of the love of God toward all women: God stepped in on the woman's behalf where He tells us in 1 Timothy 2:15 "... and she shall be saved in child-bearing." Many women are having supernatural childbirths because they have found that they have been redeemed from the curse of the law, which included some very painful deliveries. We are now under grace because of the redemptive work of Jesus Christ, the Anointed One! Jesus Christ (our Savior) died on the Cross and defeated Satan 2,000 years ago. Young women must believe that they, too, can have victory over Satan!

We must help African-American young women to discover the purpose for which they are born. Their purpose could be in the five-fold ministry gifts (the apostle, prophet, evangelist, pastor or teacher) or in a field in the secular world. The purpose should be discovered, if possible, before marriage so that God's work will be well underway. African-American young women must learn that they can do all things through Christ which strengthens them (Philippians 4:13). God always causes us to triumph (2 Corinthians 2:14)! University/Bible College/trade school education is very impor-tant because it not only prepares them for time management and for their life's purpose, but it enhances the purpose and/or skills of their mates when they get married.

In addition to their spiritual upkeep, African-American young women must keep up with the business of the secular world, so they will be prepared for victory, not mere survival. At this millennium, the world is increasingly reliant on new technologies: computers, the internet, e-mail, etc., where our young women can learn of the glories of ancient Africa, of the vitality of African-Americans and become prepared for the world of work.

The world is hostile for the most part, prejudiced; indifferent and at times very difficult. Our African-American young women may have grown up in a two-parent, single parent, extended and/or an adoptive family. In either case, they must be taught that the Word of God is their best educator/teacher in order to strive for excellence and to be successful in life. Second Timothy 2:15 states, "Study to shew thyself approved unto God, a workman that needeth not to be ashamed, rightly dividing the word of truth." The Holy Bible is God's love letter to us. An appropriate acronym for the word Bible is, "Basic Instructions Before Leaving Earth."

In conclusion, African-American young women will be taught to receive Jesus Christ as their personal Lord and Savior; follow Him; stay close to Him by praying, reading and obeying His holy Word; strive for excellence in their purpose; take care of their physical body (the temple of the Holy Spirit); use time wisely; and be the best daughter, wife, mother, sister, aunt that they can be. In addition, they will witness for Christ. They will pass this knowledge on to their children and their children's children to affect generations to come. These children ("arrows" - Proverbs 127:3-5) will make positive changes in the dual society in which they live.

The African American Church and Freedom Movement

Rev. Dr. Prathia Hall, Ph.D.

The history of African-American people is absolutely amazing. Consider the tortuous events filled with brutality and pain which tore our African ancestors away from our African homeland and planted us on American soil. It is reasonable to ask "how have we survived? The experience has included excruciating pain. The journey has also included capture, kidnap, shackles, chains, neck braces and leg irons. During the traumatic middle passage, our ancestors were packed like sardines in a can, spoon-like on top of each other with insufficient breathing space. One can also consider how they were defiled and humiliated even before they arrived at the slave docks of the Southeastern United States.

The African continent was seriously depopulated. Millions died having been literally worked to death after a few short years. This was followed by two hundred and forty-four years of chattel slavery, segregation, discrimination and the ugly and deadly reign of terror that was lynching. These events of human shame and pain are correctly characterized as the African holocaust.

Many Americans do not wish to remember this gruesome history. They believe that it divides Americans and encourages racial hostility. Yet, if we do not know our history, we will fail to understand much of our contemporary life. Both Black and White Americans need to be aware of our racial history. If we learn the important lessons of the past we can work to prevent repetition in the future. When we know the truth, the truth shall set us free.

It is very necessary to learn how we survived as a people. Indeed had God not been with us, we would have been destroyed. Most researchers agree that the African-American churches have been essential to the survival of African-American people. The Black Church has functioned as the primary institutional advocate for our people. Further, when we examine closely the history of the Black Church within the framework of the history of Black people in the United States, we find both histories interwoven in very interesting ways. Indeed, the Church's own struggle for existence was identical with the African-American freedom struggles because the Church actually emerged from the people's struggle for identity and existence.

Religion was one of the aspects of African life which the oppressors attempted to destroy. During the breaking-in process, Africans were separated from their original regional and tribal groups so that they could not speak their African languages or use their African names or practice their African religions. The early African-American sociologist, E. Franklyn Frazier, believed that the process of kidnap, capture and breaking-in were so profoundly traumatic that the slaves were totally stripped of their African cultural heritage. Therefore, they retained no memory of their African way of life, including their religious faith. Most contemporary scholars believe that Frazier was wrong. African people found a variety of ways to keep their faith alive. As slaves in the Caribbean and in South America, Blacks continued to practice African beliefs and mingled them with the Roman Catholic traditions to which they were introduced on this side of the Atlantic.

New research and archeological digs of old plantations and cemetery excavations have revealed evidence that slaves in the United States practiced their African beliefs in secret, in the slave quarters and in the woods, far from the eyes and ears of the slaveholders. Current research helps to explain the relation of African-American Christianity to Africans and the factors which make African-American Christianity different in many ways from European-American Christianity.

Africans from different regions and tribes were able to piece together some of what the slaveholders attempted to destroy. These African religious beliefs had many similarities to Christianity. Africans believed in a supreme God who was creator and ruler of everything in the universe. They also believed in other divine creatures who were emissaries for good or evil and were involved directly in the lives of human beings. Africans believed that all life was sacred. They possessed a powerful and vibrant spirituality and worshiped God with their bodies and souls in sacred dance. These beliefs and practices were compatible with Christian beliefs and practices and over a period of time were merged through the experience of slavery to form African-American Christianity.

We learn a great deal more about the African-American Christian Churches and their relation to the African-American freedom struggle when we examine the process by which the African slaves were introduced to Christianity. Slaveholders did not want their slaves to convert to Christianity if it meant that they would have to set them free. Slaveholders feared that Christianity would make the slaves bold and rebellious, stirring their deep longing for freedom. The most evil and destructive obstacle to the process of evangelization was the claim by many slaveholders that Blacks did not have souls and could not go heaven; therefore, they should not be Christianized. Those slaveholders who did permit missionaries to preach to the slaves held the belief that Christianity would make the Africans better slaves. Some of these preachers preached a distorted version of the gospel which claimed that God had ordained slavery.

The process of evangelization that led to the creation of the Black Churches was very complex and very difficult. Despite the attempts to use religion to control slaves, planters greatly feared that Christianity could not be trusted to function as a tool of oppression if the slaves were able to examine, understand and interpret it for themselves. Consequently, laws were passed which prohibited religious meetings by Black people. It was against the law to teach a Black person to read or write. Punishment for breaking these laws was very severe. Andrew Bryan, a Black pastor, preached to slaves and organized the first African Baptist Church in Savannah, Georgia. He and the church members were arrested and whipped by slave patrols, even when they had passes for worship. The pattern of harassment and abuse continued as more slaves embraced the new faith and interpreted it through their experience of slavery.

Christian faith, under such conditions, became itself an act of rebellion. The earliest form of congregational life was what E. Franklyn Frazier called the "invisible institution." Under cover of night, black women and men would "steal away" to the brush arbor or praise houses or secret praying ground in the woods. There, they heard what they called "real preaching" as opposed to what the White preachers offered. They were able to sing, shout and cry to God. They interpreted the scriptures, claimed the exodus even as their own, analyzed the Christianity of the slaveholders and found it to be false.

We can see then, that the life of the Black Church was formed as a part of the struggle for the survival of Black people. The Church had to fight for the right to exist in much the same way that African-American people had to fight. The invisible institution was the place where freedom struggles were carried out. Slaves not only sang, prayed, preached and danced in the praise house meetings, they also plotted escape and rebellion. The spirituals expressed their Christian theology and gave them solace in pain. They also contained code language by which they could communicate plans to escape by way of the underground railroad - a network of helpful friends, White and Black, who would feed and hide them along the route of their escape. "Steal Away to Jesus" was one of the popular code songs.

Independent Black churches were organized in the North and in the large cities of the South where free Blacks lived. These churches became the heartbeat of the Black movement for the abolition of slavery. Frederick Douglas, the Reverend Henry Highland Garnett and many other preachers and leaders, including such women as Maria Stewart, Harriett Tubman and Sojourner Truth, often proclaimed the message of God-ordained freedom from the pulpits of these churches. Mr. Gayraud Wilmore calls these Black churches, "The Black Church Freedom Movement." They taught what Mr. Peter Paris called "The prophetic principle" of the equality of all human beings before God. *This foundational belief and practice distinguished the Black Christian churches from the White Christian churches more profoundly than did their styles of worship.* The Black churches continued to grow and develop only as places of worship, religious education, and heart of the freedom movement.

The Black churches followed the concept of the African World-view which understood the religious and the political, the sacred and the secular, to be integrated in the pattern of life. The church was the center of the lives of Black people. Schools were organized and operated in the churches including famous historically Black colleges. Social agencies, banks, insurance agencies and civil rights organizations were organized in and by the Black churches. Following emancipation, the African- American church became the center of the work of racial uplift.

This pattern of church leadership in the social, civil and economic development struggles of the Black community continues today. Although many churches have become less active, this was also true during the civil rights movement of the 1950's and 1960's. The Movement was led by churches, but it did not have the support of all the churches. Some churches advocated a less activist, more accommodationist approach to the freedom struggle.

We can see from this brief historical survey that the roots of the Black church are planted firmly in the struggles of Black people for survival, emancipation, freedom and social development. Indeed, the church itself emerged by means of its own freedom struggle. The path to independent existence for the Black church was a path of great suffering and turmoil. This essay attempts to illumine the inseparable connection of the roots of the faith struggle and the freedom struggle. This formation of history compels the African-American church.

ACTS: THE CONTINUING WORK OF JESUS

James Estep, Ph.D.

The Acts of the Apostles is one of the important, but often neglected, books of the New Testament. While the Gospels provide ample insight into the life and teachings of Jesus, and the Epistles provide theological interaction between the early Christian leaders, especially the Apostle Paul, and the Christian community, without the Book of Acts no *historical* voice from the first-century Christian community would exist. Acts provides a window for twenty-first century Christians to look back on the infancy of the Christian faith and interact with Christians from the first-century; and come to discover that while "things" change, God doesn't.

The Value of Acts

What does the Book of Acts uniquely provide for the Christian? What makes it valuable to me or my congregation? First, it provides a pattern or paradigm for the Christian community to follow in any culture or setting. In it, we are afforded the opportunity to see the Christian faith move from a strictly Jewish context in Jerusalem, to a transcultural movement of faith present throughout the Roman world. Second, it provides a portrait of "Doing Theology," the process whereby the Christian community determines and applies its theological convictions. For example, the incidences described in Acts 6 and Acts 15 represent not only practical issues that resulted in conflict, but theologically rooted conflicts that required a theological solution to the predicament. Acts provides insight into how

the early Christian community addressed such issues, and hence providing a model for our contemporary deliberation of those issues. Third, it provides a historical link between Jesus of the Gospels and the theology of the epistles. Without Acts, we would lack these essential insights into the life, teaching, and ministry of Christians in the first-century. Consequently, Acts can provide new insights into the Christian faith that are relatively unparalleled in the rest of the New Testament.

Luke's Narrative

While the author of the Acts does not identify himself by name, the Church since its inception has accepted and supported Luke as its author. It does bear striking similarity to Luke's Gospel, with the conclusion of the Gospel and the opening of Acts "dovetailing" together rather well. Similarly, Luke 1:1-4 and Acts 1:1-2 bear striking resemblance as well to one another. As a result, Luke has provided the community of faith a two-volume set of historical narratives.

Paul identified Luke as a physician (Colossians 4:14), and later as his sole companion during the last weeks of his life (2 Timothy 4:11). As Paul's travel companion, Luke was provided a unique perspective into the early Christian community. He obviously joined Paul in his missionary endeavor and trip to Rome, as is evidenced by the use of "we" as opposed to "they" in the narrative of Acts, indicating his presence and absence in given accounts

(16:10-17, 20:5-15, 21:1-18, 27:1-28:16). In fact, the abrupt end to the text contained no stated outcome of Paul's trial, nor any information from later in the first century. It has been hypothesized, based partially on the abrupt nature of Acts' ending, that Luke may have planned an additional volume. Nevertheless, Luke narrates the events of Paul's life up to AD 63, and hence made a record of the events insofar as they had occurred.

Jesus' Work in the Church

The church is a Great Commission community, and Acts portrays it as the extension of Christ's ministry. Luke opens the Book of Acts with the statement, "The former account I made, O Theophilus, of all that Jesus began both to do and teach . . ." (1:1). If the Gospel of Luke is what "Jesus began," what is Luke implying? Is the Church, the Christian community, intended to be the continuing work of Jesus? Apparently, Luke understood the Church, as the body and bride of Christ, to be responsible for the carrying out of Jesus' ministry and Commission. In fact, the depiction of Paul at the close of Acts describes him as preaching the kingdom of God and teaching the things which concern the Lord Jesus Christ with all confidence, no one forbidding him (28:31). As one individual expressed it, perhaps your congregation is writing Acts Chapter 29!

Purpose and Pattern

Why would Luke have taken it upon himself to write such a narrative? Lewis Foster, professor emeritus of Cincinnati Bible College and Seminary, notes that Acts has five purposes:

• To present a history of the expansion of Christianity
• To give a defense of Christianity, especially to the Roman readers
• To provide a guide for the future Church to emulate
• To depict the triumph of Christianity in the face of bitter persecution
• To provide a background to Paul's epistles

As the curriculum units depict, the outline of Acts is provided by Luke in Acts 1:8, "But you shall receive power when the Holy Spirit has come upon you; and you shall be witnesses to Me in Jerusalem, and in Judea and Samaria, and to the end of the earth." Geographically, the contents of the text stretch from Jerusalem, as the religious center of Judaism and the place of Jesus' crucifixion and resurrection, to Rome, the imperial center of politics and culture in the first four centuries AD.

Chronologically, the events narrated in the text extend from AD 30 with the birth of the Church in Jerusalem to a rather abrupt end in AD 63 with Paul ministering while under house-arrest in Rome. Hence, Acts portrays the Christian faith from its inception in an upper room in Jerusalem to gaining wide acceptance and resistance throughout the entire Roman world.

Obstacles and Opportunities

Change and conflict are two sides of the same coin. Luke's narrative of the birth and expansion of the church does not present an idealized picture of the advancement of the Christian faith. He was not writing propaganda! Rather, he depicts a community of faith that faces decision, challenge, and controversy. Luke includes incidents of conflict, both from within and outside the church, personal and corporate, as well as theological and socio-cultural in nature (Acts 6:1ff, 15:39, 15:1ff, 21:20-21). As one studies the accounts of conflict in Acts, the general premise emerges that within every obstacle the community of faith must face lies an opportunity to reassert our commitment to Christ, advancing the Kingdom by redesigning ministry to match the church's context. They are able to advance the cause of Christ by securing the core values of the Christian faith, but developing relevant ministry initiative within a given culture (for example, the Grecian widows of Acts 6).

Who is the Chief Character in Acts?

Some may immediately assume the main figure in Acts to be Paul, or perhaps Peter, or perhaps even Jesus (by proxy); however, the main figure in Acts is indeed the Holy Spirit. His arrival is predicted and anticipated in Acts 1, first experienced and made evident in Acts 2, His miraculous involvement in the Church is present in Acts 7, and His approval of the Gentile's entry into the faith community is evident in Acts 10, and He is ever-present in the missionary endeavors of Paul and his companions. It is not Peter or Paul or any other figure presented in Acts, but the Holy Spirit working through them that is the central figure of the text.

Charles Albert Tindley

Charles Albert Tindley surely influenced and inspired many people as he continued Jesus' liberating work. Tindley ministered to others as a pastor and a musician; however, his name is not well known. His composition "I'll Overcome Some Day" served as the basis for the civil rights anthem "We Shall Overcome." Tindley also penned the song "Stand By Me," which became a national hit during the 1960s when Ben E. King and the Drifters sang it. The father of gospel music, Thomas A. Dorsey, considered Tindley as the originator of gospel music. Tindley's "I Do, Don't You" reportedly inspired Dorsey to begin writing gospel music.

While Tindley is one of the earliest and most influential writers of gospel music, his talents do not stop or begin with his compositions. Tindley was born in Berlin, Maryland, around 1856. He had no formal education as a child of slavery, but taught himself to read and write.

When Tindley was about 17 years old, he married Daisy Henry and moved to Philadelphia to make a better life for himself. In 1885, he worked as a sexton, or janitor, at the John Wesley Methodist Episcopal Church. He dreamed of becoming a minister, but he had no formal education. He couldn't stop working and attend school because he needed to take care of his family.

His desires and family obligations made him decide to take correspondence classes. The correspondence classes enabled him to pass the exam to become a minister; he also taught himself Hebrew and Greek. After becoming a minister, Tindley served as pastor at churches in New Jersey and Delaware. He was appointed elder of the Wilmington (Delaware) District.

Eventually, Tindley was asked to become the pastor of the church that he had cleaned when he first moved to Philadelphia. The church's name had been changed to the Bainbridge Street Methodist Church.

The church began with 200 members, but Tindley's eloquence, intellect, and spiritual singing attracted more and more members. The church grew to more than 10,000 members under his leadership. It was renamed Tindley Temple after its leader.

While serving at the church, Tindley organized a church credit club to help the members buy housing. Tindley also worked for civil rights. He especially helped Philadelphia's poor, disadvantaged, and those trying to settle into the northern lifestyle after migrating from the South.

While pastoring his extensive congregation, ministering to the needy, and fighting for social justice, the preacher-composer wrote more than 45 hymns, many of which are still sung today. Some include *We'll Understand It Better, By and By, Let Jesus Fix It For You, I Know The Lord Will Make A Way, Oh Yes He Will,* and *Some Day* (which is known as *Beams of Heaven As I Go*).

The great preacher and songwriter died in 1933. The church named after him still exists.

March 4
Bible Study Guide 1

1. Words You Should Know

A. Passion (Acts 1:3) Greek *Pascho*—The opposite of free action. Mostly suffering on behalf of someone.

B. Witnesses (v. 8) Greek *Martus*—One who remembers or who has information or knowledge of someone or something. Also used as a designation of those who have suffered death as a consequence of confessing Christ.

2. Teacher Preparation

A. Read the GENERAL INTRODUCTION and UNIT 1 INTRODUCTION pages.

B. Next, read the devotional reading and the background Scriptures for this lesson.

C. Write the KEEP IN MIND verse on the chalkboard or newsprint before class time.

D. Spend time in prayer, using the QUARTER AT-A-GLANCE outline to pray over each lesson that you will teach this quarter. Also pray for each of your students by name that they may be filled with the Holy Spirit.

3. Starting the Lesson

A. As students arrive, ask each one what they hope to learn this quarter. Write their answers on the chalkboard or newsprint for all to see.

B. Next, write the AT-A-GLANCE outline on the board or newsprint. Have several students volunteer to read the IN DEPTH according to the AT-A-GLANCE outline.

C. Read the FOCAL VERSES out loud. Ask students to write down any significant points they may have gleaned from the reading.

D. Open the class time with prayer, focusing on the KEEP IN MIND verse as the foundation of the prayer.

4. Getting into the Lesson

A. Have several students read the IN FOCUS and the BACKGROUND sections of today's lesson. Then ask students to briefly discuss each section.

B. Now ask those students who volunteered to read the IN DEPTH section of the lesson. Assign the SEARCH THE SCRIPTURES questions to correspond with the reading.

C. Have students read THE PEOPLE, PLACES, AND TIMES section and ask them to comment on what they read.

5. Relating the Lesson to Life

A. Lead the students to answer the DISCUSS THE MEANING questions and relate them to the lesson.

B. Read the BIBLE BACKGROUND scriptures. Have students divide into groups of three and work on the LESSON IN OUR SOCIETY exercise. Allow 5-10 minutes for the students to come up with answers to be shared with the class.

6. Arousing Action

A. Read the MAKE IT HAPPEN exercise and challenge students to complete it as a group.

B. Close the class with prayer.

WORSHIP GUIDE

For the Superintendent or Teacher
Theme: The Promise of the Spirit's Power
Theme Song: "Holy Spirit, Thou Art Welcome In This Place"
Scripture: Romans 8:14-17
Song: "Jesus Is All the World to Me"
Meditation: Thank You Lord for the Holy Spirit which You promise to give to me. Help me to yield to His power in my life. In Jesus' name. Amen.

THE PROMISE OF THE SPIRIT'S POWER

Bible Background • ACTS 1
Printed Text • ACTS 1:3-14
Devotional Reading • JOHN 16:7-14

LESSON AIM

By the end of the lesson, students should have explored the ministry of the Holy Spirit in the life of the church and the world, recognize whether the Holy Spirit is evident in their lives, and commit to seeking a deeper level of the Holy Spirit's ministry in their personal lives.

KEEP IN MIND

"But ye shall receive power, after that the Holy Ghost is come upon you: and ye shall be witnesses unto me both in Jerusalem, and in all Judea, and in Samaria, and unto the uttermost part of the earth" (Acts 1:8).

LESSON OVERVIEW

LESSON AIM
KEEP IN MIND
FOCAL VERSES
IN FOCUS
THE PEOPLE, PLACES, AND TIMES
BACKGROUND
AT-A-GLANCE
IN DEPTH
SEARCH THE SCRIPTURES
DISCUSS THE MEANING
LESSON IN OUR SOCIETY
MAKE IT HAPPEN
FOLLOW THE SPIRIT
REMEMBER YOUR THOUGHTS
MORE LIGHT ON THE TEXT
DAILY BIBLE READINGS

FOCAL VERSES

Acts 1:3 To whom also he showed himself alive after his passion by many infallible proofs, being seen of them forty days, and speaking of the things pertaining to the kingdom of God.

4 And being assembled together with them, commanded them that they should not depart from Jerusalem, but wait for the promise of the Father, Which, saith he, ye have heard of me.

5 For John truly baptized with water; but ye shall be baptized with the Holy Ghost not many days hence.

6 When they therefore were come together, they asked of him saying, Lord, wilt thou at this time restore again the kingdom of Israel?

7 And he said unto them, It is not for you to know the times or the seasons, which the Father hath put in his own power.

8 But ye shall receive power, after that the Holy Ghost is come upon you: and ye shall be witnesses unto me both in Jerusalem, and in all Judea, and in Samaria, and unto the uttermost part of the earth.

9 And when he had spoken these things, while they beheld, he was taken up; and a cloud received him out of their sight.

10 And while they looked steadfastly toward heaven as he went up, behold, two men stood by them in white apparel;

11 Which also said, Ye men of Galilee, why stand ye gazing up into heaven? this same Jesus, which is taken up from you in heaven, shall so come in like manner as ye have seen him go into heaven.

12 Then returned they into Jerusalem from the mount called Olivet, which is from Jerusalem a sabbath day's journey.

13 And when they were come in, they went up into an upper room, where abode both Peter, and James, and John, and Andrew, Philip, and Thomas, Bartholomew, and Matthew, James the son of Alphaeus, and Simon Zelotes, and Judas the brother of James.

14 These all continued with one accord in prayer and supplication, with the women, and Mary the mother of Jesus, and with his brethren.

IN FOCUS

Betty Willis is a faithful member of Parkside Christian Church in Little Rock, Arkansas, having served as the youth minister for the past seven years. As a single woman, Betty is determined to dedicate her life to serving the Lord by evangelizing youth in her area.

One summer, Betty and several other youth ministers of Little Rock flew to Los Angeles to participate in an evangelistic crusade in the inner city. While there, Betty met Jacob Lewis, a minister of the Los Angeles team and a very handsome man.

One night after the staff Bible Study, Jacob approached Betty and asked if she would consider having lunch with him since he was leaving for Kenya the end of the week. Betty told Jacob that she had already made a commitment to her youth group to intercede with them on behalf of the city and there was no way she would break it. Jacob was persistent and continued asking Betty, hoping to change her mind. Each time, Betty said no.

Two weeks later, Betty and the team returned to Little Rock, excited at how Jesus Christ had moved in Los Angeles. Betty was also happy that she remained faithful to the Lord and did not let down the young people who were in her care.

The following year, as Betty was leaving service one night, the pastor handed her a letter that had been written by Jacob Lewis from Kenya:

Dearest Sister Betty:

I pray this letter finds you blessed in the Lord and that your faithfulness to Jesus Christ is as strong today as it was when we first met in Los Angeles. I was so impressed by your commitment to the kingdom of God, a commitment that many believers lack. In fact, your willingness to put Jesus Christ first has brought great conviction in my own life and forced me to re-examine my faith and lack of commitment in many areas and repent of my faithlessness. Thank you for saying no. I will be returning to the States next month. My prayer is that God will allow you to say yes.

Your brother,

Jacob

Christians need power to be faithful and committed to God's kingdom. This week, we will see how the disciples remained faithful and committed to God so that they might receive power through the Promise He had for them. It is the same power we need today to be committed and faithful workers for Jesus Christ.

THE PEOPLE, PLACES, AND TIMES

Jerusalem. Under Rome, Jerusalem was conquered in 63 B.C. by Pompey and reached its pinnacle of grandeur and strength as a result of the building program of Herod the Great, whom Rome appointed king of Judea in 40 B.C. Herod strengthened the Hasmonean walls. At the top of the western hill, he built a huge palace complex for himself. Its two sections were named after his Roman benefactors, Caesar and Agrippa: The Caesarium and Agrippium. They later became the praetorium (quarters) for the prefect or procurator of Judea. Three monumental towers built into the Hasmonean wall as it curved to the south protected the palace from attacks from the north at this vulnerable corner of the city. The towers were named Mariamne (after Herod's wife), Phaesalis (after his brother), and Hippicus (after his friend). The base of Phaesalis tower, now called "The Tower of David," is still standing in the citadel area of the Old City.

The northern section of the Hasmonean wall was also vulnerable where the ridge created by the northern east-west depression disappears along its eastern half. To strengthen this and include more of the western area of the city, Herod built a second wall that circled from the middle of the first, or Hasmonean wall, to a fortress north of the Temple Mount called the Antonia. Some trace this wall as far north as the present-day Damascus Gate, where it is claimed that part of the wall has been found. Others describe the wall as turning to the Antonia just east of the Church of the Resurrection. To further strengthen this second wall, which was open to attack from the west, a quarry was opened in front of it that served as a defense moat.

Evacuations in the area of the Lutheran Church of the Redeemer have uncovered parts of this quarry. The entrance to the quarry cut into the sloping western hill. A section of this was not worth quarrying and it was left standing on the mound of limestone. It was called Golgotha, or the "skull" (John 19:17). This part of the quarry belonged to Joseph of Arimathaea, who cut his family tomb into the exposed hill of the quarry adjacent to Golgotha. This is now part of the Church of the Resurrection and probably was the burial place of Jesus.

(The Harper Bible Dictionary, San Francisco: Harper and Row Publishing Co., 1984, pp. 463-473).

BACKGROUND

The Book of the Acts was written by Luke, "the beloved physician," who also wrote the Gospel of Luke. Written approximately A.D. 63, Acts was addressed to a man named "Theophilus" (Acts 1:1) by the prompting of the Holy Spirit.

Most theologians believe that Luke wrote the book of Acts to give the Gentile church an accurate accounting of the beginning of Christianity. The development of the early church and the promised outpouring of the Holy Spirit, as well as the role He plays in establishing believers, is the primary focus of the Book.

Luke was an inspired writer who covers the first 30 years of early church history. He also traces the spread of the Gospel of Jesus Christ from Jerusalem to Rome, and gives several accounts of the supernatural power of the Holy Spirit at work in the lives of the committed believers.

Luke also describes the persecution that believers experienced because of their faith in Christ. In all, Luke helps to shape our theological perspective of the work and witness of the Holy Spirit through his adept account in the Acts of the Apostles.

We begin our Bible study with the apostles preparing for the ascension of Jesus Christ and

AT-A-GLANCE

1. The Promised Holy Spirit
(Acts 1:3-8)
2. The Promised Return of Jesus Christ
(vv. 9-11)
3. The Promised Power Through Prayer
(vv. 12-14)

their return to Jerusalem with a command from our Lord.

IN DEPTH
1. The Promised Holy Spirit (Acts 1:3-8)

After Jesus' resurrection, He remained on earth 40 days and was seen by the apostles and other followers. He also spoke with them concerning the kingdom of God. Christ had given His followers a commandment that they should not depart from Jerusalem, but that they should wait there for the promise of the Father, which was prophesied by Joel (Joel 2:28-29).

The Prophet Joel had predicted the day when God was going to pour out His Holy Spirit upon all flesh—that is, on all who called upon the name of Jesus Christ, repented of their sins, and surrendered their lives to His Lordship. The outpouring of the Holy Spirit would enable God's people to flow in the Spirit's power in order to witness for Christ, win the lost to Him, and teach them how to observe all that He had commanded.

Jesus is the One who baptizes His believers in the Holy Spirit (John 1:33). Thus, a key verse in Acts states that "ye shall receive power after that the Holy Ghost is come upon you" (v. 8). In the Greek, the word "power" is *dunamis* from which we get our English word "dynamite." The power in the life of a believer is not just strength to accomplish things in our own ability, but in the supernatural flow and power of God through His Holy Spirit. The Book of Acts (as well as the Gospel of Luke), describes how the Holy Spirit's power was used in the name of Jesus to drive out evil spirits and heal the sick. In fact, these two signs often accompanied the proclamation of the Gospel (Luke 4:14, 36; Acts 6:8; 8:4-8; 14:13). Luke affirms Jesus promised power upon the arrival of the Holy Spirit (Acts 1:8). Notice that Jesus told His disciples, who likely had already been baptized with water by John the Baptist (v. 5), that they were to wait in Jerusalem for the "promise of the Father" (Luke 24:49). The Holy Spirit's power came after Jesus ascended, which is why Jesus instructed that they wait for the promise.

We must understand why God promised to give us the gift of the Holy Spirit. God has called us to be effective witnesses for Christ, not just pew-warmers in the church. In fact, one of the definitions for "witness" (v. 8) literally means one who may suffer persecution and death for the cause of Christ. Is there any wonder we need the power of the Holy Spirit?

Jesus made it clear that the witnessing would take place "after" the Holy Ghost is upon us. How does the presence of the Holy Spirit affect the life of a believer?

a. The Holy Spirit gives us power to accomplish God's work in the world.

b. The Holy Spirit gives us grace to live godly and overcome sin in the midst of a perverse and crooked generation.

c. The Holy Spirit gives us the desire to love, honor, and submit to the lordship of Jesus Christ.

d. The Holy Spirit will witness to righteousness and truth by bringing conviction of sin in the lives of both Christians and unbelievers (John 16:8-10, 13).

e. The Holy Spirit will help us to become more like Jesus Christ in everything we do.

Therefore, when Jesus told the disciples that they would receive power, it was more than just "fire from heaven." Jesus was talking about the person of the Holy Spirit who comes to abide in us and to help us have a lifestyle that is in line with God's Holy Word, and provides divine power that changes our attitude and disposition, and develops our hunger to please the Lord in all we do.

2. The Promised Return of Jesus Christ (vv. 9-11)

After Jesus had given His disciples instructions, He was taken up into heaven. They saw Him leave the earth and received confirmation of His departure and return from "two men" (v. 10). Luke does not say these men were angels. However, we can surmise they were because they understood the purpose and reason of Jesus' departure and the nature of His return. Matthew records that Jesus shared this event with His disciples in great detail (Matthew 24:15-30). Jesus also explained that tribulation would precede His return. His second coming would be for the purpose of judging the wicked, delivering His own faithful followers and bringing about God's righteousness on the earth (Mark 13:24-37; Luke 21:25-33).

The two men reminded Peter, James, John, Andrew, Philip, Thomas, Barthlomew, Matthew, James, Alphaeus, Simon Zelotes, and Judas, the brother of James (Acts 1:13) of Jesus' teaching. Even though He ascended to heaven, one day Jesus would return for His faithful followers (John 14:1-3). This reminder of Jesus' words gave the disciples courage to wait on the promised Holy Spirit as our Saviour commanded so that they might proclaim the Gospel with power. Today, we can take comfort that one day Jesus Christ will return from heaven, as He promised, to receive us. But until He comes, we should genuinely desire the presence and power of the Holy Spirit so that we might proclaim with power the Gospel of Jesus Christ to a lost and hurting world.

3. The Promised Power Through Prayer (vv. 12-14)

In obedience to their Lord, the disciples returned from Mount Olivet to Jerusalem where they, with other believers, gathered together in an upper room to pray and wait on the promised Holy Spirit.

The experience of Pentecost involved both obedience and human responsibility. Jesus had instructed the disciples not to witness without first being baptized with the Holy Spirit. Jesus Himself was baptized and filled with the Holy Spirit in order to complete His earthly ministry (Luke 4:1, 18; Acts 10:38). Therefore, He did not want to send His followers out until they were clothed with power from on high (Luke 24:39).

Today, the church needs the power of the Holy Spirit to fulfill the responsibility of harvesting souls for Jesus Christ in these last days. However, like the early disciples, we must be in our "upper room" praying fervently that the power of the Holy Spirit will be evident in our lives, as well as the corporate life of the church (v. 14). Since Jesus was a man of prayer (Luke 3:21), we too must pray for God's blessings, power, and the manifestation of His promises in our lives.

Jesus encouraged His followers to "tarry" in the city of Jerusalem. They weren't there to have a potluck supper or a fashion show. Jesus wanted them to be on one accord, praying and seeking God for the promise (v. 14).

There are many things that can only be accomplished in God's kingdom with persistent and fervent prayer (2 Chronicles 7:14). Jesus also affirms the power of prayer in the lives of New Testament believers today. Thus, the eleven disciples "with the women, and Mary the mother of Jesus with his brethren" (v. 14) were faithful and committed to fervent prayer in the upper room until God's power was made available to them.

Through the grace of God, commitment to unity, prayer, and obedience to God's Word, we too can receive the promised power of the Holy Spirit to be effective in the work of Christ, just as His disciples were.

SEARCH THE SCRIPTURES

1. Why did Jesus command His disciples not to depart from Jerusalem? (Acts 1:4)

2. What is the primary purpose of the baptism in the Holy Spirit? (v. 8)

3. What message did the two men in white apparel give to Jesus' disciples? (v. 11)

4. The disciples returned to Jerusalem from where? (v. 12)

5. What took place in the upper room? (v. 14)

DISCUSS THE MEANING

1. The early church witnessed and experienced the beginning of the outpouring of the Holy Spirit recorded in Joel 2:28-29. As a result, they were able to witness effectively and proclaim the Gospel with the demonstration of the Holy Spirit's power. Should believers today be just as effective as they were in the early church? Why or why not? What is hindering us from having the same power?

2. The early church was committed to prayer. However, the fact that many churches today have all but eliminated prayer meetings has resulted in a loss of power. How can we begin to reestablish the ministry of prayer in the local church?

LESSON IN OUR SOCIETY

Most inner cities in America are filled with churches, while our communities are falling apart through poverty, crime, and other major problems. What did the early New Testament church possess that was able to change whole cities? What can be done to change churches that are just getting by? Although many churches today claim to have the Holy Spirit's power, the evidence is contrary. Discuss what Christians are, or should be doing, to make a difference in our urban cities.

MAKE IT HAPPEN

Make a decision to pray for a genuine filling of the Holy Spirit in your life. If your local church doesn't have a weekly prayer meeting, talk with your pastor about starting one. In the prayer meeting, be sure to pray that the Lord will fill the whole church with the power of the Holy Ghost so that every member will become an effective witness for Christ and our cities will be turned right-side up for the glory of God.

FOLLOW THE SPIRIT

What God wants me to do:

_____

_____

REMEMBER YOUR THOUGHTS

Special insights you learned:

_____

_____

MORE LIGHT ON THE TEXT
Acts 1:3-14

1:3 To whom also he showed by many infallible proofs, being seen of them forty days, and speaking of the things pertaining to the kingdom of God.

This passage from the Book of Acts is written to convince us beyond any shadow of doubt that there is compelling evidence that, indeed, Jesus is risen from the dead! The Greek word *tekmeriois* translated "proofs" means demonstrative, positive, and with certainty. In addition, the word "infallible" is used in conjunction with "proofs." Consider the following synonyms of the word "infallible:" unerring, trustworthy, reliable, perfect. Literally, we can be perfectly positive and certain that Jesus is alive! Jesus made sure that the fact that He rose from the dead could not be disputed, since the same disciples who witnessed His crucifixion also saw Him alive after His death and burial. During those appearances, Jesus made it clear that He was not a spirit—they touched Him. Jesus revealed His scarred hands and feet, declaring, "It is I myself " (Luke 24:28-43).

Through the Holy Spirit Jesus revealed Himself to the disciples, He discloses Himself to us today! The Greek word for "chose" here is *exelexato.* Jesus was specific in His selection. This was no random appearance. Jesus manifested Himself so that they might have a personal witness to give.

The only way finite man can begin to understand and recognize Jesus is that He *show* Himself. Luke uses the Greek verb *paristemi* for "show." Jesus is the active agent. He provides the revelation, instead of the disciples taking the initiative. The Greek is rendered by various English words: present, furnish, provide, assist. We must make ourselves available as vessels unto honor. Those who want to be in His presence must have "clean hands and a pure heart" (Psalm 24:4). Jesus is always able, willing and ready to show Himself alive, and prove unequivocally, that what He says is true and reliable.

4 And, being assembled together with them, commanded them that they should not depart from Jerusalem, but wait for the promise of the Father, which, saith he, ye have heard of me.

Note the greek phrase *kai sunalizomenos* translated "Being assembled together with them" indicates the movement of one or two objects to the same location.

It was according to prophecy (Micah 4:12; Isaiah 2:3) that the gospel should go forth from Jerusalem. It is very significant that Jesus told the disciples to wait, and they obeyed.

The way God deals with His people is more like following the glow of a flash light, rather than the glare of a huge street lamp or a helicopter search light. More often than not there is just enough illumination to immediately obey. As we obey, He illuminates our path further, one step at a time. Abraham waited so long for the son God promised. We are not told, but conceivably he did not fully understand God's command to sacrifice Isaac, since God had promised Abraham he would be a great nation through Isaac. Abraham followed the light, despite the pain of what God seemed to require, and he saw the fulfillment in

Isaac being spared, and God's provision of a "ram in the bush" (Genesis 22:1-14).

No doubt we, too, will be required to *wait* in our own Jerusalem. Perhaps God will call us to trust Him with beloved relationships. Just as God did for the disciples and Abraham, He will give us direction!

How should we wait for God to fulfill His promises?

1. We should *rest.* What does it mean to rest?

Cease from exerting oneself—When we experience an insurmountable problem or grief—such as the death of a loved one, an absent parent, the feeling of abandonment of an orphaned child, the suffering caused by an untrue accusation, or any negative situation that we have no control over— these things can shake the very foundations of our lives. What else can we do but obtain ease and refreshment from God's Word? This is the unique rest that God offers us through the person of the Holy Spirit. It cannot be found anywhere else!

2. *Fret not*—This means we can experience freedom from fear and worry. We can receive support from the promise that Jesus extends to us, just like the commitment He made to the disciples. God has proven Himself to be faithful to keep His Word. Just as all Jesus spoke to the disciples came to fruition, those things He says to us will also prove to be reliable.

3. *Anticipate His return, response, and instruction*— The plans that God has for us as His children are worthy of our hope. We can place our every confidence in Him. God's Word assures us: "For I know the thoughts that I think toward you, saith the Lord, thoughts of peace, and not of evil, to give you an expected end" (Jeremiah 29:11).

4. *Pray*—Jeremiah 29 continues (verse 12): "Then shall ye call upon me, and ye shall go and pray unto me, and I will hearken unto you." Waiting requires patience and confidence in the trustworthiness of God. He will fulfill—since He changes not.

5 For John truly baptized with water; but ye shall be baptized with the Holy Ghost not many days hence.

The baptism of John was unto repentance (Matthew 11; Luke 3:3). The baptism of the Holy

to Israel encompassed and was connected to the land: "For I will take you from among the heathen, and gather you out of all countries, and will bring you into your own land" (Ezekiel 36:24). The form of the Greek verb "restore" used here is *apokathistemi*, which is translated "restore to its former state." The disciples were aware of this, and their desire was to see their nation restored to the level of riches and importance it had once enjoyed. Their hope was that Christ would destroy the hated yoke imposed on them by the Roman empire. Like the rest of the nation of Israel, they longed for a political messiah. Little did they know that Jesus Christ would be Redeemer, Messiah, King of heaven and earth; one who held more power than the rulers they had become accustomed to. Instead, He would rule over the souls of men, reigning in the hearts of those who would choose to submit to His sovereignty! In order to deliver this wonderful message of hope and truth, they needed the power and edification of the Holy Spirit to see the bigger picture; they needed a new perspective — not just looking for changes in the government and society, but rather witnessing the power of lives changed from the inside out.

Spirit was unto power! At the moment we receive Christ, we become one with Him by virtue of the baptism of the Holy Spirit. The historic baptism on the day of Pentecost took place to unite all believers into one organism—the body of Christ: "For by one Spirit are we all baptized into one body, whether we be Jews or Gentiles, whether we be bond or free; and have been all made to drink into one spirit" (1 Corinthians 12:13). We can't see the Holy Spirit, but we can see Him manifested in our behavior. He enables us to become who Christ wants us to be through His power.

6 When they therefore were come together, they asked of him, saying, Lord, wilt thou at this time restore again the kingdom to Israel?

Throughout the Old Testament, God's promise

7 And he said unto them, It is not for you to know the times or the seasons, which the Father hath put in his own power.

Just as Jesus did not deny that part of God's Divine plan was to restore the kingdom (world rule) of God (a theocracy) in Israel, He has not denied or revoked any of His promises to us! However, because God is a God of consistency and order, "the times and seasons" are known only by God and will take place in His own good pleasure!

8 But ye shall receive power, after that the Holy Ghost is come upon you: and ye shall be witnesses unto me both in Jerusalem, and in all Judaea, and

in Samaria, and unto the uttermost part of the earth.

The Greek verb for "receive," *lempsesthe*, means the giving of power is simultaneous with the coming of the Holy Spirit. This is the baptism discussed in verse 5. The gift of this power is an unconditional blessing imparted by God to every believer. We do not receive this blessing on the basis of our ability, effort, or worthiness. Instead, God gives us the power to live a Christ-controlled life so that we might be strengthened and encouraged from the onset of our relationship with Him.

Jesus continues to tell us a significant purpose for the gift of the Holy Spirit: that we may be His witnesses in Jerusalem, Judea, and Samaria. As Christians in America, we can make this part of the mandate more personal, by allowing it to represent those people who would be considered less desirable, or even enemies, much the way that the Jews looked at the Samaritans. Should we ever withhold the Good News of the Gospel from someone because we didn't like their race, ethnic background, appearance or culture? God doesn't look kindly on this type of partiality! Remember Jonah and his vacation in the whale's belly? All because he did not like Nineveh or its inhabitants. (Book of Jonah)

Finally, the "uttermost part of the earth" is just that—everywhere else in the world. It's an overwhelming mandate. God equips us for any task He calls us to accomplish. We need to witness, first at home, within our community, then the world. Each of these mission fields is dear to the heart of God. Sadly, a common mistake prevalent in the church of Christ today is the tendency of pastors and lay leaders to put the ministry of others before service and ministry to their family members. David's life shows the extremely sad consequence of this well-intentioned, albeit misguided, choice in 2 Samuel 13-18.

9 And when he had spoken these things, while they beheld, he was taken up; and a cloud received him out of their sight.

The word "Beheld" here is translated "as they were looking." While He was speaking, Jesus was received into heaven by God on a cloud of glory (Shekinah). We have a challenge to also reflect God's character and glory in everything we say and do. The person of the Holy Spirit empowers us to allow Christ to live in and through us (Galatians 2:20).

10 And while they looked steadfastly toward heaven as he went up, behold, two men stood by them in white apparel;

Spiritually speaking, we must maintain our gaze toward heaven, we must keep our eyes on Jesus, "looking full in His wonderful face" for inspiration, instruction, direction, reproof, correction, comfort and "the things of earth will grow strangely dim, in the light of His glory and grace." (Helen H. Lemmel, *Turn Your Eyes Upon Jesus*, Singspiration, Inc. 1950.)

11 Which also said, Ye men of Galilee, why stand ye gazing up into heaven? This same Jesus, which is taken up from you into heaven, shall so come in like manner as ye have seen him go into heaven.

In everything there is balance! We must not be so heavenly-minded that we're no earthly good. In other words, we must apply biblical principles to contemporary life, then walk in faith. There is so much to accomplish. Once we each know God's unique objective, we must get busy, since when night comes, "no man can work" (John 9:4). Jesus will always be in heaven a personal friend and divine Saviour. We long for His promised return as we work.

12 Then returned they unto Jerusalem from the mount called Olivet, which is from Jerusalem a sabbath day's journey.

Jesus and the disciples returned to the spot where the Lord taught to begin His triumphal entry into Jerusalem at Passover (Palm Sunday), and sang a hymn after the Passover meal they shared (the Lord's Supper). Just as the disciples returned to a place that held significant memories of the Lord's working in their lives, we too must establish memorials of the great works God has done in our lives. These memorials will encourage our children and their children that God is Jehovah Jireh (our provider), Jehovah Rophe (our healer), Jehovah Shalom (our giver of peace)! We must tell the stories to establish a legacy of faith.

13 And when they were come in, they went up into an upper room, where abode both Peter, and James, and John, and Andrew, Philip, and Thomas, Bartholomew, and Matthew, James the son of Alphaeus, and Simon Zelotes and Judas the brother of James.

The disciples were identifiable. Jesus knew each of them by name. Does He know our names? Do we really know Him? Do we know His heart, desires, and commandments? Does our lifestyle reflect a knowledge of Him, and intimate relationship with Him? "I am the good shepherd, and know my sheep, and am known of mine" (John 10:14).

The upper room may be the location where the Last Supper was held, as well as where Jesus made His Resurrection appearances. Many Bible scholars believe it was at the home of Mary, the mother of John Mark. The significant thing is that the disciples had designated a place where they knew Jesus would always show up! We need to have an upper room. A specific place where we go to commune with God in solitude and concentration. A special place where we keep our prayer journal and Bible. A meeting place where God expects us, and we anticipate His presence!

14 These all continued with one accord in prayer and supplication, with the women, and Mary the mother of Jesus, and with his brethren.

The truest test of our Christianity is whether we love each other! To love our brother is not optional! Jesus remarks that the sum total of the Bible lies in the commandment to love. Loving our neighbor is the difference between practicing true spirituality and behaving religiously. In fact, God says that our love of each other is a barometer of how much we love Him: "If a man say, I love God, and hateth his brother, he is a liar: for he that loveth not his brother whom he hath seen, how can he love God whom he hath not seen? And this commandment have we from him, That he who loveth God love his brother also" (1 John 4:20-21).

The jealousy and competition the disciples showed prior to Jesus' crucifixion, when two of them wanted to be in the closest position of power and influence to Christ (Matthew 20:20-24), is gone. All of the disciples are now on *one accord.*

The phrase "with one accord" *homothumadon* in Greek, means "to have the same mind." This sameness of purpose is critical for the church to successfully accomplish God's work. The maintenance for this demeanor was, and still is, in praise and prayer. These tasks were the chief occupation for the disciples during Pentecost, and it is where true spiritual warfare is fought and won today. The work is accomplished through prayer.

The church today needs more Christians like Mary and the other women in the upper room. Workers on the cutting edge! First in commitment, humility, worship, ministry and service.

Finally, in every extended family, church, or community you can identify women whose presence is essential to the stability of the affiliation. Women can be very indispensable when they are willing to minister unto God with their substance, and are willing to use their talents, possessions, time, and energy to assist others in reproducing the character of Christ in their lives.

DAILY BIBLE READINGS

M: The Promise of the Holy Spirit
Acts 1:1-5

T: The Ascension of Jesus
Acts 1:6-11

W: Jesus Appoints the Twelve
Mark 3:13-19

T: The Acts of the Apostles Begin
Acts 1:12-20

F: The Voice of God's Spirit
Psalm 29

S: The Suicide of Judas Iscariot
Matthew 27:3-10

S: Matthias Chosen to Replace Judas
Iscariot Acts 1:22-26

TEACHING TIPS

March 11
Bible Study Guide 2

1. Words You Should Know

A. Pentecost (Acts 2:1) Greek *Pentekoste*—Fiftieth, from Passover or the feast of Pentecost.

B. Testify (v. 40) Greek *Diamarturomai*—To witness or to bear witness earnestly or repeatedly, attesting to the truth of redemption.

2. Teacher Preparation

A. Review last week's lesson and the SEARCH THE SCRIPTURES questions for this lesson.

B. Now read the IN DEPTH section of the lesson. Answer the following questions:

1. Why did God send the Holy Spirit?

2. God used Peter in the beginning of Acts. What made the difference between the Peter who denied Jesus and the Peter of this chapter?

3. How does this lesson relate to where we are today?

4. What does Peter say in Acts 2 that suggests that the Holy Spirit moves today as He did during Pentecost?

5. What would happen to believers if the Holy Spirit fell on us today as He did at Pentecost?

C. Materials needed: Bible, pencils or pens and paper for students, chalk and chalkboard or newsprint.

3. Starting the Lesson

A. As students arrive, write the lesson title and the AT-A-GLANCE outline on the chalkboard.

B. Have students discuss last week's lesson and how they applied the truths to their lives. Next, ask a student to read the BACKGROUND, FOCAL VERSES, KEEP IN MIND and devotional verses.

C. Have a student lead the class in prayer.

4. Getting into the Lesson

A. Have several students read the BACKGROUND and IN DEPTH sections of the lesson.

B. Now have students work in pairs to answer the SEARCH THE SCRIPTURES questions, which they will share later.

C. Ask students to read THE PEOPLE, PLACES, AND TIMES section of the lesson and comment on the nature of the event of Pentecost.

5. Relating the Lesson to Life

A. Ask for volunteers who will answer the SEARCH THE SCRIPTURES questions. Write their answers down on the chalkboard.

B. Allow students to work silently on the DISCUSS THE MEANING questions. Be sure to solicit answers from students who would like to share.

6. Arousing Action

A. Read the LESSON AIM. Ask students to share how close the class came to achieving each aim.

B. Remind students to read and jot down notes they may glean from the DAILY BIBLE READINGS.

C. Use the MAKE IT HAPPEN exercise as a means to get students "doing" this lesson outside of the class.

D. Have a student close the class with prayer, thanking the Lord for an opportunity to learn this week.

WORSHIP GUIDE

For the Superintendent or Teacher
Theme: The Holy Spirit Comes in Power
Theme Song: "Holy, Holy, Holy"
Scripture: 1 Corinthians 2:1-5
Song: "Holy Ghost, Wind Blowing Strong"
Meditation: "Thank You God for the Holy Spirit, the Wind from Heaven. Help me to submit my life to His Power. In Jesus' name. Amen.

THE HOLY SPIRIT COMES IN POWER

Bible Background • ACTS 2
Printed Text • ACTS 2:1-4, 37-47
Devotional Reading • JOHN 3:5-8

LESSON AIM

By the end of the lesson, students should be able to relate the events of Pentecost, explore the significance of the Holy Spirit's power during Pentecost, and commit to applying the significance of Pentecost in their own lives.

KEEP IN MIND

"Then Peter said unto them, Repent, and be baptized every one of you in the name of Jesus Christ for the remission of sins, and ye shall receive the gift of the Holy Ghost" (Acts 2:38).

FOCAL VERSES

Acts 2:1 And when the day of Pentecost was fully come, they were all with one accord in one place.

2 And suddenly there came a sound from heaven as of a rushing mighty wind, and it filled all the house where they were sitting.

3 And there appeared unto them cloven tongues like as of fire, and it sat upon each of them.

4 And they were all filled with the Holy Ghost, and began to speak with other tongues as the Spirit gave them utterance.

ACTS 2:37 Now when they heard this they were pricked in their heart, and said unto Peter and to the rest of the apostles, Men and brethren, what shall we do?

38 Then Peter said unto them, Repent, and be baptized every one of you in the name of Jesus Christ for the remission of sins, and ye shall receive

LESSON OVERVIEW

LESSON AIM
KEEP IN MIND
FOCAL VERSES
IN FOCUS
THE PEOPLE, PLACES,
AND TIMES
BACKGROUND
AT-A-GLANCE
IN DEPTH
SEARCH THE SCRIPTURES
DISCUSS THE MEANING
LESSON IN OUR SOCIETY
MAKE IT HAPPEN
FOLLOW THE SPIRIT
REMEMBER YOUR THOUGHTS
MORE LIGHT ON THE TEXT
DAILY BIBLE READINGS

the gift of the Holy Ghost.

39 For the promise is unto you, and to your children, and to all that are afar off, even as many as the Lord our God shall call.

40 And with many other words did he testify and exhort, saying, Save yourselves from this untoward generation.

41 Then they that gladly received his word were baptized: and the same day there were added unto them about a three thousand souls.

42 And they continued steadfastly in the apostles' doctrine and fellowship, and in breaking of bread, and in prayers.

43 And fear came upon every soul: and many wonders and signs were done by the apostles.

44 And all that believed were together, and had all things common;

45 And sold their possessions and goods, and parted them to all men, as every man had need.

46 And they, continuing daily with one accord in the temple, and breaking bread from house to house, did eat their meat with gladness and singleness of heart,

47 Praising God, and having favor with all the people. And the Lord added to the church daily such as should be saved.

IN FOCUS

Donald Taylor, also known as "Little D," was destined for a life of prison or an early grave. Donald was 18 and had been actively involved in gangs, drugs, and crime since he was 9 years old.

Sara, Donald's mother, prayed for him every day. But it seemed the more she prayed, the worse Donald got. Often Sara would try to share the love of Christ with her son, but Donald's response was always the same: "If Jesus Christ is real, He had better make Himself known to me one-on-one."

One night as Donald was about to leave a crackhouse, a group of young men pulled up in a car and shot at him. Several hours later, Donald awoke in a pool of blood in an alley. Suddenly, he felt the arms of a huge man surrounding him. The man smiled warmly at Donald and told him that help was on the way.

A few minutes later as the ambulance turned into the alley, the man softly whispered to Donald, "I've been sent to respond to your request. Jesus is real." Before Donald could respond, the man seemed to disappear among the crowd that had gathered in the alley. Donald began to cry. "Lord Jesus, I'm so sorry. Just let me live, and I'll serve you the rest of my life."

As they put Donald in the ambulance, one of the attendants said, "It's a miracle this boy is still alive. Somebody upstairs must really love him."

On the day of Pentecost, the miracle of God touched lives one-on-one with the power of the Holy Spirit.

THE PEOPLE, PLACES, AND TIMES

Feast of Pentecost. The feast of Pentecost is commemorated in the church as the day on which the Holy Spirit descended (Acts 2) in fulfillment of the promise of Jesus (John 16:7, 13; Acts 1:4,14). It is traditionally recognized as the birth of the church as an institution.

"Pentecost," meaning "fifty," is the Greek name for the Old Testament Feast of Weeks, which occurred on the fiftieth day (seven weeks) after Passover. Along with the feasts of Passover and Tabernacles, Pentecost was one of the three annual pilgrimage feasts among the Jews. A harvest festival, it marked the beginning of the time when the people brought their offerings of firstfruits. Leviticus 23:15-21 provides the most detailed account of the ritual observed during the feast. The observance is also known as the Feast of Ingathering (Exodus 23:16) and Day of Firstfruits (Numbers 28:26).

The coming of the Holy Spirit on the Day of Pentecost (Acts 2) implies the passing of the old system of worship, as well as the climax and fulfillment of the promises that system foreshadowed. For the church, Pentecost has become a time to celebrate God's bestowal of the gift of the Spirit.

BACKGROUND

The events in our lesson today take place after Jesus had appeared to the apostles and given them specific instructions to wait for the promised Holy Spirit, which would be given to them for effective witnessing. In obedience to Jesus' command, the apostles went to the upper room in Jerusalem and devoted themselves to prayer and supplication.

After prayer, Peter stood among the 120 believers and discussed what had happened to Judas, who betrayed the Lord. His death was a fulfillment of David's prophecy in the Old Testament (Psalm 41:9). Peter reminded the group of another passage in Psalms: "let his habitation be desolate and let no man dwell therein" (see Psalm 69:25).

Peter also suggested that Judas' office be filled by another disciple who had been an eyewitness of Jesus' ministry. Two men were appointed for the office: Joseph, called Barsabas, and Matthias. The disciples had prayed for the Lord to reveal the one who should replace Judas and cast lots. Matthias was finally chosen to serve with the other apostles. Then the apostles awaited the arrival of the Lord.

AT-A-GLANCE

1. The Holy Spirit and Pentecost (Acts 2:1-4)
2. The Holy Spirit Is for All (vv. 37-42)
3. The Holy Spirit Motivates Believers a New Life (vv. 43-47)

IN DEPTH

1. The Holy Spirit and Pentecost (Acts 2:1-4)

On the day of Pentecost, all of Jesus' disciples were assembled together and on one accord. It is important we understand this from a three-fold perspective:

a. God has a strategic timetable for His promise.

b. Christian unity in the local church is crucial to experience the full manifestation of God's presence.

c. Obedience to God is required as we wait patiently for His promise to be fulfilled.

God's promised Holy Spirit came "suddenly." Sometimes believers miss what God has for us because we are too impatient. The inability to wait on God causes us to give premature birth to a God-inspired dream in our lives.

What would have happened if the disciples had disobeyed the Lord's command and departed from Jerusalem because they didn't want to wait? They would not have experienced Pentecost and would have missed the promised Holy Spirit! Because God's Spirit came suddenly, it was imperative that they were at the right place at the right time to receive the full manifestation of His power.

Jesus told His disciples "to go into all the world and preach the Gospel (Mark 16:15-18). They needed to be baptized with the Holy Spirit, and the only way for that to be accomplished was for them to obey the Lord's command (see Luke 24:49). We, too, must be obedient to the Lord's command if we expect to receive the power of the Holy Spirit in our lives and in the church today.

Luke also affirms that the Spirit's presence "sat" upon each of the disciples who were in the upper room, including Mary, the mother of Jesus and His brethren (Acts 1:14). Everyone there had a personal encounter with God's power and no one was excluded.

As the "tongues" of fire came into the room, the Scripture declares that they were all filled with the Holy Spirit and began to speak with other tongues "as the Spirit gave them utterance" (v. 4). When there is a genuine manifestation of God's Holy Spirit in our churches, there will be unity among believers, an excitement in our worship, powerful messages in our preaching, and a shaking in our personal and corporate lives.

2. The Holy Spirit Is for All (vv. 37-42)

After the disciples received the gift of the Holy Spirit in the upper room, they were able to witness just as Jesus had said. In fact, the 120 spoke with distinct dialects so that the Jews from different regions could understand what God was doing.

The disciples also began to impact cities as well. They didn't just stay in the upper room ministering to one another, but they became witnesses unto Jesus, "both in Jerusalem, and in all Judea and in Samaria, and unto the uttermost part of the earth." The early disciples shared what they had experienced and encouraged people to repent and be baptized in order that they would also receive the baptism in the Holy Spirit.

The power and the presence of God worked mightily in the disciple's lives. When Peter proclaimed the Gospel, people were convicted, many repented of their sins and accepted Jesus Christ as Saviour and Lord. They were also baptized with water and received the baptism in the Holy Ghost. Many were healed of sickness and delivered from demons. The religious leaders became furious and were determined to stop the move of the Holy Spirit in the lives of Jesus' disciples, but they were unsuccessful.

We must understand that when the Gospel of Jesus Christ is proclaimed, signs and wonders sometimes follow to confirm the authenticity of the Gospel. Jesus Christ desires to make Himself known to us through His Holy Spirit. The same power of the Holy Spirit that the disciples experienced is available to us today.

After listening to Peter's convicting message, the Scriptures affirm that the people were ready for a change in their lives (v. 37). In essence, they told Peter "whatever that is you have, we want it in our lives today." The apostle told the people that all they had to do to receive God's power was to repent of their sins, receive Jesus Christ as their Saviour and Lord and they were instant candidates for the precious Holy Spirit.

Many people believe that Peter's words were only applicable to the people whom he addressed. But Peter made it clear that the promise of God's power is available to all who would believe in Jesus Christ throughout this age "unto you, and to your children" and the age to come "to all that are afar off, even as many as the Lord our God shall call." The Holy Spirit's presence and power for the believer did not cease at Pentecost (Acts 8:5; 10:44-46). The Holy Spirit is the birthright of every true born-again believer in Christ (Joel 2:28; Matthew 3:11; Luke 24:49).

Once the people had received Peter's word,

they continued steadfast in the apostle's doctrine. It is evident that the people needed to be taught how to live for God and how to affect change in the lives of their community and they were willing to sit at the apostles' feet to feast on the Word of God.

3. The Holy Spirit Motivates Believers to a New Life (vv. 43-47)

Once the Holy Spirit was in full manifestation among these new believers, fear came upon them. This does not mean that they were shaking in their boots. Rather, these men and women had a new reverence for the Lord. It is time for the fear of God to return to our local churches. Many of God's people no longer revere His holiness. Instead, some churches have become nothing more than social gatherings, a place for fashion and talent shows, entertainment centers, and feel-good clubs.

The altar prayers have been replaced by the "name it and claim it" game. Our testimony services have become a time to boast of our own achievements. Every local church needs a genuine outpouring of God's Holy Spirit so that we may worship the Lord in holiness and truth, where we tremble at His Word (Isaiah 66:3b-5; Acts 2:37), and experience His power like they did in the early church.

Not only was the Holy Spirit manifested in many signs and wonders by the apostles, but there was also unity among all the believers. Only the Holy Spirit can bring about unity in the Christian community.

As Christians, we are to share our blessings with others who may be less fortunate than we are and assist people in Jesus' name. The New Testament believers became givers when the Holy Spirit empowered their lives. They were willing to part with their resources so that the church would be a true evangelistic and benevolent center. Indeed, this was the real thing. Luke affirms that they "continued daily with one accord in the temple" (v. 46). The people praised God for all that He did in their lives and God continued to add to the church many more who needed the power of the Holy Spirit in their lives.

God's Spirit within a believer will prompt us to praise God. As a result, we release the favor of God in our churches and in our lives and there will be church growth that will effect change in our communities, cities, and world for the glory of God. (Acts 2:46-47). If we want our churches to grow, we must do it God's way!

SEARCH THE SCRIPTURES

1. How did the Holy Spirit come? (Acts 2:2)
2. How many had a personal encounter with the Holy Spirit? (v. 3)
3. What happened because of Pentecost? (v. 4)
4. What was the result of Peter's preaching? (Acts 2:37)
5. To whom did God promise to give the Holy Spirit? (v. 39)
6. How did God add to the church? (v. 47)

DISCUSS THE MEANING

1. The outpouring of the Holy Spirit had been prophesied many years prior to the actual event. Are there any other prophesies that have not yet been fulfilled? Discuss.
2. Why is it so important that we have a genuine outpouring of the Holy Spirit in our lives and in our churches?
3. What would happen if the fear of God returned in the same manner that was evident in the early church?
4. How important is it to be in the right place at the right time in order to receive God's blessings?

LESSON IN OUR SOCIETY

The world is looking for the real thing. In the perilous times that we live in, it is vital for every born again believer to participate in God's redemptive plan to effect change in our communities for God's glory. How can we turn our world upside down for Jesus Christ and set people free from demonic strongholds? Write out three things you will do to make this lesson real in your life. Be ready to share your action plan with the class.

MAKE IT HAPPEN

If you are a born again believer who has not yet experienced the filling and power of the Holy Ghost, now is the time to cry out to the Lord for His power. The first step is to ask and believe that God wants to fulfill His work in your life and in the lives of others through you. When you are filled with power, as the disciples were, go out and make a difference where you live. Ask your pastor or teacher what your church believes regarding the infilling of the Holy Spirit and commit yourself to being filled.

FOLLOW THE SPIRIT
What God wants me to do:

_____

_____

REMEMBER YOUR THOUGHTS
Special insights you have learned:

_____

_____

MORE LIGHT ON THE TEXT
Acts 2:1-4, 37-47

2:1 And when the day of Pentecost was fully come, they were all with one accord in one place.

The interval of time between the Passover and Pentecost is 50 days; during this time the disciples maintained their oneness of spirit and mind. Their hearts were prepared in obedient anticipation of what the Lord had promised.

2 And suddenly there came a sound from heaven as of a rushing mighty wind, and it filled all the house where they were sitting.

The sound came from heaven—loud and violent—like a hurricane or tornado. Its enormity filled the room. God provides what we need to accomplish His work! He is consistent to prove Himself on a grand scale. There is no doubt from whom or where the power comes. It is God alone. We are simply the recipients and His agents.

When we practice godly, biblical disciplines (prayer, unity of purpose, and expectant faith), then Christ is ready to respond to us. If we are anxious for His appearing today, we should practice these same disciplines. Then we can say, "even so Lord Jesus, come!"

3 And there appeared unto them cloven tongues like as of fire, and it sat upon each of them.

The word, "cloven," *diamerizo,* means "being distributed." The fire appeared as an expanse of flames, which separated and then settled on each

individual simultaneously. This is significant since it reinforces the notion of unity. Everyone who has received Christ as their personal Saviour is equally equipped. God does not show partiality. He is anxious to give His all to us. It is His desire that none perish, but all come to repentance (2 Peter 3:9).

Fire is a common representation of the Holy Spirit. The appearance of tongues of fire resting on each of them could signify God's acceptance of each individual believer's heart as His dwelling place (1 Corinthians 3:16; Ephesians 2:21,22).

4 And they were all filled with the Holy Ghost, and began to speak with other tongues, as the Spirit gave them utterance.

There were Jews present from all over the world for Pentecost. The evidence that God would, indeed, give the apostles power to reach Jerusalem, Judea, Samaria, and the uttermost parts of the earth was confirmed with the Holy Spirit "giving utterance" so that each one present could hear God's message in their own language. This dispensation further confirms the fact that God provides whatever is required and necessary for each believer to be in a right relationship with Him, and that He is "no respecter of persons" (Acts 10:34-35).

2:37 Now when they heard this, they were pricked in their heart, and said unto Peter and to the rest of the apostles, Men and brethren, what shall we do?

The audience for Peter's sermon is deeply affected by his message. The Bible reports that "they were pricked in their heart." In Greek, the word *katenugesan* translates as "to sting sharply, stun, or smite." The audience was full of remorse at the gravity of the wickedness committed by the crucifixion of the Messiah, and their blindness and inability to recognize Him.

38 Then Peter said unto them, Repent, and be baptized every one of you in the name of Jesus Christ for the remission of sins, and ye shall receive the gift of the Holy Ghost.

Peter explains the appropriate response to the Gospel:

The Gospel Requires Repentance: Man has frequently attempted to add additional conditions

and works to God's requirement. The fact remains that salvation is a total work of the triune God (Father, Son, and Holy Spirit), and there is no additional effort that we can add to re-make God's plan or provision. Salvation is strictly by grace through faith. Ephesians 2:8-9 states: "For by grace are ye saved through faith; and that not of yourselves: it is the gift of God: Not of works, lest any man should boast." To repent means "to change your mind" in regard to sin. Secularists may say, "There is no sin. Do what you want to do." However, we can also deny or dispute gravity; our disbelief does not change the fact that it exists. The truth of the matter is, what goes up must come down. Similarly, the only way to have a personal relationship with God is to accept the provision He offers. There is no "plan B."

Baptism—An Outward Confession of an Inward Reality: The next instruction Peter gives is "be baptized every one of you in the name of Jesus Christ for the remission of sins." Baptism does not add anything to our salvation. It does not wash away sin, or help to make us more worthy of the gift God has already given us. Rather, we partake of this ordinance out of love and obedience to Christ. Remember, salvation is a complete and total work of God.

The word "baptize" comes from the Greek word *baptistheto*, which means "to dip" or "submerge." The word also means "identification."

When we are baptized, we are indicating to all who witness the event that we identify with Christ in His death, burial, and resurrection. When we go under the water, it represents a "death" to our old lifestyle independent of Christ. Being raised out of the water is indicative of rising to a new life of submission to Jesus Christ. We are raised to a new way of thinking and being. In Acts, the order is never reversed. It is always "believe and be baptized." Confession must precede declaration.

To participate in baptism without repentance is to simply reduce it to a religious ritual, a vain exercise, since an individual simply goes into the water a dry sinner, only to come out a wet one!

39 For the promise is unto you, and to your children, and to all that are afar off, even as many as the Lord our God shall call.

Clearly, the promise is for the Gentile and Jew. "For as many as were far away who would receive Him to them He gave the power to become His sons" (John 1:12, paraphrased). Redemption is for all of humanity not just for the 3,000 who responded. God has made His promises available to their descendants and to all future generations.

40 And with many other words did he testify and exhort, saying, Save yourselves from this untoward generation.

"Untoward" is translated from the word *skolias* in Greek, which means "crooked, perverse." Peter exhorts his audience to reject the corruption of those who denied the truth about Jesus. This passage is particularly sobering for our generation, where so many things that are wrong (abortion, homosexuality, pornography, adultery, etc.) are justified as "lifestyle alternatives." As Christians, we must purpose that our attitudes and actions are consistent with the principles and commandments of God's Word.

41 Then they that gladly received his word were baptized: and the same day there were added unto them about three thousand souls.

Those who received redemption in Christ were baptized. The converts were instant in their obedience to the command to be baptized.

42 And they continued stedfastly in the apos-

tles' doctrine and fellowship, and in breaking of bread, and in prayers.

We must be sure to be available for those we lead to Christ! The apostles obeyed Christ's mandate to make disciples, given in Matthew 28:19. These new converts had a persistent desire to be taught the things of the Lord. They were anxious to learn more. There is a shared responsibility between those who lead and those who receive.

On one hand, the recipient must have a teachable spirit. Conversely, the person who introduces the new Christian to Christ must have a spirit of service and availability.

The commitment to help others grow in their faith is larger than just performing the role of teacher. We must be willing to share our lives. *Koinonia*, the Greek word translated here as "fellowship" means, "sharing in common interests or partnership." This collaboration involves cooperating to accomplish the work of the Gospel, ensuring each other's success, praying together, sharing meals and observing the Lord's Supper. The verb *Klao* is used to refer to breaking bread at a normal meal (Luke 24:30) and as part of the Lord's Supper (Luke 22:19). It is supposed that the early disciples attached so much significance to the "breaking of bread" (communion) at the ordinary meals, similar to our saying grace, that they followed the traditional meal with communion, a combination called "agape" (love) feasts, with great frequency.

This verse emphasizes the very important disciplines of fellowship, prayer, and communion. These disciplines are vital to our spiritual growth and maturity. No Christian should neglect them.

43 And fear came upon every soul: and many wonders and signs were done by the apostles.

A reverential fear of God is critical in helping Christians walk according to godly principles. In this situation, the fear was also felt by all of Jerusalem, giving the infant Church time to establish a tradition of unity and holiness. Jerusalem was so overwhelmed by the events and acts of the apostles that favor was bestowed, giving the disciples time to multiply and establish themselves before the inevitable tide of opposition from the established church and Roman Empire. The mir-

acles the apostles performed were done to confirm the Word, and the apostles' teaching, as Jesus had promised (Mark 16:20).

44 And all that believed were together, and had all things in common; 45 And sold their possessions and goods, and parted them to all men, as every man had need.

These verses give a picture of Christian unity. This was not communism, in the contemporary sense. Nor was it communal living. It was simply Christian charity. All of the apostles and their converts realized the importance of developing and nurturing the faith. Some who were not from Jerusalem ran out of money, so those who were "local" did what they could to make it feasible for these converts to remain nearby. The example and teachings of Jesus made it easy for the believers to share among themselves.

46 And they, continuing daily with one accord in the temple, and breaking bread from house to house, did eat their meat with gladness and singleness of heart,

The happening is a loving body of believers, still worshiping at the temple, since, as of yet, no division exists between the Jewish Christians, and their Jewish brethren. Each home was an assembly of Christian fellowship and worship. ("From house to house" means by households.) Jerusalem was ill-equipped to hold such a large group of people, and many likely stayed in surrounding villages. Mealtime was an opportunity for rejoicing without criticism or variance. The believers were single-hearted or united in motive, with a common agenda.

47 Praising God, and having favour with all the people. And the Lord added to the church daily such as should be saved.

The joy, excitement, and anticipation kept the believers in a spirit of praise and worship. The result was that they found favor with many in Jerusalem. At this juncture there was no persecution or opposition. Those who had not received Christ were impressed and attracted by the sense of community, and good works were performed by the apostles and their converts. As a result, the Lord continued to add to those who would believe on a daily basis.

TEACHING TIPS

March 18
Bible Study Guide 3

1. Words You Should Know

A. Beautiful. (Acts 3:2, 10) Greek *Horaios*—Timely, fair, proper and good timing; used in the New Testament in a figurative sense.

B. Ignorant (Acts 4:13) Greek *Idiotes*—A common man as opposite to either a man of power or a man of education and learning.

2. Teacher Preparation

A. Review last week's lesson and make appropriate notes to be used for teaching today's lesson.

B. Read the FOCAL VERSES in several translations of the Bible. Read the IN DEPTH commentary and imagine yourself as: the lame man, Peter, and John.

C. Write down some questions to ask your students based on your study.

D. Materials needed: Bible, chalkboard or 3 x 5 cards.

3. Starting the Lesson

A. As students arrive today, assign three to role play the lame man, Peter, and John.

B. Have students read the background Scriptures.

C. Next, ask a volunteer to read the FOCAL VERSES emphasizing the KEEP IN MIND verse.

D. Write the AT-A-GLANCE outline on the chalkboard and assign three other students to read the lesson following the outline.

4. Getting into the Lesson

A. Ask a student to read the IN FOCUS section of the lesson. Then ask students how this story relates to the Scriptures. What's the difference between natural power and the Holy Spirit's power?

B. Have the three volunteers read today's IN DEPTH section.

C. Ask the students to answer the SEARCH THE SCRIPTURES questions based on their reading.

5. Relating the Lesson to Life

A. Ask the three students who volunteered, to role play today's lesson. Encourage the rest of the students to comment on how the events of the Scripture lesson relate to the lame and outcast of our society.

B. Remind students that the greatest need of many people everywhere is salvation. Only a personal relationship with Jesus Christ can change lives and bring people to the level of healing and faith that can make a difference.

6. Arousing Action

A. Challenge students to read and incorporate the key points from the DAILY BIBLE READINGS into their lives.

B. Give students an opportunity to read both the LESSON IN OUR SOCIETY and MAKE IT HAPPEN sections and discuss how they plan to implement them this week.

C. Close the class with prayer, using the KEEP IN MIND verse as the basis of the prayer.

WORSHIP GUIDE

For the Superintendent or Teacher
Theme: The Holy Spirit Works with Power
Theme Song: "Holy Spirit, Thou Art Welcome in this Place"
Scripture: 2 Thessalonians 2:13-14
Song: The Power of the Holy Ghost"
Devotional Thought: Heavenly Father, we need Your power so that we might work for You. Help us to yield our lives to You so that we may be vessels through whom Your power can flow. In Jesus' name, Amen.

THE HOLY SPIRIT WORKS WITH POWER

Bible Background • ACTS 3:1—4:13
Printed Text • ACTS 3:1-10; 4:1-4, 13
Devotional Reading • 1 CORINTHIANS 1:26-31

LESSON AIM

By the end of the lesson, students should be able to describe certain evidences of the power of the Holy Spirit, list some characteristics of the Holy Spirit's power, and commit their lives to be used by the Holy Spirit's power.

KEEP IN MIND

"Now when they saw the boldness of Peter and John, and perceived that they were unlearned and ignorant men, they marvelled; and took knowledge of them, that they had been with Jesus" (Acts 4:13).

FOCAL VERSES

Acts 3:1 Now Peter and John went up together into the temple at the hour of prayer, being the ninth hour.

2 And a certain man lame from his mother's womb was carried, whom they laid daily at the gate of the temple which is called Beautiful, to ask alms of them that entered into the temple;

3 Who seeing Peter and John about to go into the temple asked an alms.

4 And Peter, fastening his eyes upon him with John, said, Look on us.

5 And he gave heed unto them, expecting to receive something of them.

6 Then Peter said, Silver and gold have I none; but such as I have give I thee: In the name of Jesus Christ of Nazareth rise up and walk.

7 And he took him by the right hand, and lifted him up: and immediately his feet and ankle bones

LESSON OVERVIEW

LESSON AIM
KEEP IN MIND
FOCAL VERSES
IN FOCUS
THE PEOPLE, PLACES,
AND TIMES
BACKGROUND
AT-A-GLANCE
IN DEPTH
SEARCH THE SCRIPTURES
DISCUSS THE MEANING
LESSON IN OUR SOCIETY
MAKE IT HAPPEN
FOLLOW THE SPIRIT
REMEMBER YOUR THOUGHTS
MORE LIGHT ON THE TEXT
DAILY BIBLE READINGS

received strength.

8 And he leaping up stood, and walked, and entered with them into the temple, walking, and leaping and praising God.

9 And all the people saw him walking and praising God:

10 And they knew that it was he which sat for alms at the Beautiful gate of the temple: and they were filled with wonder and amazement at that which had happened unto him.

ACTS 4:1 And as they spake unto the people, the priests, and the captain of the temple, and the Sadducees, came upon him.

2 Being grieved that they taught the people, and preached through Jesus the resurrection from the dead.

3 And they laid hands on them, and put them in hold unto the next day: for it was now eventide.

4 Howbeit many of them which heard the word believed; and the number of the men was about five thousand.

4:13 Now when they saw the boldness of Peter and John, and perceived that they were unlearned and ignorant men, they marvelled; and they took knowledge of them, that they had been with Jesus.

IN FOCUS

The massive power plant of Detroit Edison is located in Ecorse, Michigan, approximately 15 miles southwest of downtown Detroit. Every day,

Detroit Edison serves approximately 300 communities in a six county radius in southeastern Michigan with enough electrical power to send a space shuttle around the moon ten times and still have enough current to spare.

When the workers at Detroit Edison went on strike for more money and better working conditions, the entire area was affected. Without electrical power, very little commerce took place in metropolitan Detroit. In fact, the city and suburbs were completely shut down until the strike was settled and power restored to the communities.

"I never knew just how much power Detroit Edison had until this strike. I'm glad we didn't have to go very long without power. It would have been disastrous for everyone," said one man in Pontiac, Michigan.

Although we may take it for granted, power is one thing most of us can't do without. Our whole lifestyle is based on power being available so that we can work, learn, and play. Imagine living in a world without power. How empty and futile our technology would be.

This lesson will focus on power, but not the kind of power generated by Detroit Edison. For the power believers need comes from the Holy Spirit.

THE PEOPLE, PLACES, AND TIMES

The Temple. The religious structure in Jerusalem that was the center of Israelite national life in the biblical period, beginning with the monarchy (10th century B.C.) and continuing until its final destruction by the Roman legions in A.D. 70. Even in sixth century B.C. after the temple had lain in ruins for about seventy years as the result of the Babylonian conquest of the kingdom of Judah (586 B.C.), sacrifice took place in the temple courtyard. The Temple Mount (Mount Zion in Jerusalem) continued to symbolize, in prophecy and tradition, God's relationship with His people. Despite the fact that for over a millennium the temple's existence was nearly continuous, it did undergo two major reconstructions: one following the Exile, which began in 520 B.C. and the other as part of the enormous building projects carried out by King Herod, who reigned in Palestine 37 to 4 B.C.

The importance of the temple in religious life of Jews at this time is evident in the New Testament. The birth of John the Baptist was announced in the temple (Luke 1:11-20) and the sacrificial offering for every Jewish male child, including Jesus, was offered there (Luke 2:22-24).

The largest and grandest of the Jerusalem temples was also the shortest lived. During the Roman siege of Jerusalem, Titus and his legions set fire to the temple in A.D. 70. Today, the Muslim shrine called the "Dome of the Rock" or the Mosque of Omar stands on the Temple site.

(Harper Bible Dictionary, Paul J. Achtemeier, Gen. Ed., San Francisco: Harper and Row Publishing Co., 1984, pp. 1021-1029)

BACKGROUND

God's Holy Spirit had empowered not only 120 men who were waiting in the upper room in Jerusalem for the promise of the Father (Acts 1:4), but also the apostle Peter who preached the first sermon of the New Testament church (see Acts 2:14-36).

Why did these men wait? Jesus had told them that they would receive power after the Holy Ghost came upon them so that they would be witnesses for Jesus, in Jerusalem, Judea, Samaria and other places around the world (Acts 1:8).

On the day of Pentecost, God's power came upon these men and they spoke in languages they didn't know, and they were heard by the Jews from different provinces who were also in Jerusalem during Pentecost. By speaking "with other tongues" (Acts 2:4) and proclaiming the Good News of God's saving grace, these 120 helped to confirm Peter's message so that it was readily received by the Jews. Once Peter finished

AT-A-GLANCE

1. Peter and John Head for the Temple
(Acts 3:1-5)
2. Peter and John Yield to God's Power
(vv. 6-10)
3. Peter and John Proclaim God's Power
(Acts 4:1-4, 13)

the sermon, 3,000 souls were immediately added to the church.

This Bible Study Guide continues the focus of the Holy Spirit's power at work in the lives of the New Testament believers.

IN DEPTH

1. Peter and John Head for the Temple
(Acts 3:1-5)

It was time for God's power to be demonstrated outside the "four walls" of the upper room. After all, Jesus said that believers should be witnesses in Jerusalem after they were empowered by the Holy Spirit (Acts 24:49).

Once the church was established, Peter and John decided to go to the temple to join the prayer meeting which began around 3:00 in the afternoon. As they approached the temple, they saw a lame beggar sitting at the gate, asking for "alms" of people who entered (v. 2). Luke makes several assessments of this scene that must be emphasized:

a. This was a "certain" lame man who was born crippled. However, the Bible does not give the nature of his problem nor his emotional state at the time Peter and John approached.

b. The man was brought to the temple by others everyday so he could beg from those who went in and out. In fact, this is how the lame man survived.

c. He was laid at the "Beautiful" gate of the temple. The Greek word for "beautiful" means "proper timing." Literally speaking, God had this man's friends place him at the gate of "proper timing" so that when Peter and John came by, he would be in the right place at the right time for a miracle in his life.

d. The man asked for "alms" of all who entered the temple. The Greek definition for alms has more to do with help and mercy than it does with money. In essence, the man was asking for any type of compassion and mercy that could help ease the pain and suffering he felt. However, no one was able to help this man with what he really needed until he experienced the power of the Holy Spirit.

So often in our society, we are told that the solution for poverty is to give the poor money and programs to help pull them out of a vicious cycle. However, without the power of the Holy Spirit in their lives, they will soon return to the cycle of despair. Only God's power can change people so they can rise to their greatest potential.

As Peter and John were about to enter the temple, the lame man cried out to the disciples for help. Now was the time to see whether or not the power of the Holy Spirit really worked. Having preached such a powerful sermon where 3,000 souls were stirred to follow Jesus Christ, what was one lame man before the awesome power of the Holy Spirit?

Like a laser-guided missile, Peter and John locked on to the man's eyes and commanded that he look at them. They were ready to show to everyone entering the temple, and the lame man as well, that it was time for his life to change.

2. Peter and John Yield to God's Power
(vv. 6-10)

Peter and John knew that if they gave this lame man money he would be back begging again at the temple the next day. They decided not to give the man temporal relief. Instead, Peter commanded that the man get up from his "comfort zone" in the name of Jesus of Nazareth through the power of the Holy Spirit (v. 6).

Note that Peter did not use his own name when ministering to the man. There is no power in our name. No matter how much God uses us in the ministry, we must always focus people's attention on Jesus Christ. He is the Healer and Deliverer and we are the vessels through whom He works. Anytime we seek glory for ourselves, we are asking for trouble.

Secondly, Peter didn't just preach to the man. He took the man's hand and pulled him up on his feet from where he was sitting. It was one thing for Peter to proclaim healing in this man's life and another to demonstrate it by getting the man involved in his own healing.

As the man arose from the ground, "immediately his feet and ankle bones received strength" (v. 8). This man didn't need money or pious platitudes. What he needed was God's healing power so that he could become a contributing member of society and fulfill God's plan for his life.

Once Peter pulled him up from the ground and the Holy Spirit touched the man, he was so excited about his transformed life, that he leaped and walked into the temple to give God the praise. He was no longer a beggar, but now a worshiper. He was no longer seeking for what he could get from others, but for what he could give to God. He was no longer a liability, but a testament of the healing power of God.

When the man came into the temple, he probably let out such a shout (see Psalm 150:1-6), that the people were surprised to see him. They immediately recognized him as the lame man who had been at the Beautiful Gate for so long. Now he was ready to give God praise because the power of the Holy Spirit had touched his life.

3. Peter and John Proclaim God's Power (Acts 4:1-4, 13)

Peter and John didn't stay outside of the temple to receive praises from people for this miraculous work. Instead, they followed the man inside where Peter preached to the people about Jesus Christ, the Author of the miracle (Acts 3:11-26).

While Peter preached, many of the Jewish temple leaders were grieved because of his sermon's content. First, Peter affirmed that the Jews were responsible for Jesus' death. Secondly, Peter made it clear that the lame man was healed by the name of Jesus. Finally, Peter told the people that they could be saved and have eternal life with God only by believing in the resurrected Jesus Christ.

Perhaps it was the last statement that drove the religious leaders to action. The Sadducees laid their hands on Peter and John to stop them from ministering to the people—especially about the resurrection. Since they deny the resurrection (see Matthew 22:23; Acts 23:8), the Sadducees believed that Peter and John were heretics who had to be stopped.

The Sadducees grabbed the disciples and arrested them until they could sort out the uproar that their preaching had started. But it was too late. Because of Peter's preaching and the eye witness account of the lame man being healed, 5,000 people were converted and believed in the name of Jesus Christ.

The next day, Peter and John were released from prison and brought before the religious leaders to answer their charges. However, one night in prison didn't deter them from proclaiming Jesus' name. In fact, as they stood before the religious leaders, Peter and John were so bold that it shocked them. The religious leaders recognized that the disciples were not educated men. They had not been to rabbinical schools nor had they sat under the teachings of the Pharisees. Their only "education" was "on the job" training with Jesus.

Only Jesus can give us boldness to stand in the midst of opposition to proclaim His truths. That's why we need His presence and power to do His work.

SEARCH THE SCRIPTURES

1. Who went to the temple to pray? (Acts 3:1)

2. What time did Peter and John go to the temple? (v.1)

3. Who did the disciples see when they arrived at the temple? (vv. 2-3)

4. What happened to the man once he met Peter and John? (vv. 4-8)

5. How did the people respond after the lame man was healed? (vv. 9-10)

6. What happened to Peter and John when they entered the temple? (Acts 4:1-4)

DISCUSS THE MEANING

1. Why is it important that we point people to Jesus Christ when we minister to them?

2. Do you think God's power is available to heal people today? Why or why not?

3. Why do you think the religious leaders emphasized the fact that Peter and John were ignorant and unlearned men?

4. List some of the things we need to be used mightily by God? Does your list include seminary or Bible college training? Why or why not?

LESSON IN OUR SOCIETY

Our society is full of people who rely on social assistance. What can we learn from today's lesson that will help us become a catalyst and advocate for change in their lives?

MAKE IT HAPPEN

This week, ask the Lord to give you an opportunity to minister His power in the lives of others. Perhaps a simple task of taking an elderly person grocery shopping or reading a Bible story to a visually-impaired person in your neighborhood would be a good place to start. Whatever you do, be sure to give God the praise for using you.

FOLLOW THE SPIRIT
What God wants me to do:

_____

_____

REMEMBER YOUR THOUGHTS
Special insights you have learned:

_____

_____

MORE LIGHT ON THE TEXT
Acts 3:1-10; 4:1-4, 13

3:1 Now Peter and John went up together into the temple at the hour of prayer, being the ninth hour.

The relationship of Peter and John was long standing. They were associates in the fishing business, and were working together when Jesus called them to become "fishers of men" (Luke 5:10). The two men were also present at the Transfiguration (Matthew 17:2; Mark 9:2), which established them as part of the inner circle of the Lord's apostles, the raising of Jairus's daughter (Luke 8:41; Mark 5:22), the betrayal at Gethsemane (Luke 22:42-53), the palace of Caiaphas on that same night (John 18:15), and the empty tomb on Resurrection morning (John 20:2-4). A friendship and kinship grew, and despite the different personalities of these men, they shared a oneness in purpose. Their unity typifies the *koinonia* we have observed among the Spirit-filled believers in Acts.

As Spirit-filled believers today, our relationships should typify a similar unity and commitment to each other so that we can enjoy the success that these believers did in winning, building, and sending men for Jesus.

2 And a certain man lame from his mother's womb was carried, whom they laid daily at the gate of the temple which is called Beautiful, to

ask alms of them that entered into the temple; 3 Who seeing Peter and John about to go into the temple asked an alms. 4 And Peter, fastening his eyes upon him with John, said Look on us. 5 And he gave heed unto them, expecting to receive something of them. 6 Then Peter said, Silver and gold have I none; but such as I have give I thee: In the name of Jesus Christ of Nazareth rise up and walk. 7 And he took him by the right hand, and lifted him up: and immediately his feet and ankle bones received strength. 8 And he leaping up stood, and walked, and entered with them into the temple, walking, and leaping, and praising God. 9 And all the people saw him walking and praising God: 10 And they knew that it was he which sat for alms at the Beautiful gate of the temple: and they were filled with wonder and amazement at that which had happened unto him.

In the temple, between the Court of the Gentiles and the Court of the Women was an ornate bronze gate with gold and silver inlays. The Court of the Gentiles was as far as Gentiles were allowed to go in the temple. Women could only go as far as the Court of the Women. The Pharisees had established a long-standing tradition of using the Court of Women to present their teaching to both sexes, so it was the logical location for the new church to gather as well.

Giving to the poor and handicapped was encouraged by law, and considered by the Jews to be an important way to please God. The beggar at the gate doesn't seem to be aware of the miraculous events taking place in Jerusalem. Because of this, it was important that Peter not miss the opportunity to share the Good News of Jesus with this man, and with others who would witness this encounter.

Peter did not do the expected, which was to simply give money. Rather, he healed the man "in the name of Jesus Christ of Nazareth." Everything the apostles did was in Jesus' name. This should also be our goal. Our good works should be done to bring glory to God, not to garner any attention or accolades for ourselves.

The healing required faith on Peter's part in giving the command, and on the lame man's part by accepting Peter's out stretched hand. Faith in

The apostles taught the truth, as was verified and validated by the miracles God worked through them. The response of the listeners was overwhelming. There were many who had responded to the preaching and teaching of the apostles between the ascension of Christ and the beginning of Pentecost. This troubled the current religious leaders, the Sadducees in particular. The overwhelming response by the people crowding around the new teachers in the temple courts was a distinct annoyance. The high priest and the Sadducees thought that Jesus was dead, and they were done with Him. Now, two of His disciples were speaking out boldly and with power.

Jesus is always demonstrated actively (see Matthew 9:20-22; Mark 10:46-52; Hebrews 11).

As the others observed this miraculous healing, they were astonished! Peter responds to their amazement by saying, "Why are you so shocked? Have you forgotten who God is?" This is inferred in Acts 3:13 when Peter refers to all God has accomplished throughout the history of Israel in regard to His fulfilled promises. Peter is quick to remind all present that he is only an ambassador, a representative of Christ, and all he accomplished is through the *dunamei*, translated "supernatural power of Christ. ". . .why marvel ye at this? Or why look ye so earnestly on us, as though by our own power or holiness we had made this man to walk? The God of Abraham, and of Isaac, and of Jacob, the God of our fathers, hath glorified his Son Jesus. . ." (vv. 12-13).

4:1 And as they spake unto the people, the priests, and the captain of the temple, and the Sadducees, came upon them, 2 Being grieved that they taught the people, and preached through Jesus the resurrection from the dead.

The Pharisees and Sadducees, who usually opposed one another, had joined forces to oppose Jesus. Obviously, these religious leaders were more concerned with maintaining their status, prestige, and power than they were about establishing the truth of God. The Sadducees were fully aware of the fact that Peter was preaching and teaching the truth of Jesus' resurrection. In their "grieved state," (Greek *diaponeo*), meaning "deeply annoyed, worked-up, or indignant," the leaders had the apostles arrested, because neither the power of the Gospel, nor its teachers could be allowed to continue.

3 And they laid hands on them, and put them in hold unto the next day: for it was now eventide.

Peter and John were arrested and held overnight because it was too late to assemble the Sanhedrin council. This standard was violated in the case of Jesus.

Physical restraints are to be imposed only when there is a threat to disturb the social order. These men were only teachers, and had done nothing to deride social order, encourage or direct lawlessness, nor were they personally involved in any illegal activity. In addition, they had not broken the temple law or violated the Jewish system.

The secret motives for their arrest were jealousy and power. Since the Christian movement did not emanate from the religious status quo, the religious leaders wanted no part of it, whether it was true or not.

Our witness, both in principle (what we say we believe) and practice (how we live) should be as effective. As Christians, we should never allow anything in our lives to hinder the message of God's love and forgiveness.

4 Howbeit many of them which heard the word believed; and the number of the men was about five thousand.

The Sadducees could not stop the spread of the Gospel. We witness a similar type of persecution today. Christianity does not threaten civil law, rather, it enforces it. Submission to Christ and the virtues of Christianity produce a moral, conscientious citizenry. Yet, there are segments of society who vehemently oppose the display of the Ten Commandments in courtrooms.

4:13 Now when they saw the boldness of Peter and John, and perceived that they were unlearned and ignorant men, they marveled; and they took knowledge of them, that they had been with Jesus.

The priests and elders were shocked when they saw how bold Peter and John were. It was obvious that the two men had never attended a rabbinic school or been tutored by a great rabbi like Gamaliel. They were "unlearned" *(agramm^atoi)* and "ignorant" or common lay people. However, the Holy Spirit was the source of their inspiration, giving them the power to act and teaching them what to say.

". . . And they took knowledge of them, that they had been with Jesus." When people look at us, is it readily apparent that we spend time with the Lord? There will be a distinct correlation between how much time we invest in our relationship to God, and how much we resemble Him. Galatians 5:22-23 paints a very specific portrait of what we should look like. When you consider your character, do you see *humility,* in realizing that personal frailty brings dependence on God? *Patience and long-suffering* in waiting on God? *Quietness* to reflect on who God is? *Gratefulness* for those who serve and love you? *Self-control* that is evident in how you are able to yield your preferences in the interest of others. *Meekness,* strength under control. *Faith* to endure any trial, knowing that pain often aids us in discerning God's will? Has anyone ever told you, "You look just like your (heavenly) Father?"

Though education is important, it is not the primary thing. The most important thing we can do is to know Jesus Christ as our Saviour and Lord, and be thoroughly acquainted with His will and ways. African-Americans emphasize higher education for our children, and this should be *a* priority. However, it is not *the* priority. We must also begin to reward our children for their consistent study of God's Word. We must communicate to them that this knowledge is critical for their personal success. We must even begin to demand that they participate and establish other godly disciplines, such as a consistent prayer life or Scripture memorization. At the very top of our list of goals and aspirations should be a continuing education program that equips us for ministry that will bring glory to God.

DAILY BIBLE READINGS

M: Peter Heals a Crippled Beggar
Acts 3:11-10

T: Peter's Sermon in Solomon's Portico
Acts 3:11-16

W: Peter Calls for Repentance
Acts 3:17-21

T: Jesus Is the Promised Messiah
Acts 3:22-26

F: The Rise of Persecution
Acts 4:1-4

S: Peter and John before the Council
Acts 4:8-12

S: No Boasting in God's Presence
1 Corinthians 1:26-31

TEACHING TIPS

March 25
Bible Study Guide 4

1. Words You Should Know

A. Apostles (Acts 5:34) Greek *Apostolos*—An ambassador. The Lord chose the term to indicate the distinctive relation of the Twelve whom He chose to be His witnesses. An office as instituted by Jesus Christ.

B. Obey (v. 36) Greek *Peitho*—To entice or persuade or solicit the favor of. To prevail by persuasion.

2. Teacher Preparation

A. Read Acts 5 before studying this week's FOCAL VERSES. Write down any questions that may come to you as a result of your reading.

B. Next, read the Scriptures for the Devotional Reading and the IN DEPTH section of this Bible Study Guide.

C. Answer the SEARCH THE SCRIPTURES and DISCUSS THE MEANING questions so you will be prepared to help the students become better acquainted with today's lesson.

D. Materials needed: Bibles, paper and pencils for students, chalkboard or newsprint.

3. Starting the Lesson

A. Before the class begins, write the lesson title and the AT-A-GLANCE outline on the chalkboard or newsprint.

B. Have a student read the FOCAL VERSES. Then ask a student to read the Bible Background Scriptures.

C. Divide the class into three groups. Ask each group to be responsible for one section of the lesson as laid out in the AT-A-GLANCE outline.

D. Have a student lead the class in prayer, focusing on the KEEP IN MIND verse as the basis of the prayer.

4. Getting into the Lesson

A. Read the BACKGROUND of the lesson as well as the PEOPLE, PLACES, AND TIMES section. Ask students to discuss Gamaliel and Theudas.

B. Ask the students to read the lesson and then answer the appropriate SEARCH THE SCRIPTURES questions.

5. Relating the Lesson to Life

A. Direct the students to answer the DISCUSS THE MEANING questions and encourage each student to participate in the discussion.

B. Next, have each group discuss what they learned from their particular section of the lesson and how they plan to apply what they have learned in the week ahead.

C. Have students read the LESSON IN OUR SOCIETY section and give them an opportunity to brainstorm answers. Be willing to share your ideas with the students.

6. Arousing Action

A. Challenge students to commit themselves to complete the MAKE IT HAPPEN assignment. Be sure students record their ideas for completing the assignment in the FOLLOW THE SPIRIT and REMEMBER YOUR THOUGHTS sections of the lesson before they leave the class.

B. Challenge students to read the DAILY BIBLE READINGS which will strengthen their resolve to obey God.

C. Close the class with prayer.

MAR 25TH

WORSHIP GUIDE

For the Superintendent or Teacher
Theme: Obedient to the Spirit
Theme Song: "I Love You Lord"
Scripture: Luke 22:39-42
Song: "I'll Follow All the Way"
Meditation: Lord, help me to follow You, no matter where You lead me. Give me strength to commit my life to You. In Jesus' name. Amen.

OBEDIENT TO THE SPIRIT

Bible Background • ACTS 5:12-42
Printed Text • ACTS 5:27-32a, 33-36, 38-42
Devotional Reading • PSALM 103:15-18

LESSON AIM

By the end of the lesson, students will be able to explain why the disciples obeyed the Holy Spirit, affirm the importance of obeying the Holy Spirit, and be motivated to help others obey Him.

KEEP IN MIND

"Then Peter and the other disciples answered and said, we ought to obey God rather than men" (Acts 5:29).

FOCAL VERSES

Acts 5:27 And when they had brought them, they set them before the council: and the high priest asked them,

28 Saying, Did not we straitly command you that ye should not teach in this name? And, behold, ye have filled Jerusalem with your doctrine, and intend to bring this man's blood upon us.

29 Then Peter and the other apostles answered and said, We ought to obey God rather than men.

30 The God of our fathers raised up Jesus, whom ye slew and hanged on a tree.

31 Him hath God exalted with his right hand to be a Prince and a Saviour, for to give repentance to Israel, and forgiveness of sins.

32 And we are his witnesses of these things;

33 When they heard that, they were cut to the heart, and took counsel to slay them.

34 Then stood there up one in the council, a Pharisee named Gamaliel, a doctor of the law, had in reputation among all the people, and commanded to put the apostles forth a little space;

35 And said unto them, Ye men of Israel, take heed to yourselves what ye intend to do as touching

LESSON OVERVIEW

LESSON AIM
KEEP IN MIND
FOCAL VERSES
IN FOCUS
THE PEOPLE, PLACES, AND TIMES
BACKGROUND
AT-A-GLANCE
IN DEPTH
SEARCH THE SCRIPTURES
DISCUSS THE MEANING
LESSON IN OUR SOCIETY
MAKE IT HAPPEN
FOLLOW THE SPIRIT
REMEMBER YOUR THOUGHTS
MORE LIGHT ON THE TEXT
DAILY BIBLE READINGS

these men.

36 For before these days rose up Theudas, boasting himself to be somebody; to whom a number of men, about four hundred, joined themselves: who was slain; and all, as many as obeyed him, were scattered, and brought to nought.

5:38 And now I say unto you, Refrain from these men, and let them alone: for if this counsel or this work be of men, it will come to naught:

39 But if it be of God, ye cannot overthrow it; lest haply ye be found even to fight against God.

40 And to him they agreed: and when they had called the apostles, and beaten them, they commanded that they should not speak in the name of Jesus, and let them go.

41 And they departed from the presence of the council, rejoicing that they were counted worthy to suffer shame for his name.

42 And daily in the temple, and in every house, they ceased not to teach and preach Jesus Christ.

IN FOCUS

Charlotte's son, Bradley, had been giving her a hard time all day long. First, she tried to get him to eat some oatmeal, but he refused. Next, she told him to clean up his room, but Bradley ignored her. Finally, Charlotte demanded that Bradley do his homework, but he chose to watch his favorite television program instead.

Charlotte was adamant when she confronted Bradley. Not only would he be punished for disobeying her, but she also made him stand in the corner without speaking. When Charlotte's husband came home from work and saw Bradley in the corner, he asked her what was wrong. "Your son refused to obey me, so he will remain in that corner until I tell him to come out."

Obedience is a key principle in Christianity. In fact, the Bible says that to obey God is better than sacrifice (1 Samuel 15:22). We may not understand everything God leads us to do, but if we yield to Him and follow His voice, everything will work out in our lives as long we obey Him.

This week, we will discuss how the early disciples obeyed the Holy Spirit, despite pressures from the religious leaders of Israel.

THE PEOPLE, PLACES, AND TIMES

Gamaliel. A Pharisee in the Sanhedrin, honored by all the people, who counseled letting the apostles out of prison (Acts 5:34-49) and a teacher of the law who instructed Paul (Acts 22:3). In rabbinic literature, Gamaliel is identified as Gamaliel I or the Elder, a teacher who flourished in the mid-first century. Little is known of him reliably; the list of princes or patriarchs of Judaism lists him after Hillel.

(Harper's Bible Dictionary, 1984, San Francisco: Harper and Row Publishing Co., 1984 p. 331.)

Theudas. The leader of a messianic movement in Judah. According to Jewish historian Josephus, Theudas saw himself as a new Joshua figure who would lead his men by God's power across the Jordan and into the Holy Land to commence a new era for Israel. He was killed by the Romans ca. A.D. 44. Theudas is also mentioned in the New Testament (Acts 5:36-37), along with another revolutionary, Judas, who led his doomed rebellion about A.D. 6.

(Harper's Bible Dictionary, p. 1066.)

BACKGROUND

Peter and John were on their way to the temple when they saw a lame man sitting in front of it begging. Because Peter and John were filled with the Holy Spirit, God used them to heal the man and preach a powerful sermon that converted 5,000.

That didn't sit well with the religious leaders. Peter and John were arrested and brought before the council to answer questions about why they gave so much credit to Jesus Christ. But Peter and John didn't flinch. They knew that Jesus was Lord of all and no amount of pressure from the religious leaders would sway them from the truth.

Peter and John continued to be instrumental in the growth and development of the New Testament church with the Holy Spirit's power. God used the apostles to set church discipline (Acts 5:1-11) and heal many sick and demonized people (vv. 12-16). And, for the second time, they were arrested by the Jewish leaders because they obeyed the Holy Spirit rather than religious protocol.

AT-A-GLANCE

1. Peter Challenges Religious Leaders to Obey God (Acts 5:27-32)
2. The Religious Leaders Discuss Peter's Challenge (vv. 33-36)
3. The Apostles Rejoice in their Obedience to God (vv. 38-42)

IN DEPTH

1. Peter Challenges Religious Leaders to Obey God (Acts 5:27-32)

Peter and John were bold soldiers in the army of the Lord. Despite the opposition they experienced for proclaiming the name of Jesus Christ, the disciples refused to back down. When they were arrested by the high priest and put in prison, Peter and John didn't panic. In fact, the Bible declares that God's angel miraculously opened their prison doors and commanded them to return to the temple to preach Jesus (Acts 5:17-20).

In the meantime, the high priest called an important meeting with the religious leaders to discuss what they should do with Peter and John. Their preaching had stirred thousands of people to accept Jesus Christ; therefore, the religious leaders wanted to put a stop to these men. But when the temple captain went to the prison to get the disciples, they were not there. God wanted them before the people and no amount of coercion from the opposition would change that. Finally, the captain went to the disciples and demanded that they appear before the religious leaders so that they might reason with them.

The first question the religious leaders asked Peter and John was "did not we straitly command you that ye should not teach in this name?" (v. 28) Secondly, they accused the disciples of filling Jerusalem with false doctrine. Lastly, they challenged Peter and John for attempting to accuse them of Jesus' death.

Even under pressure, Peter refused to back down from what he believed. He let the religious leaders know that for him, God's Word is paramount over anyone or anything. Despite the charges and accusations that were thrown at him by the religious leaders, Peter made it clear that man's words mean nothing when compared to God's.

If Peter had stopped preaching in the name of Jesus, no one would have come to God through repentance and faith. The Bible says there is no other name under heaven whereby we must be saved other than the name of Jesus Christ (Acts 4:12). If we call upon the name of the Jesus, we shall be delivered from sin and receive eternal life (Romans 10:13). And we are also told that Jesus' blood cleanses us from all sin (Romans 3:25, 1 John 1:7). No matter what these religious leaders said or didn't want to hear, God's Word is true! (Psalm 119:160)

Peter had an assignment from God. His responsibility was not only to teach the people, but also to challenge the religious leaders with their false doctrine. Peter told them that they were indeed responsible for killing Jesus, but God raised Him from the dead. Secondly, Peter affirmed the doctrine of the resurrection, one of the central beliefs of the Christian faith. Jesus Christ sits at the right hand of the Father, not only as "Prince" but also as "Saviour." The word "prince" means originator, founder, chief, and leader. The word "Saviour" means deliverer and preserver. Thus, Jesus Christ is the most unique person who has ever lived. He

is the God-Man who provides salvation for Israel and the church and forgiveness of sins for all who put their trust in Him (v. 31). Peter tells the religious leaders that the disciples will obey God and continue to speak out for Him, since they were eyewitnesses of Jesus' death, burial, and resurrection.

2. The Religious Leaders Discuss Peter's Challenge (vv. 33-36)

The religious leaders were not pleased with Peter's message. In fact, they wanted to take the disciples outside of the council and have them killed. As they considered this option, Gamaliel, a respected Pharisee teacher (Acts 22:3), suggested that the disciples be excused so that the religious leaders could discuss the ongoing events in detail.

Once the disciples left the room, Gamaliel encouraged the religious leaders to rethink their position. If they chose to kill Peter and John, it would add more problems to their current dilemma. He also reminded them of an Egyptian named Theudas, who lead an uproar of men against the Romans, only to be squashed and killed (see Acts 21:38). Whatever is created by human beings will eventually come down. Only what is built and dedicated for Jesus Christ will have a lasting affect in our lives and in the lives of others.

3. The Apostles Rejoice in their Obedience to God (vv. 38-42)

Gamaliel convinced the religious leaders to leave the apostles alone and even to ignore their work. If what they were teaching was motivated by their own human intellect, the apostles wouldn't succeed. But if they were being led by the Holy Spirit, Gamaliel knew that the religious leaders would be guilty of fighting against God Himself.

We should remember this truth ourselves. God's work is inspired by the Holy Spirit. Therefore, no human or devil can stop God's movement. Our responsibility as believers is to march forward in the power of the Holy Spirit, committed to the work of Christ.

The religious leaders finally listened to Gamaliel. So they called the apostles back before the council, had them beaten and commanded them to stop speaking in the name of Jesus Christ. Peter and John left the council excited for several reasons. First, they were counted worthy to "suffer for the name of Jesus" (v. 41). Second, they were excited because no matter what the religious leaders said, they couldn't stop God's work. Finally, the disciples were excited because their obedience to the Holy Spirit made a statement to the other people in Jerusalem and gave them boldness to continue speaking and teaching for God.

We can stand in the power of God and do His work if we will obey Him. Our choice to obey God rather than men may become difficult at times and even life threatening for some. But God is faithful to His people and He will reward those who commit their will and lives to Him.

SEARCH THE SCRIPTURES

1. What questions did the high priest ask the disciples when they were brought before the council? (Acts 5:27-28)

2. How did Peter and the disciples answer the religious leaders? (v. 29)

3. What did Peter say about Jesus Christ? (vv. 30-32)

4. Who spoke to the Jewish council about the disciples? (vv. 34-35)

5. What warning did Gamaliel give the religious leaders? (vv. 38-39)

6. How did the disciples feel once they left the council? (vv. 41-42)

DISCUSS THE MEANING

1. What did Peter mean when he said "we ought to obey God rather than men?"

2. Should we rejoice when we suffer for the name of Jesus? Why or why not?

3. How do individuals fight against God? Explain.

4. Is it possible to be a witness for Jesus Christ in our hedonistic society? Why or why not?

LESSON IN OUR SOCIETY

People today find it hard to obey the laws of the land, from running traffic lights, cheating on income taxes, to stealing office products. Should we as believers do the same, or should we obey man's laws as well as God's? Discuss.

MAKE IT HAPPEN

This week, make a list of those things that cause you to stray from God and challenge your devotion to Him. As you look at your list, ask the Lord to help you in those areas where you have fallen short in obeying Him. Walk in faith that God has forgiven you once you have repented.

FOLLOW THE SPIRIT

What God wants me to do:

_____

_____

REMEMBER YOUR THOUGHTS

Special insights you learned:

_____

_____

MORE LIGHT ON THE TEXT
Acts 5:27-32a, 33-36, 38-42

5:27 And when they had brought them, they set them before the council: and the high priest asked them, 28 Saying, did not we straitly command you that ye should not teach in this name? And, behold, ye have filled Jerusalem with your doctrine, and intend to bring this man's blood upon us.

When Peter and John were brought before the Sanhedrin, they stood before its 71 members. Interestingly, the high priest avoided making any reference to how the apostles got out of jail (Acts 5:19-23). The high priest accused the apostles of starting controversy by their teaching "in this name." The high priest was so filled with contempt and guilt concerning the Lord that he could not even say the name of Jesus! The accusation that the apostles wanted to arouse uprising against the council as vengeance for the crucifixion of Jesus was slanderous, and untrue. The entire nation (those present for the judgment by Pilate) accepted responsibility for the death of Jesus (Matthew 27:22-26).

Like the apostles, we must "be ready always to give an answer to every man that asketh you a reason of the hope that is in you with meekness and fear" (1 Peter 3:15). We must be prepared to answer questions and accusations concerning our faith, and, if need be, suffer ridicule and mistreatment. The "art" of defending our faith is called *Apologetics*.

All authority is subject to the principles of God's Word. When a command is given that conflicts with God's Word, those under authority must learn how to effectively appeal. Often, the effectiveness of our appeal will depend on our attitudes of loyalty, gratefulness, humility, and diligence. This is why Scripture addresses those under authority first: "Let every soul be subject unto the higher powers. For there is no power but of God: the powers that be are ordained of God. Whosoever therefore resisteth the power resisteth the ordinance of God: and they that resist shall receive to themselves damnation" (Romans 13:1-2). If, after we make an appeal to an authority, they refuse to submit to the Word of God, only then are we justified in opposing that authority, as in the case of Peter and John.

30 The God of our fathers raised up Jesus, whom ye slew and hanged on a tree. 31 Him hath God exalted with his right hand to be a Prince and a Saviour, for to give repentance to Israel, and forgiveness of sins.

Peter contrasts the way God favored Jesus, exalting Him to His right hand as author and founder of the faith, a provision for the sin of mankind; to the way the Jewish leaders had treated Him, having tortured and crucified Him. The word "tree" *xulou* also means wood or anything made of wood. Therefore, "tree" in this context refers to the cross.

32 And we are his witnesses of these things;

We should be ready and willing to speak of Christ as His witnesses *everywhere*. If we are willingly true and unflinching in our commitment to Him, we too will suffer inconveniences and ridicule for His sake. We must be sure that any suffering is for His sake, and not a result of our own

29 Then Peter and the other apostles answered and said, We ought to obey God rather than men.

Peter does not deny receiving the directive of the Sanhedrin. However, he defers to the higher authority of Christ. By virtue of the fact that we have received Christ as Lord and Saviour, He has our primary allegiance. The Sanhedrin did not consider the apostles to be under "divine authority," so they were adamant concerning their demands for obedience and loyalty.

How should we identify the chain of command? Of course, our ultimate authority is God's Word. God has established four basic directives to provide for our protection and direction: 1. Parents/Husband; 2. Church; 3. Government Officials; 4. Employers.

lack of discretion, honesty, kindness, or the fact that we compromise His message in any way.

5:33 When they heard that, they were cut to the heart, and took counsel to slay them. 34 Then stood there up one in the council, a Pharisee named Gamaliel, a doctor of the law, had in reputation among all the people, and commanded to put the apostles forth a little space; 35 And said unto them, Ye men of Israel, take heed to yourselves what ye intend to do as touching these men. 36 For before these days rose up Theudas, boasting himself to be somebody; to whom a number of men, about four hundred, joined themselves: who was slain; and all, as many as obeyed him, were scattered, and brought to nought.

Gamaliel cautioned the council that they must proceed with caution in regard to Peter and John. Gamaliel commanded great respect, since he was able to take charge of the situation. F. F. Bruce quotes the following from the Mishnah in *The New International Commentary on the New Testament*, Acts, p.115: "When the Rabban Gamaliel died the glory of the Torah ceased, and purity and 'separateness' died." Bruce explains further that *Rabban* is an Aramaic word which means "our teacher," a title of great honor bestowed only upon the most distinguished teachers. It is interesting to note that he was probably not present on the night Jesus was tried. All of the Sanhedrin was not in attendance because of the hour. This may have been the providence of God, protecting the fledgling church in its infancy.

5:38 And now I say unto you, Refrain from these men, and let them alone: for if this counsel or this work be of men, it will come to nought: 39 But if it be of God, ye cannot overthrow it; lest haply ye be found even to fight against God.

Gamaliel reminded the Sanhedrin that self-appointed leaders had risen and fallen in the past and in the end, God always prevailed. Gamaliel continued that if the new movement was indeed of God, there would be nothing the Council could do to thwart it. This is an accurate appraisal. A move of God cannot be overthrown. It is foolish to try to use physical means to deter spiritual forces!

40 And to him they agreed: and when they had called the apostles, and beaten them, they commanded that they should not speak in the name of Jesus, and let them go. 41 And they departed from the presence of the council, rejoicing that they were counted worthy to suffer shame for his name. 42 And daily in the temple, and in every house, they ceased not to teach and preach Jesus Christ.

The apostles were able to leave the Sanhedrin rejoicing because they had suffered for Christ's sake. They understood the name of Jesus to be all inclusive of His character, nature, deity and lordship.

Obviously, no matter what the cost, the apostles were willing to obey God's Word. Obedience is a matter of the heart. In David's prayer for his son, Solomon, who was preparing to become the successor to the throne of Israel, David concentrates on Solomon's heart. He wants Solomon to be one that is willing to keep the commandments, testimonies, and statutes of the Lord.

Obedience is an act of our will. We must make a conscious decision to submit our choices to God. We must bring them under His authority, and purpose to evaluate our attitudes and actions in light of the whole counsel of God.

DAILY BIBLE READINGS

M: Ananias and Sapphira Sin and Die
Acts 5:1-11

T: The Power of the Apostles
Acts 5:12-16

W: Life and Faith of Believers
1 Thessalonians 1

T: Persecution and Relief
Acts 5:17-23

F: Arrest and Accusation
Acts 5:24-28

S: The Answer of the Apostles
Acts 5:29-32

S: The Warning of Gamaliel
Acts 5:34-42

TEACHING TIPS

April 1
Bible Study Guide 5

1. Words You Should Know

A. Ministration (Acts 6:1) Greek *diakonia*—The office of service of a deacon or minister of relief.

B. Wisdom (v. 3) Greek *sophia*—The demonstrated use of wisdom of a higher or spiritual source.

C. Were obedient (v. 7) Greek *hupakouo*—To act as a subordinate to conform to a command or authority.

2. Teacher Preparation

A. Read and meditate upon the devotional and background Scriptures. Write down any questions that you may anticipate and prepare your comments.

B. Study the FOCAL VERSES in the most popular translations used by the church in corporate worship or students in individual study. Make note of study notes and contemporary language.

C. Prepare your responses for the SEARCH THE SCRIPTURES and DISCUSS THE MEANING questions.

3. Starting the Lesson

A. Write the theme of the lesson and the AT-A-GLANCE outline on the board.

B. Engage students in discussion about the different ministries of the church and their real or perceived priorities in ministry.

4. Getting into the Lesson

A. Share WORDS YOU SHOULD KNOW with students and present the definitions as they relate to the context of the lesson.

B. Have a volunteer read the BACKGROUND text and THE PEOPLE, PLACES, AND TIMES sections. Use this information to set the tone for the lesson discussion.

C. Read the FOCAL VERSES and answer the SEARCH THE SCRIPTURES questions as a group.

5. Relating the Lesson to Life

A. Allow students to break off into small groups and answer the DISCUSS THE MEANING questions.

B. Reconvene in the larger group and reflect on the LESSON IN OUR SOCIETY.

6. Arousing Action

A. Discuss, and perhaps administer, a spiritual gifts test to identify gifts within the group.

B. Explore obedient responses to identifying and using individual spiritual gifts for the good of the body of Christ, especially to build up the group and the local church.

WORSHIP GUIDE

For the Superintendent or Teacher
Theme: Empowered to Serve
Theme Song: "A Charge to Keep
I Have"
Scripture: Micah 4:1-7
Song: "I'll Go Where You Want
Me to Go"
Devotional Thought: Lord, stir up
the gifts of the Spirit within me
that I might serve You with power
as Your Kingdom is established
on earth as it is in Heaven.

EMPOWERED TO SERVE

Bible Background • ACTS 6:1—8:3
Printed Text • ACTS 6:1-8; 7:55—8:1
Devotional Reading • MICAH 4:1-7

LESSON AIM

By the end of this lesson, students will be able to explain the process of selecting a good leader, the qualities of a good leader, and the effectiveness of a good leader by examining the life and ministry of Stephen.

KEEP IN MIND

"And the word of God increased; and the number of the disciples multiplied in Jerusalem greatly; and a great company of the priests were obedient to the faith" (Acts 6:7).

FOCAL VERSES

Acts 6:1-8 And in those days, when the number of the disciples was multiplied, there arose a murmuring of the Grecians against the Hebrews, because their widows were neglected in the daily ministration.

2 Then the twelve called the multitude of the disciples unto them, and said, It is not reason that we should leave the word of God, and serve tables.

3 Wherefore, brethren, look ye out among you seven men of honest report, full of the Holy Ghost and wisdom, whom we may appoint over this business.

4 But we will give ourselves continually to prayer, and to the ministry of the word.

5 And the saying pleased the whole multitude: and they chose Stephen, a man full of faith and of the Holy Ghost, and Philip, and Prochorus, and Nicanor, and Timon, and Parmenas, and Nicolas a proselyte of Antioch:

6 Whom they set before the apostles: and when

LESSON OVERVIEW

LESSON AIM
KEEP IN MIND
FOCAL VERSES
IN FOCUS
THE PEOPLE, PLACES, AND TIMES
BACKGROUND
AT-A-GLANCE
IN DEPTH
SEARCH THE SCRIPTURES
DISCUSS THE MEANING
LESSON IN OUR SOCIETY
MAKE IT HAPPEN
FOLLOW THE SPIRIT
REMEMBER YOUR THOUGHTS
MORE LIGHT ON THE TEXT
DAILY BIBLE READINGS

they had prayed, they laid their hands on them.

7 And the word of God increased; and the number of the disciples multiplied in Jerusalem greatly; and a great company of the priests were obedient to the faith.

APRIL 1ST

8 And Stephen, full of faith and power, did great wonders and miracles among the people.

7:55 But he, being full of the Holy Ghost, looked up steadfastly into heaven, and saw the glory of God, and Jesus standing on the right hand of God,

56 And said, Behold, I see the heavens opened, and the Son of man standing on the right hand of God.

57 Then they cried out with a loud voice, and stopped their ears, and ran upon him with one accord,

58 And cast him out of the city, and stoned him: and the witnesses laid down their clothes at a young man's feet, whose name was Saul.

59 And they stoned Stephen, calling upon God, and saying, Lord Jesus, receive my spirit.

60 And he kneeled down, and cried with a loud voice, Lord, lay not this sin to their charge. And when he had said this, he fell asleep.

8:1 And Saul was consenting unto his death. And at that time there was a great persecution against the church which was at Jerusalem; and they were all scattered abroad throughout the regions of Judaea and Samaria, except the apostles.

IN FOCUS

In March of 1981, President Ronald Reagan was

shot by John Hinckley, Jr., and was hospitalized for several weeks. Although Reagan was the nation's chief executive, his hospitalization had little impact on the nation's activity. Government continued on.

On the other hand, suppose the garbage collectors in this country went on strike, as they did in Philadelphia. That city was a literal mess; the pile of decaying trash quickly became a health hazard. A three week strike by garbage collectors nationwide would paralyze the country. Who is more important—the President or a garbage collector?

In the body of Christ, seemingly insignificant ones are urgently needed. As Paul reminds us, "the head cannot say to the feet, 'I don't need you!' On the contrary, those parts of the body that seem to be weaker are indispensable" (1 Corinthians 12:21-22).

Take a moment and think about your church's hierarchy. Each member, though in different positions, works together as a unit. When the Pastor is out of town, there is the assistant pastor (or a staff of assistant pastors) readily available to preach, pray and serve the sacrament. There are faithful, diligent, and humble servants in church, who may be regarded as the least important in day-to-day decision making and influence, but whose absence would be readily felt were they not there. How many times have we understated the importance of someone and discovered that person may not be as disposable as we thought?

In the body of Christ, everyone's gift, calling and appointment is vitally necessary for the building up of the church. Although Stephen and the other deacons were not called personally by Jesus like the Twelve, their diligence to serve food proved as effective in ministering the Gospel as the preaching ministry of the Twelve. With both the disciples and the deacons serving God and the church as needed, the church grew even the face of adversity and opposition.

THE PEOPLE, PLACES, AND TIMES

Believers. Christian converts were called believers before the ministry at Antioch (Acts 11:26). Believers included Jews and Greeks from all nations who believed the Gospel of Jesus Christ.

Stephen. The first deacon of seven, named to serve in the ministry of the New Testament church. Stephen was also the first Christian martyr; he was stoned to death for preaching the Gospel (Acts 7:59—8:1).

Persecution. Acts of imprisonment, murder, and destruction of property to discourage new believers from the Christian faith, witnessing and winning converts. Sometimes, persecution was lead by the government; at other times, it was incited by angry mobs.

BACKGROUND

The spread of the Gospel westward from Jerusalem caused the church to grow in great measure by people and regions. With Peter's leadership and ministry, many Jews heard the Gospel, believed, and were saved. Yet, God's will was such that the Word fulfilled included the Word preached also to the Gentiles. Key to this expansion was the peculiar method of persecution.

The greater the influence and effectiveness of the ministry, the more volatile the opposition became to rid the region of these believers and to silence the Gospel message. However, just as widespread persecution broke out against the church, so did widespread preaching. For every place the church went, they preached Jesus.

Significantly, just as Peter initially evangelized the Jews, the dispersement of the church through persecution also accommodated the preaching of the Gospel to the Gentiles.

AT-A-GLANCE

1. The Burden of Church Growth
(Acts 6:1-4)
2. The Blessing of Church Leaders
(vv. 5-8)
3. Beholding the Glory of God
(Acts 7:55—8:1)

IN DEPTH

1. The Burden of Church Growth (Acts 6:1-4)

As the number of believers increased, the Greeks complained that their widows were being neglected (v. 1). Because the early church had a reputation of community and love, it is a ready assumption that this problem did not evolve from any act of malicious discrimination. Instead, this problem was probably because of the language barrier between newly converted Jews and Gentiles living together for the first time in community.

The growing pains of the early church created the urgent need that the Gentile widows receive a fair distribution of food. The church viewed meeting this need as their social and spiritual responsibility. As was customary, the early church viewed the needs of one as the needs of the whole community.

In that regard, the complaints were legitimate requests and not to be regarded as contentious, attention-getting, or greedy. In this instance, complaining set in motion a ministry which facilitated an opportunity to further the Gospel—by first meeting the physical needs of the people.

To solve the problem, the Twelve asked the believers to choose seven men to distribute food so the apostles would be free to continue praying and preaching (vv. 2-4). To facilitate the phenomenal growth in the church, the Twelve extended an opportunity for developing the Christian leaders called deacons, for the express purpose of meeting the administrative needs of the people.

Before converting, the Greek widows received public assistance with food and other needs from the government. Once they became believers, their protection and provision from the government was turned into persecution and out-casting. However, the need for public assistance remained.

As the church perceived the need and the problems it had created, the Twelve set the precedent for meeting the needs of the body by going to the gifts within the body to meet the need. Making such swift and decisive action demonstrated that the Twelve understood their calling to prayer and preaching, as well as the need to empower others to fulfill the equally important calling of administration. This new problem, created through the effective preaching of the Gospel, called for radical changes in the leadership of the church.

2. The Blessing of Church Leaders (vv. 5-7)

The believers chose seven men, including Stephen and Philip, who were full of faith and of the Holy Spirit, to distribute food to the widows (vv. 5-6). The believers and the leaders took ministry to the poor as seriously as the ministry of preaching. Understanding that the job required more than just passing out food, the believers selected spiritually mature men who had demonstrated wisdom in other areas of their lives, and who could be trusted to make fair, prudent, and expedient decisions to resolve and prevent further problems.

The job description was posted: Good reputation, full of the Holy Spirit and wisdom. A good reputation was to ensure that the man's lifestyle was consistent with Christian principles. Being full of the Holy Spirit indicated the man's submission to the supernatural working of God in his life. And, full of wisdom implied that the man was not a novice in making decisions and dealing with people. These three characteristics were evident in Stephen's effectiveness as an administrator, preacher, and martyr.

Like Stephen, the other six men also possessed these leadership characteristics. After selecting the men, the Twelve exercised their ministry of prayer, affirmed by the Spirit the character of the seven, and laid hands on them. The laying on of hands symbolized the relationship of the seven for a common purpose and the transference of leadership responsibility upon them.

In addition to their administrative responsibilities, the seven seized the opportunity to evangelize. Compared to the disciple's ministry of prayer and preaching, the seven viewed their ministry as that of administration and evangelism. As they led the way to meet the needs of the widows, their service and sermons attracted even more believers.

As the Word of God continued to spread, the number of disciples, including priests, increased greatly (v. 7). With the administrative problem solved, preaching the Word of God was not hindered. As a matter of fact, the Gospel was proclaimed so well in both service and in sermon that the church grew, the numbers of disciples multiplied, and even priests traded their prestige for persecution and believed in Jesus.

As former Greek priests and religious leaders were converted, persecution against the church increased. The conversion of the priests indicated that the Gospel of Jesus Christ had not only crossed class and culture, but also threatened the core of religious and governmental leadership.

3. Beholding the Glory of God (Acts 6:8, 7:55-8:1)

Stephen performed great wonders and signs, but Jewish leaders brought him before the council where he was accused and convicted of blasphemy (6:8, 7:55-57). At the height of Stephen's ministry of administrative leadership and evangelism, he faced vehement opposition from Jewish leaders. It was evident that the Jewish leaders felt the political and social pressure of mass conversion of their priests and the Christians' ministry to the people. Therefore, they falsely accused Stephen and sentenced him to death.

The people dragged Stephen outside the city and stoned him to death, and Saul approved (7:58-8:1). When Stephen realized that death was imminent, he did not panic, curse his accusers, or try to escape. Instead, in faithful dependence upon God, Stephen looked up. As the heavens opened, Stephen saw God's glory and Jesus at His right hand. Empowered by the Holy Spirit, Stephen then interceded for his persecutors with a prayer for forgiveness and peacefully lay down into the sleep of death.

Note the similarities between Stephen and Jesus. Like Jesus: Stephen was accused of blasphemy; Stephen asked God's forgiveness for his murderers; Stephen consented to his own death. Like Jesus, Stephen's death caused a great increase in the number of Christians.

SEARCH THE SCRIPTURES

1. Which two ethnic groups made up the multitude of new believers? (Acts 6:1)

2. What are three characteristics of good spiritual leaders? (v. 3)

3. Why did the Twelve lay hands on the seven men who were chosen to serve? (v. 6)

4. List three significant results of effective Christian leadership? (v. 7)

5. What or who empowered Stephen to serve the people and worship God even at the point of persecution unto death? (Acts 6:5; 7:55)

DISCUSS THE MEANING

1. Why do you think the disciples refused to serve tables, in order to resolve the dispute regarding equality of service to both the Greek and Hebrew widows? Are there times when you, as a leader, have had to make decisions which, at first glance, may seem to be insensitive to the people's needs? Have there been times when you, as a church member, have questioned a leader's decision, but later realized that it actually served the greater good?

2. Stephen, while being stoned to death, saw the glory of God and the person of Jesus. As stones assailed his head and body, Stephen called upon God in the name of Jesus to "receive my spirit." Where else in Scripture do we see this intimate exchange between heaven and earth take place?

LESSON IN OUR SOCIETY

Bruce Larson points out some interesting facts about sandhill cranes in his book Wind and Fire. These large birds, who fly great distances across continents, have three remarkable qualities. First, they rotate leadership. No one bird stays out in front all the time. Second, they choose leaders who can handle turbulence. Finally, all during the time one bird is leading, the rest are honking their affirmation. That's not a bad model for the church. We certainly need leaders who can handle turbulence and who are aware that leadership is a responsibility that should be shared. But most of all, the church needs members who are all honking encouragement. ("IIllustrations for Preaching and Teaching" from Leadership Journal Craig Brian Larson, ed., Grand Rapids: Baker Books, 1993, p. 129.)

How is leadership modeled in your congregation? Are leaders sharing the leadership roles and responsibilities? Are followers encouraging leaders? Are strong leaders being chosen for their ability and stability? What kind of leader are you?

MAKE IT HAPPEN

The apostles resisted the temptation to do more, be more, and be seen more before the people. Instead of becoming workaholics and yielding to the proud, human tendency to consider themselves to be indispensable, they delegate authority to others. Although they may have been excellent servers, the apostles knew that their greatest gift and calling was prayer and preaching. As you take inventory of your place of leadership (at church, work, or home), which tasks could you delegate to another? To excel at your calling, what other tasks and ministries are you willing to relinquish?

FOLLOW THE SPIRIT
What God wants me to do:

_____

_____

REMEMBER YOUR THOUGHTS
Special insights you learned:

_____

_____

MORE LIGHT ON THE TEXT
Acts 6:1-8; 7:55-8:1

6:1 And in those days, when the number of the disciples was multiplied, there arose a murmuring of the Grecians against the Hebrews, because their widows were neglected in the daily ministration.

God caused the church to grow tremendously in the early days of its existence. Such growth was a sign of God's presence, power, and truth. The unbelieving world had to admit, if nothing else, that something out of the ordinary was at work. Of course, believers today understand that the church, and its growth, is fueled by the presence and power of God through the Holy Spirit (see 1 Corinthians 12:13; Acts 1:8), and by the truth found in Christ.

The believers in the church at Jerusalem (v. 7) were called "disciples" which means "learners" or "pupils" in Greek. The early church members were truly trying to learn about the new way of life which they had adopted. They were students of the ways of God as expressed through Jesus Christ.

Modern-day Christians must also become serious "pupils" who learn about God and His Word. We are to, "Study to shew thyself approved unto God, a workman that needeth not to be ashamed, rightly dividing the word of truth" (2 Timothy 2:15). If we know and understand God's Word, we will certainly be equipped and prepared to face whatever God allows to come our way (see 2 Timothy 3:16-17).

Acts 6:1 says that the Greek disciples began "murmuring" against the Hebrew disciples because Greek widows were not getting their share of the daily distribution of church services or "ministrations." In those days, the church did not just hold a worship service for a couple of hours on Sunday and Wednesday for those who wanted to attend. For the early saints, Christianity was truly an all-encompassing way of life. They were a community of people who shared property and food (see Acts 2:44-47; 4:32-35). Therefore, the "daily ministration" which was allegedly withheld from Greek widows was of serious importance.

The "murmuring" or "grumbling" was a way for Satan to destroy unity and cause a problem within the church. Satan loves to cause problems in relationships. He is in favor of whatever God is against (see John 10:10). Believers are told, "Do all things without murmurings and disputings." (Philippians 2:14). And, we are told that there should be no "divisions" nor "schisms" within the church (see 1 Corinthians 1:10; 12:25). So, when the Greeks and Jews of the early church squabbled over the treatment of each other's widows, there was fertile ground for a split in the church.

2 Then the twelve called the multitude of the disciples unto them, and said, It is not reason that we should leave the word of God, and serve tables.

Like all good church leadership, "the twelve" assembled the followers of Christ, Greeks and Hebrews, in order to prevent further problems. "The twelve" refers to the original men who followed Jesus during His earthly ministry. They were Jesus' original "disciples," excluding Judas, who was replaced by Matthias (Acts 1:25-26).

The twelve leaders suggested to the congregation that it was better for them (the leaders) to spend their time preparing and delivering sermons than on the other daily services of the church, such as passing out food, i.e., "serving tables." This was wise thinking because there were not many men, at that early point in church history, who knew as much about Jesus as those original disciples. So, it was better for them to spend time passing on what they knew rather than acting as waiters.

Though it may not always be possible for pastors to minister full-time today, a church that can support its pastor and his family puts itself in a better position to get his full devotion to study, prayer, and the delivery of God's Word. Dedicated pastors who are true to the Bible certainly deserve to be supported by those they serve (1 Corinthians 9:7-14). The disciples recognized the importance of a pastor's total dedication to ministry. And, a wise church today, which is financially able, will do the same.

3 Wherefore, brethren, look ye out among you seven men of honest report, full of the Holy Ghost and wisdom, whom we may appoint over this business.

The twelve then delegated to the congregation the responsibility of selecting seven men to whom they would, in turn, delegate responsibility for the proper distribution of daily church services. The ability to properly delegate responsibility and authority is another hallmark of good leadership. In this case, it served the function of promoting the most efficient use of time by the leaders. Delegation also can serve the function of sharing the workload so that leaders are not prematurely burned out. Moses was one of the first leaders to delegate work to prevent an overload (Exodus 18:17-26).

Another good reason for delegation of duties is to get better results due to expertise in a given area. The Holy Spirit distributes various "spiritual gifts" to everyone in the body of Christ (1 Corinthians 12:4, 11). Thus, some believers are more gifted in certain areas than others. They should be given duties in the area of their gift(s).

Finally, the twelve leaders stated the qualifications for the seven men who were to be selected by the congregation. They had to be "of good report," or have good reputations, so that the peo-

ple would respect and trust them. Furthermore, they had to be "full of the Holy Ghost" so that they had the proper servant's heart and were led by God's Spirit in their work. And, last, they had to be men of "wisdom" so that they had sound judgment and made godly decisions.

4 But we will give ourselves continually to prayer, and to the ministry of the word.

The twelve leaders restated that their primary function was to teach the Word. To gain proper spiritual insight, they had to be "continually in prayer," as all good Bible teachers must be. The "deep things of God" can only be revealed by the Holy Spirit (1 Corinthians 2:10), and an effective teacher of the Word must "pray without ceasing" that he or she will be guided by the Spirit into God's truth (see John16:13; 1 Thessalonians 5:17).

5 And the saying pleased the whole multitude: and they chose Stephen, a man full of faith and of the Holy Ghost, and Philip, and Prochous, and Nicanor, and Timon, and Parmenas, and Nicolas a proselyte of Antioch.

The congregation universally agreed to follow the recommendation of leadership, bringing both Greek and Hebrew on one accord regarding this issue. Not much is said of the seven men who were selected. Evidently, the congregation felt that they fulfilled the qualifications set forth by the leaders. But they are given the honor of being forever recorded in the annals of Scripture.

Significance is often found in the names given to people in ancient times. Nicanor means "victorious" in Greek. Timon means "valuable." and, Parmenas means "constant." Perhaps these men had shown these qualities in their lives. On the other hand, Philip means "fond of horses," and Prochous means "before the dance." Who knows what to make of that?

Two of the men, Nicolas, whose name means "victorious over the people" and Stephen, whose name means "crown," are described more fully in the text. Nicolas was probably of Greek descent and was a "proselyte," or a convert to Judaism. Now a believer in Christ, he was from the city of Antioch which was in Syria. The first Gentile church was established there (Acts 11:10- 21), and

and guidance of the Holy Spirit is evidenced by his brilliant testimony concerning God at the rigged "trial" (Acts 7:1-53). Needless to say, he was thereafter condemned to death because of his strong stance upon his faith (Acts 7:55-60).

6 Whom they set before the apostles: and when they had prayed, they laid their hands on them.

The congregation presented the seven men whom they had selected to "the twelve" leaders of the church. Those seven men were the forerunners of what now are called "deacons" (see 1 Timothy 3:10-13), and "the twelve" here are identified as the first "apostles."

At that time, the seven deacons were installed in their office in a ceremony before God. The apostles prayed for them and their new undertaking, and the apostles "laid their hands upon them." This practice was similar to the ordination ceremonies we now hold in many churches.

Antioch was where believers were first called "Christians" (Acts 11:26).

Stephen is mentioned first among the seven men and his strong spiritual qualities are emphasized. He was "full of faith and of the Holy Ghost." Both of those qualities were essential for him because he became the first Christian martyr. He was the first follower of Christ who was put to death because of his beliefs.

He was such a mighty man of God that the Jews hated him and brought him into court on phony charges (Acts 6:9-15). His treatment was reminiscent of the way Jesus was railroaded before His own death (Matthew 26:57-66). The full extent of Stephen's faith and his submission to the power

The laying on of hands by the apostles was similar to the way that the Old Testament prophet Samuel anointed Saul and David with oil when God installed them in office as kings (see 1 Samuel 10:1; 16:13). But, the actual practice of laying on of hands originated with the sacrificial system to cover sins which God instituted in Israel during Moses' time (see Leviticus 1:4; 3:2, 8, 13; 4:4). The practice was symbolic of a transfer of one's sins to the sacrificial offering. So, too, the apostles in our study text were anointing the seven deacons for the Lord's service and conducting the flow of God's power into their lives.

7 And the word of God increased; and the number of the disciples multiplied in Jerusalem greatly; and a great company of the priests were obedient to the faith.

With the potential split in the church having been averted, everything was in the proper order. Our God is the God of order and not confusion (2 Chronicles 29:35; 1 Corinthians 14:33). We understand from God's Word that there is strength in unity (see Ecclesiastes 4:9-12; Mark 3:24-25).

As a result of this newfound peace, order, and efficiency within the church at Jerusalem, tremendous fruit was borne by its ministry. Since the apostles were focused only on prayer and preaching, we are told that "the word of God increased." The apostles taught others the Word and preached with more power. We have already alluded to the fact that today's pastors can do greater works if they are true to the Bible and able to put in full-time work. The testimony of this study text proves the point of such a possibility.

Furthermore, "the number of the disciples multiplied in Jerusalem." God has said that His Word would not return to Him void, but would accomplish and prosper as He pleases (Isaiah 55:11). The preaching of the Gospel, thus, produced many new converts. It was a phenomenon similar to Jesus' parable wherein He alluded to a sowing of seed which produced ". . .fruit, some an hundredfold, some sixtyfold, some thirtyfold" (Matthew 13:8).

In modern times, we can look around our community and see thousands of people who are lost and under the heavy yoke of spiritual oppression. We see them on the street corners, in bars and dope houses, and in our jails. As Jesus said, "The harvest truly is plenteous" (Matthew 9:37a). There are enough lost souls in our communities across urban America to burst the seams of every church in sight. But, like the apostles and the early church, we must spread the Gospel message with power. Therefore, we must focus on our mission and devote ourselves to study and prayer on a regular basis.

Finally, many of the religious leaders who formerly opposed the spread of the Gospel began to accept it. This change of heart shows the awesomeness of God and his Word. The Bible says,

"Say unto God, How terrible art thou in thy works! Through the greatness of thy power shall thine enemies submit themselves unto thee" (Psalm 66:3). Truly the conversion of "a great company of the priests" confirms the truth of Scripture.

Furthermore, the fact that these men were "obedient to the faith" (see also Romans 16:26) after their conversion speaks volumes about the life-changing power of God's Word. They decided to conform their ways to that which they had previously found offensive to their understanding of the Law. Is there anything too hard for God?

8 And Stephen, full of faith and power, did great wonders and miracles among the people.

Stephen's miracles were a visual validation of God's existence and power which helped make new converts during that time. God did similar miracles before that with Peter (Acts 3:6-7) and the other apostles during that time (Acts 5:12-16).

The works of Stephen also are proof that one does not have to be a pastor or a minister to do wondrous things for God. All Stephen needed and all that we need is to be "full of faith." Our faith is founded upon the Word of God. The Bible says, "But without faith it is impossible to please him: for he that cometh to God must believe that he is, and that he is a rewarder of them that diligently seek him" (Hebrews 11:6).

Jesus said that the power of God is located within our level of faith (see Matthew 17:20; Mark 5:34; Luke 7:9-10). And the indwelling Holy Spirit also supplies us with God's power (see Luke 24:49; Acts 1:8; 1 Corinthians 2:4-5).

So, like Stephen who was "full of faith and the Holy Ghost" (v. 5), we have the capacity to perform marvelous works for God, regardless of whether we hold a high church office or not. We need only to trust in God and believe His Word. For the last words of the Gospel of Mark records Jesus as saying to His disciples before He was taken up into Heaven, "And these signs shall follow them that believe; In my name shall they cast out devils; they shall speak with new tongues; they shall take up serpents; and if they drink any deadly thing, it shall not hurt them; they shall lay hands on the sick, and they shall recover" (Mark 16:17-18).

It must be remembered, however, that the performance of "wonders and miracles," like those attributed to Stephen in Acts 6:8, is not the only manifestation of great works for God. For even though the Bible speaks of the spiritual gifts of healing and the working of miracles, both of which Stephen possessed, the Scriptures also say there are "diversities of gifts. . .(and) diversities of operations, but it is the same God which worketh all in all" (see 1 Corinthians 12:4, 6, 9-10). Therefore, we must seek to glorify God through attaining the maximum results from whatever particular spiritual gift(s) He has given us. Whether it be in teaching, exhortation, showing mercy, or giving (Romans 12:6-8), we must work to put our gifts to their best use.

7:55 But he, being full of the Holy Ghost, looked up steadfastly into heaven, and saw the glory of God, and Jesus standing on the right hand of God.

Stephen has been railroaded in a rigged trial by the Jewish leaders and condemned to die (Acts 6:12-13; 7:54). But rather than panic and cower with fear before his bloodthirsty enemies, he ". . .looked up steadfastly into heaven." "Steadfastly" in Greek means "to gaze intently" or "to fasten upon". So, Stephen glued his eyes on heaven ". . . from whence cometh (his) help" (Psalm 121:1). His example indicates that we should always look to God as a first resort.

Once again, Stephen is referred to as being "full of the Holy Ghost" (v. 55). The Bible tells us that we should ". . .be not drunk with wine, wherein is excess; but be filled with the Spirit" (Ephesians 5:18). One of the Greek translations for this "filling" means "to influence." So, just as too much wine controls us or puts us under the influence, especially when driving after drinking, we are told to let the Holy Spirit control us instead. Stephen's continual state of being "filled" allowed him to peacefully go through extreme tribulation.

Then, God did a beautiful thing. To reassure Stephen that his faith and boldness were not in vain, God allowed him to see His glory and Christ standing at His right hand. The compassionate Godhead allowed this condemned saint to experience what very, very few men ever have experienced (see Exodus 33:17-23; Luke 9:28-32).

56 And said, Behold, I see the heavens opened, and the Son of man standing on the right hand of God.

Stephen had boldly cut his enemies to pieces with God's Word during his so-called trial (see vv. 2-53). Now, after having all his beliefs confirmed by God in the vision, he boldly reported seeing the supremacy of Jesus Christ, i.e., "the Son. . .standing on the right hand of God."

God confirms His truths to us through His Word, the Bible (John 17:17). We must become familiar with His Word and be ready to boldly give an answer to anyone who challenges the truth of the Gospel (1 Peter 3:15).

57 Then they cried out with a loud voice, and stopped their ears, and ran upon him with one accord,

We must never be intimidated by lost folk who aggressively deny the truth. Like Stephen's enemies, some of the lost people we encounter will hate to even hear what we have to say. But we need the boldness of John the Baptist in delivering God's message anyway (see Matthew 3:7-10).

58 And cast him out of the city, and stoned him: and the witnesses laid down their clothes at a young man's feet, whose name was Saul.

Stephen's statement about seeing Jesus standing next to God (v. 56) was all his enemies needed in order to begin his execution. By "casting him out of the city, and stoning him," they considered themselves to be justified in his death according to the Mosaic Law against blasphemy (Leviticus 24:13-16). The young man named Saul who was looking on will go on to become the great Apostle Paul (Acts 9:20-22; 13:9; 22:20).

59 And they stoned Stephen, calling upon God, and saying, Lord Jesus, receive my spirit.

Here is another biblical example showing that we must turn to God and call upon Him at the most dire points in life. The Lord is the only one who can "preserve our souls" (Psalm 121:7-8). Thanks be to God that not even death can separate us from His love (Romans 8:38-39).

60 And he kneeled down, and cried with a loud voice, Lord, lay not this sin to their charge. And when he had said this, he fell asleep.

Stephen becomes the first Christian martyr to die for his faith as recorded in the Bible. He did not die because he had raped or killed. He did not die because he was a terrorist bomber who blew up a plane. He died for his faith in Christ, and his audacity to proclaim the Gospel in a hostile environment. If we must die for a cause, Jesus is the cause to choose.

Stephen's death also was special because of his attitude toward his murderers. His final words in life were a plea for God to be merciful unto those who unjustly killed him. There is no better example of being "Christ-like" to be found anywhere. Stephen's final act was almost exactly a duplication of what our Saviour did on the cross (Luke 23:34).

If we are to be Christ-like ourselves, we have to stop playing with the Christian life. We cannot be like Jesus in one instance, and unlike Jesus in another. We have to be prepared to take it all the way. The Bible says that we are being conformed to the image of Christ (Romans 8:29). Voluntary submission to all that God is trying to do with us will bring us closer to Christ-likeness each day.

8:1 And Saul was consenting unto his death. And at that time there was a great persecution against the church which was at Jerusalem; and they were all scattered abroad throughout the regions of Judea and Samaria, except the apostles.

Saul (who later became the Apostle Paul) was very pleased with Stephen's death. The term "consenting" means "to think well of in common" or "to feel gratified with" in Greek. Since Saul was an enemy of the doctrine of Christ at that time (Acts 8:3), killing a bold and effective spokesman such as Stephen was a real plus.

The "great persecution against the church. . .at Jerusalem," was a natural result of Stephen's murder. Proverbs 29:10 says, "The bloodthirsty hate the upright." Like sharks which circle in the water looking for prey at the smell of blood,

the enemy stepped up persecution of the church.

However, God, who can turn disaster into blessings (Genesis 50:20 and Romans 8:28), used the persecution to spread the Gospel of Jesus Christ into other areas. He kept the apostles in Jerusalem as a sort of spiritual "anchor" for His movement. The apostles trusted that He would protect them according to His purpose. But, the teachers and preachers of the Word whom they had trained were "scattered abroad. . .(into) Judea and Samaria." Gloriously, these locations precisely fit the pattern Jesus had laid out for the spread of the Word as it went into "the uttermost part of the earth" (Acts 1:8).

The modern church has to take God's message ". . .into the highways," (Matthew 22:9-10). And, as we evangelize the lost, we must anticipate stiff resistance from Satan. He wants to stop God's program in its tracks. We must expect opposition and tribulation, but we must have courage because Christ will enable us to overcome all obstacles (see John 16:33).

DAILY BIBLE READINGS

M: Chosen to Serve
Acts 6:1-7

T: Stephen Arrested
Acts 6:8-15

W: Stephen Speaks of Abraham and Isaac
Acts 7:1-8

T: Stephen Speaks of Joseph
Acts 7:9-16

F: Stephen Speaks of Moses
Acts 7:20-35

S: Stephen Speaks of God's Blessings
Acts 7:36-50

S: Stephen Martyred Before Saul
Acts 7:51 8:1

TEACHING TIPS

April 8
Bible Study Guide 6

1. Words You Should Know

A. Preaching (Acts 8:4) Greek *euaggelizo*—To announce good news, especially the Gospel.

B. Eunuch (Acts 8:27) Greek *eunouchos*—A state-officer with much influence and positional power.

C. Scripture (Acts 8:35) Greek *graphe*—The Holy Writings, generally, and specifically its contents or a statement in it.

2. Teacher Preparation

A. Read and meditate upon the devotional and background Scriptures.

B. Study the FOCAL VERSES in the most popular translations used by the church in corporate worship or students in individual study. Make note of study notes and contemporary language.

C. Recruit students ahead of class to act out in mime (silent but exaggerated expression of events and emotions) Philip's ministry in Samaria and to the Eunuch. You will need a narrator, a preacher, a few representing the possessed and infirmed, one acting as the eunuch, and a crowd (the rest of the class).

3. Starting the Lesson

A. Write the AT-A-GLANCE outline on the board.

B. Discuss powerful and unusual opportunities of ministry that you and/or students have experienced.

C. Read the IN FOCUS story as a centering devotional.

4. Getting into the Lesson

A Share the WORDS YOU SHOULD KNOW with students as an introduction to the pantomime.

B. Allow students to act out the lesson in mime and narration.

5. Relating the Lesson to Life

A. Review the KEEP IN MIND Scripture and discuss ways the class could carry out the word of God. As devoted Christians, we must make a commitment to not only "hear the word of God," but to also "be doers of God's word."

B. Put this Scripture into action and role play opportunities to lead others to Christ.

6. Arousing Action

A. After reflecting on the LESSON IN OUR SOCIETY section, encourage the students to seriously consider the ways in which they might answer the call to evangelism in their personal lives.

B. Lead a prayer for boldness as students endure the persecution of exclusion, hostility, or ridicule as believers.

APRIL 8TH

WORSHIP GUIDE

For the Superintendent or Teacher
Theme: Witnessing Beyond Jerusalem
Theme Song: "Go Tell It on
the Mountain"
Scripture: Micah 4:1-7
Song: "I Love to Tell the Story"
Devotional Thought: Father, in the name
of Jesus, I go to tell the story of Your
redemptive love and saving grace.
May the message of Your gift of Jesus
be spread abroad wherever I am sent
and obediently go.

WITNESSING BEYOND JERUSALEM

Bible Background • ACTS 8:4-40
Printed Text • ACTS 8:4-8, 26-35
Devotional Reading • MICAH 5:7-9

LESSON AIM

By the end of this lesson, students will be able to show how effective ministry takes place through Philip's broad availability and immediate obedience and they will be challenged to become better prepared and more available and obedient to tell others about the Gospel of Jesus Christ.

KEEP IN MIND

"Therefore they that were scattered abroad went every where preaching the word" (Acts 8:4).

FOCAL VERSES

Acts 8:4 Therefore they that were scattered abroad went every where preaching the word.

5 Then Philip went down to the city of Samaria, and preached Christ unto them.

6 And the people with one accord gave heed unto those things which Philip spake, hearing and seeing the miracles which he did.

7 For unclean spirits, crying with loud voice, came out of many that were possessed with them: and many taken with palsies, and that were lame, were healed.

8 And there was great joy in that city.

8:26 And the angel of the Lord spake unto Philip, saying, Arise, and go toward the south unto the way that goeth down from Jerusalem unto Gaza, which is desert.

27 And he arose and went: and, behold, a man of Ethiopia, an eunuch of great authority under Candace queen of the Ethiopians, who had the charge of all her treasure, and had come to

LESSON OVERVIEW

LESSON AIM
KEEP IN MIND
FOCAL VERSES
IN FOCUS
THE PEOPLE, PLACES, AND TIMES
BACKGROUND
AT-A-GLANCE
IN DEPTH
SEARCH THE SCRIPTURES
DISCUSS THE MEANING
LESSON IN OUR SOCIETY
MAKE IT HAPPEN
FOLLOW THE SPIRIT
REMEMBER YOUR THOUGHTS
MORE LIGHT ON THE TEXT
DAILY BIBLE READINGS

Jerusalem for to worship,

28 Was returning, and sitting in his chariot read Esaias the prophet.

29 Then the Spirit said unto Philip, Go near, and join thyself to this chariot.

30 And Philip ran thither to him, and heard him read the prophet Esaias, and said, Understandest thou what thou readest?

31 And he said, How can I, except some man should guide me? And he desired Philip that he would come up and sit with him.

32 The place of the scripture which he read was this, He was led as a sheep to the slaughter; and like a lamb dumb before his shearer, so opened he not his mouth:

33 In his humiliation his judgment was taken away: and who shall declare his generation? for his life is taken from the earth.

34 And the eunuch answered Philip, and said, I pray thee, of whom speaketh the prophet this? of himself, or of some other man?

35 Then Philip opened his mouth, and began at the same scripture, and preached unto him Jesus.

IN FOCUS

What is a Christian? In the Letter to Diognetus, which dates back to the second century B.C., an anonymous writer describes a strange people who are in the world but not of the world:

"Christians are not differentiated from other people by country, language, or customs; you see, they do not live in cities of their own, or speak some strange dialect. . . They live both in Greek and foreign cities, wherever chance has put them. They follow local customs in clothing, food and the other aspects of life. But at the same time, they demonstrate to us the unusual form of their own citizenship.

"They live in their own native lands, but as aliens. . . Every foreign country is to them as their native country, and every native land as a foreign country.

"They marry and have children just like everyone else, but they do not kill unwanted babies. They offer a shared table, but not a shared bed. They are passing their days on earth, but are citizens of heaven. They obey the appointed laws and go beyond the laws in their own lives.

"They love everyone, but are persecuted by all. They are put to death and gain life. They are poor and yet make many rich. They are dishonored and yet gain glory through dishonor. Their names are blackened, and yet they are cleared. They are mocked and bless in return. They are treated outrageously and behave respectfully to others.

"When they do good, they are punished as evildoers; when punished, they rejoice as if being given new life. They are attacked by Jews as aliens and are persecuted by Greeks; yet those who hate them cannot give any reason for their hostility. ("Illustrations for Preaching & Teaching" from *Leadership Journal*, Craig Brian Larson, ed., Grand Rapids: Baker Books, 1993, p. 18.)

A common characteristic among the first Christians was their sense of purpose. The Scripture records that their response to persecution, which caused them to be scattered among all regions, was to preach the Gospel. One might think that to dilute the Christian numbers in one place would cause them to be discouraged and complain. On the contrary, they counted all they possessed and lost as insignificant to what would be attained by the preaching of the Gospel. And so it was, that these common people of every nation, went into every nation preaching the Gospel and making disciples.

This is a model for contemporary Christians, as we live in a highly mobile society. For American Christians, we may not know religious persecution in the magnitude experienced by Christians in foreign countries; however, we may find ourselves being scattered abroad due to job changes, educational pursuits, and ministry opportunities. Whether in the course of our daily travels or with the intent of missions, we should take every opportunity given to preach the Gospel.

THE PEOPLE, PLACES, AND TIMES

Philip. An apostle of Jesus, who was also a deacon serving alongside Stephen and an evangelist who preached and baptized a eunuch.

Eunuch. A man appointed to a very powerful post in Queen Candace's court; and who, on his way from Jewish worship, was taught, converted, and baptized by Philip.

Preaching. Generally and widely understood to be taking the opportunity to expound on a particular scriptural text.

BACKGROUND

The first Christian martyr, Stephen, had given his life for the furtherance of the Gospel. With his death, the persecution of Christians intensified and caused them to be dispersed out of Jerusalem. However, by this unorthodox method—by persecution—the fulfillment of Jesus' prophecy that the church would witness of Him in Judea, Samaria, and the uttermost parts of the world (Acts 1:8) was realized.

As the believers suffered, God was glorified and the church grew through their preaching in the face of persecution. Particularly notable is that all who were scattered participated in spreading the Gospel. The task of witnessing was not solely relegated to the apostles, or the Twelve; but all who believed preached the Gospel in some manner. The Christians of the early church understood the simplicity of the message and the messengers of the Gospel. All who believe ought tell another about the saving grace of the Lord Jesus the Christ.

Perhaps the most notorious persecutor to emerge during this period of the church was a man named Saul. Although he was later converted and became known as the apostle Paul, Saul evolved from a passive observer of Stephen's stoning (Acts 7:58), to one who affirmed his death (Acts 8:1), to one who became the most feared persecutor of the first Christians (Acts 8:3).

Instead of shirking away in shame and being dispersed into silence, the Christians became bolder witnesses. Whether they were in prison or relocating after having been forced out of Jerusalem, they preached the Gospel. These homeless people were not a hopeless people, and everywhere they went they preached Christ.

AT-A-GLANCE

1. Go, Preach! (Acts 8:4-8)
2. Go, South! (Acts vv. 26-29)
3. Go, There! (Acts vv. 30-38)

IN DEPTH

1. Go, Preach! (Acts 8:4-8)

Because of persecution, many believers fled Jerusalem, preaching Christ wherever they went (v. 4). As they journeyed abroad, the Christians, whether Jews or Greeks, were forced out of the boundaries of familiar customs. This heightened their sensitivity to all who had been rejected by religion or nationality, and stirred up their concern for all who desired to belong and believe. By persecution and prophecy, Christianity broke the boundaries and bondage of religion, race, and culture.

Among those scattered was Philip, one of the seven deacons appointed along with Stephen. Philip went to Samaria, preaching Christ and demonstrating the power of the Holy Spirit (vv. 5-8). This leader, who had demonstrated the gift of administration while in Jerusalem, gained the reputation of an able preacher and performed many miracles of healing in Samaria.

Through preaching and performing miracles, the people got to hear and see the Gospel at work. Philip preached Christ and many were healed. There were many who required spiritual healing from unclean spirits. These unclean spirits suggest psychological infirmities. There were many who required physical healing from palsy and deformities. These palsies were evident physical infirmities. Through Philip's ministry, he ministered the healing Gospel—profitable for the body, mind, and spirit.

As a result, the Samaritans lived with the many who needed psychological and physical healing and realized that they were among many who needed spiritual healing. After hearing the Gospel preached and witnessing miracles performed, many believed and there was great joy in the city.

2. Go, South! (vv. 26-29)

Led to the south by an angel of the Lord, Philip encountered a high-ranking Ethiopian official who had been to Jerusalem to worship (vv. 26-27). While experiencing great revival in Samaria, Philip was led to a desert experience. There he found his next opportunity of ministry.

While on his way, Philip saw a man sitting on a chariot. That man was an Ethiopian eunuch, who was the head treasurer in the reign of Queen Candace, Queen of Ethiopia. Because the eunuch was either Jewish by birth, or a Jewish convert, he had been to Jerusalem to worship. While leaving, he was compelled to pause and ponder the Scriptures.

The Spirit directed Philip to join the Ethiopian, who was reading from the prophet Isaiah (vv. 28-29). It is this passage which describes Jesus' crucifixion as that of suffering servant and lamb for the slaughter. Given that the text was written in Hebrew, it is not unusual that a Greek translation provided an insufficient interpretation.

Obedient to the Spirit, Philip boldly approached and addressed the eunuch. Transcending national and religious differences, Philip ran and seized the opportunity to preach the Gospel to another.

3. Go, There! (vv. 29-38)

At the Ethiopian's invitation, Philip explained the scriptural text, telling the man the Good News about Jesus (vv. 30-35). Obedient to the Spirit, Philip inquires about the eunuch's level of understanding. The eunuch, eager to understand and believe, responded honestly. Although he did not know what the Scriptures meant, he had a teachable spirit and implored that Philip should interpret the Scripture for him.

Beginning at the passage where the eunuch was reading, Isaiah 53:7-8, Philip opened his mouth and began to preach the Gospel. Although they were strangers, Philip did not waste time with formalities of introduction. Why, he didn't even find it necessary to share his credentials of being one of the first deacons and his reputation of being a prolific preacher and miracle worker throughout all Samaria. Meeting the eunuch where he was, Philip preached Jesus.

His instruction and interpretation was so convincing that, upon approaching a body of water, the eunuch inquired about his suitability for baptism. Making certain that the eunuch did not confuse Christian water baptism with the Greek custom of baptizing, Philip reiterated the foundations of Christian faith as the precedent for Christian baptism namely, a belief in the Lord Jesus Christ.

The eunuch confessed his belief in the Jesus Christ as the Son of God and brought the chariot to a halt. Both men disembarked from the chariot and entered the water, where Philip baptized the eunuch into the family of God.

SEARCH THE SCRIPTURES

1. Who were they that were scattered abroad preaching the Word? (Acts 8:4)

2. What caused the people to believe Philip's message? (vv. 5-7)

3. What was the people's response to the Gospel? (v. 8)

4. Who spoke to Philip and what did Philip do? (vv. 26, 29)

5. What Scripture was the eunuch reading and desiring understanding? (vv. 32-33)

6. What Scripture did Philip use to preach Jesus to the eunuch? (v. 35)

DISCUSS THE MEANING

1. Some churches today seldom use the Old Testament for preaching, teaching, and worship. They reason that with the coming of Christ Jesus in the New Testament, that Old Testament law and purpose is insufficient in preaching the Gospel unto salvation. What might have Philip, a believer in Jesus Christ, said to the eunuch in preaching Jesus from this Old Testament passage?

2. In verse 26 it is recorded that the angel of the Lord spoke to Philip. In verse 29, it is record-

ed that the Spirit spoke to Philip. Are these voices the same? Which of these voices is the voice of God? Which phrase is most often used in your congregation to refer to hearing from God?

LESSON IN OUR SOCIETY

One day a lady criticized D. L. Moody's method of evangelism in attempting to win people to the Lord. Moody's reply was, "I agree with you. I don't like the way I do it either. Tell me, how do you do it?" The lady replied, "I don't do it." Moody retorted, "Then I like my way of doing it better than your way of not doing it." (From *Illustrations Unlimited*, James S. Hewett, ed., Wheaton: Tyndale House Publishers, Inc., 1988, p. 178)

There are some who are quite proficient in using the Bible as the sole tool to lead another to Christ. Others effectively use tracts explaining the laws of salvation and realities of heaven and hell to facilitate a conversion experience in friends and strangers alike. Some even evangelize by hosting Bible studies and prayer meetings during lunch breaks at work. Still others win souls for the kingdom by baking cookies for the new neighbors, gathering blankets for the homeless, and driving the soccer car pool.

What is your method of evangelism? As you reflect on its effectiveness, remember, it is not the method that converts, but the message.

MAKE IT HAPPEN

Philip's actions are a model of obedience. His spirit of willingness is evident whether following directions to go into the desert or to minister to a stranger. The next time you hear the voice of God, prompting you to change directions and approach a stranger, will you be as prepared and as obedient as Philip to preach Jesus unto them? Where has God told you to go? To whom has God told you to minister? Have you done it?

FOLLOW THE SPIRIT

What God wants me to do:

_____

_____

REMEMBER YOUR THOUGHTS
Special insights you learned:

_____

_____

MORE LIGHT ON THE TEXT
Acts 8:4-8, 26-35

8:4 Therefore they that were scattered abroad went every where preaching the word.

There is an old saying in our churches that goes something to the effect that, "If you truly have Jesus, you just can't keep quiet. You have to tell somebody about Him." That appears to be what happened with those early saints from Jerusalem (v. 1) who were "scattered abroad."

Jesus had made it clear to the apostles in Acts 1:8 that they were to be "witnesses unto me." And, what we call The Great Commission in Matthew 28:19-20 presupposes that Christianity will spread into all nations only by means of believers opening their mouths and telling others. Therefore, going "everywhere (and) preaching the word" was exactly what God wanted from those early saints—and from us today.

5 Then Philip went down to the city of Samaria, and preached Christ unto them.

The Samaritans were looked down upon by the Hebrews or Jews who considered themselves to be of purer blood. There was a racial tension between them. When Jesus dealt with the Samaritan woman by the well she reminded Him, ". . .the Jews have no dealings with the Samaritans" (John 4:9). Jesus' encounter with that woman was proof that "God is no respecter of persons" (Acts 10:34). Therefore, the Spirit of God led Philip into Samaria to cut across all social barriers in order to bring the Gospel to "all nations" (Matthew 28:19).

6 And the people with one accord gave heed unto those things which Philip spake, hearing and seeing the miracles which he did.

Philip, the deacon chosen with six others by the Jerusalem church congregation (Acts 6:5), had apparently attained a high degree of favor with God and the people of God in the church (1 Timothy 3:13). God used him to give the same proof to the Samaritans that He had given to the Jewish people who believed on Christ in Jerusalem. Just as Stephen, Peter, and other apostles performed wonders and miracles to draw those in Jerusalem (Acts 5:12-16; 6:8), Philip performed miracles in Samaria.

As Jesus had pointed out during His earthly ministry, the miraculous works were intended to indicate that God was the One who sent the miracle-worker (see John 5:36). Thus, no one who harbored prejudice against the Samaritans could continue to look down upon them, or claim that God had not provided His full array of salvation experiences for them (Acts 8:14-17).

Philip's audience was wise enough to believe him and "with one accord (they) gave heed unto those things which Philip spake." Those Samaritans were just as "saved" as any other group of people (Mark 16:15-16).

7 For unclean spirits, crying with loud voice, came out of many that were possessed with them: and many taken with palsies, and that were lame, were healed.

The miracles that God performed through Philip were just as authentic, both in nature and quantity, as those which were performed in Jerusalem by the apostles (Acts 5:15-16), and by the Lord (see Matthew 9:2, 6-7; 12:22). So, God did not perform "lesser" miracles for the Samaritans.

8 And there was great joy in that city.

In Luke 10:20, Jesus said, ". . .Rejoice, because your names are written in heaven." And that is exactly what the new Samaritan Christians did. They had found a Saviour and eternal life. With belief in Christ came the prospect of new hope and spiritual blessings in their lives.

We must frequently take time to reflect on how God has saved us and how He has wrought so many great works in our lives. In spite of the noise and activities of the world that distract us and pull at us, frequently we must take the time to tell the Lord how much we love Him and how glad we are to be His children.

8:26 And the angel of the Lord spake unto Philip, saying, Arise, and go toward the south

unto the way that goeth down from Jerusalem unto Gaza, which is desert.

Philip can now truly be said to have the gift of evangelism based upon his work in Samaria (see Ephesians 4:11). God used an angel to deliver His message to Philip. The message was one of direction. God will always direct us if we are willing to follow Him. Proverbs 3:6 says "In all thy ways acknowledge him, and he shall direct they paths." In Matthew 7:7, Jesus said, ". . .seek, and ye shall find."

While God rarely uses angels to give us direction in modern times, His Word is certainly "profitable" for such a purpose (2 Timothy 3:16-17). If we let it, God's Word will be ". . .a lamp unto (our) feet" (Psalm 119:105), and the Holy Spirit is also available to us for whatever direction we may need (John 16:13).

God led Philip south into the desert of Judah. A desert is vast and empty. It is not the kind of place where an evangelist can find lots of people to whom he can witness. But, like Philip, we must always trust the omniscience and sovereignty of God's direction for our lives.

27 And he arose and went: and, behold, a man of Ethiopia, an eunuch of great authority under Candace queen of the Ethiopians, who had the charge of all her treasure, and had come to Jerusalem for to worship.

Philip did not waste time questioning God's instructions, as we sometimes do to our own detriment. Philip was immediately obedient. "He arose and went." And, when Philip, the evangelist, followed God's will he was given the opportunity to use his spiritual gift. Behold, God had arranged an encounter with a man from Ethiopia to whom He wanted the Gospel message delivered.

This Ethiopian was no ordinary man. Long before that day, David wrote in Psalm 68:31: ". . . Ethiopia shall soon stretch out her hands unto God." So, it was not a coincidence that Philip met this man of "great authority under Candace queen of Ethiopia" who also must have thirsted to know about the One True God because ". . .(he) had come to Jerusalem for to worship." Presumably, this man was a proselyte, or convert to Judaism, since Jerusalem was the seat of that religion.

When we consider all these facts together, we can see that it was God's plan to use Philip to instruct this man in the truth. God could use this man of "great authority" in his home country to spread a true understanding of Jesus Christ to the African culture.

The word "eunuch" does mean a "castrated man" in Greek, but it also means "a chamberlain," or state officer. The fact that he "had charge of all of (Candace's) treasure," implies that he was probably far from being poor himself. Here again we see God's lack of preferential treatment. Both rich and poor men need Jesus. And obviously, all races of men need Jesus because here God is dealing with a Black man, just as He dealt with the Samaritans and the Greeks (Acts 6:1).

28 Was returning, and sitting in his chariot read Esaias the prophet.

The Ethiopian official stopped his chariot to read the Book of Isaiah on his way home. He did not know it, but God had a man right there who was going to reveal the greatest knowledge in the world to him.

Believers today must remember that we are not victims of luck, chance, coincidence, nor fortune. God chose us and ordains things in our lives (John 15:16; Ephesians 2:10). God "orders our steps" in His Word (Psalm 133:119). But, like Philip, we must be obedient to benefit from it. God is in control.

29 Then the Spirit said unto Philip, Go near, and join thyself to this chariot. And Philip ran thither to him, and heard him read the prophet Esaias, and said, Understandest thou what thou readest?

Philip shows no hesitation to obey the Spirit of God; he "ran" over to the Ethiopian. Philip's question to the man was not meant to embarrass him. His question was an "icebreaker" to get him into a conversation where he could witness about the Lord. Jesus used such an icebreaker on the Samaritan woman at the well when he asked her for a drink of water (John 4:7). If we are going to witness effectively today, we must be sensitive to the leading of the Holy Spirit to initiate conversation with strangers we meet along life's way.

31 And he said, How can I, except some man should guide me? And he desired Philip that he would come up and sit with him.

The Ethiopian's response, "How can I unless some man should guide me?" and his invitation for Philip to join him was like begging to be told about Jesus! In our conversations with those we do not know, we must be careful to show a pleasantness which will make them want to respond in the same fashion. At that point, we will have our foot in the door, so to speak. As we witness more and more, we will gain practice and experience. Thus, our natural fear of speaking to others about Christ will dissipate.

The more obedient we are, the more we will be "filled," or controlled, by the Holy Spirit (Ephesians 4:30; 5:18; 1 Thessalonians 5:19). The Holy Spirit will lead us as we witness in conversation with others. He will speak to us just as He spoke to Philip (v. 29).

32 The place of the Scripture which he read was this, He was led as a sheep to the slaughter; and like a lamb due before his shearer, so opened he not his mouth: 33 In his humiliation his judgment was taken away: and who shall declare his generation? For his life is taken from the earth.

Perhaps the Ethiopian had heard this passage in the Jewish service in Jerusalem. Or, perhaps he had heard someone preaching the Gospel of Jesus Christ in the city and was intrigued by it. At any rate, the wonderful workings of God had the man reading what we now call a "Messianic prophecy." Such Old Testament prophecies were given by God, through the prophets He anointed, in order to foretell of the coming of the Messiah, Jesus Christ (Psalm 22:1, 16-18; Isaiah 9:6).

34 And the eunuch answered Philip, and said, I pray thee, of whom speaketh the prophet this? of himself, or of some other man?

The Ethiopian was ready to hear the Good News of Salvation through Jesus Christ. His questions indicate that the Holy Spirit was illuminating his mind, so that he could gain an understanding of the Gospel which, previously, would have seemed like foolishness to him (Hebrews 10:32; 1 Corinthians 2:10-11;12:3). At the same time that the Spirit was turning the light on in his previously darkened mind, his heart was becoming "good ground" where the planting of the Word of God would take hold and bear fruit (Matthew 13:8, 23).

One way that we can overcome a fear of witnessing is by remembering our responsibility in the process of salvation. Jesus merely told us to "witness" about Him; we cannot "save" people. "Salvation belongeth unto the Lord" (Psalm 3:8), not us. All we are required to do is "sow the seeds" of the Gospel (Matthew 13:3-9). If our audience rejects the Gospel of Jesus Christ, then they have not rejected us, but they have rejected God (1 Samuel 8:7).

35 Then Philip opened his mouth, and began at the same Scripture, and preached unto him Jesus.

Philip did what God had led him through the desert to do. He did that which God has commanded us to do. He "opened his mouth" and told the Ethiopian about Jesus.

DAILY BIBLE READINGS

M: Philip Preaches in Samaria
Acts 8:4-8
T: Simon the Magician
Acts 8:9-13
W: Peter Confronts Simon the Magician
Acts 8:14-25
T: Philip and the Ethiopian Official
Acts 8:26-31
F: Those Excluded from the Assembly
Deuteronomy 23:1-7
S: The Suffering Servant
Isaiah 53
S: An Ethiopian Converted and Baptized
Acts 8:32-40

TEACHING TIPS

April 15
Bible Study Guide 7

1. Words You Should Know

A. Assayed (Acts 9:26) Greek *peirao*—Implies that Paul timidly tested whether he would be accepted by the disciples as he attempted to be identified as a new preacher of the Gospel.

B. Declared (v. 27) Greek *diegeomai*—To relate or to fully explain as in defense of one.

C. Preached Boldly (v. 27) Greek *parrhesiazomai*—To be confident in spirit and demeanor, particularly in preaching the Gospel.

D. Rest (v. 31) Greek *loipoy*—Indicates a period without significant persecution where the church was allowed to rest or remain undisturbed.

2. Teacher Preparation

A. Read and meditate upon the devotional and background Scriptures.

B. Study the FOCAL VERSES in the most popular translations used by the church in corporate worship or students in individual study. Make note of study notes and contemporary language.

C. Write out answers to the SEARCH THE SCRIPTURES questions.

3. Starting the Lesson

A. Write the AT-A-GLANCE outline on the board.

B. Discuss the WORDS YOU SHOULD KNOW. Invite students to share thoughts or stories about people who used to persecute Christians but who have now been converted.

C. Read the IN FOCUS story as a centering devotional, and use the LESSON AIM as a guide for discussion.

4. Getting into the Lesson

A. Have the students read The PEOPLE, PLACES, AND TIMES section.

B. Lead a discussion about the conversion experiences of well-known preachers and church leaders.

5. Relating the Lesson to Life

A. Break off into small groups to answer the DISCUSS THE MEANING questions.

B. Reconvene the larger group and share reflections and discoveries.

6. Arousing Action

A. Reflect on the LESSON IN OUR SOCIETY.

B. Devise strategies to respond to the MAKE IT HAPPEN assignment.

C. Secure the students' commitment to read and meditate upon the DAILY BIBLE READINGS this week.

APR 15TH

PROCLAIMING THE RISEN LORD

Bible Background • LUKE 24:1-12; ACTS 9:1-31
Printed Text • LUKE 24:1-10; ACTS 9:19-20, 26-28, 31
Devotional Reading • JOHN 20:1, 11-18

LESSON AIM

By the end of this lesson, students will be able to narrate the story of Jesus' resurrection and the story of Paul's conversion.

KEEP IN MIND

"Why do you look for the living among the dead? He is not here, but is risen" (Luke 24:5).

FOCAL VERSES

Luke 24:1 Now upon the first day of the week, very early in the morning, they came unto the sepulchre, bringing the spices which they had prepared, and certain others with them.

2 And they found the stone rolled away from the sepulchre.

3 And they entered in, and found not the body of the Lord Jesus.

4 And it came to pass, as they were much perplexed thereabout, behold, two men stood by them in shining garments:

5 And as they were afraid, and bowed down their faces to the earth, they said unto them, Why seek ye the living among the dead?

6 He is not here, but is risen: remember how he spake unto you when he was yet in Galilee,

7 Saying, The Son of man must be delivered into the hands of sinful men, and be crucified, and the third day rise again.

8 And they remembered his words,

9 And returned from the sepulchre, and told all these things unto the eleven, and to all the rest.

10 It was Mary Magdalene, and Joanna, and Mary the mother of James, and other women that

were with them, which told these things unto the apostles.

Acts 9:19 And when he had received meat, he was strengthened. Then was Saul certain days with the disciples which were at Damascus.

20 And straightway he preached Christ in the synagogues, that he is the Son of God.

9:26 And when Saul was come to Jerusalem, he assayed to join himself to the disciples: but they were all afraid of him, and believed not that he was a disciple.

27 But Barnabas took him, and brought him to the apostles, and declared unto them how he had seen the Lord in the way, and that he had spoken to him, and how he had preached boldly at Damascus in the name of Jesus.

28 And he was with them coming in and going out at Jerusalem.

9:31 Then had the churches rest throughout all Judea and Galilee and Samaria, and were edified; and walking in the fear of the Lord, and in the comfort of the Holy Ghost, were multiplied.

IN FOCUS

Paul's testimony is repeated over and over again as persons respond in faith to God's gift of salvation, receive His Spirit, and become new creations in Jesus Christ. I heard of such a miracle recently. The American Red Cross was gathering supplies, medicine, clothing, food and other necessities for the suffering people of Biafra. Inside one of the boxes that showed up at the collecting depot one day was a letter. It said, "We have recently been converted and because of our conversion we want to try to help. We won't ever need these again. Can you use them for something?" Inside the box were several Ku Klux Klan sheets. The sheets were cut down to strips and eventually used to bandage the wounds of Black people in Africa. This example could hardly be more dramatic—from symbols of hatred to bandages of love because of the new creation. Nothing else matters, says Paul. (Maxie Dunnam, "Commentary on Galations," from *Illustrations Unlimited,* James S. Hewett, ed., Wheaton: Tyndale House Publishers, Inc., 1988, p. 51.)

"I couldn't believe my eyes!" This exclamation befits an observation contrary to what was previously known or considered possible. The disciples, upon hearing that Saul had been converted, possibly exclaimed, "I can't believe my eyes; I can't believe my ears!" And certainly, Saul must have understood, as his heinous reputation for persecuting Christians preceded him.

As Christians, it is not with our eyes and ears that we should seek to affirm or question one's conversion. It is with our hearts and spirits. The inward conversion soon follows with an outward transformation. For as with Saul, once converted, Paul's zealous energy was transformed from hate to love, from persecutor to preacher, from despiser to disciple.

THE PEOPLE, PLACES AND TIMES

Women. Although outcast from the center of Jewish worship, women were central to the spread of the Gospel. A popular Jewish prayer in the first century was, "Blessed be God that He did not make me a Gentile, a slave, or a woman."

Saul. The Hebrew name for the apostle Paul (Greek name), most widely used before his conversion to Christianity and transformation from a persecutor of Christians to a prolific preacher of Christ.

Preachers. Men who were not unfamiliar to the people, from the days of Noah to the Day of Pentecost and thereafter, preachers proclaimed the Word of God and the Gospel of Jesus Christ.

BACKGROUND

Disbelief is the common element in the following stories. First, the women at the tomb could not believe their eyes (Luke 24:1-5). The tomb was unsealed, Jesus' body was missing, and they were frightened by the sight of angels appearing as men. Similarly, the disciples at Jerusalem could not believe their eyes (Acts 9:26-28). The chief persecutor of Christians stood before them, professing Jesus as the Son of God, and they were afraid of Saul for his reputation preceded him.

Both the women and the disciples could not believe their eyes, nor their ears. Jesus had died. Saul was a persecutor. But now, could it be that Jesus was risen? And Saul, a disciple? It took the affirmation of angels and others for the women and the disciples to believe. But the truth became clear: He who was dead is now alive; and he who had persecuted Christians now preaches Christ.

AT-A-GLANCE

1. The Resurrection Messengers
(Luke 24:1-10)
2. A Messenger's Transformation
(Acts 9:19-20, 26-28)
3. The Kingdom's Expansion
(v. 31)

IN DEPTH

1. The Resurrection Messengers (Luke 24:1-12)

The women who went to prepare Jesus' body found it missing from the tomb (Luke 24:1-3).

Jesus had died. The women, the disciples, and the crowd all saw Him die—crucified at Calvary. The men who loved the Lord requested His body that they might give Him a proper burial. The women who loved the Lord came early on the morning of the third day, as was their custom, to bring embalming spices to dress the Lord's body.

When the women came to the tomb, they were certainly surprised to see that the stone seal had been rolled away. Perplexed, but undaunted, they entered the tomb, still expecting to minister to the One they loved. But, His body was gone.

Focused on his purpose, Saul's thought and path was interrupted by the presence of a great light and commanding voice. It was the presence and voice of Jesus, holding Saul accountable for his persecution of the church.

Although Saul's companions saw no one, they heard the dialogue between Saul and Jesus. And Saul, stricken blind, was led into the city for further instructions in ministry. After three days of blindness and fasting, a servant of the Lord, Ananias, laid hands on Saul. Immediately, Saul regained his sight, was water baptized, and ate a hearty meal.

Thus began Saul's preaching ministry. Instead of arriving at Damascus as a persecutor, Saul enters Damascus demonstrating his faith in Jesus Christ. Saul stayed with the disciples at Damascus to learn from them for a few days. . . then they went out into the synagogues to preach Jesus as the Son of God.

Two men in dazzling clothes announced that Jesus had risen, and they reminded the women that Jesus had foretold what would happen (vv. 4-7). Two angels, appearing as men, announced that Jesus was risen and alive and reminded them of His prophecy in Galilee. The women's fear dissipated, as they remembered the Lord's words. Their fear was replaced with great joy!

The women reported to the disciples what had happened (vv. 8-10). Overjoyed, they ran to tell the good news of the Gospel to the eleven and to all who believed.

Many who heard him were amazed; they had known and feared Saul as the most zealous and ruthless persecutor of the Christian church. They reminded themselves, each other, and all who would listen of Saul's reputation. But Saul, increased in knowledge and boldness, confounded the crowd by his conversion.

When the disciples in Jerusalem were afraid of Saul, Barnabas affirmed Saul's conversion and he was accepted (vv. 26-28). Saul's ministry and conversion was so convincing to the masses, that the religious and governmental leaders decided to kill him—much like they had sanctioned the

2. A Messenger's Transformation (Acts 9:19-20, 26-28)

While spending several days with the disciples in Damascus, Saul proclaimed Jesus as the Son of God (Acts 9:19-20). On the way to Damascus to persecute the church, Saul was converted.

deaths of Stephen and Jesus. However, the disciples at Damascus devised a plan to save Saul's life. Shrouded by night, they lowered him over the city wall in a basket that he might escape to Jerusalem. Saul's escape from Damascus was successful, but his acceptance by the disciples in Jerusalem was suspect.

They legitimately feared the man who had planned the mass persecution of the Christians. They feared for their lives and the lives of those in the Christian community. They probably suspected that talk of Saul's conversion was the latest arsenal for infiltrating and dispersing the church at Jerusalem.

3. The Kingdom's Expansion (v. 31)

During the peaceful period that followed, the churches were built up and increased in numbers (v. 31). As Saul, now Paul, went about with the disciples preaching and teaching the Gospel, he preached with such boldness to the Greek community that some set out, again, to kill him. When the disciples at Jerusalem learned of this plot, they arranged to relocate Paul to another region for ministry.

With Paul sent forth on his first Christian missionary journey, the church experienced rest from persecution. Instead, during this season of peace, the church continued to increase spiritually and numerically.

SEARCH THE SCRIPTURES

1. Who were the first to come to the tomb and why were they there? (Luke 24:1-3, 10)

2. What was the first post-resurrection sermon and who preached it? (vv. 6-7, 10)

3. Where was Paul's first sermon preached? (Acts 9:20)

4. Who doubted Paul's conversion and why? (v. 26)

5. How did the church benefit from Paul's conversion? (v. 31)

DISCUSS THE MEANING

1. Why do you think the disciples doubted Paul's conversion and continued to fear him? Have there been times when you doubted another's conversion? Have you ever experienced the grief and alienation that Paul might have felt when the disciples doubted his conversion and sought to exclude him from ministry and fellowship?

LESSON IN OUR SOCIETY

C. S. Lewis fell into grace. But instead of simply entering a monastery, he did worse. He ended up publicly explaining and openly defending his personal God to millions of listeners and readers. Such undignified behavior embarrassed the hierarchy at Oxford college and cost Lewis his chance of ever advancing to a higher position on the faculty there. Lewis learned that if you speak about beauty, truth, or goodness, and about God as a great spiritual force, people will remain friendly. But he found that the temperature drops when you discuss a God who gives definite commands, who does definite acts, who has definite ideas and character. (Kathryn Lindskoog in *Illustrations Unlimited,* James S. Hewett, ed., Wheaton: Tyndale House Publishers, Inc., 1988, p. 51.)

As the women at Jesus' tomb and C. S. Lewis discovered, there is a time to break out of the mold of what is culturally proper and socially acceptable in order to preach the Gospel. Both faced the risk of ridicule by telling others that Jesus is risen, that the Lord is alive! The women risked being ignored and rejected as viable messengers of the Gospel. Lewis gave up temporal prestige and professional success at a point when peer influence could determine his career. Yet, both chose to break out of the proverbial box and preach the Gospel of Jesus Christ.

MAKE IT HAPPEN

When you have been wronged by another, it may be difficult to forgive their offenses and forget their reputation. This is probably how the disciples felt when Paul confessed his conversion—they couldn't believe their ears and feared for their lives. Think about someone who has made a confession unto Christ. How have you received them? How will you encourage them, rather than exclude them, in their transformation from darkness to light?

FOLLOW THE SPIRIT
What God wants me to do:

_____

_____

REMEMBER YOUR THOUGHTS
Special insights you learned:

_____

_____

MORE LIGHT ON THE TEXT
Luke 24:1-10; ACTS 9:19-20, 26-28, 31

24:1 Now upon the first day of the week, very early in the morning, they came unto the sepulchre, bringing the spices which they had prepared, and certain others with them.

In the days of Jesus, there were no funeral parlors with machines to pump embalming chemicals into dead bodies. Jesus had been wrapped in linen with some spices (John 19:40) and placed in the sepulchre, or tomb (Luke 23:50-53). The women who loved and honored Jesus during His life wanted to anoint His head and face, and perhaps his wounded feet, hands, and side, with spices and oils they had prepared two days before. Since Jesus had not received any type of mourning service or funeral, it was a way of showing their love for Him.

Under Jewish law and tradition the women could not do any work on the previous day because it was the Sabbath which was "the seventh day" (Genesis 2:3; Exodus 16:23; Deuteronomy 5:14). Saturday, the Jewish Sabbath day, was to be a holy day, the Lord's Day. However, gradually "the church," which was established after the Resurrection and to which all born-again believers belong, began to observe Sunday, the first day, as the Lord's Day. In this passage, the women rested on the Sabbath and came to the tomb on the first day of the week with other women who also cared about Jesus.

2 And they found the stone rolled away from the sepulchre.

In Matthew 27:60, the stone which covered the entrance to the tomb is described as a "great stone" which had to be "rolled" into place (also Mark 15:46). And, the passage reveals that Jesus' enemies took care to "seal the stone" (v. 66) and

place guards there to watch the tomb so that no disciples could steal the body (vv. 64-66). They wanted to thwart Jesus' prophecy that He would rise on the third day (v. 64).

When the women got to the tomb and "found the stone rolled away," they must have been amazed that such a "great stone" was just pushed aside. This was especially significant since guards had been placed there to prevent anyone from stealing Jesus' body. However, the power of God was at work. In Matthew 28:2, we learn that "the angel of the Lord" moved the stone.

3 And they entered in, and found not the body of the Lord Jesus.

The women must have felt further amazement to find Jesus' dead body now missing. If human knowledge and logic tells us anything, it is that a dead body stays put. The dead do not get up and walk away, except in horror movies. However, we learn from John 20:6-7, that the linen clothes which were wrapped around Jesus' body were still in place in the tomb, along with a "napkin" which had been around His head. Again, human knowledge tells us that a dead body could not undress itself either. This is further evidence of a supernatural event.

4 And it came to pass, as they were much perplexed thereabout, behold, two men stood by them in shining garments:

As the women's heads were swimming from their discoveries, and as their hearts were pounding with excitement, fear, doubt, wonder, and other emotions, "two men" appeared. They were obviously angels based upon their outer appearance, "in shining garments" and their sudden arrival out of nowhere, i.e., "behold. . .two men stood by them."

God cared about those women who loved Jesus so much. He was no longer going to leave them "much perplexed" and in a quandary about what was going on. God always monitors our emotions. He knows what we can bear (1 Corinthians 10:13). Many times He will directly intervene in circumstances that He knows will overwhelm us. It is His divine providence that affects the affairs of men. Many a saint can testify how they were in a situation where death seemed imminent and unavoidable, but God. . . .

5 And as they were afraid, and bowed down their faces to the earth, they said unto them, Why seek ye the living among the dead?

Fear at the sight of angels is a common and understandable reaction (Matthew 28:3-4; Luke 1:11-12, 30; 2:9). So it was with these women. However, they "bowed down their faces to the earth." They had enough composure to recognize an act of God, and they assumed an attitude of worship. God is always worthy of our worship, especially when He manifests His power before our very eyes (see Exodus 4:29-31; Judges 6:22-24; 7:15; 1 Samuel 1:27-28). A good question for many Christians might be whether we know an act of God when we see it. Can we recognize God's hand in our lives today?

The angels asked the women, "Why seek ye the living among the dead?" The question was heaven's first proclamation that the Son of God was risen. It was God's first announcement of final victory over death and sin (1 Corinthians 15:55-57).

6 He is not here, but is risen: remember how he spake unto you when he was yet in Galilee, 7 Saying, the Son of man must be delivered into the hands of sinful men, and be crucified, and the third day rise again.

The angels made it clear that Christ indeed was alive, "He is not here, but is risen." There was no hoax about the absence of His body. No political plot was afoot to further the influence of the disciples, as His enemies feared (Matthew 27:64). No, God was making everything crystal clear by His Word for all men, just in case all the physical evidence was not enough.

Then the angels reminded the women of Jesus' prophecies when He was alive (Mark 8:31; 9:31). Jesus had said that He "must" be delivered, killed, and rise again. In other words, those events were absolutely essential to God's plan for salvation. That is why Jesus delivered the famous, "Get thee behind me, Satan," comment to Peter (Matthew 16:21-23). God's plan for the salvation of mankind encompassed and culminated in the events of the day of His resurrection (John 10:17).

8 And they remembered his words.

The angels' statement jogged the memories of the women. They recalled the words of Jesus. That remembrance helped them to believe even stronger because Jesus' words obviously had come true.

God has now blessed all modern believers to carry around His "reminding system" wherever we may go. He is called the Holy Ghost. Jesus said, "He shall teach you all things, and bring all things to your remembrance, whatsoever I have said unto you" (John 14:26).

Unfortunately, too many of us today do not study the Bible frequently enough, as we are commanded in 2 Timothy 2:15. Thus, we are unfamiliar with "whatsoever" Jesus has said unto us. And, we cannot "do whatsoever" Jesus has commanded us (John 15:14), nor can we keep His commandments (John 14:15). Therefore, it is difficult for us to become like "wise men" who "heareth these sayings of (Jesus), and doeth them," in order to build the foundation of our lives "upon a rock." (Matthew 7:24-25).

If we do not study and mentally absorb the principles that Jesus left us in the Bible, along with all the other principles and doctrines in the Word, then the Holy Ghost will have little to "bring (back). . . to our remembrance." We have to ingest and digest God's Word within our minds and spiritual systems, in order to provide raw material for the work of the Holy Spirit.

Satan loves biblical illiteracy. He can have quite a time with Christians who live on their opinions, speculations, or what others have said. A lack of spiritual knowledge helps Satan in his war against us (Hosea 4:6).

9 And returned from the sepulchre, and told all these things unto the eleven, and to all the rest. 10 It was Mary Magdalene, and Joanna, and Mary the mother of James, and other women that were with them, which told these things unto the apostles.

The women were used by God to spread the message of the glorious Resurrection of Jesus Christ. The first people to know of this great event were the men who had walked the earth with Jesus, but who became so scarce at the end. Presumably, most of them were hiding where Jesus

Himself found them "the same day at evening. . .where (they) were assembled for fear of the Jews" (John 20:19). Peter and John, "the disciple whom Jesus loved," were the first ones that Mary Magdalene ran into. Then they "ran both together" to inspect the tomb for themselves (John 20:2-8).

The Bible names several of the women in this group who made the initial discovery. Over the years since that day, there has been interesting discussion over the absence of men. Apparently, no men took it upon themselves to go and say a final farewell to Jesus nor anoint His body the way those women did. The fact that the disciples are described as hiding for "fear of the Jews" (John 20:19) does not make the male followers look good.

Throughout the history of African-American churches, Black women have made up the highest percentage of members. Women have worked hard to sustain the programs and ministries of the Black church. We thank God for the dedication and hard work of Black women for so long but we must continually pray for Black men to take on more active roles in the work of God's Kingdom.

Acts 9:19 And when he had received meat, he was strengthened. Then was Saul certain days with the disciples which were at Damascus.

The same Saul who was present for the death of Stephen was converted to the faith by Jesus Himself on the Damascus road (Acts 7:58; 8:1; 9:3-6). He had been fasting for three days in Damascus (Acts 9:9), "and when he had received meat, he was strengthened."

After regaining his physical strength, Saul decided to stay "certain days with the disciples which were at Damascus." He fellowshiped and ate with the same people he had been persecuting so harshly (Acts 9:1-2). He talked with the disciples about the faith, went to their meetings, prayed, and worshiped with them.

This relationship must have been strange for Saul and the disciples. He now felt love for those whom he so violently hated just days before. They now were led to welcome a former adversary into their midst and share all that they had with him. Yes, God moves in ways which seem mysterious to us (Isaiah 55:8). But once a former enemy comes to Christ, we become members of the same family.

God expects that believers will love each other no matter what our past histories or relationships may have been. Jesus said, "By this shall all men know that ye are my disciples, if ye have love one to another" (John 13:35). We cannot profess to love God but hate another brother (1 John 4:20-21). So it was with Saul and the disciples at Damascus.

20 And straightway he preached Christ in the synagogues, that he is the Son of God.

"Straightway" means "directly; at once; soon; immediately" in Greek. Paul was so filled with the Spirit of God that he immediately went about preaching that which he used to refute, "that he (Jesus) is the Son of God." And, he had the boldness to go up into the Jewish synagogues to preach it. The synagogue was the central place where the Christian doctrine was rejected. It was the place where Saul probably used to rail the loudest against Christ.

God can make the most timid person bold through His Spirit. Men like Paul and John the Baptist had such a bold and zealous streak in them that they did not need much more than an opportunity to step forth aggressively. Proverbs 28:1 says, "The wicked flee when no man pursueth: but the righteous are bold as a lion." As we grow in Christ, we should become bolder advocates for Christ. God will always be there to support us (Hebrews 13:5-6).

9:26 And when Saul was come to Jerusalem, he assayed to join himself to the disciples: but they were all afraid of him, and believed not that he was a disciple.

Because of his bold preaching of Christ to Jews, many of them plotted to kill Saul in Damascus, but the other Christians helped him get out of town (Acts 9:22-25). He went to Jerusalem and tried to join the brethren there. However, he met with a much different reception than the one in Damascus.

The Jerusalem disciples had not heard of Saul's conversion and bold preaching. Therefore, they exercised caution because they feared he was trying to infiltrate them to cause serious mischief. The Bible does warn us to be careful about who we listen to, saying, "Beloved, believe not every spirit, but try the spirits whether they are of God: because many false prophets are gone out into the world" (1 John 4:1). The disciples' general opinion about Paul was that he looked like a Christian-killer before; he walked like a Christian-killer before; he talked like a Christian-killer before, so he must be a Christian-killer now.

27 But Barnabas took him, and brought him to the apostles, and declared unto them how he had seen the Lord in the way, and that he had spoken to him, and how he had preached boldly at Damascus in the name of Jesus.

It is not revealed how Barnabas came to know about Saul's exploits in Damascus, but he stepped forward and spoke up for Saul. Barnabas went to the church leaders, the apostles. He knew that if the apostles accepted Saul, the congregation would follow.

Barnabas told the apostles about Saul's conversion and his preaching ministry. Barnabas had the respect of the apostles. Had he not been a man "of good report" (1 Timothy 3:7), it is unlikely that the apostles would have taken his recommendation so easily. But Barnabas knew that the apostles trusted him. The apostles had changed his name from Joseph to Barnabas (Acts 4:36), and knew he was of the Levite tribe from Cyprus. Barnabas means "the son of consolation," and he lived up to that name in Saul's case.

Barnabas' defense of Saul, and the fact that he did all he could to have Saul accepted in the community of believers is an example to us all. New converts or believers who come into a new church home must be made to feel accepted and shown love. If they are not, the risk is that they will fall away from the body and "forsake the assembling of ourselves together" (Hebrews 10:25). Then they will miss the essential edification, or spiritual "building up" process that the body of Christ provides (Romans 15:2; 1 Corinthians 14:12).

28 And he was with them coming in and going out at Jerusalem.

The apostles accepted Barnabas' testimony. Saul became a member of that body of believers. He was involved in all their functions, "coming in and going out (with them) at Jerusalem."

9:31 Then had the churches rest throughout all Judea and Galilee and Samaria, and were edified; and walking in the fear of the Lord, and in the comfort of the Holy Ghost, were multiplied.

Saul could not help but preach boldly on behalf of Christ, even when running into difficulty with some Hellenic or Greek Jews who tried to kill him (v. 29). But his new church family managed to get him out of town to Tarsus (v. 30).

Then God provided a period of calm and ease for the church. "The churches had rest throughout all Judea..." and the believers were edified, or "built up." The members began to grow spiritually. Their lives were obedient and fruitful because they "walked in the fear of the Lord, and in the comfort of the Holy Ghost." They took God seriously and reverenced Him as they should. They allowed the Holy Spirit to operate in and through them. As a result of their individual spiritual progression, the congregation grew, "they were multiplied."

DAILY BIBLE READINGS

M: The Empty Tomb
Luke 24:1-10
T: The Conversion of Saul
Acts 9:1-9
W: Ananias, A Reluctant Witness
Acts 9:10-19a
T: Saul Preaches and Leaves Damascus
Acts 9:19b-25
F: Saul in Jerusalem
Acts 9:26-31
S: Peter Heals Aeneas and Raises Tabitha
Acts 9:32-43
S: Have Faith! God Will Provide
Psalms 63

TEACHING TIPS

April 22
Bible Study Guide 8

1. Words You Should Know

A. Fasting (Acts 10:30) Greek *nesteuo*—To abstain from food for religious or spiritual purposes.

B. Baptized (v. 47) Greek *baptizo*—A ceremonial ordinance of Christianity; practiced as a public testimony to identify new believers.

C. Commanded (v. 48) Greek *prostasso*—Implies instructions from one in authority that plans should be made to carry out a particularly ordinance.

2. Teacher Preparation

A. Read and meditate upon the devotional and background Scriptures.

B. Study the FOCAL VERSES in the most popular translations used by the church in corporate worship or students in individual study. Make note of study notes and contemporary language.

C. Write out answers to the SEARCH THE SCRIPTURES questions and your personal responses to the DISCUSS THE MEANING questions.

3. Starting the Lesson

A. Write the AT-A-GLANCE outline on the board.

B. Read the IN FOCUS story as a centering devotional.

4. Getting into the Lesson

A. Read the FOCAL VERSES in the context of the AT-A-GLANCE outline.

B. Break up into small groups to answer the SEARCH THE SCRIPTURES questions and discover insights.

C. Reconvene into large group and share doctrinal insights and practices.

5. Relating the Lesson to Life

A. Read THE PEOPLE, PLACES, AND TIMES.

B. Create student teams to present both sides of the argument that might have ensued over whether or not to water-baptize the newly converted Gentiles.

C. Reflect on testimonial in LESSON IN OUR SOCIETY and make individual and group decisions to include all who profess Christ and resist every temptation to exclude others because of feelings of superiority.

6. Arousing Action

A. Discuss the MAKE IT HAPPEN reflections.

B. Brainstorm ideas to affirm and welcome new converts.

C. Encourage students to plan to welcome and bring a new convert or an outsider to the group for the next class.

WORSHIP GUIDE

For the Superintendent or Teacher
Theme: Gentiles Receive the Spirit
Theme Song: "Welcome Holy Spirit"
Scripture: Galatians 3:11-14
Song: "Sweet, Sweet Spirit"
Devotional Thought: Lord God, it is not by might, nor by power, but by Your Holy Spirit that I am saved and sanctified. I yield to Your Spirit for filling, baptizing, and in-dwelling that You might be known through me to those seeking to believe.

GENTILES RECEIVE THE SPIRIT

Bible Background • ACTS 10:1—11:18
Printed Text • ACTS 10:30-39, 44-48
Devotional Reading • GALATIANS 3:11-14

LESSON AIM

By the end of this lesson, students will be able to observe the work of the Holy Spirit transcends race, culture, and gender.

KEEP IN MIND

"Then Peter opened his mouth, and said, Of a truth I perceive that God is no respecter of persons: But in every nation he that feareth him, and worketh righteousness, is accepted with him" (Acts 10:34-35).

FOCAL VERSES

Acts 10:30 And Cornelius said, Four days ago I was fasting until this hour; and at the ninth hour I prayed in my house, and, behold, a man stood before me in bright clothing,

31 And said, Cornelius, thy prayer is heard, and thine alms are had in remembrance in the sight of God.

32 Send therefore to Joppa, and call hither Simon, whose surname is Peter; he is lodged in the house of one Simon a tanner by the sea side: who, when he cometh, shall speak unto thee.

33 Immediately therefore I sent to thee; and thou hast well done that thou art come. Now therefore are we all here present before God, to hear all things that are commanded thee of God.

34 Then Peter opened his mouth, and said, Of a truth I perceive that God is no respecter of persons:

35 But in every nation he that feareth him, and worketh righteousness, is accepted with him.

36 The word which God sent unto the children of Israel, preaching peace by Jesus Christ: (he is Lord of all:)

LESSON OVERVIEW

LESSON AIM
KEEP IN MIND
FOCAL VERSES
IN FOCUS
THE PEOPLE, PLACES,
AND TIMES
BACKGROUND
AT-A-GLANCE
IN DEPTH
SEARCH THE SCRIPTURES
DISCUSS THE MEANING
LESSON IN OUR SOCIETY
MAKE IT HAPPEN
FOLLOW THE SPIRIT
REMEMBER YOUR THOUGHTS
MORE LIGHT ON THE TEXT
DAILY BIBLE READINGS

37 That word, I say, ye know, which was published throughout all Judea, and began from Galilee, after the baptism which John preached;

38 How God anointed Jesus of Nazareth with the Holy Ghost and with power: who went about doing good, and healing all that were oppressed of the devil; for God was with him.

39 And we are witnesses of all things which he did both in the land of the Jews, and in Jerusalem; whom they slew and hanged on a tree:

10:44 While Peter yet spake these words, the Holy Ghost fell on all them which heard the word.

APRIL 22ND

45 And they of the circumcision which believed were astonished, as many as came with Peter, because that on the Gentiles also was poured out the gift of the Holy Ghost.

46 For they heard them speak with tongues, and magnify God. Then answered Peter,

47 Can any man forbid water, that these should not be baptized, which have received the Holy Ghost as well as we?

48 And he commanded them to be baptized in the name of the Lord. Then prayed they him to tarry certain days.

IN FOCUS

One Mercedes Benz TV commercial shows their car colliding with a cement wall during a safety test. Someone then asks the company spokesman why they do not enforce their patent on the Mercedes

Benz energy-absorbing car body, a design evidently copied by other companies because of its success. He replies matter-of-factly, "Because some things in life are too important not to share."

How true. In that category also falls the Gospel of salvation, which saves people from far more than auto collisions.

When Peter preached, "But in every nation he that feareth him [God], and worketh righteousness, is accepted with him," he preached a Gospel to the Gentiles that was too important not to share. And while Peter preached, the Holy Spirit came upon the Gentiles as evidence of their acceptance into the family of God.

But the Christian Jews were amazed as the Gentiles began to speak in tongues and worship God in a manner formerly known only by Jewish believers. As they questioned the validity of the experience of the outpouring of the Holy Ghost, Peter advanced the preaching of the Gospel which included all who believed. He told the gathering that just as the Gentiles had been baptized in the Spirit, they should also receive baptism by water as had the Jewish believers.

God's gift of salvation is freely and fully given to all who believe. The church must resist excluding any privileges from believers with other cultural backgrounds.

THE PEOPLE, PLACES, AND TIMES

Cornelius. The first Gentile cited in Scripture to hear the Gospel, receive salvation, and influence many to believe.

Fasting and Praying. A Jewish custom to bring synergy with mind, body, and spiritual matters; used by believers for increasing faith and preparation for good works.

Peter. One of the Twelve first named as Jesus' apostles who preached to the Gentiles.

Gentiles. Commonly known as Greeks who had not heard or believed the Gospel of Jesus Christ.

BACKGROUND

Acts 10 opens with the conversion of a significant governmental official. Cornelius was a Roman centurion, a high-ranking army official who adhered to Jewish custom. Evidence of his piety was in the conversion of his whole household, giving alms to the poor, and praying to God in accordance with the Jewish ritual.

However, because he was not a circumcised Jew, he could not worship in the inner sanctuary of the Jewish synagogue. He worshiped God on the fringes of his religious culture. But, Cornelius worshiped God, and God heard his prayers (v. 4).

God used Cornelius to minister to Peter, one of Jesus' disciples. Peter struggled with the cultural divisions between the Jews and Gentiles. Although he had heard Jesus preach salvation to all nations, Peter struggled to think outside the boundaries of exclusion and inclusion. The conflict between the Jew and the Gentile was too great and was buttressed by many barriers—culture, language, prejudicial hatred, and geographical barriers.

In a vision at a time of fasting and prayer, the Lord spoke to Peter. After showing Peter animals given for food of all species, God commands Peter to rise, kill, and eat. However, as a devout Jew, Peter refuses to eat that which his culture has deemed common and unclean. The Lord rebukes Peter, declaring that which God calls clean is no longer subject to its common perspective.

Peter did not understand the meaning of the vision; and as he thought about it more, the Spirit of the Lord gave him revelation. Through instruction to join Cornelius's entourage, the Lord helps Peter understand that His gift of salvation is available to the Jews, the Greeks, and all who believe. From this revelation, Peter avows never again to call any man common, unclean, or unworthy of the Gospel.

AT-A-GLANCE

1. The Vision (Acts 10:30-33)
2. The Witnesses (vv. 34-39)
3. The Baptisms (vv. 44-48)

IN DEPTH

1. The Vision (Acts 10:30-33)

Cornelius sent for Peter in response to a vision

(vv. 30-33). He tells Peter of the visitation of the angel of the Lord during his time of prayer and fasting andhow he sent his servants to fetch Peter. Cornelius blesses Peter's obedience and explains to Peter that he has been brought there to preach to him and his household.

And for the first time Peter, a Jew and commoner, has the opportunity to preach to Cornelius, a Greek aristocrat.

2. The Witnesses (vv. 34-39)

Peter declared that God shows no partiality but accepts all people who revere Him and do what is right (vv. 34-35). The same Peter who rendered non-Jews, and especially Greeks, as unclean now stands preaching the Gospel to a Greek congregation. He confessed the truth that God does not play cultural favorites, but that He favors every nation that reverences Him and is righteous.

Peter preached the Good News of Christ to the people gathered with Cornelius (vv. 36-39). He told them of the Gospel, water baptism, the anointing of the Holy Spirit and of the good works, healings, and triumph over demonic works which would follow.

3. The Baptisms (vv. 44-48)

While Peter was preaching, the Holy Spirit came upon the people who heard him (v. 44). Peter was not simply speaking to them about cultural differences and conflicts. He preached the Gospel unto salvation.

As the Word was preached, the hearers believed and were filled with the Holy Spirit.

The Jewish believers saw that the Gentiles had received the Holy Spirit and were amazed (vv. 45-46). The evidence of the presence of the Holy Spirit being poured out on the Gentiles could not be denied. Peter's companions were astonished as they watched the Gentiles speak in tongues and worship God.

As the Jewish believers witnessed this supernatural phenomena, they questioned the possibility of regarding the Gentiles as full members of the Christian church—namely, including them in the ceremony of baptism. To this inquiry, Peter responded that any who received baptism in the Holy Spirit could not be denied the baptism by water. The baptism in the Spirit was indicative of an inward conversion; the baptism by water was indicative of an outward inclusion into the family of God. And Peter commanded that Cornelius, his family and his friends—the Gentile converts—be baptized with water in the name of Jesus as they had been baptized by the Holy Spirit.

After they were baptized, Cornelius invited Peter and his companions to stay over a few days that they might be taught more about the Christian life and experience.

SEARCH THE SCRIPTURES

1. Was Cornelius's vision a hallucination or a true visitation from an angel of the Lord? (Acts 10:30-32)

2. How did Simon Peter respond upon hearing of Cornelius's vision? (v. 33)

3. What happened as the people listened to Peter preach? (vv. 44-45)

4. After the Gentiles were baptized in the Holy Spirit, evidenced with speaking in tongues and magnifying God, what question arose among the believers? (vv. 47-48)

DISCUSS THE MEANING

Divisions in the church are usually formed over interpretation of Scripture and formation of doctrine. Often, these divisions have led to the formation of new denominations, or worse, schisms within the professing body of Christ that dilute our unified testimony and the preaching the Gospel. The circumcised Jewish believers questioned the extension of water baptism to Gentile believers who had been baptized in the Holy Spirit. What do you believe are the purposes of the water baptism and baptism in the Holy Spirit? What does your church/denomination practice as doctrine regarding them both?

LESSON IN OUR SOCIETY

The article "What Good is A Tree?" in *Reader's Digest* explained that when the roots of trees touch, there is a substance present that reduces competition. In fact, this unknown fungus helps link roots of different trees—even of dissimilar species. A whole forest may be linked together. If one tree has access to water, another to nutrients, and a third to sunlight, the trees have the means to share with one another.

Like trees in a forest, Christians in the church need to support one another. When we find Christians of dissimilar races, cultures, classes, genders, callings and expressions of worship, we should become like a forest of trees and link up to nourish one another in the faith. Through our inclusion of all believers, we are fortified that God might be glorified. Instead of excluding Christians who do not look like us or worship like us, we must extend our roots of righteousness to give what we have and get what we need to grow into the church for which Christ will return.

MAKE IT HAPPEN

When was the last time you, or your church, had worship or fellowship with another body of Christian believers that you know has doctrinal differences? A good place to begin to know others in the body of Christ is through neighborly relationships. If someone in your family, at work, or neighborhood belongs to a different church or denomination, ask them if you might accompany them to a fellowship or worship, and extend a reciprocal invitation. Resist the temptation to compare or condemn the various styles of expressions of worship; but rather, seek to experience God through the eyes of another.

FOLLOW THE SPIRIT

What God wants me to do:

_____

_____

REMEMBER YOUR THOUGHTS

Special insights you learned:

_____

_____

MORE LIGHT ON THE TEXT
Acts 10:30-39, 44-48

10:30 And Cornelius said, Four days ago I was fasting until this hour; and at the ninth hour I prayed in my house, and, behold, a man stood before me in bright clothing,

Cornelius was a Roman centurion or a captain in the army. The Bible says he was a "devout man,"

which means he tried to be godly in his ways and gave God due reverence. His godliness was evident by the fact that he positively influenced all those in his house, and he gave money to the poor while praying to God "alway" (Acts 10:1-2).

Cornelius recounted to Peter how God had given him a vision to send for Peter. The man who wore "bright clothing" was identified as an angel in the actual vision (v. 3). The study verse also indicates that Cornelius was given to fasting and prayer. As a result of this Gentile man's efforts to know God, he was blessed with the vision which would start a series of events leading to his salvation.

31 And said, Cornelius, thy prayer is heard, and thine alms are had in remembrance in the sight of God.

The angel in the vision let Cornelius know that God had been watching him and his actions, and also listening to his prayers. Proverbs 11:27 says, "He that diligently seeketh good procureth favour." Hebrews 11:6 says, ". . .He (God) is a rewarder of them that diligently seek him."

The angel was letting Cornelius know that his efforts to please God and come closer to Him were not in vain. James 4:8 says, "Draw nigh to God, and he will draw nigh to you. Cleanse your hand, ye sinners; and purify your hearts, ye double minded." God was now drawing nigh to Cornelius.

32 Send therefore to Joppa, and call hither Simon, whose surname is Peter; he is lodged in the house of one Simon a tanner by the sea side: who, when he cometh, shall speak unto thee.

Cornelius recounted his vision to Peter in order to explain why he had sent for him. God had instructed him to do so. The omniscient God knew exactly where Peter was, just as He knows where all of our blessings are. He should know. After all, He is the One who placed them there (see James 1:17). The glorious gift that God had for Cornelius was that Peter would "speak unto thee." It was the gift of the Gospel message.

33 Immediately therefore I sent to thee; and thou hast well done that thou art come. Now therefore are we all here present before God, to hear all things that are commanded thee of God.

Cornelius dared not hesitate to act upon God's command to "Send therefore to Joppa. . . (for) Peter." He was not about to fool around and possibly miss the season of his blessing. Procrastination and slothfulness can cause precisely that. So, Cornelius told Peter, "Immediately therefore I sent to thee."

Now, Cornelius thanked Peter for coming. But what Cornelius did not know was that God gave Peter a vision just before Cornelius's messengers arrived. And, in Peter's vision, God dealt with Peter's feelings of prejudice toward Gentiles, while telling Peter to go with Cornelius's messengers (Acts 10:9-20).

The mighty providence of God works everything out. God can weave a tapestry of people and events in our lives which appear to be unrelated. Or, those people and events are totally unknown to us. Then, when the time is right, God will pull all the pieces together so that we are blessed with something He has been preparing for us for some time.

Cornelius showed his love for his household by having everyone gathered to hear Peter's words. His example shows that we should not be selfish with God's Word of salvation. We should see to it that all of our relatives and friends get to hear it, whether it comes from us or someone else. We owe it to the ones we love to see that they get a chance to hear the Gospel and receive the gift of salvation through Jesus Christ our Lord.

34 Then Peter opened his mouth, and said, Of a truth I perceive that God is no respecter of persons. 35 But in every nation he that feareth him, and worketh righteousness, is accepted with him.

Peter knew why he was there, so he went right to work. And, he began by acknowledging the truth which God had shown him in his own vision. The truth is that Jesus was not kidding when He told Peter and the other original disciples to take the Gospel to "all nations" and to "the uttermost part of the earth" (see Matthew 28:19; Acts 1:8).

The truth of God is that He does not care what color a person is nor what language he speaks. God sent Jesus to die on the cross for "whosoever" would believe (John 3:16). As a result of believing in Christ, God said that "whosoever" would not perish (John 3:15). "Whosoever shall call upon the name of the Lord shall be saved" (Romans 10:13). And, in the event at Cornelius's house, God was using a formerly prejudiced Peter to initiate opening up the invitation of the Gospel to Gentiles everywhere.

36 The word which God sent unto the children of Israel, preaching peace by Jesus Christ: (he is Lord of all:)

Peter began to lay out the chronological progression of the Gospel. He told his audience that God started by sending Jesus (who is "Lord of all") to preach to the Jews first (Romans 1:16).

37 That word, I say, ye know, which was published throughout all Judea, and began from Galilee, after the baptism which John preached;

Peter encouraged them by saying that they already knew about some aspects of the message which had been spread to areas beyond Jerusalem. He indicated that the ministry of Jesus began in Galilee after His baptism by John the Baptist. John preached a message of repentance from sin and water baptism (Mark 1:4).

38 How God anointed Jesus of Nazareth with the Holy Ghost and with power: who went about doing good, and healing all that were oppressed of the devil; for God was with Him.

Peter then told his audience about the earthly ministry of Jesus. He said that Jesus was "anointed . . .with the Holy Ghost and with power" (Matthew 3:16). Then Jesus did good and miraculous works, such as healing people with all sorts of ailments (Matthew 8:2-3, 13, 14-16; 9:20-22, 32-33; 12:10-13; John 9:1-7; 11:43-44). And, that God Himself expressed that He was with Jesus, saying, "This is my beloved Son, in whom I am well pleased; hear ye him" (Matthew 17:5).

39 And we are witnesses of all things which he did both in the land of the Jews, and in Jerusalem; whom they slew and hanged on a tree.

Next, Peter gave verification of all the events in Jesus' ministry by asserting his own presence on those occasions, saying, "We are witnesses of all things which he did." Peter gave eyewitness testimony of Jesus' ministry. Finally, Peter indicated that Christ was killed and took on our sins, saying, "Whom they slew and hanged on a tree." Under Mosaic Law anyone who died that way was "accursed," so Christ became "accursed" for us (Deuteronomy 21:22-23; Galatians 3:13; 1 Peter 2:24).

10:44 While Peter yet spake these words, the Holy Ghost fell on all them which heard the word.

Peter covered Jesus' resurrection, His appearance to certain people thereafter, and His command to spread the Gospel (vv. 40-42). He explained that the Old Testament prophets had pointed to Jesus' appearance as the Messiah (v. 43). Peter then mentioned that salvation came from belief in Christ (v. 43), and as he was saying this, ". . .the Holy Ghost fell on all them which heard the word." Apparently, the Gentile audience of Cornelius's household believed on Jesus at that moment, because the Holy Ghost came (1 Corinthians 12:3).

45 And they of the circumcision which believed were astonished, as many as came with Peter, because that on the Gentiles also was poured out the gift of the Holy Ghost.

Six of the Jewish believers from Joppa had gone with Peter to Cornelius's house (Acts 10:23; 11:12). There is no doubt that they were Jewish because they were "of the circumcision" (Genesis 17:9-10). Though Peter had confronted and resolved his own prejudice through a vision from God, apparently these other Jews still felt a modicum of superiority. They "were astonished. . .that on the Gentiles also was poured out the gift of the Holy Ghost."

God is not "a respecter of persons" (v. 34), and He plays no favorites. Since God was opening up salvation to "all nations," this inaugural event with the Gentiles of the world was to have all the signs which the Jews experienced at Pentecost (Acts 2:1-4). The Jews could not say that Gentiles had a lesser salvation and, thus, not be as close to God.

46 For they heard them speak with tongues, and magnify God. Then answered Peter, 47 Can any man forbid water, that these should not be bap-

tized, which have received the Holy Ghost as well as we?

These verses show the completion of God's stamp of authenticity on the Gentiles' conversion to Christ. For, they spoke in tongues just like the Jews at Pentecost (Acts 2:4). Then Peter challenged his Jewish brethren to give a reason why the Gentiles should not be baptized, just they themselves were baptized at Pentecost (Acts 2:41).

48 And he commanded them to be baptized in the name of the Lord. Then prayed they him to tarry certain days.

Obviously, none of the Jews could object to the baptism of the Gentile believers. Rejecting Gentile believers would have meant fighting against God's purpose. God's purpose will always be achieved because His Word will not return to Him void (Isaiah 55:11).

Peter baptized the Gentiles, and their conversion to Christ was complete. There was even a similar feeling afterwards to what occurred at Pentecost. Cornelius's household asked Peter to stay and fellowship with them for a few days. This was similar to the "fellowshiping" and "breaking of bread" among the Jewish converts (Acts 2:42).

DAILY BIBLE READINGS

M: Cornelius Sends for Peter
Acts 10:1-8
T: Peter's Vision
Acts 10:9-16
W: The Men at the Gate
Acts 10:17-22
T: Peter Goes to Caesarea
Acts 10:23-33
F: Gentiles Hear the Good News
Acts 10:34-43
S: Gentiles Receive the Holy Spirit
Acts 10:44-48
S: Peter's Report in Jerusalem
Acts 11:1-18

TEACHING TIPS

April 29
Bible Study Guide 9

1. Words You Should Know

A. Persecution (Acts 11:19) Greek *diogmos*—Implies great pressure from trials and tribulations.

B. Christian (Acts 11:26) Greek *christianos*—A follower of Christ.

C. Separate (Acts 13:2) Greek *aphorizo*—To sever common, familiar relationships to appoint to a particular task.

2. Teacher Preparation

A. Study and meditate upon the devotional and background Scriptures.

B. Study the FOCAL VERSES in the most popular translations used by the church in corporate worship or students in individual study. Make note of study notes and contemporary language.

C. Prepare your answers for the SEARCH THE MEANING and DISCUSS THE SCRIPTURES questions.

3. Starting the Lesson

A. Write the AT-A-GLANCE outline on the board.

B. Discuss student's definitions and understandings of calling, commissioning, and making disciples.

4. Getting into the Lesson

A. Share the WORDS YOU SHOULD KNOW with students as these terms relate to the lesson.

B. Have volunteers read the BACKGROUND and THE PEOPLE, PLACES, AND TIMES sections to set the tone for discussion for the lesson.

C. Read the FOCAL VERSES and answer the SEARCH THE SCRIPTURES questions as a group.

5. Relating the Lesson to Life

A. Allow students to break off into small groups and answer the DISCUSS THE MEANING questions.

B. Reconvene in the larger group and reflect on the LESSON IN OUR SOCIETY section.

6. Arousing Action

A. Examine corporate and individual practices of evangelism. Ask students to discuss various situations with which they are familiar. Compare these experiences of evangelism emphasizing the importance of prayerful consideration before we attempt to evangelize for Christ.

B. Brainstorm ways of improving or broadening the evangelistic efforts of your group or church. Plan to do your part in winning new converts.

THE CHURCH IN ANTIOCH

Bible Background • ACTS 11:19-30; 13:1-3
Printed Text • ACTS 11:19-30; 13:1-3
Devotional Reading • EPHESIANS 3:7-12

LESSON AIM

By the end of this lesson, students will be able to explain how discipleship multiplies the effectiveness of the ministry, even in the face of persecution.

KEEP IN MIND

"As they ministered to the Lord, and fasted, the Holy Ghost said, Separate me Barnabas and Saul for the work whereunto I have called them" (Acts 13:2).

FOCAL VERSES

Acts 11:19-30 Now they which were scattered abroad upon the persecution that arose about Stephen traveled as far as Phoenicia, and Cyprus, and Antioch, preaching the word to none but unto the Jews only.

20 And some of them were men of Cyprus and Cyrene, which, when they were come to Antioch, spake unto the Grecians, preaching the Lord Jesus.

21 And the hand of the Lord was with them: and a great number believed, and turned unto the Lord.

22 Then tidings of these things came unto the ears of the church which was in Jerusalem: and they sent forth Barnabas, that he should go as far as Antioch.

23 Who, when he came, and had seen the grace of God, was glad, and exhorted them all, that with purpose of heart they would cleave unto the Lord.

24 For he was a good man, and full of the Holy

LESSON OVERVIEW

LESSON AIM
KEEP IN MIND
FOCAL VERSES
IN FOCUS
THE PEOPLE, PLACES, AND TIMES
BACKGROUND
AT-A-GLANCE
IN DEPTH
SEARCH THE SCRIPTURES
DISCUSS THE MEANING
LESSON IN OUR SOCIETY
MAKE IT HAPPEN
FOLLOW THE SPIRIT
REMEMBER YOUR THOUGHTS
MORE LIGHT ON THE TEXT
DAILY BIBLE READINGS

Ghost and of faith: and much people was added unto the Lord.

25 Then departed Barnabas to Tarsus, for to seek Saul:

26 And when he had found him, he brought him unto Antioch. And it came to pass, that a whole year they assembled themselves with the church, and taught much people. And the disciples were called Christians first in Antioch.

27 And in these days came prophets from Jerusalem unto Antioch.

28 And there stood up one of them named Agabus, and signified by the Spirit that there should be great dearth throughout all the world: which came to pass in the days of Claudius Caesar.

29 Then the disciples, every man according to his ability, determined to send relief unto the brethren which dwelt in Judea:

30 Which also they did, and sent it to the elders by the hands of Barnabas and Saul.

13:1 Now there were in the church that was at Antioch certain prophets and teachers; as Barnabas, and Simeon that was called Niger, and Lucius of Cyrene, and Manaen, which had been brought up with Herod the tetrarch, and Saul.

2 As they ministered to the Lord, and fasted, the Holy Ghost said, Separate me Barnabas and Saul for the work whereunto I have called them.

3 And when they had fasted and prayed, and laid their hands on them, they sent them away.

IN FOCUS

Carl Lundquist in *Silent Issues of the Church*, writes:

"Henry Wingblade used to say that Christian personality is hidden deep inside us. It is unseen, like the soup carried in a tureen high over a waiter's head. No one knows what's inside—unless the waiter is bumped and he trips!"

Just so, people don't know what's inside us until we've been bumped. But if Christ is living inside, what spills out is the fruit of the Spirit.

What was inside the persecuted Christians? When they were bumped from the comforts of community, they scattered abroad to spread the Gospel; some to the Jews and others to the Gentiles. What spilled out of the persecuted Christians was a message of salvation and hope in which a great number believed.

What was inside the Jerusalem church? When it was bumped, the encourager Barnabas spilled out to the church at Antioch. And, like the martyr Stephen, Barnabas was full of the Holy Ghost and faith. Through his ministry of encouragement, many more believed.

What was inside the church at Antioch? When they were bumped with the news of impending famine and persecution of the church in Judea, they sent monetary and material relief. Each household gave as they were able, in order to meet the needs of believers in a foreign land.

What was inside the early church? When they were bumped, out spilled that of which they were full—the Holy Spirit, faith, and good works.

THE PEOPLE, PLACES, AND TIMES

The Church at Antioch. Comprised of Jewish Christians who were fleeing persecution and Greek Christians who had responded to the Gospel. The church at Antioch was known for their sensitivity to the Spirit of God; and it was from there that Paul was sent on three of his missionary journeys.

The Days of Claudius Caesar. A time wrought with an intensified persecution of the Christians. Jewish authorities sought to frustrate the

advancement of the Gospel. Yet, with the death of Stephen, the conversion of Paul, and Peter's revelation that the Gospel is for the Gentiles also, the church prospered.

BACKGROUND

The news spread far and wide. Peter had preached to the Gentiles, the Holy Spirit fell upon them and they were, at Peter's command, water-baptized into the family of God.

Although this was a great victory for the Christian church—the Gentile community had been introduced to and invaded by the Gospel message—there were Jewish Christians who questioned Peter's actions. These ultraconservative Christians adhered more fiercely to ceremonial law than those who rejoiced over Peter's ministry to the Gentiles. The Christians who protested against Peter's ministry objected more to the fact that he had eaten with a Gentile, than the fact that Peter had preached Christ to them. They believed that Christianity was to be practiced within the confines of Judaism; an assumption which excluded any other than Jews.

Peter sought to convince them of his righteousness through obedience. He told them of his vision and of the vision of Cornelius. Peter corroborated his story with the presence of his six companions. He reminded them of the Lord's revelation of baptism in the Holy Spirit to follow the practice of John's water baptism. He finally implored their sympathies, "what was I, that I could withstand God?" (Acts 11:17)

The devout, ultraconservative Jewish Christians listened, learned, and in their silent affirmation, acknowledged their error of judgment by praising

AT-A-GLANCE

1. Making Believers
(Acts 11:19-21)
2. Calling them Christians
(vv. 22-26)
3. Partners in Ministry
(vv. 27—Acts 13:1-3)

God for His extension of grace to include the Gentile believers as full members of the family of God.

IN DEPTH

1. Making Believers (Acts 11:19)

Believers who fled from persecution preached to Jews living outside Judea (11:19). This observation is the same recorded in Acts 8:4 wherein Stephen's persecution and death catalyzed the scattering of the Christians out of Jerusalem into surrounding areas. These displaced believers preached to the Jews gathered in these places.

In Antioch, believers from Cyprus and Cyrene preached to Greeks, many of whom believed the Gospel (Acts 11:20-21). This opportunity might have been delayed or never afforded had it not been for the persecution in Jerusalem. And it was the metropolitan city of Antioch which became the center of Christian activity for the next season of church growth.

Because of the boldness of the early church, many Jews and Greeks heard the Gospel, believed in the Lord, and converted to Christianity.

2. Calling them Christians (vv. 22-26)

When the news of these Greek believers reached Jerusalem, the church sent Barnabas to Antioch (v. 22). With the growth of the church at Antioch, the mother church at Jerusalem knew that good leadership would be crucial in mobilizing the ministry there. The apostles then called Barnabas, a man with a good reputation, full of the Holy Ghost, and faith; and commissioned him to go lead the Christians at Antioch.

Barnabas rejoiced to see the Gospel spread to the Greeks and enlisted Saul to help him in the work in Antioch (vv. 23-26). Although called as the senior pastor, as such, to the Antioch church, Barnabas discerned his need for an able assistant to lead the people. He called for Saul of Tarsus, the one now called Paul, to join him in this endeavor. And for a year, Barnabas and Saul ministered to the congregation at Antioch.

It was at Antioch that the disciples were first called Christians; the name given to all who believe in Christ.

3. Partners in Ministry (v. 27 13:1-3)

Agabus predicted a famine, and the Christians in Antioch sent an offering to the church in Jerusalem (vv. 27-30). With word that a famine was upon a foreign land, the Christians at Antioch instituted an emergency relief fund to assist the Christians affected by the famine. Every household gave out of their substance. Not equal giving, but equal sacrifice.

As important as it was that the Antioch Christians respond with support, they also demonstrated that the ministry of support must be handled by the church leaders. Barnabas and Paul were sent forth as bearers of the tidings of relief and encouragement.

Barnabas and Saul were called by the Holy Spirit and sent out by the church in Antioch as missionaries (Acts 13:1-3). As the five named prophets and teachers at Antioch gathered for worship and fasting, the Spirit of the Lord spoke to them. He commanded the commissioning of Barnabas and Paul for a specialized ministry away from the church at Antioch. And when the prophets and teachers had finished praying and fasting, they laid their hands on Barnabas and Paul and let them go to the next place where God was calling them to ministry.

SEARCH THE SCRIPTURES

1. As a paradox to persecution, what were the benefits of causing the believers to scatter? (Acts 11:19-21)

2. Using information from prior lessons, identify three foundational characteristics of a good leader that appear in Barnabas. (v. 24)

3. The community of believers were previously identified by the city in which they resided. What was the church at Antioch named after Barnabas's and Saul's ministry there? (v. 6)

4. What ritual of calling and commissioning did the prophets and teachers perform after being told by the Spirit to separate Barnabas and Saul for their work in the ministry? (Acts 13:3)

DISCUSS THE MEANING

1. In the first lesson this month, we learned of Stephen, a martyr for Christ. Several chapters and months later, the effect of Stephen's life and death

was still being felt—many believed and turned to the Lord. What effect does the persecution of the church have in today's society?

LESSON IN OUR SOCIETY

Fred Craddock, in an address to ministers, caught the practical implications of consecration: "To give my life for Christ appears glorious. To pour myself out for others . . . to pay the ultimate price of martyrdom—I'll do it. I'm ready, Lord, to go out in a blaze of glory."

We think giving our all to the Lord is like taking a $1,000 bill and laying it on the table—"Here's my life, Lord. I'm giving it all." But the reality for most of us is that God sends us to the bank and has us cash in the $1,000 for quarters. We go through life putting out 25 cents here and 50 cents there: Listen to the neighbor kid's troubles instead of saying, "Get lost." Go to a committee meeting. Give a cup of water to a shaky old man in a nursing home.

Usually, giving our life to Christ isn't glorious.

It's done in all those little acts of love, 25 cents at a time. It would be easy to go out in a flash of glory; it's harder to live the Christian life little by little over the long haul.

In our age of mass media, even the Christian community has succumbed to the making of celebrities and superstars. Surrounded by glitz and glamour, fame and infamy, Christians have begun to measure God's favor and their own effectiveness by the number of television stations or appearances they make, by the number of persons who come to their church, or by the size of their building projects.

However, it is most consistent with the life of Christ, that Christian ministry is in the everyday, common life experiences that glorify God. Just as Jesus went about doing good, Christians today need to be refocused on doing good every day instead of accumulating wealth and worldly exposure.

How have you spent the moments in your day blessing another in the love of the Lord?

MAKE IT HAPPEN

When the prophets from Jerusalem came to Antioch and told the Christians of a great need in another part of the country, the disciples gave. The Bible records that "every man according to his ability" gave in this relief effort. What news have you heard of a need far away, and how have you responded? With the mass arson of Black churches during 1996-98, did you, or your church, send relief according to your ability? Will you lead your class, Sunday School, or Bible Study group in sending aid to Christians in need, whether near or far?

FOLLOW THE SPIRIT

What God wants me to do:

_____

_____

REMEMBER YOUR THOUGHTS

Special insights you learned:

_____

_____

MORE LIGHT ON THE TEXT
Acts 11:19-30; 13:1-3

11:19 Now they which were scattered abroad upon the persecution that arose about Stephen traveled as far as Phoenicia, and Cyprus, and Antioch, preaching the word to none but unto the Jews only.

Stephen had died approximately five or six years before the time of this highlighted text. The persecutors had hoped to be rid of the Gospel message but God used their flight as an opportunity to spread out the seeds of the Gospel. Again, He turned intended evil into good (Genesis 50:20; Romans 8:28). They went northward into Phoenicia, and up to the island of Cyprus, and into the chief Syrian city of Antioch.

Rather than letting opposition silence them, they kept up their preaching. They did not stop working for the Lord. It is a good reminder to today's Christian that we must take our faith wherever we go because God can use us anywhere and everywhere.

Even though Peter explained the opening of the door to Gentiles upon his return to Jerusalem from Cornelius's house in Caesarea (Acts 11:1-18), the believers who had fled upon Stephen's death had not heard of it. Thus, they continued to preach to "none but unto the Jews only." As far as they knew that was still God's pattern.

20 And some of them were men of Cyprus and Cyrene, which, when they were come to Antioch, spake unto the Grecians, preaching the Lord Jesus.

The evangelists from Cyprus and Cyrene were probably African Jews, or "Grecians," themselves. So they chose to preach to those of their own country in Antioch. There was much mingling of cultures in those days because Cyrene was located on the northern edge of Africa, past Egypt, and where Libya is today. Cyprus, on the other hand, was located up in the Mediterranean Sea. In spite of the co-mingling of ideologies, Jesus and Christians remained distinct and were known by the society at large to be this.

The evangelists preached one message. It was and is the only message on earth worth preaching (1 John 4:3). We need to know no other message ". . . save Jesus Christ, and him crucified" (1 Corinthians 2:2).

21 And the hand of the Lord was with them: and a great number believed, and turned unto the Lord.

The "hand" of the Lord means the "power" of the Lord was with them. God will put His "power" behind any preaching which is true to Scripture. When we submit to any other doctrine or philosophy, not based on the Gospel of Jesus Christ, we are on our own and giving place to Satan and his ministers of falsity (2 Corinthians 11:12-15).

Being true to the Bible will produce fruit unto God. In the Book of Acts this truth was established because ". . .a great number believed, and turned unto the Lord," as a result of preaching Christ.

22 Then tidings of these things came unto the ears of the church which was in Jerusalem: and they sent forth Barnabas, that he should go as far as Antioch.

The Jerusalem church received word of what was happening to the north, and, Barnabas, who was a Levite from Cyprus, was sent to Antioch. His mission was to lay a firm doctrinal foundation for the church there. As an anointed elder of the church, he could "set in order the things that (were) wanting" (Titus 1:5). God expects the more spiritually mature among us to set things right.

23 Who, when he came, and had seen the grace of God, was glad, and exhorted them all, that with purpose of heart they would cleave unto the Lord.

There is rejoicing in heaven whenever a lost soul comes to Christ (Matthew 18:11-14). Similarly, Barnabas was glad when he saw the wonderful results of the grace of God in Antioch. He did what we must do with all those who are newly come to Christ, he "exhorted them all" to be sincere in coming closer to Christ.

Christians must "purpose in our hearts," or "be determined," that we will "cleave" or "glue" ourselves to the Lord. We must get to the point where we are totally dependent on Him. We must get so close to Him that He is always our closest and best friend. "Cleaving" represents the kind of intimate and personal relationship that a husband should share with a wife (Genesis 2:24).

We can't fool God because He knows the thoughts of our hearts (Genesis 6:5). We must "draw nigh" to Him (James 4:8), and, like Barnabas, we must encourage others to do the same.

24 For he was a good man, and full of the Holy Ghost and of faith: and much people was added unto the Lord.

There was a reason for Barnabas's positive and inspirational reaction to what he saw in Antioch. "He was a good man, and full of the Holy Ghost and of faith." Such a person can always appreciate the works of God. Such a person can always rejoice over the way God blesses the lives of people.

Barnabas was sent to Antioch to help lay a solid foundation for the church. His attitude and demeanor did just that because ". . .much people was added unto the Lord." Many Christians should ask themselves whether their walk turns people on to Christ or whether they are turned off. Barnabas knew that he was an ambassador for Christ (2 Corinthians 5:20). Accordingly, his manner of living before the people of Antioch was important to him, and was reflective of Christ. He was warm, caring, encouraging, self-sacrificing, and loving in the same way that Christ would have been. That is the essence of our being Christlike.

25 Then departed Barnabas to Tarsus, for to seek Saul: 26 And when he had found him, he brought him unto Antioch. And it came to pass, that a whole year they assembled themselves with the church, and taught much people. And the disciples were called Christians first in Antioch.

Barnabas knew of Saul's zeal and preaching power, and he decided that Saul could really help get the Antioch church off the ground. So Barnabas went to Tarsus and brought Saul back. Such a move gave a further glimpse into Barnabas's makeup. He realized that Saul might outshine him in preaching and teaching, and become more popular in the eyes of impressionable men. However, Barnabas did not succumb to the snares of pride and jealousy. He knew that the agenda which God had for those people was the number one priority.

Many times we retard the development of the church and foster divisions within it because too many leaders are afraid of sharing the spotlight. The Bible says we are to be humble and submissive to each other, allowing God to choose whom He would use and when (1 Peter 5:5-6). Jesus alone is the Founder of the church, not men (Matthew 16:18). Thus, Jesus is to be the only "star" that people see. Barnabas understood that when he decided to bring in Saul.

Barnabas and Saul labored for a whole year setting up the Antioch church. It was to be a solid church for that region and show stability, just as the Jerusalem church did in Judea. As part of that process, the people had to become knowledgeable in the Word. So, Barnabas and Saul "taught much people" (1 Timothy 5:17; Matthew 28:19).

Hearing and believing the Gospel message for our salvation is only the first step. People must then receive the whole counsel of God, which the Bible offers, in order to learn how to walk a victorious and godly life. Jesus said God must be worshiped "in spirit and in truth" (John 4:24). Some churches overflow with praise and "spirit," but they are lacking in sharing the "truth."

The Word of God is the "milk" by which we are to grow spiritually mature (1 Peter 2:2). Those whom God has entrusted with teaching the Word to others are vital to the role of the "perfecting of the saints. . .and the edifying of the body of Christ" (Ephesians 4:11-12). We must grow to the point where we are ready for "strong meat" rather than "milk" (Hebrews 5:12-14).

Finally, the church at Antioch took a giant step toward forging unity within the body of Christ. There was no strong opposition in Antioch. This was important for many reasons, including the fact that enemies of the disciples had taken it upon themselves to call the disciples derisive names like "the Nazarenes" (see Acts 24:5). So, the disciples must have felt secure in taking it upon themselves to adopt the name "Christians" for the first time in history.

Being a Christian showed their identification and relationship with Christ the way that "Roman" did with Rome, or "Grecian" did with Greece. Living under the single banner of "Christian" also did away with the divisive potential which the labels "Jew," "Gentile," "Greek," "proselyte," etc. generated. Galatians 3:26-29 indicates that Christ unifies all of His people, and they need not look to other identifying factors. All Christians are one in Jesus Christ.

27 And in these days came prophets from Jerusalem unto Antioch. 28 And there stood up one of them named Agabus, and signified by the Spirit that there should be great dearth throughout all the world: which came to pass in the days of Claudius Caesar.

Prophets and prophecy were gifts from the Holy Spirit to the New Testament church (see 1 Corinthians 12:10; Ephesians 4:11-12). Those prophets were enabled "by the Spirit" to foresee coming events. The test for whether God sent a prophet was, and is, whether their prophecies would come true (see Deuteronomy 18:22; Jeremiah 28:9). Prophets offer tremendous guidance to the church.

During the year that Barnabas and Saul were in Antioch, some prophets came from Jerusalem.

Agabus was one of them, and he forecast a widespread famine, i.e., "a great dearth throughout all the world." His prophecy indeed came true "in the days of Claudius Caesar" and the famine lasted two or more years. Later, in Acts 21:10-11, this same Agabus prophesied that Paul would be imprisoned.

29 Then the disciples, every man according to his ability, determined to send relief unto the brethren which dwelt in Judea: 30 Which also they did, and sent it to the elders by the hands of Barnabas and Saul.

Those in Antioch who heard this prophecy of famine were touched by Christian love and decided to share all that they could spare with their mother church in Judea. This was a self-sacrifice since the prophet said that the famine would be worldwide. It was in keeping with the spirit of sharing which was begun by the Jerusalem church in the beginning (Acts 4:32-37). It was in keeping with what we are told in Galatians 6:10, "As we have therefore opportunity, let us do good unto all men, especially unto them who are of the household of faith."

The believers in Antioch did more than determine, or make a decision to give; they carried their plan forward with action and sent money by way of Barnabas and Saul "to the elders" so that resources would be distributed according to the leading of the Spirit. Many times we pay lip-service to the need for doing things for others with a lot of spiritual-sounding talk. However, too often there is a lack of follow-through on these promises. The commitment of the church at Antioch is a good example for us to follow in terms of keeping our word.

13:1 Now there were in the church that was at Antioch certain prophets and teachers; as Barnabas, and Simeon that was called Niger, and Lucius of Cyrene, and Manaen, which had been brought up with Herod the tetrarch, and Saul.

The church at Antioch was blessed with great men of instruction. Acts 13:1 mentions five of them: Barnabas, Simeon, Lucius, Manaen, and Saul. They were gifted to receive special messages from heaven as prophets, and were inspired teachers of doctrine. Perhaps, these were the kind of men Jesus told the Pharisees He would send during an occasion when He chastised the Pharisees for the killings of past prophets of God (Matthew 23:34).

Barnabas and Saul had worked a year to get the church firmly established at Antioch. Not much is known about the other three men beyond what is revealed in the verse. Simeon "that was called Niger" was probably from Cyrene in northern Africa. "Niger" means "black" in Greek and infers that Simeon may have been a Black man. Lucius "of Cyrene" was definitely from northern Africa. The Apostle Paul fondly referred to Lucius as "my kinsman" at the close of the Epistle to the Romans (Romans 16:21). And, Manaen is said to have been "brought up with Herod the tetrarch," probably as a foster brother. This Herod was also known as Herod Antipas, the ruler who had John the Baptist beheaded (Matthew 14:3,10). So, Manaen grew up in a regal and courtly situation, but God moved him away from Herod's influence to be used in the service of the Lord.

2 As they ministered to the Lord, and fasted, the Holy Ghost said, Separate me Barnabas and Saul for the work whereunto I have called them.

"Ministering to the Lord" simply means that those men served Christ to the fullest. They were about the business of building His kingdom. That is the responsibility of every born-again believer (Romans 14:17-18; Ephesians 2:10, Colossians 3:24). Like these men, we must also take some time to "fast", or deny our flesh, in order to be more receptive to the Spirit of God.

During their time of fasting, the Holy Spirit instructed them that it was time for Barnabas and Saul to move into another area of God's service. Saul already may have had an idea that this service was to carry the Word to the Gentiles (Acts 9:15; 22:21), but he did not force the move on his own. He waited until this moment when the Holy Ghost gave God's command. Ecclesiastes 3:1 says, "To every thing there is a season, and a time to every purpose under the heaven." God knows the perfect time for what He wants us to do.

Likewise, Barnabas probably had an idea that he would someday be sent forth as a missionary to the Gentiles. He was always "full of the Holy Ghost and of faith" (Acts 11:24), which would have kept him in a position to receive plenty of impressions from God. Furthermore, during his close association with Saul at Antioch, he undoubtedly felt the Lord preparing him to go in that direction. If we are walking righteously in an intimate relationship with God and in His service, we will frequently feel His leading in a particular direction.

3 And when they had fasted and prayed, and laid their hands on them, they sent them away.

Though Barnabas and Saul had long been ministers of God, this new commission required a special ordination service by their fellow prophets and teachers (v. 1). Again, we see that fasting and praying was an essential first step in receiving clarity in God's instructions.

The "laying on of the hands" of the fellow prophets was God's way of transmitting His clear directions and sanctioning them for the mission before them. Those who have been blessed with great insight from God are told in 2 Timothy 2:2 to "commit (the same) to faithful men, who shall be able to teach others also." Thus, having been properly prepared and anointed, Barnabas and Saul embarked on what is known as their First Missionary Journey.

DAILY BIBLE READINGS

M: The Church in Syrian Antioch
Acts 11:19-24

T: Barnabas and Saul in Antioch
Acts 11:25-30

W: James Killed and Peter Imprisoned
Acts 12:1-5

T: Peter Delivered from Prison
Acts 12:6-19

F: Barnabas and Saul Commissioned
Acts 12:24 13:3

S: Paul, a Prisoner for Christ Jesus
Ephesians 3:1-6

S: Paul's Ministry to the Gentiles
Ephesians 3:7-13

TEACHING TIPS

1. Words You Should Know

A. Shook off the dust (Acts 13:51) *ektinasso* (shook)—To shake violently, to shake off. This action symbolized cleansing oneself from the impurity of sinners who did not worship God. The expression goes back to Jesus' time (Mark 10:14; 6:11; Luke 10:11). The kingdom was preached by these messengers. The dust was left behind as a witness that will testify on the last day that the messengers were there but the message was rejected.

B. Ordained (v. 48) Greek *tasso*—To place, to set, appoint, order to dispose, adapt, set in order, with detailed instructions.

C. Blaspheming (v. 45) *Blasphemeo*—To speak with irreverence concerning God; especially to revile God and divine things.

2. Teacher Preparation

A. Begin preparing for the lesson by reading Acts 13. Then read THE PEOPLE, PLACES, AND TIMES and the BACKGROUND sections to give yourself a good framework for the lesson.

B. Read over the LESSON IN OUR SOCIETY section. Keep this in mind as you prepare the lesson and think about your students and their needs.

3. Starting the Lesson

A. Open with prayer. Ask one of the students to read the LESSON AIM and pray with this in mind.

B. This week's lesson deals with a very difficult witnessing experience that Paul and Barnabas had. In fact, they were run out of the city because they dared to explain the truth of the Gospel. Allow one or two students to testify about a difficult experience they have had. You may want to assign this to someone ahead of time.

4. Getting into the Lesson

A. Divide the class into small groups and assign each group a section of the lesson to read and pre-pare for presentation, (THE PEOPLE, PLACES, AND TIMES, BACKGROUND, etc.) .

B. Read the FOCAL VERSES, IN FOCUS, and the IN DEPTH commentary. Then allow each group time to present their part of the lesson to the class.

5. Relating the Lesson to Life

A. Call on the group that has SEARCH THE SCRIPTURES and DISCUSS THE MEANING sections first. Encourage others in the class to add their comments and insights. Have the group assigned to THE PEOPLE, PLACES, AND TIMES section give their report next.

B. Allow those who had the LESSON IN OUR SOCIETY to give the final report.

C. Ask students to share what they consider to be the most challenging part of the lesson and why.

6. Arousing Action

A. Read the questions in the MAKE IT HAPPEN section. Challenge the students to examine their hearts. You may want to share at this point what God spoke to you about as you went through the lesson.

WORSHIP GUIDE

For the Superintendent or Teacher
Theme: Mission to the Gentiles
Theme Song: "Make me a Blessing"
Scripture: Acts 13:14-15, 42-52
Song: "This Little Light of Mine"
Devotional Thought: Father, thank You
that You have opened our eyes to the
truth about the Gospel of Christ. Now
help us to be bold and sensitive to others
who need to hear this truth.

MISSION TO GENTILES

Bible Background • ACTS 13:4—14:28
Printed Text • ACTS 13:14-15, 42-52
Devotional Reading • PSALM 96

LESSON AIM

By the end of this lesson, students should be able to explain the difficulty Paul and Barnabas had in spreading the Gospel in Asia Minor and become more determined to participate in evangelism in spite of challenging obstacles.

KEEP IN MIND

"For so hath the Lord commanded us, saying, I have set thee to be a light of the Gentiles, that thou shouldest be for salvation unto the ends of the earth" (Acts 13:47).

FOCAL VERSES

Acts 13:14 But when they departed from Perga, they came to Antioch in Pisidia, and went into the synagogue on the sabbath day, and sat down.

15 And after the reading of the law and the prophets the rulers of the synagogue sent unto them, saying, Ye men and brethren, if ye have any word of exhortation of the people, say on.

13:42 And when the Jews were gone out of the synagogue, the Gentiles besought that these words might be preached to them the next sabbath.

43 Now when the congregation was broken up, many of the Jews and religious proselytes followed Paul and Barnabas: who, speaking to them, persuaded them to continue in the grace of God.

44 And the next sabbath day came almost the whole city together to hear the word of God.

45 But when the Jews saw the multitudes, they were filled with envy, and spake against those things which were spoken by Paul, contradicting and blaspheming.

LESSON OVERVIEW

LESSON AIM
KEEP IN MIND
FOCAL VERSES
IN FOCUS
THE PEOPLE, PLACES, AND TIMES
BACKGROUND
AT-A-GLANCE
IN DEPTH
SEARCH THE SCRIPTURES
DISCUSS THE MEANING
LESSON IN OUR SOCIETY
MAKE IT HAPPEN
FOLLOW THE SPIRIT
REMEMBER YOUR THOUGHTS
MORE LIGHT ON THE TEXT
DAILY BIBLE READINGS

46 Then Paul and Barnabas waxed bold, and said, It was necessary that the word of God should first have been spoken to you: but seeing ye put it from you, and judge yourselves unworthy of everlasting life, lo, we turn to the Gentiles.

47 For so hath the Lord commanded us, saying, I have set thee to be a light of the Gentiles, that thou shouldest be for salvation unto the ends of the earth.

48 And when the Gentiles heard this, they were glad, and glorified the word of the Lord: and as many as were ordained to eternal life believed.

49 And the word of the Lord was published throughout all the region.

50 But the Jews stirred up the devout and honourable women, and the chief men of the city, and raised persecution against Paul and Barnabas, and expelled them out of their coasts.

51 But they shook off the dust of their feet against them, and came unto Iconium.

52 And the disciples were filled with joy, and with the Holy Ghost.

MAY 6TH

IN FOCUS

The youth group at Second Baptist Church in Joliet, Illinois, during the 1970's was no ordinary "meet on Sunday—have Bible study—then go home and watch television" group. They did the usual plays, programs, special youth Sunday presentations, and they met together on Sunday afternoons for youth group meetings like most churches. However, when a few of the people in the youth group became concerned when they understood the truth of the Gospel, these ordinary activities were not enough.

The group began to pray about and discuss ways to reach people with the Gospel of Jesus Christ. They were committed to sharing Christ where ever they went: at school, in their neighborhoods, family gatherings, church conferences, and even at the mall. In addition to their personal evangelistic efforts, they also did group evangelism. On a regular basis, they met at different times of the week for food, fun, and fellowship. Unsaved friends and loved ones were invited and warmly welcomed. This promoted a comfortable atmosphere for unsaved persons to ask questions and hear the Gospel in a place other than church.

One night a member of the youth group was propositioned by a prostitute on his way to one of the fellowship meetings. Instead of just telling her "no thank you" and moving on, he picked her up and brought her to the fellowship meeting. She did not come to Christ that night, but everyone knew it was a night she would never forget.

One Saturday after a inspiring youth rally meeting, the group decided to go and evangelize to the local motorcycle club that night. The musician set up his keyboard in a parking lot across the street and the youth choir sang a few selections. Then the group divided up among the motorcyclists and talked to them about Jesus.

The church members were divided about these activities. Some believed the youth should stop doing such bizarre things and stick to the regular youth programs, while others were extremely pleased to see the fresh excitement for the Gospel and encouraged the group to do more.

As you will see from today's lesson, if this youth group existed in Paul's time they would have fit in perfectly. He would not only have encouraged their efforts, he would have been leading the way.

THE PEOPLE, PLACES, AND TIMES

Jews. A nation of people joined together by a common bond. This was a title that was reassured for God's choice, elect people—Israel.

Gentiles. A nation or people referred to as heathens. This referred to anyone who was not a Jew.

Proselytes. A foreigner or stranger who comes from his own people to another. They are people who came to dwell among the Jews and embrace their religion. A convert from heathenism to Judaism.

Pisidia. A mountain province in central Asia Minor, in the region of Phrygia. It was on a plateau some 3600 feet high. The road to reach Pisidia was steep, rocky, and infested with bandits. The city was founded by one of Alexander the Great's successors in about 300 BC. The population was a mixture of Jews, Greeks, Romans, and a few of the native Phrygians. Pisidia is often referred to as Pisidian Antioch, which more accurately should be interpreted as Antioch near Pisidia.

BACKGROUND

For the first two years after the coming of the Holy Spirit, the Gospel was spread mainly in Jerusalem to the Jews, primarily under the guidance of Peter. In Acts 8, the focus of the evangelistic outreach changed. The primary leader was Philip, and for the next 13 years the target region was Judea and Samaria, the area surrounding Jerusalem. For the most part, both of these outreach efforts involved Jewish people or proselytes, who were non-Jewish people familiar with and accustomed to adhering to the Jewish traditions. The proselytes were Gentiles who converted to Judaism and had gone through all the necessary ceremonies and committed themselves to following Jewish laws and traditions.

In Acts 13, another shift was made in the church's evangelistic outreach. Paul was appointed by God and assigned to go minister to the Gentile world. Paul and Barnabas were in Antioch when the Holy Spirit gave this command, "Separate for me Barnabas and Saul for the work to which I have called them for myself" (Acts 13:2) It was approximately 49 A.D. when Paul and Barnabas left Antioch, the Christian headquarters, and began expanding the ministry to include the Gentiles beyond Jerusalem, Judea, and Samaria. For the next 14 years, Paul heavily evangelized this group of people who were not Jews nor desiring to become Jewish proselytes. His ministry was very successful. Many Gentiles turned from their heathen beliefs to Christianity. However, the Jews did not like the idea of these heathen people now thinking that because of Christ they were just as worthy as the Jews of all God's blessings. They argued with Paul and tried to convince the Gentiles that he was wrong. This kind of conflict continued throughout Paul's ministry. His first major confrontation was in Pisidia, the city in which today's lesson takes place.

AT-A-GLANCE

1. Paul Preached in Pisidia
(Acts 13:14-15)
2. Paul Persecuted by the Jews
(vv. 42-49)
3. Paul Was Put Out of the City
(vv. 50-51)

IN DEPTH

1. Paul Preaches in Pisidia (Acts 13:14-15)

Before Paul arrived in Pisidia, he and Barnabas were in Pamphylia. Some scholars believe, even though there is no scriptural evidence, that Paul left Pamphylia because he caught malaria there. Pisidia was a high region in which he could recuperate in the mountain air; therefore, he made that his next stop. In order to get to Pisidia, one had to travel up a ragged mountain. This territory was also famous for robbers who would hide amongst the rocks and take advantage of those traveling to the city.

When Paul and Barnabas arrived in Pisidia, they found lodging and rested up from their journey. After a time of refreshment, Paul and Barnabas sought out the Jewish leaders in the city and evidently talked with them prior to the Sabbath. On the Sabbath, Paul and Barnabas went to the temple. After the opening prayers were presented and sections from the law and the prophets were read, the elders asked Paul to speak. If there were spiritually educated persons in the audience like Paul and Barnabas, the leaders of the synagogue would allow them to teach. It was uncommon for learned men to come to town.

In this synagogue, Paul presented his message to a mixed congregation, both Jews and Gentiles (10:2). He reviewed the Jewish history to emphasize God's chosen people, Israel. He pointed out how God provided her with land and a succession of rulers, that ended with Jesus the Saviour. Paul addressed God's fulfillment of His promise by raising Christ from the dead, and how in Christ alone is forgiveness and justification. Paul concluded by challenging the hearers not to be like the unbelieving Israelites who refused the message of the Old Testament prophets.

2. Paul Persecuted by the Jews (vv. 42-49)

Paul's message in the synagogue on his first Sabbath in Pisidia was received well by all. The elders invited Paul and Barnabas then to come and teach the congregation again the following Sabbath. As the two men were leaving the synagogue, people flocked to them. Some could not wait a whole week to hear more of this marvelous truth. Paul encouraged them to remain "faithful to the grace of God." This indicated that those people who attended the service already trusted in the grace of God as they had come to know it through the Old Testament. Paul challenged them to now continue in that basic attitude by believing in Jesus as the One through whom God's promises were being brought to fulfillment.

In just seven days, the word had spread around the city, especially among the Gentiles. The proselytes were telling all their non-Jewish friends that Paul said they could become believers without becoming Jews first and following the Jewish laws. Virtually the whole city turned out that next Sabbath listen to Paul. The synagogue was crowded with more Gentiles than Jews, eagerly wanting to hear the Good News about Christ.

The popularity of Paul and Barnabas caused some Jews to become envious. They argued against Paul's message. Conflict was common in this city because of the mixture of people (Jews, Greeks, Romans, and native Phrygians). Down throughout history, Jews made a distinction between themselves and the rest of the Gentiles. Up until that time, according to the Jews, not one of God's privileges referred to the Gentiles—only to the Jews. Paul's teaching upset the city. He was truthfully stating that Gentiles could receive and were entitled to God's blessings as well as the Jews. This infuriated the Jews.

The opposition caused Paul and Barnabas to be bolder and more open. They declared their determination to take the message to the Gentiles. They had fulfilled their duty of first going to the Jews. The Jews as a body had said, "no!" They did not want any part of the Gospel if it meant sharing their promises and blessings with the Gentile world. Like spoiled children they whined, "If I have to share my bag of candy with the boy next door, I don't want any candy at all." Paul responded like a wise parent, "Fine, if you don't want to share, I'll give the whole bag to the boy next door and you won't have any." Because the Jews could not accept the truth about the Gentiles they disqualified themselves from eternal life. This rejection from the Jews freed Paul to take the Gospel exclusively to the Gentiles, and he plainly told them that this was his intention.

Paul also quoted Old Testament Scripture to reinforce his teaching, "I have made you [Jesus] a light for the Gentiles, so that all the world may be saved" (Isaiah 49:5, Today's Contemporary Version). Jesus was light and salvation for the whole world, not just the Jews. God wanted the Jews to accept His Son, Jesus, and also accept the mission of the Messiah. That mission was to bring the Gospel to all the world. The Jews were to be the leaders of world evangelism. But they failed to carry out their mission. It has been said, "The Jews saw the heathen as chaff to be burned; Jesus saw them as a harvest to be reaped for God."

The Gentiles eagerly and heartily accepted the message Paul and Barnabas preached. They rejoiced and praised God for His Word. Not all the Gentiles accepted the message. Those who believed are described as those who "were ordained to eternal life." This phrase has been interpreted different ways, but most believe it simply means those within the crowd who placed their faith in the truth of the Gospel. The new Gentile Christians were excited about their new found faith and spread it throughout the region. Paul and Barnabas continued to minister among the Gentiles for about six months. Paul's journey did not involve rushing from place to place, converting small groups of people and moving on.

Paul and his companions would stay and work with the new converts, teaching and encouraging them until they were rooted in their faith. Then Paul would move on to another city.

3. Paul Put Out of the City (vv. 50-52)

As excitement about the Gospel traveled among the region of the Gentiles, great opposition was brewing among the Jews as well. They were increasingly unhappy about this new teaching and the overwhelming response. They did not like the idea that eventually more Gentiles would be involved in Christianity than Jews. Their leadership and Jewish distinction was being threatened. They felt something had to be done. Paul had to be stopped. The Jews could not refute the truth of what Paul was preaching with Scripture so they resorted to scheming and violence.

They decided to use influential women connected with the synagogue to do their dirty work. The Jewish religion had always been attractive to women, especially those who were not Jews. In the ancient world, there was much sexual immorality. Family life was broken down and the worst sufferers were women. The Jewish religious leaders preached a high standard of sexual purity and valued family. Many women gathered around the synagogues; this crowd often included women of high social position, who found what they longed for within the Jewish way of life. Many of these women became proselytes. If they did not convert, some of them still believed in God and feared Him rather than worshiping the idols in their cities. The Jews persuaded these women, whose husbands were often men in influential positions, to take steps against the Christian preachers.

Pisidia became unsafe for Paul and Barnabas. The Jews were intent on keeping their Jewish privileges to themselves and were going to any number of lengths to stop Paul and Barnabas from teaching. Eventually, this persecution forced Paul and Barnabas to leave the city.

Although Paul and Barnabas had to leave town, many of the Gentiles in Pisidia accepted the salvation through faith in Christ as a result of their ministry there. This newly formed Christian group separated from the synagogue. They became the first of the Christian churches of Galatia.

Before Paul and Barnabas left the city, they performed a symbolic action; they "shook the dust off their feet." It was customary for Jews to shake off the dust of a pagan town when they returned to their own land as a symbol of cleansing themselves from the impurity of sinners who did not worship God. For Paul to do this to his fellow Jews, demonstrated that who they had rejected the Gospel and drove out the missionaries were no better than unbelievers.

SEARCH THE SCRIPTURES

1. When Paul went to the synagogue on the Sabbath what took place? (Acts 13:14-15)

2. What occurred the following Sabbath and why? (vv. 44-45)

3. Who was responsible for putting Paul out of the city, and why did they think this was necessary? (v. 45)

4. What was the disciples' response to the rejection? (vv. 50-51)

DISCUSS THE MEANING

1. What are some reasons why you believe Paul's ministry was rejected?

2. What do you think about the disciples' response to this rejection?

LESSON IN OUR SOCIETY

In our society, many people have experienced painful rejection. Parents have pushed their children away for careers. Married persons have pushed their spouses away for intimate relationships with others. Children have pushed their elderly parents away because it interrupts their lifestyle to have them around.

When a person has experienced one of these losses or some other kind of rejection, they are very leery about putting themselves in a vulnerable position again. If you attempt to talk to a nonbeliever about Christ—at sometime in your experience—you will be rejected. You may even lose close friends. This is the reason why many people refuse to share Christ in their neighborhoods, on their jobs, or other challenging or difficult places.

However, the Scripture makes it clear that we are to go into the world and tell them about Jesus Christ. Remember the Holy Spirit, the Comforter,

will be there to comfort us whenever we have been hurt or rejected.

MAKE IT HAPPEN

Think back, if you can, on any difficult witnessing experiences you may have had. What happened and why? Were you being loving and understanding or too aggressive and forceful? Were you prepared? How often are you sharing your faith now? Why? Do you need to learn how to share your faith? Do you need to join a team that goes out regularly? Plan this week to become more evangelistic in your thinking and living.

FOLLOW THE SPIRIT

What God wants me to do:

_____

_____

REMEMBER YOUR THOUGHTS

Special insights you learned:

_____

_____

MORE LIGHT ON THE TEXT
Acts 13:14-15, 42-52

13:14 But when they departed from Perga, they came to Antioch in Pisidia, and went into the synagogue on the sabbath day, and sat down.

Perga is located in Pamphylia, a province of the south coast of Asia Minor. As a leading city located in the Plain of Pamphylia, it is best known as the place where the temple of the goddess Diana (also known as Artemis Pergaia) is erected.

We do not know what Paul and Barnabas did while in Perga. We are told only that John Mark separates from their group, returns to Jerusalem, and Paul and Barnabas go on to Pisidian Antioch. This is a part of their first missionary journey. Many scholars believe the churches found in this area are those addressed by Paul in Galatians.

Pisidian Antioch is located in the mountainous region in the south central part of Asia Minor. It is not the same as Syrian Antioch, the place they originally leave (Acts 13:1). Pisidian Antioch is bounded by Pamphylia on the south, Lycia on the west, Phrygia on the north, and Isauria on the east.

While in Pisidian Antioch, Paul and Barnabas went to the synagogue on the Sabbath day and sat down. Paul and Barnabas continued the custom of Jesus. For it was Jesus' custom to worship in the synagogue on the Sabbath day (Luke 4:16).

"Synagogue" is a Greek word for the place of assembly used by Jewish communities primarily for public worship and instruction, or the assembly itself. The Sabbath day refers to the Jewish Sabbath day, which is the seventh day of the week, Saturday. It was a day of weekly repose from secular avocations, when all physical labor was considered taboo. One of the reasons why the Pharisees conspired to destroy Jesus was because he healed a man on the Sabbath day (Mark 3:1-6). However, Jesus informed them that ". . .The Sabbath was made for man, and not man for the Sabbath: Therefore the Son of man is Lord also of the Sabbath" (Mark 2:27-28).

Paul, knowing that Jesus is the Lord of the Sabbath, eventually convinces the Gentile Christians to shift the Sabbath from Saturday to Sunday, because Jesus rose from the grave on the first day of the week, Sunday. Thus, the Christian Sabbath is celebrated on Sunday, the first day of the week.

15 And after the reading of the law and the prophets the rulers of the synagogue sent unto them, saying, Ye men and brethren, if ye have any word of exhortation for the people, say on.

The Jewish leaders of the synagogue performed the usual liturgical worship service held in the synagogue. This included prayer, praise, reading of Scripture and preaching. They read the Scripture lesson for the week, that is, a portion of the Old Testament law and the writings of the prophets. Following the Scripture reading, the leaders of the synagogue invited Paul and Barnabas to address the congregation by expounding on the Scriptures.

Reading the Scriptures is not enough. Teaching and explaining the Scriptures helps people understand the meaning, thus enabling them to apply it to their lives.

13:42 And when the Jews were gone out of the synagogue, the Gentiles besought that these words might be preached to them the next sabbath.

Paul brought the Gospel—the Good News about Jesus Christ—first, to the Jews and proselytes, but he did not direct his attention to the Gentiles. Some Jews and Jewish converts rejected this message. They got up and left the synagogue. They wanted no part of Paul's new doctrine.

However, the Gentiles in the assembly were willing to hear what Paul had to say. In fact, they invited Paul to return on the following Sabbath and continue his message. They begged Paul to preach the message of salvation, that is, forgiveness of sins through Christ.

Many people come to church on a regular basis. They hear the message of salvation over and over again. Yet, they fail to understand the message. They are like the people Jesus described in Luke 13:10-17. They watch and hear Jesus with their physical eyes and ears, but they are not capable of understanding the truth because their hearts are wicked and they have rejected Jesus. However, God desires that none should perish, and salvation is offered and available to them through Jesus Christ the Lord.

43 Now when the congregation was broken up, many of the Jews and religious proselytes followed Paul and Barnabas: who, speaking to them, persuaded them to continue in the grace of God.

Not all the Jews and proselytes rejected Paul's message. Some followed Paul and Barnabas, and they believed God's message of salvation. Paul and Barnabas urged these new converts to continue to trust and stand fast in the grace of God. Grace is the unmerited favor and blessing of God.

44 And the next sabbath day came almost the whole city together to hear the word of God.

"The next Sabbath day the whole city gathered to hear the Word of God concerning the attainment through Christ of salvation in the kingdom of God" (v. 44, Amplified Bible).

Some came out of curiosity. Others wanted to

see how the dissenting Jews would react at this second gathering. Yet, there were those who wanted to really hear the Word of God through Paul's preaching.

Not everyone comes to church for the same reason. Some come to be seen; others come to see. Yet, there are those who come to seek God and hear His Word.

45 But when the Jews saw the multitudes, they were filled with envy, and spake against those things which were spoken by Paul, contradicting and blaspheming.

"But when the Jews saw the crowds, filled with envy and jealousy they contradicted what was said by Paul, and reviled and slandered him" (Amp.). They did not want to receive the Gospel themselves, nor did they want others to embrace the message of Jesus Christ. When the kingdom of heaven opened, they would not go in themselves, but were angry with those that did. This was the same spirit the Pharisees had toward Jesus Christ. Jesus said, ". . .unless your uprightness and your right standing with God is more than that of the scribes and Pharisees, you will never enter the kingdom of heaven" (Matthew 5:20, Amp.).

The Jewish leaders contradicted everything Paul said. Nothing would silence them. They contradicted for contradiction's sake. They spoke against Jesus Christ and His Gospel, blaspheming Him and the truth of salvation. "Commonly, those that begin with contradiction end with blaspheming."

46 Then Paul and Barnabas waxed bold, and said, It was necessary that the word of God should first have been spoken to you: but seeing ye put it from you, and judge yourselves unworthy of everlasting life, lo, we turn to the Gentiles.

The Jews had been given the first offer to receive salvation. Jesus Christ sent out the 12 disciples charging them to "Go nowhere among the Gentiles . . . But go rather to the lost sheep of the house of Israel" (Matthew 10:5-6, Amp). Jesus, then, further instructs the disciples to preach to all nations, but begin in Jerusalem

(Luke 24:47).

Since the Jewish leaders refused to receive the Gospel of Jesus Christ, Paul and Barnabas turned their attention to the Gentiles—those who will receive the Word of God. God gives His Word to all who will freely receive it. If one will not, another will.

47 For so hath the Lord commanded us, saying, I have set thee to be a light of the Gentiles, that thou shouldest be for salvation unto the ends of the earth.

Paul and Barnabas justify their actions by saying they were acting by divine warrant as foretold by the Old Testament prophet, Isaiah: "And he said, It is a light thing that thou shouldest be my servant to raise up the tribes of Jacob, and to restore the preserved of Israel: I will also give thee for a light to the Gentiles, that thou mayest be my salvation unto the end of the earth" (Isaiah 49:6, KJV).

Jesus Christ's offer of salvation extends to the ends of the earth. Jesus is our salvation. Wherever the Gospel is preached, God's light of salvation shines and the souls of all who receive His message of Good News are saved.

48 And when the Gentiles heard this, they were glad, and glorified the word of the Lord: and as many as were ordained to eternal life believed.

And when the Gentiles heard this, they rejoiced with praise and thanksgiving for the Word of God; and believed and relied on Jesus as their Saviour (The Amplified Bible).

The Gentiles cheerfully embraced what the Jews had scornfully rejected. Through the Gospel of Jesus Christ, which had been rejected by the Jews, salvation, admission to God, and the knowledge of God's Word were now available to the Gentiles.

Through their newfound faith in Jesus Christ and their belief in Him as the risen Saviour, they were saved (Romans 10:9).

49 And the word of the Lord was published throughout all the region.

"And the Word of the Lord concerning eternal salvation through Jesus Christ scattered and spread throughout the whole region" (Amp). They told everyone they knew! They were saved, and they wanted everyone they knew to be saved.

What an excellent example of evangelism for believers of today to follow! We are not saved to keep the Gospel to ourselves, but we are saved to spread the Good News of salvation through Jesus Christ. We are saved to save somebody!

50 But the Jews stirred up the devout and honourable women, and the chief men of the city, and raised persecution against Paul and Barnabas, and expelled them out of their coasts.

The Jews stirred up the devout women of high rank. These women were zealous in the Jewish faith. Yet, they opposed the Gospel of Jesus Christ. Devotion and zeal are wonderful characteristics. However, misdirected devotion and zeal, especially against the Word of God, can result in eternal damnation. The Jewish leaders stirred up the chief men of the city, the magistrates and the rulers who were in power, and set them against the apostles. Because of this violent persecution, Paul and Barnabas were banished out of their coast.

51 But they shook off the dust of their feet against them, and came unto Iconium.

Paul and Barnabas shook off the dust from their feet against the unbelieving Jews, left Antioch, Persidia, and went to Iconium.

They followed Jesus' instructions on how to deal with persecution: "But when they persecute you in this city, flee ye into another" (Matthew 10:23a). Jesus Christ also instructed the disciples by saying: "And whosoever shall not receive you, nor hear your words, when ye depart out of that house or city, shake off the dust of your feet as a testimony against them" (Matthew 10:14; Mark 6:11).

The Jews, by banishing Paul and Barnabas from their coast, intended to stop the spread of their new doctrine. However, their plans backfired. The persecution and expulsion of the disciples from their coasts made people inquisitive

about who they were and what they did. This perhaps raised more interest in the disciples and the Gospel of Jesus Christ.

52 And the disciples were filled with joy, and with the Holy Ghost.

"And the disciples were continually filled throughout their souls with joy and the Holy Spirit" (Amp). When the new converts witnessed the courage demonstrated by Paul and Barnabas, they were filled with the joy of Jesus Christ, and with the Holy Spirit. They now knew that the joy of the Lord was their strength. The Holy Spirit revealed this to them.

Matthew Henry's Commentary sums it up in this manner: "The more we relish the comforts and encouragement we meet with in the power of godliness, the fuller our hearts are of them, the better prepared we are to face the difficulties we meet within the profession of godliness."

The psalmist says, "The Lord is my light and my salvation; whom shall I fear? The Lord is the strength of my life; of whom shall I be afraid?" (Psalm 27:1)

DAILY BIBLE READINGS

M: The Apostles Preach in Cyprus
Acts 13:4-12
T: The Apostles in Pisidian Antioch
Acts 13:13-25
W: Paul Preaches About the Messiah
Acts 13:26-41
T: Responses to Paul's Sermon
Acts 13:42-52
F: Paul and Barnabas in Iconium
Acts 14:1-7
S: Paul and Barnabas in Lystra and Derbe
Acst 14:8-20
S: Return to Syrian Antioch
Acts 14:21-28

TEACHING TIPS

May 13
Bible Study Guide 11

1. Words You Should Know

A. Circumcised (Acts 15:2) Greek *peritemno* —To cut around, cut off. Jews were to cut the foreskins of their male children at eight days old. This symbolized a distinctive, marked difference from other nations and tribes in biblical times.

B. Fornication (v. 20) Greek *porneia*—Sexual intercourse outside of marriage or within marriages between two near relatives.

2. Teacher Preparation

A. Read over the entire lesson. If you have a commentary or a Bible encyclopedia, look up the Jerusalem Council. Note any additional insight you discover and add it to your lesson, if you wish.

B. Begin preparing for the lesson by reading the entire 15th chapter of Acts.

C. The key words for this lesson are in the WORDS YOU SHOULD KNOW section. You also need to read THE PEOPLE, PLACES, AND TIMES and the BACKGROUND sections. Both of these sections will give you a good framework for the lesson.

D. Read over the LESSON IN OUR SOCIETY and MAKE IT HAPPEN sections. Be sure you think these questions over for yourself and be ready to share your personal experiences.

3. Starting the Lesson

A. Take the LESSON AIM and break it up into several parts. Stop and pray for each part.

B. Explain to the students that this week's lesson focuses in on a very important meeting during the development of the New Testament Church.

4. Getting into the Lesson

A. Have a student read the IN FOCUS story.

B. Briefly summarize the BACKGROUND, THE PEOPLE, PLACES, AND TIMES sections.

C. Have several students read the FOCAL VERSES aloud.

5. Relating the Lesson to Life

A. As you read through the IN DEPTH section, have the class answer the SEARCH THE SCRIPTURES and DISCUSS THE MEANING questions.

B. Read the LESSON IN OUR SOCIETY. Ask if anyone has believed in one of the ways listed and how they came to understand the truth of the Gospel.

6. Arousing Action

A. Read the questions in the MAKE IT HAPPEN section. Challenge the students to examine their hearts. You may want to share, at this point, what God spoke to you as you went through the lesson.

B. Remind students to use the DAILY BIBLE READINGS and to fill in the REMEMBER YOUR THOUGHTS and FOLLOW THE SPIRIT sections of the lesson. This will help them to have a focus for the week.

THE JERUSALEM CONFERENCE

Bible Background • ACTS 15:1-35
Printed Text • ACTS 15:1-2, 6-15, 19-20
Devotional Reading • ROMANS 3:21-26

LESSON AIM

By the end of this lesson, students should be able to explain what happened at the Jerusalem Council and express their desire to stand for the truth of the Gospel in the same way.

KEEP IN MIND

"Wherefore my sentence is, that we trouble not them, which from among the Gentiles are turned to God"(Acts 15:19).

FOCAL VERSES

Acts 15:1 And certain men which came down from Judea taught the brethren, and said, Except ye be circumcised after the manner of Moses, ye cannot be saved.

2 When therefore Paul and Barnabas had no small dissension and disputation with them, they determined that Paul and Barnabas, and certain other of them, should go up to Jerusalem unto the apostles and elders about this question.

15:6 And the apostles and elders came together for to consider of this matter.

7 And when there had been much disputing, Peter rose up, and said unto them, Men and brethren, ye know how that a good while ago God made choice among us, that the Gentiles by my mouth should hear the word of the Gospel, and believe.

8 Now God, which knoweth the hearts, bare them witness, giving them the Holy Ghost, even as he did unto us;

9 And put no difference between us and them, purifying their hearts by faith.

LESSON OVERVIEW

LESSON AIM
KEEP IN MIND
FOCAL VERSES
IN FOCUS
THE PEOPLE, PLACES, AND TIMES
BACKGROUND
AT-A-GLANCE
IN DEPTH
SEARCH THE SCRIPTURES
DISCUSS THE MEANING
LESSON IN OUR SOCIETY
MAKE IT HAPPEN
FOLLOW THE SPIRIT
REMEMBER YOUR THOUGHTS
MORE LIGHT ON THE TEXT
DAILY BIBLE READINGS

10 Now therefore why tempt ye God, to put a yoke upon the neck of the disciples, which neither our fathers nor we were able to bear?

11 But we believe that through the grace of the Lord Jesus Christ we shall be saved, even as they.

12 Then all the multitude kept silence, and gave audience to Barnabas and Paul, declaring what miracles and wonders God had wrought among the Gentiles by them.

13 And after they had held their peace, James answered, saying, Men and brethren, hearken unto me:

14 Simeon hath declared how God at the first did visit the Gentiles, to take out of them a people for his name.

15 And to this agree the words of the prophets;

15:19 Wherefore my sentence is, that we trouble not them, which from among the Gentiles are turned to God:

20 But that we write unto them, that they abstain from pollutions of idols, and from fornication, and from things strangled, and from blood.

IN FOCUS

Victoria grew up in the church. Her parents were active leaders in the church. Victoria thought she had done everything necessary to become a Christian. She had a mental check list, and as far as she was concerned all the criteria was met:

Believed in Jesus.
Joined the church.
Been baptized.

Attending and being an active participant in church functions.

Attempting to be a good person and asking God to forgive her sins.

Because she had met all these criteria Victoria thought, "I'm a Christian. I'm on my way to heaven." However, as a teenager, she was challenged by a youth group leader. "If you are trusting in anything else beside Jesus and His death on the cross, you are not a Christian." She went on to explain, "Joining the church, being baptized, being a good person, all that is good, but none of that saves you. It is only as you trust Christ and Him alone are you on your way to heaven."

This challenged Victoria's thinking. For the first time in her life, she realized she was not a Christian because she was trusting all these additional things to get her into heaven. After listening to more of what the youth leader had to say and examining the Scriptures for herself, Victoria decided to trust Christ and Him alone for her salvation. She became a Christian. She no longer had a check list.

Victoria was excited about her newly discovered faith and did not keep quiet about it. When Victoria began to share her new understanding, she realized several people in the church did not agree with her. Even though some of them were active in the church or even leaders and teachers in the church, they still had their list of criteria that would get them into heaven. Like Victoria, they thought they were Christians, because of what they did, not because of what Christ had done.

However, even when she talked about this newfound truth with some of the people in the church and the Scriptures were clearly explained, they insisted on keeping their lists. Sometimes, when Victoria spoke out about her new belief, it often caused conflict with those who were keeping their lists and were not Christians.

One day Jesus confronted Paul and helped him understand that he had a list. When Paul trusted Christ alone for his salvation, like Victoria he was excited and shared his newfound faith. He, too, encountered those who insisted on keeping their lists instead of accepting the free gift of grace in Jesus Christ.

THE PEOPLE, PLACES, AND TIMES

Judaizers. They belonged to a sect of the Pharisees. The word "Pharisee" means "separated one." They had separated themselves from people in one life-long attempt to keep every last detail of the Law.

The Jerusalem Church. The capital of Judea was in Jerusalem. When David was king, he made Jerusalem the worship center for the people. David and the other kings of the Southern Kingdom who followed his example lived and set up their administration in Jerusalem.

The setting of the first few chapters of Acts was Jerusalem. Jesus gave instructions and the order in which the Gospel was to go out (Acts 1:8). It was to start in Jerusalem. The city became the center of Christian activity because after the Day of Pentecost, the eleven apostles made it their headquarters; they left from Jerusalem to preach the Gospel and returned there after their journeys. However in Acts 13, there is a shift from Jerusalem to Antioch. The missionaries were then sent forth from Antioch and also returned there with their reports.

BACKGROUND

At the birth of the New Testament Church, most of the Christians were Jews. They all had been circumcised as babies or as adults, if they were proselytes. Proselytes were Gentiles who became Jews and kept all the laws. They were considered to be the same as other Jews, except that they were not born into Jewish families. So when a number of the Jews believed in Jesus, a number of proselytes believed the Gospel as well. For approximately 15 years, this did not present a problem for the New Testament church. The proselytes were already circumcised like the Jews and adhered to the Jewish laws and traditions without question and without any problem. They continued to keep the dietary laws (such as abstaining from pork or other meats considered unclean). They still observed the Sabbath (Saturday) as well as the Lord's Resurrection Day (Sunday). They still regarded the Ten Commandments as their standard for living.

After the persecution of Stephen, the revival in

Samaria, the conversion of Saul and Cornelius, and Paul's missionary journeys which extended beyond Jerusalem, Judea, and Samaria, hundreds of non-Jewish or Gentile believers were pouring into the church. Many did not know the teachings of the Old Testament. They had not been circumcised (circumcision was extremely important to the Jews. It indicated entrance into the community as God's people). Many had immoral, heathen habits and their lifestyles needed plenty of correction.

The conservative Jews at Jerusalem watched Gentiles pour into the church at Antioch. They heard about Paul's successful ministry among the former pagans. They knew that before long the Gentiles in the Christian community would outnumber the Jews. They were concerned that the immoral ways of the Gentiles would weaken the moral standards of the entire church.

These issues had to be resolved before the Christian church could continue in unity and truth. It was decided that a meeting would take place in Jerusalem and the matter would be settled there once and for all.

AT-A-GLANCE

1. The Conflict (Acts 15:1-2)
2. The Testimonies (vv. 6-11)
3. The Resolution (vv. 12-15, 19-20)

IN DEPTH

1. The Conflict (Acts 15:1-2)

Acts 15 opens with a group of unnamed persons from Judea who traveled to Antioch and confronted the Christian leaders and the new Christian converts saying, "If you are not circumcised according to the practice of Moses, you cannot be saved." These ultra-conservative Jews were saying, "it's okay to believe in Jesus Christ, but in order to be truly saved and accepted by God into His family, one must also be circumcised and carefully keep all the traditions and old symbolic ceremonies of Jewish law." The legalistic Jews refused

to eat meals (including the Lord's Supper) with Gentiles unless they had been circumcised, and prepared their meals according to Jewish rituals of cleansing.

The ultra-conservative Jews, the Judaizers, asked the question, "If the Gentile believers are not circumcised, how can we be brethren?" In the Old Testament, God continually warned the Jews to stay away from the heathen because He wanted them to be distinct from all other nations in the world. Now Paul and other leaders in the church were teaching, because of Christ, this unclean person can now sit next to the Jews in worship and eat with them, without adhering to any of the Jewish instructions and rituals. Many of the ultra-conservative Jewish Christians said "No!" They felt they had to insist that the new Gentile Christians become proselytes and convert to Judaism as well as Christianity. Therefore, the Gentile Christians, according to their understanding, must be circumcised and agree to keep all the symbolic ceremonies of Jewish ritual, including all the extra traditions imposed by the Jewish rabbis down through the years.

Paul replied to these men by asking the question, "If outward laws must be added to salvation, why did Christ have to die?" Paul tried to make it clear to these Jewish leaders that once a person receives new life through faith in Christ, this individual is now free not only from guilt and sin, but they are also released from ritual. The law was given to the Jews to point them to Jesus; now that Jesus had come, it was no longer necessary to keep the ritual law to be righteous.

Paul emphasized in his teaching that what is important is not the keeping of outward laws, but the daily inner working and power of the Holy Spirit. The Holy Spirit is to direct the new believer each day, convicting them of wrongdoing, reminding them of Christ's words, encouraging them to do things God's way. Then the Holy Spirit supplies the power for the Christian to live his life in a way that is pleasing to the Lord. Moses put the Ten Commandments into the hands of God's people. When Jesus came, He insisted that law must be written in our hearts. He affirmed the law by summarizing it in love.

Paul and Barnabas did not back down with

their stand on the truth. The Judaizers stood just as firm in their beliefs. It was obvious that this issue was going to divide the church. A meeting of the apostles and church leaders was essential to settle the matter. This historic meeting was called the Jerusalem Council. The Antioch Christians selected a group of leaders to attend the meeting in Jerusalem. Paul, Barnabas, and Titus were sent. As Paul and his companions traveled 300 miles back to Jerusalem, they visited and encouraged several fellow Christians along the way.

2. The Testimonies (vv. 6-11)

The Jerusalem Council met in 48 or 49 A.D. Three major sessions took place. The first was a public session. As soon as Paul and the other representatives from Antioch arrived, they were received open-heartedly by the apostles, James, and the group of Jewish Christians there (Acts 15:4). Paul and Barnabas gave their missionary report and affirmed God's work among the Gentiles. However, the Judaizers were present and interrupted the testimony service and began to argue with them (v. 5). This meeting had to be adjourned because of the heated discussion.

The second meeting took place in private. Paul and Barnabas met alone with the Jewish leaders (v. 6). In this private meeting, many Israelites who were followers of law referred to the Old Testament. They did not understand how Jesus Christ fulfilled them. They insisted that the Jewish laws were still binding and valid.

Paul used the Old Testament as well. Paul was very learned in the Scriptures, and he himself had seriously acknowledged them all his life. At the same time, Paul had witnessed first-hand God's transforming power in the lives of the Gentiles as they placed their faith in Christ alone.

Peter backed up Paul's point by telling about his experience with Cornelius and his household. God had commanded Peter to accept the Gentiles and then manifested the Holy Spirit to these uncircumcised people the same way He did with the Jews on the Day of Pentecost. Peter also pointed out that the traditional rules of conduct were a heavy burden to the Jews; he did not want this same burden around the neck of the Gentiles. Peter echoed Paul's conclusion: by grace of the

Lord Jesus Christ alone we are all saved! After Peter spoke, it seemed the arguments of the Judaizers were quieted.

Also in this private session there was a discussion of the Gentiles contributing to the poor Christians in Jerusalem. The Christians in Jerusalem were suffering because of the persecution. Many of them had suffered major material (houses, business, etc.) loss because of their new found faith. The apostles asked that the Gentiles remember the poor brethren and help them financially. This would also contribute to a tighter bond of unity between the two groups. Paul eagerly agreed to this request (Galatians 2:10) and later it was fulfilled (1 Corinthians 16:1-3; 2 Corinthians 8-9).

3. The Resolution (vv. 12-15, 19-20)

The third meeting of the Jerusalem Council brought the whole church together again. This was to be the summary and the final conclusion. Paul and Barnabas gave a report again regarding their successful ministry among the pagan Gentiles. This time the Judaizers did not interrupt their presentation.

James, the chairman of the meeting, stood up to summarize what had been said and stated the resolution of the conflict. He referred back to Peter's testimony about Cornelius's new birth. God had spoken, the new birth could take place without the ritual of circumcision (Acts 15:13-14). James's next point was from the Old Testament. God said, "That the residue of men (non-Jews) might seek after the Lord and all the Gentiles upon whom My Name is called." It was God's plan and intention for the Gentiles to seek after Him and come to know Him.

He made it clear that there would be no more attempts to impose the Jewish rite of circumcision, Jewish traditions, and dietary laws on the Gentile converts.

The way of salvation was the same for the circumcised Jew or the heathen Gentile. God's gift of grace was undeserved by both but made available by God to the believer who chooses to accept that Christ died and rose again to atone for their sins.

Although James had made these clear and conclusive statements, there were still problems to resolve. What was supposed to happen when Jews and non-Jews ate together? What about the ungodly habits of some of the Gentiles? James, therefore, went on to make an appeal to the Gentiles for the sake of unity among the new converts. He asked that the Gentiles refrain from eating "food offered to idols," "meat with blood," and "animals killed by strangulation." James also said that the Gentiles should keep themselves from sexual immorality.

It was also decided that some men from the group would be the spokesmen and take a letter back to Antioch, along with Paul and Barnabas, to let the church know what was decided. This meeting had great theological significance. Had the leaders of the church agreed to the Judaizers' demands for the Gentiles to be circumcised, the truth of the Gospel message would have been destroyed. We are saved by God's grace through faith. "It is not the result of your own efforts, but God's gift, so that no one can boast about it" (Ephesians 2:8-9, Good News Bible).

SEARCH THE SCRIPTURES

1. _____ _____ was held to resolve issues concerning the Gentiles and the Jewish law. (Acts 15:1-2)

2. _____ testified about the coming of the Holy Spirit upon the Gentile believers. (vv. 7-9)

3. _____ and _____ gave a report about their work among the Gentiles. (v. 12)

4. _____ gave the concluding summary and decision about the matter. (v. 13)

5. Guidelines were given to the Gentiles concerning _____ and _____ . (vv. 19-20)

DISCUSS THE MEANING

1. Why did the Judaizers raise such an uproar about what was being taught to the Gentiles?

2. What was Peter's stand about the matter? Why was he so firm in his belief?

3. What was concluded about the Gentiles and salvation?

4. List the four items James asked the Gentiles to refrain from doing for the sake of unity in the Christian church. Why were these chosen?

LESSON IN OUR SOCIETY

You have to be baptized. You have to speak in tongues. You have to go through catechism classes. You have to take the sacraments. You have to keep the Ten Commandments. These are "add on's" in our society's religious system. Down through history, various denominations have added on religious rules. If the rule or several rules were not kept, many people believed they would not make it into heaven.

But it must be remembered that salvation is by grace. There is nothing anyone can do to qualify for heaven, and there is nothing that God requires other than placing trust in Jesus Christ and His finished work on Calvary that paid for our individual sins.

MAKE IT HAPPEN

Paul and his companions were very upset and moved to action when they realized that people were adding to the Gospel by teaching that there were other things one must do in order to be saved. When was the last time you heard someone talk like that? What did you do? What should you have done? How will you take a stand for the truth?

FOLLOW THE SPIRIT

What God wants me to do:

_____
_____

REMEMBER YOUR THOUGHTS

Special insights you learned:

_____
_____

MORE LIGHT ON THE TEXT
Acts 15:1-2; 6-15; 19-20

15:1 And certain men which came down from Judaea taught the brethren, and said, Except ye be circumcised after the manner of Moses, ye cannot be saved.

Some say these certain men were (1) proselytes to the Jewish religion, (2) the Pharisees, or (3) priests who were obedient to the Jewish faith. Whoever they were, they were recent Jewish converts to Christianity.

The men arrived in Antioch from Judea pretending to be sent by the apostles at Jerusalem. They came to Antioch (because it was the headquarters of those who preached to the Gentiles). They preached a doctrine different from what Paul, Barnabas, and the other leaders of Christianity taught. Their message to the Gentile Christians at Antioch obligated them to submit to circumcision and the Jewish ceremonial law. They taught that unless people were circumcised after the manner of Moses and bound themselves to all the observances of the Jewish ceremonial law, they were not saved.

Although many of the Jews embraced Christianity, they did not want to release their Jewish heritage and customs. Not only did they continue to observe Jewish rituals and laws, but they also wanted to impose these requirements on the Gentile Christians.

Tradition can be hard to break. "We've always done it this way. If it works, why are we changing?" The need for change often forces us to consider whether or not our actions have been wrong in the past. Most people do not want to admit the error of their ways. Change does not necessarily mean that we were wrong, it could mean that God is introducing a new idea.

God is the same yesterday, today, and forever (Hebrews 13:8). Yet, God is forever revealing His will and power to us in various ways. For God says, "Behold, I will do a new thing" (Isaiah 43:19a).

Sometimes, we suffer disappointment when events do not occur as we envision them. Perhaps this is what the Jewish Christian converts were experiencing. They expected the Messiah to return to the Jews and set up His temporal kingdom in favor of the Jewish nation. Yet, salvation through Christ is offered to the Gentiles, and Christ's kingdom is established in the hearts of both Jewish and Gentile believers. What a disappointment this must have been to some Jewish Christians.

2 When therefore Paul and Barnabas had no small dissension and disputation with them, they determined that Paul and Barnabas, and certain other of them, should go up to Jerusalem unto the apostles and elders about this question.

Paul, Barnabas, and the other leaders of the Gentile Christians, would not see the truth betrayed or distorted. They taught: (1) Christ came to free us from the yoke of ceremonial law, (2) Jews and Gentiles were united in Christ, and (3) salvation comes by belief in Jesus Christ. Baptism and the Lord's Supper were the two ritual instructions given to the church. Paul and the other leaders could not bear to hear of circumcising the Gentile converts because God had already affirmed the acceptance of Gentiles by filling them with the Holy Spirit.

Those members of the house of Israel who came with this doctrine claimed they came at the directions of the apostles and elders at Jerusalem. Therefore, the church at Antioch appointed Paul and Barnabas to go the Jerusalem to present this case to the apostles and elders. Since the apostles and elders established Christianity in Jerusalem, their opinion in this matter was very crucial. It was necessary to hear what they had to say in order to put an end to the controversy, and to silence these teachers and false apostles.

15:6 And the apostles and elders came together for to consider of this matter.

At the Jerusalem Council, the apostles and elders gathered by consent to consider this matter. They came to reason together. They did not give their judgment separately or rashly, but they considered the matter. The apostles, although of higher authority than the elders, did not exclude the elders.

Here is an example to the leaders of churches, pastors in particular, when disputes arise (and they will): come together in solemn meeting for mutual advice and encouragement. Bring all together to present their positions so that the church can act in concert and come to the best decision for all involved.

7 And when there had been much disputing, Peter rose up, and said unto them, Men and brethren, ye know that a good while ago God made choice among us, that the Gentiles by my mouth should hear the word of the Gospel, and believe.

After much discussion on both sides, the

Apostle Peter stood to address the group. Peter was the first apostle to preach to the Gentiles (the conversion of Cornelius: Acts 10:1; 11:18). He reminded them of his call and commission to preach the Gospel to the Gentiles. When Peter reported his experience to the Jerusalem church, everyone rejoiced and no one said a word about circumcision (see Acts 11:1-18).

8 And God, which knoweth the hearts, bare them witness, giving them the Holy Ghost, even as he did unto us;

Peter recounted his vision while in Joppa (Acts 11:5-10). He explained to the council that afterwards, three men (Gentiles) from Caesarea came to the house of Joppa where he lodged. The Holy Spirit instructed Peter to accompany them without hesitation. He and six other men accompanied the three men. They went into Cornelius's house.

Cornelius, a Gentile, described to Peter how an angel of the Lord instructed him to send men to Joppa for Simon Peter. The angel told the man that Peter would explain a method by which he and his entire household would be saved. As Peter began to speak, the Holy Spirit fell on the Gentile man and the others, just as He did in the upper room (Acts 2:1-4).

"God knows the heart of a person" is an expression used by Luke in association with Peter in Acts 1:24. We often judge a person by their outer appearance, but God looks on the inside, at the heart. "As a person thinks in his heart, so is he" (Proverbs 23:7a).

God bore witness to the Gentiles by giving them the Holy Spirit, the same Spirit that Peter and the others received on the Day of Pentecost. To whom God gives the Holy Spirit, God bears witness that they belong to God. Hence, the Holy Spirit of promise (John 14:16), the Spirit of God, seals us to God. The Spirit of God is available to everyone who is in Christ.

Let us not confuse the giving or filling of the Holy Ghost with the baptism of the Holy Spirit. In John 20:22, Jesus breathed on them, filled them and said, "Receive the Holy Spirit." Baptism of the Holy Spirit means the Holy Spirit is the one performing the baptism (Acts 1:5),

and that one is baptized by the Holy Spirit, and filled with the Spirit of God. In Acts 2:7, 11:15-18, 19:1-7, we witness a special appearance of the Holy Spirit.

9 And put no difference between us and them, purifying their hearts by faith.

Peter went on to say that since God did not make a difference between the Gentiles and the Jews, they should not make any difference. The Gentiles were as welcome to the grace of Jesus Christ as were the Jews.

Paul reiterated this point to the church at Galatia. God is not a respecter of persons. He would not deny anyone who believes in Jesus Christ access to the Holy Spirit (Galatians 3:28). There is no distinction between Christians in Christ. One group of Christians should not flaunt their customs over another.

The Gentiles now had direct access to God by the purification of their hearts by faith in Jesus Christ. By faith, the heart is purified. By faith, we are justified, made right with God. By faith, the sanctification process begins.

10 Now therefore why tempt ye God, to put a yoke upon the neck of the disciples, which neither our fathers nor we were able to bear?

He reproved those who wanted to bring the Gentiles under the obligation of the law of Moses. In his indictment against the Jewish leaders he asked, "Why tempt God by calling into question what God has already settled?" You could not keep the laws, and neither could our forefathers. Now you want to impose this impossible task on the Gentiles?"

The Jewish ceremonial law was a heavy yoke that no one could keep. Jesus Christ came to set us free from the yoke of the law. Jesus said, "Take my yoke upon you and learn of me, for I am gentle and humble in heart, and you will find rest for your souls" (Matthew 11:29, NIV).

11 But we believe that through the grace of the Lord Jesus Christ we shall be saved, even as they.

Peter reminds them that salvation comes by the grace of Jesus Christ, not by circumcision or uncircumcision, but by grace through faith in Jesus Christ. This was the same doctrine the Gentiles practiced and believed.

12 Then all the multitude kept silence, and gave audience to Barnabas and Paul, declaring what miracles and wonders God had wrought among the Gentiles by them.

"Then the whole assembly remained silent, and they listened attentively as Paul and Barnabas rehearsed signs and wonders God had performed through them among the Gentiles" (Acts 15:12, Amp.).

Their accounts are found in Acts 14 and 15. During these occasions, their preaching of the pure Gospel did not include the Law of Moses. To include the Law of Moses now would subvert what God had already done.

13 And after they had held their peace, James answered, saying, Men and brethren, hearken unto me:

When Paul and Barnabas finished talking, James, the brother of Jesus, and the leader of the Jerusalem church, stood up to speak. He waited until Paul and Barnabas finished. He did not interrupt them. He appealed to the good nature of all the men present by calling them his brothers.

14 Simeon hath declared how God at the first did visit the Gentiles, to take out of them a people for his name.

James referenced Peter's account concerning the conversion of the Gentiles. He concluded that God visited the Gentiles in Caesarea. God redeemed those who were not Jews. God called a group of people who would glorify His name. It did not matter to God if these people were Jew or Gentile. If it does not matter to God, why should it matter to us?

15 And to this agree the words of the prophets;

James confirmed his statement with an Old Testament quotation (Amos 9:11-12). The Amos passage refers to a time when God would deal directly with Gentiles and bring them salvation.

Since Gentiles were now believing in Christ, Amos' prophecy was being fulfilled.

15:19 Wherefore my sentence is, that we trouble not them, which from among the Gentiles are turned to God:

James' judgment represented the conclusion of the general church. He gave his opinion that obstacles should not be put in the way of those Gentiles who turn to God.

20 But we write unto them, that they abstain from pollutions of idols, and from fornication, and from things strangled, and from blood.

It would please the Jews if the Gentile converts abstained from fellowshiping with idolaters or worshiping of idols, and from eating meat that has been strangled and tasting of blood, that is, meat sacrificed to idols. The precept of abstaining from eating meat strangled and tasting of blood was given to Noah before the Mosaic Law (Genesis 9:4).

DAILY BIBLE READINGS

M: Paul and Barnabas in Jerusalem
Acts 15:1-5

T: Questions and Responses
Acts 15:6-12

W: James Cites Scripture
Acts 15:13-18

T: Decision About Gentiles
Acts 15:19-29

F: Response to the Letter
Acts 15:30-35

S: Paul and Barnabas Separate
Acts 15:36-41

S: Timothy Joins Paul and Silas
Acts 16:1-5

TEACHING TIPS

May 20
Bible Study Guide 12

1. Words You Should Know

A. Baptized (Acts 16:15) Greek *baptizo*—To immerse, submerge for religious reasons. Token of purification from sin and spiritual pollution. Baptism symbolizes union with Christ.

B. Saved (v. 30) Greek *sozo*—To deliver from danger or suffering. Salvation is granted to those who believe in the Lord Jesus Christ and the redemptive work which He performed on our behalf. God also delivers from the bondage of sin.

2. Teacher Preparation

A. To gain more knowledge of Lydia, take time to read about her in a book on women in the Bible.

B. Read over the FOCAL VERSES, BACK-GROUND, and the IN DEPTH commentary to get a good understanding of the course of events.

C. Jot down your answers to SEARCH THE SCRIPTURES and DISCUSS THE MEANING questions.

D. Materials Needed: a board or newsprint and a Bible.

3. Starting the Lesson

A. Before the students arrive, write AT-A-GLANCE outline on the board. Then open the class with a prayer which includes the LESSON AIM.

B. Before you begin the lesson, read the IN FOCUS story aloud to the class.

C. Ask someone to read the LESSON IN OUR SOCIETY. Briefly discuss what "church burnout" is and why people have it.

4. Getting into the Lesson

A. Break the class into two groups. Have one group act out the scene at the river with the women and the other group act out the scene with the jailer. If possible, let the women in the class do the first one and the men in the class do the second.

B. After the skit, have them answer the SEARCH THE SCRIPTURES questions.

5. Relating the Lesson to Life

A. Solicit answers to the DISCUSS THE MEANING questions adding relative comments.

B. Ask the students to recall your earlier question from the LESSON IN OUR SOCIETY section. Ask the class to tell what is, in their opinion, the number one reason for "church burnout."

C. Emphasize the fact that Paul followed God's instructions. There were plenty of needs all around him, and he could have went his own way and become burned out and tired. But Paul went God's way, therefore he had the energy, wisdom, and knowledge to accomplish God's will.

6. Arousing Action

A. Have the students read the MAKE IT HAPPEN section and brainstorm about what they plan to do differently—this week, this month, this year.

B. Close the class with prayer asking God to strengthen the class and their efforts to put God's word into action in their lives.

WORSHIP GUIDE

For the Superintendent or Teacher
Theme: Reaching into Macedonia
Theme Song: "People Need the Lord"
Scripture: Acts 16:9-15, 27-33
Song: "Thank You Lord, for Saving My Soul"
Devotional Thought: Creator God, thank You for our salvation. May our hearts overflow with gratitude and cause us to reach out to others, but only as You lead and guide us. Amen.

REACHING INTO MACEDONIA

Bible Background • ACTS 16:6-40
Printed Text • ACTS 16:9-15, 27-33
Devotional Reading • PHILIPPIANS 1:3-11

LESSON AIM

By the end of this lesson, students should be able to relate the events surrounding the conversion of Lydia and the Philippian jailer, and have a clearer understanding of how God meets the needs of people and how he desires to use each of us.

KEEP IN MIND

"Come over to Macedonia, and help us" (Acts 16:9b).

FOCAL VERSES

Acts 16:9 And a vision appeared to Paul in the night; There stood a man of Macedonia, and prayed him, saying, Come over into Macedonia, and help us.

10 And after he had seen the vision, immediately we endeavored to go into Macedonia, assuredly gathering that the Lord had called us for to preach the gospel unto them.

11 Therefore loosing from Troas, we came with a straight course to Samothracia, and the next day to Neapolis;

12 And from thence to Philippi, which is the chief city of that part of Macedonia, and a colony: and we were in that city abiding certain days.

13 And on the Sabbath we went out of the city by a river side, where prayer was wont to be made; and we sat down, and spake unto the women which resorted thither.

14 And a certain woman named Lydia, a seller of purple, of the city of Thyatira, which worshipped God, heard us: whose heart the Lord opened, that she attended unto the things which were spoken of Paul.

15 And when she was baptized, and her house-

LESSON OVERVIEW

LESSON AIM
KEEP IN MIND
FOCAL VERSES
IN FOCUS
THE PEOPLE, PLACES, AND TIMES
BACKGROUND
AT-A-GLANCE
IN DEPTH
SEARCH THE SCRIPTURES
DISCUSS THE MEANING
LESSON IN OUR SOCIETY
MAKE IT HAPPEN
FOLLOW THE SPIRIT
REMEMBER YOUR THOUGHTS
MORE LIGHT ON THE TEXT
DAILY BIBLE READINGS

hold, she besought us, saying, If ye have judged me to be faithful to the Lord, come into my house, and abide there. And she constrained us.

16:27 And the keeper of the prison awaking out of his sleep, and seeing the prison doors open, he drew out his sword, and would have killed himself, supposing that the prisoners had been fled.

28 But Paul cried with a loud voice, saying, Do thyself no harm: for we are all here.

29 Then he called for a light, and sprang in, and came trembling, and fell down before Paul and Silas,

30 And brought them out, and said, Sirs, what must I do to be saved?

31 And they said, Believe on the Lord Jesus Christ, and thou shalt be saved, and thy house.

32 And they spake unto him the word of the Lord, and to all that were in his house.

33 And he took them the same hour of the night, and washed their stripes; and was baptized, he and all his, straightway.

IN FOCUS

I have always been fascinated by the biblical character, Lydia. She stands out because she was not a typical housewife; rather, the Bible portrays her as a powerful, successful, single, wealthy, businesswoman. This describes many women in our day. In fact, just recently I met a young woman named Lydia. I could not believe how similar she was to the biblical character in the Book of Acts.

MAY 20TH

In high school she took a real interest and enjoyment in the area of business. She went on to get her MBA in college, and after graduation worked only a short time in a major corporation before opening her own business. This modern-day Lydia is married and since her husband is a college professor who has no interest in business, she completely manages her own business affairs. She won't reveal to anyone how much she is worth financially, but it is obvious from the size of her home, the make of her car, and her constant financial generosity that she is most likely a millionaire.

Just like Lydia in the Bible, this modern-day Lydia not only has one large home in which she lives, but she owns several others. She uses them for places of refuge for women who are going through a difficult time after a separation, divorce, or death of a loved one. They go there for counseling and rest, going home eventually to better face their challenges with renewed vigor. The modern-day Lydia is a strong Christian woman who takes her faith seriously and challenges everyone around her to do the same.

Today as we will learn more about the biblical Lydia, hopefully more modern-day Lydias will come forth in this generation and help those in need spiritually and financially.

THE PEOPLE, PLACES, AND TIMES

Lydia. A Gentile who was a worshiper of the true, living God. A native of Thyatira of western Asia Minor, who presently was conducting her business and living in Philippi, a city east of Macedonia. Lydia's customers included Babylonian buyers who bought the purple cloth for temple curtains, costumes in which to dress their idols, and for members of the Roman imperial family who wore the imperial purple on state occasions. This made Lydia a very popular and wealthy woman. No husband was mentioned, so she may have been a widow who inherited her husband's business.

Macedonia. Philippi was the chief city of Macedonia. After a significant battle in 167 B.C., the Romans divided Macedonia into four politically separated parts. Philippi was the first part. It was largely inhabited by Romans. The city was located near chief rivers and connected with coastal cities by several good roads; therefore, trade was enjoyed and was financially lucrative.

BACKGROUND

Following the historic Jerusalem Council (Acts 15) in Jerusalem, several leaders returned to Antioch to share the decisions of the counsel meeting. They let the Gentiles know that the leaders of the church did not believe it was necessary for them to be circumcised and follow Jewish law. Their personal acceptance of Christ alone was sufficient to make them right and pleasing before God. Paul and Barnabas stayed in Antioch for a while teaching the Christians there and drawing new converts.

After a while, Paul and Barnabas decided to take the news about the Jerusalem Council to the newly-established churches they had planted in southern Galatia. At this point, however, a sharp disagreement arose between Paul and Barnabas concerning John Mark (Acts 15:36-39). John Mark had abandoned them on an early missionary trip, and Paul did not want to take him along. Barnabas disagreed. The two men decided to split up and travel in different directions.

Barnabas ended up taking John Mark with him. Paul picked up a new companion, Silas (his Jewish name, and Silvanus, his Roman name). He was a Roman citizen and member of the Jerusalem church. He first appeared as one of the two messengers sent by Jerusalem leaders to carry the letter containing the results of the Jerusalem Council's decree to Antioch (Acts 15:22, 32).

AT-A-GLANCE

1. Paul's Call to Macedonia
(Acts 16:9-12)
2. Paul's Ministry to Lydia (vv. 13-15)
3. Paul's Ministry to the Jailer (vv. 27-33)

IN DEPTH

1. Paul's Call to Macedonia (Acts 16:9-12)

Paul and Silas were sent out from the church in

Antioch with the letter containing the decisions of the Jerusalem Council. Paul wanted to go back to the churches he had started in southern Galatia and report the news to the Gentiles. Before the Council's decision, there had been much turmoil and disagreement among some of the Jewish leaders and those spreading the Gospel to the Gentiles. It would be a relief for the Gentiles to know they were no longer pressured into being circumcised and following Jewish law as a requirement of their faith in Christ.

Instead of traveling by boat, Paul and Silas decided to walk from Syria to Cilicia. They read the letter there and moved on to Paul's hometown, Tarsus. After leaving Tarsus they climbed the steep narrow gorge leading to Derbe. This was the first city in southern Galatia where Paul preached. From there they moved on to Lystra, where Paul had been stoned and where Timothy and his family had been converted. Paul added Timothy to his missionary team at this point.

After visiting the converts in South Galatia and seeing how wonderfully God was working among the new churches, Paul desired to continue westward to Ephesus. Surely God wanted him to strengthen the converts there with the letter from the Jerusalem Council and minister in the same way he had done in Galatia. However, Paul was forbidden, in some way, by the Holy Spirit to speak the word in Asia. They traveled northward and tried to go into Bithynia. Again, the Spirit didn't permit them to go in and minister there, so they ended up in Troas, uncertain of which way to go.

While in Troas, Paul had a vision. He saw a Macedonian man standing and calling to him, "Come over to Macedonia and help us." Paul now understood why God had blocked their way. God had a better plan and purpose for their ministry at this time. What an opportunity Paul would have missed if he insisted on going his own way. The church in Macedonia became one of the most importune achievements of Paul's ministry.

Immediately, Paul obeyed the leading of the Lord and sought passages in order to cross over to Macedonia. The "we" in verse 10 is Luke's, the writer of the Book of Acts; he was present with Paul, Silas, and Timothy in Macedonia and was an eyewitness to the events which took place there.

2. Paul's Ministry to Lydia (vv. 13-15)

It took from two to five days for Paul and his team to travel from Troas to Macedonia. The first colony they visited in Macedonia was Philippi. For once they were not greeted by hostile Jews; in fact, there was no synagogue there at all. It took ten Jewish male believers to be a recognized synagogue. Obviously the Jewish population and the desire to worship the One True God was extremely low. Jews had been expelled from Rome under the ruler Claudius, hence the low Jewish population.

The only Jewish worship Paul heard about was a small group of women who met down by the river of Gangites, a mile from the wall of the city. They were probably all proselytes, Gentiles who had embraced the Jewish God and followed their laws and traditions.

It can be assumed that this little prayer group, of which Lydia was a member, had asked for guidance. God had sent Paul in response to their prayers. Although they were small in number and no men were present, they were strong in the Spirit of God. Imagine the surprise and excitement of these women as Paul and the three other men approached their place of worship! The men introduced themselves as teachers and took turns instructing the women. It must have amazed the Jewish women when these four missionaries did not despise them as women or even preach a sermon to them, but instead "sat down and talked with them" of the things concerning Christ.

Lydia was a Gentile convert, who worshiped the One True God of the Jews. Lydia was a wealthy, successful business woman. She owned a purple dye industry. No doubt most of her Gentile friends and acquaintances were worshiping other gods. The god in Thyatira was a sun god called Tyrimnas, but it had no hold on Lydia. She had traveled to the river on the Sabbath and was seeking to know the true and living God. Lydia had a longing to know the truth.

The phrase "kept hearing" implies that Lydia may not have been converted on the first Sabbath. However, she listened with an open heart and she eventually received the truth. Lydia became the first convert in Europe. Not only was she baptized, but her entire household was baptized as well.

Lydia invited the four missionaries to stay in her home. Paul hesitated at first, but Lydia "constrained" them. Her home became the first church at Philippi. It was here that this church was born and grew. Paul later referred to the Philippian church as his "joy and crown" (Philippians 4:1). Lydia also became one of Paul's financial supporters and was a loyal helper in his ministry.

3. Paul's Ministry to the Philippian Jailer (vv. 27-33)

The Spirit of God was moving mightily in Philippi. Only in the letter to the Philippians does Paul so freely pour out his innermost feelings with joy, thankfulness, and deep affection. His initial contact with Philippi was a very pleasant and rewarding experience.

However, whenever the Holy Spirit powerfully moves among men and women, there will always be a counter-attack from the powers of evil. While in Philippi, Satan used a girl under demonic influence, who was being used for profit, to shout after Paul and his companions, "These men are the servants of the most high God, which show unto us the way of salvation" (v. 17).

Day after day, this girl continued to shout after Paul and his companions. Paul recognized that this was not God's voice, but instead was from an evil source. Paul rebuked the demons and set the girl free. Her owners, seeing their profit was lost, were very upset. They incited a mob who accused Paul of turning the city from the worship of idols and causing disloyalty to the Roman government.

Paul and Silas were the victims of a vicious attack. There was a trial, and the two men were not given the opportunity to defend themselves. Paul and Silas were stripped of their clothing (a terrible humiliation to a Jew), beaten with rods, flung bleeding and exhausted into a prison, their feet shackled down with iron cuffs.

They encouraged each other and the prisoners around them by singing and praising God out loud. They felt it a privilege to suffer for the cause of Christ. Suddenly, around midnight there was an earthquake. The prison was shaken, the doors were opened wide, and the chains fell loose from the walls. This was a perfect time for the prisoners to escape, but not one attempted to run out. The jailer came running to the jail, assuming the prisoners had escaped, which would have meant certain death for him. Roman law dealt severely with any jailer who was unable to produce prisoners. The jailer would have been promptly executed. As he drew his sword to take his own life, Paul shouted, "No! We are all here!" (v. 28)

The shock of the earthquake and the amazing conduct of the prisoners was enough for the jailer to realize that God was moving in this situation. After calling for a light and securing the other prisoners, the jailer fell down before Paul and Silas asking, "What shall I do to be saved?" (v. 30) The two men gladly told him that he must believe on the Lord Jesus Christ. The jailer and his entire household believed and were saved. The jailer demonstrated his inward change by tending to the wounds of Paul and Silas.

Acts chapter 16 ends on a positive note. The magistrates must have connected the earthquake to Paul and Silas and sent a message for them to be released. Paul wisely used this opportunity to protect the new believers and the Philippian church. He exposed the fact that he was a Roman citizen and had been beaten and imprisoned without a trial. The magistrates panicked and asked Paul and his companions to leave the city. This helped protect the new believers and gave a measure of freedom to the newly-formed church which met in Lydia's home.

When Paul, Silas, and Timothy moved on to the next city, Luke was left behind to continue to minister to the new converts. After this first experience and gradually over the years, the church in Philippi became most dear and precious to Paul's heart. He said in his letter to the Philippian church, "I thank my God upon every remembrance of you always in every prayer of mine for you all making request with joy, for your fellowship in the Gospel from the first day until now" (Philippians 1:3-5, NAS).

SEARCH THE SCRIPTURES

Match the person with the correct description.
1. Paul
a. Had a vision to go to Macedonia.
2. Silas

b. Came to Christ as a result of Paul's imprisonment.

3. The jailer

c. One of the first Christian converts in Macedonia.

4. Lydia

d. One of Paul's companions who was imprisoned with Paul.

DISCUSS THE MEANING

1. Why do you think God led Paul to Macedonia to the women at the river, but forbid him to go other places?

2. Compare and contrast the conversion of Lydia and the jailer. God uses a variety of ways to bring people to Himself. Describe other biblical and present-day examples of various ways that God works.

LESSON IN OUR SOCIETY

The term "burnout" is commonly used in our society. It means "to cease or stop operation." Those working in the social service field probably have large numbers of burnout victims. Dealing with people on a daily basis who have very little hope and many problems with few practical solutions can be exhausting. Even in the church, meeting the needs of families in the community can be overwhelming. In fact, the government is calling on the church to step up and meet more of the needs that welfare used to supply. This can be an overwhelming task, especially for a small church in a needy community.

We can study Paul's example to learn how to handle ourselves when there are pressing needs all around us and we are unsure which way to turn. Paul waited on clear direction from the Lord. He did not attempt to minister to everyone in need, only to those whom God specifically directed.

MAKE IT HAPPEN

Have you experienced "church burnout"? Are you trying to attend to as many needs as you possibly can? Maybe God is trying to show you a new way to minister, not just going wherever there is a need, but going only when God wants you to go. Maybe you need to take some time and evaluate your gifts, calling, and involvements, and seek God's direction for your life. We need to make sure that we are not going on our agenda but according to God's plans. How do you intend to make some changes in this area this week? This month? This year?

FOLLOW THE SPIRIT

What God wants me to do:

_____

_____

REMEMBER YOUR THOUGHTS

Special insights you learned:

_____

_____

MORE LIGHT ON THE TEXT
Acts 16:9-15, 27-33

16:9 And a vision appeared to Paul in the night; There stood a man of Macedonia, and prayed him, saying, Come over into Macedonia, and help us.

Paul had a vision while he was in Troas. Troas was a city in Mysia in northwest Asia Minor, on the shore of the Aegean Sea. This was Paul's first visit to Troas. Later, we learn that he visited Troas at least three times, but never stayed long.

In this vision a man from Macedonia appeared and asked him to come there to help them. Some say that this man was an angel (a messenger from God) sent by God to direct Paul to do the will of God.

What is the difference between a vision and a dream? A vision occurs when a person is awake; a dream occurs when a person is asleep.

How did Paul know this man was from Macedonia? Perhaps Paul knew by the man's dialect, his dress, or his habit.

The man asked Paul to come to Macedonia to help them, that is, "Come to preach the Gospel to us."

10 And after he had seen the vision, immediately we endeavoured to go into Macedonia, assuredly gathering that the Lord had called us for to preach the Gospel unto them.

Paul concluded that God wanted him to go to Macedonia to preach the Gospel to them. Paul knew that if God called them to go and preach the Gospel, God would direct them where to go. Ministers of the Gospel ought to be ready to go and preach the Gospel whenever, wherever, and to whomever God directs.

Scholars propose that this verse begins the first of the "we passages." They state that Luke (who is the credited writer of the Book of the Acts of the Apostles) joins Paul and Silas in Troas and travels with them to Macedonia.

11 Therefore loosing from Troas, we came with a straight course to Samothracia, and the next day to Neapolis;

Paul had the vision, but he told it to his companions who obligingly followed him. They traveled promptly to the island of Samothracia and stayed overnight. The next day, they sailed to Neapolis.

12 And from thence to Philippi, which is the chief city of that part of Macedonia, and a colony: and we were in that city abiding certain days.

Some scholars say that Philippi was the chief city in Macedonia. Still others say it was a "city of the first district of Macedonia, and a colony" of which Paul and his companions first came to after leaving Troas.

It was a Roman colony; mostly Romans populated it. Here they enjoyed self-government and the right of Roman citizenship. It was named after Philip, king of Macedon, the father of Alexander the Great.

Paul and his companions lodged in the city for several days. No one contacted them. In the past, when the apostles entered new territory, someone was there to meet and greet them (Acts 11).

13 And on the sabbath we went out of the city by a river side, where prayer was wont to be made; and we sat down, and spake unto the women which resorted thither.

There was no synagogue of the Jews in Philippi, and Paul and his companions dared not go to the idol temples of the Gentiles. On the Sabbath day (Sunday, the first day of the

week), they asked for the location of the place of worship of the true God.

The meeting took place at a river, located outside the city. At the riverside, they found a small group of proselytized women praying. The women were happy and thankful to have Paul give them a sermon.

Paul, Silas, and Luke sat down and instructed the women. They encouraged them to continue to worship the true God, but to worship God through the knowledge of Jesus Christ.

14 And a certain woman named Lydia, a seller of purple, of the city of Thyatira, which worshipped God, heard us: whose heart opened, that she attended unto the things which were spoken of Paul.

Lydia was one of the women in the group. She worshiped God according to the knowledge she had. When she heard the truth of the Gospel, the Lord opened her heart, and she wanted to know more about it. She was the first convert in Philippi.

She was born and raised in the city of Thyatira, which was located a far distance from Philippi. We are not sure why she now lived in Philippi. She could have moved there after getting married, or her profession could have brought her there. Whatever the reason, it was in God's divine providence that she hear the Word of the Lord through Paul's ministry.

Lydia sold purple-purple dye or purple cloth. This was a noble profession. This demonstrates that successful, professional people are also called to serve Christ. One should not let their professional responsibilities deter them from worship.

The women prayed, and God heard their prayers. Paul preached, and the women heard the Word of the Lord. Preaching is a part of worship. People are saved by the foolishness of preaching (I Corinthians 1:21). If we want God to hear and answer our prayers, we must hear and obey the Word of the Lord. Lydia heard the Word of the Lord, and the Lord opened her heart.

It is not enough to worship God the Father. We must believe in Jesus Christ the Son. Jesus said, "I am the way, the truth, and the life: no man or woman comes to the Father, but by me" (John 14:6). There is no coming to God, but through Jesus Christ as Mediator.

Only God can save us. God offers us salvation by His grace through faith in Jesus Christ. Jesus said, "Behold, I stand at the door, and knock: if any man hear my voice, and open the door, I will come in to him, and will sup with him, and he with me" (Revelation 3:20). Jesus stands at the door to our heart. It is up to each individual to open their heart to Jesus Christ. The opening is on the inside; the choice is ours.

God touched Lydia's heart, and she believed the Gospel of Jesus Christ. Matthew Henry says when a sinner is effectually persuaded to embrace Jesus Christ:

• The understanding is opened to receive divine light
• The will is opened to receive divine law
• The affection is opened to receive the divine love
• The ear is opened to receive God's Word
• The lips are opened in prayer
• The hands are opened in charity
• The steps are enlarged in all manner of Gospel obedience

15 And when she was baptized, and her household, she besought us, saying, If ye have judged me to be faithful to the Lord, come into my house, and abide there. And she constrained us.

Lydia's baptism and that of her household marked the beginning of the Philippian church.

She was very grateful to Paul, Silas, and Luke, and wanted to show her gratitude. Therefore, she invited them to stay in her home with her and her family. In addition, by having them stay with her, she could continue learning from them. They were at first reluctant because they did not want to impose. However, she insisted that they stay.

16:27 And the keeper of the prison awaking out of his sleep, and seeing the prison doors open, he drew out his sword, and would have killed himself, supposing that the prisoners had been fled.

Paul and Silas were thrown in prison after being beaten with rods for healing a demon-possessed slave girl (Acts 16:16-23). They were placed in the dungeon. Their punishers inflicted this treatment to discourage them from preaching the Gospel.

As believers in Jesus Christ, we will undergo persecution. However, Jesus comforts us by saying, "Blessed are you when people persecute you and say all kinds of evil things against you falsely on my account" (Matthew 5:11).

While Paul and Silas were in jail, they cheerfully started praying and singing hymns of praise to God (Acts 16:25). They prayed together. They sang together. They encouraged one another. As the praises went up, the blessings came down.

It does not matter what condition we find ourselves in, we should still praise God. There is no condition or problem too difficult for God. If we diligently serve, God will diligently supply our needs. Even in adversity, resolve to serve God. Tell yourself, "The enemy may try to slay me, but I will still trust and serve God."

At midnight, a violent earthquake shook the foundation of the prison. The prison doors flew open, and all the constraints that confined the prisoners fell off.

God signaled Paul and Silas through the earthquake. God assured them that He heard their praying and singing, and that He was with them. In our times of trouble, God is with us. Knowing that God is with us, we have the assurance that help is on the way. Hold on! Don't give up!

The earthquake awakened the sleeping jailer. Seeing the opened prison doors, he assumed the prisoners had all escaped. His job was to keep all the prisoners safely secured. Knowing he would probably die a humiliating death for his neglect, he drew his sword to commit suicide.

28 But Paul cried with a loud voice, saying, Do thyself no harm: for we are all here. 29 Then he called for a light, and sprang in, and came trembling, and fell down before Paul and Silas,

Paul shouted to the jailer, "Do not take your

life. We are all still here." The jailer called for a light and rushed in, and trembling and terrified he fell down before Paul and Silas" (Amplified Bible).

30 And brought them out, and said, Sirs, what must I do to be saved?

"He brought them out of the dungeon and said, Men, what is necessary for me to do that I may be saved?" (Amplified Bible) Notice how respectful he was to Paul and Silas. He fell down before them. Perhaps he now believed that they were indeed servants of the Most High God. He gave them a title of respect, "Sirs." He became concerned about his own salvation—"What must I do to be saved"? He realized that he must do something in order to correct his situation and obtain salvation.

Salvation is personal. Romans 10:10 says, "For with the heart man believeth unto righteousness; and with the mouth confession is made unto salvation." If you want salvation, then you must ask God for it personally–with your heart and your mouth. Salvation does not come via proxy. You must come in at the door—like the jailer.

31 And they said, Believe on the Lord Jesus Christ, and thou shalt be saved, and thy house.

"And they answered, Believe in the Lord Jesus Christ [give yourself up to Jesus Christ, take yourself out of your own keeping and entrust yourself into Jesus Christ's keeping] and you will be saved, [and this applies both to] you and your household as well" (Amp.).

Paul and Silas answered the jailer with the same directions they gave to the others, "Believe in the Lord Jesus Christ, and you shall be saved and your house." They did not ask him to apologize for beating them. They just answered his question. They were expedient in their response. They did not put him off until another time but quickly finished the work that God had begun in him. God touched his heart, the jailer's heart was opened, and Paul and Silas led him to Jesus Christ. Paul and Silas effectively demonstrated how ministers of the Gospel should lead others to Jesus Christ.

32 And they spake unto him the word of the Lord, and to all that were in his house.

"And they declared the Word of the Lord (the doctrine concerning the attainment through Christ of eternal salvation in the kingdom of God) to him and to all who were in his house" (v. 32, Amp.).

They taught him and his family the doctrine of Jesus Christ.

33 And he took them the same hour of the night, and washed their stripes; and was baptized, he and all his, straightway.

"And he took them the same hour of the night and bathed [them because of their bloody] wounds, and he was baptized immediately and all [the members of] his [household]" (Amp.).

The jailer showed respect to Paul and Silas by washing their wounds, taking them to his house, and he probably fed them. Immediately, the jailer and his family were baptized, and they became members of the church of Jesus Christ.

DAILY BIBLE READINGS

M: Paul's Vision About Macedonia
Acts 16:6-10

T: In Philippi: The Conversion of Lydia
Acts 16:11-15

W: Paul and Silas in Prison
Acts 16:16-24

T: Songs at Midnight
Acts 16:25-29

F: The Only Condition for Salvation
Acts 16:30-34

S: An Invitation to Abundant Life
Isaiah 55:1-11

S: Public Exoneration
Acts 16:35-40

TEACHING TIPS

May 27
Bible Study Guide 13

1. Words You Should Know

A. Humility (Acts 20:19) Greek *tapeino phrosune*—freedom from pride, meek, modest.

B. Serving (v. 19) Greek *douleuo*—To be in the position of a servant and acting accordingly. To be subject to or in bondage to.

C. Grievous Wolves (v. 29) Greek *lukoi Bareis*—used to describe heretical teachers who would enter and cause destruction in the church. Paul's concern was that these teachers would come from other cities and lead the local congregation astray, especially after he was no longer present.

2. Teacher Preparation

A. Read the Devotional Reading and Bible Background Scriptures in preparation for this lesson. Pray that God will make the subject of humility clear to you as you study.

B. Read and study the FOCAL VERSES. If you have a modern translation or an Amplified Bible, it could be helpful to read the verses from one of them.

C. Read THE PEOPLE, PLACES, AND TIMES and the BACKGROUND sections to give you a good framework for the lesson.

D. Materials Needed: Bibles, paper, and pencils. Optional Materials: a picture of a wolf and a sheep.

3. Starting the Lesson

A. Ask students to write down the characteristics of a wolf and a lamb. Talk briefly about the kind of personal characteristics and attitude God wants us to have. Compare them to those listed for each animal.

B. Read the IN FOCUS story and the LESSON AIM. Have a couple of students pray with these goals for the lesson in mind.

4. Getting into the Lesson

A. Have volunteers read the FOCAL VERSES. In order to understand the background and the people involved, assign one person to explain the BACKGROUND and another person to explain, THE PEOPLE, PLACES, AND TIMES.

B. Before opening the lesson discussion, read the IN DEPTH section. Then answer the SEARCH THE SCRIPTURES questions.

5. Relating the Lesson to Life

A. Allow plenty of time to answer DISCUSS THE MEANING questions. Encourage the students to be as honest and truthful as they can be.

B. Have one person read the LESSON IN OUR SOCIETY section aloud and another one explain what they believe it means.

6. Arousing Action

A. Ask each student to look at the list of words in the MAKE IT HAPPEN section, then circle the one which describes them and cross out those words that do not. Ask a few students to discuss any changes that may be needed in their lives and what they specifically plan to do.

403

SERVING WITH HUMILITY

Bible Background • ACTS 20:13-38
Printed Text • ACTS 20:18-32
Devotional Reading • CORINTHIANS 15:1-11

LESSON AIM

By the end of this lesson, students should be able to retell the specifics of Paul's humble visit to the elders of Ephesians, understand the importance of his humility, and strive to follow his example in their attitude and actions.

KEEP IN MIND

"But none of these things move me, neither count I my life dear unto myself, so that I might finish my course with joy, and the ministry, which I have received of the Lord Jesus, to testify the gospel of the grace of God (Acts 20:24).

FOCAL VERSES

Acts 20:18 And when they were come to him, he said unto them, Ye know, from the first day that I came into Asia, after what manner I have been with you at all seasons.

19 Serving the Lord with all humility of mind, and with many tears, and temptations, which befell me by the lying in wait of the Jews:

20 And how I kept back nothing that was profitable unto you, but have shewed you, and have taught you publickly, and from house to house,

21 Testifying both to the Jews, and also to the Greeks, repentance toward God, and faith toward our Lord Jesus Christ.

22 And now, behold, I go bound in the spirit unto Jerusalem, not knowing the things that shall befall me there:

23 Save that the Holy Ghost witnesseth in every city, saying that bonds and afflictions abide me.

24 But none of these things move me, neither

LESSON OVERVIEW

LESSON AIM
KEEP IN MIND
FOCAL VERSES
IN FOCUS
THE PEOPLE, PLACES,
AND TIMES
BACKGROUND
AT-A-GLANCE
IN DEPTH
SEARCH THE SCRIPTURES
DISCUSS THE MEANING
LESSON IN OUR SOCIETY
MAKE IT HAPPEN
FOLLOW THE SPIRIT
REMEMBER YOUR THOUGHTS
MORE LIGHT ON THE TEXT
DAILY BIBLE READINGS

count I my life dear unto myself, so that I might finish my course with joy, and the ministry, which I have received of the Lord Jesus, to testify the Gospel of the grace of God.

25 And now, behold, I know that ye all, among whom I have gone preaching the kingdom of God, shall see my face no more.

26 Wherefore I take you to record this day, that I am pure from the blood of all men.

27 For I have not shunned to declare unto you all the counsel of God.

28 Take heed therefore unto yourselves, and to all the flock, over the which the Holy Ghost hath made your overseers, to feed the church of God, which he hath purchased with his own blood.

29 For I know this, that after my departing shall grievous wolves enter in among you, not sparing the flock.

30 Also of your own selves shall men arise, speaking perverse things, to draw away disciples after them.

31 Therefore watch, and remember, that by the space of three years I ceased not to warn every one night and day with tears.

32 And now, brethren, I commend you to God, and to the word of his grace, which is able to build you up, and to give you an inheritance among all them which are sanctified.

IN FOCUS

Wolves are large, erect-eared, bushy-tailed, doglike predatory mammals. They are destructive to game and livestock and may on occasion, especially in a pack, attack man. Wolves are considered extremely dangerous, fierce animals. They spend most of their time hunting for food and eating anything they can catch. The wolf is a quick and clever animal who hunts mostly at night, roaming until they find their prey. When they catch an animal, they make it bleed until it is weakened, although they can kill an animal in a few minutes. Most people avoid wolves at all costs.

A sheep's nature is just the opposite of that of a wolf. Sheep are domestic mammals. They eat grain, hay, shrubs, and bark—never another animal. They flock together to make it hard for other animals to harm them. The sheep is a calm, peaceful animal. It is often one of the animals in a petting zoo for children because of its mild, non-aggressive manner. Their appearance is soft because of their woolly fur. They make a gentle murmuring sound. Sheep who are left on their own are defenseless and timid. A shepherd is needed to care for the sheep.

Today's lesson examines Paul's encouragement to the elders to become humble like shepherds who protect the church from the wolves (false teachers). Hopefully, our attitudes and actions are more sheep-like than wolf-like.

THE PEOPLE, PLACES, AND TIMES

Asia. Ephesus was a principal Roman city of Asia. It was both a strategic commercial city and a major religious center famous for its magnificent temple of Diana. The temple of Diana was considered to be one of the seven wonders of the world. The practice of magic and the local economy were related to this temple. Paul remained in Ephesus for three years on his third missionary journey. The word was spread throughout that region. Paul's ministry hurt the sale of magical items and images which lead to a huge uproar. After this, Paul left and went to Macedonia and returned only for a brief visit with the elders several miles outside the city. Paul's letter to the Ephesian church was written while Paul was imprisoned in Rome.

Elders. A name given to the leaders of the church. Paul describes their function as guardians, overseers, or bishops of the church. Their task was to care for the church. The word "elder" was often used by Paul in reference to himself.

BACKGROUND

Paul finished writing the book of Romans at a friend's home in Corinth in the spring of 58 A.D. After completing his writing, he collected a contribution from all the Gentile churches throughout the region for the poor among the Christian Jews of Jerusalem (Romans 15:25-28). Paul planned to take this contribution back to Jerusalem in time for Passover.

As Paul journeyed to Jerusalem, he went back through the Macedonian cities, along the Asian ports, and then through Syria and Caesarea and visited the various congregations along the way. Paul knew this was his final journey. He was certain that either death or prison would put a halt to his traveling evangelistic ministry. The Holy Spirit had already revealed that his future would be filled with persecution and hardships (Acts 20:23). Therefore, his visits had a sense of urgency and his words and actions had a final, farewell tone. Paul delivered crucial messages, touching last appeals, and shed many tears. On several occasions, such as his visit to the elders in Ephesus, there were desperate attempts by those who loved him to keep him from going to Jerusalem. But in spite of what Paul knew he would ultimately have to face, he continued on.

Paul did not make this journey back to Jerusalem alone. There were at least eight men who represented several of the Gentile churches traveling with Paul: Sopater, Aristarchus, and Secundus (Macedonia), Gaius (Galatia), Timothy (Lystra), Tychicus and Trophimus (Asia), and Luke. Seven of the men sailed to Troas and met

AT-A-GLANCE

1. **Paul's Past Record** (Acts 20:18-21)
2. **Paul's Future Afflictions** (vv. 22-24)
3. **Paul's Present Exhortation** (vv. 25-32)

Paul there. In the meantime, Paul visited Macedonia with Luke. The company of men made Miletus their next stop. When Paul arrived there, he called the elders of Ephesus to come and meet him. He made one of his best final exhortations at this stop.

IN DEPTH

1. Paul's Past Record (Acts 20:18-21)

On Paul's way to Jerusalem to the feast of Pentecost, he desired to visit the church at Ephesus. As he got close to the city, he decided not to go all the way in and meet with the congregation there. Paul loved the Ephesian church so much that he knew if he went into the city of Ephesus and spent time with the converts, he would be tempted to stay a long time and might not make it to Jerusalem in time for the feast. He was also concerned that the ship he was on might set sail without him, and he did not want to take that risk. So Paul sent a message to Ephesus (30 miles away) and asked the elders to meet him at Miletus.

This meeting with the Ephesian elders at Miletus provides us with one of Paul's most moving passages. Paul talked about his ministry among the Ephesians, and he challenged the leadership to remember how he had lived and served among them.

The first characteristic of ministry among the Ephesian church was humility. Paul did not think more highly of himself than he ought and he refused to claim anything to himself (Romans 12:3). He knew without a doubt that it was the Holy Spirit who operated through him in order for the Lord's work to be accomplished.

The second characteristic Paul points out was his personal concern for the believers. The tears he displayed demonstrated his care and compassion for the converts. For a man to allow his deeply felt emotions to produce a show of tears was a true demonstration of Paul's humility and earnest love for the believers there.

The third characteristic Paul points out was patience with fortitude. Paul's entire ministry was filled with one trial and challenge after the other. The Jews severely persecuted Paul and vigorously opposed him. Yet, he continued to work despite the temptation to give up.

The fourth major characteristic Paul displayed in his ministry was diligence. He never watered down his message or met with Jews or Gentiles in secret hiding places. He went from house to house preaching and teaching the truth, or he presented the Gospel in a public hall. Paul did not fear the Jews who were constantly coming against him. He declared openly the truth about the need for one to turn from their sins to God and believe in the Lord Jesus. Paul defied the odds and stood tall against the opposition. Paul desired to "do his work as unto the Lord," joyously and triumphantly.

2. Paul's Future Afflictions (vv. 22-24)

Paul was making this trip to Jerusalem out of necessity. The Scripture says Paul was constrained by the Holy Spirit to go (Acts 16:6; 19:21). Even though the Holy Spirit led him to go, it was also a trip full of uncertainty. The Spirit did not reveal to Paul the exact purpose of the journey or let him know what specifically would happen there. The Holy Spirit did let him know, however, that persecution and imprisonment were in his future. Whether these events would lead to Paul's death, he did not know.

However, the thought of these life threatening situations does not cause Paul to hesitate. Paul was unstoppable. He continued to move forward, determined to finish the work God had given him to do. He was prepared for whatever God had for him. On several occasions, Paul declared that he did not regard his own life as something precious to be preserved. What held utmost importance to him was that God's message of the grace given through Jesus Christ be spread all over. Paul, as well as the other disciples, believed that once the known world was evangelized, Jesus would return. So each one of them worked with fervence to see that the Good News went out to the ends of the earth.

3. Paul's Present Exhortation (vv. 25-32)

Paul realized this visit to Ephesus might be his last one. He knew he might never see these elders again. Paul also believed the mission God had sent him there to accomplish, in the earlier years when he established the church there, had been fulfilled. He preached the kingdom to them. The church at Ephesus was able to stand strong and clear in their beliefs because of Paul's ministry among them. Paul claims that no man's blood can be laid on him. Paul faithfully presented the Gospel and warned the unbelievers of the consequences. He was not guilty nor to be held responsible if an unbeliever ignored the truth and refused to accept the facts concerning Christ's death, burial, and resurrection. Paul had earnestly and clearly proclaimed God's Word. He had done his part, and he believed God was pleased with his work there.

Paul moved from focusing on his responsibility to challenging the elders with their obligations. Paul, first of all, offered himself as an example of one who declared the whole counsel of God. This was important because Paul knew the false teachers would attempt to infiltrate the congregation. He reminded them not to emphasize or teach one portion of God's Word and ignore others. All of it was important to understand and heed.

Paul goes on to describe how they should conduct themselves when he was no longer there. "Keep watch over yourselves" (v. 28, Good News Bible) was Paul's initial exhortation. How can the congregation remain faithful to the Lord if the leadership is changing? Paul encouraged them strongly to pay attention to themselves and their own spiritual condition.

Paul, then, exhorts them to "watch over the flock which the Holy Spirit has placed in their care" (v. 28, Good News Bible). The church was referred to as a "flock" meaning, God's people. The leaders are shepherds or pastors. They are to be guardians, giving spiritual input and pastoral care to the congregation. They are to act as shepherds, lovingly protecting the sheep. The church belongs to God. He bought it with the great price of His Son's blood.

Paul was concerned about the "fierce wolves" who would enter and cause havoc and destruction among the congregation. The wolves are the false teachers who come from the outside and spread erroneous lies, leading the people astray. Unfortunately, Paul had witnessed this

kind of devastation in other churches (Corinth and Galatia, for example). Paul also mentioned the possibility of people embracing false ideas and erroneous teaching coming from within the church to lead the people astray. Watch! Watch! Watch! Paul's stern warning is that leaders must constantly be on the alert, like shepherds keeping awake to watch for wolves at night.

Paul adds one more example from his ministry among the Ephesians—hard work. When he was there, he worked day and night. Paul did not live off of the offering from the saints. He made tents so he did not have to depend on the church financially. Paul wanted to be sure that they understood that working in ministry was not all glamour and being a leader did not mean sitting back giving others orders. Paul rolled up his sleeves and did whatever was necessary to get the Gospel out and to build up the believers. He desired for the elders to do the same.

SEARCH THE SCRIPTURES

Circle the correct answer:

1. The main message Paul gave to the Ephesians was (v. 21)
a) Turn from their sins to God and believe in Jesus Christ.
b) Be baptized.
c) Join the church.
d) Stop doing wrong things.

2. Paul was on his way to (v. 22)
a) Jerusalem.
b) Jericho.
c) Rome.
d) Troas.

3. Paul warned the elders to keep watch over (v. 28)
a) themselves.
b) the flock.
c) the disciples.
d) a and b.

4. Paul wanted them to watch out for (v. 29)
a) false teachers from the outside.
b) false teachers that may arise from the congregation.
c) grievous wolves.
d) all of the above.

407

DISCUSS THE MEANING

1. What made Paul's ministry among the Ephesian church so successful?

2. Why was Paul concerned about this congregation?

3. How can we be sure we are not spreading false teaching?

4. What was Paul teaching us about humility?

LESSON IN OUR SOCIETY

"Be aggressive. Be bold. Speak your mind. Be proud. Get ahead even if that means stepping on somebody else to get there." These are the kinds of messages that are prevalent in our society. Humility, servanthood, and putting the needs of others first are not encouraged. And yet, this is the example Jesus left for us. In fact, He was referred to several times as a humble servant. Is that how people we live with, work with, and fellowship with would describe us?

MAKE IT HAPPEN

Humility is not something that we are born with, nor something that surrounds our living environment. Therefore, we need to ask the Lord to teach us how to be humble. First, in our inner attitude toward Him, and then in our outer actions toward other people.

Look up as many of the words below as you can, then use these definitions to prayerfully examine your attitude and actions toward God and others.

Lowly, meek, modest, submissive, unassuming, peaceful, mild, calm.

FOLLOW THE SPIRIT

What God wants me to do:

_____

_____

REMEMBER YOUR THOUGHTS

Special insights you learned:

_____

_____

MORE LIGHT ON THE TEXT

Acts 20:18-32

20:18 And when they were come to him, he said unto them, Ye know, from the first day that I came into Asia, after what manner I have been with you at all seasons,

While Paul was in Ephesus, he presided over the affairs of the church. Now he appeals to the elders at Ephesus concerning his work, his life, and doctrine. They had witnessed his deportment, character, and conversation as he served the Lord.

19 Serving the Lord with all humility of mind, and with many tears, and temptations, which befell me by the lying in wait of the Jews:

Even in the midst of opposition against the Jews, he remained tender, affectionate, and compassionate among them. He cried often in his service to God. Yet, he continued his work for the Lord.

As servants of God, we will suffer persecution. However, we must continue to be diligent in our service. For we know that, "Weeping may endure for a night, but joy comes in the morning light."

20 And how I kept back nothing that was profitable unto you, but have shewed you, and have taught you publickly, and from house to house,

He taught them everything he knew about the Gospel of Jesus Christ—the unadulterated Gospel. His aim was to preach that which was true and profitable. He preached publicly to the congregations and taught privately from house to house.

21 Testifying both to the Jews, and also to the Greeks, repentance toward God, and faith toward our Lord Jesus Christ.

He was a universal preacher, in that, he constantly and earnestly preached to both Jews and Greeks (although he was called to be the apostle to the Gentiles). He preached the nature and necessity of faith and repentance. He preached faith towards our Lord Jesus Christ as our only way to God—for there is no coming to God except through Jesus Christ (John 14:6). He preached repentance towards God. Repentance is only possible through grace offered in Christ. Everyone needs to repent. Because all have sinned and gone away from God, we must turn towards God and ask for forgiveness.

22 And now, behold, I go bound in the spirit unto Jerusalem, not knowing the things that shall befall me there:

Paul here calls them to open their eyes and see. They must see with their spiritual eyes, with the eye of the heart, what he is feeling within.

He was compelled to go to Jerusalem. The Holy Spirit was leading his spirit to Jerusalem. Paul was a man who obeyed the Holy Spirit. He knew he had to go to Jerusalem, although, he foresaw trouble awaiting him there. When Paul says, "I go bound in the Spirit" the phrase suggests a certain heaviness of Spirit resulting from an uneasy revelation.

23 Save that the Holy Ghost witnesseth in every city, saying that bonds and afflictions abide me.

The use of the phrase the "Holy Ghost witnesseth" suggests that their witness was not casual. It was a solemn swearing by the Spirit that this experience would be so. The word translated "witness" implies a total and complete self-giving of someone, thus meaning that the Spirit had given their witness with earnestness.

The Holy Spirit had clearly and emphatically revealed to him through prophecy on several occasions that imprisonment and persecution awaited him. Though Paul did not know, the Holy Spirit being God knew. The word "save," which we find in the King James Version, comes from the greek "plen" which simply means "except." This is a way of saying, "I may not know, but the Spirit knows."

24 But none of these things move me, neither count I my life dear unto myself, so that I might finish my course with joy, and the ministry, which I have received of the Lord Jesus, to testify the Gospel of the grace of God.

In verse 24, Paul in his typical manner states, "but none of these things move me." Paul's letter to the Romans, chapter eight, truly captures the sense of his communication here. When Paul says "nothing moves me" one may ask, "what if your life was at stake?" He responds, "neither do

I count my life dear unto myself." It is interesting here that Paul uses "logos" for the word "count" and for life; not the normal greek word "zoe" but the hebraic soul "psychi." Paul says that he does not even count his soul dear unto himself. One must remember that turning against his tradition came with the threat of being cut off completely from Israel. So Paul was willing to be considered lost. He ends the passage by giving his rationale. First, "That I might finish my course with joy." Second, that he might finish his ministry received from Jesus. Third, that he might testify to the Gospel and the grace of God. For these three things Paul would gladly be bound in chains.

Nevertheless, knowing that trouble awaited him, he resolved to go on to Jerusalem. Paul only concerned himself with finishing his ministry with joy and remaining faithful to the ministry of Jesus Christ to which he was called. His job was to save the souls of men and women. As a minister for Jesus Christ, he testified to the world about God's grace (God's unmerited favor) to them. To this cause, Paul wanted to remain faithful.

Paul saw his life as a race, and the race ended at death. Like Paul, while running the race of life, we should not be idle. Often the flesh becomes weak. However, it is during these times that our spirit should become strong. Our strength must come from the Lord Jesus Christ. Paul says, ". . .for when I am weak, then I am strong" (2 Corinthians 12:10b).

25 And now, behold, I know that ye all, among whom I have gone preaching the kingdom of God, shall see my face no more.

This was Paul's farewell statement to the elders at Ephesus. He told them they would never see his face again. He had finished his work at Ephesus. Note how Paul has moved from not knowing what was going to happen to him to a bold statement of, "I know that ye all. . . ."

26 Wherefore I take you to record this day, that I am pure from the blood of all men. 27 For I have not shunned to declare unto you all the counsel of God.

He appealed to them concerning the faithful discharge of his ministry among them. He challenged them to prove him unfaithful in his ministry to them. He was not responsible for any among them who were not saved, because he had faithfully preached the saving grace of Jesus Christ. He did not leave out any parts of the Gospel. He preached nothing but the counsel of God, and he preached the whole counsel of God.

28 Take heed therefore unto yourselves, and to all the flock, over the which the Holy Ghost hath made you overseers, to feed the church of God, which he hath purchased with his own blood.

Paul charged the ministers to be diligent in their work. He committed the care of the church at Ephesus into their hands. This appointment did not come from him, but it came from the Holy Spirit. The church was now in their hands. As overseers of the church of God, they were to feed the flock, the church of God. He reminded them that the church belongs to God, because God purchased it with the blood of Jesus Christ.

29 For I know this, that after my departing shall grievous wolves enter in among you, not sparing the flock.

Paul warned the elders that their trouble would not stop at his departure. Therefore, they should be careful and watchful of those Jews who preach salvation through circumcision and ceremonial law. During times of persecution, leaders must take extra care of the people of God.

30 Also of your own selves shall men arise, speaking perverse things, to draw away disciples after them.

Paul admonished them to be careful because some from among them (heretics) will pervert the Gospel of Jesus Christ. They will grow proud, conceited, and opinionated.

31 Therefore watch, and remember, that by the space of three years I ceased not to warn every one night and day with tears.

Paul told them to stay alert, and to consider the pain he went through over the past three years in planting this church. He was faithful—working day and night.

32 And now, brethren, I commend you to God, and to the word of his grace, which is able to build you up, and to give you an inheritance among all them which are sanctified.

Paul committed them to the care of God. He encouraged them to hope in God. He put them in the hands of Jesus Christ. Paul knew that the grace of God was able to sustain them.

DAILY BIBLE READING

M: Paul in Athens
Acts 17:16-34
T: Paul in Corinth
Acts 18:1-11
W: Paul in Ephesus
Acts 19:1-10
T: Paul in Macedonia and Greece
Acts 20:1-6
F: Paul in Troas and Miletus
Acts 20:7-16
S: Paul speaks to the Ephesian Elders
Acts 20:17-24
S: Paul's Summary and Farewell
Acts 20:25-38

INTRODUCTION TO JUNE 2001 QUARTER

GENERAL INTRODUCTION

This quarter's lessons follows Israel's history from Solomon's death and the division of the united kingdom to the northern kingdom's fall in 722 B.C. During this time period, both Israel and Judah struggled for political power and security. Injustice and oppression were prevalent as the children of Israel violated the covenant made between God and their ancestors. God used prophets to warn, rebuke, and call the Israelites to repentance.

The Quarter at-a-Glance

UNIT 1. A KINGDOM DIVIDED

The first unit of study traces the division of the united kingdom following King Solomon's death and the subsequent development of the northern kingdom. Our first session highlights Rehoboam's unwise decision that led to the united kingdom's split, which had been foretold. The second lesson presents the prophet Elijah's appearance to Israel and the third lessons showcases his challenge for Israel to be faithful to God and not Baal. The fourth session in this unit focuses on the prophet Micaiah's courageous loyalty to deliver God's word.

LESSON 1: June 3
Rehoboam: An Unwise Decision
1 Kings 12:3-4, 6-11, 13, 16

The first lesson describes the events that led to the division of the united kingdom. After Solomon's death, Jeroboam and Israel ask Solomon's son, Rehoboam, to make their work load lighter. In exchange, they will give him loyal service (vv. 3-4). Rehoboam asks two sets of people for advice. The older men tell him that if he grants the people's wishes, they will serve him forever (vv. 6-7). The younger men advise him to

increase their burdens, and Rehoboam follows their advice (vv. 8-11, 13). The people of Israel decide to separate from Rehoboam and the house of Judah (v. 16).

This lesson centers around making wise choices. Your students will be able to empathize with wanting to make decisions that affect their lives and following leaders who appreciate their contributions. They also are familiar with being influenced by their peers. And while many of them have trouble following leaders who discount their expressed needs, they usually follow leaders who are compassionate. Some people also are not always eager to adopt the same style of leadership used in the past. This lesson should make them more determined to choose wisely.

LESSON 2: June 10
Elijah: A Prophet Appears
1 Kings 17:1-5, 8-16

In this session, one of the greatest prophets of Israel appears on the scene to rebuke King Ahab and the Israelites, who have rejected God and turned to Baal. Elijah tells Ahab that a severe drought will strike Israel (v. 1). During the drought, God instructs Elijah to go to a brook, where God will provide food and water for him (vv. 2-5). When the brook dries up, God sends the prophet to a widow (vv. 8-9). The widow however tells Elijah that she only has a small portion of food for herself and her son, and she is preparing it for their last meal (vv. 10-12). Elijah promises the widow that God will provide if she obeys (vv. 13-14). After the widow follows Elijah's instructions, God supplies her with food until the drought is over (vv. 15-16).

One of the main points in this lesson is following instructions. Some of your students have the courage to stand up and declare what they believe is right as Elijah did when he confronted Ahab. Some of them can also relate to helping others even though they have limited resources. They probably struggle with setting priorities in life, much like the widow. However, they too know that if they set their priorities appropriately, their basic needs will be met. Many times we have to sacrifice now to attain future goals.

LESSON 3: June 17
Israel: Called to Decide
1 Kings 18:20-21, 30-39

Elijah confronts and challenges the Israelites in today's lesson. He commands King Ahab to gather the people at Mount Carmel to decide who really is God (vv. 20-21). After Baal's prophets try without success to persuade their god to ignite a sacrifice, Elijah rebuilds an altar in the name of the Lord (vv. 30-32). Elijah drenches the sacrifice with water and then calls on the Lord to set fire to the sacrifice (vv. 33-37). When the people see how the Lord responds with a consuming fire, they fall on their faces and acknowledge that the Lord is God (vv. 38-39).

Staying committed to God is a central theme in this lesson. Some students may struggle with conflicting loyalties and search for evidence of a higher power in the world. They want to know how to find direction for their lives and many want to be loyal to their commitments. Your students can also relate to responding negatively when they realize they've been deceived by their leaders.

LESSON 4: June 24
Micaiah: Courageous Prophet
1 Kings 22:15-23, 26-28

This session focuses on the prophet Micaiah's courage. When Micaiah tells King Ahab what he wants to hear, Ahab demands that the prophet speak the truth that the Lord has told him (vv. 15-16). Micaiah proceeds to tell the king about a vision that depicts Israel's defeat and Ahab becomes angry (vv. 17-18). Micaiah also tells the king that God has permitted a lying spirit to take over Ahab's prophets so they can lead the king into war and defeat (vv. 19-23). Because of his unfavorable prophecy, King Ahab orders Micaiah to be placed in prison until the war is

over and he returns (vv. 26-27). Micaiah sticks by his prophecy and tells the people that if Ahab returns in peace, God has not spoken to him (v. 28).

Speaking the truth is the main point in this lesson. Your students probably are tempted to speak falsely sometimes to please others. Many of them, however, value truthfulness although they are sometimes afraid to hear the truth. While most adults know people who may compromise the truth in order to advance or further their ambitions, they admire people who courageously declare the truth despite possible negative consequences.

UNIT 2. PROPHECIES OF JUDGMENT

Unit 2 shows God's warnings through the prophets Amos, Hosea, and Micah. God commands the prophets to tell the people that unless they repent, they will be judged and punished. The first session in this unit presents Amos' message of judgment to Israel and Judah. The second session focuses on Amos' verbal chastisement against the people's empty offerings to God. In the third and fourth sessions, Hosea proclaims God's love and compassion for Israel. The fifth session summarizes what God requires from the people.

LESSON 5: July 1
Judgment on Judah and Israel
Amos 2:4-10

The lesson focuses on Amos' prophecy to Judah and Israel. He tells Judah that God's judgment will come because they have violated God's law and have followed the negative patterns set by their ancestors (vv. 4-5). Amos tells Israel that judgment will come on them because of their unjust treatment of others, their sexual immorality, and their idolatry (vv. 6-8). Through the prophet, God reminds the unfaithful Israelites that God destroyed the Amorites and brought Israel out of Egypt to possess their land (vv. 9-10).

This lesson focuses on the consequences of disobedience. Some people live as though their violation of established laws will not be punished. Others have experienced injustice and oppression. And while they recognize the injustices in today's society, many don't see how they participate in executing the injustices. Some of your students are distressed by reports of corruption from leaders and the ambiguous sexual standards of today's society. However most adults are strong advocates for integrity and for justice of the oppressed. Students should be encouraged to live obedient lives even when the consequences of disobedience appear to be far away.

LESSON 6: July 8
Empty Offerings
Amos 4:2-5; 5:20-24

This lesson continues with Amos' pronouncement of God's judgment on the unfaithful people. Amos reminds the people that God's judgment is coming and that the people of the northern kingdom will be deported (vv. 2-3). Through Amos, God denounces the fake worship practices that multiply the people's sins (vv. 4-5). Amos tells them that the Day of the Lord will be a terrible day of judgment (5:20). Amos informs the people that God despises the worship they've offered and that God requires justice and righteousness.

The focus of today's lesson is empty offerings, which happens when our actions do not follow the laws of the God we worship. Some people act as if they are not accountable for their actions. Others have difficulty distinguishing between empty rituals and meaningful practices. Still other adults are impressed when they see examples of integrity in relationships. From today's lesson, we should recognize that regular church attendance is not a substitute for just and righteous behavior. Many youth criticize hypocritical behavior in adults. Students should work to avoid being mechanical in their worship participation so they will not present empty offerings to God.

LESSON 7: July 15
God's Love for Israel
Hosea 1:2-9; 2:1-4

In this session God uses Hosea to illustrate

God's love for the unfaithful Israel. God uses Hosea's marriage to an unfaithful woman to show Israel that they have been unfaithful to their God (1: 2). After Hosea marries Gomer, she gives birth to Jezreel, whose name is a reminder to Israel that God will punish the house of Jehu and end the kingdom of Israel (vv. 3-5). After Jezreel, Gomer has a daughter, Loruhamah, whose name is a reminder to Israel that God will no longer have pity on them but God will save the kingdom of Judah (vv. 6-7). The last child born to Gomer is Lo-ammi, whose name reminds Israel that they are no longer God's people (vv. 8-9). Hosea asks the children to plead with their mother to stop her immoral ways (2:1-2). He continues by telling Israel that if Gomer (and Israel) does not turn away from her sinful ways, God will expose her shameful deeds and devastate her (vv. 3-4).

The central theme of this lesson is broken vows. Some students do not acknowledge that faithfulness to commitments is important. Others have experienced and observed devastating results when vows of commitment are broken. Fortunately, some adults have experienced a renewal of commitments. Your students should realize that their personal morality is a contributing factor to community morality. While they may find marriage difficult, they will take the responsibility seriously and determine not to break their vows to each other or to God.

LESSON 8: July 22
God's Compassion for Israel
Hosea 11:1-9

This lesson highlights God's unrequited love and compassion for Israel. The more God reaches out to the chosen nation, the more the people turn their backs on God and worshiped false gods (vv. 1-2). But God tenderly nurtures Israel as a loving parent nurtures a child (vv. 3-2). However, their continuous unfaithfulness can not go unpunished and they will be led into captivity and ruled by the Assyrians (vv. 5-6). Because of the people's waywardness, God does not answer their prayers. God grieves over their condition and promises to show compassion (vv. 8-9).

Rejected love is the main theme in today's lesson. Many adults take expressions of love for granted instead of accepting them with genuine gratitude. Others are conscious of the positive influence of people in their lives. Still more adults know the pain of having their kind and loving acts rejected. Some have found a nurturing love through their families and churches. Most do know the tension created when they refuse to give up on people they love who have rebelled against them and their values. Through this lesson, your students should be prepared to mediated God's love to persons who feel rejected and are not connected with the church.

LESSON 9: July 9
What God Requires
Micah 3:9-12; 6:6-8

We study God's requirements for God's people in today's lesson. The prophet Micah accuses the leaders of Judah and Israel of unjust, inhumane, and corrupt practices while simultaneously professing that God would protect them from harm (3:9-11). Amos tells them that because of the leaders' corruption, judgment, and destruction will fall upon Jerusalem (v. 12). He emphasizes that God requires justice, kindness, and humility more than ritual and sacrifices (6:6-8).

The focus of this lesson is on how God expects us to act as children of God. We are often cynical about leaders because of some of the unscrupulous practices that have come to light; we are therefore sometimes confused by misleading messages from certain leaders. And sometimes we experience hardship because of the wrongs we've done. Many times we want to know what God expects and what religious activities are genuinely important to our God. As today's lesson demonstrates, our God is pleased when we sincerely treat others justly and kindly and we walk humbly with our Lord.

UNIT 3. DECLINE AND FALL
The final unit of this quarter highlights the events that led to the prophesied fall of Israel in 722 B.C. Judah also plays a role in the line of

events. The first lesson presents God's call to Isaiah and the prophet's response. The second unit focuses on Isaiah's encounter with Ahaz and the prophet's counsel to the king. The third and fourth sessions deal with the announcement of doom to both Israel and Judah and the fall of Israel to the Assyrians, respectively.

LESSON 10: August 5
Isaiah's Call
Isaiah 6:1-12

This lesson presents the circumstances surrounding Isaiah's call. In the year that King Uzziah died, Isaiah experienced God's presence in the temple (v. 1). Isaiah saw seraphs attending God and praising God's holiness and glory (vv. 2-4). The prophet felt lost and frightened, and he confessed both his impurity and the people's impurity (v. 5). Isaiah was purified and his sins were forgiven after a seraph touched his lips with a burning coal from the altar (vv. 6-7). Isaiah heard God's call for a faithful servant and volunteered to deliver God's word (v. 8). God gave Isaiah a message of despair and desolation for a people who would not adhere to God's warnings and laws.

We focus on answering God's call in today's lesson. Just as Isaiah felt upon entering God's presence, many of us feel guilty and desire to be forgiven. Many of us also have life-changing spiritual experiences while others wonder how people know they've been called to spread God's Word. Some of those who've heard God's call have surrendered their lives to do God's will. And no doubt they have felt the disappointment of having their warnings ignored. As you contemplate your call, remember that many will gladly proclaim a message of hope yet few are willing to proclaim a message of despair.

LESSON 11: August 12
Isaiah and Ahaz: A Challenge to Rely on God
Isaiah 7:1-6, 10-17

God gives the King of Judah a sign of deliverance in today's lesson. King Ahaz and the people fear an impending attack from both Aram and Israel, who've joined forces (vv. 1-2). God tells Isaiah to go to Ahaz and tell him not to fear the plans of his enemies (vv. 3-6). The Lord even tells Ahaz to ask for a sign, but the king refuses because he says he does not want to tempt God (vv. 10-12). Despite Ahaz's disobedience, God tells him that before a child yet to be born is old enough to know right from wrong, Judah's enemies will be destroyed (vv. 13-17).

This lesson is about trusting God's care. Your students will probably understand how it feels to have their welfare threatened by other people, institutions, or circumstances. They should also know how it feels to be reassured by the encouragement of others, and some of them will have experienced God's presence while facing difficult times. It is common for adults to look for reasons and signs that point to hope for the future. Through this lesson, they should realize that their hope should be in God and the Lord's promise to always take care of them.

LESSON 12: August 19
Pronouncement of Doom
Isaiah 5:1-7

After much pleading with the unfaithful people, God sends Isaiah to pronounce doom on the nations. Isaiah compares God's beloved to a vineyard that is carefully tended and cultivated yet it yields wild grapes (vv. 1-2). He asks the people of Judah to judge between God and the vineyard, and he asks them what more could have been done to help the vineyard produce good fruit (vv. 3-4). Now God says he will destroy the vineyard by allowing it to become overgrown and deserted (vv. 5-6). God says that Judah is the vineyard; the good grapes that God expected were justice and righteousness, instead they produced bloodshed and oppressed others (v. 7).

This lesson deals with accepting God's judgment. Your students should be familiar with the suffering associated with rejection from people they love and are concerned about. They are probably well acquainted with the disappointment of not receiving positive results in spite of their best efforts. On the other hand, some adults do not accept objective assessment of their behavior and fail to learn valuable lessons. Therefore, they experience great losses because they do not heed warnings or take advice. Others believe that they do not deserve the trials and tribulations they have in life. By the end of this lesson your students will recognize that God will punish our continuous rejection of the Lord's law and commandment.

LESSON 13: August 26
Israel Taken Into Captivity
2 Kings 17:6-16

Today's lesson is the result of many ignored warnings to the people of Israel. Assyria invades, besieges, and conquers the capital city of Samaria; the northern kingdom of Israel is forced into captivity (v. 6). Their captivity is their punishment for sinning against God and worshiping other gods (vv. 7-8). God sent many prophets to tell the people to turn from their evil ways, but the people continued to serve the idols (vv. 9-13). They did not heed the warnings of the prophets; instead they rejected the covenant God made with their ancestors and followed the forbidden practices of foreign nations.

It is tough when we are called to deal with sin's consequences; however, we can all attest to circumstances and situations that lead to consequences. Sometimes many of us wonder if wrong conduct truly brings about unpleasant consequences. While others are able to accept the consequences of their actions. At some point, most people are willing to change behavior that brings despair and pain. And many people are actually reluctant to consider new ways when they treasure the good that has been passed on to them from older generations. Your students may be willing to defend right in spite of opposition, and they should be ready to resist influence of the majority's attitudes and behaviors in order to live by their own principles.

Teaching The Bible From An African American Perspective

Rev. Luke Benton, III, Th.D.

If a picture be worth a thousand words, better yet can a picture etch a point of view on the mind of the viewer? Can that view last a thousand, even thousands of years? The answer to these questions is a resounding yes! Just last night, I listened to a well-known minister as he preached to the Cherokee Nation, he answered the question put to him on many occasions "Why should I worship the White man's God?" referring to the blonde-haired, blue-eyed depiction posed on many church walls throughout this country. His answer, "Get that off the wall and out of the church, Jesus was not White." Has this happened to many thousands of Africans Americans, because someone hung a depiction of a White Christ on a church wall? The issue is: can you believe what you see? For many years I viewed a White Christ on many Black church walls, saw numerous pictures of biblical characters displayed as European, yet I asked myself, "Is it so?" I am happy today to report that we have awakened out of darkness and can see the marvelous light and truth of God, that He loved the world so much He put on flesh like mine, Black, came to earth, not just to save me but all mankind. It is great that most of us today are using study Bibles that have no pictures!

Nevertheless, removing the depiction from the church walls is only the beginning; we must remove the damage from the minds of our brothers and sisters, as well as ourselves. We begin by taking a hard look at the damage done and with a life-long commitment to repair all of us, all people, of all colors! We must teach the truth of the Bible, with its history that is much like that of the African-American, we must say as Moses said to Pharaoh, "Let my people go."

When a people have been denied their history, culture, and accomplishments, they are deprived of worth, pride, purpose and self-esteem, becoming dysfunctional and relegated to less than human beings. In his project/dissertation, *Hope in the Glory of God, A Hermeneutic Discourse for Black Liberation*, Dr. Harrison Edward Benton, Jr., states, "according to Bernal, the perceptions of "racial" differences were at the center of the thought of English philosophers such as John Locke and David Hume, whom he would consider as racist today. In their attempt to justify slavery in America, a scheme was developed to classify the Africans and Native Americans as sub-human. Bernal asserts that it was Locke's nominalism (his denial of an objective validity of "species" and view of them as subjective concepts) that made it easy for that type of thinking to take place. Thus, by the 1680's, it was a widespread opinion that Negroes were only a link above the apes (p. 203).

Bernal states:

It is certain that Locke and most 18th century English-speaking thinkers like David Hume and Benjamin Franklin were racists: They openly expressed popular opinions that dark skin color was linked to moral and mental inferiority. In Hume's case, racism so transcended conventional religion that he was a pioneer of the view that there had been not one creation of man but many different ones, because "Such a uniform and constant difference could not happen in so many countries and ages, if nature had not made an original distinction betwixt these breeds of men (pp. 203-204).[1]

It was out of this context that racism entered human history, and with its negative connotations, it became the major player in the development of a methodology of historiography that has willfully and knowingly distorted human history along racial lines. More importantly, its authors have used the Christian faith to justify their actions. Thus God's story of salvation which is a story of human liberation has been used indirectly as a tool of racial oppression. This line of negative thinking that was developed into a new discipline called "Science of Antiquity" gave birth to what Bernal calls the "Aryan Model" and Copher identifies as the "New Hamitic Hypotheses." However, ancient scholars had a different view. Both Copher and Bernal stress the significance of the views of ancient Greek scholars such as Homer and Herodotus (known as the father of history) who had no problems accepting the historical truths of the great contributions of the Black people of ancient Egypt to Greek culture and human civilization. Copher points out that even in Western thought, for four centuries (1400-1800), the Black person was considered to be an inhabitant of the biblical world. The so-called "Aryan Model" or the "New Hamitic Hypothesis" are latecomers to the table of "universal belief" concerning the history of human civilization. Yet, as we enter into the twenty-first century, the average person knows nothing, or very little, about earlier historical views or beliefs set forth in the "Ancient Model" or "Old Hamitic Hypothesis" centuries before the inception of the Aryan Model during the 19th century.

According to Bernal the old model was destroyed for what historians of science call "externalist" reasons. He explains:

The "Ancient Mode" fell not because of any new developments in the field but because it did not fit the prevailing world-view. To be more precise, it was incompatible with the paradigms of race and progress of the early 19th century (Bernal, p. 316). [2]

We have established that the practice of racial hierarchy and oppression did not exist in the ancient context. The people of antiquity were not categorized according to color differences. Neither was color and race used to politically or ideologically enslave, oppress, or negate the humanity of people in the ancient world of the Bible.

Hence, the Euro-American recasting of the biblical story of ancient Israel as their own story and its system of "racial hierarchy" has had a profound effect on the self-esteem of all people of color and has greatly undermined the accuracy of human history. Therefore, most of what we accept today as accurate historiography and hermeneutics are in fact slanted and distorted research produced for the specific purpose of elevating the Caucasian (White) race at the expense of people of color—specifically Africans. It is this system of devaluing Black people that forced African-Americans to address the issues of racism and oppression during the 1960s. African-American theologians such as James H. Cone, J. Deotis Roberts, Joseph R. Washington, Gayraud S. Wilmore, Albert B. Cleage and others, were confronted with the critical question of "Black Identity." As they wrestled to make sense of what it meant to be Black, Christian, and free, they realized that our identity as Black people could not be transcended or ignored; rather, it had to be enthusiastically embraced at every point.

The 1960 Civil Rights movement was a time of struggle, a time of confrontation, and a time of anger; yet on the other hand, it was a time of challenge, a time of solidarity, and a time of liberation. Specifically, it was a unique time for Black America that demanded a response. This period can best be defined as a *Kairos* time—a crucial point in a given time offered by providence. In his letter to the Romans, the Apostle Paul wrote:

Why all this stress on behaviour? Because, as I think you have realized, the present time is of the highest importance—it is time to wake up to reality. Every day brings God's salvation nearer. The night is nearly over, the Day has almost dawned. Let us therefore fling away the things that men do in the dark, let us arm ourselves for the fight of the Day! (Romans 13:11-12).[3]

To this end, whenever and wherever the Bible is taught, it should be taught truthfully and it will be if it is taught under the influence of the Holy Spirit; when the teacher is not concerned with self nor has selfish motives. There should be only one concern in the teacher's mind, the salvation of all people, which will come throughout knowing the truth in the Word of GOD! To teach is to learn twice, first to know it for one's self, that is, to adopt for sure, in your life, that set of values or principle you want others to have; and second to believe enough to assist someone in accepting those values or principles that will ultimately change their lives.

Let me suggest a beginning point of preparation in teaching the Scriptures; Joseph Johnson, Jr., who was a Black biblical scholar and bishop in the Christian Methodist Episcopal Church, recorded some principles of scriptural interpretation that were conveyed to him as a legacy by his father. He suggests the use of imagination in teaching to evoke a picture that will correspond to the scriptural text. The Bible can come to life through the images used by a spirit-filled teacher; after all, we as people of color are the imagery of our Creator as embedded in Christ Jesus. These principles suggest a way of preparation for the imaginative use of Scripture:

1. Prepare yourself with devotion and prayer prior to your encounter with the Scriptures.

2. Read the entire chapter in which the text is located.

3. Become acquainted with all of the stories, which lead up to the text and those that follow.

4. What were the problems and the situation of the participants in the story?

5. Read the biblical passages aloud, and as the hearer of the Scripture, permit them to speak to you.

6. Discover the human element and the Divine element in the situation.

7. You must see what the writer saw, feel what the participants in the story felt, and hear what they heard.

8. Use your imagination and put yourself in the place of the writer and participants of the story.

9. Assume the different roles of the principle characters in the story and act as if you were present when the story was first told.

10. Ask yourself this question, "What special message does this passage of Scripture bring to your people for their healing and renewal?"

11. Then wait for God to speak.[4]

Carlyle once received a letter from a young man that read like this: "Mr. Carlyle, I wish to be a teacher. Will you tell me the secret of successful teaching?" Carlyle immediately wrote back: "Be what you would have your pupils be. All other teaching is unblessed mockery and apery."—Dr. F. Russell Purdy

A people deprived of their history will be deprived of their future, as well as their self-worth. It is paramount for all preachers, as well as teachers of God's Word, to tell the truth of the Word in it's proper perspective—as it relates from God to His people. The Word of God is written to men, women, boys, and girls where they are and as they are! Our God is a God of color! Paint a picture of the truth. Free us to see the God that created color, who created us all in His image of color.

Speak Lord, your teachers will hear!

1. Martin Bernal, Black Athena: The Afroasiatic Roots of Classical Civilization, vol. 1. New Jersey: Rutgers University Press, 1984.
2. Ibid,
3 J.B. Phillips, LETTERS TO YOUNG CHURCHES, A Translation of the New Testament Epistles, New York: The Macmillan Company, 1952, 30.
4. Joseph A. Johnson, Jr., Proclamation Theology (Shreveport, La.: Fourth Episcopal District Press, 1977, 46-47.

African American Christian Worship

Carlyle Fielding Stewart, III

African-American Christian worship has been the source of spiritual vitality and spiritual power for Africans since the beginning of time. Corporate worship has historically been a reference point for clarity, sanity, transformation and wholeness for Africans in the midst of continuing racial holocaust.

Moreover, worship for African-Americans is not only a celebration of their relationship with Christ and the victories they have won both individually and collectively, but it is a corporate expression of hope, faith, and renewal.

Worship provides a context in which the African-American community recalls its tragic and triumphal sojourn in this strange land and creates an arena for the perfection and ceremonial practice of the ritual dramas of Black life. Facilitating the discovery, cultivation and reinforcement of systems of meaning and value, it also helps the community embrace and celebrate a "God of our weary years and a God of our silent tears who has brought us thus far along this way."

I have stated in my book, *African-American Church Growth*, that three hallmarks of Black worship are: celebration, invitation, and information. This means that African-American Christian worship should unapologetically celebrate the risen and living Christ through the nuances of Black culture. Melva Wilson-Costen reminds us that African-American Christian worship helps African-Americans establish solid belief systems in response to a culture that has marginalized them. We should then, celebrate the trials we've endured, the mountains we've climbed and the obstacles we've overcome. Who but God could have brought us through the agony and ecstasy, the terror and tumult of our American odyssey? The unique culture and ethos created by the Black experience in America is celebrated in the worship experience. This culture also becomes the primary aesthetic for the idioms of Black worship.

Invitation means giving people an opportunity to belong to a caring fellowship of believers by enabling them to participate in the worship experience and in the total life of the church. Something in worship should compel the stranger back to Christ and the church. Inviting people to serve, witness, and belong to the community of believers are important aspects of the African-American church's code of hospitality. Often the worship experience will be the first and only contact a visitor has with a particular church. If nothing in worship invites them to belong and participate, incites their interest, or kindles their enthusiasm for the church, they may not return.

Equally significant is information. How does the worship experience inform worshipers of a living, loving, liberating Christ? What vehicles of information have we established within worship that will reach people where they are, transform and touch them at the core of their ultimate concerns? Preaching, teaching, and outreaching through proclamation, music, witnessing, testimonials, and other idioms are also important venues. Is the information provided in the worship experience, spiritually and intellectually challenging, inspiring and motivating? Does it prompt people to seek God, transform their lives, and be transforming witnesses for Christ? Do we tell the stories in ways that are culturally, spiritually, and relationally relevant to the real needs of the people we serve? Worship gives us a chance to not only learn about God but to receive vital information about ourselves, about our possibilities and disabilities, thereby unlocking life's most inscrutable mysteries.

Celebration, invitation, and information should

be accompanied by what I call the three c's of worship. African-American Christian worship should provide a theater for comforting the afflicted, creatively confronting sin and the evil of this world, and clarifying Blacks as people of God in their quest for hope, redemption, and spiritual vitality.

A saving element of African-American Christian worship has been the way in which a people dehumanized, ravaged, and oppressed by slavery and racism have found comfort, hope, and joy in Christ through the worship experience. When the world despised and rejected them, the Word of God comforted them. When the outer Anglo community ostracized them, the inner community of Black believers embraced them.

Black worship has always had a therapeutic or medicinal value because Blacks have often been healed in the experience of worship. The pharmaceutical value of Black worship cannot be undervalued for we observe the forms of therapy, catharsis, and healing in everything from the Sunday morning shout, to passionate preaching and singing, to the time of witnessing and testimonials. These elements of worship have always brought a measure of comfort to Blacks who could not access other forms of mental or physical health care in the larger society. In fact, these were the predominant forms of spiritual health care in African-American communities. If you couldn't go to the psychiatrist you could shout it out on Sunday morning and find a similar sweet relief from the sorrow and pain of this life.

Creative confrontation of evil and sin is also an essential part of Black worship. This means confronting the corporate and individual sin of White racism as well as the sin of personal omission and commission. The primary motivation for such confrontation is love of God, others, and self, and a fervent desire to bring healing and justice to self and community. Confronting evil openly and honestly helps the healing process and calling evil out is a vital proclamatory component in African-American Christian worship.

The Black preacher thus becomes the personification of power in his capacity to tell the devil off in the name of Jesus, which galvanizes the poor sinner in the pew to put his armor on and do similar battle. The ability to confront individual and corporate sin openly in worship helps the individual to confront sin in the personal realm. What the slave could not say to "massa" personally could be verbalized to Satan by the preacher in the worship experience and thus some measure of resolution was achieved.

The same is true today. What is not expressed to evil doers directly is voiced vicariously through the Black preacher who is the symbol of power and authority in the Black community. Worship also emboldens believers to confront evil themselves head on, to tell the devil off personally or speak the truth against sin generally, and not live obliquely through the preacher as an emblem of liberation and justice.

Finally, clarification is an important dimension of African-American Christian worship. In a society that has perpetually exploited, dehumanized, and devalued their worth, African-Americans have needed consistent clarification that they were people of inherent value. To counteract the juggernaut of racial denigration, Black people had to cultivate a forum to be clarified individually and collectively. Worship provided an opportunity where the person who was nobody during the week could become somebody on Sunday morning. The soul that was devalued in the eyes of White community could be revalued in the eyes of God and other sojourners in Christ. Where one couldn't find freedom of expression in the larger society, one could freely express oneself as a whole person in the worship experience. Whatever humanity denied Blacks could be reaffirmed and clarified within the celebration of worship. "You are okay. You are a child of God. God loves you when nobody else does. You are not niggers . . . ." These are messages that clarify a person's value and worth theologically and spiritually and help them over the "humps" of dehumanization.

Celebration, invitation, and information as well as clarification, comfort, and creative confrontation have been great strengths of African-American Christian worship and continue to be cohesive structures binding the African-American community in its struggle for freedom, wholeness, and vitality. This is simply one point of view.

THEMATIC ESSAY

DIVISION AND DECLINE

Youssouf Dembele, Ph.D.

The birth process of Israel as God's people began with the call of Abram (Genesis 12:1-3), the deliverance from the bondage of Egypt (Exodus 3), the covenant at Sinai (Exodus 19:5-6), and culminated with the entrance into the Promised Land (Joshua 1:1-4; 24:1-31). Out of all the nations of the earth Israel was meant to be God's treasured possession, a kingdom of priests, and a holy nation (Exodus 19:5-6). A triple bond should hold strongly the individuals together: one blood, one God, and one land. The Israelites lost sight of the purpose of their election. They rejected God as their King and asked for a human king to lead them like all the other nations (1 Samuel 8:5-7; 9:1; 1 Kings 11).

Beginning with Rehoboam, Solomon's son and successor, God's one nation was divided into two rival kingdoms: Judah in the south and Israel in the north, and remained so for more than two hundred years. Nineteen kings succeeded over the throne of Israel until its fall in 722 B.C. Sin caused the division and the division increased sin. Jeroboam, the first king of Israel, made two golden calves, built shrines, appointed priests, and instituted his own religious service calendar. He even offered sacrifices, a function that belonged to the priests alone (1 Kings 12:33). His motivation proceeds from political calculation and from distrust in God and in the people he ruled. He wanted to prevent the kingdom from reverting to David's house and the people from giving their allegiance to David's successors again (1 Kings 12:26-33). God sent a prophet to Bethel to pronounce a judgment against Jeroboam's

idolatry and to lead him to repentance, but this was to no avail (1 Kings 13:1-10). Coup d'etat, assassination, and machinations became the normal way of getting power and of maintaining it. A dense spiritual darkness engulfs the land. The people of God rejected God's covenant, breaking down His altars. The air rang with the shouts of a multitude of false prophets while God's prophets were reduced to silence and put to death with the sword (1 Kings 1:10). All the high places of the Holy Land were covered and polluted with the smoke of idolatrous incenses and sacrifices (1 Kings 11:4-9). Prophets were deceiving prophets (1 Kings 13:11-33).

In spite of this spiritual disaster, God was never left without witnesses, without men and women who stand before Him to listen and execute His will (1 Kings 17:1; 2 Kings 3:14). Besides the many prophets who exercised their public ministry at this difficult time (some of these prophets are Elijah, Elisha, Micaiah, Obadiah, Joel, Jonah, Amos, Hosea, Isaiah, Micah), the Bible mentions men and women of faith who shined like stars in the darkness (1 Kings 17:9-24; 18:7-16; 2 Kings 4:1, 8-37). They stand as the remnant of God's people, as a vivid expression of God's grace, faithfulness, and judgment (1 Kings 19:18).

The exhausting taxation and forced labor to build and maintain the temple and the royal palace and the arrogance of Solomon's son Rehoboam are the immediate causes of the division of God's chosen people. Its deep, real cause, however, was God's judgment against Israel's sin. The Book of 1 Kings forcefully presents the division and decline of Israel as coming from God, as a punishment of the detestable, abominable, and crude ungodliness that provoked God's anger in the Holy Land (1 Kings 11:1-3, 9-10, 11-42). Sin led to the downfall and destruction of Jeroboam's house (1 Kings 13:34), and to the decline of the whole kingdom. The Lord used Assyria as His agent of judgment against the kingdom of Israel in 722 B.C. (Isaiah 10:5).

The Apostle Paul laconically presents the significance of the Exodus event for the church in these words: "Now all these things happened to them as examples, and they were written for our admonition, upon whom the ends of the ages have come" (1 Corinthians 10:11, RSV). This same purpose fits the period of the divided kingdom. What do we learn from the things written about the divided kingdom for our warning and instruction?

The events of the divided kingdom period reveal a God who is holy, loving, patient, jealous, and just. Because of His holiness and jealousy God cannot tolerate sin or share His glory with other gods (Exodus 20:5; 34:14; Isaiah 42:8), but because of His love and patience He gives time and opportunities to the sinners to repent (Romans 2:4). All the happenings of the period gain greater significance in the light of these divine attributes.

What happened to Israel warns us that the exclusion of God from the political arena and the tolerance of sin are pregnant with serious, fatal consequences: anarchy, chaos, and decline. Surprisingly enough, in many churches and for many Christians, God is becoming peripheral and sin is losing it gravity. Jesus, the builder and source of life of the church, is standing at the door of many churches and knocking (Revelation 3:20). The same cause producing the same effect, sin and the marginalization of God resulted in the weakening, downfall, and decline of Israel (1 Kings 13:34). They will produce the same effect in the church. However, as in Israel God preserved a remnant, likewise "the gates of hell will not prevail against the church" (Matthew 16:18). Is God at the center or on the brink of the life of your church?

The history of the divided kingdom communicates the pertinent lesson that individual sin may have corporate implications. The leader's sin affects the whole community (1 Kings 14:16). Because we live in a morally decaying society, a society that praises open-mindedness and condonation of all kinds of evil, are not we becoming more sensitive to these requirements than to our role of salt and light of the world? God's judgment and punishment of sin begins here and now. Because of the dullness of our spiritual discernment, are not we unable to see them?

The account of the events of the divided kingdom is a call to maintain the unity of the new people of God, the church. This must be done by putting God again at the center of our individual and corporate life and by pursuing sanctification without which no one will see the Lord (Hebrews 12:14). We are not allowed to lower God's standard.

BLACK PERSONALITY

Susie Baker King Taylor

1848-1912

Many African Americans played valiant roles in the American Civil War. Although women were barred from serving as soldiers, they worked as laundresses, nurses, and teachers assisting the armed forces. Susie King Taylor served as all of these, beginning at only fourteen years of age. She also wrote of hundreds of African American women assisting Union soldiers by hiding them and helping them to escape, sneaking food to the prison stockades prisoners while risking their own lives.

Susie was born in the South where it was illegal for a Black, slave or free, to learn how to read and write, but somehow she managed to learn through several teachers. Because of her ability to read and write, she was able to make a written record of the contributions and tribulations of African Americans during the Civil War.

When Susie Baker was just a child she was able to receive an education from an elderly Black woman. The children attending her school had to arrive at different times so their education would not be discovered. It was illegal to teach Blacks to read, because education would clearly introduce African Americans to dangerous ideas of freedom! Young Susie Baker continued her education with another woman until she had learned all she could from her and then she convinced a White playmate to teach her more. After this her landlord's son continued her education.

When the Civil War moved close to Susie Baker's home in Savannah, Georgia, her family escaped to St. Simon's Island, to cast their lot on the side they felt would give them freedom. Her parents disappeared and were never heard from again. The remaining male members of her family were ready to fight for the Union. When the Commodore heard of Susie's education, he asked her to teach the children on the island to read. Susie asked for some books and when the books arrived she began teaching forty-two children, besides some adults who were eager to learn.

Susie was the official laundress for the First Regiment of South Carolina Volunteers, the first Black unit to fight in the Civil War. This unit had the enormous responsibility of blockading the entire Southern coast to keep supplies and equipment from reaching the Confederates. They raided inland targets and attacked plantations freeing slaves to join the fight.

Susie assisted with nursing duties for wounded and sick soldiers, though she had no formal training in nursing. But she did such an outstanding job that even Clara Barton took note of her work.

In addition to her laundering, teaching, and nursing activities, she became close friends to Edward King, one of the Black soldiers. This friendship blossomed into marriage and then a son and so in addition to her responsibilities to the unit, she had duties as a wife and mother.

After the Civil War, Edward King was unable to find work as a carpenter, due to the racism of Savannah, and so he began a hazardous job as a loader on the docks. One day Susie was brought the news that he had fallen and died. Susie was now without any support. The Army denied her the usual pension due to nurses, because she had not had formal training. So she moved to Boston and went back to working as a laundress. She married again, this time to Russell Taylor. Her son was growing up to be the kind of man she could be proud of, but she could not forget how her prayers and faith had sustained her through her days of service in the Civil War. And so she wrote her record and we now know of Susie King Taylor, the first African American Army nurse.

TEACHING TIPS

June 3
Bible Study Guide 1

1. Words You Should Know

A. Made our yoke grievous (1 Kings 12:4) Hebrew *qasheh*—hard servitude, difficult, unfeeling, cruel, harsh, inflexible, obstinate, stubborn. The general meaning of this term sprang from the farm. They put heavy yoke on oxen to force them to pull plows. These were very hard to bear, and sometimes the oxen rebelled.

B. Counsel (v. 8) Hebrew *yaats*—to advise, admonish, or direct; to resolve, consult with one another, or counsel together.

2. Teacher Preparation

A. Spend some time in prayer before you begin this lesson. If you are not familiar, or your students are not familiar, with this period of the kings, sometimes the names of people and places can be quite confusing.

B. Read the UNIT INTRODUCTION in the BIBLE STUDY GUIDE.

C. Read the Bible Background, preferably in more than one Bible translation.

D. Go back and look specifically at the FOCAL VERSES.

E. Read the commentary in Bible Study Guide and be sure you can answer SEARCH THE SCRIPTURES and DISCUSS THE MEANING questions.

3. Starting the Lesson

A. Have the class read the AT-A-GLANCE outline together.

B. Read the LESSON AIM and pray that by the end of class each one will have a good understanding.

C. Before beginning the lesson summarize the unit.

D. Materials Needed: Bible, chalkboard or newsprint.

4. Getting into the Lesson

A. Read the IN FOCUS story.

B. Write the word "wisdom" on the board and ask the class to suggest one word, or short phrase, definitions. Write down their answers on the board or on the newsprint.

C. To get a basic understanding of the lesson have students take turns reading BACKGROUND and THE PEOPLE, PLACES, AND TIMES.

D. Have students take turns reading FOCAL VERSES and IN DEPTH, and answer the SEARCH THE SCRIPTURE questions in between.

5. Relating the Lesson to Life

A. Go through the DISCUSS THE MEANING questions, and feel free to encourage the discussion with some of your own questions, allowing time for the personal experiences of the students.

B. Have someone read the LESSON IN OUR SOCIETY article. Ask how many in the class are guilty of this kind of decision-making as well.

6. Arousing Action

A. Encourage all the students to take the test in the MAKE IT HAPPEN section. Allow them to share some of their answers.

B. Ask the students to make specific plans of how they are going to make changes in the way they make decisions in important, life-changing events and in small, daily, seemingly insignificant events.

WORSHIP GUIDE

For the Superintendent or Teacher
Theme: Rehoboam: An Unwise Decision
Theme Song: Guide Me O Thy Great Jehovah
Scripture: 1 Kings 12:3-4, 6-11, 13, 16
Song: Savior Like a Shepherd Lead Us
Meditation: Thank you, Lord, that wisdom is available to us through Your Son Jesus Christ.

REHOBOAM: AN UNWISE DECISION

Bible Background • 1 KINGS 12; 2 CHRONICLES 10:1—11:12
Printed Text • 1 KINGS 12:3-4, 6-11, 13, 16
Devotional Reading • MATTHEW 11:27-30

LESSON AIM

By the end of this lesson, the students should be able to recall the events that led to the division of the nation of Israel as a result of Rehoboam's unwise choices, and to be motivated to be wiser in times of decision-making.

KEEP IN MIND

"If you will be a servant to this people today and serve them, and speak good words to them when you answer them, then they will be your servants forever" (1 Kings 12:7).

FOCAL VERSES

1 Kings 12:3 They sent and called him. And Jeroboam and all the congregation of Israel came, and spake unto Rehoboam, saying,

4 Thy father made our yoke grievous: now therefore make thou the grievous service of thy father, and his heavy yoke which he put upon us, lighter, and we will serve thee.

12:6 And King Rehoboam consulted with the old men, that stood before Solomon his father while he yet lived, and said, How do ye advise that I may answer this people?

7 And they spake unto him, saying, If thou wilt be a servant unto this people this day, and wilt serve them, and answer them, and speak good words to them, then they will be thy servants forever.

8 But he forsook the counsel of the old men, which they had given him, and consulted with the young men that were grown with him, and which

LESSON OVERVIEW

LESSON AIM
KEEP IN MIND
FOCAL VERSES
IN FOCUS
THE PEOPLE, PLACES,
AND TIMES
BACKGROUND
AT-A-GLANCE
IN DEPTH
SEARCH THE SCRIPTURES
DISCUSS THE MEANING
LESSON IN OUR SOCIETY
MAKE IT HAPPEN
FOLLOW THE SPIRIT
REMEMBER YOUR THOUGHTS
MORE LIGHT ON THE TEXT
DAILY BIBLE READINGS

stood before him:

9 And he said unto them, What counsel give ye that we may answer this people, who have spoken to me, saying, Make the yoke which thy father did put upon us lighter?

10 And the young men that were grown up with him spake unto him, saying, Thus shalt thou speak unto this people that spake unto thee, saying, Thy father made our yoke heavy, but make thou it lighter unto us; thus shalt thou say unto them, My little finger shall be thicker than my father's loins.

11 And now whereas my father did lade you with a heavy yoke, I will add to your yoke: my father hath chastened you with whips, but I will chastise you with scorpions.

12:13 And the king answered the people roughly, and forsook the old men's counsel that they gave him.

12:16 So when all Israel saw that the king hearkened not unto them, the people answered the king, saying, What portion have we in David? neither have we inheritance in the son of Jesse: to your tents, O Israel: now see to thine own house, David. So Israel departed unto their tents.

IN FOCUS

Bertha had agreed to drive Mother Mason, one of the elderly women at the church, to a town a couple of hours away. Mother Mason wanted to go to her sister's house to help prepare for an upcoming family reunion. Mother Mason was one of the best cooks in the family, and she was anxious to get there to prepare some of the family's favorite dishes.

On the way over to pick up Mother Mason, Bertha tuned in to the local weather and traffic radio station. "There's been a major accident on Highway 30," the radio announcer reported. "Traffic is backed up, and it may take hours to clear the road. Avoid this area, if at all possible."

"Oh no," Bertha sighed to herself. Highway 30 was the only way to travel to Mother Mason's sister's home.

"Sorry, Mother Mason," Bertha said when she arrived at the house. "I'll have to take you later this afternoon or tomorrow. But no way are we going to get into all that traffic." Mother Mason agreed.

"I'll just go ahead and make some dishes and desserts here at home and wrap them up and take them tomorrow."

God used the traffic report to help Bertha and Mother Mason make a wise decision in the same way God uses the Bible, the prompting of the Holy Spirit, circumstances, and wise counsel from godly people to help His children make wise decisions. When we ignore what God has said, when we rely on our own wisdom and do as we please, we often find ourselves in a major traffic jam.

THE PEOPLE, PLACES, AND TIMES

Jeroboam. The son of Nebat. From the northern large tribe of Ephraim. Solomon recognized his leadership skills and placed him as supervisor over a major building project. He was young, industrious, and a mighty man of valor. Later, he rebelled against Solomon and sought refuge in Egypt. After Solomon died and Rehoboam, Solomon's son, took the throne, the prophecy of a divided nation came true. The nation became divided into two nations, and Jeroboam became king over the northern kingdom for 22 years. He was the first king to lead the people into idolatry, which continued for the next 200 years.

Rehoboam. Solomon's son. He became king over the southern kingdom after his father died; he was 41 years old. He was responsible for splitting the kingdom by making an unwise decision.

He ruled in Judah for 17 years. He was rebellious and led Judah into the sin of idolatry.

Israel. Saul, David, and Solomon ruled as kings over one nation—Israel. The tribes in the north and the south had conflicts from time to time, but for the most part they were one nation. After Solomon died, Israel split into two nations—the Southern Kingdom, Judah, and the Northern Kingdom, Israel.

BACKGROUND

The northern tribes and the southern tribes were sometimes at odds. When David was first crowned king it was by the southern tribes. The northern tribes remained loyal to Saul and his son, who took the throne for a short time. Eventually David was crowned king over all the tribes. During his reign, he managed to keep the tribes loosely unified. However, even during David's reign, there were outbreaks of rebellion and a temporary split in the nation.

When Solomon took the throne, the two tribes moved closer together. In his later years, Solomon inflamed rebellion by his oppressive policies of taxation and hard labor. At the time of his death there was murmuring among the people about establishing a separate nation and government.

When King David ruled Israel, the nation became a world power. The nations all around Israel could not overcome David's military genius. He conquered most of the known world. When he turned the kingdom over to his son, Solomon, the nation was strong and secure. David had also designed the temple that Solomon constructed.

Solomon became king and immediately sought the Lord's guidance for leading the people. He built the temple and continued to build Israel as one of the greatest and most powerful nations in the known world. He was considered the wisest man who ever lived.

However, Solomon married many foreign women who eventually turned his heart from God. He began to worship their gods, and this made God very angry. God told Solomon, "Because you have done this, and you have not kept My covenant and my statutes. . . I will surely tear the kingdom from you, and will give it to your servant . . . I will give one tribe to your son for the sake of

My servant David" (1 Kings 11:11-13, New American Standard). After Solomon's death this prophecy was fulfilled. The nation was divided. Judah, the largest tribe, became the southern kingdom and remained under the leadership of David's successors. Israel, ten tribes united together, became the northern kingdom, and various leaders were appointed king in that area.

IN DEPTH
1. The Northern Tribes' Request
(1 Kings 12:3-4)

The history of the division of Israel begins with Jeroboam, a faithful servant in Solomon's administration. He was highly respected and was placed over all the forced labor involved in a major building project. Nevertheless, Jeroboam eventually rebelled. The reason is not spelled out in the passage, but some scholars believe Jeroboam thought Solomon was working the people too hard and treating them unfairly.

Whatever the reason, Jeroboam left Israel and went to Egypt to escape punishment for his rebellion. While he was on his way to Egypt, the prophet Ahijah stops him and tells him that the nation of Israel will eventually divide, splitting into the northern and southern tribes. The prophet Ahijah tells Jeroboam that he will become the first king of the northern kingdom. Jeroboam continues on to Egypt and stays there until he hears of Solomon's death. The next time Jeroboam surfaces is when the tribes come together to make Rehoboam, Solomon's son, the official king of the entire nation.

Rehoboam traveled to Shechem, an ancient national meeting place. He must have sensed trouble with the northern tribes even before he took the throne. For him to travel to Shechem was highly unusual. After all, Jerusalem was the capital of Israel at the time and also the established residence of the king. Rehoboam went to Shechem and attempted to mend shaky relationships between the northern and southern tribes.

Jeroboam was in the crowd when Rehoboam presented himself before the people. It is not clear if Jeroboam had already reported the prophecy by Ahijah, and the northern tribes were waiting for an opportunity to make him their king, or if Jeroboam was alone, waiting on the Lord to work out His promises. Either way, Jeroboam was wise at this point—he waited. He did not cause an uprising among the people. He allowed Rehoboam to have his say and watched for the hand of God.

The congregation of Israel came together and spoke to Rehoboam, saying, "Thy father made our yoke grievous: now therefore make thou the grievous service of thy father, and his heavy yoke which he put upon us, lighter, and we will serve thee" (1 Kings 12:4). Solomon had demanded great performance from the people to build and maintain the splendor of his court. He had taxed the people greatly, demanded forced labor, and required military service. The people had been abused and misused by the last king. They were requesting relief. At this point they were not requesting independence or threatening to rebel. They simply wanted more leniency from the burdens Solomon had placed on them. Rehoboam did not answer the request of the people right away. He agreed to appear before the people again with his answer in three days.

2. The Elders' Advice (vv. 6-7)

During the three day waiting period, Rehoboam consulted the old men of Israel. They told him to go easy on the people to make the burden of taxation lighter. The elders assured him if this change were made the people would be loyal to the king's administration.

Rehoboam also consulted the young men. These men were advisers in his court that were around his age (Rehoboam became king at 41). The young men gave Rehoboam the opposite advice. They recommended not only continuing the heavy yoke Solomon had placed upon the people, but increasing it even further.

Rehoboam should have consulted the Lord. This is what his father had done and Solomon experienced great success in the early part of his administration. Rehoboam, however, looked to his advisers and then did what he thought was best.

3. Rehoboam's Foolish Decision (vv. 8-11, 13, 16)

Rehoboam returned to the people and reported that he planned to be even harder on the people than his father. "My father beat you with whips; I shall beat you with scorpions." To scourge them with scorpions meant beating them with a whip with nails and bits of metal and glass on the ends. This ripped the flesh and made gaping wounds.

When the people heard his answer they were outraged. Rehoboam was being harsh and insensitive. They said, "What do we have to do with David's family anymore? To your tents, Israel. Let David's family take care of themselves." The only people left were Rehoboam and his own tribe, Judah, and the smaller tribe adjacent to Judah, Benjamin. The rest of the tribes banded together to make Jeroboam their king.

The people's request had been reasonable. They suffered enough under Solomon and were increasingly burdened. The people's request was for leniency, not independence. It appeared that the people may have supported Rehoboam had he decided to be fair.

Rehoboam immediately gathered an army to fight and bring the nation back together, but the prophet Shemaiah warned him not to fight against his brother. This division of the nation was part of God's plan.

SEARCH THE SCRIPTURES

1. _____ , Solomon's son, went to the people to secure his kingship over all of Israel. (1 Kings 12:3)

2. The people said Solomon made their yoke _____ and they were asking for Rehoboam to make it _____ . (v. 4)

3. Rehoboam consulted the _____ and the _____ _____ who offered conflicting advice. (vv. 6-11)

4. Rehoboam answered the people _____

and forsook the counsel of the elders. (v. 13)

DISCUSS THE MEANING

1. Why do you think Rehoboam listened to the young men and not the elders?

2. What happens when we do not consult the Lord in our decision-making process?

LESSON IN OUR SOCIETY

A simple definition of godly wisdom is obtaining insight or direction from God. This insight and direction often influences major and minor decisions that are made in the lives of His people. In our society, however, very few people make decisions this way. Therefore, foolishness, not wisdom, permeates our country. People are making more and more decisions without the wisdom of God. This makes no sense and is even harmful to our nation.

MAKE IT HAPPEN

Evaluate the last major decision you made.

1. I talked with God on a regular basis concerning all areas of my life, not just this particular decision. (Yes) (No)

2. I had a heart that was willing to follow whatever way He directed, even when it seemed contrary to what I thought or felt about the matter. (Yes) (No)

3. I waited until I was sure God had spoken, even if it was an uncomfortable amount of time. (Yes) (No)

4. I studied the Scriptures on a regular basis and when I needed to make a decision I was already in the Word looking for God to speak. (Yes) (No)

5. I consulted some godly Christian people to pray with me about the decision and to give me wise advice. (Yes) (No)

If you answered yes to most of the questions, you are walking in wisdom with your decisions. If you answered "no" to most of the questions, you need ask God to help you to make your decisions.

FOLLOW THE SPIRIT

What God wants me to do:

_____

_____

REMEMBER YOUR THOUGHTS
Special insights you learned:

_____

_____

MORE LIGHT ON THE TEXT
1 Kings 12:3-4, 6-11, 13, 16

12:3 That they sent and called him. And Jeroboam and all the congregation of Israel came, and spake unto Rehoboam saying,

Jeroboam had fled to Egypt, because the prophet Ahijah foretold that the Lord, Yahweh, was going to split the kingdom and give Jeroboam charge over ten of the twelve tribes. When Solomon got word of this, he sought to kill Jeroboam. Earlier Solomon had given Jeroboam great authority, and Jeroboam's influence was increasing. He was one of Solomon's mightiest warriors. The Greek version of the Bible presents an account where Jeroboam actually attempted to overthrow Solomon with an army of three hundred chariots. The Hebrew version of the Bible does not contain this account. But something happened which caused Jeroboam to flee from Israel until Solomon's death. The signs of change were becoming apparent.

Word reached Jeroboam that Solomon had died, and his son, Rehoboam, was going to be crowned king over all of Israel. This information was probably sent by supporters of Jeroboam, who would rather have seen him as king. On the day of the coronation of Rehoboam, all of Israel gathered together for this historic occasion. Under the leadership of Jeroboam, a challenge was posed to Rehoboam's authority over the people.

4 Thy father made our yoke grievous: now therefore make thou the grievous service of thy father, and his heavy yoke which he put upon us, lighter, and we will serve thee.

King Solomon had imposed heavy taxation upon the people, taking great amounts of their income and produce to fund the massive building projects he had initiated throughout the country. Even their labor was taken for these projects, leaving them little time to tend to their own fields. This situation went on for a period of more than twenty years. It took quite a toll on the families

and the households for at least a generation. There was no end in sight, unless except a new king might change this policy. Thus, when Rehoboam was about to be made king, they informed him of the conditions upon which he might have their loyal service.

12:6 And King Rehoboam consulted with the old men, that stood before Solomon his father while he yet lived, and said, How do ye advise that I may answer this people?

These conditions to Rehoboam's rule must have come as quite a shock! But he took it quiet seriously, because his kingship was dependent upon the response he would give. So Rehoboam took time to seek advice. First, he sought the counsel of the old men. This designation "old" does not necessarily indicate their age, but probably does correlate with the fact that they served as Solomon's counsel. They were definitely older than Rehoboam.

7 And they spake unto him, saying, If thou wilt be a servant unto this people this day, and wilt serve them, and answer them, and speak good words to them, then they will be thy servants forever.

The old men advised Rehoboam, Be a servant to the people, and they will serve you. This was the model that Solomon had handed down. He had asked the Lord for understanding that he might serve the people well. At least this was how Solomon began his rule of Israel. Perhaps by the time Rehoboam was old enough to see his father interact with the people, and to begin to evaluate and integrate such information, Solomon had changed. Thus, Rehoboam may only have seen his father as a harsh ruler, a role which he hoped to assume.

The old men advised Rehoboam to "speak good words." This meant that he should speak to the people in a peaceful, kindly tone, in addition to giving them a favorable response. A hostile, arrogant tone might do as much to turn the people away from Rehoboam's authority as a negative response. This response should be cautious and diplomatic, aiming to gain the loyal following of the people.

8 But he forsook the counsel of the old men, which they had given him, and consulted with the young men that were grown up with him, and which stood before him:

Rehoboam decided that he did not like the advice that the old men had given him. It went against his own instincts. He wanted to hear something that was in agreement with his own thinking. So he consulted next with men of his own age, who served as his counsel. They grew up together and had experienced the world in much the same way. He trusted their perceptions more, because they were like his own.

9 And he said unto them, What counsel give ye that we may answer this people, who have spoken to me, saying, Make the yoke which thy father did put upon us lighter?

So Rehoboam put the matter before these young men to see what they would advise. He restated the condition that the people requested. It is interesting that in Rehoboam's restatement, he left off the consequence that the people gave

with the condition. This reveals something of the mind set of Rehoboam. He took the loyalty of the people for granted. How dare they even think they would not serve him as they had served his father? Who were they to dictate to the king? As the young men considered their response, they were not to entertain any possibility the people might not serve the king. These young men may have been present at the original event, but they were only to consider whether the people had a right to make such a statement to a king.

10 And the young men that were grown up with him spake unto him, saying, Thus shalt thou speak unto this people that spake unto thee, saying, Thy father made our yoke heavy, but make thou it lighter unto us; thus shalt thou say unto them, My little finger shall be thicker than my father's loins.

The tone of the response offered by the young men was arrogant and insolent. The statement "my little finger shall be thicker than my father's loins" is hyperbolic, an exaggeration. It is more akin to the kind of things one says when playing the dozens, than the diplomatic statement the old men had in mind. This statement has given translators difficulty. The Hebrew simply says "my little one," which has been reconstructed as "my little finger." The Syriac translators found difficulty with the comparison of the finger to the loins, and so they changed the word "loins" to "thumb."

Solomon's virility was widely known. With so many wives, one might easily make the leap that he was endowed in a special way, if not in size, definitely in stamina. Whether Rehoboam was comparing fingers or genitalia, it is clear that he intended to exhibit more strength than his father did.

11 And now whereas my father did lade you with a heavy yoke, I will add to your yoke: my father hath chastised you with whips, but I will chastise you with scorpions.

Rehoboam opted to deny the people's request. Not only would he not lighten their yoke, he would make it heavier. Moreover, the whips that Solomon had used to chastise and urge the people to work harder would be exchanged for scorpions. This probably did not refer to the little poisonous arachnid but to lashes, or rods, which had spikes fitted into them. These would provide a more painful blow, but not unto death.

12:13 And the king answered the people roughly, and forsook the old men's counsel that they gave him;

The king had made his decision to ignore the advice of the old men. He took the advice of the young men, and responded in a harsh tone and in an insolent manner, completely disregarding the people and their complaint. If they thought Solomon was bad, Rehoboam would be much worse. Rehoboam did not view himself as a servant of the people, but the people as his servants.

12:16 So when all Israel saw that the king hearkened not unto them, the people answered the king, saying, What portion have we in David? neither have we inheritance in the son of Jesse: to your tent, O Israel: now see to thine own house,

David. So Israel departed unto their tents.

When the congregation heard that Rehoboam had no intention of easing their burden, they seceded from the tribal federation and returned to their respective territories and homes. Each tribe had been given an independent portion of land, except the Levites, as an inheritance when they settled in the land of Canaan. This land was to remain within the tribal inheritance, in spite of marriages across tribal lines. It was against God's wish that they asked for a king to rule over them, but they united their strength and resources to become a strong nation in the region. Now, after only three kings, they decided they had enough. So the ten land-holding tribes withdrew and left Rehoboam to rule over his own tribe, Judah. Thus the prophecy of Ahijah came to pass.

The reference to David's "house" is clearly pointing to the palace. The reference to the "tents" of the other tribes may indicate that most of the building and modernizing Solomon did was primarily in his own territory of Judah. Thus, the other tribes had been greatly taxed, but did not see much benefit in their respective territories.

DAILY BIBLE READINGS

M: Jeroboam Versus Rehoboam
1 Kings 12:1-9
T: An Unwise Decision Made
1 Kings 12:6-15
W: The Northern Tribes Secede
1 Kings 12:16-24
T: Jeroboam's Golden Calves
1 Kings 12:25-33
F: Revolt Against Rehoboam
2 Chronicles 10:1-11
S: Division of the Kingdom
2 Chronicles 10:12-19
S: Judah and Benjamin Fortified
2 Chronicles 11:1-12

TEACHING TIPS

June 10
Bible Study Guide 2

1. Words You Should Know

Oil (1 Kings 17:12) Hebrew *shemen*—grease, liquid, olive oil. Oil had multiple purposes in the Bible: cooking, lighting lamps, perfume, sacrificial ointment, initiation for leaders, cleansing rituals, medications, and a preservative. In the New Testament, it signified the Holy Spirit.

2. Teacher Preparation

A. Reading the DAILY BIBLE READINGS during the week is a good place to start the lesson.

B. Read the FOCAL VERSES and the commentary for Bible Study Guide 2.

C. Materials needed: Bibles, a writing board or newsprint. Optional, a little jar of oil and a handful of cornmeal or flour.

3. Starting the Lesson

A. Before class put the oil and flour out in a place where everyone can see it. Write this formula on the board: oil + flour + a little bit of faith = God's consistent provision. Also write on the board: faith + obedience = the blessings of God. When the students are seated, ask if any of them have a formula that goes along with the lesson. Record their responses on the board.

B. Have one person read the LESSON AIM and the AT-A-GLANCE outline. Have that person pray based on the goals and the subject of the lesson.

4. Getting into the Lesson

A. Read the IN FOCUS story. Assign one person to summarize the BACKGROUND section, and have several people summarize THE PEOPLE, PLACES, AND TIMES section.

B. Divide the class into three groups. Give each group one of the three sections of the lesson. Have them read the verses and the commentary pertaining to their section and answer the true and false questions in SEARCH THE SCRIPTURES.

C. After each group has presented their section, review the DISCUSS THE MEANING questions.

D. Be sure to allow time for LESSON IN OUR SOCIETY. Emphasize the importance of following God to enjoy His blessings.

5. Relating the Lesson to Life

A. Read the DISCUSS THE MEANING questions and encourage students to give their responses tying in how God finds ways to gain our attention and provide direction for our lives today.

6. Arousing Action

A. Ask the class to sit with their eyes closed and prayerfully ask themselves these questions.

B. Optional: Sing a verse of "I Surrender All" or "Have Thine Own Way Lord." Ask the students to pray short prayers on how God spoke to them through the lesson.

WORSHIP GUIDE

For the Superintendent or Teacher
Theme: Elijah: A Prophet Appears
Theme Song: Lead Me, Guide Me
Scripture: 1 Kings 17:1-5, 8-16
Song: I Have Decided To Follow Jesus
Meditation: Thank You Lord, that we don't have to go through this life, which at times can be very dark, alone. You constantly extend Your guiding hand and shine Your guiding light along our path.
Amen.

ELIJAH: A PROPHET APPEARS

Bible Background • 1 KINGS 17
Printed Text • 1 KINGS 17:1-5, 8-16
Devotional Reading • JOB 36:5-11

JUNE
10TH

LESSON AIM

By the end of this lesson, the students should be able to identify God's leading in specific incidents of Elijah's life and realize how God's guidance was a great benefit for him. This should motivate believers to follow God closely like Elijah.

KEEP IN MIND

"And the barrel of meal wasted not, neither did the cruse of oil fail, according to the word of the Lord, which he spake by Elijah" (1 Kings 17:16, KJV).

FOCAL VERSES

1 Kings 17:1 And Elijah the Tishbite, who was of the inhabitants of Gilead, said unto Ahab, As the Lord God of Israel liveth, before whom I stand, there shall not be dew nor rain these years, but according to my word.

2 And the word of the Lord came unto him, saying,

3 Get thee hence, and turn thee eastward, and hide thyself by the brook Cherith, that is before Jordan.

4 And it shall be, that thou shalt drink of the brook; and I have commanded the ravens to feed thee there.

5 So he went and did according unto the word of the Lord: for he went and dwelt by the brook Cherith, that is before Jordan.

17:8 And the word of the Lord came unto him, saying,

9 Arise, get thee to Zarephath, which belongeth to Zidon, and dwell there: behold, I have com-

LESSON OVERVIEW

LESSON AIM
KEEP IN MIND
FOCAL VERSES
IN FOCUS
THE PEOPLE, PLACES, AND TIMES
BACKGROUND
AT-A-GLANCE
IN DEPTH
SEARCH THE SCRIPTURES
DISCUSS THE MEANING
LESSON IN OUR SOCIETY
MAKE IT HAPPEN
FOLLOW THE SPIRIT
REMEMBER YOUR THOUGHTS
MORE LIGHT ON THE TEXT
DAILY BIBLE READINGS

manded a widow woman there to sustain thee.

10 So he arose and went to Zarephath. And when he came to the gate of the city, behold, the widow woman was there gathering sticks: and he called to her, and said, Fetch me, I pray thee, a little water in a vessel, that I may drink.

11 And as she was going to fetch it, he called to her, and said, Bring me, I pray thee, a morsel of bread in thine hand.

12 And she said, As the Lord thy God liveth, I have not a cake, but an handful of meal in a barrel, and little oil in a cruse: and, behold, I am gathering two sticks, that I may go in and dress it for me and my son, that we may eat it, and die.

13 And Elijah said unto her, Fear not; go and do as thou has said: but make me thereof a little cake first, and bring it unto me, and after make for thee and for thy son.

14 For thus saith the Lord God of Israel, The barrel of meal shall not waste, neither shall the cruse of oil fail, until the day that the Lord sendeth rain upon the earth.

15 And she went and did according to the saying of Elijah: and she, and he, and her house, did eat many days.

16 And the barrel of meal wasted not, neither did the cruse of oil fail, according to the word of the Lord, which he spake by Elijah.

IN FOCUS

Elijah was a man who followed God's instructions; therefore, God used him to:

• Confront Ahab a powerful, violent, evil king

• Cause a nationwide drought throughout Israel and other regions

• Meet the needs of a Gentile, poverty-stricken widow and her son

• Raise a child from the dead

• Challenge an idolatrous nation to take a stand for God

• Cause fire to come down from heaven to consume an altar and also to consume soldiers

Elijah stayed close to God and followed His instructions. He went down in history as a man of prayer, who skipped death and went heaven in a chariot of fire; and he was also one of the most powerful prophets who ever lived.

King Ahab was a man who followed his own fleshly desires and his evil wife Jezebel's instructions; therefore, Satan used him to:

• Do more evil than all the kings before him

• Marry one of the most evil women in biblical history

• Serve Baal and worship him

• Build a temple to Baal in the center of Israel's capital city, Samaria

• Attempt to convert God's people into Baal worshipers

• Steal, murder, lie, and trust in self and other men for help

King Ahab went down in history as one of Israel's worst kings. He spent most of his life in rebellion toward God.

Elijah and Ahab were two powerful men. One was led and directed by God, and the other one was influenced and directed by Satan. In today's lesson we will see the importance of following God's instruction.

THE PEOPLE, PLACES, AND TIMES

Elijah. The name means "My God is Yahweh." He was an inhabitant of Tishbe of Naphtah, which was located in the region of Gilead. He was commissioned by God as a prophet and was also regarded as a man of prayer. He prophesied during the wicked, ungodly era of King Ahab.

Ahab. The seventh king of Israel. Asa and Jehoshapaht ruled at separate times in Judah while Ahab ruled in Israel. He was married to

Jezebel, one of the wicked women named in Scripture. She was from Tyre and her goal was to turn Israel into Baal worshipers and to completely wipe out the worship of the true and living God in Israel. She greatly influenced her husband in evil and destructive ways.

BACKGROUND

The nation of Israel divided, after King Solomon's death, into the Northern Kingdom (Israel) and the Southern Kingdom (Judah). The Northern Kingdom continued for the next two hundred years, then in 722 B. C., the nation of Assyria destroyed the Northern Kingdom and took it completely over. Before this happened nineteen kings reigned in the Northern Kingdom. No godly kings ruled in the Northern Kingdom. Not one! All of them "walked in the way of Jeroboam," Israel's first king. Jeroboam led the nation into idolatry and each king after him continued this practice.

The Southern Kingdom lasted one hundred and thirty years longer than the Northern Kingdom. Judah, however, eventually was carried into captivity by Babylon and the people were in bondage in Babylon for seventy years. In Judah's history, nineteen kings and one queen ruled. Several of them were ungodly just like the kings in the North. However, there were also several good kings. They followed in the ways of King David and sought after God.

The Northern Kingdom's sixth king was Omri. He was more wicked than the five kings before him. "Omri wrought evil in the eyes of Jehovah, and did worse than all that were before him." He continued the worship of Jeroboam's golden calves and added new idols and practices of his own.

Ahab, Omri's son, took the throne when his father died. Ahab exceeded the wickedness of his father. "Ahab did more to provoke Jehovah the God of Israel to anger than all the kings of Israel that were before him." One of the many sins Ahab committed was to marry Jezebel. She was the daughter of Ethbaal, king of the Zidonians, within the Canaanite nation. God's people were strictly forbidden to intermarry with the people in the corrupt Canaanite nation. God was concerned about the Canaanites causing the Israelites to turn away from serving Him. This is exactly what happened during Ahab's reign. Jezebel launched an all-out campaign to rid Israel of God's prophets and replace them with Baal's prophets. She intended to wipe out all traces of God in Israel and turn the nation into one that worshiped Baal. Ahab built a temple to Baal in their residence of Samaria and appointed several priests to oversee the worship.

AT-A-GLANCE

1. Elijah Predicted a Drought
(1 Kings 17:1)
2. Elijah Provided for by Ravens
(vv. 2-5)
3. Elijah Provided for by a Widow
(vv. 8-16)

IN DEPTH

1. Elijah Predicted a Drought (1 Kings 17:1)

When Ahab became king, he ushered in one of the worst periods of time for the nation of Israel. However, when great wickedness abounds, God makes His presence abound as well. Elijah was one of the most powerful prophets in history. He was called by God to confront the evil king, his false god Baal, and Baal's prophets. Elijah was also called to challenge the nation of Israel to take one side or the other—serve God or Baal. God no longer allowed this nation to straddle the fence.

Elijah was considered one of the most influential leaders since Moses and Samuel, yet very little is known about him. He appeared dramatically without any introduction. It was as if Elijah came out of the unknown and appeared right before the face of King Ahab and Jezebel, who lived in Samaria. He boldly stated, "It will not rain until I say so." Elijah gives no personal credentials, no reasons for the drought, and no conditions for mercy. The drought, which would lead to a famine, was punishment for Ahab's idolatry and leading the nation into the sin of idolatry.

Elijah delivered the message of doom and walked away. This was a bold step. In Israel, Ahab and Jezebel exterminated the prophets of God so the prophets of Baal could take over. Elijah knew the danger. Ahab could have seized him and had him killed right there on the spot.

However, Elijah followed God's instructions. God had a plan for him to fulfill, therefore, no harm was done to Elijah.

No rain in Samaria was quite unusual for this region. Generally rains fell between late October and early January and then more rain between April and early May. For no rain to fall for three and a half years was truly an act of God. Dew and rain were the main sources of moisture in ancient Israel. The lack of rain affected crops, grazing land, orchards, farm animals, and drinking supplies. Lack of rain could also affect the moods of people, causing them to be discouraged and depressed. One can imagine the devastating impact three and a half years of drought produced.

The drought also slapped Baal in the face. Baal was the god of rain. It proved that God was greater and mightier than this Canaanite god.

2. Elijah Provided for by Ravens (vv. 2-5)

After Elijah confronted king Ahab about the coming drought, God sent Elijah to a safe place to protect his life. God also shielded Elijah from Ahab's pleas and threats to bring back the rain.

God directed Elijah to a stream flowing into the east bank of the Jordan, the brook of Cherith. While Elijah resided there, God miraculously provided for him. Ravens delivered bread and meat twice a day. Ravens are unclean meat-eating birds. God used the raven, not a sparrow or a dove, to supply Elijah's food. That makes this miracle even more extraordinary. Possibly God used this supernatural event at this point in Elijah's ministry to build up his faith to meet the challenges ahead. It would be a constant reminder of God's provision in the midst of a difficult time. The period time Elijah spent here and in the next place he resided, Zarephath, totaled about two years.

3. Elijah Provided for by a Widow (vv. 8-16)

In time, the drought worsened and the Brook Cherith dried up. God directed Elijah to go one hundred miles north to the home of a widow in the Phoenician coastal city of Zarephath, about seven miles south of Sidon. This Phoenician area was controlled by Jezebel's father. Elijah visited enemy territory and demonstrated the power of God in an area where only Baal was worshiped.

Here Elijah found a poverty-stricken widow, suffering the deprivation of the drought, with a son she was attempting to feed. Obviously, the drought and famine had affected not only Israel but had infiltrated other nations surrounding it. Elijah saw a widow picking up sticks when he first entered the city. Elijah might have uttered a prayer to ask His divine guidance. Elijah asked the widow for water and something to eat. Before she responded to Elijah's request, the widow said, "As Jehovah thy God liveth." Even though Elijah was in a nation whose god was Baal, he had found a believer in the true and living God. This assured him that he had come to the right widow. Even though she lived in a Gentile city filled with the worship of Baal, she knew and believed in Yahweh (v. 12 and Luke 4:26). God had never made a covenant with any other nation besides Israel, but He did accept and use many Gentile individual believers for His purposes.

The widow also recognized Elijah as an Israelite and a man of God, probably from the way he looked and the way in which he was dressed.

The second thing the widow did to assure Elijah he had found the right woman was her exercise of faith in God's word. When Elijah asked her to bring him some water and a little cake to eat, the widow replied, "I don't have any bread. All I have is a handful of flour in a bowl and a bit of olive oil in a jar . . ." (v. 12, Good News).

Elijah assured her, "Don't worry. Go home and do as you have said, but first make me a small loaf from what you have and bring it to me, and then prepare the rest for you and your son." This is what the Lord, the God of Israel, had spoken to Elijah: "The bowl will not run out of flour or the jar run out of oil before the day that I, the Lord, send rain."

The widow believed what Elijah said. She prepared him a cake. Here is another indication she

was the widow God was sending Elijah to take care of his needs during the remainder of the drought. Not only was she able to take care of Elijah, but God took care of her and her son as well. Just as Elijah had spoken, the oil and flour did not run out.

SEARCH THE SCRIPTURES
True/False

1. Elijah the Tishbite confronted King Ahab and told him that it would not rain until he repented from his sins. (1 Kings 17:1)
(T) (F)

2. Elijah went to the brook Cherith and commanded the sparrows to feed him there. (vv. 3-4)
(T) (F)

3. Elijah went to Zarephath and met a widow with three handfuls of meal; she took that and prepared something for him to eat. (vv. 10-12)
(T) (F)

4. The oil and flour provided by the Lord did not run out until Elijah left her home. (v. 16)
(T) (F)

DISCUSS THE MEANING

1. Why did God use the problem of no rain in Israel? How did this aid His cause against Baal?

2. How does looking at Elijah and how God provided for him change your perspective on God's provisions?

LESSON IN OUR SOCIETY

How many Christmas Eve stories have we heard like this one: A parent purchases a bike, train, racetrack, or some kind of item that needs assembling for a child. Parent "A," usually the father, proceeds to put the item together on Christmas Eve. As they pull the material from the box, parent "B," usually the mother, says very kindly, "Here's the instruction booklet, Dear. Don't you need this?"

Parent "A" replies, "I don't need those; this looks easy." Several hours later, pieces and parts are all over the floor. Parent "A" calls out, "Honey, what did you do with those instructions?"

It is human nature to want to do things our own way and not follow instructions. However,

God created each one of us. The Bible is our instruction manual. When we do not follow His ways, expect something worse to occur in your life than a Christmas Eve toy disaster.

MAKE IT HAPPEN

When God gives instructions He is attempting to protect and take care of us. When we follow His instructions we are safe. When we disregard them we suffer and experience chaos and confusion in our lives. This will eventually lead to unfulfillment and unhappiness. "Blessed is the man who walks in the ways of the Lord."

When God makes His will clear to you, do you follow it? Do you wait until God's will is clear to you or do you live in a fog? Do you know when God is speaking to you? The study of God's Word is one way to be sure of God's voice. Are you studying on a regular basis or do you desperately search the Scriptures when your life is falling apart?

FOLLOW THE SPIRIT

What God wants me to do:

_____

_____

REMEMBER YOUR THOUGHTS

Special insights you learned:

_____

_____

MORE LIGHT ON THE TEXT

1 Kings 17:1-5, 8-16

17:1 And Elijah the Tishbite, who was of the inhabitants of Gilead, said unto Ahab, As the Lord God of Israel liveth, before whom I stand, there shall not be dew nor rain these years, but according to my word.

Elijah was native of Tishbe, a town east of the Jordan River. While he was dwelling in Gilead, the prophet was instructed to go to Samaria to deliver a word of the Lord to Ahab, the King of Israel. There was going to be a great drought and famine in the land. He did not specify how many years the region would be without rain. Even the morning dew would not appear to provide moisture, except as the prophet spoke by Yahweh's

instructions. The reason for the drought was that King Ahab had done worse than Solomon and Jeroboam in leading the people of Yahweh astray by incorporating the worship of Baal into Israel. Ahab married a Zidonian princess named Jezebel and built an altar to the House of Baal in the capital of the northern tribes, Samaria. Ahab provoked God to anger more than any of the kings before him (1 Kings 16:31-33). Since Ahab led the Israelites to worship Baal, the Canaanite storm-god, they would have a good opportunity to call upon him to save them from the drought.

2 And the word of the Lord came unto him, saying,

This is a frequently used phrase used to introduce an instruction or conversation directly from God. This stands in contrast to the prophet quoting what God has told him, which is indicated by "Thus saith the Lord."

3 Get thee hence, and turn thee eastward, and hide thyself by the brook Cherith, that is before Jordan.

Get out of Samaria now! The king would probably seek to kill the prophet who delivered such a word of impending doom. Yahweh instructed Elijah to go hide and himself east of the Jordan River. The precise location of the brook Cherith is unknown. Elijah could not return home, because that would be the first place the king would search for him.

4 And it shall be, that thou shalt drink of the brook; and I have commanded the ravens to feed thee there.

This would be a time of great trust for Elijah. While the nation of Israel suffered under the drought and the resulting famine, Elijah would have water and provisions provided for him by Yahweh. Elijah would not have to hunt or scrounge for food, because the ravens would bring food for him. The raven was considered an unclean bird (Leviticus 11:15) and was not to be eaten by Elijah. But Yahweh commanded these birds to bring food to Elijah twice a day.

In time, even this brook would dry up. The brooks, or *wadis,* were flourishing riverbeds during the rainy season. Afterwards, they were as dry and barren as the desert.

5 So he went and did according unto the word of the Lord: for he went and dwelt by the brook Cherith, that is before the Jordan.

Elijah was obedient and followed the Lord's instructions to the letter. His survival depended upon his obedience to the Lord. Likewise, Israel's survival was dependent upon obedience to Yahweh, but their king led them away from Yahweh to Baal.

17:8 And the word of the Lord came unto him, saying,

Again, Elijah received instructions directly from God.

9 Arise, get thee to Zarephath, which belongeth to Zidon, and dwell there: behold I have commanded a widow there to sustain thee.

It was time to leave the first place of hiding. The Lord had made other arrangements for Elijah's survival. This time God's instructions took Elijah right into the midst of the worshipers of Baal. Zarephath was a coastal Phoenician city south of Zidon, the principal city of Baal worship. This was out of Ahab's territory. The time for confrontation had not yet arrived.

Elijah was to live there and be sustained by the poorest of the poor, a widow woman. This may represent a slight improvement over the wilderness arrangements. Without a husband to provide for them, widows fell quickly into poverty, being reduced to begging. In Israel, the commandments urged the local priesthood or palace to include widows and orphans under their care. This may not have been the case in Phoenicia.

10 So he arose and went to Zarephath. And when he came to the gate of the city, behold, the widow woman was there gathering sticks: and he called to her, and said, Fetch me, I pray thee, a little water in a vessel, that I may drink.

Once again Elijah obeyed the Lord's instructions. When he arrived at the entrance to the city, immediately he saw a widow woman gather-

ing sticks for a fire. But how would he be sure whether she was the one God commanded to sustain him. Surely she was not the only widow in the city. He called to her and politely asked her to get him a drink of water in a vessel. The expression "I pray thee" is one of great humility, usually used when an inferior speaks to a superior. After all, he was the stranger. She would have had to draw this water from a well, supplied by underground springs, because there had been no rain.

The whole encounter raises questions about hospitality. Usually men and women did not address one another in public places. It is even more unusual for Elijah, a stranger to the city, to approach a woman. Normally men were assigned near the gate of the city. It was their job to check out strangers to determine whether they were friend or foe. Friends would be welcomed into the city, and shown the utmost hospitality. Foes would be escorted out. This unusual behavior was Elijah's way of testing to see if she was the one whom Yahweh commanded.

11 And as she was going to fetch it, he called to her, and said, "Bring me, I pray thee, a morsel of bread in thine hand.

Instead of fleeing from this stranger, the widow went to get him the water he had requested. No telling how far he had come without water. Her instinct for caring took over her sense of fear. When she responded in this way, Elijah was more confident that she was indeed the one. Before she could fulfill his first request, he called to her with a second request. Again very politely, he asked her for a small portion of bread. Again he was very humble in his request. He did not ask for much and was willing to accept the food from her hand.

12 And she said, As the Lord thy God liveth, I have not a cake, but a handful of meal in a barrel, and a little oil in a cruse: and, behold, I am gathering two sticks, that I may go in and dress it for me and my son, that we may eat it, and die.

The widow recognized that Elijah was a worshiper of the Lord, Yahweh, and not of Baal. She even acknowledged that Yahweh was a living god, not a god of wood or stone formed by men (perhaps her knowledge of Yahweh came through an undescribed encounter when He commanded her to provide sustenance for an approaching Israelite). Then she confessed to Elijah, she was at the end of her supplies and could not foresee how she could provide for herself and her son. She had planned to prepare this last meal for herself and for her son, then they would die of starvation in a few days. The amount she had was not sufficient for the two of them, she must have thought; now this man wants to eat of it also.

13 And Elijah said unto her, Fear not; go and do as thou hast said: but make me thereof a little cake first, and bring it unto me, and after make for thee and for thy son.

Elijah gave her assurance, "Fear not." He told the widow to go ahead as she had planned, only make a small cake for him first and bring it to him. Then she could prepare for herself and her son. Elijah was asking her to put her trust in him and his God. If she would be willing to do this act of kindness first, demonstrating obedience and trust in Yahweh, then she could go on with her plan. But Elijah had more to offer her than words of assurance. He also had a promise from God!

14 For thus saith the Lord God of Israel, The barrel of meal shall not waste, neither shall the cruse of oil fail, until the day that the Lord sendeth rain upon the earth.

Elijah told the widow of Yahweh's promise to sustain them throughout the drought. The barrel of meal which contained only a handful, would be filled and would never spoil. Even the container of oil, which had only a few drops, would never fail to supply their need until the time that Yahweh caused the rain to return to the earth. She would be sustained better during this drought than she had been before, if only she would trust in the man of God and obey what Yahweh had commanded her.

15 And she went and did according to the saying of Elijah: and she, and he, and her house did eat many days.

The widow woman decided to trust and obey Yahweh, a god foreign to her. Her faith in Baal did not keep her from the brink of starvation, but she experienced the power of Yahweh for herself. And thus, she and Elijah and her son ate for a long time from the food that Yahweh supplied. Surely others must have noticed how well-fed she and her household looked, while others looked malnourished.

16 And the barrel of meal wasted not, neither did the cruse of oil fail, according to the word of the Lord, which he spake by Elijah.

Because of her obedience, Yahweh fulfilled His promise. This was the very lesson that Yahweh wanted Israel to learn, but they were too busy putting their trust in Baal.

DAILY BIBLE READINGS

M: Omri Reigns over Israel
1 Kings 16:21-28
T: Ahab Reigns over Israel
1 Kings 16:29-34
W: Elijah Predicts a Drought in Israel
1 Kings 17:1-7
T: The Prayer of Faith
James 5:13-18
F: The Widow of Zarephath
1 Kings 17:8-16
S: Elijah Revives the Widow's Son
1 Kings 17:17-24
S: God's Goodness
Job 36:5-11

TEACHING TIPS

June 17
Bible Study Guide 3

1. Words You Should Know

A. Halt (1 Kings 18:21) Hebrew *pacach* (Pakak)—falter, limp, hop, dance, or leap. To waver, fluctuate.

B. Opinions (v. 21) Hebrew *caiph* (Kayif)— speaks of clefts, branches, for example in a tree limb or in a road. A divided opinion, division, opposites.

2. Teacher Preparation

A. There are quite a few commentaries about Elijah and his life and ministry. You might want to pick one up from your local Christian bookstore and skim through it to pick up more information about him which you can pass on to your class.

B. Read the Bible Background. It's important to understand how God set the stage for this extraordinary miracle.

C. Read through the FOCAL VERSES and the commentary. Be sure you have completed the puzzle in the SEARCH THE SCRIPTURES section.

D. You will need Bibles and a small prize.

3. Starting the Lesson

A. Have a contest to see who can complete the puzzle in the SEARCH THE SCRIPTURES section of the lesson the fastest. Give him/her the prize. Explain that this week's lesson is also about a contest between the false god and the true and living God. The puzzle contest is not that important but the contest between Baal and God was very important and significant.

B. Have the class read the LESSON AIM and the AT-A-GLANCE outline. Have a time of silent prayer and ask each student to pray that God would speak to their needs.

4. Getting into the Lesson

Go around the room and have each student read aloud a paragraph from the IN FOCUS section, a verse from the FOCAL VERSES, a paragraph from the IN DEPTH section, a person or place from the BACKGROUND and THE PEOPLE, PLACES, AND TIMES section.

5. Relating the Lesson to Life

A. Take time to answer the DISCUSS THE MEANING questions. If there is time, encourage students to share personal experiences. Be sure you have some of your own to share.

B. Have someone read the LESSON IN OUR SOCIETY article.

6. Arousing Action

A. Summarize the MAKE IT HAPPEN section.

B. Go around the room and ask each student what they plan to do differently this week as a result of this lesson.

WORSHIP GUIDE

For the Superintendent or Teacher
Theme: Israel: Called to Decide
Theme Song: Jesus is Tenderly Calling
Scripture: 1 Kings 18:20-21, 30-39
Song: I'm on the Battle Field
Meditation: Thank You Lord, for Your Holy Spirit which is a searchlight in my life. Show me any areas of compromise. Then give me the stillness to allow You to dig up the root and get rid of the sin in my life.

ISRAEL: CALLED TO DECIDE

Bible Background • 1 KINGS 18
Printed Text • 1 KINGS 18:20-21, 30-39
Devotional Reading • JOSHUA 24:14-18

LESSON AIM

By the end of this lesson, the students should be able to review the great historical event on Mount Carmel when Elijah challenged the prophets of Baal and be convinced of how powerful God be can if we remain on His side.

KEEP IN MIND

"And Elijah came unto all the people, and said, How long halt ye between two opinions? If the Lord be God, follow him: but if Baal, the follow him. And the people answer him not a word" (1 Kings 18:21, KJV).

FOCAL VERSES

1 Kings 18:20 So Ahab sent unto all the children of Israel, and gathered the prophets together unto Mount Carmel.

21 And Elijah came unto all the people, and said, How long halt ye between two opinions? If the Lord be God, follow him: but if Baal, the follow him. And the people answered him not a word.

18:30 And Elijah said unto all the people, Come near unto me. And all the people came near unto him. And he repaired the altar of the Lord that was broken down.

31 And Elijah took twelve stones, according to the number of the tribes of the sons of Jacob, unto whom the word of the Lord came, saying, Israel shall be thy name:

32 And with the stones he built an altar in the name of the Lord: and he made a trench about the altar, as great as would contain two measures of seed.

LESSON OVERVIEW

LESSON AIM
KEEP IN MIND
FOCAL VERSES
IN FOCUS
THE PEOPLE, PLACES, AND TIMES
BACKGROUND
AT-A-GLANCE
IN DEPTH
SEARCH THE SCRIPTURES
DISCUSS THE MEANING
LESSON IN OUR SOCIETY
MAKE IT HAPPEN
FOLLOW THE SPIRIT
REMEMBER YOUR THOUGHTS
MORE LIGHT ON THE TEXT
DAILY BIBLE READINGS

33 And he put the wood in order, and cut the bullock in pieces, and laid him on the wood, and said, Fill four barrels with water, and pour it on the burnt sacrifice, and on the wood.

34 And he said, Do it the second time. And they did it the second time. And he said, Do it the third time. And they did it the third time.

35 And the water ran round about the altar; and he filled the trench also with water.

36 And it came to pass at the time of the offering of the evening sacrifice, that Elijah the prophet came near, and said, Lord God of Abraham, Isaac, and of Israel, let it be known this day that thou art God in Israel, and that I am thy servant, and that I have done all these things at they word.

37 Hear me, O Lord, Hear me, that this people may know that thou art the Lord God, and that thou hast turned their heart back again.

38 Then the fire of the Lord fell, and consumed the burnt sacrifice, and the wood, and the stones, and the dust, and licked up the water that was in the trench.

39 And when all the people saw it, they fell on their faces: and they said, The Lord, he is God; the Lord he is God.

IN FOCUS

What is the power of Almighty God?

This is the God who flung out a universe—made from nothing.

He created water, land, lighting, the tiniest microorganism, and the intricacies of the human body.

How did God create?

What were His methods?

What was time before there was time?

These are God's secrets.

We only know that God spoke.

And it happened.

The rest is veiled.

Occasionally, in history, God draws aside that veil and lets us see for a moment, an image of His power.

Miracles occur . . .

Elijah lived in such a time.

And God used Elijah as a mirror of His power.

(From Characters and Kings by Carolyn Nystrom)

Elijah mirrored the power of God. When people look at you, what do you mirror?

THE PEOPLE, PLACES, AND TIMES

Mount Carmel. This mountain was on the border of Israeli and Phoenician territory. It was considered a place of worship for both nations. It has a low range of mountains running northwest to southeast from the Mediterranean Sea to the fertile Plain of Esdraelon.

Baal. A Canaanite god of the storm and fertility. The word itself means a partner or ally. It is used to indicate mastery or ownership. Droughts indicated that Baal was either dead or temporarily captive. When he came back, fields, flocks, and families flourished. The people were taught to act out a magical ritual of sacred marriage in order to insure the fertility of the earth. The worship of Baal included sexual orgies, with homosexuality, and child sacrifice.

Asherah. A major Canaanite goddess associated with passion and the sea. During the time of King Ahab and Jezebel, Asherah and Baal were being worshiped together. When Elijah confronted the 450 prophets of Baal at Mount Carmel, the 400 prophets of Asherah were summoned by Elijah but did not attend the event.

BACKGROUND

Jezebel was a native of Phoenicia. The Phoenicians were noted for their skills and business aptitude, but they were devoted worshipers of Baal. King Ahab allowed Jezebel to place the prophets of Baal in influential positions in Israel. Her plan was to replace the worship of God with the worship of Baal.

The Phoenicians lived on a narrow strip of land northwest of Palestine on the eastern shore of the Mediterranean Sea. Two of the main places in Phoenicia mentioned in the Bible are Tyre and Sidon. The area is now known as Lebanon and coastal Syria. These people once occupied the land of Canaan, but they were driven out by Israel and crowded into a narrow strip of coastline.

At one time, the Phoenicians had a good working relationship with Israel. Hiram, of Tyre, was a friend of David and Solomon. He helped Israel equip its merchant fleet. However, over the centuries these friendly relations led to sin for the nation of Israel. The Phoenician religion was a carryover from the Canaanite worship system which included child sacrifice. Baal became the main god.

The New Testament mentioned Tyre and Sidon. Jesus healed a demon-possessed girl from that area. Early Christian believers witnessed in Phoenicia after leaving Jerusalem. Paul often traveled through this area.

Throughout biblical history God allowed His people to associate with Phoenicia. This incident on Mount Carmel was not the first time, nor would it be the last, when God called Israel and its people to recognize Him and forsake their false gods.

AT-A-GLANCE

1. Elijah's Challenge to the People
(1 Kings 18:20-21)
2. Elijah Called on God
(vv. 30-37)
3. Elijah's God was Victorious
(vv. 38-39)

IN DEPTH

1. Elijah's Challenge to the People
(1 Kings 18:20-21)

In the third year of Elijah's stay at the widow in Zarapheth's home, God spoke to Elijah. He told him to go back and confront Ahab. God was about to send rain upon the land again. The three-year drought and famine had not been enough to convince King Ahab to turn from his idolatrous worship. It was time to call the nation into repentance and come back to serving the one true and living God.

When Elijah appeared before Ahab, the king called him a "troubler of Israel." He saw Elijah as the problem, not his own rebellion against the Lord.

Elijah boldly replied to Ahab, "It is not I who have brought Israel into trouble, but thou and thy family . . . ye have foresaken the commandments of Jehovah, and thou goes after Baal." Elijah challenged Ahab to gather the 450 prophets of Baal and the 400 prophets of Asherah to come to Mount Carmel.

Elijah challenged the prophets of Baal in one of the most dramatic events in biblical history. This one prophet challenged a whole nation to return to God, then he proceeded to wipe out the opposition. Elijah called not only for a commitment to the true and living God but a public declaration of their faith in Him. This was spoken in the face of Ahab and Jezebel, who were attempting to turn this nation into one that was completely dedicated to Baal. Elijah stepped up to the plate for God and defeated Baal.

The people of Israel were also present at Mount Carmel as well as the prophets of Baal. Elijah boldly challenged the people in the presence of these false prophets, "How long will you go on limping or wavering between two opinions?" This can be interpreted to mean hobbling between two forks, denoting tree branches or crossroads. Elijah was asking, How long will you "sit on the fence?" He wanted them to exclusively worship Baal or Yahweh. It was impossible to follow both. The people would not answer a word. They knew in their hearts God's law required complete loyalty to Him. Yet they lived in an environment in which the leaders were killing people who proved disloyal to Baal. To be committed to God might cost them their lives.

2. Elijah Called on God (vv. 30-37)

On Mount Carmel, Elijah gave the prophets of Baal all the advantages. The Baal prophets choose the sacrifice. Elijah allowed them to pray for as long as they wished. The proof of God's power or Baal's power was to be fire. Baal was supposed to be the god of the sun, and the god of the storm. For him to show up and produce fire should have been easy.

The worshipers of Baal danced wildly around the altar. After a while, when there was no response from Baal, Elijah began to mock and taunt the Baal worshipers. "Is your god gone on a trip? Has he gone to the bathroom? Is he asleep? Maybe you should call louder." The prophets became more earnest and intense in their worship. They began to cut themselves. The practice of self-inflicted wounds aroused a deity's pity or response. They bathed in their own blood. They ranted and raved. After all of this performance, after calling out to him all day, Baal did not appear.

By late afternoon, Elijah decided it was his turn. He called the people near. He wanted no questions or accusations from the people about trickery or clever games. They gathered around the altar of Jehovah which was broken down. Elijah restored it. Evidently an altar was already on Mount Carmel. The Baal worshipers probably destroyed it. Prior to the building of Solomon's temple, several places in Israel had altars to the Lord.

Elijah built up 12 stones, according to the number of the tribes of Jacob. Even though the nation was now divided—the Northern Kingdom, Israel, consisted of ten tribes and the Southern Kingdom, Judah, consisted of two—Elijah still used the stones to symbolize God's people as twelve tribes. The division was not what God wanted and intended for His people from the beginning. Therefore, in God's mind, the nation was still united. The priest of Judah still carried a symbol of the twelve tribes. Even in the New Testament, the nation is talked about as the twelve tribes of Israel, in spite of the division.

Elijah built a trench around the altar and then arranged the sacrifice upon the altar. Four pails of water were poured three times upon the burnt-offering. The water flowed around the alter in the trench. The prophet wanted no doubt that this was God working and no deception on the part of Elijah. False prophets had been known to set fire to the wood of the sacrifices from spaces underneath the altar in order to make people believe that the sacrifice had been set on fire by their false god.

After the altar was prepared and drenched with water, Elijah calmly prayed. This must have been anticlimactic in comparison to the ravings of the previous worshipers. He called on the God of Abraham, Isaac, and Jacob. "Prove now that you are the God of Israel and that I am your servant and have done all this at your command. Answer me, Lord, answer me, so that this people will know that you, the Lord, are God and that you are bringing them back to yourself" (vv. 36-37, Good News). Elijah prayed not only for a miracle but for the conversion of Israel.

3. Elijah's God was Victorious (vv. 38-39)

After Elijah's quiet and simple prayer, the fire from Jehovah fell and consumed the burnt offering and the altar. It also consumed the stones of the altar and licked up the water in the trench. God proved Himself to be present and mighty.

After this great demonstration the people pledged their allegiance to Him. The people cried out, "The Lord, He is God!" "Yahweh is Elohim!" Those words in Hebrew were actually Elijah's name! "Yah is El!"

Take note. The fire did not fall down on the wicked king and queen, the prophets of Baal, or the doubting congregation. The fire came down on the sacrifice. What a picture of Calvary! God did not take out his wrath on those who did wrong but on His Son to demonstrate His mercy to the sinful.

At this point, the prophets of Baal could have confessed their wrong and joined the people of God. However, they did not confess and repent. Therefore, Elijah called for the slaughter of the prophets of Baal. Elijah commanded that they be seized and slain. Not for revenge but to carry out the Old Testament Law. The Law stated that false prophets should be destroyed (Deuteronomy 13:5). The prophets were led down to the Brook

of Kishon. This water way connected to a waterway in Phoenicia. The blood of the prophets traveled back to their home where it belonged.

One would think after this kind of demonstration of God's power, Ahab and Jezebel would have given up. But they continued to challenge Elijah. Jezebel even threatened his life. Their hearts were truly hardened against the Lord.

SEARCH THE SCRIPTURES
Complete the puzzle:

Down
1. Those who represent a deity. (1 Kings 18:20)
2. A popular false god. (v. 21)
3. The 7th king of Israel. (v. 20)
Across
4. A powerful prophet sent by God during Ahab's time. (v. 36)
5. A mountain in-between two nations, spelled backwards.

DISCUSS THE MEANING
1. Why did Ahab think Elijah was the cause of the problem?
2. What does it mean to "halt between two opinions?" How were the Israelites doing this? How do we do this today?
3. God gave a mighty demonstration of His power on Mount Caramel. Do we have any prophets today like Elijah? Any Mount Caramel experiences? Why or why not?
4. What was the outcome of the showdown on Mount Caramel? Is this always the result when God shows Himself powerfully?
LESSON IN OUR SOCIETY

News reporters are not supposed to indicate what they believe. In fact, some even practice controlling their eyebrows so they do not indicate they are partial to one side or another. No one should ever know their commitment about anything.

Many people live like these reporters. They don't commit to one thing or another, especially when it concerns spiritual matters. However, when it comes to Jesus, He challenges us to get on one side or the other. "No one can serve two masters; for either he will hate the one, and love the other, or else he will be loyal to the one and despise the other. You cannot serve God and mammon" (Matthew 6:24).

MAKE IT HAPPEN

"Compromise" means to settle differences with a mutual agreement. Many times Christians will agree when someone says, "We are all going to heaven," or "It doesn't matter what you believe as long as you believe in some kind of religion," and "Jesus is not the issue as long as you believe in God." Sometimes, to keep the peace, we nod our heads in agreement, even when we know what the person has said is wrong.

Have you ever had a Mount Carmel experience? Do you need to? How can we challenge false teachings and ideas in our present situations?

FOLLOW THE SPIRIT

What He wants me to do:

_____

_____

REMEMBER YOUR THOUGHTS

Special insights you learned:

_____

_____

MORE LIGHT ON THE TEXT
1 Kings 18:20-21, 30-39

18:20 So Ahab sent unto all the children of Israel, and gathered the prophets together unto Mount Carmel.

Elijah had been hiding in Phoenicia, showing the power of the Lord, Yahweh, to the believers of Baal. Some were converted. Now Elijah had been instructed by the Lord to come out of hiding and

to return to Israel and show himself to King Ahab. When he did, Elijah told the king that the trouble Israel was experiencing was due to their worship of Baal and the other Zidonian gods; they had abandoned the commandments of Yahweh. It was now time for a direct confrontation. Elijah taunted the king and told him to gather all of Israel together at Mount Carmel, including the 450 prophets of Baal and the 400 prophets of the grove. Thus, the stage was set for a showdown.

Mount Carmel is near the western coast of Israel, at the entrance to the Jezreel Valley. It was located at the outer edge of Ahab's territory. This mountain had been a center for the cult of Baal until about 1000 B.C. The prophets of the grove are not mentioned anywhere else in the Bible. They were probably associated with the growing of particular trees, which were used in the fertility worship of Baal and Asherah.

21 And Elijah came unto all the people, and said, How long halt ye between two opinions? If the Lord be God, follow him: but if Baal, then follow him. And the people answered him not a word.

When the people had gathered around Mount Carmel, Elijah spoke directly to the people. He described their spiritual dilemma as "limping around" like a lame animal, between two belief systems. Rather than standing firm on one belief system, they hobbled back and forth between two. Elijah asked them how long they intended to remain in this quandary? His intention was to bring them to an immediate decision.

These belief systems were mutually exclusive. Either Yahweh was the God of all things, or Baal and his other gods were the gods of parts of things. They people were being forced to choose one or the other. Elijah's statement stunned them. Perhaps they were not ready to choose. Maybe they had not thought of it in those terms. They could not answer. How could they decide who was the real God? Elijah had a contest in mind.

18:30 And Elijah said unto all the people, Come near unto me. And all the people came near unto him. And he repaired the altar of the Lord that was broken down.

Elijah told the people to come closer. He wanted them to clearly see all what he was about to do. The altar of Yahweh had been neglected and unused. Under David and Solomon, Jerusalem became the worship center for Israel. When the nation divided, the kings of the northern tribes were not able to sustain the sole worship of Yahweh. This allowed some to return to their previous worship practices. Then Ahab's queen, Jezebel, killed many of the prophets and priests of Yahweh. The altar was probably smashed to break down the morale of any remaining Yahwists. So Elijah's first act was to restore the altar of Yahweh.

31 And Elijah took twelve stones, according to the number of the tribes of the sons of Jacob, unto whom the word of the Lord came, saying, Israel shall be thy name:

Elijah gathered 12 stones, one for each tribe. Twelve was the original number of the sons of Jacob, the ancestor whose name Yahweh had changed to "Israel" (Genesis 35:10). Each of Jacob's sons became the head of a tribe, which bore his ancestral name. But the corporate name under which all the tribes united was Israel. The political split under Jeroboam had drawn ten of the twelve tribes apart, but they retained the name Israel.

When Joshua was crossing the Jordan, he instructed the priests to set up 12 stones as a testimony to the mighty works of Yahweh, works they had experienced from the crossing of the Red Sea to the crossing of the Jordan. Perhaps Elijah wanted to remind the people of their roots, of their heritage under the theocracy of Yahweh. If they connected with their heritage, surely they would turn back to the Lord.

32 And with the stones he built an altar in the name of the Lord: and he made a trench about the altar, as great as would contain two measures of seed.

Elijah built this altar in the name of Yahweh, not to Baal. In addition, he dug a trench around the altar. The reference to two measures of seed could have indicated the amount of land over which two measures of seed could be strewn (approximately 1568 square meters). Thus a trench would have been dug around that area.

33 And he put the wood in order, and cut the bullock in pieces, and laid him on the wood, and said, Fill four barrels with water, and pour it on the burnt sacrifice, and on the wood.

Elijah arranged the wood, cut the bull into pieces, and laid them upon the wood on the altar, according to the instructions that Yahweh had given to the Levitical priesthood. This served as a reminder of the Yahwistic traditions of Israel's heritage. In addition, Elijah did an unusual thing. He ordered water to be poured upon the sacrifice and upon the wood. This would increase the difficulty of a fire igniting it. Not even the priests of Baal were expected to do this.

The burnt sacrifice (*korban*) was one of several types of sacrifice that Israel was instructed to offer to Yahweh (Leviticus 1). The English translation of the word simply indicates the process by which it is to be offered, while the Hebrew word emphasizes that it was an offering brought from one's herd.

34 And he said, Do it the second time. And they did it the second time. And he said, Do it the third time. And they did it the third time.

As if the first four barrels of water were not enough to thoroughly soak the meat and the wood, Elijah ordered eight more barrels to be poured upon them. Thus a total of twelve barrels of water were poured upon the offering and the wood, one for each tribe. This increased the level of difficulty that Yahweh would have to overcome to win back the hearts of his people.

35 And the water ran around about the altar; and he filled the trench also with water.

The entire area of the altar was wet. The meat was soaked; the wood was soaked; the stones were wet; even the ground around the altar was soaked by the runoff. As if that was not enough, Elijah filled the trench itself with water. If Yahweh could start a blaze here, there would be no room for doubt of His greatness.

36 And it came to pass at the time of the offering of the evening sacrifice, that Elijah the prophet came near, and said, Lord God of Abraham,

Isaac, and of Israel, let it be known this day that thou art God in Israel, and that I am thy servant, and that I have done all these things at thy word.

Presumably, Elijah had begun this whole dramatic event in the morning, as the priests of Baal had done. He built the altar, arranged the wood and the meat, and soaked it all with water. He gave it time to soak deeply into the wood, into the flesh, and into the ground. Unlike the priests of Baal, he did not spend the entire day calling upon his God. No, he patiently waited until the time of the evening sacrifice (around 3 p.m.). Then he spoke to God. He did not cry out in a loud voice, as if God was too far to hear him. He simply said what he needed to say.

Elijah called upon the name of his God, Yahweh, and identified Him as the God of their ancestors, Abraham, Isaac, and Israel. Normally, the formulation of the names of the ancestors is Abraham, Isaac, and Jacob. But Elijah was making a political statement regarding the identity of this people; they were named by Yahweh in the first place, not by Baal. "Let it be known today"—do not let another day pass—"that You are God in Israel. Let the Zidonians have Baal, but prove that You are God in Israel."

Elijah also asked Yahweh to prove his legitimacy as a servant of Yahweh. Many of the prophets of Yahweh had been killed, had gone into hiding, or had perhaps become prophets of Baal to escape death. Elijah wanted to be sure that the people knew where he stood. The things he did on that day were in accordance with Yahweh's word.

37 Hear me, O Lord, Hear me, that this people may know that thou art the Lord God, and that thou hast turned their heart back again.

Elijah pleaded for the Lord to hear him, and to act, so that the people of Israel would know that Yahweh was their true God. Let this demonstration be enough to turn their hearts, and their loyalty back to you.

38 Then the fire of the Lord fell, and consumed the burnt sacrifice, and the wood, and the stones, and the dust, and licked up the water that was in the trench.

As soon as Elijah had finished his plea to the Lord, an intense fire fell from the sky. It was so hot that it consumed everything, the meat, the wood, the stones, and the dust of the earth. The fire was so hot that it even vaporized the water in the surrounding trench.

39 And when all the people saw it, they fell on their faces: and they said, The Lord, he is God; the Lord, he is God.

The fire came so quickly and was so fierce that the people bowed down in fear and respect for the presence and power of Yahweh. Baal had failed to burn the sacrifice and the wood, which was dried from the drought. Though it was easy to burn as kindling, it did not burn. It would have only required a tiny spark. But Yahweh burned up everything, including the rocks and the water. It was enough to prove to the people the awesome power of Yahweh. And they emphatically declared that Yahweh "the Lord, He is God!"

DAILY BIBLE READINGS

M: Elijah Is Sent to Ahab
1 Kings 18:1-5
T: Elijah Meets and Challenges Ahab
1 Kings 18:7-19
W: Elijah and the Prophets of Baal
1 Kings 18:20-29
T: Choose Whom You Will Serve
Joshua 24:14-18
F: Elijah's Triumph for God
1 Kings 18:30-40
S: The Drought Ends
1 Kings 18:41-46
S: Elijah Flees, Then Meets God
1 Kings 19:1-18

TEACHING TIPS

June 24
Bible Study Guide 4

1. Words You Should Know

A. Prophesy (1 Kings 22:18) Hebrew *Naba*—to cause to bubble up, to pour forth words abundantly, to be inspired, to speak or sing as a prophet by divine power.

B. Lying Spirit (v. 22) Hebrew *sheqer*—the spirit sent to entice, trick, or deceive. An untruth, lie, lying words. A way contrary to God.

2. Teacher Preparation

A. Read the Bible Background and 2 Chronicles 18, preferably in more than one Bible translation, to get a full picture of this incident.

B. Go back and look specifically at the FOCAL VERSES.

C. Read the commentary for Bible Study Guide 4 and be sure you can answer SEARCH THE SCRIPTURES and DISCUSS THE MEANING questions.

3. Starting the Lesson

A. Have the class read the AT-A-GLANCE outline together.

B. Read the LESSON AIM and pray that by the end of class each one will have a good understanding.

C. Materials needed: Bible, chalkboard or newsprint.

4. Getting into the Lesson

A. Call everyone's attention to the IN FOCUS cartoon.

B. Ask a couple of people to be honest and tell the last time they had to tell a lie or a half-truth, or relate an incident in which God told them to speak up on a matter and they did not. Allow the class some time to discuss the circumstances and feelings involved. Read the LESSON AIM and have an opening prayer.

C. To get a basic understanding of the lesson take turns reading BACKGROUND and THE PEOPLE, PLACES, AND TIMES.

D. Have students take turns reading FOCAL VERSES, IN DEPTH, and then answer the SEARCH THE SCRIPTURES questions in-between the reading.

5. Relating the Lesson to Life

A. Go through the DISCUSS THE MEANING questions and feel free to encourage the discussion with more of your own questions and allowing time for personal experiences of the students.

B. Have someone read the LESSON IN OUR SOCIETY article.

6. Arousing Action

A. Break up into couples and go over the MAKE IT HAPPEN section.

B. After making a decision, have the couples pray together.

C. Encourage the students to study for next week's lesson and be sure to read their Daily Devotions.

WORSHIP GUIDE

For the Superintendent or Teacher
Theme: Micaiah: Courageous Prophet
Theme Song: Stand Up, Stand Up for Jesus
Scripture: 1 Kings 22:15-23, 26-28
Song: We Are Soldiers In the Army
Meditation: Thank You Lord, that we can know the truth that is revealed to us in Your Word. Help us to stand for truth even in times when it is not popular.

MICAIAH: COURAGEOUS PROPHET

Bible Background • 1 KINGS 22:1-40
Printed Text • 1 KINGS 22:15-23, 26-28
Devotional Reading • PROVERBS 12:13-22

LESSON OVERVIEW

LESSON AIM
KEEP IN MIND
FOCAL VERSES
IN FOCUS
THE PEOPLE, PLACES, AND TIMES
BACKGROUND
AT-A-GLANCE
IN DEPTH
SEARCH THE SCRIPTURES
DISCUSS THE MEANING
LESSON IN OUR SOCIETY
MAKE IT HAPPEN
FOLLOW THE SPIRIT
REMEMBER YOUR THOUGHTS
MORE LIGHT ON THE TEXT
DAILY BIBLE READINGS

JUNE 24TH

LESSON AIM

By the end of this lesson, the students should be able to recall the encounter between God's prophet, Micaiah, and King Ahab, understand that speaking the truth is better than popularity, and desire to speak the truth for God no matter how difficult it may be.

KEEP IN MIND

"As the Lord liveth, what the Lord saith unto me, that will I speak" (1 Kings 22:14, KJV).

FOCAL VERSES

1 Kings 22:15 So he came to the king. And the king said unto him, Micaiah, shall we go against Ramoth-gilead to battle, or shall we forbear? And he answered him, Go, and prosper: for the Lord shall deliver it into the hand of the king.

16 And the king said unto him, How many times shall I adjure thee that thou tell me nothing but that which is true in the name of the Lord?

17 And he said, I saw all Israel scattered upon the hills, as sheep that have not a shepherd: And the Lord said, These have no master: let them return every man to his house in peace.

18 And the king of Israel said unto Jehoshaphat, Did I not tell thee that he would prophesy no good concerning me, but evil?

19 And he said, Hear thou therefore, the word of the Lord: I saw the Lord sitting on his throne, and all the host of heaven standing by him on his right hand and on his left.

20 And the Lord said, Who shall persuade Ahab, that he may go up and fall at Ramoth-gilead? And one said on this manner, and another said on that manner.

21 And there came forth a spirit, and stood before the Lord, and said, I will persuade him.

22 And the Lord said unto him, Wherewith? And he said, I will go forth, and I will be a lying spirit in the mouth of all his prophets. And he said, Thou shalt persuade him, and prevail also: go forth, and do so.

23 Now, therefore, behold, the Lord hath put a lying spirit in the mouth of all these thy prophets, and the Lord hath spoken evil concerning thee.

22:26 And the king of Israel said, Take Micaiah, and carry him back unto Amon, the governor of the city, and to Joash, the king's son;

27 And say, Thus saith the king, Put this fellow in the prison, and feed him with bread of affliction and with water of affliction, until I come in peace.

28 And Micaiah said, If thou return at all in peace, the Lord hath not spoken by me. And he said, Hearken, O people , every one of you.

"I PROMISE TO TELL THE TRUTH IF YOU PROMISE NOT TO SPANK ME."

IN FOCUS

"I promise to tell the truth if you promise not to spank me."

If only what this little boy is asking could apply whenever we have to tell the truth. Speaking out boldly, especially on spiritual matters to unbelievers, usually has consequences and they are not always pleasant.

THE PEOPLE, PLACES, AND TIMES

Micaiah. Name means "who is like Yahweh?" Some say he is the unnamed prophet in 1 Kings 20:35.

Ramoth-Gilead. A border city between Aram and Israel, modern Tel ar-Ramith. It was lost to the Syrians later by Jehu (2 Kings 10:32-33).

Jehoshaphat. Son of Asa. He reigned as king in Judah for 25 years. He was Judah's fourth king. He took the throne in the fourth year of Ahab's reign in Israel. He was regarded as one of Judah's most godly kings.

BACKGROUND

God had given Ahab victory over Benhadad, the king of Damascus, on two separate occasions. God gave him these victories to show Ahab mercy, to demonstrate His power, and to draw Ahab and sinful Israel back to Himself. Instead of embracing the Lord and His ways, Ahab made an alliance with Benhadad. The Damascus king bribed him with riches and promises. After three years the promises had not been fulfilled. Once again Ahab wanted to go to war against this country.

When Jehoshaphat, King of Judah (the

Southern Kingdom), visited Ahab in Samaria, Ahab asked Jehoshaphat to join him in battle against Benhadad. Jehoshaphat unwisely agreed. Up to this point Jehoshaphat sought God concerning matters of his kingdom and Judah was at peace and prospering. For no apparent reason Jehoshaphat befriended this evil king and began to make political alliances with him. He even allowed his son to marry Ahab and Jezebel's daughter, Athailiah.

As the two kings sat at the kings' gate they were surrounded by Ahab's prophets who were reporting nothing but success for this battle against Benhadad. Jehoshaphat, however, must have sensed that these prophets were loyal to Ahab and desired the king's favor; they were not necessarily speaking the truth. These prophets were probably new ones since the old prophets of Baal had been killed after Elijah's challenge on Mount Caramel. Jehoshaphat was not a Baal worshiper; he wanted to seek Yahweh's word and to hear from one of God's prophets.

AT-A-GLANCE

1. Micaiah's Prophecy
(1 Kings 22:15-17)
2. Micaiah Exposes the False Prophets
(vv. 18-23)
3. Micaiah Imprisoned
(vv. 26-28)

IN DEPTH

1. Micaiah's Prophecy (1 Kings 22:15-17)

After deciding to go into battle with King Ahab of Israel, King Jehoshaphat of Judah, requested that an inquiry be made about God's will in the matter. Jehoshaphat asked, "Is there not here a prophet of the Lord besides, that we might inquire of him?"

Ahab replied, "There is yet one man . . . by whom I may inquire of the Lord. But I hate him, for he doth not prophesy good concerning me, but evil." All the other prophets were interested in being with favor with the king, but there was one prophet, Micaiah, who did not avoid God's words even if they which were sometimes unwelcome, discouraging, or negative.

The official who escorted Micaiah to the kings warned him to agree with the other prophets concerning the success of the war. Micaiah's reply reflected his character, "By the living Lord I promise that I will say what He tells me to!" No matter if it cost him his life, Micaiah was committed to being true to God and His Word.

When Micaiah first came before the kings, he agreed with the prophecies of the false prophets. Maybe he did this to be sarcastic, or maybe he was trying to test Ahab's sincerity to see if he really wanted to hear the truth. Ahab sternly admonished Micaiah, "In the name of the Lord" speak the truth.

Micaiah reported the opposite of what the false prophets had been saying. He told Ahab that he would be killed and his army scattered. This battle, according to Micaiah who spoke on behalf of the Almighty God, would be a disaster.

Ahab looked over to Jehoshaphat and said, "Didn't I tell you that he never prophesies anything good for me? It is always something bad." Although Ahab asked for a true word from God when it was spoken he pushed it aside and blamed the prophet for always being against him.

2. Micaiah Exposes the False Prophets (vv. 18-23)

Micaiah not only prophesies negatively about the outcome of the war, he goes on to identify the prophets around him as liars. This further prophecy was given to confirm what Micaiah was saying as true, and it was an attempt to save the life of Ahab and many soldiers.

Micaiah saw the Lord seated upon His throne. All the army of heaven was around Him. The Lord said, "Who will persuade Ahab to go up and fall at Ramoth in Gilead?" One spirit came forth and said, "I will persuade him. I will go out and be a lying spirit in the mouth of all his prophets." Then Jehovah gave him permission to go and do so. Micaiah boldly accused all the prophets around him of being a liar.

This so upset the prophets that one stepped forward and slapped Micaiah on the face. This vio-

lence did not cause Micaiah to back down, "Indeed, you shall see on that day when you go into an inner chamber to hide!" He was referring to the time after the battle and King Benahadad's success.

3. Micaiah Imprisoned (vv. 26-28)

Micaiah was returned to the custody of Amon and Joash. He was being held under arrest. Amon is identified as the governor of Samaria, but Joash is not known. Ahab was attempting to silence the word of God. Micaiah gave a final warning, "If you return safely . . . then the Lord has not spoken through me!" (Today's Contemporary Bible). He also added an extra word of encouragement for everyone. Micaiah was not just trying to prove he was right, but he wanted the people to see the fallacy of the false prophets and to turn back to following the true and living God.

Once again God gives Ahab a chance to repent and to follow His instructions, but he does not take it. This, however, was his last chance. Just as Micaiah had predicted, Ahab does not come back alive. His army was defeated and King Ahab died in battle.

SEARCH THE SCRIPTURES

1. _____ gave King Ahab positive news at first. (23:15)

2. According to Micaiah's prophecy, _____ would be scattered upon the hills. (v. 17)

3. Micaiah informed the king that a _____ spirit led Ahab's prophets to give false prophecy. (vv. 19-23)

4. Ahab ordered Micaiah to be placed in _____. (v. 27)

DISCUSS THE MEANING

1. Why did Micaiah lie at first?

2. Why wouldn't Ahab believe Micaiah?

3. What might have been the outcome if these two kings had listened to God's prophet? And why do you think they did not?

LESSON IN OUR SOCIETY

We live in a society that encourages, excuses, and glorifies lies. When someone tells the truth, especially biblical truth, most people do not want to hear it. People who want to live in lies and deception often lash out at the person telling the truth. Sometimes it hurts to hear the truth because then we might have to admit we are wrong or confess a sin. To stand for the truth in a difficult situation can be hard. Many times God is the only one pleased with our honest decision.

MAKE IT HAPPEN

Micaiah was called to deliver some hard truth. He spoke boldly but also spoke with love for the king and love for the people. Truth must be spoken, yet the Scripture exhorts us to "speak the truth in love." It is also necessary to pray and ask God for the best time to speak the truth. God directed Micaiah at this particular time to speak to these kings. When we decide to speak the truth, let's make sure that God—not our flesh, or our desire to get back at someone, or our need to dump on someone—is the motivation prompted by the Holy Spirit.

Is there something you've been holding back that God wants you to say? What's your next step?

FOLLOW THE SPIRIT

What God wants me to do:

_____

_____

REMEMBER YOUR THOUGHTS

Special insights you learned:

_____

_____

MORE LIGHT ON THE TEXT

1 Kings 22:15-23, 26-28

22:15 So he came to the king. And the king said unto him, Micaiah, shall we go against Ramoth-gilead to battle, or should we forbear? And he answered him, "Go, and prosper: for the Lord shall deliver it unto the hand of the king.

King Ahab of Israel was planning to join forces with King Jehoshaphat of Judah to fight against the Syrians to take back the city of Ramoth in Gilead. Four hundred prophets had been queried, and had all agreed that this battle would turn out favorable for these allied kings.

However, King Jehoshaphat wanted to be sure they had consulted with all the prophets, so he asked if there were any besides these? Weren't 400 enough? Didn't they get the answer they wanted to hear? How often does one find such a large group of people agreeing unanimously? So Ahab sent for the prophet, Micaiah, the son of Imlah, to add his voice to the 400 prophets who had been consulted.

Perhaps this is what signaled a problem to King Jehoshaphat. One of the criteria for distinguishing false prophets from true prophets was that the false prophet told the king what he wanted to hear, while the true prophet told the king what was difficult or unfavorable. When Micaiah arrived, he answered the king in the same manner as the other prophets. This alerted King Ahab that there might be a problem, because Micaiah had never been agreeable. As King Ahab had done many things to anger the Lord. Under his leadership, altars were built for foreign gods. Micaiah was one of the few prophets who dared to speak out against the king's behavior.

16 And the king said unto him, How many times shall I adjure thee that thou tell me nothing but that which is true in the name of the Lord?

Micaiah's response must have sounded completely insincere to King Ahab, too agreeable, and too sweet. Verse 8 indicates that Micaiah and Ahab's relationship had been conflictual to the point that the king hated this prophet. His opinion would not have even been sought if it were not for King Jehoshaphat. Ahab did not care to hear what Micaiah had to say, because he knew it would not be good. Ahab knew he must be lying, if Micaiah agreed with the others.

King Ahab, in his most pious sounding voice, said, "How often must I tell you to only speak that which is true in the name of Yahweh?" This from the mouth of a king who built altars to Baal!

17 And he said, I saw all Israel scattered upon the hills, as sheep that have not a shepherd: And the Lord said, These have no master: let them

return every man to his house in peace.

So Micaiah revealed what the Lord had truly said. He had seen a vision of the army scattered upon the hills in Gilead, confused and wandering aimlessly. The vision was confirmed by the word of the Lord saying, "They have no master." This meant that King Ahab would be killed in the battle, and that his death would bring an end to the war. They would not make peace, but the loss of their king would end their desire to fight.

18 And the king of Israel said unto Jehoshaphat, Did I not tell thee that he would prophesy no good concerning me, but evil?

King Ahab was correct. Micaiah's prophecy regarding him was terrible, as expected. That was why he avoided Micaiah. What a demoralizing prophecy to go into battle with. Ahab did not wish to hear anything like this. Not only would they lose, but he would also be killed. With the support of his other prophets, King Ahab was certain he would achieve the victory.

19 And he said, Hear thou therefore the word

of the Lord: I saw the Lord sitting on his throne, and all the host of heaven standing by him on his right hand on his left.

King Ahab had not yet heard all that the Lord had to say concerning him. Micaiah continued by telling him what the Lord had really said. Micaiah began to describe an anthropomorphic vision of God. God, the King of Heaven, was seated on His heavenly throne, with His heavenly army standing around him.

This scene is reminiscent of the vision Isaiah described (Isaiah 6). Here, too, the Lord is seated upon His throne, delivering unfavorable news to the nation, sending forth seraphim (fiery angels) to dull the spiritual sensibilities of the people.

20 And the Lord said, Who shall persuade Ahab, that he may go up and fall at Ramoth-gilead? And one said on this manner, and another said on that manner.

According to the vision, the Lord inquired amongst the heavenly host to see if any might have a strategy to convince Ahab to go into battle, in order that he might meet his end there. The word *petah*, translated "persuade," carries the sense of causing one to be deceived, or enticed. Various ones answered with differing approaches. But none came up with an acceptable plan to Yahweh.

21 And there came forth a spirit, and stood before the Lord, and said, I will persuade him.

As in Isaiah 6, the Lord was preparing to dispatch an agent to accomplish His will. It is believed that the "spirit" referred to here was the Spirit of Prophecy who inspired prophets to speak truth or lies. This part of the story also reminds one of the story of Job whom Satan sought to harm, but could not do so without God's permission. However, it is not useful to think of the agent here as Satan. At this point in Israel's history, evil had not yet been conceived as an independent entity. God was responsible for the origin of good and of evil. Thus God could be thought of as being responsible for the deception of Ahab. Ahab was not a righteous king. So here we find God participating in his demise, instead of offering protection.

22 And the Lord said unto him, Wherewith? And he said, I will go forth, and I will be a lying spirit in the mouth of all his prophets. And he said, Thou shalt persuade him, and prevail also: go forth, and do so.

The Lord wanted to know the details of how this spirit hoped to achieve the results. His response was that he would inspire all of Ahab's prophets to lie. Thus, they would all agree with one voice. This seemed like a good plan, so the Lord gave this spirit permission to do as he had said.

23 Now, therefore, behold, the Lord hath put a lying spirit in the mouth of all these thy prophets, and the Lord hath spoken evil concerning thee.

So concluded Micaiah's story, explaining how it was that all the other prophets agreed upon the plan for battle. It must have required a lot of courage to be the lone dissenting voice when Micaiah knew what King Ahab wanted to hear. Micaiah was already very unpopular with the king, but he never changed the word that he was supposed to deliver from the Lord.

22:26 And the king of Israel said, Take Micaiah, and carry him back unto Amon, the governor of the city, and to Joash the king's son;

When Micaiah had finished his prophecy, King Ahab was furious with him. Ahab was expecting a negative word, but this was a bit too much. Perhaps it was the story itself that the king found insulting. Could 400 men all be lying, and Micaiah be the only one telling the truth? In his fury, King Ahab ordered that Micaiah be arrested and taken back to the capital, Samaria. He was to be jailed in the palace, under the custody of the governor and the king's son. No independent documents have been found that indicate Ahab had a son named Joash. However, evidence has been found that king's son was the title of a high-ranking office. Originally, a son of the king may have filled the office, but in time the title just stuck.

27 And say, Thus saith the king, Put this fellow in the prison, and feed him with bread of afflic-

tion and with water of affliction, until I come in peace,

The king ordered that Micaiah be thrown into the palace dungeon. The bread and water of affliction referred to prison food, which was probably most unpleasant.

Ahab planned to return shortly from the battle, and then gloat in Micaiah's face. He said, ". . . until I come in peace" in defiance of Micaiah's prophecy. If he returned, Micaiah would appear the fool and would be discredited forever. Ahab figured that would put an end to this pesky prophet. If he did not return, then Micaiah would die in prison.

28 And Micaiah said, If thou return at all in peace, the Lord hath not spoken by me. And he said, Hearken, O people, every one of you.

Micaiah's reputation as a prophet of the Lord, and his life, were at stake. Yet he did not back down from what he knew to be the truth. King Ahab would not return. Micaiah called for the attention of everyone around, so that they would be witnesses to the words that were spoken. Thus, even in death, Micaiah would be vindicated.

DAILY BIBLE READINGS

M: Israel and Judah Become Allies
1 Kings 22:1-5
T: The Lying Prophets of Ahab
1 Kings 22:5-12
W: Bad Advice for Jehoshaphat
2 Chronicles 18:4-11
T: Micaiah Predicts Failure
1 Kings 22:13-28
F: Micaiah's True Answer
2 Chronicles 18:12-27
S: Defeat and Death of Ahab
1 Kings 22:29-40
S: Jehoshaphat, Jehoram, and Ahaziah's Reign
1 Kings 22:41-53

TEACHING TIPS

July 1
Bible Study Guide 5

1. Words You Should Know

A. Transgressions (Amos 2:4) Greek *poneros*—sin, evil, godless.

B. Righteous (v. 6) Greek *dikaiosyne*—speaks of God's righteous provision of salvation for sinners.

C. Meek (v. 7) Greek *prautes and praotes*—denotes inward attitude of submission to God and His Word.

2. Teacher Preparation

A. Study the FOCAL VERSES for today's lesson. Understand and focus on the type of person Amos was and why God could use Him. Stress to your students that God sometimes use ordinary people to do very important tasks. Also, concentrate on the sins that Israel and Judah had committed and why they kindled the anger of God.

B. Read Bible Study Guide 5 and write down your answers to the SEARCH THE SCRIPTURES and DISCUSS THE MEANING questions.

C. Materials needed: a chalkboard and a Bible.

3. Starting the Lesson

A. Before the class enters, write the AT-A-GLANCE outline and the words "transgressions, righteousness, and meek" on the chalkboard. Make sure you have a clear grasp of these words and can explain them concisely to your students.

B. After the students have entered and settled, take prayer requests and pray. Be sure to include the LESSON AIM in your prayer.

C. Now discuss the words that you have written on the board. Allow your students an opportunity to give their own definitions. Remind them that these words play a very important part in today's lesson.

D. Read the IN FOCUS section. Discuss with your class allowing them to give input as well.

4. Getting into the Lesson

A. To help the students gain a better understanding of today's lesson, ask for volunteers to read the BACKGROUND section and THE PEOPLE, PLACES, AND TIMES articles. Take time to discuss the information given in both.

B. Now assign students to read selected portions of the FOCAL VERSES commentary according to the AT-A-GLANCE outline. After each section, review the appropriate SEARCH THE SCRIPTURES questions and discuss.

5. Relating the Lesson to Life

A. Use the DISCUSS THE MEANING questions to help students relate the lesson to our lives today. Encourage them to share their own experiences.

B. Read and discuss the LESSON IN OUR SOCIETY article to help students see how the lesson applies to our modern day society.

6. Arousing Action

A. Sum up the lesson with the KEEP IN MIND verse. Remind the students that God expects His children to obey His commands. He does give mercy again and again, but there will come a time when He will be our judge.

B. Read the MAKE IT HAPPEN section and challenge the students to follow through on the assignment. Remind them that even though we might not have all that we want, we still have many reasons to be thankful.

C. Encourage your students to do their DAILY BIBLE READINGS.

D. Ask for prayer requests and close the class with prayer.

WORSHIP GUIDE

For the Superintendent or Teacher
Theme: Judgment on Judah and Israel
Theme Song: The King Is Coming
Scripture: Amos 2:4-10
Song: Let's Just Praise the Lord
Meditation: Dear God, Thank You for Your many blessings. Most of all, thank You for your Son, Jesus! Amen.

JULY 1ST

JUDGMENT ON JUDAH AND ISRAEL

Bible Background • AMOS 1—2
Printed Text • AMOS 2:4-10
Devotional Reading • HEBREWS 10:26-30

LESSON AIM

By the end of the lesson, students will know that there is a penalty for sinning against God.

KEEP IN MIND

"Thus saith the Lord; For three transgressions of Judah, and for four, I will not turn away the punishment thereof; because they have despised the law of the Lord, and have not kept his commandments, and their lies caused them to err, after which their fathers have walked." (Amos 2:4, KJV).

FOCAL VERSES

Amos 2:4 Thus saith the Lord; For three transgressions of Judah, and for four, I will not turn away the punishment thereof; because they have despised the law of the Lord, and have not kept his commandments, and their lies caused them to err, after which their fathers have walked:

5 But I will send a fire upon Judah, and it shall devour the palaces of Jerusalem.

6 Thus saith the Lord; For three transgressions of Israel, and for four, I will not turn away the punishment thereof; because they sold the righteous for silver, and the poor for a pair of shoes;

7 That pant after the dust of the earth on the head of the poor, and turn aside the way of the meek: and a man and his father will go in unto the same maid, to profane my holy name:

8 And they lay themselves down upon clothes laid to pledge by every altar, and they drink the wine of the condemned in the house of their god.

LESSON OVERVIEW

LESSON AIM
KEEP IN MIND
FOCAL VERSES
IN FOCUS
THE PEOPLE, PLACES, AND TIMES
BACKGROUND
AT-A-GLANCE
IN DEPTH
SEARCH THE SCRIPTURES
DISCUSS THE MEANING
LESSON IN OUR SOCIETY
MAKE IT HAPPEN
FOLLOW THE SPIRIT
REMEMBER YOUR THOUGHTS
MORE LIGHT ON THE TEXT
DAILY BIBLE READINGS

9 Yet destroyed I the Amorite before them, whose height was like the height of the cedars, and he was strong as the oaks; yet I destroyed his fruit from above, and his roots from beneath.

10 Also I brought you up from the land of Egypt, and led you forty years through the wilderness, to possess the land of the Amorite.

IN FOCUS

Some time ago, an article in a local newspaper reported that in one middle-size city in the U.S., more than seven million people had boarded the city's two casino boats in their first 23 months of operation. It also reported that when these seven million people left the boats, they were $432 million dollars poorer. This article failed to mention, however, that more and more cities are seeking economic salvation through gambling, and they are attracting mostly senior citizens and women on welfare, who cannot afford to lose. When they lose, many children do not eat.

The news media tells us that our economy is good; prosperity is here; people are living better than they ever have, yet some people, especially children in single parent homes, live in poverty. Drug and alcohol use is on the rise, the lottery and gambling boats are plentiful, and men's hearts are becoming harder to the Word of God.

Even the President of the United States is not immune from trouble because he's supposed to have violated God's moral rules of conduct. Some defend him, however, as they feel he is doing nothing anymore wrong than so many other politicians.

God needs prophets like Amos to stand against sin, to live, preach, and teach His standards of behavior. He needs people who are willing to uphold His standards no matter how hot the fires of condemnation become.

Just as the wealthy people of Israel and Judah were enjoying peace and prosperity, worshiping idols after abandoning real faith in God, and complacent when it came to the sacred things of God, we find our society, too, falling into the same mold. So many people are well off materially but are depraved spiritually. So many are greedy and unjust toward the poor, and *God is still not pleased.*

Even today the rich in our society are reported to be getting richer while the poor are getting poorer. More and more people are locked into poverty, crime, violence, hopelessness, and despair. Those who can help unlock the doors to justice and equality often refuse to do so; God is still not pleased.

Today He is calling ordinary people like Amos to speak frankly about the condition of our world and denounce sin. He is calling for our country to take the lead in repenting and believing on the Lord Jesus Christ so that we can be saved!

Many churches have also abandoned true worship of God for programs and politics. Those who are hurting mentally, physically, and spiritually often cannot find the balm in Gilead to save the sin-sick soul because religiosity and churchianity have taken the place of a true personal relationship with God.

Will you be one of God's Amoses today? The harvest is white but the laborers are few.

THE PEOPLE, PLACES, AND TIMES

The Times. Amos' prophecy is said to have been delivered on a visit to Bethel about 30 years before the fall of Israel. King Uzziah reigned. It had been about 200 years since the ten tribes had set up the northern kingdom (Israel). The southern kingdom was Judah. The people of Israel had adopted Baal worship as its religion and calf worship. Many of the practices of Canaanite idolatry, which God warned against, were still rampant. God had already sent Elijah, Elisha, and Jonah, but the people did not hear and obey them. They were rapidly heading toward their own ruin when God sent Amos to make a final effort to get them to hear and to heed. His patience, however, was running out.

Samaria. The capital of the northern kingdom situated on a hill 300 feet high and surrounded by mountains. The city had luxurious beautiful palaces that were built from the blood of the poor (Amos 2:6, 7; 3:10; 5:11).

The People. The people of Israel were rich, pampered, and they lived on gains acquired by oppressing the poor. It is said that the Assyrians led their captives with hooks through their lip. Even the religious leaders were said to be pitiless in their cruelty to the poor and yet very religious. God noted all of these actions and heard the cries and prayers of the less fortunate. He is a mighty deliverer!

BACKGROUND

What happens when a society or nation becomes so selfish, materialistic, promiscuous, and turns its back on the one true and living God? Today's lesson gives us the answer. Judah and Israel are no longer in slavery. They are, in fact, enjoying prosperity and peace. A life of luxury has caused them to forget about God, who delivered their ancestors out of 400 years of bondage in Egypt and led them to the Promised Land, Canaan. God calls an ordinary man, Amos, to do an important work for Him. Amos is a shepherd, a fig grower from Judah, a lay-person. God calls Amos to pronounce His judgment upon Judah and Israel.

God calls Amos to talk to the rich about their sins against the poor and against God Himself. There are only two classes of people in Israel at the time of Amos' assignment, the rich and the poor. There is no middle class. The wealthy people are enjoying themselves in luxury by oppressing the poor. Some of the less fortunate are even sold into slavery to benefit the wealthy. Needless to say, God is not pleased. Neither is He pleased with the fact that the cares of the world and riches have stolen the hearts of these people. They are evil, unfaithful, and will pay a price for their transgressions.

God's judgment is going to take the place of His mercy.

AT-A-GLANCE

1. Amos Proclaims God's Judgment on Judah and Israel (Amos 2:4-6)
2. God Condemns Judah and Israel for Five Specific Sins (vv. 7-8)
3. God Speaks of How He Blessed Israel in the Past (vv. 9-10)

IN DEPTH

1. Amos Proclaims God's Judgment on Judah and Israel (Amos 2:4-6)

Amos is a man of God. His life is devoted to serving the true and living God. As Amos tends his sheep, God sees that he is available for His service. God gives this humble servant a vision of the future, and tells him to take His message to the people of Judah and Israel. Amos obeys. He speaks with frankness to the people and does not try to gloss over their sins. Of course, he collides with the religious leaders of his day, but he is not intimidated by the priest or the king. After all, Amos represents a higher authority who gives him boldness as he speaks on truth, goodness, justice, and righteousness.

2. God Condemns Judah and Israel for Five Specific Sins (vv. 7-8)

God's anger is kindled against Israel and Judah for five specific sins: (1)They enslave poor people who can not pay their debts. God tells them in Deuteronomy 15:7-8 how to treat the poor. He tells them to be generous and lend them whatever they need. He tells them not to be hard-hearted or tight-fisted toward them. The rich, however, do just the opposite.

(2) They exploit and take advantage of those less fortunate. God tells them in Deuteronomy 16:18-20 to let true justice prevail and to appoint judges and officials for each of their tribes in the new land. He tells them to judge the people fairly throughout the land and not to twist justice or show partiality. However, they do the opposite. Righteousness and justice take a backseat to greed.

(3) They are sexually promiscuous. God tells them in Leviticus 20:10-20 how to conduct themselves sexually . . . the dos and don'ts. They break His rules time and time again. Oftentimes, they put away their Jewish wives and intermarry with foreigners after God told them specifically not to do this. In today's lesson, God cites the fact that a man and his father go to the same woman and engage in sex (v. 7). This is an abomination to Him. He will not tolerate this behavior.

(4) They practice usury or collect illegal collateral for loans from the poor. God tells them in Exodus 22:26-27 what to do. He says that if they take a poor neighbor's cloak as a pledge of repayment, they must return it by sundown because the neighbor will need it to keep warm through the night. God warns them that if the poor cry out to Him for help because of what the rich are doing, He will be merciful to them. The rich do not obey God.

(5) They engage in the worship of idol gods. This is definitely a no-no! In Exodus 20:3-5, God tells them not to worship any other gods except Himself. Again they disobey. They break their covenant relationship with Him (Exodus 19:5) time and time again. In this covenant, He tells them if they obey His voice and keep His covenant, then they will be a peculiar treasure to Him above all people.

In today's lesson, God refuses to look the other way as the people continue to sin. Their unfaithfulness will no longer be tolerated. It is time for His justice. He is going to send down His fire and consume them (v. 5) if they do not repent and change their wicked ways.

3. God Speaks of How He Blessed Israel in the Past (vv. 9-10)

God reminds the Israelites of His covenant relationship with them and how He has always been faithful. He wants them to think of all He has done for His people in the past. God reminds them of the bridges that they crossed to the Promised Land. He reminds them how He fought their battles and subdued their enemies. He reminds them how he rescued them from Egypt, how He led them through the wilderness after 40 years, how He fed them, quenched their thirst, and saw that their clothes and shoes did not wear out. He reminds them because prosperity and peace have caused them to forget who is their supplier. God sends Amos to remind them that their time has run out. He will no longer tolerate their insolence. Enough is enough!

SEARCH THE SCRIPTURES

1. Why was the Lord going to punish Judah? (Amos 2:4)

2. What had Israel done to the poor? (v. 6)

3. What sexual sins had they committed? (v. 7)

4. God reminded the people of what past blessings? (vv. 9-10)

DISCUSS THE MEANING

1. How does God really feel about the poor?

2. Why does religiosity and churchianity cause hurting souls to turn away from the church?

LESSON IN OUR SOCIETY

Why is it that good times often cause us to forget about God as the source of all our blessings? Instead of having a thankful heart, oftentimes we see ourselves as the supplier of our own health, job, and other resources. Some historians have coined the phrase, "This is an ungrateful generation." They usually apply it to Generation X. Yet we know that generations past have been just as ungrateful in so many ways. We have thumbed our nose at God and almost dared Him to do anything about it. We should be grateful that He is still applying His mercy and not His judgment.

MAKE IT HAPPEN

This week, take time to prayerfully consider some of God's blessings to you. In fact, to help you recall, look around and jot as many as you can on a sheet of paper. Then thank God for His mercy, His grace, and His love.

FOLLOW THE SPIRIT

What God wants me to do:

_____

_____

REMEMBER YOUR THOUGHTS

Special insights you learned:

_____

_____

MORE LIGHT ON THE TEXT
Amos 2:4-10

2:4 Thus saith the Lord; For three transgressions of Judah and for four, I will not turn away the punishment thereof; because they have despised the law of the Lord, and have not kept his commandments, and their lies caused them to err, after which their fathers have walked.

According to Amos, Judah, the Southern Kingdom, has transgressed, trespassed, rebelled, or gone against what God has commanded. The Hebrew word *peh-shah* denotes this moving away from, or going against, God. The phrase "for three transgressions and for four" is a Hebrew numeric parallelism. The numbers are not quantitative, but poetic devices. The phrase indicates that the sins of Judah are innumerable, so many that they are hard to count (see also Amos 1:3, 6, 9, 11, 13; 2:1).

This monarchy is not accused of committing wrongs against other countries, or against each other, but their indictment is based on a threefold sin against the Lord, or Adonai. First, they have despised, rejected, or had disdain for the Law or Torah. *Maw-as* is the Hebrew word that expresses a pungent ill-feeling or strong dislike for the laws of God. "Torah" means teaching. It can refer to humans instructing each other or to God instructing Israel. It refers also to a set of regulations, i.e. Exodus 12, which contains the Law regarding the Passover. Frequently the Old Testament states that Moses received the Law (Deuteronomy 30:10). This became the phrase "the Law of Moses." This Law, as dictated by God, became the standard from which interpretation was made. The Law was the property of the priests who were to teach its precepts and follow its regulations (Deuteronomy 17:8-11). Because of Israel's constant disobedience, the prophets looked for a time when once again the Law, directly from God, would go forth from Jerusalem. Amos notes such disobedience to the Law, or Torah, in this verse.

Secondly, Judah is accused of not keeping or obeying the commandments (*khoke*) of God. The word *shaw-mar* means to keep, guard, protect, or hold fast. *Khoke* in the Hebrew language refers to a decree or statute. In other words, Judah has disregarded the decrees meted down by its Creator and has not kept them. They have not considered these statutes sacred or worthy of safekeeping. The commandments have been treated vainly.

The third part of the accusation against Judah can be broken down into two parts: lying, and erring as a result of such lying. Amos concludes the indictment by informing Judah that the apple does not fall far from the tree. Their fathers engaged in similar actions, and now the children. The sins of the father have been borne on the children.

5 But I will send fire upon Judah, and it shall devour the palaces of Jerusalem

Amos is prophesying before the destruction of Israel in 722 B.C. by the Assyrians. Since the Lord addresses how Jerusalem will be burned, one can assume that the Northern Kingdom of Israel is still in existence during the time of Amos' prophecy. Like his contemporary prophet, Hosea, Amos delivered his message primarily to the Northern Kingdom.

6 Thus saith the Lord; For three transgressions of Israel, and for four, I will not turn away the punishment thereof; because they sold the righteous for silver, and the poor for a pair of shoes.

Having indicted the enemies of Israel not related to her (1:3, 6, 9), the enemies of Israel related to her (1:11, 13; 2:1), and Israel's sibling kingdom of Judah (2:4), the Lord now informs Israel that she is not without sin. The phrase "for three transgressions . . . and for four" is repeated to show the seriousness and intensity of the violation against God. Such repetition also shows the degree of God's anger. The phrase is also a rhetorical device assisting Amos in making his argument.

Israel is accused, not of sinning against God as Judah did, but of mistreating her own kind. They enslaved each other due to nonpayment of debts and have allowed greed to overlook

human care and concern. Such an indictment is ironic in light of Israel's own previous enslavement at the hands of the Egyptians (Exodus 1-14).

7 That pant after the dust of the earth on the head of the poor, and turn aside the way of the meek: and a man and his father will go in unto the same maid, to profane my holy name:

Israel is accused of having little or no regard for the poor. They trample the head of the poor into the earth, meaning they provide no means for the poor to better themselves. Instead, Israel is accused of wanting the poor to remain poor for their own benefit and personal gain. They also push the meek or afflicted out of the way and do not give alms, or any type of assistance, whether it be financial, social or physical.

Not only have the Israelites committed wrongs externally, but the Lord accuses them of internal family sins. The accusation of incest is presented, which was condemned in Leviticus (18:15; 20:12). There is also the possibility that men may have been exploiting girls. Such acts profane, defile, or stain the Lord's holy name. The Hebrew word *khaw-la* expresses the hideous act of desecrating that which belongs to God. It is making unholy that which is deemed holy. The Israelites are particularly accused of defiling, or staining, the Lord's name through sexual and social sins. Such defamation goes against the commandment forbidding one to take the Lord's name in vain as handed down in the Ten Commandments (Exodus 20:7).

8 And they lay themselves down upon clothes laid to pledge by every altar, and they drink the wine of the condemned in the house of their god.

Amos continues to show how Israel has sinned. Now he begins to explain how they have sinned against God like Judah. However, Israel has not only desecrated the Lord's name, but has also desecrated the Lord's holy place or house. House, or *bah-yith* in Hebrew, also means temple. Thus, Israel has misused the Lord's dwelling place. The glory of the Lord, the presence of God, and the incense or prayers of the righteous filled the Temple. The psalmist also expresses the nature of the temple by stating, "The Lord is in the holy temple. Let all the earth keep silence" (Psalm 11:4). Israel has disrespected and dishonored this high and holy place. They have taken from the temple and given to themselves that which was to be offered to God. Their sin is similar to Belshazzar who, a century later, took vessels out of the temple in Jerusalem for this own pleasure and worshiped the gods of gold, silver, brass, and iron. Because of his transgression and defamation, Belshazzar was made like a beast to dwell among wild asses (Daniel 5).

9 Yet destroyed I the Amorite before them, whose height was like the height of the cedars, and he was strong as the oaks; yet I destroyed his fruit from above and his roots from beneath.

Amos warns Israel that nothing is beyond the reach of God. No king or kingdom is beyond God's span or reach. Just as God was able to rescue them from the Amorites, so is the same God able to destroy them because of sin. God as Creator is entitled to do with creation as He wills.

The Amorites were a western Semitic Black people who lived in the hill country (Exodus 3:8; Numbers 13:29). Israel needed to travel northeast in order to get to Canaan. However, the king of Amorites, Sihon, refused to let Israel pass. A battle occurred and eventually all of Sihon's land, including his main city of Heshbon, was captured. Israel settled in the land of the Amorites and dispossessed them as well (Numbers 21:21-31).

Thus, God reminded Israel that the same can happen to it if they continued to disobey him. Israel was not beyond God's punishment. If they were obedient, God would take care of them and find favor with them as was done during the battle with the Amorites. Yet if God's people continued in their disobedience and irreverence, they would receive the same destruction as any enemy of God who attempts to thwart the divine plan.

10 Also I brought you up from the land of Egypt, and led you forty years through the wilderness to possess the land of the Amorite.

God through Amos again reminds Israel of the grace that has been bestowed upon them. The people are to remember that it was God who did great things for them (Deuteronomy 8). They must not forget. The Deuteronomist constantly urges Israel to write it on their doorposts and to teach their children all that the Lord has done for them (Deuteronomy 9). From the beginning when they were slaves in Egypt, to the parting of the Red Sea, to the wilderness, and to the defeat of Sihon and the Amorites, Israel is called to remember that God was in the midst of all of their activities. From the past to the present, it has been the all-seeing eye of God and His powerful hand that has sustained them.

The use of such historical recollection is also a rhetorical device by Amos to assist Israel in seeing the error of their ways and to enable to see how far from God they have come. This is the climax of Amos' argument. By indicting Israel last, he reminds them that God has "invested" so much in this kingdom. God has been with them from their infancy and has guided and directed their path. Israel needed to remember all of the battles God had fought for them and all the miracles performed in their presence. God had done much for them, and, lest they forget, their fate would be similar to their enemies.

DAILY BIBLE READINGS

M: Prophecy Against Syria
Amos 1:1-5
T: Judgment on Damascus
Jeremiah 49: 23-27
W: Prophecy Against Gaza and Tyre
Amos 1:6-10
T: Prophecy Against Edom and Ammon
Amos 1:11-15
F: Prophecy Against Moab and Judah
Amos 2:1-5
S: Prophecy Against Israel
Amos 2:6-3:2
S: Penalties for Disobedience
Leviticus 26:14-22

TEACHING TIPS

July 8
Bible Study Guide 6

1. Words You Should Know

The meaning of "transgression" and "righteousness," discussed in last week's lesson, is carried over in our discussion today. Make sure that your students understand these words and how they apply to today's lesson.

A. Transgression (Amos 2:4; 4:4) Greek *poneros*—sin, evil, godless.

B. Righteous-sin (Amos 5:24) Greek *dikaiosyne*—speaks of God's righteous provision of salvation for sinners.

C. Holiness (Amos 4:2) Greek *hagios* and *hagiosyne*—denotes a basic separation from what is common and unclean, and is then consecrated to God.

D. Sacrifices (v. 5) Greek *thysia*—means to kill.

2. Teacher Preparation

A. Begin preparing for this lesson by studying the Devotional Reading. This passage of another prophet, Malachi, brought warning to God's people, trying to get them to mend their broken relationship with Him.

B. Study the FOCAL VERSES for today's lesson. Understand why God was displeased with the Israelites and how Amos' message was very urgent.

C. Read Bible Study Guide 6 and write down your answers to the SEARCH THE SCRIPTURES and DISCUSS THE MEANING questions.

D. Materials needed: chalk, chalkboard, a Bible, and offering plate.

3. Starting the Lesson

A. Before the students arrive, place an offering plate on a table in front of the class. Then write on the board the title of today's lesson and the AT-A-GLANCE outline.

B. Begin your class time with prayer. Be sure to pray the LESSON AIM. Then, go over the "Words You Should Know" with them. Allow them to give their own definitions as well. Discuss. Tie everything in with our giving, using the offering plate to talk about one form of giving. Stress that God does not want our leftover time, money, and energy.

C. Read the IN FOCUS story.

4. Getting into the Lesson

A. Assign several students to read the BACKGROUND information and THE PEOPLE, PLACES, AND TIMES article. Discuss and tie into the lesson.

B. Assign three students to read the FOCAL VERSES according to the AT-A-GLANCE outline. Then, go through the IN DEPTH commentary and highlight these sections. Allow students to share and discuss, reminding them of the main point that God wants our very best and not our left-overs.

5. Relating the Lesson to Life

A. Direct the students' attention to the LESSON IN OUR SOCIETY article and allow for discussion.

B. Review and discuss the DISCUSS THE MEANING questions. This should help them to realize how today's lesson applies to their own personal life.

6. Arousing Action

A. Direct the students to the MAKE IT HAPPEN suggestions and challenge them to put the suggestions into practice this week.

WORSHIP GUIDE

For the Superintendent or Teacher
Theme: Empty Offerings
Theme Song: What Shall I Render To God For All His Blessings?
Scripture: Amos 4:2-5; 5:20-24
Song: esus Paid It All!
Meditation: Father, help us always to make you first in our life, giving you our very best. Amen.

EMPTY OFFERINGS

Bible Background • AMOS 4—5
Printed Text • AMOS 4:2-5; 5:20-24
Devotional Reading • MALACHI 1:6-14

LESSON AIM

By the end of the lesson, students will know that God wants us to obey His Word. He wants our spiritual leaders to lead and not be stumbling blocks because of their own sins. Our relationship to Him is to be the utmost in importance to us. He wants to be first in our life, and He wants our very best everyday.

KEEP IN MIND

"But let judgment run down as waters, and righteousness as a mighty stream" (Amos 5:24, KJV).

FOCAL VERSES

Amos 4:2 The Lord God hath sworn by his holiness that, lo, the days shall come upon you, that he will take you away with hooks, and your posterity with fishhooks.

3 And ye shall go out at the breaches, every cow at that which is before her; and ye shall cast them into the palace, saith the Lord.

4 Come to Bethel, and transgress; at Gilgal multiply transgression; and bring your sacrifices every morning, and your tithes after three years:

5 And offer a sacrifice of thanksgiving with leaven, and proclaim and publish the free offerings: for this liketh you, O ye children of Israel, saith the Lord God.

5:20 Shall not the day of the Lord be darkness, and not light? Even very dark, and no brightness in it?

21 I hate, I despise your feast days, and I will not smell in your solemn assemblies.

22 Though ye offer me burnt offerings and your meat offerings, I will not accept them: neither will I

LESSON OVERVIEW

LESSON AIM
KEEP IN MIND
FOCAL VERSES
IN FOCUS
THE PEOPLE, PLACES, AND TIMES
BACKGROUND
AT-A-GLANCE
IN DEPTH
SEARCH THE SCRIPTURES
DISCUSS THE MEANING
LESSON IN OUR SOCIETY
MAKE IT HAPPEN
FOLLOW THE SPIRIT
REMEMBER YOUR THOUGHTS
MORE LIGHT ON THE TEXT
DAILY BIBLE READINGS

regard the peace offerings of your fat beasts.

23 Take away from me the noise of thy songs; for I will not hear the melody of thine viols.

24 But let judgment run down as waters, and righteousness as a mighty stream.

IN FOCUS

A disgruntled parent called in to a Christian Radio Program in June of 1998. "They have taken prayer out of the schools," she accused. "Now look what is happening! Kids are killing their parents, kids, and their teachers; violence is everywhere!"

JULY 8TH

In fact, the news media reported that our supposed Christian nation was bombarded with more than 40 incidents of violence and murder across the country just this year. Many Christians are wondering if we, like Israel, have failed to learn from God's warnings. They have concluded that we are reaping what we have sown, paying the penalty for our unfaithfulness to a faithful, loving, living God, who demands our loyalty, respect, and reverence.

A noted author wrote a book on protecting our children from pornography on the Internet. He concluded that "smut," which used to be just found on newsstands, has now invaded the privacy of our bedrooms via our personal computers. Because of this, some children are being lured away from home by predators who want to abuse them. This is indeed a sign of the times.

Again, religious leaders of our day see a parallel between the rise in crime in our nation to our overall lukewarm worship and devotion to God. No matter how God warns us that He is not pleased with our actions as a whole, we have not heeded His warnings. Like Israel, we have taxed His patience. We are counting on His mercy to save us and that mercy will someday come to an end.

We have forgotten that one day we will come face to face with a God who will be our judge. We must then give Him an account for our complacency and negligence.

THE PEOPLE, PLACES, AND TIMES
Amos' Contemporaries:
The Prophet Jonah. Amos probably knew Jonah and heard him tell of his visit to Nineveh and how he ended up in the belly of a whale because of his own disobedience. Jonah was older and passing off the stage when Amos entered with his message or warning from God to the Israelites.

The Prophet Joel. Joel was probably Amos' contemporary or predecessor according to theologians. It is believed that Amos referred to Joel's plague of locusts in 4:9.

The Prophet Hosea. Hosea was younger than Amos and was believed to be a co-worker with him. They knew each other well. Hosea could have been in Bethel at the time Amos prophesied against Judah and Israel; he continued to work after Amos left the scene.

BACKGROUND
On a visit to Bethel, the prophet Amos delivered his message to the Northern kingdom (Israel) and to the Southern kingdom (Judah) about 30 years before Israel met destruction. Uzziah was the king of Judah (787-735 B.C.), and Jeroboam II was king of Israel (790-749 B.C.).

Israel was enjoying great prosperity and peace. At the same time, these successes caused the people to become selfish, materialistic, and complacent toward God and His sacred things.

The Israelites (God's chosen people) failed to heed the warnings of the Prophets Elijah, Elisha, and Jonah who spoke to them before Amos. In fact, they became hardened in their wickedness and their ruin was imminent. They were a hard-headed, stiff-necked people. God called Amos, a herdsman, a lowly fig grower who did not come from a long line of priests, to address the wealthy of Samaria, the capital of the Northern kingdom. He was to tell them in blatant terms—no holds

barred— of God's displeasure and His coming judgment. Amos brought God's final warning.

He stated God's indictments against eight nations: Syria, Philistia, Phoenicia, Edom, Ammon, Moab, Judah, and Israel. Afterwards, Amos centered his attention on Israel.

IN DEPTH

AT-A-GLANCE

1. Israel's Failure to Learn
(Amos 4:2-5)
2. God's Complaint Against Judah and
Israel (vv. 2-3)
3. Warnings of Coming Judgment
(5:20-24)

1. Israel's Failure to Learn (Amos 4:2-5)
The prophet Amos' mission was to boldly confront Israel (the northern kingdom) and Judah (the southern kingdom) with their sins . . . their outright disobedience to God's commands, in a hope to restore their relationship with God. Their relationship with Him was broken, shattered, because of their own doings.

God had been faithful to the Israelites. He had kept His part of the covenant made back in Egypt to their ancestors (Exodus 19:5) to be their God if they would be His people. He loved them as a husband loves his wife (Jeremiah 31:32). Yet they often went whoring after other gods . . . idols. God was tired of their unfaithfulness! He was tired of their sin!

2. God's Complaint Against Judah and Israel (vv. 2-3)
The prophet Amos, a layman, herdsman, and dresser of sycamore trees, warned the people in sometimes harsh and brash language to prepare to meet their God because their sins were so brazen against God. He especially addressed the pampered ladies of Samaria (vv. 2-3).

God saw how the people were living such a sumptuous or prosperous life on the backs of the poor. These wealthy women, in fact, were called "fat cows." It displeased God when they supported their lavish lifestyles by being unfair to the needy and so glibly took from them without a second thought.

The punishment of the people for their transgressions would be severe. Within a few years, they would be led away into slavery with hooks through their lips by the Assyrians.

The false, hypocritical worship by the people to God was an abomination to Him. They no longer honored Him and sacrificed their best . . . perfect animals. They gave Him their leftovers. This showed their real attitude toward Him. This showed the depraved spiritual condition of their heart.

Even their tithes and offerings were given just for outward show . . . so they could brag about it (v. 5). In fact, God despised the worship offered to Him by the Israelites (5:21-23). They also took part in idol worship. God will not share His place with anyone or anything else.

3. Warnings of Coming Judgment (5:20-24)

The Israelites were looking forward to the Lord's coming, thinking He would bring mercy. Instead Amos warned them that the day of the Lord would bring His judgment on them. They would meet their God they be weighed in the balance and found wanting. That would be a dark and hopeless day for them (v. 20) because the people of the northern kingdom would be deported (4:2-3). It would be a time of no joy nor hope because God hated their hypocrisy as shown in their religious festivals and the assemblies given with a divided heart (5:21-23). Even their hymns of praise did not come out of faithfulness and loyalty to Him. It was no more than religiosity, lip service in place of heart-felt worship. They were concerned with the outward show while God looks on the heart. He looks at our attitude toward Him and requires justice and righteousness from His people (v. 24). God was and is still calling His people to repentance. God was and is still calling His people to righteousness or right living, not to make empty offerings to Him from a sinful heart.

SEARCH THE CRIPTURES

1. Who would take the wealthy Samaritans away with hooks? (Amos 4:2)

2. The people transgressed at _____ and _____. (v. 4)

3. After offering a sacrifice, what did the people do? (v. 5)

4. The day of the Lord would be _____ and not _____ for them. (5:20)

5. God _____their feast days. (v. 21)

6. God would order his _____ to run down like waters and _____ as a mighty stream. (v. 24)

DISCUSS THE MEANING

1. In delivering God's prophetic message to Judah and Israel, Amos often used harsh words. Why do you think that was necessary? When is the time to be frank or candid with others?

2. God condemned the Israelites for their hypocrisy and empty offerings. How can we make sure that we don't fall into the same grievous behaviors?

LESSON IN OUR SOCIETY

Some ministers no longer say "We will take your offering" during that part of the worship service. Instead they say, "We will receive your offering," denoting that God's people are freely giving back their tithes and offerings to Him out of a cheerful heart. They are gladly being obedient to His edicts.

Some churches also clap during offering time and allow each member to bring their gift to the front of the church where ushers are stationed with the trays. Again, this denotes a thankful and worshipful time.

God does not like hypocrisy as we have discovered in today's lesson. He wants our very best. Whatever we do for Him should be because we reverence and respect a Holy God, who loved us so much that He sent His only Son to die so that we might be saved. May our offerings to God never be empty!

MAKE IT HAPPEN

If you have not already done so, commit today to always worship God with your whole heart. As you share in today's services, focus on God and His goodness to you. Bring to Him a pure heart of thanksgiving and praise. If you are unable to do so, ask Him to help you to correct anything that needs correcting in your life.

Even in your giving, give out of a grateful heart. Tell Him how thankful you are that you have been blessed by Him with money, energy, and health that you freely offer up to Him. Also, commit to giving Him your very best in service, devotion, and praises.

FOLLOW THE SPIRIT
What God wants me to do:

_____

_____

REMEMBER YOUR THOUGHTS
Special insights you learned:

_____

_____

MORE LIGHT ON THE TEXT
Amos 4:2-5; 5:20-24

4:2 The Lord God hath sworn by his holiness that lo, the days shall come upon you, that he will take you away with hooks and your posterity with fishhooks.

The socialites of Bashan, previously referred to as cows, will be treated like cows or cattle by the captors of Samaria. Bashan was a region in northern Transjordan known for its numerous cattle. Amos uses agricultural language, familiar to the people to foretell their fate. Those who herd and use cattle for their own wealth will soon be oppressed and treated like cattle. The Lord warns those who are materially wealthy who do not come to the aid of the less fortunate that not only will they be taken away, there will not remain a remnant. The present generation would be taken into captivity and future generations would be nonexistent. The Hebrew word *naw-saw* denotes not only taking away, but also to lift up or uproot. Thus, there will not even be a foundation for Israel. There will be nothing left to indicate that it ever existed. As with anything that does not have a foundation, it is blown away and tossed to and fro.

The prophet Amos uses "Lord God" *Adonay Elohim* as a proper name to show God's sovereignty. To avoid the risk of taking the Lord's name in vain, Jews substituted the word *adonay* for the proper name *YHWH*. This occurs some 6,000 times in the Hebrew Bible (Old Testament). The title is used to refer to the supreme God only. It is

an intensive plural or plural of majesty. By examining the actual Hebrew script one can see that YHWH is similar to the Hebrew word " to be." YHWH is *hwhy* and the verb "to be" is *hyh* (hah-yah). Thus the plural denotes that God can be many things to many different people. YHWH appears mainly in the Psalms, Lamentations, and later prophetic works of Hosea, Isaiah, and Micah. Many pastors and church educators often misuse YHWH and refer to it as "Yahweh." This however is semantically and theologically incorrect.

3 And ye shall go out at the breaches, every cow at that which is before her; and ye shall cast them into the palace, saith the Lord.

The oppressors in Samaria will be treated as slaves. "Through the breaches" indicates the manner in which slaves and cattle were sold individually, meaning "each one straight ahead." They will be cast, or thrown out, of their *Harmon*, i.e., comfort places or palaces. The actual meaning of *Harmon* is uncertain. The word "cast," *shalak* in Hebrew means to hurl, pluck, or throw. In other words, these uncaring socialites in Samaria will be harshly removed from their upper class positions. Again Amos implies a type of uprooting due to sin and disobedience. God will not simply move those who transgress, but they will be violently cast aside.

4 Come to Bethel, and transgress; at Gilgal multiply transgression; and bring your sacrifices every morning, and your tithes after three years.

The prophet asserts that socialites in Samaria have confused worship with sin. They have convinced themselves that their sin, wrongdoing, and transgression are okay in the eyes of the Lord. They have committed so much wrong that they believe it is pleasing to God. Amos refers to Bethel (house of God), the place where Jacob dreamed of angels ascending and descending, and to Gilgal, the place where circumcision became an important Jewish ritual and a sign of God's relationship with Israel. There were also traditional sanctuaries, or places of holy gathering, at Bethel and Gilgal (Genesis 28:10-22; Joshua 5:2-9). Naming these two places, which were vital to Jewish worship, Amos shows how far off these people are from worshiping God due to their transgressions. "Transgress" from the Hebrew word *paw-shah*, means to rebel, revolt, offend, or break away from. Thus the people give the Lord God transgression, rebellion, and revolution as an offering. Sin is not just what they give as an offering to God, but it is what Israel presents as God's tithe.

A tithe, *mah- as-ar*, or one-tenth, was not unique with Israel in the ancient Near East. It was practiced by Egyptians and Mesopotamians. It was first introduced when Abram paid a tithe to Melchizedek after receiving priestly benediction from him (Genesis 14:20). What was to be tithes, as outlined in Leviticus 27, included vegetation, animals, and money. A tithe was to be given to the priests (Numbers 18:21-32). Here the Levites were given a tithe from the inheritance of the Israelites as a reward for their service. In return, the Levites were to give one-tenth (tithe) of the tithe that had been given to them. The place where the tithe was to be given was the central sanctuary site in Jerusalem. It was not to be offered in every place (Deuteronomy 12: 3). In the presentation of the tithes and offerings there was to be a sacred meal in which the Levite was to share.

According to Amos the upper class of Samaria had desecrated this tradition of tithing by giving out of spite and selfishness and not offering out of thanksgiving.

5 And offer a sacrifice of thanksgiving with leaven, and proclaim and publish the free offerings: for this liketh you, O ye children of Israel, saith the Lord God.

Continuing his ironic statements, which declare how worship and transgression have become synonymous among the upper class, the prophet Amos refers to sacrifices, or offerings, which were integral parts of Israelite worship. There were drink offerings, peace offerings, guilt offerings, and whole offerings integrated in Jewish religious custom. Amos refers to a burnt or incense offering, a *kaw-tar*, used in the act of worship. He includes other elements of worship, the leavened bread, which symbolizes the Passover, and free offerings, or *ned-aw-baw*, which is a spontaneous or voluntary gift over that which is required. The prophet says the people love to engage in these ritualistic acts. The word love

derives from *aw-hab* to have affection for. The range of meaning extends from God's love for people to the carnal appetites of a lazy glutton. Here Amos says that the people have fooled themselves into believing they like worship when they are really content with their foolishness and transgressions. This is what they love or have affection for.

5:20 Shall not the day of the Lord be darkness, and not light? Even very dark and no brightness in it?

The "day of the Lord" refers to the time of God's judgment. Amos continues to forewarn the people of the repercussions of their wrongdoing. This day of doom and destruction emanates from God's anger and disapproval at sin and disobedience. Metaphorical language refer to this day as dark, cloudy, and thick and indicate the seriousness of the transgression and the depth of God's wrath. Ezekiel 30:1-4 and Joel 2 also refer to the "day of the Lord" as a time of decimation. The prophets, including Amos, desired to stress how God would punish sinners for evil actions. Amos also asks a rhetorical question to suggest that the people were quite aware of their having to pay for breaking this covenantal relationship with their Creator.

21 I hate, I despise your feast days, and I will not smell in your solemn assemblies.

Contrary to the Jews' delight and exuberance in their worship and sacrifices (4:4, 5), Amos declares that God is not pleased with such empty activities. The Hebrew word *maw-as* (to despise) expresses God's loathing, contempt, and disdain for impure, hypocritical worship. The assemblies or *ats-eh-reth* are also not pleasing to God. Such assemblies for festival gatherings were incorporated in Jewish worship. They included both regular and unscheduled gatherings for prayer, sacrifice, and celebration. There were Passover feasts/festivals, the Festival of Booths, and the Jubilee which were celebrated among the Jews. God declares through Amos that no aspect of worship, or any of these festivals for whatever reason, is receptive because the people mistreat and abuse one another.

22 Though ye offer me burnt offerings and

your meat offerings, I will not accept them: neither will I regard the peace offerings of your fat beasts.

The three common types of Hebrew sacrifices are burnt, grain, and well/peace; all are rejected by God. The burnt offering, or *o-law*, is a gift of ascension or going up. A portion is given to the priest to offer to God and the remaining is consumed or burned. It is the base word for "holocaust." The grain offering, sometimes called the meat offering, comes from the Hebrew word *min-khaw*. It is a bloodless offering and is also voluntary. It is sometimes called the cereal offering and is usually given after the burnt offering. The third offering mentioned by Amos is the peace offering from the word *shalem*. It is called a peace offering because *shalem* resembles the word *shalom* or peace. This offering is a family or community sacrifice and is the most common type of offering. A portion of this offering is burnt; a portion is given to the priest, and the last portion is eaten.

God through Amos declares that even the most common or simplest form of worship is despised because of the sin of the people. No high and lofty forms of praise, nor everyday utterances, to the Lord God will be received because He is angry with the sin of Israel.

23 Take away from me the noise of thy songs; for I will not hear the melody of thine viols.

Not only will festivals, celebrations, sacrifices, and offerings be rejected, but the God of Israel will not receive or accept ANY form or praise. Vocal and instrumental praise offered by the viols, or harps, are cacophony to God's ear because the people transgress and rebel in their hearts. The word *shamar* (to hear) also means to pay attention to and consider. Thus, God will ignore and disregard any songs of praise that stem from a hard heart and a disobedient spirit. The Lord considers such sacred music rendered under these circumstances as mere noise.

24 But let judgment run down as waters, and righteousness as a mighty stream.

God does not desire festivals, songs, or worship when the rich mistreat the poor. The Creator does not listen to celebrations or smell offerings when the upper class shows lack of concern for the socially marginalized. What the Lord God requires is justice and righteousness. Amos mentions these two words in tandem also in 5:7 and 6:12. Justice, from the Hebrew word *mish-pawt* means judgment or a right sentence. It is the establishment of right and of the person in the right through fair and legal procedures in accordance with the will of God. Righteousness, from *tsed-aw-kaw*, is the quality of life in relationship with others in the community that gives rise to justice.

Thus, the Lord requires people to behave according to the stability and rightness in the community and therefore produce environments indicative of such rightness and justice.

The phrase "roll down" comes from *gaw-lal*, meaning to commit, seek occasion, trust, or wallow. In others words, the people are to passionately and actively seek justice and make every effort to make sure it is administered. Their way of life must be committed to attaining justice for the decentralized.

DAILY BIBLE READINGS

M: Prophet's Privilege and Responsibility
Amos 3:3-8

T: The Doom of Samaria
Amos 3:9-4:5

W: Israel Rejects Correction
Amos 4:6-13

T: A Call to Repentance
Amos 5:1-15

F: The Day of the Lord
Amos 5:16-20

S: God Despises Worship without Righteousness
Amos 5:21-27

S: Corruption of the Priesthood
Malachi 1:6-14

TEACHING TIPS

July 15
Bible Study Guide 7

1. Words You Should Know

A. Mercy (Hosea 1:6-7) Greek Septuagint *eleos*—motherly compassion, God's goodness, particularly toward those in trouble.

B. Adultery(Hosea 2:2) Greek *porneia*—includes all lewdness and sexual irregularity, sexual intercourse of a married person with someone other than his/her married partner.

2. Teacher Preparation

A. Prepare for the lesson by studying the Devotional Reading. Understand what the writer is saying to believers about truly worshiping God. Then read the Bible Background and the DAILY BIBLE READINGS to get more insight into today's lesson.

B. Go back and read the FOCAL VERSES for Bible Study Guide 7. Keep in mind that God told Hosea to marry Gomer, and Hosea did so believing that an all-wise God would keep and protect him no matter how hard the valley experience became as he dealt with an unfaithful wife. He believed that God was still in control of the situation and had a higher purpose. Hosea was willing to be used by God to get the job done.

C. Materials needed: Bible, chalk, chalkboard, a picture of a bride and groom.

3. Starting the Lesson

A. Before the students arrive, write the title of today's lesson and the AT-A-GLANCE outline on the board.

B. To help focus the students' attention, ask them to join in a discussion on certain attributes of a good marriage, pointing out how God ordained it, that it is holy, and that it is a threefold covenant relationship between the bride, the groom, and God.

C. Read the IN FOCUS story, and start your class by taking prayer requests and prayer.

4. Getting into the Lesson

A. Ask for volunteers to read the BACKGROUND and THE PEOPLE, PLACES, AND TIMES sections of *The Student Manual*.

B. Assign students to read selected portions of the FOCAL VERSES commentary according to the AT-A-GLANCE outline. After each section, review the appropriate SEARCH THE SCRIPTURES questions.

5. Relating the Lesson to Life

A. Focus on the picture of the bride and groom you have as a visual aid. Ask your students to discuss the IN FOCUS couple's experiences with those of the new bride and groom in the picture. Now tie both couples' experiences in with Hosea and Gomer's. Compare and contrast. Finally, tie everything in with the relationship between Israel and God, the Israelites being the bride married to God who broke their vows.

6. Arousing Action

A. Direct the students' attention to the MAKE IT HAPPEN suggestions. Ask them to discuss some reasons why once faithful believers may no longer be actively participating in the worship services. Also, discuss what may be done to win them again.

JULY 15TH

WORSHIP GUIDE

For the Superintendent or Teacher
Theme: God's Love for Israel
Theme Song: O How He Loves You and Me
Scripture: Hosea 1:2-9; 2:1- 4
Song: I Love Him
Meditation: Dear Lord, help us to always come before You with hearts of thanksgiving and praises. Help us to be faithful to You and remember that You are always faithful to us. Amen.

GOD'S LOVE FOR ISRAEL

Bible Background • HOSEA 1–2
Printed Text • HOSEA 1:2-9; 2:1-4
Devotional Reading • PSALM 100

LESSON AIM

By the end of the session, students should know that the relationship between the church and God is like a marriage; God expects believers (His bride) to be faithful to their vows and commitments to Him, and His mercy and His patience will not always be with us when we refuse to hear Him and turn from our wicked ways.

KEEP IN MIND

"But I will have mercy upon the house of Judah, and will save them by the Lord, their God. . ." (Hosea 1:7, KJV).

FOCAL VERSES

Hosea 1:2 The beginning of the word of the Lord by Hosea. And the Lord said to Hosea, Go, take unto thee a wife of whoredoms and children of whoredoms: for the land hath committed great whoredom, departing from the Lord.

3 So he went and took Gomer the daughter of Diblaim; who conceived, and bore him a son.

4 And the Lord said unto him, Call his name Jezreel; for yet a little while, and I will avenge the blood of Jezreel upon the house of Jehu, and will cause to cease the kingdom of the house of Israel.

5 And it shall come to pass at that day, that I will break the bow of Israel in the valley of Jezreel.

6 And she conceived again, and bore a daughter. And God said unto him, Call her name Loruhamah: for I will no more have mercy upon the house of Israel; but I will utterly take them away.

7 But I will have mercy upon the house of Judah, and will save them by the Lord, their God, and will not save them by bow, nor by sword, nor by battle, by horses, nor by horsemen.

LESSON OVERVIEW

LESSON AIM
KEEP IN MIND
FOCAL VERSES
IN FOCUS
THE PEOPLE, PLACES, AND TIMES
BACKGROUND
AT-A-GLANCE
IN DEPTH
SEARCH THE SCRIPTURES
DISCUSS THE MEANING
LESSON IN OUR SOCIETY
MAKE IT HAPPEN
FOLLOW THE SPIRIT
REMEMBER YOUR THOUGHTS
MORE LIGHT ON THE TEXT
DAILY BIBLE READINGS

8 Now when she weaned Lo-ruhamah, she conceived, and bore a son.

9 Then said God, Call his name Lo-ammi: for ye are not my people, and I will not be your God.

2:1 Say ye unto your brethren, Ammi; and to your sisters, Ruhamah.

2 Plead with your mother, plead: for she is not my wife, neither am I her husband: let her, therefore, put away her whoredoms out of her sight, and her adulteries from between her breasts;

3 Lest I strip her naked, and set her as in the day that she was born, and make her as a wilderness, and set her like a dry land, and slay her with thirst.

4 And I will not have mercy upon her children; for they are the children of whoredoms.

IN FOCUS

Genesis 2:23-25 tells how God instituted or ordained marriage. It speaks of how God gave marriage as a gift to Adam and Eve, and they were made perfect for each other, to complement each other. Eve was Adam's bride as the church is Christ's. Therefore, marriage is sacred. It is holy.

Ephesians 6: 28-29, NIV says, "Husbands ought to love their wives as they love their own bodies. He who loves his wife loves himself." This is one of the models that God gives to married couples in His Word. A successful marriage will display these attributes.

Throughout the Bible, God uses the faithful marriage between a man and a woman to show how Christ loves His church, His people. He also uses

Christ's love for the church to show how special that relationship is. It is so special that God was willing to send His only Son to die for sinful mankind to bridge the gap between man and Himself, a gap brought about when Adam and Eve broke their covenant relationship with God in the garden.

Bill and Ada knew the agape love that God talks about in His Word, the love that is unconditional, love that exists in spite of shortcomings. They knew how to pull together in the best of times and the worst of times. They knew how to truly love each other. In fact, after honoring their marriage vows for over 50 years, their seven children decided to give them a special wedding anniversary party. It was one to remember as they renewed their covenant to each other.

Many eyes teared as friends and loved ones watched this cherished couple who had loved each other through the ups and downs of life, the strains and stresses, the having and not having! Bill and Ada started out on their marital journey with little in material possessions, but now they enjoyed much. Most of all, they enjoyed their love. They enjoyed their faithfulness and loyalty to each other. They took their vows seriously—to heart.

God wanted that faithfulness and loyalty from Israel, His chosen people. He often showed it to them, but they played the harlot, the prostitute, the fool. They cheated and trampled on their vows to God again and again. Unlike Bill and Ada, Israel could not look back on many years of marriage to God and smile. They could only see regrets.

In today's lesson, God uses Hosea and his unfaithful wife, Gomer, to show how Israel's unfaithfulness to Him has hurt their personal relationship with God, their marriage. Our unfaithfulness to God also hurts our relationship to Him. Yet He is willing to forgive! He is willing to restore!

THE PEOPLE, PLACES, AND TIMES

Hosea. One of the minor prophets. He was an Old Testament prophet of the eighth century; called by God from the northern kingdom. He prophesied about the last 40 years before the fall of the northern kingdom, warning the Israelites to return to God before it was too late. He was an older contemporary of Isaiah and Micah, and began His ministry at a time when Israel was prosperous and powerful under King Jeroboam II (790-749 B.C.).

The Times. The children of Israel were committing abominable sins against God. Two hundred years before Hosea's time, the ten tribes had set up their own independent kingdom. They worshiped the golden calf as their official national god. They also worshiped Baal. They would not listen to the warnings of the prophets Elijah, Elisha, Jonah, and Amos who brought God's message before Hosea. They were a hard-headed, stiff-necked, adulterous people.

BACKGROUND

The Israelites had violated their sacred holy vows in today's lesson. They had broken their covenant relationship with God by worshiping idols, whoring after false gods in the Promised Land, Canaan. One of the gods they worshiped was Baal, a god who supposedly looked over the weather and farming. To illustrate Israel's broken relationships to Him, Almighty God told Hosea to marry a wife who would be guilty of adultery, prostitution, and unfaithfulness. He told Hosea beforehand that Gomer would commit these acts that would violate the marriage and that some of their children would not be his.

The Book of Hosea was written by the prophet Hosea. His name meant "The Lord Saves." In this book Hosea told about his life and the ministry given to him by God. The book itself is a tragic love story. Hosea represented faithful God, and Gomer represented unfaithful Israel.

Hosea received the prophecy about unfaithful Israel from God seven years after Amos became a prophet. He was a prophet to the northern kingdom of Israel and served from 753 to 715 B.C. His ministry continued after Assyria captured the northern kingdom.

A number of kings reigned in Judah during Hosea's prophetic period. Some were Uzziah, Jotham, Ahaz, and Hezekiah (Hosea 1:1). Ahaz was an extremely evil king who caused Israel to move further and further away from God.

God wanted Hosea to give a "show and tell lesson" to the Children of Israel. They could watch the marriage of Hosea and Gomer unfold right before their eyes. As they watched the sufferings of Hosea, they would be reminded of their own broken vows, their own sin. They would know that if they did not return to the one and only true God,

471

they would lose His blessings and suffer His punishment. God wanted them to repent and be restored to Him who would still show them mercy.

Even though Hosea experienced much pain in his marriage to Gomer, he was still obedient to God. He did just what God told him to do. He knew that an all-knowing God would protect him in the end. Hosea had been asked to suffer by a loving faithful God so that his pain might benefit others (Israel).

AT-A-GLANCE

1. God Calls Hosea to Speak to Israel for Him (Hosea 1:2)
2. Hosea's Wayward Wife and His Children (Hosea 1:2-9)
3. Charges Against Gomer, the Unfaithful Wife (Hosea 2:2-4)

IN DEPTH

1. God Calls Hosea to Speak to Israel for Him (Hosea 1:2)

God is indeed merciful. He called the prophet Hosea to speak to the wayward Israelites after they continued to break their covenant vows with Him. Israel is considered to be the wife of God as they are in a covenant relationship. They are His chosen people. Yet, as they prospered materially, the people were spiritually depraved, they committed spiritual adultery. They were greedy. The rich had their feet on the neck of the poor, and many worshiped idol gods. As Hosea was brokenhearted in dealing with Gomer, his unfaithful wife, so was God in dealing with the Israelites. God wanted them to know that He suffered as well when His children are rebellious, stiff-necked, and hard-headed. Israel was all these things and more.

Like Amos, Hosea told the people to repent of their sins and to turn back to the God who loved them unconditionally. If they did not, there would be a time of retribution or punishment.

Just as Hosea tenderly dealt with Gomer, in spite of her sins, God tenderly dealt with Israel. He was merciful and forgiving. Yet His patience did run out. Then He brought His judgment.

2. Hosea's Wayward Wife and His Children (Hosea 1:2-9)

God told Hosea to go and marry Gomer, even though God knew she would be unfaithful, and Hosea did just that. He knew beforehand what kind of woman he was marrying. God did not keep it a secret. Hosea put his faith in God, whom he believed would not forsake him in his time of need all that he had to go through dealing with Gomer. He trusted God to shield him while he was in pain. This pain would benefit others and not Hosea.

Gomer was unfaithful to Hosea, just as Israel was to God. She openly committed adultery against Hosea; she had no shame. In fact, Hosea bore his shame just as God did when the Israelites flaunted their brazen adultery against God (v. 2).

Gomer became pregnant with her first child, Jezreel. God even told Hosea what to name the child and why (vv. 3-4). Israel was going to be punished. God was going to break Israel's stronghold of power in the Jezreel Valley (v. 5).

Gomer had her second child, a girl. Again, God told Hosea what to name her, "Lo-ruhamah." There is meaning in a name and this one meant "not loved" (v. 6). God wanted the Israelites to know that He had been showing them love. In fact, they had been enjoying His love, even while they hurt Him and broke His commandments. He was tired of them. He would no longer show pity, neither would He continue to forgive their unfaithfulness (v. 6). Instead, He would show love to the people of Judah. He would personally rescue these people from their enemies without using weapons or armies. They would witness His might and power in their rescue because they had been faithful. He would show them that He needed no man to carry out His plan. He is God all by Himself!

In verse 8, Gomer had yet another son, "Lo-ammi." His name meant "not my people." This was to let Israel know that because of their disobedience and unfaithfulness to God, He would not even consider them His people anymore, His Bride. He would not be their God—their husband (v. 9). God was dissolving the covenant or vows He made with them in Jeremiah 7:23. Israel had abandoned their marriage to God, and He was abandoning them. He was tired! He was fed up!"

3. Charges Against Gomer, the Unfaithful Wife (Hosea 2:2-4)

Hosea dealt in these verses with Israel's punishment and restoration. These people, as Gomer, had been weighed in the balance and found wanting. They, as Gomer, came to trial and were found guilty. After they were punished, however, God was still willing to take them back as Hosea did with Gomer. After her whoring, Hosea's heart was still tender towards her. He still loved her unconditionally. He loved her as His bride, so he joyfully and tenderly welcomed her back. God did the same to Israel. He does the same to us.

SEARCH THE SCRIPTURES

1. Who told Hosea to marry Gomer? (Hosea 1:2)

2. Was Hosea obedient to God's command? (v. 3)

3. What does the name "Lo-ru-ha-mah" mean? (v. 6)

4. What does the name "Lo-am-mi" mean? (v. 9)

5. What was Gomer to do with her whoredom? (Hosea 2:2)

6. What would her punishment be? (vv. 3-4)

DISCUSS THE MEANING

1. If God tells Christians not to be unequally yoked with unbelievers (marry someone who is not a Christian, 2 Corinthians 6:14), why would He tell Hosea to marry unfaithful Gomer?

2. Why did Hosea, who was faithful to God, have to suffer so much pain when he, himself, did not commit sin?

3. When Hosea took Gomer back as His wife, even after her unfaithfulness, this act demonstrated God's what towards Israel?

LESSONS IN OUR SOCIETY

Our country once led the way in going to other countries as missionaries. Many souls were saved under the tutelage of these spiritual leaders for God. However, many theologians tells us today that the United States is a fertile field for missions. We have legislated prayer out of the public schools; we have commercialized and taken Christ out of Christmas, and we have violated many of God's spiritual and moral rules. Bible scholars feel that our nation is losing much of its spiritual heritage and is reaping the consequences in crime, violence, and other societal decay.

God is sending ministers from all denominations to warn us of our shaky footing.

Bishop T.D. Jakes, Billy Graham, Joyce Meyer, Dr. Charles Stanley, Dr. Arthur M. Brazier, Dr. Millicent Thompson, and many others are begging us to get ready because time is winding up. Jesus is coming back again, and this time He is coming as our judge. How much longer will God let us worship idols and be unfaithful to Him as His bride?

MAKE IT HAPPEN

Think of someone who used to come to church, but you have not seen them in a while. Make an effort to contact him/her during the week to see how they are, if they have a need, and invite them to attend next Sunday. Pray for that person all during the week and ask God to bless them mentally, physically, and spiritually!

FOLLOW THE SPIRIT

What God wants me to do:

_____

_____

REMEMBER YOUR THOUGHTS

Special insights you learned:

_____

_____

MORE LIGHT ON THE TEXT

Hosea 1:2-9; 2:1-4

1:2 The beginning of the word of the Lord by Hosea. And the Lord said to Hosea, Go take unto thee a wife of whoredoms and children of whoredoms: for the land hath committed great whoredom, departing from the Lord.

Hosea is the first of the minor prophets. He is a minor prophet because of the size of his prophecy, not due to a lack of importance. Hosea means "salvation." Like Amos, he spoke to the Jews of the northern kingdom of Israel to warn them of their faithlessness to God. Unlike Amos, Hosea was resident of the northern kingdom. Whereas Amos pronounced judgment upon a rebellious people, Hosea's marriage to a harlot was used to physically exemplify the unfaithful relationship Israel had with God.

Hosea is told to take a wife, or *ish-shaw*, which can also be interpreted as adulteress. Here the paradigm is established with Israel being labeled as the adulteress. The wife is to be from whoredom, or *zaw-naw*, which figuratively means to commit idolatry with the Jews who were the wife of God. This is exactly God's complaint against Israel; they have worshiped other gods and been faithful to other husbands. The marriage of Hosea is a metaphor for Israel's involvement with the religion of the surrounding culture and its sexual rites, which ensured the fertility of the land. Scholars argue that since Hosea is told to take a wife of whoredom from the land of whoredom, it is unclear of the character and identity of Gomer.

The children are to be "children of whoredom" or children from the land of the people who are committing whoredom. Yet the text also states that the children are from Hosea and Gomer. Perhaps the term "whoredom" means that Gomer and the children belong to a people who are religiously promiscuous. They chose many different gods to engage in spiritual relations and religious intercourse and frenzies.

3 So he went and took Gomer the daughter Diblaim; who conceived and bore him a son.

Hosea's wife is identified as the daughter of Diblaim which says nothing about her identity as a wife of whoredom. Thus biblical scholars question whether Gomer was actually a harlot or if her people practiced idolatrous adultery. Some say that Gomer's role was simply to be the mother of children who bear symbolic or representative names.

4 And the Lord said unto him, Call his name Jezreel; for yet a little while, and I will avenge the blood of Jezreel upon the house of Jehu, and will cause to cease the kingdom of the house of Israel.

In this context, Jezreel refers to a plain in the central section of Israel and to a city on its perimeter associated with the bloody violence and the greedy politics practiced by the kings of Israel to gain the throne and wealth (1 Kings 21 and 2 Kings 9-10). Jezreel is considered to be a legitimate son of Hosea and Gomer because she conceived and bore him.

The Lord promises to avenge the blood of Jezreel on the house of Jehu. Jeroboam II, who was king during Hosea's time (770-725 B.C.), was a descendent of the house of Jehu. Thus Jeroboam is to be punished for all of his bloodshed and his evil military and political undertakings. The Hebrew word for "avenge," *paw-kad*, means to punish, hurt, bring judgment, or visit with hostile intent. The kingdom of Israel would come to an end through the same bloodshed its leaders used to obtain power.

5 And it shall come to pass at that day, that I will break the bow of Israel in the valley of Jezreel.

Break, or *shaw-bar*, means to crush, destroy, quench or tear. The idiom "to break the bow" is a military term for the destruction of a state's military power. Thus, Hosea prophesies about Israel's imminent destruction and captivity by the Assyrians in 722 B.C.

6 And she conceived again, and a bore a daughter. And God said unto him, Call her name Lo-ruhamah: for I will no more have mercy upon the house of Israel; but I will utterly take them away.

Lo-ruhamah contains the Hebrew verb *raw-kham*, which means to have compassion, love, or show mercy. It also connotes the manner in which one bonds to a child and feels connected or attached to a kin or needy person. *Lo* in Hebrew means "not, no." Thus, Lo-ruhamah means the Divine Parent who no longer feels any attachment to the sons and daughters of Israel. It is this sense of displacement and lack of feeling which allows the Lord to forewarn Israel of His intent to take them away, or lift them up, or displace them. Amos used the same Hebrew verb *naw-saw* (4:2) to describe how these same inhabitants of the northern kingdom would be punished.

7 But I will have mercy on the house of Judah, and will save them by the Lord, their God, and will not save them by bow, nor by sword, nor by battle, by horses, nor by horsemen.

Hosea contrasts the destruction of Israel with the salvation of Judah. The northern kingdom of Israel will be punished for its adulterous behavior, but the southern kingdom of Judah will be unharmed.

Here the word "salvation" comes to play. *Yaw-shah* means to rescue, keep safe, or save. It connotes freedom from distress and the ability to pursue one's own objectives. To move from distress to safety requires deliverance or salvation. In the Hebrew tradition it is God who saves and thus becomes the "Saviour." God saved the Israelites from defeat in military battles (1 Samuel 4:6; 17:47). The people were saved from oppression by God (Exodus 14:30). Often God uses human agents to bring salvation, yet sometimes the *Jehovah-Nissi*, "God of the Banner," intervenes (Proverbs 21:31). Salvation is not only offensive but it is also defensive. In this case, God is a refuge of deliverance and salvation (Psalm 62:7), hence the terms which refer to God as "the shield of salvation" (Psalm 18:35), "the garments of salvation" (Isaiah 61:10), and "the helmet of salvation" (59:17). Isaiah also refers to the city of God whose walls are "salvation" (60:18). This city is for the righteous and provides security (26:1).

Hosea also provides a second contrast for Israel and Judah. Whereas Israel will be destroyed by military force, Judah will not be saved due to military prowess or battle. Instead the Lord will save Judah without any army or forceful presence.

8 Now when she had weaned Lo-ruhamah, she conceived and bore a son.

After giving birth to a child who represents the lack of mercy God will show on Israel, Gomer and Hosea give birth to another son. This occurs after the weaning period of Lo-ruhamah, indicating the span of at least a year.

9 The said God, Call his name Lo-ammi: for ye are not my people, and I will not be your God.

For the second instance (the first in verse 7), Hosea refers to the Divine Creator as God. *Elohim* is the plural of *eloah* and is the described as a plural of majesty and not intended as a true plural when used toward God. It occurs 2570 times in the Scripture, and it functions as the subject of all divine activity revealed to humankind as the object of true reverence and fear. The term *elohim* is often used in titles. One category relates to God creative work, "God of heaven who made the sea and dry land (John 1:9) and "God himself who formed the Earth (Isaiah 45:18). Expressions of God's sovereignty include "God of all flesh" (Jeremiah 32:27), "God in Heaven" (II Chronicles 20:6) and" God most high" (Psalm 57:2). As sovereign God, *elohim* is sometimes described as "God is Judge" (Psalm

50:6). Titles pertaining to God's majesty or glory include "everlasting God" (Isaiah 40:28), and "God of truth" (Isaiah 65:16). The most frequent category of titles relates to Saviour God, "The God of Abraham" (Genesis 26:24), and "Their God" (Genesis 17:8). Sometimes in these titles the personal name Yahweh, *adonai*, is added. There are also titles expressing the intimacy of God with humankind: "God at hand" (Jeremiah 23:23), "thy God in whom thou trustest" (2 Kings 19:10), "God of my righteousness" (Psalm 4:1), and "God of my strength" (Psalm 43:2). It is this last category of intimacy that Hosea uses in showing how such closeness is no longer available to the people of Israel who have played the whore.

The people are no longer God's people (Hebrew *am*). They are not under God's care or protection. They are not God's flock. In addition, God no longer is their Sovereign Authority, nor their Salvation. Nor is God their Deliverer. God is no longer their God.

2:1 Say ye unto your brethren, Ammi; and to your sisters, Ruhamah.

Now the Lord, through Hosea, identifies the Israelites as "my people" or "Ammi." They are also described as "having mercy" or "Ruhamah." In 1:8-9 the Hebrew negative *lo* indicated that due to the sin of Israel and their unfaithfulness to God, they were not worthy of God's mercy. This changes in chapter 2; the Lord God gives those who were "not his people" and without mercy an opportunity to repent and become "God's people" and receive "God's mercy."

Chapter two also begins the theme of the wife of whoredom. Lord God explains the guilt of Israel and His plan for punishment and reconciliation. This allegorical speech has the Lord God as the faithful husband and the Israel as the unfaithful wife.

2 Plead with your mother, plead: for she is not my wife, neither am I her husband: let her, therefore, put away her whoredoms out of her sight, and her adulteries from between her breasts;

The word "plead" in Hebrew is *roob*. It means to complain, plead, or grapple. It is also a term for the process of accusation, argument, and persuasion aimed at settling a conflict. Hosea uses this word twice in this verse emphatically. It is used to stress God's telling Hosea to beg Israel to recognize its transgression and wrongdoing.

A second metaphor, or allegorical, phrase is employed in that individual daughters and sons of Israel are to plead with Mother Israel—the political and religious leaders—to return to the Lord's favor. The phrase "not by wife" does not connote divorce but merely implies that sin has spiritually separated the marriage relationship of God and Israel. Hosea makes it clear that not only has Israel committed whoredoms, *zaw-naw*, but they also have sinned by engaging in adulteries. *Nah-af-oof* describes adultery as one married person engaging in "non-kosher" relationships with another. Israel has paid tribute to idols and has done so while being religiously and spiritually committed to the Lord God.

The phrase "between her breasts" form a literary and rhetorical stance and intensifies the feminine imagery of Israel as wife. In a cultural sense it refers to the place where devotees of Baal wore jewelry, on their heads and between their breasts. Again Hosea emphasizes the unfaithfulness of Israel to God, and her playing the whore with another god.

3 Lest I strip her naked, and set her as in the day that she was born, and make her as a wilderness, and set her like a dry land, and slay her with thirst.

There are many allusions of God's relationship to history in this verse. First, Hosea warns the people of God's threat to strip Israel to nakedness. *Aw-rome* denotes partial or complete nakedness. This is significant because Genesis records how Adam and Eve were ashamed of their nakedness after they disobeyed God and ate of the tree of the knowledge of good and evil (Genesis 3:7-10). Adam and Eve hid from God because they were embarrassed about their nudity and tried to hide themselves from their Creator by covering themselves with leaves. Thus, there is established a negative connotation for nakedness, a complete openness and a sense of being exposed and vulnerable.

A second reference to God's relationship to history is in the word "wilderness." Exodus 16:35 and Deuteronomy 8:2 describe how the Children of Israel were made to wander in the wilderness for 40 years because of sin. They were totally depen-

dent on God during this time and ate manna God provided from heaven. They also were guided by God with a cloud by day and fire by night. Hosea reminds Israel of this time in their journey with God and how God placed them in the wilderness long ago for sin and threatens to do the same because of their current rebellion.

4 And I will not have mercy upon her children; for they are the children of whoredoms.

Hosea cannot stress enough to Israel the seriousness of her sin of idolatry and unfaithfulness. Such unfaithfulness leads to distrust and a breach in relationships. Not only is Mother Israel affected by her sin but the sins of the parents are also borne on the children and thus become the children's sins. Reference to the daughter Lo-ruhamah is made again in this verse. The mother or wife will not receive mercy, nor will the children. Because the people have engaged in whoredom or idolatry, the children become children of whoredom and idolatry.

DAILY BIBLE READINGS

M: The Prophet Hosea's Symbolic Marriage
Hosea 1:1-5

T: The Births of Lo-ruhamah and Lo-ammi
Hosea 1:6-9

W: Blessings Followed by Chastisement
Hosea 1:10-2:7

T: Israel's Humiliation and Punishment
Hosea 2:8-13

F: The Lord's Hope for His People
Hosea 2:14-18

S: Unfaithful Israel to Be Restored
Hosea 2:19-23

S: Invitation to Praise
Psalm 100

TEACHING TIPS

July 22
Bible Study Guide 8

1. Words You Should Know

A. Yoke (Hosea 11:4) Hebrew *Owl* **(obe)** Greek *Zygos*—a wooden frame placed over the neck of slaves and oxen to restrain them.

B. Repentings (v. 8) Greek *metanoia, metameloma*— change of mind, change of attitude, turn from sin.

2. Teacher Preparation

A. Begin preparing for this lesson by reading the Devotional Reading and the FOCAL VERSES at least three times using a different translation for each reading. Also refer to Scripture commentaries and footnotes.

B. Read Bible Study Guide 8 and answer all the SEARCH THE SCRIPTURES and DISCUSS THE MEANING questions.

C. Materials needed: Bible, chalk, and chalkboard.

3. Starting the Lesson

A. Before the class begins, write the words, "Yoke" and "Repentance" on the board with their definitions.

B. After students have arrived and are settled, take prayer requests and pray. Then key in on the two words on the board. Discuss the words and their meanings. Then, read the IN FOCUS story and tie it in with these words.

C. Allow students to give their own definitions to the terms on the board and discuss the IN FOCUS story.

4. Getting into the Lesson

A. To help the students understand the context for today's lesson, read the BACKGROUND information and THE PEOPLE, PLACES, AND TIMES articles.

B. Discuss those readings in context of today's LESSON AIM.

C. Ask for volunteers to read the FOCAL VERS-ES according to the AT-A-GLANCE outline. You may discuss verse by verse, or wait until the entire text has been read.

D. After each student has completed a section of the reading, ask the corresponding SEARCH THE SCRIPTURES questions.

5. Relating the Lesson to Life

A. To help students understand how the lesson applies to today's society, direct their attention to the LESSON IN OUR SOCIETY article. Allow time for discussion and debate tying in to the LESSON AIM.

B. Review the DISCUSS THE MEANING questions. Again, allow time to discuss each question.

C. Ask students what they have learned from today's lesson that might personally impact their life.

6. Arousing Action

A. Review the MAKE IT HAPPEN suggestion and challenge the students to put the suggestion into practice this week.

JULY 22ND

B. Challenge the students to do the DAILY BIBLE READINGS. Tie in these readings with today's lesson.

C. Ask for prayer requests and close with prayer.

WORSHIP GUIDE

For the Superintendent or Teacher
Theme: God's Compassion for Israel
Theme Song: Jesus Is Tenderly Calling Today
Scripture: Hosea 11:1-9
Song: Count Your Blessings, Name Them One By One
Meditation: Father, thank You for Your love, mercy, and discipline. Help us to learn the lessons You are trying to teach us because they are for our good. Amen.

GOD'S COMPASSION FOR ISRAEL

Bible Background • HOSEA 11
Printed Text • HOSEA 11:1-9
Devotional Reading • PSALM 103:8-14

LESSON AIM:

By the end of the lesson, students will know that God is indeed a merciful and compassionate God, that He constantly reaches out to us to return to Him when we are unfaithful, that He loves us in spite of our shortcomings.

KEEP IN MIND

"I drew them with cords of a man, with bands of love: and I was to them as they that take off the yoke on their jaws, and I laid meat unto them" (Hosea 11:4, KJV).

FOCAL VERSES

Hosea 11:1 When Israel was a child, then I loved him, and called my son out of Egypt.

2 As they called them, so they went from them: they sacrificed unto Baalim, and burned incense to graven images.

3 I taught Ephraim also to go, taking them by their arms, but they knew not that I healed them.

4 I drew them with cords of a man, with bands of love: and I was to them as they that take off the yoke on their jaws, and I laid meat unto them.

5 He shall not return into the land of Egypt, but the Assyrian shall be his king, because they refused to return.

6 And the sword shall abide on his cities, and shall consume his branches, and devour them, because of their own counsels.

7 And my people are bent to backsliding from me: though they called them to the most High, none at all would exalt him.

8 How shall I give thee up, Ephraim? How shall I deliver thee, Israel? How shall I make thee as

LESSON OVERVIEW

LESSON AIM
KEEP IN MIND
FOCAL VERSES
IN FOCUS
THE PEOPLE, PLACES,
AND TIMES
BACKGROUND
AT-A-GLANCE
IN DEPTH
SEARCH THE SCRIPTURES
DISCUSS THE MEANING
LESSON IN OUR SOCIETY
MAKE IT HAPPEN
FOLLOW THE SPIRIT
REMEMBER YOUR THOUGHTS
MORE LIGHT ON THE TEXT
DAILY BIBLE READINGS

Admah? How shall I set thee as Zeboim? Mine heart is turned within me, my repentings are kindled together.

9 I will not execute the fierceness of mine anger, I will not return to destroy Ephraim: for I am God, and not man; the Holy One in the midst of thee: and I will not enter into the city.

IN FOCUS

A noted minister, Novel Hayes, told of his love for his wayward daughter, Zona, in his book *Stand in the Gap For Your Children* (Harrison House Publishers, 1991). Even though Zona grew up in a God-fearing and God-honoring home all of her life, and her father went across the country teaching and preaching God's Word, she chose to rebel in her teen years. Her father prayed for her, talked to her, prodded, pleaded, and prayed again for her soul.

Zona was like the prodigal son of the parable in Luke's Gospel (15:11-32), who took all of his inheritance and went away from his loving home to a foreign land to do his own thing. His own thing included sinful living, which took almost all that he had mentally, physically, and spiritually. Yet Zona, as the prodigal son, one day came to herself and found her way back to her father and to her God, who still loved her unconditionally. She repented and was restored. Today she ministers to others.

There are many Zonas in our society, many children who are rebelling and forgetting their spiritual roots for a season, even though they have been trained up in the way they should go. The lure of the world is pulling after them, and many are too weak to refuse. Their parents, and God, are brokenhearted over their departure and care for them with loving kindness. Of course, the parents and other saints must engage in spiritual warfare to take them back from Satan. This includes praying, fasting, standing on God's promises, and praying some more.

Israel is that wayward child in today's lesson. They are Zona. God reminds the Israelites through Hosea of His love, His mercy, and His kindness to them in spite of their transgressions. He is also tenderly calling today, "Come home! Come home! You who are weary, come home!" Do you need to come home to God today? Do you know someone who does? His loving arms are outstretched to you and to all who will believe on the Lord Jesus Christ and be saved.

THE PEOPLE, PLACES, AND TIMES

God's Judgment. Hosea, in his prophetic ministry, warned Judah not to follow in the same footsteps as Israel. However, they did not obey either. Instead, the people broke their covenant, turned away from God, and forgot about His goodness. The consequences they suffered were a devastating invasion and exile.

God's Love. God did not give up on Israel or Judah. In fact, He pursued and pursued them, trying to get them to change their wicked ways. Because His love is tender, faithful, unchanging, and forever, He loved them still. Yet their actions proved that they did not love God.

Restoration. God was more than willing to restore His wayward children. In fact, His love and mercy were extended to them. He just wanted them to repent, to have a heartfelt sorrow for their sins and return to Him. Then He would accept them back into the fold. His offer was good even when their enemies overtook them. He was willing to forgive them. Instead of restoration, however, they reaped a whirlwind of despair because of their continued disobedience.

BACKGROUND

The last four chapters of Hosea focus on God's love for His stubborn children, the Israelites. He was tired of pleading with them to repent and return to Him. They must now suffer the conse-quences of their sin. He had already offered to restore them if they would only turn back to Him, but they refused to obey God. Therefore, their doom was sealed. The northern kingdom would be destroyed. They would be disciplined in the hand of an angry God!

There was, however, a faithful few who would still walk with God and be spared. They would return to Jerusalem and await the Messiah who would come to pardon and restore them. Then they would faithfully follow Him.

God always nurtured and loved the Israelites, but they were ungrateful. They did not thank Him for His many blessings and kindnesses to them, they did not even acknowledge His goodness to them. Often they were hypocritical in their worship of Him, and God despised their pretending. Therefore, He had to discipline them to teach them, and us; He had to show His love for them through the rod of correction.

The northern kingdom survived for only two centuries after they seceded from Jerusalem. They did not hear the warnings of the prophet Hosea, just as they did not hear Amos and the others before him. Some of their evil kings also did not help people mend their broken relationship with God, so they never repented as a nation. Therefore in 722 B.C., Israel fell at the hands of the Assyrians. Judah also was captured, but a remnant returned to the homeland.

Because Judah did have some good kings—including Asa, Jehosphaphat, Joash, Amaziah, Azariah (Uzziah), Jotham, Hezekiah, and Josiah—the priests were able to wipe out some of their idol worship. This allowed Judah to survive more than 150 years after the fall of Israel. The remnant of faithful souls, who survived the fall, returned to restore their land and temple. God always has a people who will be faithful and worship Him.

AT-A-GLANCE

1. Israel's Sins Against God
(Hosea 11:1-5)
2. God Pronounces Punishment (v. 6)
3. God Tells of His Love for Israel Still
(vv. 8-9)

IN DEPTH

1. Israel's Sins Against God (Hosea 11:1-5)

God reminded Israel how He loved him even as a child, yet he was stubborn and always breaking God's rules. These infractions, or transgressions, had consequences. God heard the cries of his ancestors and led them out of Egypt with a strong hand. Yet these ancestors repaid God's love and mercy just as the new generation did, by being unfaithful to Him. God called this rebellion (v. 2).

This rebellion took the form of worshiping idol gods; Baal was one. They also worshiped other idols, images, and the golden calf. This was breaking their covenant relationship with God—His commandments. He had promised to be their God if they would be His people. God always kept His promises to the Israelites. They, however, always seemed to break theirs.

God showed Himself to be a tender Father, leading the Children of Israel by the hand, teaching them how to walk with Him, how to serve Him, how to honor Him (v. 3). He took care of them, supplying their needs in every way, mentally, physically, and spiritually.

In verse 4, God referred back to how He showed kindness and unconditional love to them when their ancestors were in the wilderness for 40 years. He fed them with food from heaven. When they were thirsty, He supplied the water. Their clothes and shoes did not wear out because God saw to it that they didn't. Yet they complained and were unfaithful to Him. It was God's kindness and mercy that allowed the remnant to survive the desert experience. Yet the Israelites forgot their history in the Promised Land, Canaan. They forgot the love of the one and only true God. It was God who freed them from bondage and they forgot (v. 5).

In fact, in verse 7, God acknowledged that the Israelites did not worship Him with a pure heart. He felt by their actions that they were determined to leave Him and whore after idols. God will not share His glory with anyone.

2. God Pronounces Punishment (v. 6)

There is a penalty for sin and usually it is death. A merciful loving God, however, does not want anyone to be lost. This was true with the Israelites.

He had been more than patient with them. Yet His chosen people refused to listen, refused to repent, refused to turn back to God. Therefore in verse 6, God pronounced His judgment. He would discipline them. His love dictated that He take this action.

God's mercy will not last always. Because the Israelites refused to hear the prophets even Hosea, God dictated that they go back into bondage, slavery. This time they would be captured by the Assyrians. They would be at war, and many would be destroyed. The Israelites' sin led to Israel's downfall in 722 B.C.

3. God Tells of His Love for Israel Still (vv. 8-9)

Even though the Israelites must be disciplined by God at the hands of their enemies, still God did not get any enjoyment out of this action. He knew that it was best for them, but still it broke His heart. In verse 8, He lamented over His chosen people. He did not want to give them up or see them destroyed. In fact, it was tearing God's heart apart to see so many of His children die because of their own wickedness. He was not sending them to hell. They were sending themselves.

Though God was angry with His wayward children, still He did not give them what they deserved. His love for them caused God to still show mercy. In verse 9, God decided not to destroy Israel totally. There was a remnant who were still faithful. They would be spared. They would be allowed to rebuild and continue to cultivate their personal relationship with a faithful, loving, and merciful God!

SEARCH THE SCRIPTURES

1. God loved Israel even when he was a _____. (Hosea 11:1)

2. How did God draw Israel? (v. 4)

3. What will happen to Israel because of his continued disobedience? (v. 5)

4. Because of God's love and mercy, He decided that He would not do what? (v. 9)

DISCUSS THE MEANING

1. Why does God sometimes find it necessary to discipline His children?

2. What does discipline do?

3. What happens when we continue to be disobedient after He warns us again and again?

4. Does God get any enjoyment out of disciplining His children?

LESSON IN OUR SOCIETY

Bible scholars continuously tell us that the signs of the time indicate that it will not be long before Jesus Christ returns. He has already come as our Saviour. God has given us ample time to hear the Gospel and believe on the Lord Jesus Christ and be saved. Yet our world is becoming weaker and wiser. More and more, people are turning their back on the true and living God and are being lured by the world into its mold.

Some churches are into programs and entertainment, instead of ministries to win the lost. People are searching for answers to their problems and needs, but there are few laborers in the field. Are you willing to minister in your home, neighborhood, on the job, or wherever you are? If so, God can also use you.

MAKE IT HAPPEN

This week determine that you will witness to someone wherever you may be. Share the Good News of salvation with them. Also, remember to pray for them and yourself as you go out to do God's work.

FOLLOW THE SPIRIT

What God wants me to do:

REMEMBER YOUR THOUGHTS

Special insights you learned:

MORE LIGHT ON THE TEXT
Hosea 11:1-9

11:1 When Israel was a child, then I loved him and called my son out of Egypt.

Until this time Hosea has been informing Israel of God's disappointment with her idolatry and adultery with other gods. Israel has played the harlot and has forsaken and forgotten her first and true love, the Lord God. Now Hosea reminds Israel how much God still loves her despite her wrongdoing. Hosea uses language of call and election to cause the Hebrews to remember that God has been their God from the beginning, even in their youth and embryonic stages of life. The prophet uses the rhetorical strategy of "corporate personality," that is he speaks to the whole nation of Israel as if it were an individual. Israel, as a nation, was God's firstborn when they were in Egypt (Exodus 4:22). This parallels with the Matthean account of how Jesus, as God's firstborn Son, was also called out of Egypt (Matthew 2:15).

Hosea employs the words "loved" and "called" to exemplify God's election of Israel as the people of God. "Love" in the Hebrew language is *aw-hab*, to have affection, to like, or befriend. The intensity of the meaning ranges from God's infinite affection for his people to the carnal appetites of a lazy glutton. Hosea uses this word not only to speak of God's interest in Israel, but also to refer to Israel's adulterous relationships (2:5-13). *Aw-hab* is often used to describe love between human beings as between fathers and sons (Genesis 22:2), a slave and his master (Exodus 21:8), neighborly or communal love (Leviticus 19:18), the love of a stranger (Deuteronomy 10:19), and international friendship or political kinship (1 Kings 5:1). The love between Ruth and Naomi is also expressed by this verb (Ruth 4:15).

This word is also used to show how people have affection for things, i.e., savory meat (Genesis 27:4), oil (Proverbs 21:17), silver (Ecclesiastes 5:9), and gifts (Isaiah 1:23). Love for God's commandments is illustrated in the Psalms (119:47, 97, and 119).

The second verb Hosea uses to demonstrate Israel's election is "called" or *kaw-raw*. It means to call out, to call forth, to cry out, to pronounce, or to publish. This verb represents naming as an indication of God's power and sovereignty over that which the Lord calls. If such a "calling" is by sound of voice, then the word means "to call to," i.e. Abner calls to Joab (2 Samuel 2:26). As a declaration or pronouncement *kaw-raw* is also used as "attention" (Genesis 41:43) or "unclean, unclean" (Leviticus 13:45). In prophetic literature, this verb means to proclaim the Word of the Lord (1 Kings

13:32; Isaiah 40:2 and Jeremiah 2:2).

This verb also refers to calling to Adonai, or the Lord. In this sense it means to cry out to or shout unto God. This connotation is found some 98 times throughout the Bible, half of which are located in the Psalms (3:5; 27:7; 56:10; 102:3 and 116:2). The meanings range from giving praise and thanks to calling for help and lamenting.

Hosea uses *kaw-raw* in the sense of "drawing someone's attention in order to establish contact." Consequently, the one who is summoned must respond, or hear, such a calling. Other examples of God's calling and seeking a response are found in Isaiah 50:2; Jeremiah 7:13; Zechariah 7:13; Job

5:1; Proverbs 1:28 and Song of Solomon 5:6.

2 As they called them, so they went from them: they sacrificed unto Baalim, and burned incense to graven images.

Hosea shows the antithetical response of Israel to God's calling her. Instead of the people bringing themselves and offering their goods to the One who summoned them, they sacrificed and presented offerings to gods who cannot speak or hear them respond. The word "sacrifice" in Hebrew is *zaw-bakh* meaning to kill, offer, or slay. The word is mainly used in connection with slaying animals for sacrifice. Sacrifices were often linked with the various types of offerings. The pertinence of sacrifices is seen early in Genesis. Noah sacrificed clean animals after the Flood (Genesis 8:20-21). Abram made a sacrifice at Shechem (Genesis 12:7-8), and Isaac and Jacob offered to God at Beersheba and Bethel (Genesis 26:25; 35:7). Such acts of worship continued from Moses on to Solomon. Yet God often warned Israel that obedience was honored more than sacrifices (1 Samuel 15:22). The Hebrews were often tempted to offer to other gods what was restricted to the God of their ancestors (Exodus 34:13; Deuteronomy 7:5). Offerings to Baal were numerous (Judge 6:30 and 1 Kings 16:32). Baal was a deity worshiped at local shrines scattered throughout the land into which Israel came. Hosea accuses Israel of sacrificing to Baal.

Israel is also guilty of burning incense to graven images. They have disobeyed the second commandment, "Thou shalt not make unto thee any graven image, or any likeness of anything that is in heaven above, or that is in the earth beneath, or that is in the water under the earth" (Exodus 20:4). Graven image is *pes-eel* or idol, quarry, that which is made or created by human hands. The burnt, or incense, offering is a *kaw-tar* offering used in the act of worship. It means to smoke or turn into fragrance by fire, especially as an act of worship. It not only denotes the burning of offerings, but it can also refer to the burning of incense as suggested by Hosea. The chronicler also refers to this (1 Chronicles 13:11). The purpose of such burning is to render the thing offered into smoke which would ascend to God as a sweet-smelling savor. Isaiah mentions such incense burning (6:4). In Exodus God instructed the people to burn incense with their morning and evening offerings and during the annual atonement offering (Exodus 30). Such holy incense was to be ignited only by coals from the altar of burnt incense (Isaiah 6:6). Use of other strange fire was punishable by death (Leviticus 10:1-2).

3 I taught Ephraim also to go, taking them by their arms, but they knew that I had not healed them.

Hosea continues the personification of Israel as a child in God's loving care. Israel is young and needing the Lord's guidance and support. The imagery of being taken by the arm expresses Israel's dependence on God and the necessity of the Lord's support.

Just as parents teach children and impart knowledge to them so has the Lord taught Israel. The Hebrew word *torah* (tow-rah) means teaching. It can refer to humans instructing each other or to God instructing Israel. It also refers to a set of regulations, i.e. Exodus 12 which contains the law regarding the Passover.

Hosea infers that although Israel had been taught some things, they were still young and immature. The people had grown up too soon and still needed additional instruction. His implication is similar to Paul's dilemma centuries later with the church at Corinth whom he desired to feed meat, but who still needed milk (1 Corinthians 3: 1-2).

4 I drew them with cords of a man, with bands of love: and I was to them as they that take off the yoke on their jaws, and I laid meat unto them.

God, through Hosea, proclaims that the Divine led Israel with cords of human kindness. Because of this parental imagery one cannot help but bring to mind the image of umbilical cords that feed and nurture babies in the womb. Umbilical cords transfer nutrients and oxygen from the mother to the infant in order that the baby may grow and develop. The cord, or *khay-bel*, to which Hosea is referring functions similarly. This type of cord ties people together so that they are not separated. Thus God and Israel were joined together so that nothing, or no one, could supposedly come between the Parent or child.

Not only did God attempt stay close to Israel with a spiritual chord, but the Lord also reached down to her. The meaning of "take off the yoke on their jaws" is an agricultural metaphor demonstrating the closeness of God to Israel. In order to remove a yoke the farmer must get close to the animal or beast of burden. There is a sense of touching, feeling, and being near the animal. Thus God has been close to, and very near, Israel, a very present help to them.

The final image is that of laying meat unto them or bending down to feed. God used a cord so that nothing would separate the Parent and the child; the Lord attempted to stay close to Israel by caressing, touching, and being near. Now Hosea shows how the Lord has been Israel's provider, Jehovah *Jireh*, the Lord who sees to it. God has fed Israel. This is reminiscent of God providing Israel with manna from heaven during its sojourn in the wilderness (Exodus 16:35 and Deuteronomy 8:2).

5 He shall not return into the land of Egypt, but the Assyrian shall be his king, because they refused to return.

Hosea now prophecies how Israel will be punished for its sin and transgressions. They will not be put into bondage under the Egyptians as had been their previous lot. Instead they will experience slavery and defeat at the hands of the Assyrians. Here Hosea foretells of the upcoming Assyrian conquest.

The Assyrians were people named after the city of Asshur on the upper Tigris and named after its national god. They were Akkadian and northwest-semiotician origin and were primarily tent dwellers or semi-nomadic people. From their very beginning they pursued a vigorous policy of commercial expansion to the north and northwest. It was their leader Tiglath-pileser who inaugurated their revival from 745-727 B.C.E. Internal fighting and the lack of support from Egypt forced Israel into battle with the Assyrians. After the death of Tiglath-pileser, Shalmaneser and Sargon II succeeded him and enabled the Assyrians to capture Samaria, a key city-state of the northern kingdom. After a two-year delay, Sargon II finally took Samaria in 722 B.C.E. and some 27,000 were deported (2 Kings 17).

Hosea insists this was due to Israel's refusal to return to their Divine Parent, God, the Lord, *Adonai*.

6 And the sword shall abide on his cities, and shall consume branches his branches, and devour them, because of their own counsels.

Hosea alludes to some details regarding the Assyrian capture of Israel. Since Jeroboam, Israel had had five kings. There was debauchery, sexual licentiousness, and a corrosive national character. Such was the nature of the internal disasters of

Israel. Furthermore, political mistakes were also made. Pekah, one of Israel's leaders (737-732 B.C.E.) formed an alliance with Syria against Assyria. Such ill counsel forced Israel to pay tribute to the Assyrians, and the nation was nearly destroyed. Of all of Israel's territory only a small portion remained which could only be run as a vassal state with the Assyrians watching every move.

As stated by Hosea, the sword that raged and consumed the cities was the Assyrian army. The counsel, schemes, and plots that allowed them emanated from Israel's own leaders and their selfish ambitions.

7 And my people are bent to backsliding from me: though they called them to the most High, none at all would exalt him.

Hosea again refers to the idolatry of Israel. The nation was full of sexual deviance, cannibalism, and a lack of internal cohesion. Offerings and sacrifices to Baal were the order of the day. There was no acknowledgment of the mighty hand of God throughout the history of Israel. Sin and transgression, under the aegis of religion, was considered the norm and the right thing to do.

Again Hosea establishes an irony in which it is God who calls Israel. They were not summoned by Baal or other gods, but their Lord God called them out and called them forth. Yet Israel runs from the One who calls her to the one who cannot receive her response in praise and worship. The prophet intensifies the extent of the wrongdoing by saying that none, not one of the children of God, would praise or exalt their Maker. According to Hosea, the people are determined, insistent, and have a proclivity for doing what is wrong in the eyes of God. They are bent on backsliding and disobedience.

8 How shall I give thee up, Ephraim? How shall I deliver thee, Israel? How shall I make thee as Admah? How shall I set thee as Zeboim? Mine heart is turned within me, my repentings are kindled together.

God, as the Divine Parent, struggles to neglect and destroy the chosen child. Hosea shows God as needing to punish Israel for sins. Yet the love or *aw-*

hab, of God is so strong that even God toils with the idea of chastisement. Hosea's rhetorical use of questions also shows the extreme dilemma that God encounters in deciding what to do with a wayward, disobedient child. Israel is again referred to as Ephraim (11:3), one of the sons of Joseph who became part of the twelve tribes of Jacob. Such a reference to Ephraim displays the youthful nature of Israel and how God cannot turn away from that which is so young and needy. The reference to Admah and Zeboim is based on Deuteronomy 29:23. These were two cities, like Sodom and Gomorrah, on the Jordan plain which were destroyed by the Lord's fierce anger. The Lord does not want to bring such destruction on Israel like the calamity which was brought on these cities. Yet the Lord admits that evil must be brought down.

Hosea personifies God and shows how God's heart is heavy. The Lord's emotions, feelings, and compassion for Israel are causing Him to possibly reconsider the punishment for the crime. The heart, in Hebrew psychology, was the organ of thinking and deciding. To say that the Lord's heart "is turned" is to imply that it is possibly changing. The Hebrew word for "turned" is *haw-fak*. It means to change, overturn, be converted, or overthrow. God speaks through Hosea and demonstrates the Divine indecisiveness over that which is near and dear to God.

The word for "repentings," *nee-khoom*, also means compassion and comfort. Again Hosea is informing us that God is struggling over the necessary punishment because the Lord cares so much about Israel.

9 I will not execute the fierceness of mine anger, I will not return to destroy Ephraim: for I am God, and not man; the Holy One in the midst of thee: and I will not enter into the city.

God through Hosea now proclaims that Israel will not receive the penalty due them. God desires so much for Israel to repent and change that another opportunity has been granted them. The Lord's rationalization for withholding judgment is that the Lord is God, not a human being. Hosea implies that humans always engage in an eye for eye resolution. Yet God does not behave in such a manner because God is God. Reference can be made to

Numbers 23:19 which states, "God is not a human being that God should lie." Hosea informs Israel that God is not like her. Just because she has incited the anger of the Lord, the Lord does not have to succumb to such anger. For God's thoughts are not our thoughts nor are God's way our ways (Isaiah 55:8).

God is referred to as the Holy One. *Kaw-doshe* in Hebrew is the Holy One, Holy, or saint. It connotes that which is distinct from the common or profane. Because God is holy, God is free from the moral imperfections and frailties common to humankind. God is thus faithful to what God has promised. The title "the Holy One of Israel" is applied to God numerous times in Hebrew texts, but especially in Isaiah. It places the sin of the people in contrast to the moral perfection of God and expresses God's absolute separation from evil. That which is holy is not only distinct from the profane but in opposition to it as well. God hates and punishes sin (Joshua 24:19 and Isaiah 5:16). In light of God's holiness, Isaiah saw himself and his people as sinners (Isaiah 6:3, 5).

God, in this verse of Hosea, states that because the city is unclean, defiled, and full of sin, the Lord cannot enter into it. God is holy, it is unholy. The two cannot occupy the same space.

DAILY BIBLE READINGS

M: A Call to Repentance
Hosea 6:1-6
T: God's Love for Israel
Hosea 11:1-7
W: God's Great Compassion
Hosea 11:8-12:1
T: Thanksgiving for God's Mercies
Psalm 103:8-14
F: The Long History of Rebellion
Hosea 12:2-14
S: Judgment on Israel
Hosea 13:4-16
S: A Plea for Repentance
Hosea 14

TEACHING TIPS

1. Words You Should Know

A. Iniquity (Micah 3:10) Hebrew *owlah* **(o-law)** Greek *adikia*—unrighteousness; *anomia*lawlessness.

B. Transgression (Micah 6:7) *Peshua*—moral or religious revolt; Greek *poneros*—evil, godless.

2. Teacher Preparation

A. Begin preparing for this lesson by studying the Devotional Reading, Bible Background, and the DAILY BIBLE READINGS listed at the end of the lesson. As you study, keep in mind the LESSON AIM.

B. Read the FOCAL VERSES for Bible Study Guide 9. Read with understanding by consulting different translations and the footnotes at the end of the passages. Key in on what God expects from His people and why He is not pleased with the Israelites.

3. Starting the Lesson

A. After your students are settled, take prayer requests and pray. Also include the LESSON AIM in your request.

B. Before the students arrive, write the title of today's lesson and the AT-A-GLANCE outline on the board as well as the Words You Should Know.

C. Ask your students to give their own definitions of the Words You Should Know. Then give the definitions and discuss.

D. Read the IN FOCUS story.

4. Getting into the Lesson

A. Ask for volunteers to read the BACKGROUND section and THE PEOPLE, PLACES, AND TIMES article. Discuss during or after each reading, tying it in with the theme.

B. Assign the FOCAL VERSES according to the AT-A-GLANCE outline. Discuss and relate to today's LESSON AIM. After each section, review

the SEARCH THE SCRIPTURES question.

5. Relating the Lesson to Life

A. Read and discuss the LESSON IN OUR SOCIETY article. Key in on what God requires of His children in serving Him and each other.

B. Tie reading into today's LESSON AIM.

6. Arousing Action

A. Direct students to the MAKE IT HAPPEN suggestion. Explain that our leaders are especially attacked by Satan because he knows that if he can cause the shepherd to fall, he can scatter the sheep. Also stress that oftentimes, our leaders need encouragement too.

B. Challenge the students to suggest ways that they might encourage their leaders.

C. Encourage them to use the DAILY BIBLE READINGS as part of their daily devotions.

D. Close the class with prayer.

WORSHIP GUIDE

For the Superintendent or Teacher
Theme: What God Requires
Theme Song: I Surrender All
Scripture: Micah 3:9-12; 6:6-8
Song: Is Your All on the Altar?
Meditation: Dear Father, thank You for
Your instructions and guidance on how to
serve You and others. Help us to obey.
Amen.

WHAT GOD REQUIRES

Bible Background • MICAH 3; 6:1-8
Printed Text • MICAH 3:9-12; 6:6-8
Devotional Reading • PROVERBS 21:2-3

LESSON AIM

By the end of the session, students should know that God looks on our heart and at our motives for serving Him and the good we do. He requires a pure heart and pure motives, and He wants us to do what is just and right rather than substitute empty sacrifices.

KEEP IN MIND

"He hath shown thee, O man, what is good; and what doth the Lord require of thee, but to do justly, and to love mercy, and to walk humbly with thy God?" (Micah 6:8, KJV).

FOCAL VERSES

Micah 3:9 Hear this, I pray you, ye heads of the house of Jacob, and princes of the house of Israel, that abhor judgment, and pervert all equity.

10 They build up Zion with blood, and Jerusalem with iniquity.

11 The heads thereof judge for reward, and the priests thereof teach for hire, and the prophets thereof divine for money: yet will they lean upon the Lord, and say, Is not the Lord among us? none evil can come upon us.

12 Therefore shall Zion for your sake be plowed as a field, and Jerusalem shall become heaps, and the mountain of the house as the high places of the forest.

6:6 Wherewith shall I come before the Lord, and bow myself before the High God? Shall I come before him with burnt offerings, with calves of a year old?

LESSON OVERVIEW

LESSON AIM
KEEP IN MIND
FOCAL VERSES
IN FOCUS
THE PEOPLE, PLACES, AND TIMES
BACKGROUND
AT-A-GLANCE
IN DEPTH
SEARCH THE SCRIPTURES
DISCUSS THE MEANING
LESSON IN OUR SOCIETY
MAKE IT HAPPEN
FOLLOW THE SPIRIT
REMEMBER YOUR THOUGHTS
MORE LIGHT ON THE TEXT
DAILY BIBLE READINGS

7 Will the Lord be pleased with thousands of rams, or with ten thousands of rivers of oil? Shall I give my firstborn for my transgression, the fruit of my body for the sin of my soul?

8 He hath shown thee, O man, what is good; and what doth the Lord require of thee, but to do justly, and to love mercy, and to walk humbly with thy God?

IN FOCUS

Over a year ago, the headlines ran in many newspapers and the same was reported on TV that some Chicago alderman were being indicted for taking bribes, or kickbacks, from companies, individuals who were seeking to do business with the city.

The operation was called "Silver Shovel," and the federal government sent some of these men to jail. Even before that bit of news hit the media, a senator from Chicago was indicted for bribes and kickbacks as well and spent time in federal prison. Also policemen across the country have been found guilty of breaking laws, shaking down drug dealers, abusing inmates, and even staging robberies of stores. All this came on the back of reports that some priests in different parishes across the country have been brought up on charges for sexually molesting some of their altar boys for more than 40 years. Many of the victims are still suffering from the effects.

The list of injustices go on and on. In most societies leaders are held to a higher standard than those they serve. They are expected not only to

JULY
29TH

obey the laws of God, but the laws of the land as well. They are expected to have compassion and respect for the people they serve. However, time and time again, greed and corruption have caused many to fall into a cesspool of crime and broken vows.

This is expecially devastating when God's ministers and teachers succumb to Satan's traps. It is most heartbreaking when they do not serve the people out of a love for them and God, but because of what they can materially gain from the people.

Today's lesson tells us that God is not pleased when leaders refuse to lead by His standards or when His people do not stand on His Word. He warns and warns, but sooner or later, He will judge His people. Examine your own heart and actions to see if your motives in serving God and others are pleasing to Him. Remember that an all-seeing and all-knowing God will be the judge. He does not want empty sacrifices but pure hearts that love Him and appreciate what He did on Calvary.

THE PEOPLE, PLACES, AND TIMES

The Injustices of the People The people of the northern kingdom (Israel) and the southern kingdom (Judah) were guilty of many sins. They plotted evil to steal land, houses, and inheritance from the poor by fraud and violence (Micah 2:1-2). God accused them of stealing the shirt right off the backs of those who trusted them. They evicted women from their homes and stripped their children of all their God-given rights (v. 9). They hated good and loved evil (Micah 3:1-2) even when they were supposed to know right from wrong. They despised justice, distorted what was right (v. 9) by taking bribes (v. 11), and they murdered (v. 10) to take what was not theirs.

The Prophet Micah. Lived about 750-680 B.C. at the same time of the prophet Isaiah. Called by God to minister mainly to Judah (the southern kingdom), he also spoke to Israel (the northern kingdom). He spoke of their sins, their coming destruction if they did not return to God, and their restoration after the fall of Jerusalem.

Micah prophesied during the reign of three kings: Jotham, Ahaz, and Hezekiah. At the time, Judah enjoyed great prosperity, but this had turned their hearts away from God. They forgot about His blessings, His deliverance, and His mercy. Micah's mission was to warn the people before God judged them.

BACKGROUND

Micah became a prophet in 742 B.C., eight years after Hosea and two years before Isaiah. God called him to tell Israel and Judah that His judgment was coming and to offer pardon to those who repented and turned back to Him.

As stated previously, Micah prophesied during the reign of three kings: Jotham, Ahaz, and Hezekiah (742-687 B.C.). Jotham and Hezekiah were good kings, but Ahaz was evil. Evil leaders often assisted in driving the people further and further away from God as they did not pull down idolatry but condoned evil and wicked deeds.

Micah emphasized God's hate of sin and love for the sinner. He told how God stands as a righteous Judge over all mankind. He is ready to punish those who break His commands. Micah also stressed God's love. God loved us so much that He sent His one and only Son to die for all our sins. He sent Jesus to save and accept judgment in our place.

Micah denounced the leaders of his time and the selfish, wicked priests who led the people astray. He predicted their ruin and also denounced the oppression of the poor by the rich. Micah predicted that a new King was coming. This King would bring strength and peace to His people. This King would restore His people. His name is Jesus, but He did not to come until hundreds of years after Micah ministered.

Because the people and their leaders did not heed God's continuous warnings from Micah,

AT-A-GLANCE

1. The Leaders Sin Against God and His People (Micah 3:9-11)

2. Judgment Against Israel and Her Leaders (v. 12)

3. The Lord's Case Against Israel (Micah 6:6-8)

Jerusalem was destroyed in 586 B.C. when Nebuchadnezzar and the Babylonian army attacked the city (2 Kings 25).

IN DEPTH

1. The Leaders Sin Against God and His People (Micah 3:9-11)

The prophet Micah was called by God for a special purpose. As the prophets before him, he was to plead with and warn the Israelites of their impending doom if they did not repent of their sins and turn back to the true and living God. Micah ministered to them and warned them that God's judgment was coming. He offered pardon to anyone who would repent of their sins.

Micah was direct in his indictments of the leaders of the northern kingdom (Israel) and the southern kingdom (Judah). He warned the unfair judges, the wicked priests, and the false prophets who were supposed to be serving God's chosen people that they had better change their evil ways. God was not pleased with them at all. They served the people, but their motives were wrong. They oppressed the downtrodden.

The leaders were accused by God of hating justice and perverting it. In fact, they twisted all that was right (v. 9) by accepting bribes. Money influenced their decisions. Justice could be bought if the price was right.

Judah was finally destroyed because of the injustices of her leaders. This injustice also caused Jerusalem to be built on a foundation of murder and corruption (v. 10).

When these leaders in the land perverted justice for a price, it not only corrupted them but the whole justice system. This caused the people to lose faith in their leaders and the system. Many others also joined in the corruption instead of taking a stand against it.

The priests were also guilty of evil motives in performing their spiritual duties. They would not prophesy unless they were paid (v. 11). Therefore, they did not serve the people out of love for God nor for those they led, but for greed. This proved to Micah, and the people, that these priests were not depending on God to meet their needs, but on what they could get from the people.

2. Judgment Against Israel and Her Leaders (v. 12)

The penalty for sin is often death. This was the case in today's lesson. In verse 12, God pronounced the penalty. Because of their sins, Jerusalem would be destroyed as Samaria. In 586 B.C., Nebuchadnezzar and the Babylonian army attacked the city (2 Kings 25), and it fell. The time of warning was over. The time of mercy was over. Judgment was exacted. The people and their leaders had been weighed in the balance and found wanting. It was time to reap what they had sown. God would prosecute them to the full extent of His laws.

3. The Lord's Case Against Israel (Micah 6:6-8)

Before Jesus Christ (the perfect sacrifice) came and gave His life and paid the penalty for our sins, the Israelites made sacrifices of perfect animals for their sins. The prophet Micah, however, let them know that they could no longer bring offerings of yearling calves, or thousands of rams, or tens of thousands of rivers of olive oil for their sins (vv. 6-7). God didn't want their empty sacrifices when their hearts were far from Him. They were just pretending. He is an all-knowing and all-seeing God; He knew the condition of their hearts. Their sacrifices would be simply trying to buy God's appeasement. They were not truly repentant, nor were they sorry for their sins. God cannot be bribed. He cannot be bought. To try to do so is an insult to Him.

Therefore Micah told the people that God had already told them what was right and good (v. 8). He did not leave them in the dark. He had already shown them His ways, but they were a disobedient, hard-headed, stiff-necked people. God wanted them to do what was right, to love mercy and walk humbly before Him.

He wanted them to be His people in their hearts, to love Him with all their heart, mind, and strength.

SEARCH THE SCRIPTURES

1. The leaders were accused of perverting _____equity. (Micah 3:9)

2. They built up _____ with _____, and Jerusalem with _____.

(v. 10)

3. Why did the leaders judge? (v. 11)

4. Why did the priest teach? (v. 11)

5. What did God decree as Israel's punishment for their sins? (v. 12)

6. What did God want from his people? (Micah 6:8)

DISCUSS THE MEANING

1. What can happen to people's hope when they have corrupt leaders?

2. When leaders pervert justice, what usually happens to the people's respect for the justice system? Why?

3. When a church leader serves God's people without compassion and love for them, what usually happens to the congregation? What will eventually happen to that leader?

LESSON IN OUR SOCIETY

One of the most devastating and heart wrenching trials that a congregation can go through is dealing with a fallen leader, someone they have trusted, esteemed, and expected to teach them and preach God's Word. Dr. Millicent Thompson, pastor of the Baptist Worship Center in Philadelphia, Pennsylvania, shared her experiences and tests of faith in her book, *Don't Die in the Winter, Your Season Is Coming,* (Treasure House, 1995.) She co-pastored, with her husband, who backslid. Not only did she suffer many reeling attacks from the forces of darkness, Satan and his demons, but from their church as well.

Dr. Thompson and her congregation had to learn how to console each other and to lean on God with all they had to survive these attacks. Since Dr. Thompson had two children, she learned what it meant to depend on no one else but God.

Many churches have suffered the heartaches of the downfall, or betrayal, of an unfaithful leader. Some young converts and lukewarm Christians do not survive the ordeal.

Truly, we need to pray for our pastors and other leaders, those rule over us. Since they are God's shepherds, Satan works overtime to destroy their testimonies.

MAKE IT HAPPEN

Make a commitment to pray for your church leaders this week. Ask God to give them His wisdom and knowledge on how to better serve His people as well as have a servant heart. Also, pray for their families who must support them.

Then, commit to helping your leaders in some tangible way. Maybe you could ease their load by one day inviting one, or some of them, to breakfast, lunch, or dinner. Even a phone call to let them know that you are praying could be very reassuring.

FOLLOW THE SPIRIT

What God wants me to do:

_____

_____

REMEMBER YOUR THOUGHTS

Special insights you learned:

_____

_____

MORE LIGHT ON THE TEXT
Micah 3:9-12; 6:6-8

3:9 Hear this, I pray you, ye heads of the house of Jacob, and princes of the house of Israel, that abhor judgment, and pervert all equity.

The prophet Micah, a contemporary of Isaiah, speaks to the southern kingdgom of Judah. At this time, Israel, the northern kingdom, has been under threat of destruction and will eventually fall into the hands of the Assyrians in 722 B.C.E. Micah's warning to Judah is that the same could happen to them if they continue in their evil ways.

Micah particularly addresses the political and religious groups of Judah. He calls out the heads and princes who are responsible for establishing the religious and political moral standards for the people. Instead of the leaders practicing justice and righteousness, the Lord, through Micah, accuses them of hating or abhoring what is just. Justice, from the Hebrew word *mish-pawt,* means judgment or a right sentence. It is the establishment of right through fair and legal procedures in accordance with the will of God. The word "abhor," or *taw-ab,* means to loathe, detest, or make abominable and is a strong indication of how far those who rule over the Hebrews have fall-

practice such honesty.

10 They build up Zion with blood, and Jerusalem with iniquity.

The prophet continues to personalize the accusation against Judah. In the name of religion and sacrifice to God, the people have erected buildings using perverse and deceitful means. Instead of using tithes and offerings to establish places of worship, the religious leaders have taken from the poor and, in some instances, killed to expand Jerusalem. Archaeology testifies to the building activities underway in Jerusalem during Micah's prophecy. Such capitol activities were performed at the expense of the oppressed and less fortunate. Jeremiah makes reference to similar activities by mentioning those who build their homes by unrighteousness (22:13). The prophet Habakkuk (2:12) also records about official building with bloodshed.

The name "Zion" refers to the hill between the Kidron and Tyropean valleys that David captured from the Jebusites (2 Samuel 5:7). Subsequently, it became known as the city of David. With the building of the temple to the north, the hill became known as Mount Zion. Zion may specifically refer to the temple vicinity or to Jerusalem in general. From the time of Solomon, who built the Temple, Zion became the center of the Lord's activity. Zion frequently refers to the temple area where Yahweh dwells. Thus, Micah's reference to the people building Zion up with blood shows how this holy habitation had been defamed and desecrated.

11 The heads thereof judge for reward, and the

en from God. They are not instructing people with fairness. On the contrary, such leaders are seeking their own gain and pursing personal ambitions and agendas.

Not only do these rulers and chiefs abhor justice, but they also pervert, turn against, equity. *Yaw-shawr* is that which is straight, right or just. It also denotes fairness and that which is honest and aboveboard. Those who rule over Judah do not

priests thereof teach for hire, and the prophets thereof divine for money: yet will they lean upon the Lord, and say, Is not the Lord among us? none evil can come upon us.

Micah again compels Judah to reexamine its political and social ethics. The rulers who govern civic and state affairs are corrupt. The priests who dictate religious standards practice evil. The prophets who speak the Word of the Lord only do it for money. Micah contends that Judah's leadership, who are responsible for directing people in all social, political, and religious affairs have turned away from the Lord. Those who are in power only want to be compensated by humankind for what God has gifted and instructed them to do. Rulers give judgment for a bribe, priests teach for a price, and prophets give oracles for money. Micah stresses the greed and insatiable materialism that has pervaded Judah.

These leaders, however, believe that what they do is good and pleasing in the eyes of the Lord. They are convinced that since Zion is the dwelling place of God and that since the Hebrews are God's chosen seed, all is well and their transgressions can be overlooked. Speaking rhetorically Micah states that those in authority did not lean upon the Lord. The word "lean," or *shaw-an*, means to lie, rely on, rest on, particularly God. Isaish makes reference to this phrase in stating how Judah must depend on God (48:2). Such leaning implies a need to find favor and obtain support from that which is leaned upon. Judah wishes to engage in wrongdoing while depending on the Lord to provide safety and security. The secular and religious leaders, despite their unscrupulous conduct, believe that God will protect them on the based on His faithfulness and His promises. The people do not see the error of their ways. They are so obstinate and spiritually blind that they are convinced that because the Lord dwells in Zion, no harm can befall them even when they sin against God.

12 Therefore shall Zion for your sake be plowed as a field, and Jerusalem shall become heaps, and the mountains of the house as the high places in the forest.

Because Judah has become prideful and sinful, the Lord, through Micah, predicts its ensuing destruction and decimation. The crassness of the leaders will result in the leveling of Jerusalem and its temple. Micah made a similar pronouncement by stating that Samaria would be a heap and a place for planting vineyards, i.e., a waste, a barren land (1:6). Jeremiah repeated this prophecy a century later when he was actually observing its fulfillment (26:18-19). Both prophets were foretelling the captivity of Judah by the Babylonians and the exile afterward. Judah, during Micah's time, was already a vassal state of the Assyrians; further enslavement was the next step.

Again the prophet specifically names Zion and Jerusalem, the center of Jewish worship, as places to be destroyed. No place was beyond God's wrath when evil had been committed. Micah personalizes the message and the plans of God to show Judah's leaders their ill behavior.

6:6 Wherewith shall I come before the Lord, and bow myself before the High God? Shall I come before him with burnt offerings, with calves of a year old?

Micah uses personification (giving human qualities to non-human things) to establish a courtroom setting in which the Lord is the Accuser (Plaintiff) who charges Israel the accused (defendant) with social and religious injustice. Judah attempts to respond to God's indictment by asking how can it approach God who is so high and mighty under the shadow of its own sin and transgressions.

The act of bowing (*kaw-faf*) means to pay homage or respect to one who is a royal personage or someone with regal power. It is similar to the Greek word *pros-koo-nay-o*, which means to lie prostrate as a form of worship. Judah acknowledges the royal and lofty nature of God and realizes that the King of Kings is worthy to receive their obeisance. Yet they have not paid God the respect and honor the Divine deserves because of the greed of the religious and political leadership.

Not only does God deserve their honor as a Royal Being, God must be offered sacrifices, particularly burnt offerings. The burnt offering, or *o-law*, offering is a gift of ascension or going up. A portion is given to the priest to offer to God and the remaining is consumed or burned. It is the base word for "holocaust." The offering is dedicated completely to God. Young calves, or any animal less than a year old, were often sacrificed to render this type of offering. By their question Judah knows it should have been engaging in these sacrifices. Yet their questions also indicate how far they have strayed from the Lord's covenant or promise.

7 Will the Lord be pleased with thousands of rams, or with ten thousands of rivers of oil? shall I give my first-born for my transgression, the fruit of my body for the sin of my soul?

Judah continues an arrogant defense of their crimes by sarcastically asking what does the Lord require. The people know that sacrifices of rams are pleasing to the Lord. Yet they exaggerate how many sacrifices should be given to God by asking if thousands of rams will do. The Hebrews are aware that oil is used in anointing royalty and in presenting gifts to God. Yet they are overzealous in their need to repent and ask if many rivers, not vials of oil, will suffice. Micah again uses this rhetorical line of reasoning to show how far the people are removed from God. They are not aware how much repentance needs to occur.

The line of questioning and sarcasm continues with Judah even offering its firstborn as restitution for sin. Micah alludes to the importance of the Lord receiving the firstfruits of the harvest for sacrifice. This passage also alludes to God delivering the firstborn of the Hebrew children from the angel of death during Israel's enslavement in Egypt (Exodus 12). This giving of the firstborn also refers to human sacrifices practiced in Judah under kings Ahaz (2 Kings 16:3) and Manasseh (2 Kings 21:6).

8 He hath shown thee, O man, what is good; and what doth the Lord require of thee, but to do justly, and to love mercy, and to walk humbly with thy God?

Micah now offers a response to the questions of verses 6 and 7. None of what Judah has offered is what the Lord desires. God does not seek sacrifices, offerings, or rituals. The Lord wants the people to treat each other fairly and to walk according to His way. Obedience is better than sacrifice (1 Samuel 15:22).

To do justly or to carry out justice comes from the Hebrew word *mish-pawt*. It means judgment or a right sentence. It is the establishment of right through fair and legal procedures in accordance with the will of God. Mercy is translated from the Hebrew word *ches-ed*. It is pity, lovingkindnes, or showing good deeds. It is synonymous with New Testament concept of grace. Some scholars distinguish grace as favor which God bestows "just because," whereas mercy is favor "in spite of" sinful behavior. It is the punishment God withholds despite our guilt. The idea of walking humbly with God mentioned in light of Judah's arrogance and refusal to lean on the Lord as mentioned in Micah 3:11. Because the people have allowed their lust for money to interfere with their relationship with God, and because they have chosen their own selfish gain, Micah warns them that the Lord wants them to submit, to return to the commandments and to the way of the Lord. God resists the proud and gives grace to the humble (1 Peter 5:5).

DAILY BIBLE READINGS

M: Wicked Rulers and Prophets
Micah 3
T: Peace and Security through Obedience
Micah 4:1-5
W: Restoration Promised after Exile
Micah 4:6-5:1
T: The Ruler from Bethlehem
Micah 5:2-6
F: Future Role of the Remnant
Micah 5:7-15
S: God Challenges Israel
Micah 6:1-5
S: What God Requires
Micah 6:6-16

TEACHING TIPS

August 5
Bible Study Guide 10

1. Words You Should Know

A. Seraphim (Isaiah 6:2) Hebrew *srafim*—a fiery serpent, angel that flies, speaks, and stands reverently in the presence of God and dramatizes His Word.

B. Holiness, Holy (v. 3) Greek *hagios and hagiosyne*—means separation from what is common or unclean, a consecration to God.

2. Teacher Preparation

A. Begin preparing for this lesson by studying the Devotional Reading and the Daily Bible Readings.

B. Read the Bible Background Scripture in several translations, especially from a study Bible. Reflect on the condition of the peoples' hearts and the mercy of God as He sent yet another prophet to them to attempt to get them from their sins to turn to Him. Also, concentrate on the fact that Isaiah had to be cleansed himself before he could go to the unclean people.

3. Starting the Lesson

A. Before the students arrive, write the title of today's lesson and the AT-A-GLANCE outline on the board.

B. To help focus the students' attention, ask them to help you list on the board some works that God may call us to do. Discuss your list.

C. Read the IN FOCUS story, and open the class in prayer.

4. Getting into the Lesson

A. To help the students gain a better understanding of the context for today's lesson, ask for a volunteer to read the BACKGROUND section, and another to read THE PEOPLE, PLACES, AND TIMES article.

B. Have volunteers read a selected portion of the FOCAL VERSES commentary according to the AT-A-GLANCE outline. After each section, review the appropriate SEARCH THE SCRIPTURES question. Engage in discussion, making sure that your class understands what is happening in the lesson and God's point of view.

5 Relating the Lesson to Life

A. To help the students see how the lesson applies to our modern day society, direct them to read and discuss the LESSON IN OUR SOCIETY article.

C. Ask the students to share any insights they may have received from today's lesson.

6. Arousing Action

A. Direct your students to the MAKE IT HAPPEN suggestions, and ask them to share their call into God's service. Also, discuss why it is so important that we work where God wants us to work and where He places us. Tell them that we do not have to be jealous of others' gifts because when God calls us, He will make a place for us to use our gifts.

B. Encourage the students to use the DAILY BIBLE READINGS as a part of their daily devotions. Ask them to tie the readings in with the lesson of that week.

C. Close with prayer.

WORSHIP GUIDE

For the Superintendent or Teacher
Theme: Isaiah's Call
Theme Song: Jesus Is Tenderly Calling Today
Scripture: Isaiah 6:1-12
Song: Where He Leads Me I Will Follow
Meditation Thought: Precious Lord, let me hear Your voice when You call. And let me say, "Here I am, send me." Do what You must in my life to make me ready for Your service.

ISAIAH'S CALL

Bible Background • ISAIAH 6
Printed Text • ISAIAH 6:1-12
Devotional Reading • ACTS 26:12-20

LESSON AIM

By the end of the lesson, students should know that God uses ordinary people to carry out His programs, that we must be cleansed by God before He uses us to do His Holy work, and that any successful task for God requires God in the equation.

KEEP IN MIND

"Also I heard the voice of the Lord, saying, Whom shall I send, and who will go for us? Then said I, Here am I; send me" (Isaiah 6:8, KJV).

FOCAL VERSES

Isaiah 6:1 In the year that King Uzziah died I saw also the Lord sitting upon a throne, high and lifted up, and his train filled the temple.

2 Above it stood the seraphim: each one had six wings; with twain he covered his face, and with twain he covered his feet, and with twain he did fly.

3 And one cried unto another, and said, Holy, holy, holy, is the Lord of hosts: the whole earth is full of his glory.

4 And the posts of the door moved at the voice of him that cried, and the house was filled with smoke.

5 Then said I, Woe is me! For I am undone; because I am a man of unclean lips, and I dwell in the midst of a people of unclean lips: for mine eyes have seen the King, the Lord of hosts.

6 Then flew one of the seraphim unto me, having a live coal in his hand, which he had taken with the tongs from off the altar:

7 And he laid it upon my mouth, and said, Lo,

LESSON OVERVIEW

LESSON AIM
KEEP IN MIND
FOCAL VERSES
IN FOCUS
THE PEOPLE, PLACES, AND TIMES
BACKGROUND
AT-A-GLANCE
IN DEPTH
SEARCH THE SCRIPTURES
DISCUSS THE MEANING
LESSON IN OUR SOCIETY
MAKE IT HAPPEN
FOLLOW THE SPIRIT
REMEMBER YOUR THOUGHTS
MORE LIGHT ON THE TEXT
DAILY BIBLE READINGS

this hath touched thy lips; and thine iniquity is taken away, and thy sin purged.

8 Also I heard the voice of the Lord, saying, Whom shall I send, and who will go for us? Then said I, Here am I; send me.

9 And he said, Go, and tell this people, Hear ye indeed, but understand not; and see ye indeed, but perceive not.

10 Make the heart of this people fat, and make their ears heavy, and shut their eyes; lest they see with their eyes, and hear with their ears, and understand with their heart, and convert, and be healed.

11 Then said I, Lord, how long? And he answered, Until the cities be wasted without inhabitant, and the houses without man, and the land be utterly desolate,

12 And the Lord have removed men far away, and there be a great forsaking in the midst of the land.

AUG 5TH

IN FOCUS

Michael knew that God called him to minister as a preacher of the Gospel. He knew it without a doubt. God planted the idea in his mind and heart, and he could not get rid of it. Even when he graduated from college and went into business, he knew he was in the wrong field. God wanted Michael to declare His Word, and he was out of God's will pursuing any other career choice. God wanted Michael to serve Him full-time through winning lost souls to the kingdom of God. Michael had a divine calling and he had to deal with that calling.

In fact, Michael's restlessness persisted for over twenty years. He even went through a time of outright rebellion against God, turning his back on God and the church, trying to get away from His calling. He just felt so empty, so unfulfilled in his chosen vocation. Yet he would not acquiesce to God's command.

Being in the world did not bring the peace and contentment he craved. So, one day, running from his problems and himself, Michael confessed his sins, and surrendered his life to the Lord again. He knew that he could not escape his destination. He had to do what God wanted him to do.

After attending Bible College, he declared his ministry. God allowed him to sit under a senior pastor who did not feel threatened by his calling and gifts. In fact, he welcomed Michael.

Finally, Michael was in his right place in life, serving where God called him. Now he had the peace and contentment that surpasses all understanding.

THE PEOPLE, PLACES, AND TIMES

The People. The people of Judah had a form of godliness, but their hearts were far from God. They expected God to reward them for serving Him half-heartedly instead of sending His judgment and destruction on them. They could have been rescued from their sins, their moral and spiritual decay, if they had listened to Isaiah's warnings and the hope given through turning to God. However, they grew angry with Isaiah's messages and wanted to take his life.

Isaiah One of the greatest prophets of his time. He had a vision of God and was called by God to do God's work bringing his nation to repentance in order to save it from a whirlpool of destruction. His very name means "Yahweh is (the source) of salvation" (*Wycliffe's Bible Dictionary*, Charles F. Pfeiffer, Howard F. Vos, and John Rea, Hendrickson Publishers, 1998, p. 855).

Isaiah came to the people with messages of judgment tempered with hope. He ministered for 60 years or more and prophesied during the reign of five kings: Uzziah, Jotham, Ahaz, Hezekiah, and Manasseh.

He pleaded with the people to turn from their wicked ways back to a loving God who would forgive and restore them. Isaiah saw the deliverance of Jerusalem from her enemies, the Assyrians. It was through his prayers and by the intervention of God that Jerusalem was spared from being destroyed.

Many of the promises God gave through Isaiah have been fulfilled in Jesus Christ (adapted from the *Life Application Study Bible*, New Living Translation, Tyndale House Publishers, Inc. Wheaton, Ill, 1996, pp. 1055-1056).

BACKGROUND

God speaks to His people in many ways: through His Word, through others, through visions and dreams, etc. In today's lesson, He speaks to the Messianic prophet, Isaiah, through visions. Isaiah, considered to be the greatest prophet, believes that his nation is to be a Messianic nation to the whole world. He believes that it will be used by God to bless all nations. This blessing will be when God sends His one and only Son, Jesus Christ, to die for all mankind. Jesus would come through these chosen people.

The prophet Isaiah is the son of Amoz. He is speaking and writing in the southern kingdom (Judah), mainly in Jerusalem, to call the nation of Judah back to God and to tell the people of God's salvation through the coming Messiah, Jesus Christ. As a spokesman for God, He comes warning and condemning the people for their sins.

Many of the people do not receive God's message through Isaiah. In fact, they are angry, insulting, and threatening. Yet Isaiah still teaches God's commands and promises. He tells them to turn from their lives of sin (repent), and warns them of God's judgment and punishment if they continue to disobey Him.

After attacking Israel, the Assyrians move on to Judah. They destroy 46 walled cities and take many of the people into slavery. It is not until 701 B.C., when Isaiah is an old man, that the Assyrians are stopped by an angel of God before the walls of Jerusalem. Thereafter, Isaiah spends the rest of his life under the threatening Assyrian power. He, himself, is an eyewitness to the fall of his entire nation at the hands of their enemy. Only Jerusalem survives.

Isaiah prophesies from 745-695 B.C., at a time when the northern kingdom (Israel) is being destroyed by the Assyrians because of their many sins against God. In fact, the Assyrians take many of the people of Israel into bondage. Their capital, Samaria, falls 13 years later. Then, the rest of Israel falls at the hands of the enemy.

Isaiah also offers a message of hope, hope to be found in accepting Jesus Christ as Lord and Saviour by faith. He preaches turning from sin to God! God wants to redeem His chosen people.

AT-A-GLANCE

1. Isaiah's Vision
(Isaiah 6:1-4)
2. Isaiah's Cleansing and Call
(vv. 5-9)
3. Isaiah's Message to the People
(vv. 10-12)

IN DEPTH

1. Isaiah's Vision (Isaiah 6:1-4)

God calls Isaiah to be His spokesman at a time in Judah's history when the people are still sinning against God by worshiping idols, intermarrying with foreign women, and disobeying His commands. It is the year King Uzziah dies, one of the five kings that reigns during Isaiah's ministry.

King Uzziah is considered to be one of the good kings with a long and prosperous reign. Many of the people, however, turn away from God. They do not repent and seek His forgiveness. Therefore, in verse one, God is calling Isaiah to be His messenger to His wayward, stiff-necked, hardheaded chosen people. He comes to Isaiah in a vision or dream.

This is a difficult mission for Isaiah. He is to tell people who have a form of godliness but whose hearts are far from God, that they are corrupt and that God is going to destroy them because of their disobedience.

In verses 1-4, Isaiah gives us a description of God's greatness, His holiness, His mystery, and His power. When we compare ourselves with Him then we see how undone, how sinful, how unholy we are. Isaiah sees all these things. Therefore, as Isaiah, we need God's forgiveness to cleanse us from all unrighteousness. This forgiveness comes through accepting Jesus Christ as our own personal Saviour through faith.

In verses 1-3, Isaiah sees God high and lifted up. He sees His moral perfection and purity. He sees how far Israel has fallen from God's standards.

2. Isaiah's Cleansing and Call (vv. 5-9)

Isaiah cannot do the work that God calls Him to do until He is personally cleansed. When he beholds the holiness of God, God has to do a work on Isaiah in his heart to get him ready for the mission. Isaiah's sins have to be forgiven before he can tell the people of their own sins and the forgiveness to be found in accepting the coming Messiah, Jesus Christ. In fact, Isaiah has to go through a painful cleansing process with live coals. The sin has to be burned out of him. It has to be burned out of Israel as well, and this can be done only through their turning to God. They have to commit to God's control. We all have to do the same if we are going to be used by Him in His service, if we are going to do His will.

Isaiah also sees that he is powerless without God. He is aware that he, himself, is inadequate to do anything of lasting value for God no matter how much he may want it. Isaiah cannot carry God's message to the sinful people without God's help. Even though he wants God to send Him out, Isaiah needs God to go with him and to give His anointing.

3. Isaiah's Message to the People (vv. 10-12)

Now that Isaiah has been purified, made ready to do the will of God, God tells Isaiah what he has to face in dealing with a rebellious people. In other words, God does not send Isaiah on the mission without preparing him for what he is to face.

God tells Isaiah that the people will not repent and turn from their wickedness as Isaiah warns them (v. 9). He tells him that the people's hearts have become hardened to their own sins. God, in fact, has abandoned them to their rebellion. This is the reason they are in such a state.

God is growing tired of the people sinning against Him. He is growing tired of their disobedience, but because of His mercy He is still trying to warn them. Yet a holy God is no longer patient with them. He is no longer tolerating their sins. Instead, He is about to judge and destroy them.

SEARCH THE SCRIPTURES

1. Isaiah saw God sitting on His throne _____ and _____ _____. (Isaiah 6:1)

2. The seraphim cried out that God is _____   _____ _____. (v. 3)

3. When Isaiah saw the holiness of God, he cried, "_____ _____ _____! (v. 5)

4. The seraphim cleansed Isaiah with a _____ _____. (v. 6)

5. The seraphim put the coal on Isaiah's _____. (v. 7)

6. Isaiah wanted God to send _____. (v. 8)

DISCUSS THE MEANING

1. Why did God keep calling and sending prophets to His chosen people when He already knew that they would not repent?

2. Since Isaiah was called by God, why did he have to be cleansed before he could do the work?

LESSON IN OUR SOCIETY

The news media have bombarded us with accounts of ministers who fell in their walk with

God. The latest account is of the head of the Baptist Movement, who was indicted on many counts of wrongdoing. Jim Baker, another noted Christian leader, was indicted several years ago for income tax evasion, and other infractions of the law, and served time in jail. Jimmy Swaggart, a renowned TV evangelist and singer, also fell when he was caught frequenting prostitutes. It was just reported that a Methodist minister was arrested for attempting to elicit sex from minors over the Internet. What does this say to us? It should warn us that Satan is a very real adversary and he is after God's chosen people, especially those called to lead. He knows that the most harm can be done to God's people when a noted leader falls. Therefore, a daily, close walk with God is imperative.

We need to pray for our leaders, we need to ask God to put a hedge of protection around them and cover them with His blood as they work in His vineyard.

MAKE IT HAPPEN

God calls us out of darkness into light. He calls us into His service, and He calls His church to be His witness. If you have not answered His calls, then do so today. Once you have given your heart to God, go on to seek what His will is for your life. Ask Him. He will tell you through prayer and reading His Holy Word. Do not sit on the bench in these last days, but get up and work in the service of your God. Make sure, however, you are where He wants you to be. Let your light so shine so that others can see your good works and glorify your Father who is in heaven and is also living in and through you.

FOLLOW THE SPIRIT

What God wants me to do:

_____

_____

REMEMBER YOUR THOUGHTS

Special insights you learned:

_____

_____

MORE LIGHT ON THE TEXT
Isaiah 6:1-12

6:1 In the year that king Uzziah died I saw also the Lord sitting upon a throne, high and lifted up, and his train filled the temple.

It is often after the loss of a loved one, a well-known celebrity, or a high ranking government official, that we feel a deep sense of loss, insecurity, fear, helplessness, and even hopelessness. Many times, consciously and subconsciously, we put more trust and give more honor to people than we do to God.

When those who are the most important to us are taken away from us, we often seek the Lord as never before. How vast is the mercy of our Lord who accepts our cries for help even when we make Him the last resort.

When all of the idols and other distractions are removed and we truly make God the King of our lives, we can see the presence and witness the power of the Almighty God whose glory far outshines that of anyone or anything else that we could ever give our time and attention.

The throne of the Lord is high and lifted up above all others; truly He is the King of kings and the Lord of lords. He is the sovereign, universal ruler of the eternal kingdom, and He is always available and eager to reveal Himself and to develop a personal relationship with each of His children.

2 Above it stood the seraphim: each one had six wings; with twain he covered his face, and with twain he covered his feet, and with twain he did fly.

The seraphim are angelic creatures who are a part of the heavenly host. Although they are not often mentioned in Scripture, they are involved in the worship of God and are different from the cherubim who surround the throne of God (Revelation 4:6-8). The seraphim stand above the throne of God.

It is believed that the word "seraphim" is a noun taken from the root verb *saraph* which means to burn with fire. Fire is symbolic of purification. In verse 6, we will see that it is one of the seraphim that purifies the lips of the prophet Isaiah with a burning coal.

3 And one cried unto another, and said, Holy, holy, holy, is the Lord of hosts: the whole earth is full of his glory.

In the Hebrew language, to say the word "holy" twice is the same as saying "most holy." In this verse the seraphim describe the Lord as being "holy, holy, holy," which indicates that the holiness of the Lord is indescribable. Words fall short in their attempt to capture the magnificent glory of the Creator of the universe. If the seraphim, who stand above the throne of God and worship Him continually, cannot fully describe His holiness, then we as mortals surely cannot fully describe the glory of His holiness. In spite of our limited understanding, the Creator of the universe expresses Himself to each of us and reveals to us as much of Himself as we are able to handle.

4 And the posts of the door moved at the voice of him that cried, and the house was filled with smoke.

God's holiness is so awesome and so powerful that even the doors of the heavenly temple are shaken in response to His holiness. How much more shall the temple of our bodies be shaken in His presence? In the presence of the Lord everything that can be shaken is shaken and all that remains is that which brings glory to His name. We all have an awesome opportunity to praise and worship the Lord in the beauty of holiness, yet too often we fail to do so. Oh that we would remove all of the distractions, distortions, and disturbances in our lives and worship the Lord in spirit and in truth.

5 Then said I, Woe is me! For I am undone; because I am a man of unclean lips, and I dwell in the midst of a people of unclean lips: for mine eyes have seen the King, the Lord of hosts.

In the presence of the Lord, truth is revealed. All of our attempts to appear to be more or less than we truly are fail drastically. No lie can stand in the presence of the God of truth, and no imitation can bear His inspection. We must always remember that God is looking for worshipers, and they that worship Him must worship Him in spirit and in truth.

In the presence of the Lord, Isaiah saw the truth about himself and those around him. The light of God's holiness penetrated through everyone and everything in Isaiah's life and he could plainly see his sin and the sins of those around him. In the next verse, we see how Isaiah's penitence brought about his purification.

6 Then flew one of the seraphim unto me, having a live coal in his hand, which he had taken with the tongs from off the altar:

In the temple the coals which were used for the altar of incense had to be taken from the altar of sacrifice, which symbolizes that because of the sacrifice of the Lord Jesus Christ, we are able to pray to, and have a personal relationship with, our heavenly Father. Although Isaiah lived before Christ was born, the temple and all that was in it was a foreshadowing of the finished work of Christ.

7 And he laid it upon my mouth, and said, Lo, this hath touched thy lips; and thine iniquity is taken away, and thy sin purged.

How wonderful it is to know that the God of creation is a personal Saviour. Though there are billions of people in the world, He is willing to meet each of us at our deepest point of need. Isaiah confessed to the Lord that he was a man of unclean lips, and the Lord provided a way for him to be forgiven and cleansed from his unrighteousness.

The Lord is ready, willing, and able to do the same for us. Whatever the sin is our lives, Jesus Christ has already paid the price and paved the way for our forgiveness by becoming the sacrifice whose blood has washed away our sins.

8 Also I heard the voice of the Lord, saying, Whom shall I send, and who will go for us? Then said I, Here am I; send me.

Once Isaiah confessed his sins and received his forgiveness and cleansing, he could clearly hear the voice of the Lord. If we listen carefully, we too will hear the voice of the Lord calling each of us to represent Him wherever we are and whatever we are doing. We all must be willing, as Isaiah was, to allow the Master of the universe to cleanse us and prepare us to do the work that we were created to do on the earth.

When Isaiah heard the voice of the Lord, he did not hesitate. He responded, "Here am I, send me."

Let each of us examine ourselves to see how we respond to the call of God on our lives. Do we constantly come up with excuses? Is there any good reason not to heed the call of God in our lives? I think not.

9 And he said, Go, and tell this people, Hear ye indeed, but understand not; and see ye indeed, but perceive not.

When Isaiah answered the call of God and allowed the Lord to prepare him for service, the Lord Himself gave him specific instructions. God instructed Isaiah to go to a particular group of people. God told Isaiah in advance that the people would hear but not heed his message; they would see but not believe. In spite of their hardness of heart, the mercy of the Lord was extended to them. Even though the nation would not listen, God sent His message to the remnant who would hear and obey His Word.

10 Make the heart of this people fat, and make their ears heavy, and shut their eyes; lest they see with their eyes, and hear with their ears, and understand with their heart, and convert, and be healed.

Because of the hardness of their hearts, this rebellious nation became insensitive to God's will; their ears were dull of hearing His voice; their eyes became dim and unable to see the plan of God. They were unwilling to receive the presence and the power of God in their lives. As a result, they were unable to receive all of the many blessings that God had in store for them, and the nation suffered.

11 Then said I, Lord, how long? And he answered, Until the cities be wasted without inhabitant, and the houses without man, and the land be utterly desolate,

How sad it is that in spite of all of the many blessings that the Lord has provided for each of His children, and in spite of all of the suffering that the Lord Jesus Christ has gone through on our behalf, we, like the Children of Israel, turn away from our Saviour and choose the ways of sin.

The Bible teaches that rebellion is as the sin of witchcraft. When we refuse to follow the Lord and yield to His plan for our lives, we are giving ourselves over to Satan and his schemes which only lead to death and destruction.

12 And the Lord have removed men far away, and there be a great forsaking in the midst of the land.

The rebellion of the people of God led to their captivity at the hands of their enemies and to the land of their enemies. When we are consistently rebellious to the will of the Lord for our lives, we become vulnerable to the wiles of the devil who wants to isolate us from every positive influence and from those who truly love us. Satan wants to do all that he can to keep us from the land of promise. Although the Lord allowed the people to be removed far from their homeland, we must understand that it was after He had given them many opportunities to yield to His will and abide under the shelter of His protection. When they continually refused to obey the voice of the Lord, He allowed them to do things their way which led to their captivity. Whenever we refuse to follow the path that the Lord has prepared for us, we will find ourselves in the hands of the enemy. Many never get out.

DAILY BIBLE READINGS

M: The Wickedness of Judah
Isaiah 1:1-9
T: Isaiah's Transforming Vision
Isaiah 6:1-8
W: Daniel's Vision of God's Glory
Daniel 10:1-11
T: John's Vision of Christ
Revelation 1:9-18
F: Isaiah's New Commission
Isaiah 6:9-13
S: A Prayer of Trust
Psalm 25:1-10
S: Paul Tells of His Conversion
Acts 26:12-20

TEACHING TIPS

1. Words You Should Know

A. Virgin (Isaiah 7:14) Hebrew *Almah*—veiled-damsel; Greek *parthenos*—one who has never had sexual intercourse.

B. Immanuel (v. 14) Hebrew *Emmanuel*—God is with us.

2. Teacher Preparation

A. Begin preparing for this lesson by studying the Devotional Reading. Then read the Background Scripture. This will give you an account of the times and what the people faced.

B. Read the FOCAL VERSES from at least three different translations, especially a study Bible that has footnotes and references.

C. Read Bible Study Guide 11 and answer the SEARCH THE SCRIPTURES and DISCUSS THE MEANING questions.

3. Starting the Lesson

A. Before the class begins, write the words "virgin" and "Immanuel" on the board. Also write the AT-A-GLANCE outline.

B. After the students have arrived and are seated, ask for prayer requests and then pray also asking for God's anointing as you discuss the lesson.

C. Read the IN FOCUS story. Explain that today's lesson explores how God offers hope and deliverance to believers through having faith in Him to do what He has already promised.

D. Direct their attention to the definitions on the board and explain that God has promised to deliver his people from sin by believing on His Son, Jesus, who is Immanuel—"God with us." God used a virgin to bring His Son into this world for one purpose and one purpose only—to deliver us from sin by dying on the Cross.

4. Getting into the Lesson

A. Write the word "challenge" on the board. Then ask the question, "Have you ever been challenged by God to do or not do something?" Allow a brief time for discussion.

B. Explain that King Ahaz was presented with a challenge by none other than God Himself. In today's lesson, we will find out how he responded to the challenge.

C. Have them read the BACKGROUND information, and THE PEOPLE, PLACES, AND TIMES articles.

D. Have volunteers read the FOCAL VERSES according to the AT-A-GLANCE outline. You may engage in discussion during the reading or wait until all the verses are read. Then, ask the corresponding SEARCH THE SCRIPTURES questions.

5. Relating the Lesson to Life

A. To help students understand how the lesson applies to today's society, direct their attention to the LESSON IN OUR SOCIETY article. Allow them time for discussion and debate.

B. Review the DISCUSS THE MEANING questions and allow time for discussion.

6. Arousing Action

A. Review the MAKE IT HAPPEN suggestions and challenge them to follow through.

B. Challenge them to do their DAILY BIBLE READINGS.

C. Close with prayer and thanksgiving for God's Word.

WORSHIP GUIDE

For the Superintendent or Teacher
Theme: Isaiah and Ahaz: A Challenge to Rely on God
Theme Song: Trust and Obey
Scriptures: Isaiah 7:1-6, 10-17
Song: It Is No Secret What God Can Do
Meditation: Lord, help us to trust and obey You in all that we say and do.

502

ISAIAH AND AHAZ: A CHALLENGE TO RELY ON GOD

Bible Background • ISAIAH 7; 2 KINGS 16; 2 CHRONICLES 28
Printed Text • ISAIAH 7:1-6, 10-17
Devotional Reading • PSALM 33:4-12

LESSON AIM

By the end of the session, students will know that God is indeed our Saviour and Deliverer; He is worthy of trust and praise; He is faithful and His word is dependable, and He is holy and unchangeable.

KEEP IN MIND

"Therefore the Lord himself shall give you a sign; Behold, a virgin shall conceive, and bear a son, and shall call his name Immanuel" (Isaiah 7:14, KJV).

FOCAL VERSES

Isaiah 7:1 And it came to pass in the days of Ahaz, the son of Jotham, the son of Uzziah, king of Judah, that Rezin, the king of Syria, and Pekah, the son of Remaliah, king of Israel, went up toward Jerusalem to war against it, but could not prevail against it.

2 And it was told the house of David, saying, Syria is confederate with Ephraim. And his heart was moved, and the heart of his people, as the trees of the wood are moved with the wind.

3 Then said the Lord unto Isaiah, Go forth now to meet Ahaz, thou, and Shear-jashub, thy son, at the end of the conduit of the upper pool in the highway of the fuller's field;

4 And say unto him, Take heed, and be quiet; fear not, neither be fainthearted for the two tails of these smoking firebrands, for the fierce anger of Rezin with Syria, and of the son of Remaliah.

5 Because Syria, Ephraim, and the son of

LESSON OVERVIEW

LESSON AIM
KEEP IN MIND
FOCAL VERSES
IN FOCUS
THE PEOPLE, PLACES, AND TIMES
BACKGROUND
AT-A-GLANCE
IN DEPTH
SEARCH THE SCRIPTURES
DISCUSS THE MEANING
LESSON IN OUR SOCIETY
MAKE IT HAPPEN
FOLLOW THE SPIRIT
REMEMBER YOUR THOUGHTS
MORE LIGHT ON THE TEXT
DAILY BIBLE READINGS

Remaliah have taken evil counsel against thee, saying,

6 Let us go up against Judah, and vex it, and let us make a breach therein for us, and set a king in the midst of it, even the son of Tabeal:

7:10 Moreover the Lord spake again unto Ahaz, saying,

11 Ask thee a sign of the Lord, thy God; ask it either in the depth, or in the height above.

12 But Ahaz said, I will not ask, neither will I tempt the Lord.

13 And he said, Hear ye now, O house of David; Is it a small thing for you to weary men, but will ye weary my God also?

14 Therefore the Lord himself shall give you a sign; Behold, a virgin shall conceive, and bear a son, and shall call his name Immanuel.

15 Butter and honey shall he eat, that he may know to refuse the evil, and choose the good.

16 For before the child shall know to refuse the evil, and choose the good, the land that thou abhorrest shall be forsaken by both her kings.

AUG 12TH

17 The Lord shall bring upon thee, and upon thy people, and upon thy father's house, days that have not come, from the day that Ephraim departed from Judah; even the king of Assyria.

IN FOCUS

The doctor said the dreaded words, "Melanoma, cancer." Ruth already had the feeling deep within her that the report was not going to be good, and she was in for the long haul—a trial that would test her faith to the maximum. Sure enough, the doctors advised her that six months of chemotherapy was in order and 36 treatments of radiation.

Fear of the worse kind set in. Panic dotted her countenance. Yet a small voice whispered within her, "Trust God. Put yourself in His care and trust Him."

In stead of reading all the literature on chemotherapy and radiation that were given to her by her doctors, that same small voice advised Ruth to go to God in prayer and ask for His wisdom, His strength, and His support.

As Ruth lay in the dark radiation chamber all by herself time and time again, God whispered to her spirit, "By my stripes, you are healed." His presence filled the room.

As they pumped the chemo through her, that same small voice offered words of comfort and hope to her reminding her of Scriptures previously read. Instead of losing weight, she gained. In stead of losing hair, her hair shone silky and healthy. Even the chemotherapy doctor wanted to know what was going on. One day Ruth testified to her, "I am trusting God for my healing! I am putting myself in His care." And she did!

THE PEOPLE, PLACES, AND TIMES

King Ahaz. A very wicked king who was the son of Jotham and the grandson of Uzziah. Ahaz was the 12th king of Judah and started his reign when he was 20 years old. He governed for 16 years (732-716 B.C.). In fact, he was one of Judah's worst kings as he led the people in idol worship and even sacrificed his own son to pagan gods. In the end Ahaz chose the Assyrians to help him in his battle with Syria and Israel rather than God. The Assyrians did help Judah by destroying Syria and Israel, but they turned on Ahaz later. As a result, 120,000 soldiers lost their lives, and 200,000 citizens of Judah were taken into captivity. Ahaz led his people to their destruction and spent his last days as an ineffective king.

The People Israel and Judah. (The Northern and Southern kingdom.) After the death of King Solomon, the nation of Israel split into two kingdoms. The Northern kingdom (Israel) consisted of ten tribes. The Southern kingdom (Judah) con-

sisted of two tribes and the city of Jerusalem. The two kingdoms were frequently at odds, and sometimes fought against each other.

BACKGROUND

The prophet Isaiah, perhaps the greatest Old Testament prophet, was cleansed by God (in the previous lesson) and now is on a mission for God. He has been given the task as God's messenger to tell the king of Judah, Ahaz, that God has a challenge for him. This challenge was simple. Would Ahaz rely on an all-knowing, all-powerful, all-seeing God, or an outsider to deliver him and his people?

Because of the people's sins, Judah is now experiencing the full-force attack of an enemy. Satan has fixed it so that Israel and Judah are at odds with each other. The reigning king, Ahaz, knows that an alliance has formed between Syria and Israel to unseat him; he is afraid. He knows that if they attack, many people will be killed and others taken captive.

However, God has a message of hope for Ahaz. Since God can see into the future, He sends His spokesman, Isaiah, to the king to encourage him. He tells Ahaz that Judah will not fall to the enemy at this time. Instead, deliverance will come. The sign of Immanuel, Jesus Christ, will be a sign of deliverance for them. God indeed can be counted on to be faithful to carry out His promises because He cannot lie. He is consistent, and He is mighty!

AT-A-GLANCE

1. The Problem (Isaiah 7:1-2)
2. A Message for Ahaz from God (vv. 3-7)
3. A Sign of Hope (vv. 10-17)

IN DEPTH

1. The Problem (Isaiah 7:1-2)

In today's lesson, we learn how war is declared on Judah by Syria and Israel. Even though Israel was one united with Judah, the northern kingdom now allies with Judah's enemies to unseat King Ahaz. Yet God is merciful. He is willing to give Judah a chance. Through the prophet Isaiah, God reassures King Ahaz. If he and the people trust in God, everything will be all right. The challenge is made, Ahaz is to pick up the ball.

2. A Message for Ahaz from God (vv. 3-7)

Judah is guilty of many sins against God, religiosity and hypocrisy. The people are guilty of appalling wickedness especially their king. This is why God's judgment came upon them. God wants genuine repentance and obedience from His chosen people. Instead, He gets continuous rebellion. Therefore, they now find themselves reaping the consequences of their actions.

King Ahaz now fears the future. In verse 3, God tells Isaiah to take his son Shear-jashub, and meet with Ahaz. God has a word for the king.

The name of Isaiah's son, Shear-jashub means "a remnant will return" (*The Life Application Bible,* Tyndale House Publishers, Inc., Wheaton, IL, 1996, p. 1056). This name is given by God to represent hope for the people in their dire situation. This is to let them know that God will have mercy on them even after He judges them. A remnant is going to survive. A remnant is going to be redeemed.

Shear-jashub's mere existence reminds the people that God is faithful. He is their Savior and Deliverer. He is trustworthy and dependable. He is holy and unchangeable.

God tells Isaiah in detail where to find King Ahaz (v. 3) and tells him what to say to him (v. 4). This demonstrates that when God calls His people to do a work, He prepares, instructs, goes before and with that person.

Isaiah predicts the break up of Israel's alliance with evil counsel, namely Syria (vv. 4-7). God is going to divide the enemy so that Judah can survive the attack. In fact, because Israel chooses to ally himself against God's people, it will be destroyed by the Assyrians. God will see to it. He will also see to it that Judah, at a later date, is punished for its sins as well.

3. A Sign of Hope (vv. 10-17)

God sends King Ahaz a sign of hope in the midst of King Ahaz's despair. A virgin and her son, Immanuel (God with us), is a sign intended to reassure a frightened king that God is all-powerful and very capable of delivering Judah if only he

and the people have faith.

Yet King Ahaz does not listen to God through Isaiah. He does not accept the challenge. Instead, he goes to another enemy, the Assyrians. Ahaz tries to buy the Assyrians, help with silver and gold. The Assyrians, however, bring more trouble than help. In 722 B.C., Samaria, the capital of Israel (the northern kingdom) is destroyed. Baal (idol) worship is widespread, because this is one of the Assyrians' gods.

Isaiah tells King Ahaz that God will bring a terrible curse on him, his nation, and his family because of his disobedience and for not accepting God's challenge (v. 17). The Assyrians will turn on Judah. The snake (Assyria) will bite them, too! Faith in man as opposed to faith in God is doomed to failure.

SEARCH THE SCRIPTURES

1. Who was Ahaz's father and grandfather? (Isaiah 7:1)

2. Who is Ephraim? (v. 2)

3. Who was Isaiah to take with him to meet Ahaz? (v. 3)

4. What did Syria and Israel want to do to King Ahaz's government? (v. 6)

5. What was God's sign to King Ahaz that He would deliver? (v. 14)

DISCUSS THE MEANING

1. What happens when God's people ally with evil men?

2. Why was God still willing to help King Ahaz and Judah, even though they had sinned against Him continuously?

LESSON IN OUR SOCIETY

In verse 5 of today's lesson, we read of how God talks about Ephraim. Israel has allied itself with "evil counsel," Syria. As the story unfolds, this evil counsel or men will lead to Israel's complete destruction. It will also lead to Judah's destruction when it allies with the Assyrians. Only a remnant will be saved.

Throughout our country's history, the U.S. has sometimes allied with evil counsel . . . evil men and women bent on the destruction of others. In fact, from the country's inception, we find some of the founding fathers, (George Washington, John

Quincy Adams, etc.) owning and participating in slavery, the captivity of a people which has robbed African Americans of almost all of their dignity, pride, and self-esteem.

When this land we call America was taken, or stolen, from the Native Americans, many were killed and only a remnant was spared and forced to live on reservations. In fact, just a few years ago, when the U.S. regaled Russia for its inhumane treatment to its citizenry, the Russians used America's ill treatment of the Indians as a rebuttal. America found itself ashamed and speechless.

We still find institutionalized racism rampant in our country. For instance, before the white regime toppled in South Africa, U.S. Corporations supported the status quo. These corporations held vast monetary interest in the success of institutions which maintained racial divisions.

Many of the problems we face in our country today—drugs, child abuse, poverty, racism, etc.—can be traced back to seeds of discord sown early in history. Now we are reaping a harvest of despair. Before we can be healed, America, as the Israelites, must turn to God, repent, and ask Him for forgiveness. Then redemption and restoration can truly take place.

MAKE IT HAPPEN

Think of a time when you have faced a difficulty in your life which brought you to your knees. Concentrate on how God walked and counseled you through that valley experience. If you are led, share your testimony with the class. Stress how you maintained hope by keeping your faith in Almighty God rather than in man.

FOLLOW THE SPIRIT:

What God wants me to do:

_____

_____

REMEMBER YOUR THOUGHTS:

Special insights you learned:

_____

_____

MORE LIGHT ON THE TEXT
Isaiah 7:1-6, 10-17

7:1 And it came to pass in the days of Ahaz, the son of Jotham, the son of Uzziah, king of Judah, that Rezin, the king of Syria, and Pekah, the son of Remaliah, king of Israel, went up toward Jerusalem to war against it, but could not prevail against it.

In 734 B.C. Judah was attacked by the northern kingdom of Israel and Syria. Ahaz, king of Judah, was troubled at the possibility of his nation being overthrown and his people being killed and taken away as slaves. However, the alliance was unable to conquer Judah.

We, too, go through times in our lives when it seems as though everything and everyone is against us. We feel like we are being attacked from every direction. As soon as we find the solution to one problem, another one arises. The fear of failure torments us to such a degree that we often lose hope and want to surrender to our enemies, but if we are obedient to His Word, God will not allow our enemies to prevail against us.

2 And it was told the house of David, saying, Syria is confederate with Ephraim. And his heart was moved, and the heart of his people, as the trees of the wood are moved with the wind.

Just as Ahaz was overcome with fear at the thought of his enemies conspiring against him, we, too, are overwhelmed when those who are against us form unholy alliances against us for the purpose of destroying us and taking that which belongs to us.

We all face periods in our lives when it seems like failure is unavoidable. Sometimes we are shaken to the very core of our being, and we barely have the strength to stand, especially when there are others whom we love and are responsible for who will be affected negatively if we fail.

3 Then said the Lord unto Isaiah, Go forth now to meet Ahaz, thou, and Shear-jashub, thy son, at the end of the conduit of the upper pool in the highway of the fuller's field;

How blessed we are, especially in times of hopelessness, to hear a word from the Lord. God sent His servant Isaiah to the troubled Ahaz with a word of encouragement. Not only did God tell Isaiah to go to Ahaz, but He also told Isaiah to bring his son Shear-jashub with him. The name Shear-jashub means "a remnant will return." It is also interesting that the name Isaiah means "Yahweh is salvation," and the name Ahaz means "he has grasped."

God was not only sending Ahaz a verbal message, but He was also sending Ahaz a visual message. When Ahaz saw Isaiah ("Yahweh is salvation") and his son Shear-jashub ("a remnant will return"), he should have grasped the message that Yahweh is going to save a remnant who will return to their homeland from the captivity of their oppressors. Unfortunately, Ahaz did not live up to his name (he has grasped) since he didn't grasp the message that God sent to him.

4 And say unto him, Take heed, and be quiet; fear not, neither be fainthearted for the two tails of these smoking firebrands, for the fierce anger of Rezin with Syria, and of the son of Remaliah.

The first thing that Ahaz was told to do was to "take heed." How many times have we heard the word of the Lord in times of distress as well as in times of peace and failed to take heed to all that the Lord said? Many times the word that the Lord gives us seems inadequate to meet the challenges that we faced. Therefore, we come up with our own plans and procedures that may work for a while. Ultimately these plans fail, and we find ourselves in more trouble than when we began.

The second thing that Ahaz was told to do was to "be quiet," meaning be calm. When we are under serious attack from our enemies and the welfare of those we love is at stake, it is hard to be calm. Too often we respond to the situation rather than to the Saviour. Our heavenly Father promised to keep us in perfect peace if we will keep our minds on Him.

Next, Ahaz was told "fear not, neither be fainthearted." Fear is the opposite of faith. When we follow the instructions of the Lord there is no need to fear. Who is able to defeat the Almighty God? All of the armies of the world with all of their sophisticated weapons combined are no match against the power of one word from the Lord our God. The word that the Lord sent to Ahaz is an admonition also for us: Tust in God.

5 Because Syria, Ephraim, and the son of Remaliah, have taken evil counsel against thee, saying, 6 Let us go up against Judah, and vex it, and let us make a breach therein for us, and set a king in the midst of it, even the son of Tabeal:

The name Tabeal means "good for nothing."

The enemies of Ahaz came together and plotted out a threefold strategy: (1) cause vexation, (2) make a breach in their defenses, (3) set a new king over them who is good for nothing.

Satan uses the same strategy against us. He will send anyone, and anything, our way that will cause vexation. He knows that vexation is designed to steal our joy, weaken us, and cause us to lose our focus. When we lose focus, we become vulnerable and susceptible to subtle invasions of enemy forces, which are designed to cause a breach in our relationship with the Lord and with the people of the Lord. When our relationship with our heavenly King is breached, Satan attempts to set a new king in our lives who is good for nothing. Whatever, and whoever, takes the place of the Lord Jesus Christ in our lives is our new king; nothing good can come from them. The Bible teaches us that "every good gift and every perfect gift is from above, and cometh down from the Father of lights, with whom is no variableness, neither shadow of turning" (James 1:17).

Jesus Christ is our personal Saviour, and we must be sure that we never let anyone, or anything, interfere with our personal time alone with the Lord in prayer and in studying His Word. We must be obedient to the Word of our King.

7:10 Moreover the Lord spake again unto Ahaz, saying,

Jehovah is merciful even in spite of our disobedience and doubt. He is willing to give us a sign to assure us that it is He who is speaking to us and to demonstrate to us the infallibility of His Word. Often the Lord has to speak to us several times, and in various ways, before we believe and obey Him. Often, in spite of His attempts, we still rebel against Him and His Word.

11 Ask thee a sign of the Lord, thy God; ask it either in the depth, or in the height above.

God was willing to demonstrate His universal power to Ahaz by performing not only whatever sign Ahaz chose, but God was also willing to perform this sign wherever Ahaz wanted it to be seen, either in the deepest depths or in the highest heights. This was a great opportunity for Ahaz to test the power of God. Only the Master of the universe has the power to allow a mortal, sinful man to use his imagination and chose the sign, and the location of the sign anywhere in the universe, and perform it just to prove that He is God, and His Word is true.

12 But Ahaz said, I will not ask, neither will I tempt the Lord.

Ahaz refused God's offer. Rather than trust in the God of the universe, Ahaz put his trust in the Assyrians, their military might and their gods. How many times has God wanted to demonstrate His power in our lives only to be rejected because of our trust in that which is mortal, material, or mystic.

13 And he said, Hear ye now, O house of David; Is it a small thing for you to weary men, but will ye weary my God also?

Isaiah said to Ahaz, in essence: It is not enough for you to try the patience of men, but are you so arrogant that you would even try the patience of the Almighty God by refusing His message and His offer to prove Himself to you personally?

14 Therefore the Lord himself shall give you a sign; Behold, a virgin shall conceive, and bear a son, and shall call his name Immanuel.

Although Ahaz refused God's offer to show him a sign of his choice, the prophet Isaiah informed him that God was going to give a sign not only for Ahaz but for the whole world. In spite of the rebellion of Ahaz, who was a descendant of David, God was going to manifest Himself and His power through One who would also be a descendant of David.

15 Butter and honey shall he eat, that he may know to refuse the evil, and choose the good.

Butter and honey is considered to be good food. The land will be so desolate that butter and honey will be in abundance to the remnant who remain. This verse is saying that before the Child is able to eat butter and honey (which is about two years of age), he will know to refuse evil and choose good.

16 For before the child shall know to refuse the evil, and choose the good, the land that thou abhorrest shall be forsaken by both her kings.

Isaiah is saying that before the Child is approximately two years of age and able to refuse evil and choose good, the land of the two kings Ahaz dreads will be forsaken.

This prophecy has immediate significance to Ahaz. At the same time, it has a broader and a more important significance to the line of David and to the whole world. Here is a prophecy concerning the Saviour of the world, Jesus Christ.

17 The Lord shall bring upon thee, and upon thy people, and upon thy father's house, days that have not come, from the day that Ephraim departed from Judah; even the king of Assyria.

"The day that Ephraim departed from Judah" refers to the division of the kingdom into northern and southern tribes after the death of King Solomon in 931 B.C. "The king of Assyria" is the one through whom the destruction of Israel will come.

Approximately two years after Isaiah's prophecy to Ahaz, Syria was overthrown by Assyria (732 B.C.) and Pekah was no longer in power in Israel. Within a decade Israel was also overthrown by Assyria.

DAILY BIBLE READINGS

M: Isaiah Reassures King Ahaz
Isaiah 7:1-9
T: The Great Sign
Isaiah 7:10-17
W: Ahaz Reigns over Judah
2 Kings 16:1-8
T: The Assyrians Take Damascus
2 Kings 16:9-20
F: Ahaz' Apostasy Leads to Defeat
2 Chronicles 28:1-7
S: Intervention of Obed
2 Chronicles 28:8-15
S: Invasion of Judah and Ahaz' Death
2 Chronicles 28:16-27

TEACHING TIPS

August 19
Bible Study Guide 12

1. Words You Should Know

A. Vineyard (Isaiah 5:1) Hebrew *Kerem (Kereem)*; Greek *ampelon*—a plantation of grapevines for producing grapes for wine or other uses.

B. Hosts (v. 7) Hebrew *Sabooth;* Greek *xenos*—God is recognized as the divine Commander of the armies of Israel on earth and especially of the heavenly bodies.

2. Teacher Preparation

A. Begin preparing for this lesson by studying the DEVOTIONAL READING and the DAILY BIBLE READINGS.

B. Read the FOCAL VERSES from at least three different translations, especially a study Bible that has footnotes and references.

C. Read Bible Study Guide 12 and answer all the SEARCH THE SCRIPTURES and DISCUSS THE MEANING questions.

D. Materials needed: Bible, 3x5 index cards.

3. Starting the Lesson

A. Before the class begins, write the words "vineyard" and "hosts" on the board. Also write the AT-A-GLANCE outline.

B. After the students have arrived and are seated, ask for prayer requests and pray asking for God's anointing as you discuss the lesson.

C. Read the IN FOCUS story. Explain that today's lesson explores how God's beloved people are compared to a vineyard, carefully tended and cultivated, but yielding wild grapes. God wants to know why the vineyard is bringing forth wild grapes. In other words, He wants to know why they rebelled.

D. Direct their attention to the definitions on the board and engage in a brief discussion of these terms.

4. Getting into the Lesson

A. Write the phrase "People will know us by our fruit" on the board. Then ask the class to list on an index card some good fruit in our life and then on the back, some bad fruit (attitudes & behavior).

B. Discuss some of the examples that they gave. Ask them to tell what impact our lives have on a lost world who is watching our behavior. Then ask, "Can the world see Jesus in you?"

C. Have them read the BACKGROUND information, and THE PEOPLE, PLACES, AND TIMES articles.

D. Have volunteers read the FOCAL VERSES according to the AT-A-GLANCE outline. You may engage in discussion during the reading or wait until all the verses are read. Then ask the corresponding SEARCH THE SCRIPTURES questions.

5. Relating the Lesson to Life

A. To help students understand how the lesson applies to today's society, direct their attention to the LESSON IN OUR SOCIETY article. Allow them time for discussion and debate.

B. Review the DISCUSS THE MEANING questions and allow time for discussion.

6. Arousing Action

A. Review the MAKE IT HAPPEN suggestions, and challenge them to follow through.

B. Challenge them to do their DAILY BIBLE READINGS.

C. Close with prayer and thanksgiving for God's word.

WORSHIP GUIDE

For the Superintendent or Teacher
Theme: Pronouncement of Doom
Theme Song: Take Time To Be Holy
Scriptures: Isaiah 5:1-7
Song: Stand Up, Stand Up For Jesus!
Meditation: Lord, help us to let our lives so shine that others will see our good works and glorify You.

AUG 12TH

509

PRONOUNCEMENT OF DOOM

Bible Background • ISAIAH 5
Printed Text • ISAIAH 5:1-7
Devotional Reading • MARK 12:1-9

LESSON AIM

By the end of the lesson, students will know that God expects us to obey His will and His Word. He warns us when we are disobedient, and finally, He judges and punishes us to teach and correct our behavior.

KEEP IN MIND

"Woe unto them that call evil good and good evil; that put darkness for light, and light for darkness; that put bitter for sweet, and sweet for bitter" (Isaiah 5:20, KJV).

FOCAL VERSES

Isaiah 5:1 Now will I sing to my well-beloved a song of my beloved touching his vineyard. My well-beloved hath a vineyard in a very fruitful hill:

2 And he fenced it, and gathered out the stones thereof, and planted it with the choicest vine, and built a tower in the midst of it, and also made a winepress therein: and he looked that it should bring forth grapes, and it brought forth wild grapes.

3 And now, O inhabitants of Jerusalem, and men of Judah, judge, I pray you, betwixt me and my vineyard.

4 What could have been done more to my vineyard, that I have not done in it? Wherefore, when I looked that it should bring forth grapes, brought it forth wild grapes?

5 And now go to; I will tell you what I will do to my vineyard: I will take away the hedge thereof, and it shall be eaten up; and break down the wall thereof, and it shall be trodden down:

LESSON OVERVIEW

LESSON AIM
KEEP IN MIND
FOCAL VERSES
IN FOCUS
THE PEOPLE, PLACES,
AND TIMES
BACKGROUND
AT-A-GLANCE
IN DEPTH
SEARCH THE SCRIPTURES
DISCUSS THE MEANING
LESSON IN OUR SOCIETY
MAKE IT HAPPEN
FOLLOW THE SPIRIT
REMEMBER YOUR THOUGHTS
MORE LIGHT ON THE TEXT
DAILY BIBLE READINGS

6 And I will lay it waste: it shall not be pruned, nor digged; but there shall come up briers and thorns: I will also command the clouds that they rain no rain upon it.

7 For the vineyard of the Lord of hosts is the house of Israel, and the men of Judah his pleasant plant: and he looked for judgment, but behold oppression; for righteousness, but behold a cry.

IN FOCUS

A pressing problem in a local church almost consumed it. The children of God knew that one of the leaders engaged in sexual sins, which God warned against, and had done so for a long period of time. Some newborn Christians fell to the wiles of this leader while more mature Christians simply talked among themselves, lamenting over the situation, but did nothing.

Finally, the elders could procrastinate no longer. They could not idly stand by and tolerate Satan's continuous attack on the church. They could no longer call "right wrong and wrong right." Something had to be done, or the whole church would be destroyed. Therefore, these elders called a meeting to address the problem. Their brother had broken God's commands of conduct on sexual sins, and he had to be dealt with before God's judgment came down on the whole body.

After much prayer and fasting, the elders decided that this brother had to give up his position in the church for a season, until he repented and was restored. Collectively, this was agreed upon and carried out. The fallen leader knew that they were right and accepted his fate. He cooperated in repenting and being restored. Therefore, the entire church was blessed and so was he!

THE PEOPLE, PLACES, AND TIMES

The Vineyard. The main cash crop of the Israelites was grapes. Therefore, it is understandable why God used this parable to show the people of their sins and His forthcoming judgment and punishment.

The vines were usually planted on a hill that often had a terrace and protective walls made of stone and bushes. There was a stone watchtower that housed a watchman who guarded the ripening grapes during the vintage season. These vineyards were cultivated by their owners or hired hands.

Oftentimes, the owners left a portion of the crops for resident aliens, widows, and orphans. Therefore, the poor were fed as well (adapted from *Wycliff's Bible Dictionary*, Charles F. Pfeiffer, Howard F. Vos, John Rea, Hendrickson Publishers, Inc., 1998, p. 1778).

The Times. On a whole, the people of Israel and Judah had engaged in all sorts of evil practices, which displeased God. The Lord's patience had come to an end. His anger was stirred against His rebellious children. The leaders, especially, ignited His anger because they upheld the wrong; they called wrong right and right wrong.

BACKGROUND

In today's lesson, God called the prophet Isaiah to warn his chosen people (Israel and Judah) again about their disobedience and sins against Him. He used the vineyard, something very familiar to their culture, to show what had happened in their relationship with God. This parable also parallels the one given in Mark's Gospel where Jesus, Himself, told the parable of the evil farmers (12:1-9). In both stories, God demonstrated that He had high hopes for His rebellious children. They were to take the lead in moral and spiritual purity. However, they betrayed their loving and merciful Father. They broke His commands time and time again, exploiting others, engaging in drunkenness, taking pride in the wrong they did, confusing moral standards by calling wrong right and right wrong, being conceited in the sins they perpetrated, and perverting justice for all through bribes.

Because of these transgressions, God prepared to strike a blow against Israel by letting its enemies, the Assyrians, capture and destroy many of the people. Some would be taken captive and go back into servitude to another nation. A similar fate awaited Judah. God's patience with His people, when they continuously sin against Him, will not last always!

> ### AT-A-GLANCE
>
> 1. How the Lord Cared for His Vineyard (Isaiah 5:1-2)
> 2. The Sins of Israel and Judah (vv. 3-4)
> 3. God's Judgment and Punishment of Israel and Judah (vv. 5-7)

IN DEPTH

1. How the Lord Cared for His Vineyard (Isaiah 5:1-2)

God meticulously cared for His vineyard, Israel and Judah, His chosen people. Throughout their history, His hands were upon them: leading, guiding, protecting, and nurturing. This seed of Abraham was blessed by God, chosen by Him to bear the lineage of God's One and Only Son.

As far back as Abraham, when God gave him and Sarah a son, Isaac, after many barren years, God let His people know what conduct He expected. He would be their God if they would be His people. In fact, God kept all of His promises to them, but they broke their covenant relationship with Him again and again. They had been delivered from 400 years of slavery in Egypt and from 40 years in the wilderness, and yet they disobeyed God. Even in today's lesson, they continued to sin by breaking His rules. Therefore, this song, about the Lord's vineyard where the vineyard represents Israel and Judah (Isaiah 5:1-2), began with how God cared, and had mercy on His people. He loved and nurtured them for hundreds of years. They were not just any old grapevine, but a "choice vine." They were a chosen people, a special people. They were so special, in fact, that God's Son would be sent through their lineage, King David's line.

After all God's goodness, mercy, and caring, He waited for the good fruit from a good people. He waited for sweet grapes (v. 2). He waited for His people to honor Him to love, adore, and worship Him only. He is still waiting!

2. The Sins of Israel and Judah (vv. 3-4)

Instead of a grateful people showing the proper respect to a Holy God, showing gratitude to a loving and merciful, living God they rebelled. They engaged in sexual sins, whored after other gods, intermarried with foreign women, perverted justice by bribing officials, and did horrendous things in God's sight. These grapes (Israel and Judah) were not sweet at all, but wild and sour. The people broke the heart of God because they were a hardheaded, stiff-necked generation as their fathers and forefathers had been. They kindled His anger; they tried His patience to the breaking point.

God sent prophet after prophet to warn the people, but they hated the messengers because of the negative message they brought concerning God's coming judgment and punishment. Often the religious leaders killed the messenger as they killed Jesus, God's Son. Now Israel and Judah must suffer the consequences of their actions.

3. God's Judgment and Punishment of Israel and Judah (vv. 5-7)

God grew tired of warning. A rebellious people had to be punished for their sins by a holy God. Therefore, He told Isaiah to tell them that He was going to let their enemies, the Assyrians, destroy them because of their unrighteousness, injustice, and rebellion.

This song about the Lord's vineyard was indeed a sad song about God's people, a song that broke God's heart. He did not want to punish them. He wanted them to repent and be restored.

He tried to lead them in this direction, but they would not follow. They chose the path of death and destruction.

SEARCH THE SCRIPTURES

1. Who is Isaiah's well-beloved? (Isaiah 5:1)
2. Who do the wild grapes represent? (v. 2)
3. What will God do to His vineyard? (vv. 5-6)
4. What were some of the sins of Israel and Judah? (v. 7)

DISCUSS THE MEANING

1. In Matthew 7:20 it says we can identify a person by the fruit that is produced? What does this mean?
2. Why did God use Israel's enemy, Assyria, to destroy it?

LESSON IN OUR SOCIETY

The Vietnam War, over 30 years ago, was like no other war that our country has engaged. Many Americans disagreed with sending our young people thousands of miles from home to fight in a war they deemed unjust. Yet our officials held that we were fighting for democracy and striking a blow against communism on foreign soil.

America was not used to fighting a war such as the one fought in Vietnam. Many Vietnamese children fought in this war and had to be killed as they hurled bombs at our soldiers. The American public could not understand why our soldiers were killing children. Yet our soldiers knew it was kill or be killed. After all, they were there.

Many of these young soldiers returned home damaged in mind and body, and their country did not respect them for fighting a war that had so many tragedies. Our country was beginning to turn its back on God, and we lost this war in more ways than one. As Israel and Judah, we did not know that the winning side is with Jesus.

MAKE IT HAPPEN

Examine your own life and see what kind of fruit you are producing. Ask God in prayer and in reading His word to show you. Then ask the question, "If I died right now, where would I spend eternity?"

FOLLOW THE SPIRIT

What God wants me to do:

_____

_____

REMEMBER YOUR THOUGHTS
Special insights you learned:

_____

_____

MORE LIGHT ON THE TEXT
Isaiah 5:1-7

5:1 Now will I sing to my well-beloved a song of my beloved touching his vineyard. My well-beloved hath a vineyard in a very fruitful hill:

This is a parable of an unfruitful vineyard. In this parable the beloved is the Lord and the vineyard is Israel. The style of this parable resembles that of the Song of Solomon, but this is a poem of judgement. In these verses the prophet tells the people of their sin and of God's judgement upon them. Judah is portrayed as a well-tended vineyard that has been placed "in a very fruitful hill." With such an advantageous location and with God himself as the keeper of the vineyard, there should be no excuse for the vineyard not to bring forth much fruit.

2 And he fenced it, and gathered out the stones

thereof, and planted it with the choicest vine, and built a tower in the midst of it, and also made a winepress therein: and he looked that it should bring forth grapes, and it brought forth wild grapes.

In this verse, we get a clear picture of how the Lord Himself took exceptional care of His vineyard (His children). "He fenced it" is a picture of the Lord's possession. He "gathered out the stones thereof" is a picture of the Lord's purification and preparation for productivity. He "planted it with the choicest vine" is a picture of the Lord's preferential provisions and His pleasure in the prosperity of His vineyard. He "built a tower in the midst" of the vineyard is a picture of the Lord's watchful protection. He "also made a winepress therein" is a picture of the Lord's plan for us to mature in order to meet our potential, to fulfill His purpose for our lives and to partake of His goodness and the fruit of His labor.

After the Lord had made all of these provisions for His children, "He looked that it should bring forth grapes, and it brought fourth wild grapes." The term "wild grapes" means "stinking things." How sad it is that our Heavenly Father gives us everything that we need to be fruitful. Yet so many people are living unfruitful and defeated lives, all because of disobedience and rejection of God's plan for our lives.

3 And now, O inhabitants of Jerusalem, and men of Judah, judge, I pray you, betwixt me and my vineyard.

God is telling His people to be the judge. He is drawing their attention to themselves and to their disobedience of Him in spite of all that He has done for them. God is also telling them to consider their ways. He wants them to realize that it is their own rebellion that has put them in the position they now find themselves in—living defeated and unfruitful lives.

4 What could have been done more to my vineyard, that I have not done in it? Wherefore, when I looked that it

should bring forth grapes, brought it forth wild grapes?

God is pointing out to His people that He has blessed them with everything that they could ever need to be abundantly fruitful, yet they are shamefully unfruitful. There is nothing more that God could have done to insure their productivity. By an act of their will they chose to sin against the Creator of the universe, and as a result, they will be punished.

One would think that since we have written accounts of the effects of disobedience to the will and to the Word of God, we would never find ourselves in the situation like Israel. The truth of the matter is we have no right to put Israel down, as if we are better than they were. Each of us, in one way or another has found ourselves in gross disobedience to the will of God for our lives.

What more could the Lord do that He has not already done on our behalf?

5 And now go to; I will tell you what I will do to my vineyard: I will take away the hedge thereof, and it shall be eaten up; and break down the wall thereof, and it shall be trodden down:

This is a prophecy. God was telling His people that He was going to remove the blessings of protection, provisions, and prosperity from them, and their enemies would have their way with them. They were about to learn a very painful lesson, one that would effect every aspect of their lives. When God removes His hedge of protection from us, we become an open target for all of the wiles of the devil. God's chosen people went from being a vineyard to being a barren land. God offered them prosperity, and they chose poverty. God offered them fruit, and they chose failure. God offered them victory, and they chose vices. The same holds true today.

6 And I will lay it waste: it shall not be pruned, nor digged; but there shall come up briers and thorns: I will also command the clouds that they rain no rain upon it.

Not only did God withdraw His blessings from His disobedient children, but He made sure that no one, and nothing, else would come along and bless them. God allowed them to suffer as a result of their refusing the abundant provisions that He had offered them.

7 For the vineyard of the Lord of hosts is the house of Israel, and the men of Judah his pleasant plant: and he looked for judgment, but behold oppression; for righteousness, but behold a cry.

Here the parable is explained in greater detail. As stated earlier the vineyard is Israel. The pleasant plant is the men of Judah. God had blessed them tremendously, yet they sinned against Him. God expected much more from them than He received. He expected them to be His representatives on the earth. He also wanted to have fellowship with them on a continual basis. God had given them many precious promises, but they refused them. As a result they found themselves in bitter bondage.

Let us readily accept the lessons that Israel learned the hard way. Must we find ourselves in poverty, fear and bondage before we are willing to truly surrender our lives to the Almighty God of the universe? He has not withheld any good thing from those of us who are willing to obey His commands.

DAILY BIBLE READINGS

M: The Song of the Vineyard
Isaiah 5:1-7

T: Woe unto Extortioners and Playboys
Isaiah 5:8-17

W: Woe unto Scoffers
Isaiah 5:18-23

T: Foreign Invasion Predicted
Isaiah 5:24-30

F: The Anger of the Almighty
Isaiah 9:11-10:4

S: Assyria Also Judged
Isaiah 10:5-12

S: Wicked Tenants of the Vineyard
Mark 12:1-9

TEACHING TIPS

August 26
Bible Study Guide 13

1. Words You Should Know

A. Sin (2 Kings 17:7) Hebrew *Chata (Khawtaw)*; Greek *poneros*—evil, godless, transgression of God's laws.

B. Heathen (v. 8) Hebrew *Croyim;* Greek *ethnos*—all nations other than the Jewish.

2. Teacher Preparation

A. Begin preparing for this lesson by studying the DEVOTIONAL READING and the DAILY BIBLE READINGS.

B. Read the FOCAL VERSES from at least three different translations, especially a study Bible that has footnotes and references.

C. Read Bible Study Guide 13, and answer all the SEARCH THE SCRIPTURES and DISCUSS THE MEANING questions.

D. Materials needed: Bible, chalk, chalkboard, pens or pencils, and 3x5 index cards.

3. Starting the Lesson

A. Before the class begins, write the words "sin" and "heathen" on the board. Also write the AT-A-GLANCE outline.

B. After the students have arrived and are seated, ask for prayer requests and pray asking for God's anointing as you discuss the lesson.

C. Read the IN FOCUS story. Explain that today's lesson tells us of the punishment that God allowed Israel to go through because of its disobedience to God's commands. Stress that God was no longer tolerating Israel's disobedience, and it was time for them to suffer the consequences of their actions.

D. Direct their attention to the definitions on the board and engage in a brief discussion of these terms.

4. Getting into the Lesson

A. Write the words "secret sins" and "public sins" on the board. Then ask the class to list on an index card some examples of secret sins in our society and then on the back some public sins.

B. Discuss some of the examples that they gave. Ask them to tell what impact our lives have on a lost world who is watching our behavior. Then ask, "Can the world see Jesus in you?" Now discuss some possible punishments for these sins.

C. Have them read the BACKGROUND information, and THE PEOPLE, PLACES, AND TIMES articles.

D. Have volunteers read the FOCAL VERSES according to the AT-A-GLANCE outline. You may engage in discussion during the reading or wait until all verses are read. Then ask the corresponding SEARCH THE SCRIPTURES questions.

5. Relating the Lesson to Life

A. To help students understand how the lesson applies to today's society, direct their attention to the LESSON IN OUR SOCIETY article. Allow them time for discussion and debate.

B. Review the DISCUSS THE MEANING questions and allow time for discussion.

6. Arousing Action

A. Review the MAKE IT HAPPEN suggestions and challenge them to follow through.

B. Challenge them to do their DAILY BIBLE READINGS.

C. Close with prayer and thanksgiving for God's Word.

WORSHIP GUIDE

For the Superintendent or Teacher
Theme: Israel Taken into Captivity
Theme Song: Revive Us Again
Scripture: 2 Kings 17:6-16
Song: Guide Me, O Thou Great Jehovah!
Meditation: Lord, help us to listen to
Your voice and obey Your commands so
that there will be no
need for punishment for our sins.

AUG 26TH

515

ISRAEL TAKEN INTO CAPTIVITY

Bible Background • 2 KINGS 17:1-23
Printed Text • 2 KINGS 17:6-16
Devotional Reading • EXODUS 20:1-6

LESSON AIM

By the end of this session, students will know that sin has consequences; God's warnings against willfully committing sin will not go on forever; a Holy God will not tolerate His people continuing to break His commands; and God's punishment for sin is just.

KEEP IN MIND

"Therefore, the Lord was very angry with Israel, and removed them out of his sight: there was none left but the tribe of Judah only" (2 Kings 17:18, KJV).

FOCAL VERSES

2 Kings 17:6 In the ninth year of Hoshea, the king of Assyria took Samaria, and carried Israel away into Assyria, and placed them in Halah and in Habor by the river of Gozan, and in the cities of the Medes.

7 For so it was, that the children of Israel had sinned against the Lord their God, which had brought them up out of the land of Egypt, from under the hand of Pharaoh, king of Egypt, and had feared other gods.

8 And walked in the statues of the heathen, whom the Lord cast out from before the children of Israel, and of the kings of Israel, which they had made.

9 And the children of Israel did secretly those things that were not right against the Lord their God, and they built them high places in all their cities, from the tower of the watchmen to the fenced city.

10 And they set them up images and groves in

LESSON OVERVIEW

LESSON AIM
KEEP IN MIND
FOCAL VERSES
IN FOCUS
THE PEOPLE, PLACES,
AND TIMES
BACKGROUND
AT-A-GLANCE
IN DEPTH
SEARCH THE SCRIPTURES
DISCUSS THE MEANING
LESSON IN OUR SOCIETY
MAKE IT HAPPEN
FOLLOW THE SPIRIT
REMEMBER YOUR THOUGHTS
MORE LIGHT ON THE TEXT
DAILY BIBLE READINGS

every high hill, and under every green tree:

11 And there they burnt incense in all the high places, as did the heathen whom the Lord carried away before them; and wrought wicked things to provoke the Lord to anger:

12 For they served idols, whereof the Lord had said unto them, Ye shall not do this thing.

13 Yet the Lord testified against Israel, and against Judah, by all the prophets, and by all the seers, saying, Turn ye from your evil ways, and keep my commandments and my statutes, according to all the law which I commanded your fathers, and which I sent to you by my servants, the prophets.

14 Notwithstanding, they would not hear, but hardened their necks, like to the neck of their fathers, that did not believe in the Lord their God.

15 And they rejected his statutes, and his covenant that he made with their fathers, and his testimonies which he testified against them: and they followed vanity, and became vain, and went after the heathen that were round about them, concerning whom the Lord had charged them, that they should not do like them.

16 And they left all the commandments of the Lord their God...

IN FOCUS

In a book entitled *The Bible Promise Book* (Barbour and Company, 1985, pp. 48-49), different Scriptures are quoted on God's faithfulness. One of these Scriptures is Deuteronomy 7:9 which says, "Know, therefore, that the Lord thy God, he is God, the faithful God, which keepeth covenant and mercy with them who love him and keep his commandments to a thousand generations."

This Scripture tells us that Almighty God cannot lie and is faithful in His promises to His children. Unlike Israel and us, He has not forsaken those who trust in Him. Therefore, God will not break His covenant or alter what He says. If He speaks it, He will bring it to pass. He will do just what He says.

This is also true of His punishment. If He tells us not to do something and we continue to do it, He warns us, and warns us, and warns us again, telling us of upcoming judgment and punishment for sin. He means what He says. In today's lesson, Israel sees that God is faithful to His Word and this can involve good and bad consequences.

THE PEOPLE, PLACES, AND TIMES

The Assyrians. The Assyrian Empire destroyed the kingdom of Israel. They deported the conquered people to other lands in order to destroy their sense of nationalism. In fact, according to *Halley's Bible Handbook* (Zondervan Publishing House, 1994, p. 209) "they (the Assyrians) built their state on the loot of other peoples. They practiced cruelty, including skinned their prisoners alive, cut off their hands, feet, noses, ears, tongues, and made mounds of human skulls, all to inspire terror."

BACKGROUND

The Israelites, God's chosen people, were to honor Almighty God and to be a light to a dark, sinful world. However, throughout their history, they chose a different path from what God had laid out for them. They chose the path of sure destruction, a path that dishonored God as they took on the behaviors of the godless nations around them.

God made a covenant with the Israelites, after rescuing them from 400 years of slavery in Egypt; He would be their God if they would be His people. He warned them that He would not tolerate them worshiping idol gods. He was to be their only God—the center of their lives (Exodus 20:3).

God also warned them that He does not leave unpunished the sins of those who hate Him. In fact, He punishes the sins of their parents to the third and fourth generations.

In today's lesson, judgment day has passed; punishment and God's wrath is upon the Israelites. He had instructed and warned them through the prophets but in vain. His patience with the northern kingdom, Israel, has come to an end. It was time for them to reap the consequences of their actions. They had broken many of God's rules, now God was going to break them.

Even though the new king, King Hosea, paid tribute to the king of Assyria, he still made a secret alliance with King So of Egypt. Again, this was against God's command. In retaliation, the Assyrians under King Shalmaneser V and Sargon II attacked the northern kingdom. Samaria, the capital, fell. The people were then taken into captivity after 200 years of freedom. God allowed the Israelites' enemies to invade and conqueror them.

AT-A-GLANCE

1. What Happened When Samaria Fell
(2 Kings 17:6)
2. The Sins of Israel
(vv. 7-16)

IN DEPTH

1. What Happened When Samaria Fell
(2 Kings 17:6)

In today's lesson, Assyria, Israel's enemy, made a third and final invasion of Israel. The first two were to warn them. If Israel had paid money faithfully and had not rebelled, the Assyrians would not have invaded a third time. However, Israel decided to ally with Egypt, which angered the Assyrians. This also angered God, who had freed their forefathers from Egyptian bondage. In essence, Israel allied with one enemy to fight another enemy. They were not depending on God.

When Assyria found out what the Israelites had done, they invaded. During Hosea's ninth year reign as king, Samaria fell. The people were then exiled. Their sense of nationalism was destroyed. Because they had disobeyed God, they paid a heavy price.

2. The Sins of Israel (vv. 7-16)

A. Idolatry. The sins that got Israel into this predicament were numerous. Their greatest transgression was worshiping idol gods (v. 7). In fact, the people often took on the religious practices of surrounding pagan nations. They forgot about the covenant that God made with their ancestors, that He would be their God if they would be His people. Time and time again, they dishonored their vows by whoring with idols.

B. Took on the Practices of Pagan Nations. Instead of the Israelites winning the pagan nations to God, oftentimes the pagan nations won the Israelites to their way of life—sin. God had driven these pagans from the land when the Israelites settled, but the Israelites forgot their heritage (v. 8). Even some of the kings influenced the Israelites into idolatry.

C. Secret Sins. The Israelites engaged in many secret sins that were displeasing to God. They built pagan shrines to aid them in their idol worship and followed the rituals of incense burning and other ungodly practices (vv. 9-12).

God sent many warnings through the prophets, including Isaiah, Hosea, and Micah, to tell the Israelites that God would not continue to tolerate their wickedness, that God's mercy would not last always, that God's patience was coming to an end. They should repent, turn to God, and be restored (v. 13).

The Israelites would not hear God's messengers. They would not listen to the prophets. Often they killed the messengers because of the negative messages from God. They were warned to obey God's commands and laws, but because they were a hardheaded, stiff-necked people, as their forefathers, they had a harsh fate (v. 14).

When the Israelites rejected God by worshiping idols, they sealed their demise (vv. 15-16).

SEARCH THE SCRIPTURES

1. Who captured Israel? (2 Kings 17:6)
2. What had Israel done? (v. 7)
3. The Israelites walked in whose statutes? (v. 8)
4. What did they set up in the high hills? (v. 10)
5. Who did they serve? (v. 12)
6. What had the prophets told the Israelites? (v. 13)

DISCUSS THE MEANING

1. Why do you think the Lord allowed Assyria three invasions before Israel finally fell?
2. God warned Israel because of its public and secret sins. Why are secret sins just as destructive as public ones?

LESSON IN OUR SOCIETY

Over 30 years ago, the U.S. government commissioned a study on race relations in our American society. From this study came a report called "The Kerner Commission Report," which said, "Our society is moving toward two distinct separate societies, one black, one white— separate and unequal" (*Black Enterprise*, Earl G. Graves Publishing Co. Inc., New York, NY, May 1988, p. 35).

This report warned our government and society of the devastation that could be caused by a divided America: poverty, crime, segregation, drug abuse, child abuse, etc. The report implored our government and society to act because the situation was so urgent.

As the Israelites did not heed God, the American society did not listen to the Kerner Report or to God's just rules of conduct on how to treat each other. Instead, evil prevailed. Right was called wrong and wrong right. Here at the beginning of the 21st century, we are realizing our worse nightmare. Seeds of division along racial lines have reaped a harvest of evil that threatens to destroy our very existence as we know it. In fact, a 49-year-old Black man from a small Texas town was beaten by two White men, chained to their truck, and dragged for over two miles until his body was torn asunder and unrecognizable. One of the White men had a White supremacist symbol on his torso.

Israel was taken hostage by its enemies because of its disobedience to God. America is fighting its enemies, trying to remain united and free because it, too, has broken many of God's commands.

MAKE IT HAPPEN

Think of some secret sins in your own life. Remember that they can hinder your walk with God just as much as public ones. Ask God to forgive you for these sins and help you to be an overcomer.

Then ask God to remind you of anything that is displeasing in your life as you daily walk with Him.

FOLLOW THE SPIRIT

What God wants me to do:

_____

_____

REMEMBER YOUR THOUGHTS

Special insights you learned:

_____

_____

MORE LIGHT ON THE TEXT
2 Kings 17:6-16

17:6 In the ninth year of Hoshea, the king of Assyria took Samaria, and carried Israel away into Assyria, and placed them in Halah and in Habor by the river of Gozan, and in the cities of the Medes.

In 725 B.C. Shalmaneser V invaded and attacked Samaria and held it under siege for three years until it fell in 722 B.C. The northern kingdom of Israel was then led into captivity.

7 For so it was, that the children of Israel had sinned against the Lord their God, which had brought them up out of the land of Egypt, from under the hand of Pharaoh, king of Egypt, and had feared other gods,

In spite of the centuries of cruel bondage that Israel experienced while captive in Egypt, they deliberately turned away from the almighty God who had miraculously delivered them from the hand of Pharaoh. God protected and provided for the Children of Israel in the wilderness and led them into the promised land. Nevertheless, they turned away from the true God, and chose to worship false gods.

Why is it that after we have been rescued from hurt, harm, and danger we feel and act as though we no longer need the Lord as much as we did when we were in trouble? The truth of the matter is that we need the Lord just as much when things are going well as we do when things are in an uproar.

8 And walked in the statutes of the heathen, whom the Lord cast out from before the children of Israel, and of the kings of Israel, which they had made.

Israel was so rebellious that it deliberately sinned against the God of their fathers and worshiped the gods of their enemies. The children of Israel were no different than many of us today who, from time to time, choose the ways of sin rather than follow the ways of righteousness. When we decide to disobey God and do that which we know is wrong, we are opening ourselves to the forces of evil. Many times, when we choose the ways of darkness, God allows us to suffer the consequences of the choices we make. Often we blame God for the pain that we suffer as a result of our rebellion, when in fact we are the ones who have chosen the path that leads to destruction.

9 And the children of Israel did secretly those things that were not right against the Lord their God, and they built them high places in all their cities, from the tower of the watchmen to the fenced city.

How can anyone hide anything from God who is omniscient (all knowing), omnipresent (everywhere all the time), and omnipotent (all powerful)? It is as if we think that because we cannot see God, He cannot see us either. How foolish. There is nothing that we can hide from the true God. He is our Creator and our Father. He knows our thoughts before we think them; there are no secrets to God. When we continually disobey the Word of God we gradually become deaf and blind. When we refuse His warnings and instructions, we find ourselves in the hands of our enemies. Often we think that God has left us, when, in fact, we have left Him.

10 And they set them up images and groves in every high hill, and under every green tree:

The children of Israel had become so insensitive to the voice of God that their sins became

children, were sacrificed on the altars of the high places.

12 For they served idols, whereof the Lord had said unto them, Ye shall not do this thing.

Although God had warned and commanded the children of Israel not to serve the idols of the heathens, they ignored Him. Whenever the Lord tells us anything there is a good reason for it. It's not that He is trying to make life difficult or keep us from enjoying ourselves. It is because He knows the suffering that comes as a result of sin, and He wants us to avoid it. God was very clear in His instructions to the children of Israel. He told them, in no uncertain terms, "Ye shall not do this thing." Yet they ignored Him.

13 Yet the Lord testified against Israel, and against Judah, by all the prophets, and by all the seers, saying, Turn ye from your evil ways, and keep my commandments and my statutes, according to all the law which I commanded your fathers, and which I sent to you by my servants, the prophets.

God had given the children of Israel many warnings in many different ways. One of the ways that God warned them was through the prophets and seers. Prophets and prophetesses receive a direct word from God through the Holy Spirit and gave this word to the people. There are several words in Hebrew to describe these people: *Ro'eh* and *rozeh* are translated "seer" and the word nabi is usually translated "prophet," which means "one who has been called to speak."

God had also given the Children of Israel many warnings through commandments and statutes and the Law which He gave to their fathers. Yet they rejected God and chose the ways of the heathens. Again this is true today; many people would rather get advice from a psychic than to listen to the many men and women that have been called by God to speak to His people. God has done everything to make His ways known to His people, and for us to refuse to obey Him only makes us vulnerable to the attacks of Satan.

14 Notwithstanding, they would not hear, but hardened their necks, like to the neck of their

more and more prevalent. They became so involved with the ways of darkness that they worshiped images that they carved themselves. They built places to worship these false gods "in every high hill, and under every green tree." The very people whom God had chosen rudely disrespected Him and rejected Him to worship wicked spirits. They became as corrupt as the heathens.

The same is true today. Many Christians try to relate to the world by trying to be like the world in many ways. This is an indication that we are more impressed with the world than the world is with us. Our focus must always be on the true God. The results of a godly lifestyle will produce more fruit than any other lifestyle.

11 And there they burnt incense in all the high places, as did the heathen whom the Lord carried away before them; and wrought wicked things to provoke the Lord to anger:

Incense was a mixture of spices used in the offering of sacrifices. The high places were elevated sites such as a mountain or a hill where false worship took place. The high places usually had an altar, stone pillars, wooden poles and a structure of some sort. Animals, and sometimes fathers, that did not believe in the Lord their God.

Every generation is plagued by people who reject God, His people and His law. The results are devastating. We serve a God who is loving, compassionate, and eager to bless us. When we reject God, we reject His love, compassion, and blessings. Whether we believe it or not we are turning our lives over to Satan who is determined to steal, kill, and destroy us and everything that pertains to us. Satan's desire is to use each of us in any way that he can to help him in his many schemes that ultimately end in death.

15 And they rejected his statutes, and his covenant that he made with their fathers, and his testimonies which he testified against them; and they followed vanity, and became vain, and went after the heathen that were round about them, concerning whom the Lord had charged them, that they should not do like them.

We often look at the Children of Israel and think, "How could anyone who has witnessed the power and mercy of God in so many miraculous ways and for such a long period of time be so foolish to totally reject His commandments, ignore His desires, and commit themselves to the gods of sinful, wicked men and women? Sadly we have no right to point out their sin, for we, too, in this and every other society, have been guilty of the same. The times have changed and the situations are different, but the sin is the same. We, too, are or have been guilty of rebellion against God, His Son, and His Spirit. Samuel told Saul, "Hath the Lord as great delight in burnt offerings and sacrifices, as in obeying the voice of the Lord? Behold, to obey is better than sacrifice, and to hearken than the fat of rams. For rebellion is as the sin of witchcraft, and stubbornness is as iniquity and idolatry. Because thou hast rejected the word of the Lord, he hath also rejected thee from being king" (1 Samuel 15:22-24).

God, through His Son the Lord Jesus Christ, has given His children authority over all of the works of the devil. We have been born into His holy kingdom and have been appointed and anointed to be kings for His glory. When we rebel against our King and His Word, we deliberately refuse and reject the position, power, protection, and privileges of kingship.

16 And they left all the commandments of the Lord their God, and made them molten images, even two calves, and made a grove, and worshiped all the host of heaven, and served Baal.

Man has been designed for worship. Everyone worships someone or something. It may be a celebrity, money, cars, sex, sports, career, self, etc. Worship comes naturally to everyone because God created us to be worshipers. God desires, and is seeking for, our worship of Him. Lucifer was the worship leader in heaven before he was kicked out. He was kicked out of heaven because his pride kept him from worshiping God. Jesus told the woman at the well, "But the hour cometh, and now is, when the true worshipers shall worship the Father in spirit and in truth: for the Father seeketh such to worship Him. God is a Spirit and they that worship Him must worship him in spirit and in truth" (John 4:23-24).

Let us not become vain, as did Lucifer, and allow our vanity and pride to replace our true worship of the Father. When we stop worshiping the Father we automatically begin to worship someone or something else because we were made for worship.

The question is not, "Will you worship?" The question is, "Who or what will you worship?"

DAILY BIBLE READINGS

M: Assyria Defeats King Hosea
2 Kings 17:1-6

T: Israel Sinned and Disobeyed God
2 Kings 17:7-13

W: Reasons for Israel's Captivity
2 Kings 17:14-18

T: Summary of Israel's Iniquity
2 Kings 17:19-23

F: Assyria Resettles Samaria
2 Kings 17:24-28

S: Pagan Worship Prevails in Samaria
2 Kings 17:29-41

S: The One True God
Exodus 20:1-6

NOTES

NOTES

NOTES

NOTES

NOTES

NOTES

_____

_____

_____

_____

_____

_____

_____

_____

_____

_____

_____

_____